W9-CSM-411

William Shakespeare

THE COMPLETE WORKS

William Shakespeare
THE COMPLETE WORKS

VOLUME 2

. . .

THE COMEDIES II / ROMANCES / POEMS

The Complete Works of William Shakespeare, Volume 2

This edition published by Tess Press, an imprint of
Black Dog & Leventhal Publishers, Inc.
151 West 19th Street, New York, NY 10011

Design by Edstudio Design
Manufactured in China

ISBN-10: 1-57912-653-7
ISBN-13: 978-1-57912-653-7

h g f e d c b a

Table of Contents

MEASURE FOR MEASURE

MEASURE FOR MEASURE

DRAMATIS PERSONAE

VINCENTIO, the Duke.
ANGELO, Deputy.
ESCALUS, an ancient Lord.
CLAUDIO, a young gentleman.
LUCIO, a fantastic.
Two other gentlemen.
PROVOST.
THOMAS, friar.
PETER, friar.
A Justice.
VARRIUS.
ELBOW, a simple constable.
FROTH, a foolish gentleman.
POMPEY, servant to Mistress Overdone.
ABHORSON, an executioner.
BARNARDINE, a dissolute prisoner.
ISABELLA, sister to Claudio.
MARIANA, betrothed to Angelo.
JULIET, beloved of Claudio.
FRANCISCA, a nun.
MISTRESS OVERDONE, a bawd.
Lords, Officers, Citizens, Boy, and Attendants.

SCENE: *Vienna.*

ACT ONE SCENE ONE

An apartment in the DUKE'S *palace.*

Enter DUKE, ESCALUS, Lords *and* Attendants.

DUKE
Escalus.
ESCALUS
My lord.
DUKE
Of government the properties to unfold,
Would seem in me to affect speech and discourse;
Since I am put to know that your own science
Exceeds, in that, the lists of all advice
My strength can give you: then no more remains,
†But that to your sufficiency . . . .
. . . . as your worth is able, [1]
And let them work. The nature of our people,
Our city's institutions, and the terms
For common justice, you're as pregnant in
As art and practise hath enriched any
That we remember. There is our commission,
From which we would not have you warp. Call hither,
I say, bid come before us Angelo.
[*Exit an Attendant.*
What figure of us think you he will bear?
For you must know, we have with special soul
Elected him our absence to supply,
Lent him our terror, dress'd him with our love,
And given his deputation all the organs
Of our own power: what think you of it?
ESCALUS
If any in Vienna be of worth
To undergo such ample grace and honour,
It is Lord Angelo.
DUKE
Look where he comes.

Enter ANGELO.

ANGELO
Always obedient to your grace's will,
I come to know your pleasure.

DUKE
Angelo,
There is a kind of character in thy life,
That to the observer doth thy history
Fully unfold. Thyself and thy belongings
Are not thine own so proper as to waste
Thyself upon thy virtues, they on thee.
Heaven doth with us as we with torches do,
Not light them for themselves; for if our virtues
Did not go forth of us, 'twere all alike
As if we had them not. Spirits are not finely touch'd
But to fine issues, nor Nature never lends
The smallest scruple of her excellence
But, like a thrifty goddess, she determines
Herself the glory of a creditor,
Both thanks and use. But I do bend my speech
To one that can my part in him advertise;
Hold therefore, Angelo:— [2]
In our remove be thou at full ourself;
Mortality and mercy in Vienna
Live in thy tongue and heart: old Escalus,
Though first in question, is thy secondary.
Take thy commission.

ANGELO
Now, good my lord,
Let there be some more test made of my metal,
Before so noble and so great a figure
Be stamp'd upon it.

DUKE
No more evasion:
We have with a leaven'd and prepared choice
Proceeded to you; therefore take your honours.
Our haste from hence is of so quick condition
That it prefers itself and leaves unquestion'd
Matters of needful value. We shall write to you,
As time and our concernings shall importune,
How it goes with us, and do look to know
What doth befall you here. So, fare you well:
To the hopeful execution do I leave you
Of your commissions.

ANGELO
Yet give leave, my lord,
That we may bring you something on the way.

DUKE
My haste may not admit it;
Nor need you, on mine honour, have to do
With any scruple; your scope is as mine own,
So to enforce or qualify the laws
As to your soul seems good. Give me your hand:
I'll privily away. I love the people,
But do not like to stage me to their eyes:
Through it do well, I do not relish well
Their loud applause and Aves vehement;
Nor do I think the man of safe discretion
That does affect it. Once more, fare you well.

ANGELO
The heavens give safety to your purposes!

ESCALUS
Lead forth and bring you back in happiness!

DUKE
I thank you. Fare you well. [*Exit.*

ESCALUS
I shall desire you, sir, to give me leave
To have free speech with you; and it concerns me
To look into the bottom of my place:
A power I have, but of what strength and nature
I am not yet instructed.

ANGELO
'Tis so with me. Let us withdraw together,
And we may soon our satisfaction have
Touching that point.

ESCALUS
I'll wait upon your honour. [*Exeunt.*

ACT ONE SCENE TWO

A Street.

Enter LUCIO *and two Gentlemen.*

LUCIO
If the duke with the other dukes come not to composition with the King of Hungary, why then all the dukes fall upon the king.

FIRST GENTLEMAN
Heaven grant us its peace, but not the King of Hungary's!

SECOND GENTLEMAN
Amen.

LUCIO
Thou concludest like the sanctimonious pirate, that went to sea with the Ten Commandments, but scraped one out of the table.

SECOND GENTLEMAN
'Thou shalt not steal'?

LUCIO
Ay, that he razed.

FIRST GENTLEMAN
Why, 'twas a commandment to command the captain and all the rest from their functions: they put forth to steal. There's not a soldier of us all, that, in the

GENTLEMAN I believe thee; for I think thou never wast where grace was said.

thanksgiving before meat, do relish the petition well that prays for peace.

SECOND GENTLEMAN

I never heard any soldier dislike it.

LUCIO

I believe thee; for I think thou never wast where grace was said. 19

SECOND GENTLEMAN

No? a dozen times at least.

FIRST GENTLEMAN

What, in metre?

LUCIO

In any proportion or in any language.

FIRST GENTLEMAN

I think, or in any religion.

LUCIO

Ay, why not? Grace is grace, despite of all controversy: as, for example, thou thyself art a wicked villain, despite of all grace.

FIRST GENTLEMAN

Well, there went but a pair of shears between us. [3]

LUCIO

I grant; as there may between the lists and the velvet. Thou art the list. 29

FIRST GENTLEMAN

And thou the velvet: thou art good velvet; thou'rt a three-piled piece, I warrant thee: I had as lief be a list of an English kersey as be piled, as thou art piled, for a French velvet. Do I speak feelingly now?

LUCIO

I think thou dost; and, indeed, with most painful feeling of thy speech: I will, out of thine own confession, learn to begin thy health; but, whilst I live, forget to drink after thee. 37

FIRST GENTLEMAN

I think I have done myself wrong, have I not?

SECOND GENTLEMAN

Yes, that thou hast, whether thou art tainted or free.

LUCIO

Behold, behold. where Madam Mitigation comes! I have purchased as many diseases under her roof as come to—

SECOND GENTLEMAN
To what, I pray?
LUCIO
Judge.
SECOND GENTLEMAN
To three thousand dolours a year.
FIRST GENTLEMAN
Ay, and more. 46
LUCIO
A French crown more.
FIRST GENTLEMAN
Thou art always figuring diseases in me; but thou art full of error; I am sound.
LUCIO
Nay, not as one would say, healthy; but so sound as things that are hollow: thy bones are hollow; impiety has made a feast of thee.

Enter MISTRESS OVERDONE.

FIRST GENTLEMAN
How now! which of your hips has the most profound sciatica?
MISTRESS OVERDONE
Well, well; there's one yonder arrested and carried to prison was worth five thousand of you all.
SECOND GENTLEMAN
Who's that, I pray thee?
MISTRESS OVERDONE
Marry, sir, that 's Claudio, Signior Claudio.
FIRST GENTLEMAN
Claudio to prison? 'tis not so.
MISTRESS OVERDONE
Nay, but I know 'tis so: I saw him arrested, saw him carried away; and, which is more, within these three days his head to be chopped off. 62
LUCIO
But, after all this fooling, I would not have it so. Art thou sure of this?
MISTRESS OVERDONE
I am too sure of it: and it is for getting Madam Julietta with child.
LUCIO
Believe me, this may be: he promised to meet me two hours since, and he was ever precise in promise-keeping.
SECOND GENTLEMAN
Besides, you know, it draws something near to the speech we had to such a purpose.
FIRST GENTLEMAN
But, most of all, agreeing with the proclamation. 73
LUCIO
Away! let's go learn the truth of it.
[*Exeunt Lucio and Gentlemen.*

MISTRESS OVERDONE
Thus, what with the war, what with the sweat, what with the gallows and what with poverty, I am custom-shrunk.

Enter POMPEY.

How now! what's the news with you?
POMPEY
Yonder man is carried to prison.
MISTRESS OVERDONE
Well; what has he done?
POMPEY
A woman.
MISTRESS OVERDONE
But what's his offence? 82
POMPEY
Groping for trouts in a peculiar river.
MISTRESS OVERDONE
What, is there a maid with child by him?
POMPEY
No, but there's a woman with maid by him. You have not heard of the proclamation, have you?
MISTRESS OVERDONE
What proclamation, man?
POMPEY
All houses in the suburbs of Vienna in the suburbs be pulled down?
MISTRESS OVERDONE
And what shall become of those in the city? 90
POMPEY
They shall stand for seed: they had gone down too, but that a wise burgher put in for them.
MISTRESS OVERDONE
But shall all our houses of resort in the suburbs be pulled down?
POMPEY
To the ground, mistress.
MISTRESS OVERDONE
Why, here's a change indeed in the commonwealth!
What shall become of me?
POMPEY
Come; fear you not: good counsellors lack no clients: though you change your place, you need not change your trade; I'll be your tapster still.
Courage! there will be pity taken on you: you that have worn your eyes almost out in the service, you will be considered.
MISTRESS OVERDONE
What's to do here, Thomas tapster? let's withdraw.
POMPEY
Here comes Signior Claudio, led by the provost to prison; and there's Madam Juliet. [*Exeunt.*

Enter PROVOST, CLAUDIO, JULIET, *and* Officers.

CLAUDIO
Fellow, why dost thou show me thus to the world?
Bear me to prison, where I am committed.

PROVOST
I do it not in evil disposition,
But from Lord Angelo by special charge.

CLAUDIO
Thus can the demigod Authority
Make us pay down for our offence by weight
The words of heaven; on whom it will, it will; [4]
On whom it will not, so; yet still 'tis just.

Re-enter LUCIO *and two* Gentlemen.

LUCIO
Why, how now, Claudio! whence comes this restraint?

CLAUDIO
From too much liberty, my Lucio, liberty:
As surfeit is the father of much fast,
So every scope by the immoderate use
Turns to restraint. Our natures do pursue,
Like rats that ravin down their proper bane,
A thirsty evil; and when we drink we die.

LUCIO
If I could speak so wisely under an arrest, I would send for certain of my creditors: and yet, to say the truth, I had as lief have the foppery of freedom as the morality of imprisonment. What's thy offence, Claudio? [5]

CLAUDIO
What but to speak of would offend again.

LUCIO
What, is't murder?

CLAUDIO
No.

LUCIO
Lechery?

CLAUDIO
Call it so.

PROVOST
Away, sir! you must go.

CLAUDIO
One word, good friend. Lucio, a word with you.

LUCIO
A hundred, if they'll do you any good.
Is lechery so look'd after?

CLAUDIO
Thus stands it with me: upon a true contract
I got possession of Julietta's bed:
You know the lady; she is fast my wife,
Save that we do the denunciation lack
Of outward order: this we came not to,
Only for propagation of a dower [6]
Remaining in the coffer of her friends,
From whom we thought it meet to hide our love
Till time had made them for us. But it chances
The stealth of our most mutual entertainment
With character too gross is writ on Juliet.

LUCIO
With child, perhaps?

CLAUDIO
Unhappily, even so.
And the new deputy now for the duke—
Whether it be the fault and glimpse of newness,
Or whether that the body public be
A horse whereon the governor doth ride,
Who, newly in the seat, that it may know
He can command, lets it straight feel the spur;
Whether the tyranny be in his place,
Or in his emmence that fills it up,
I stagger in:—but this new governor
Awakes me all the enrolled penalties
Which have, like unscour'd armour, hung by the wall
So long that nineteen zodiacs have gone round
And none of them been worn; and, for a name,
Now puts the drowsy and neglected act
Freshly on me: 'tis surely for a name.

LUCIO
I warrant it is: and thy head stands so tickle on thy shoulders that a milkmaid, if she be in love, may sigh it off. Send after the duke and appeal to him.

CLAUDIO
I have done so, but he's not to be found.
I prithee, Lucio, do me this kind service:
This day my sister should the cloister enter
And there receive her approbation:
Acquaint her with the danger of my state:
Implore her, in my voice, that she make friends
To the strict deputy; bid herself assay him:
I have great hope in that; for in her youth
There is a prone and speechless dialect,
Such as move men; beside, she hath prosperous art
When she will play with reason and discourse,
And well she can persuade.

LUCIO
I pray she may; as well for the encouragement of the like, which else would stand under grievous imposition, as for the enjoying of thy life, who I would be sorry should be thus foolishly lost at a game of tick-tack. I'll to her.

CLAUDIO
I thank you, good friend Lucio.

LUCIO
Within two hours.

CLAUDIO
Come, officer, away! [*Exeunt.*

ACT ONE SCENE THREE

A monastery.

Enter DUKE *and* FRIAR THOMAS.

DUKE
No, holy father; throw away that thought;
Believe not that the dribbling dart of love
Can pierce a complete bosom. Why I desire thee
To give me secret harbour, hath a purpose
More grave and wrinkled than the aims and ends
Of burning youth.

FRIAR THOMAS
May your grace speak of it?

DUKE
My holy sir, none better knows than you
How I have ever loved the life removed
And held in idle price to haunt assemblies
Where youth, and cost, and witless bravery keeps.
I have deliver'd to Lord Angelo,
A man of stricture and firm abstinence,
My absolute power and place here in Vienna,
And he supposes me travell'd to Poland;
For so I have strew'd it in the common ear,
And so it is received. Now, pious sir,
You will demand of me why I do this?

FRIAR THOMAS
Gladly, my lord.

DUKE
We have strict statutes and most biting laws.
The needful bits and curbs to headstrong weeds,
Which for this nineteen years we have let slip;
Even like an o'ergrown lion in a cave,
That goes not out to prey. Now, as fond fathers,
Having bound up the threatening twigs of birch,
Only to stick it in their children's sight
For terror, not to use, in time the rod
Becomes more mock'd than fear'd; so our decrees,
Dead to infliction, to themselves are dead;
And liberty plucks justice by the nose;
The baby beats the nurse, and quite athwart
Goes all decorum.

FRIAR THOMAS
It rested in your grace
To unloose this tied-up justice when you pleased:
And it in you more dreadful would have seem'd
Than in Lord Angelo.

DUKE
I do fear, too dreadful:
Sith 'twas my fault to give the people scope,
'Twould be my tyranny to strike and gall them
For what I bid them do: for we bid this be done,
When evil deeds have their permissive pass
And not the punishment. Therefore indeed, my father,
I have on Angelo imposed the office;
Who may, in the ambush of my name, strike home,
And yet my nature never in the fight
To do in slander. And to behold his sway, [7]
I will, as 'twere a brother of your order,
Visit both prince and people: therefore, I prithee,
Supply me with the habit and instruct me
How I may formally in person bear me
Like a true friar. Moe reasons for this action
At our more leisure shall I render you;
Only, this one: Lord Angelo is precise;
Stands at a guard with envy; scarce confesses
That his blood flows, or that his appetite
Is more to bread than stone: hence shall we see,
If power change purpose, what our seemers be.
[*Exeunt.*

ACT ONE SCENE FOUR

A nunnery.

Enter ISABELLA *and* FRANCISCA.

ISABELLA
And have you nuns no farther privileges?

FRANCISCA
Are not these large enough?

ISABELLA
Yes, truly; I speak not as desiring more;
But rather wishing a more strict restraint
Upon the sisterhood, the votarists of Saint Clare.

LUCIO
[*Within*] Ho! Peace be in this place!

ISABELLA
Who's that which calls?

FRANCISCA
It is a man's voice. Gentle Isabella,
Turn you the key, and know his business of him;
You may, I may not; you are yet unsworn.
When you have vow'd, you must not speak with men
But in the presence of the prioress:
Then, if you speak, you must not show your face,
Or, if you show your face, you must not speak.
He calls again; I pray you, answer him. [*Exit.*

ISABELLA
Peace and prosperity! Who is't that calls

Enter LUCIO.

LUCIO
Hail, virgin, if you be, as those cheek-roses
Proclaim you are no less! Can you so stead me

As bring me to the sight of Isabella,
A novice of this place and the fair sister
To her unhappy brother Claudio? 22

ISABELLA
Why 'her unhappy brother'? let me ask,
The rather for I now must make you know
I am that Isabella and his sister.

LUCIO
Gentle and fair, your brother kindly greets you:
Not to be weary with you, he's in prison.

ISABELLA
Woe me! for what?

LUCIO
For that which, if myself might be his judge,
He should receive his punishment in thanks:
He hath got his friend with child.

ISABELLA
Sir, make me not your story.

LUCIO
It is true. 33
I would not—though 'tis my familiar sin
With maids to seem the lapwing and to jest,
Tongue far from heart— play with all virgins so:
I hold you as a thing ensky'd and sainted.
By your renouncement an immortal spirit,
And to be talk'd with in sincerity,
As with a saint.

ISABELLA
You do blaspheme the good in mocking me.

LUCIO
Do not believe it. Fewness and truth, 'tis thus:
Your brother and his lover have embraced: 43
As those that feed grow full as blossoming time
That from the seedness the bare fallow brings
To teeming foison, even so her plenteous womb
Expresseth his full tilth and husbandry.

ISABELLA
Some one with child by him? My cousin Juliet?

LUCIO
Is she your cousin?

ISABELLA
Adoptedly; as school-maids change their names
By vain though apt affection.

LUCIO
She it is.

ISABELLA
O, let him marry her.

LUCIO
This is the point.
The duke is very strangely gone from hence;
Bore many gentlemen, myself being one,
In hand and hope of action: but we do learn
By those that know the very nerves of state,
His givings-out were of an infinite distance
From his true-meant design. Upon his place,
And with full line of his authority,
Governs Lord Angelo; a man whose blood
Is very snow-broth; one who never feels
The wanton stings and motions of the sense,
But doth rebate and blunt his natural edge 65
With profits of the mind, study and fast.
He—to give fear to use and liberty,
Which have for long run by the hideous law,
As mice by lions— hath pick'd out an act,
Under whose heavy sense your brother's life
Falls into forfeit: he arrests him on it;
And follows close the rigour of the statute,
To make him an example. All hope is gone,
Unless you have the grace by your fair prayer
To soften Angelo: and that's my pith of business 76
'Twixt you and your poor brother.

ISABELLA
Doth he so seek his life?

LUCIO
Has censured him
Already; and, as I hear, the provost hath
A warrant for his execution.

ISABELLA
Alas! what poor ability's in me
To do him good?

LUCIO
Assay the power you have.

ISABELLA
My power? Alas, I doubt—

LUCIO
Our doubts are traitors
And make us lose the good we oft might win
By fearing to attempt. Go to Lord Angelo,
And let him learn to know, when maidens sue,
Men give like gods; but when they weep and kneel, 91
All their petitions are as freely theirs
As they themselves would owe them.

ISABELLA
I'll see what I can do.

LUCIO
But speedily.

ISABELLA
I will about it straight;
No longer staying but to give the mother
Notice of my affair. I humbly thank you:
Commend me to my brother: soon at night
I'll send him certain word of my success.

LUCIO
I take my leave of you.

ISABELLA
Good sir, adieu. [*Exeunt.* 102

ACT TWO SCENE ONE

A hall in ANGELO'S *house.*

Enter ANGELO, ESCALUS, *and a* Justice, Provost, Officers, *and other* Attendants, *behind.*

ANGELO
We must not make a scarecrow of the law,
Setting it up to fear the birds of prey,
And let it keep one shape, till custom make it
Their perch and not their terror.

ESCALUS
Ay, but yet
Let us be keen, and rather cut a little,
Than fall, and bruise to death. Alas, this gentleman,
Whom I would save, had a most noble father!
Let but your honour know,
Whom I believe to be most strait in virtue,
That, in the working of your own affections,
Had time cohered with place or place with wishing,
Or that the resolute acting of your blood
Could have attain'd the effect of your own purpose,
Whether you had not sometime in your life
Err'd in this point which now you censure him,
And pull'd the law upon you.

ANGELO
'Tis one thing to be tempted, Escalus,
Another thing to fall. I not deny,
The jury, passing on the prisoner's life,
May in the sworn twelve have a thief or two
Guiltier than him they try. What's open made to justice,
That justice seizes: what know the laws
That thieves do pass on thieves? 'Tis very pregnant,
The jewel that we find, we stoop and take't
Because we see it; but what we do not see
We tread upon, and never think of it.
You may not so extenuate his offence
For I have had such faults; but rather tell me,
When I, that censure him, do so offend,
Let mine own judgment pattern out my death,
And nothing come in partial. Sir, he must die.

ESCALUS
Be it as your wisdom will.

ANGELO
Where is the provost?

PROVOST
Here, if it like your honour.

ANGELO
See that Claudio
Be executed by nine to-morrow morning:
Bring him his confessor, let him be prepared;
For that's the utmost of his pilgrimage.
[*Exit Provost.*

ESCALUS
[*Aside*] Well, heaven forgive him! and forgive us all!
Some rise by sin, and some by virtue fall:
Some run from brakes of ice, and answer none: [8]
And some condemned for a fault alone.

Enter ELBOW, *and* Officers *with* FROTH *and* POMPEY.

ELBOW
Come, bring them away: if these be good people in a commonweal that do nothing but use their abuses in common houses, I know no law: bring them away.

ANGELO
How now, sir! What's your name? and what's the matter?

ELBOW
If it please your honour, I am the poor duke's constable, and my name is Elbow: I do lean upon justice, sir, and do bring in here before your good honour two notorious benefactors.

ANGELO
Benefactors? Well; what benefactors are they? are they not malefactors?

ELBOW
If it please your honour, I know not well what they are: but precise villains they are, that I am sure of; and void of all profanation in the world that good Christians ought to have.

ESCALUS
This comes off well; here's a wise officer.

ANGELO
Go to: what quality are they of? Elbow is your name? why dost thou not speak, Elbow?

POMPEY
He cannot sir; he's out at elbow.

ANGELO
What are you, sir?

ELBOW
He, sir! a tapster, sir; parcel-bawd; one that serves a bad woman; whose house, sir, was, as they say, plucked down in the suburbs; and now she professes a hothouse, which, I think, is a very ill house too.

ESCALUS
How know you that?

ELBOW
My wife, sir, whom I detest before heaven and your honour,—

ESCALUS
How? thy wife?

ELBOW
Ay, sir; whom, I thank heaven, is an honest woman,—

ESCALUS
Dost thou detest her therefore?

ELBOW
I say, sir, I will detest myself also, as well as she, that this house, if it be not a bawd's house, it is pity of her life, for it is a naughty house.
ESCALUS
How dost thou know that, constable?
ELBOW
Marry, sir, by my wife; who, if she had been a woman cardinally given, might have been accused in fornication, adultery, and all uncleanliness there.
ESCALUS
By the woman's means?
ELBOW
Ay, sir, by Mistress Overdone's means: but as she spit in his face, so she defied him.
POMPEY
Sir, if it please your honour, this is not so.
ELBOW
Prove it before these varlets here, thou honourable man; prove it.
ESCALUS
Do you hear how he misplaces?
POMPEY
Sir, she came in great with child; and longing, saving your honour's reverence, for stewed prunes; sir, we had but two in the house, which at that very distant time stood, as it were, in a fruit-dish, a dish of some three-pence; your honours have seen such dishes; they are not China dishes, but very good dishes,—
ESCALUS
Go to, go to: no matter for the dish, sir.
POMPEY
No, indeed, sir, not of a pin; you are therein in the right: but to the point. As I say, this Mistress Elbow, being, as I say, with child, and being great-bellied, and longing, as I said, for prunes; and having but two in the dish, as I said, Master Froth here, this very man, having eaten the rest, as I said, and, as I say, paying for them very honestly; for, as you know, Master Froth, I could not give you three-pence again.
FROTH
No, indeed.
POMPEY
Very well: you being then, if you be remembered, cracking the stones of the foresaid prunes,—
FROTH
Ay, so I did indeed.
POMPEY
Why, very well; I telling you then, if you be remembered, that such a one and such a one were past cure of the thing you wot of, unless they kept very good diet, as I told you,—
FROTH
All this is true.
POMPEY
Why, very well, then,—
ESCALUS
Come, you are a tedious fool: to the purpose. What was done to Elbow's wife, that he hath cause to complain of? Come me to what was done to her.
POMPEY
Sir, your honour cannot come to that yet.
ESCALUS
No, sir, nor I mean it not.
POMPEY
Sir, but you shall come to it, by your honour's leave. And, I beseech you, look into Master Froth here, sir; a man of fourscore pound a year; whose father died at Hallowmas: was't not at Hallowmas, Master Froth?
FROTH
All-hallond eve.
POMPEY
Why, very well; I hope here be truths. He, sir, sitting, as I say, in a lower chair, sir; 'twas in the Bunch of Grapes, where indeed you have a delight to sit, have you not?
FROTH
I have so; because it is an open room and good for winter. [9]
POMPEY
Why, very well, then; I hope here be truths.
ANGELO
This will last out a night in Russia,
When nights are longest there: I'll take my
leave.
And leave you to the hearing of the cause;
Hoping you'll find good cause to whip them all.
ESCALUS
I think no less. Good morrow to your lordship.
[*Exit Angelo.*
Now, sir, come on: what was done to Elbow's wife, once more?
POMPEY
Once, sir? there was nothing done to her once.
ELBOW
I beseech you, sir, ask him what this man did to my wife.
POMPEY
I beseech your honour, ask me.
ESCALUS
Well, sir; what did this gentleman to her?
POMPEY
I beseech you, sir, look in this gentleman's face.
Good Master Froth, look upon his honour; 'tis for a good purpose. Doth your honour mark his face?
ESCALUS
Ay, sir, very well.

POMPEY
Nay, I beseech you, mark it well.

ESCALUS
Well, I do so.

POMPEY
Doth your honour see any harm in his face?

ESCALUS
Why, no.

POMPEY
I'll be supposed upon a book, his face is the worst thing about him. Good, then; if his face be the worst thing about him, how could Master Froth do the constable's wife any harm? I would know that of your honour.

ESCALUS
He's in the right. Constable, what say you to it?

ELBOW
First, an it like you, the house is a respected house; next, this is a respected fellow; and his mistress is a respected woman.

POMPEY
By this hand, sir, his wife is a more respected person than any of us all.

ELBOW
Varlet, thou liest; thou liest, wicked varlet! the time is yet to come that she was ever respected with man, woman, or child.

POMPEY
Sir, she was respected with him before he married with her.

ESCALUS
Which is the wiser here? Justice or Iniquity? Is this true?

ELBOW
O thou caitiff! O thou varlet! O thou wicked Hannibal! I respected with her before I was married to her! If ever I was respected with her, or she with me, let not your worship think me the poor duke's officer. Prove this, thou wicked Hannibal, or I'll have mine action of battery on thee.

ESCALUS
If he took you a box o' the ear, you might have your action of slander too.

ELBOW
Marry, I thank your good worship for it. What is't your worship's pleasure I shall do with this wicked caitiff?

ESCALUS
Truly, officer, because he hath some offences in him that thou wouldst discover if thou couldst let him continue in his courses till thou knowest what they are.

ELBOW
Marry, I thank your worship for it. Thou seest, thou wicked varlet, now, what's come upon thee: thou art to continue now, thou varlet; thou art to continue.

ESCALUS
Where were you born, friend?

FROTH
Here in Vienna, sir.

ESCALUS
Are you of fourscore pounds a year?

FROTH
Yes, an't please you, sir.

ESCALUS
So. What trade are you of, sir?

POMPEY
A tapster; a poor widow's tapster.

ESCALUS
Your mistress' name?

POMPEY
Mistress Overdone.

ESCALUS
Hath she had any more than one husband?

POMPEY
Nine, sir; Overdone by the last.

ESCALUS
Nine! Come hither to me, Master Froth. Master Froth, I would not have you acquainted with tapsters: they will draw you, Master Froth, and you will hang them. Get you gone, and let me hear no more of you.

FROTH
I thank your worship. For mine own part, I never come into any room in a tap-house, but I am drawn in.

ESCALUS
Well, no more of it, Master Froth: farewell.

[*Exit Froth.*

Come you hither to me, Master tapster. What's your name, Master tapster?

POMPEY
Pompey.

ESCALUS
What else?

POMPEY
Bum, sir.

ESCALUS
Troth, and your bum is the greatest thing about you; so that in the beastliest sense you are Pompey the Great. Pompey, you are partly a bawd, Pompey, howsoever you colour it in being a tapster, are you not? Come, tell me true: it shall be the better for you.

POMPEY
Truly, sir, I am a poor fellow that would live.

ESCALUS
How would you live, Pompey? by being a bawd? What do you think of the trade, Pompey? Is it a lawful trade?

POMPEY
If the law would allow it, sir.

ESCAL

But the law will not allow it, Pompey; nor it shall not be allowed in Vienna. 222

POMPEY

Does your worship mean to geld and splay all the youth of the city?

ESCAL

No, Pompey.

POMPEY

Truly, sir, in my poor opinion, they will to't then. If your worship will take order for the drabs and the knaves, you need not to fear the bawds.

ESCALUS

There are pretty orders beginning, I can tell you: it is but heading and hanging.

POMPEY

If you head and hang all that offend that way but for ten year together, you'll be glad to give out a commission for more heads: if this law hold in Vienna ten year, I'll rent the fairest house in it after three-pence a bay: if you live to see this come to pass, say Pompey told you so.

ESCALUS

Thank you, good Pompey; and, in requital of your prophecy, hark you, I advise you, let me not find you before me again upon any complaint whatsoever; no, not for dwelling where you do: if I do, Pompey, I shall beat you to your tent, and prove a shrewd Caesar to you; in plain dealing, Pompey, I shall have you whipt: so, for this time, Pompey, fare you well.

POMPEY

I thank your worship for your good counsel: [*Aside*] but I shall follow it as the flesh and fortune shall better determine.

Whip me? No, no; let carman whip his jade:
The valiant heart is not whipt out of his trade.
[*Exit.*

ESCALUS

Come hither to me, Master Elbow; come hither, Master constable. How long have you been in this place of constable?

ELBOW

Seven year and a half, sir.

ESCALUS

I thought, by your readiness in the office, you had continued in it some time. You say, seven years together?

ELBOW

And a half, sir.

ESCALUS

Alas, it hath been great pains to you. They do you wrong to put you so oft upon 't: are there not men in your ward sufficient to serve it?

ELBOW

Faith, sir, few of any wit in such matters: as they are chosen, they are glad to choose me for them; I do it for some piece of money, and go through with all.

ESCALUS

Look you bring me in the names of some six or seven, the most sufficient of your parish.

ELBOW

To your worship's house, sir?

ESCALUS

To my house. Fare you well. [*Exit Elbow.*
What's o'clock, think you? 268

JUSTICE

Eleven, sir.

ESCALUS

I pray you home to dinner with me.

JUSTICE

I humbly thank you.

ESCALUS

It grieves me for the death of Claudio; But there's no remedy.

JUSTICE

Lord Angelo is severe.

ESCALUS

It is but needful:
Mercy is not itself, that oft looks so;
Pardon is still the nurse of second woe:
But yet,—poor Claudio! There is no remedy.
Come, sir. [*Exeunt.*

ACT TWO SCENE TWO

Another room in the same.

Enter PROVOST *and a* Servant.

SERVANT

He's hearing of a cause; he will come straight:
I'll tell him of you.

PROVOST

Pray you, do. [*Exit Servant.*] I'll know
His pleasure; may be he will relent. Alas,
He hath but as offended in a dream!
All sects, all ages smack of this vice; and he
To die for't!

Enter ANGELO.

ANGELO

Now, what's the matter. Provost?

PROVOST

Is it your will Claudio shall die tomorrow?

ANGELO

Did not I tell thee yea? hadst thou not order?
Why dost thou ask again?

PROVOST
Lest I might be too rash:
Under your good correction, I have seen,
When, after execution, judgment hath
Repented o'er his doom.
ANGELO
Go to; let that be mine:
Do you your office, or give up your place,
And you shall well be spared.
PROVOST
I crave your honour's pardon.
What shall be done, sir, with the groaning Juliet?
She's very near her hour.
ANGELO
Dispose of her
To some more fitter place, and that with speed.

Re-enter Servant.

SERVANT
Here is the sister of the man condemn'd
Desires access to you.
ANGELO
Hath he a sister?
PROVOST
Ay, my good lord; a very virtuous maid,
And to be shortly of a sisterhood,
If not already.
ANGELO
Well, let her be admitted. [*Exit Servant.*
See you the fornicatress be removed:
Let her have needful, but not lavish, means;
There shall be order for't.

Enter ISABELLA *and* LUCIO.

PROVOST
God save your honour!
ANGELO
Stay a little while. [*To Isabella.*
You 're welcome: what's your will?
ISABELLA
I am a woeful suitor to your honour,
Please but your honour hear me.
ANGELO
Well; what's your suit?
ISABELLA
There is a vice that most I do abhor,
And most desire should meet the blow of justice;
For which I would not plead, but that I must;
For which I must not plead, but that I am
At war 'twixt will and will not.
ANGELO
Well; the matter?
ISABELLA
I have a brother is condemn'd to die:
I do beseech you, let it be his fault,
And not my brother.
PROVOST
[*Aside*] Heaven give thee moving graces!
ANGELO
Condemn the fault, and not the actor of it?
Why, every fault's condemn'd ere it be done:
Mine were the very cipher of a function,
To fine the faults whose fine stands in record,
And let go by the actor.
ISABELLA
O just but severe law!
I had a brother, then. Heaven keep your honour!
LUCIO
[*Aside to Isabella*] Give't not o'er so: to him again, entreat him;
Kneel down before him, hang upon his gown:
You are too cold; if you should need a pin,
You could not with more tame a tongue desire it:
To him, I say!
ISABELLA
Must he needs die?
ANGELO
Maiden, no remedy.
ISABELLA
Yes; I do think that you might pardon him,
And neither heaven nor man grieve at the mercy.
ANGELO
I will not do't.
ISABELLA
But can you, if you would?
ANGELO
Look, what I will not, that I cannot do.
ISABELLA
But might you do't, and do the world no wrong,
If so your heart were touch'd with that remorse
As mine is to him?
ANGELO
He's sentenced; 'tis too late.
LUCIO
[*Aside to Isabella*] You are too cold.
ISABELLA
Too late? why, no; I, that do speak a word.
May call it back again. Well, believe this,
No ceremony that to great ones 'longs,
Not the king's crown, nor the deputed sword,
The marshal's truncheon, nor the judge's robe,
Become them with one half so good a grace
As mercy does.
If he had been as you and you as he,
You would have slipt like him; but he, like you,
Would not have been so stern.

ANGELO
Pray you, be gone.
ISABELLA
I would to heaven I had your potency,
And you were Isabel! should it then be thus?
No; I would tell what 'twere to be a judge,
And what a prisoner.
LUCIO
[*Aside to Isabella*] Ay, touch him; there's the vein.
ANGELO
Your brother is a forfeit of the law,
And you but waste your words.
ISABELLA
Alas, alas!
Why, all the souls that were were forfeit once;
And He that might the vantage best have took
Found out the remedy. How would you be,
If He, which is the top of judgment, should
But judge you as you are? O, think on that;
And mercy then will breathe within your lips,
Like man new made. [10]
ANGELO
Be you content, fair maid;
It is the law, not I condemn your brother:
Were he my kinsman, brother, or my son,
It should be thus with him: he must die tomorrow.
ISABELLA
To-morrow! O, that's sudden! Spare him, spare him!
He's not prepared for death. Even for our kitchens
We kill the fowl of season: shall we serve heaven
With less respect than we do minister
To our gross selves? Good, good my lord, bethink you;
Who is it that hath died for this offence?
There's many have committed it.
LUCIO
[*Aside to Isabella*] Ay, well said.
ANGELO
The law hath not been dead, though it hath slept: [11]
Those many had not dared to do that evil,
If the first that did the edict infringe
Had answer'd for his deed: now 'tis awake
Takes note of what is done; and, like a prophet,
Looks in a glass, that shows what future evils,
Either new, or by remissness new-conceived,
And so in progress to be hatch'd and born,
Are now to have no successive degrees,
But, ere they live, to end.
ISABELLA
Yet show some pity.
ANGELO
I show it most of all when I show justice;
For then I pity those I do not know,
Which a dismiss'd offence would after gall;
And do him right that, answering one foul wrong,
Lives not to act another. Be satisfied;
Your brother dies to-morrow; be content.
ISABELLA
So you must be the first that gives this sentence,
And he, that suffers. O, it is excellent
To have a giant's strength; but it is tyrannous
To use it like a giant.
LUCIO
[*Aside to Isabella*] That's well said.
ISABELLA
Could great men thunder
As Jove himself does, Jove would ne'er be quiet,
For every pelting, petty officer
Would use his heaven for thunder;
Nothing but thunder! Merciful Heaven,
Thou rather with thy sharp and sulphurous bolt
Split'st the unwedgeable and gnarled oak
Than the soft myrtle: but man, proud man,
Drest in a little brief authority,
Most ignorant of what he's most assured,
His glassy essence, like an angry ape,
Plays such fantastic tricks before high heaven
As make the angels weep; who, with our spleens,
Would all themselves laugh mortal.
LUCIO
[*Aside to Isabella*] O, to him, to him, wench! he will relent;
He's coming; I perceive 't.
PROVOST
[*Aside*] Pray heaven she win him!
ISABELLA
We cannot weigh our brother with ourself:
Great men may jest with saints; 'tis wit in them,
But in the less foul profanation.
LUCIO
Thou'rt i' the right, girl; more o' that.
ISABELLA
That in the captain's but a choleric word,
Which in the soldier is flat blasphemy.
LUCIO
[*Aside to Isabella*] Art avised o' that? more on 't.
ANGELO
Why do you put these sayings upon me?
ISABELLA
Because authority, though it err like others,
Hath yet a kind of medicine in itself,
That skins the vice o' the top. Go to your bosom;
Knock there, and ask your heart what it doth know

That's like my brother's fault: if it confess
A natural guiltiness such as is his,
Let it not sound a thought upon your tongue
Against my brother's life.

ANGELO
[*Aside*] She speaks, and 'tis
Such sense, that my sense breeds with it. Fare you well.

ISABELLA
Gentle my lord, turn back.

ANGELO
I will bethink me: come again tomorrow.

ISABELLA
Hark how I'll bribe you: good my lord, turn back.

ANGELO
How! bribe me?

ISABELLA
Ay, with such gifts that heaven shall share with you.

LUCIO
[*Aside to Isabella*] You had marr'd all else.

ISABELLA
Not with fond shekels of the tested gold,
Or stones whose rates are either rich or poor
As fancy values them; but with true prayers
That shall be up at heaven and enter there
Ere sun-rise, prayers from preserved souls,
From fasting maids whose minds are dedicate
To nothing temporal.

ANGELO
Well; come to me to-morrow.

LUCIO
[*Aside to Isabella*] Go to; 'tis well; away!

ISABELLA
Heaven keep your honour safe!

ANGELO
[*Aside*] Amen:
For I am that way going to temptation,
Where prayers cross. [12]

ISABELLA
At what hour to-morrow
Shall I attend your worship?

ANGELO
At any time 'fore noon.

ISABELLA
'Save your honour!

[*Exeunt Isabella, Lucio, and Provost.*

ANGELO
From thee, even from thy virtue!
What's this, what's this? Is this her fault or mine,
The tempter or the tempted, who sins most?
Ha!
Not she; nor doth she tempt: but it is I
That, lying by the violet in the sun,
Do as the carrion does, not as the flower,
Corrupt with virtuous season. Can it be
That modesty may more betray our sense
Than woman's lightness? Having waste ground enough,
Shall we desire to raze the sanctuary
And pitch our evils there? O, fie, fie, fie!
What dost thou, or what art thou, Angelo?
Dost thou desire her foully for those things
That make her good? O, let her brother live:
Thieves for their robbery have authority
When judges steal themselves. What, do I love her,
That I desire to hear her speak again,
And feast upon her eyes? What is't I dream on?
O cunning enemy, that, to catch a saint,
With saints dost bait thy hook! Most dangerous
Is that temptation that doth goad us on
To sin in loving virtue: never could the strumpet,
With all her double vigour, art and nature,
Once stir my temper: but this virtuous maid
Subdues me quite. Even till now,
When men were fond, I smiled and wonder'd how.

[*Exit.*

ACT TWO SCENE THREE

A room in a prison.

Enter, severally, DUKE *disguised as a friar, and* PROVOST.

DUKE
Hail to you, provost! so I think you are.

PROVOST
I am the provost. What's your will, good friar?

DUKE
Bound by my charity and my blest order,
I come to visit the afflicted spirits
Here in the prison. Do me the common right
To let me see them and to make me know
The nature of their crimes, that I may minister
To them accordingly.

PROVOST
I would do more than that, if more were needed.

Enter JULIET.

Look, here comes one: a gentlewoman of mine,
Who, falling in the flaws of her own youth, [13]
Hath blister'd her report: she is with child;
And he that got it, sentenced; a young man

More fit to do another such office
Than die for this.

DUKE
When must he die?

PROVOST
As I do think, to-morrow.
I have provided for you: stay awhile, [*To Juliet.*
And you shall be conducted.

DUKE
Repent you, fair one, of the sin you carry?

JULIET
I do; and bear the shame most patiently. 21

DUKE
I'll teach you how you shall arraign your conscience,
And try your penitence, if it be sound,
Or hollowly put on.

JULIET
I'll gladly learn.

DUKE
Love you the man that wrong'd you?

JULIET
Yes, as I love the woman that wrong'd him.

DUKE
So then it seems your most offenceful act
Was mutually committed?

JULIET
Mutually.

DUKE
Then was your sin of heavier kind than his.

JULIET
I do confess it, and repent it, father.

DUKE
'Tis meet so, daughter: but lest you do repent, 34
As that the sin hath brought you to this shame,
Which sorrow is always towards ourselves, not heaven,
Showing we would not spare heaven as we love it,
But as we stand in fear,—

JULIET
I do repent me, as it is an evil,
And take the shame with joy.

DUKE
There rest.
Your partner, as I hear, must die to-morrow,
And I am going with instruction to him.
Grace go with you, Benedicite! [*Exit.*

JULIET
Must die to-morrow! O injurious love, [14]
That respites me a life, whose very comfort 47
Is still a dying horror!

PROVOST
'Tis pity of him. [*Exeunt.*

ACT TWO SCENE FOUR

A room in ANGELO'S *house.*

Enter ANGELO.

ANGELO
When I would pray and think, I think and pray
To several subjects. Heaven hath my empty words;
Whilst my invention, hearing not my tongue,
Anchors on Isabel: Heaven in my mouth,
As if I did but only chew his name;
And in my heart the strong and swelling evil
Of my conception. The state, whereon I studied
Is like a good thing, being often read,
Grown fear'd and tedious; yea, my gravity, [15]
Wherein—let no man hear me—I take pride,
Could I with boot change for an idle plume,
Which the air beats for vain. O place, O form,
How often dost thou with thy case, thy habit,
Wrench awe from fools and tie the wiser souls
To thy false seeming! Blood, thou art blood:
Let's write good angel on the devil's horn:
'Tis not the devil's crest.

Enter a SERVANT.

Now now! who's there?

SERVANT
One Isabel, a sister, desires access to you.

ANGELO
Teach her the way. [*Exit Servant*] O heavens!
Why does my blood thus muster to my heart,
Making both it unable for itself,
And dispossessing all my other parts
Of necessary fitness?
So play the foolish throngs with one that swoons;
Come all to help him, and so stop the air
By which he should revive: and even so
The general, subject to a well-wish'd king,
Quit their own part, and in obsequious fondness
Crowd to his presence, where their untaught love
Must needs appear offence.

Enter ISABELLA.

How now, fair maid?

ISABELLA
I am come to know your pleasure. 33

ANGELO
That you might know it, would much better please me
Than to demand what 'tis. Your brother cannot live.

ISABELLA
Even so. Heaven keep your honour!

ANGELO
Yet may he live awhile; and, it may be,
As long as you or I: yet he must die.

ISABELLA
Under your sentence?
ANGELO
Yea.
ISABELLA
When, I beseech you? that in his reprieve,
Longer or shorter, he may be so fitted 42
That his soul sicken not.
ANGELO
Ha! fie, these filthy vices! It were as good
To pardon him that hath from nature stolen
A man already made, as to remit
Their saucy sweetness that do coin heaven's image
In stamps that are forbid: 'tis all as easy
Falsely to take away a life true made
As to put metal in restrained means
To make a false one.
ISABELLA
'Tis set down so in heaven, but not in earth. 52
ANGELO
Say you so? then I shall pose you quickly.
Which had you rather, that the most just law
Now took your brother's life; or, to redeem him,
Give up your body to such sweet uncleanness
As she that he hath stain'd?
ISABELLA
Sir, believe this,
I had rather give my body than my soul.
ANGELO
I talk not of your soul: our compell'd sins
Stand more for number than for accompt.
ISABELLA
How say you?
ANGELO
Nay, I'll not warrant that; for I can speak
Against the thing I say. Answer to this: 64
I, now the voice of the recorded law,
Pronounce a sentence on your brother's life:
Might there not be a charity in sin
To save this brother's life?
ISABELLA
Please you to do't,
I'll take it as a peril to my soul,
It is no sin at all, but charity.
ANGELO
Pleased you to do't at peril of your soul,
Were equal poise of sin and charity.
ISABELLA
That I do beg his life, if it be sin,
Heaven let me bear it! you granting of my suit, 76
If that be sin, I'll make it my morn prayer
To have it added to the faults of mine,
And nothing of your answer.
ANGELO
Nay, but hear me.
Your sense pursues not mine: either you are ignorant,
Or seem so craftily; and that's not good.
ISABELLA
Let me be ignorant, and in nothing good,
But graciously to know I am no better.
ANGELO
Thus wisdom wishes to appear most bright
When it doth tax itself; as these black masks
Proclaim an enshield beauty ten times louder 87
Than beauty could, display'd. But mark me;
To be received plain, I'll speak more gross:
Your brother is to die.
ISABELLA
So.
ANGELO
And his offence is so, as it appears,
Accountant to the law upon that pain.
ISABELLA
True.
ANGELO
Admit no other way to save his life,—
As I subscribe not that, nor any other,
But in the loss of question,—that you, his sister,
Finding yourself desired of such a person, 98
Whose credit with the judge, or own great place,
Could fetch your brother from the manacles
Of the all-building law; and that there were
No earthly mean to save him, but that either
You must lay down the treasures of your body
To this supposed, or else to let him suffer;
What would you do?
ISABELLA
As much for my poor brother as myself:
That is, were I under the terms of death, 107
The impression of keen whips I'ld wear as rubies,
And strip myself to death, as to a bed
That longing have been sick for, ere I'ld yield [16]
My body up to shame.
ANGELO
Then must your brother die.
ISABELLA
And 'twere the cheaper way:
Better it were a brother died at once,
Than that a sister, by redeeming him,
Should die for ever.
ANGELO
Were not you then as cruel as the sentence
That you have slander'd so? 118
ISABELLA
Ignomy in ransom and free pardon
Are of two houses: lawful mercy
Is nothing kin to foul redemption.

ANGELO
You seem'd of late to make the law a tyrant;
And rather proved the sliding of your brother
A merriment than a vice.
ISABELLA
O, pardon me, my lord; it oft falls out,
To have what we would have, we speak not what we mean:
I something do excuse the thing I hate,
For his advantage that I dearly love.
ANGELO
We are all frail.
ISABELLA
Else let my brother die,
If not a feodary, but only he
Owe and succeed thy weakness.
ANGELO
Nay, women are frail too.
ISABELLA
Ay, as the glasses where they view themselves;
Which are as easy broke as they make forms.
Women! Help Heaven! men their creation mar
In profiting by them. Nay, call us ten times frail;
For we are soft as our complexions are,
And credulous to false prints.
ANGELO
I think it well:
And from this testimony of your own sex,—
Since I suppose we are made to be no stronger
Than faults may shake our frames,—let me be bold:
I do arrest your words. Be that you are,
That is, a woman; if you be more, you're none;
If you be one, as you are well express'd
By all external warrants, show it now,
By putting on the destined livery.
ISABELLA
I have no tongue but one: gentle my lord,
Let me entreat you speak the former language.
ANGELO
Plainly conceive, I love you.
ISABELLA
My brother did love Juliet,
And you tell me that he shall die for it.
ANGELO
He shall not, Isabel, if you give me love.
ISABELLA
I know your virtue hath a licence in't,
Which seems a little fouler than it is,
To pluck on others.
ANGELO
Believe me, on mine honour,
My words express my purpose.
ISABELLA
Ha! little honour to be much believed,
And most pernicious purpose! Seeming, seeming!
I will proclaim thee, Angelo; look for't:
Sign me a present pardon for my brother,
Or with an outstretch'd throat I'll tell the world aloud
What man thou art.
ANGELO
Who will believe thee, Isabel?
My unsoil'd name, the austereness of my life,
My vouch against you, and my place i' the state,
Will so your accusation overweigh,
That you shall stifle in your own report
And smell of calumny. I have begun,
And now I give my sensual race the rein:
Fit thy consent to my sharp appetite;
Lay by all nicety and prolixious blushes,
That banish what they sue for; redeem thy brother
By yielding up thy body to my will;
Or else he must not only die the death,
But thy unkindness shall his death draw out
To lingering sufferance. Answer me to-morrow,
Or, by the affection that now guides me most,
I'll prove a tyrant to him. As for you,
Say what you can, my false o'erweighs your true.
[*Exit.*

ISABELLA
To whom should I complain? Did I tell this,
Who would believe me? O perilous mouths, [17]
That bear in them one and the self-same tongue,
Either of condemnation or approof;
Bidding the law make court'sy to their will;
Hooking both right and wrong to the appetite,
To follow as it draws! I'll to my brother:
Though he hath fall'n by prompture of the blood,
Yet hath he in him such a mind of honour.
That, had he twenty heads to tender down
On twenty bloody blocks, he 'ld yield them up,
Before his sister should her body stoop
To such abhorr'd pollution.
Then, Isabel, live chaste, and, brother, die:
More than our brother is our chastity.
I'll tell him yet of Angelo's request,
And fit his mind to death, for his soul's rest.
[*Exit.*

ACT THREE SCENE ONE

A room in the prison.

Enter DUKE *disguised as before,* CLAUDIO, *and* PROVOST.

DUKE
So then you hope of pardon from Lord Angelo?

DUKE So; then, you hope of pardon from Lord Angelo?

CLAUDIO
The miserable have no other medicine
But only hope:
I've hope to live, and am prepared to die.
DUKE
Be absolute for death; either death or life
Shall thereby be the sweeter. Reason thus with life:
If I do lose thee, I do lose a thing
That none but fools would keep: a breath thou art,
Servile to all the skyey influences,
That dost this habitation, where thou keep'st,
Hourly afflict: merely, thou art death's fool;
For him thou labour'st by thy flight to shun
And yet runn'st toward him still. Thou art not noble;
For all the accommodations that thou bear'st
Are nursed by baseness. Thou'rt by no means valiant;
For thou dost fear the soft and tender fork
Of a poor worm. Thy best of rest is sleep,
And that thou oft provokest; yet grossly fear'st
Thy death, which is no more. Thou art not thyself;
For thou exist'st on many a thousand grains
That issue out of dust. Happy thou art not;
For what thou hast not, still thou strivest to get,
And what thou hast, forget'st. Thou art not certain;
For thy complexion shifts to strange effects,
After the moon. If thou art rich, thou'rt poor;
For, like an ass whose back with ingots bows,
Thou bear's thy heavy riches but a journey,
And death unloads thee. Friend hast thou none;
For thine own bowels, which do call thee sire,
The mere effusion of thy proper loins,
Do curse the gout, serpigo, and the rheum,
For ending thee no sooner. Thou hast nor youth nor age,
But, as it were, an after-dinner's sleep,
Dreaming on both; for all thy blessed youth
Becomes as aged, and doth beg the alms
Of palsied eld; and when thou art old and rich,
Thou hast neither heat, affection, limb, nor beauty,
To make thy riches pleasant. What's yet in this

That bears the name of life? Yet in this life
Lie hid moe thousand deaths: yet death we fear,
That makes these odds all even.

CLAUDIO
I humbly thank you.
To sue to live, I find I seek to die;
And, seeking death, find life: let it come on.

ISABELLA
[*Within*] What, ho! Peace here; grace and good company!

PROVOST
Who's there? come in: the wish deserves a welcome.

DUKE
Dear sir, ere long I'll visit you again.

CLAUDIO
Most holy sir, I thank you.

Enter ISABELLA.

ISABELLA
My business is a word or two with Claudio.

PROVOST
And very welcome. Look, signior, here's your sister.

DUKE
Provost, a word with you.

PROVOST
As many as you please.

DUKE
Bring me to hear them speak, where I may be concealed. [*Exeunt Duke and Provost.*

CLAUDIO
Now, sister, what's the comfort?

ISABELLA
Why,
As all comforts are; most good, most good indeed.
Lord Angelo, having affairs to heaven,
Intends you for his swift ambassador,
Where you shall be an everlasting leiger:
Therefore your best appointment make with speed;
To-morrow you set on.

CLAUDIO
Is there no remedy?

ISABELLA
None, but such remedy as, to save a head,
To cleave a heart in twain.

CLAUDIO
But is there any?

ISABELLA
Yes, brother, you may live:
There is a devilish mercy in the judge,
If you'll implore it, that will free your life,
But fetter you till death.

CLAUDIO
Perpetual durance?

ISABELLA
Ay, just; perpetual durance, a restraint,
Though all the world's vastidity you had,
To a determined scope.

CLAUDIO
But in what nature?

ISABELLA
In such a one as, you consenting to't,
Would bark your honour from that trunk you bear,
And leave you naked.

CLAUDIO
Let me know the point.

ISABELLA
O, I do fear thee, Claudio; and I quake,
Lest thou a feverous life shouldst entertain,
And six or seven winters more respect
Than a perpetual honour. Darest thou die?
The sense of death is most in apprehension;
And the poor beetle, that we tread upon,
In corporal sufferance finds a pang as great
As when a giant dies.

CLAUDIO
Why give you me this shame?
Think you I can a resolution fetch
From flowery tenderness? If I must die,
I will encounter darkness as a bride,
And hug it in mine arms.

ISABELLA
There spake my brother; there my father's grave
Did utter forth a voice. Yes, thou must die:
Thou art too noble to conserve a life
In base appliances. This outward-sainted deputy,
Whose settled visage and deliberate word
Nips youth i' the head and follies doth emmew
As falcon doth the fowl, is yet a devil
His filth within being cast, he would appear
A pond as deep as hell.

CLAUDIO
The prenzie Angelo! [18]

ISABELLA
O, 'tis the cunning livery of hell,
The damned'st body to invest and cover
In prenzie guards! Dost thou think, Claudio?
If I would yield him my virginity,
Thou mightst be freed.

CLAUDIO
O heavens! it cannot be.

ISABELLA
Yes, he would give't thee, from this rank offence,
So to offend him still. This night's the time
That I should do what I abhor to name,
Or else thou diest to-morrow.

CLAUDIO
Thou shalt not do't.
ISABELLA
O, were it but my life,
I'ld throw it down for your deliverance
As frankly as a pin.
CLAUDIO
Thanks, dear Isabel.
ISABELLA
Be ready, Claudio, for your death to-morrow.
CLAUDIO
Yes. Has he affections in him,
That thus can make him bite the law by the nose,
When he would force it? Sure, it is no sin,
Or of the deadly seven, it is the least.
ISABELLA
Which is the least?
CLAUDIO
If it were damnable, he being so wise,
Why would he for the momentary trick
Be perdurably fined? O Isabel!
ISABELLA
What says my brother?
CLAUDIO
Death is a fearful thing.
ISABELLA
And shamed life a hateful.
CLAUDIO
Ay, but to die, and go we know not where;
To lie in cold obstruction and to rot;
This sensible warm motion to become
A kneaded clod; and the delighted spirit
To bathe in fiery floods, or to reside
In thrilling region of thick-ribbed ice;
To be imprison'd in the viewless winds,
And blown with restless violence round about
The pendent world; or to be worse than worst
Of those that lawless and incertain thought
Imagine howling: 'tis too horrible!
The weariest and most loathed worldly life
That age, ache, penury and imprisonment
Can lay on nature is a paradise
To what we fear of death.
ISABELLA
Alas, alas!
CLAUDIO
Sweet sister, let me live:
What sin you do to save a brother's life,
Nature dispenses with the deed so far
That it becomes a virtue.
ISABELLA
O you beast!
O faithless coward! O dishonest wretch!
Wilt thou be made a man out of my vice?
Is't not a kind of incest, to take life
From thine own sister's shame? What should I think?
Heaven shield my mother play'd my father fair!
For such a warped slip of wilderness
Ne'er issued from his blood. Take my defiance!
Die, perish! Might but my bending down
Reprieve thee from thy fate, it should proceed:
I'll pray a thousand prayers for thy death,
No word to save thee.
CLAUDIO
Nay, hear me, Isabel.
ISABELLA
O, fie, fie, fie!
Thy sin's not accidental, but a trade.
Mercy to thee would prove itself a bawd:
'Tis best thou diest quickly.
CLAUDIO
O hear me, Isabella!

Re-enter DUKE.

DUKE
Vouchsafe a word, young sister, but one word.
ISABELLA
What is your will?
DUKE
Might you dispense with your leisure, I would by and by have some speech with you: the satisfaction I would require is likewise your own benefit.
ISABELLA
I have no superfluous leisure; my stay must be stolen out of other affairs; but I will attend you awhile.
[*Walks apart.*
DUKE
Son, I have overheard what hath passed between you and your sister. Angelo had never the purpose to corrupt her; only he hath made an essay of her virtue to practise his judgment with the disposition of natures: she, having the truth of honour in her, hath made him that gracious denial which he is most glad to receive. I am confessor to Angelo, and I know this to be true; therefore prepare yourself to death: do not satisfy your resolution with hopes that are fallible: to-morrow you must die; go to your knees and make ready.
CLAUDIO
Let me ask my sister pardon. I am so out of love with life that I will sue to be rid of it.
DUKE
Hold you there: farewell. [*Exit Claudio.*] Provost, a word with you!

Re-enter PROVOST.

PROVOST
What's your will, father?

DUKE

That now you are come, you will be gone. Leave me awhile with the maid: my mind promises with my habit no loss shall touch her by my company.

PROVOST

In good time. [*Exit Provost. Isabella comes forward.*

DUKE

The hand that hath made you fair hath made you good: the goodness that is cheap in beauty makes beauty brief in goodness; but grace, being the soul of your complexion, shall keep the body of it ever fair. The assault that Angelo hath made to you, fortune hath conveyed to my understanding; and, but that frailty hath examples for his falling, I should wonder at Angelo. How will you do to content this substitute, and to save your brother?

ISABELLA

I am now going to resolve him; I had rather my brother die by the law than my son should be unlawfully born. But, O, how much is the good duke deceived in Angelo! If ever he return and I can speak to him, I will open my lips in vain, or discover his government.

DUKE

That shall not be much amiss: yet, as the matter now stands, he will avoid your accusation; he made trial of you only. Therefore fasten your ear on my advisings: to the love I have in doing good a remedy presents itself. I do make myself believe that you may most uprighteously do a poor wronged lady a merited benefit; redeem your brother from the angry law; do no stain to your own gracious person; and much please the absent duke, if peradventure he shall ever return to have hearing of this business. 223

ISABELLA

Let me hear you speak farther. I have spirit to do anything that appears not foul in the truth of my spirit.

DUKE

Virtue is bold, and goodness never fearful. Have you not heard speak of Mariana, the sister of Frederick the great soldier who miscarried at sea?

ISABELLA

I have heard of the lady, and good words went with her name. 231

DUKE

She should this Angelo have married; was affianced to her by oath, and the nuptial appointed: between which time of the contract and limit of the solemnity, her brother Frederick was wrecked at sea, having in that perished vessel the dowry of his sister. But mark how heavily this befell to the poor gentlewoman: there she lost a noble and renowned brother, in his love toward her ever most kind and natural; with him, the portion and sinew of her fortune, her marriage-dowry; with both, her combinate husband, this well-seeming Angelo.

ISABELLA

Can this be so? did Angelo so leave her?

DUKE

Left her in her tears, and dried not one of them with his comfort; swallowed his vows whole, pretending in her discoveries of dishonour: in few, bestowed her on her own lamentation, which she yet wears for his sake; and he, a marble to her tears, is washed with them, but relents not.

ISABELLA

What a merit were it in death to take this poor maid from the world! What corruption in this life, that it will let this man live! But how out of this can she avail?

DUKE

It is a rupture that you may easily heal: and the cure of it not only saves your brother, but keeps you from dishonour in doing it.

ISABELLA

Show me how, good father.

DUKE

This forenamed maid hath yet in her the continuance of her first affection: his unjust unkindness, that in all reason should have quenched her love, hath, like an impediment in the current, made it more violent and unruly. Go you to Angelo; answer his requiring with a plausible obedience; agree with his demands to the point; only refer yourself to this advantage, first, that your stay with him may not be long; that the time may have all shadow and silence in it; and the place answer to convenience. This being granted in course,—and now follows all,—we shall advise this wronged maid to stead up your appointment, go in your place; if the encounter acknowledge itself hereafter, it may compel him to her recompense: and here, by this, is your brother saved, your honour untainted, the poor Mariana advantaged, and the corrupt deputy scaled. The maid will I frame and make fit for his attempt. If you think well to carry this as you may, the doubleness of the benefit defends the deceit from reproof. What think you of it?

ISABELLA

The image of it gives me content already; and I trust it will grow to a most prosperous perfection.

DUKE

It lies much in your holding up. Haste you speedily to Angelo: if for this night he entreat you to his bed, give him promise of satisfaction. I will presently to Saint Luke's: there, at the moated grange, resides this dejected Mariana. At that place call upon me; and dispatch with Angelo, that it may be quickly. 283

ISABELLA

I thank you for this comfort. Fare you well, good father. [*Exeunt severally.*

ACT THREE SCENE TWO

The street before the prison.

Enter, on one side, DUKE *disguised as before; on the other,* ELBOW, *and* Officers *with* POMPEY.

ELBOW
Nay, if there be no remedy for it, but that you will needs buy and sell men and women like beasts, we shall have all the world drink brown and white bastard.

DUKE
O heavens! what stuff is here?

POMPEY
'Twas never merry world since, of two usuries, the merriest was put down, and the worser allowed by order of law a furred gown to keep him warm; and furred with fox and lambskins too, to signify, that craft, being richer than innocency, stands for the facing. [19]

ELBOW
Come your way, sir. 'Bless you, good father friar.

DUKE
And you, good brother father. What offence hath this man made you, sir? [20]

ELBOW
Marry, sir, he hath offended the law: and, sir, we take him to be a thief too, sir; for we have found upon him, sir, a strange picklock, which we have sent to the deputy.

DUKE
Fie, sirrah! a bawd, a wicked bawd!
The evil that thou causest to be done,
That is thy means to live. Do thou but think
What 'tis to cram a maw or clothe a back
From such a filthy vice: say to thyself,
From their abominable and beastly touches
I drink, I eat, array myself, and live.
Canst thou believe thy living is a life,
So stinkingly depending? Go mend, go mend.

POMPEY
Indeed, it does stink in some sort, sir; but yet, sir, I would prove—

DUKE
Nay, if the devil have given thee proofs for sin,
Thou wilt prove his. Take him to prison, officer:
Correction and instruction must both work
Ere this rude beast will profit.

ELBOW
He must before the deputy, sir; he has given him warning: the deputy cannot abide a whoremaster: if he be a whoremonger, and comes before him, he were as good go a mile on his errand.

DUKE
That we were all, as some would seem to be,
†From our fault as faults from seeming, free! [21]

ELBOW
His neck will come to your waist,—a cord, sir.

POMPEY
I spy comfort; I cry bail. Here's a gentleman and a friend of mine.

Enter LUCIO.

LUCIO
How now, noble Pompey! What, at the wheels of Caesar? art thou led in triumph? What, is there none of Pygmalion's images, newly made woman, to be had now, for putting the hand in the pocket and extracting it clutched? What reply, ha? What sayest thou to this tune, matter and method? Is't not drowned i' the last rain, ha? What sayest thou, Trot? Is the world as it was, man? Which is the way? Is it sad, and few words? or how? The trick of it?

DUKE
Still thus, and thus; still worse!

LUCIO
How doth my dear morsel, thy mistress? Procures she still, ha?

POMPEY
Troth, sir, she hath eaten up all her beef, and she is herself in the tub.

LUCIO
Why, 'tis good; it is the right of it; it must be so: ever your fresh whore and your powdered bawd: an unshunned consequence; it must be so. Art going to prison, Pompey?

POMPEY
Yes, faith, sir.

LUCIO
Why, 'tis not amiss, Pompey. Farewell: go, say I sent thee thither. For debt, Pompey, or how?

ELBOW
For being a bawd, for being a bawd.

LUCIO
Well, then, imprison him: if imprisonment be the due of a bawd, why, 'tis his right: bawd is he doubtless, and of antiquity too; bawd-born. Farewell, good Pompey. Commend me to the prison, Pompey: you will turn good husband now, Pompey; you will keep the house.

POMPEY
I hope, sir, your good worship will be my bail.

LUCIO
No, indeed, will I not, Pompey; it is not the wear. I will pray, Pompey, to increase your bondage: If you take it not patiently, why, your mettle is the more. Adieu, trusty Pompey. 'Bless you, friar.

DUKE
And you.

LUCIO
Does Bridget paint still, Pompey, ha?

ELBOW
Come your ways, sir; come.

POMPEY
You will not bail me, then, sir?

LUCIO
Then, Pompey, nor now. What news abroad, friar? what news?

ELBOW
Come your ways, sir; come.

LUCIO
Go to kennel, Pompey; go. [*Exeunt Elbow, Pompey and Officers.*] What news, friar, of the duke? 81

DUKE
I know none. Can you tell me of any?

LUCIO
Some say he is with the Emperor of Russia; other some, he is in Rome: but where is he, think you?

DUKE
I know not where; but wheresoever, I wish him well.

LUCIO
It was a mad fantastical trick of him to steal from the state, and usurp the beggary he was never born to. Lord Angelo dukes it well in his absence; he puts
transgression to 't. 90

DUKE
He does well in 't.

LUCIO
A little more lenity to lechery would do no harm in him: something too crabbed that way, friar.

DUKE
It is too general a vice, and severity must cure it.

LUCIO
Yes, in good sooth, the vice is of a great kindred; it is well allied: but it is impossible to extirp it quite, friar, till eating and drinking be put down. They say this Angelo was not made by man and woman after this downright way of creation: is it true, think you?

DUKE
How should he be made, then?

LUCIO
Some report a sea-maid spawned him; some, that he was begot between two stock-fishes. But it is certain that when he makes water his urine is congealed ice; that I know to be true: †and he is a motion generative; that's infallible.

DUKE
You are pleasant, sir, and speak apace. 106

LUCIO
Why, what a ruthless thing is this in him, for the rebellion of a codpiece to take away the life of a man! Would the duke that is absent have done this? Ere he would have hanged a man for the getting a hundred bastards, he would have paid for the nursing a thousand: he had some feeling of the sport: he knew the service, and that instructed him to mercy.

DUKE
I never heard the absent duke much detected for women; he was not inclined that way.

LUCIO
O, sir, you are deceived. 116

DUKE
'Tis not possible.

LUCIO
Who, not the duke? yes, your beggar of fifty; and his use was to put a ducat in her clack-dish: the duke had crotchets in him. He would be drunk too; that let me inform you.

DUKE
You do him wrong, surely.

LUCIO
Sir, I was an inward of his. A shy fellow was the duke: and I believe I know the cause of his with-
drawing. 125

DUKE
What, I prithee, might be the cause?

LUCIO
No, pardon; 'tis a secret must be locked within the teeth and the lips: but this I can let you understand, the greater file of the subject held the duke to be wise.

DUKE
Wise! why, no question but he was.

LUCIO
A very superficial, ignorant, unweighing fellow.

DUKE
Either this is the envy in you, folly, or mistaking: the very stream of his life and the business he hath helmed must upon a warranted need give him a better proclamation. Let him be but testimonied in his own bringings-forth, and he shall appear to the envious a scholar, a statesman and a soldier. Therefore you speak unskilfully; or if your knowledge be more it is much darkened in your malice.

LUCIO
Sir, I know him, and I love him.

DUKE
Love talks with better knowledge, and knowledge
with dearer love. 143

LUCIO
Come, sir, I know what I know.

DUKE
I can hardly believe that, since you know not what you speak. But, if ever the duke return, as our prayers are he may, let me desire you to make your answer before him. If it be honest you have spoke, you have courage to maintain it: I am bound to call upon you; and, I pray you, your name?

LUCIO

Sir, my name is Lucio; well known to the duke. 152

DUKE

He shall know you better, sir, if I may live to report you.

LUCIO

I fear you not.

DUKE

O, you hope the duke will return no more; or you imagine me too unhurtful an opposite. But indeed I can do you little harm; you'll forswear this again.

LUCIO

I'll be hanged first: thou art deceived in me, friar. But no more of this. Canst thou tell if Claudio die to-morrow or no? 160

DUKE

Why should he die, sir?

LUCIO

Why? For filling a bottle with a tun-dish. I would the duke we talk of were returned again: the ungenitured agent will unpeople the province with continency; sparrows must not build in his house-eaves, because they are lecherous. The duke yet would have dark deeds darkly answered; he would never bring them to light: would he were returned! Marry, this Claudio is condemned for untrussing. Farewell, good friar: I prithee, pray for me. The duke, I say to thee again, would eat mutton on Fridays. He's not past it yet, and I say to thee, he would mouth with a beggar, though she smelt brown bread and garlic: say that I said so. Farewell. [*Exit.*

DUKE

No might nor greatness in mortality Can censure 'scape; back-wounding calumny The whitest virtue strikes. What king so strong Can tie the gall up in the slanderous tongue? But who comes here? 178

Enter ESCALUS, PROVOST, *and* Officers *with* MISTRESS OVERDONE.

ESCALUS

Go; away with her to prison!

MISTRESS OVERDONE

Good my lord, be good to me; your honour is accounted a merciful man; good my lord.

ESCALUS

Double and treble admonition, and still forfeit in the same kind! This would make mercy swear and play the tyrant.

PROVOST

A bawd of eleven years' continuance, may it please your honour. 186

MISTRESS OVERDONE

My lord, this is one Lucio's information against me. Mistress Kate Keepdown was with child by him in the duke's time; he promised her marriage: his child is a year and a quarter old, come Philip and Jacob: I have kept it myself; and see how he goes about to abuse me!

ESCALUS

That fellow is a fellow of much licence: let him be called before us. Away with her to prison! Go to; no more words. [*Exeunt Officers with Mistress Overdone.*

Provost, my brother Angelo will not be altered; Claudio must die to-morrow: let him be furnished with divines, and have all charitable preparation. if my brother wrought by my pity, it should not be so with him.

PROVOST

So please you, this friar hath been with him, and advised him for the entertainment of death.

ESCALUS

Good even, good father.

DUKE

Bliss and goodness on you!

ESCALUS

Of whence are you?

DUKE

Not of this country, though my chance is now 204
To use it for my time: I am a brother
Of gracious order, late come from the See
In special business from his holiness.

ESCALUS

What news abroad i' the world?

DUKE

None, but that there is so great a fever on goodness, that the dissolution of it must cure it: novelty is only in request; and it is as dangerous to be aged in any kind of course, as it is virtuous to be constant in any undertaking. There is scarce truth enough alive to make societies secure; but security enough to make fellowships accurst: much upon this riddle runs the wisdom of the world. This news is old enough, yet it is every day's news. I pray you, sir, of what disposition was the duke? [22]

ESCALUS

One that, above all other strifes, contended especially to know himself.

DUKE

What pleasure was he given to?

ESCALUS

Rather rejoicing to see another merry, than merry at any thing which professed to make him rejoice: a gentleman of all temperance. But leave we him to his events, with a prayer they may prove prosperous; and let me desire to know how you find Claudio prepared. I am made to understand that you have lent him visitation.

DUKE

He professes to have received no sinister measure from his judge, but most willingly humbles himself to the determination of justice: yet had he framed to himself, by the instruction of his frailty, many deceiving promises of life; which I by my good leisure have discredited to him, and now is he resolved to die.

ESCALUS

You have paid the heavens your function, and the prisoner the very debt of your calling. I have laboured for the poor gentleman to the extremest shore of my modesty: but my brother justice have I found so severe, that he hath forced me to tell him he is indeed Justice.

DUKE

If his own life answer the straitness of his proceeding, it shall become him well; wherein if he chance to fail, he hath sentenced himself.

ESCALUS

I am going to visit the prisoner. Fare you well.

DUKE

Peace be with you! [*Exeunt Escalus and Provost.*
He who the sword of heaven will bear [23]
Should be as holy as severe;
Pattern in himself to know,
Grace to stand, and virtue go; [24]
More nor less to others paying
Than by self-offences weighing.
Shame to him whose cruel striking
Kills for faults of his own liking!
Twice treble shame on Angelo,
To weed my vice and let his grow!
O, what may man within him hide,
Though angel on the outward side!
How may likeness made in crimes, [25]
Making practise on the times,
To draw with idle spiders' strings
Most ponderous and substantial things!
Craft against vice I must apply:
With Angelo to-night shall lie
His old betrothed but despised;
So disguise shall, by the disguised,
Pay with falsehood false exacting,
And perform an old contracting. [*Exit.*

ACT FOUR SCENE ONE

The moated grange at ST. LUKE'S.

Enter MARIANA *and a* BOY.

BOY *sings.*

Take, O, take those lips away, [26]
That so sweetly were forsworn;
And those eyes, the break of day,
Lights that do mislead the morn:
But my kisses bring again, bring again;
Seals of love, but seal'd in vain, seal'd in vain.

MARIANA

Break off thy song, and haste thee quick away:
Here comes a man of comfort, whose advice
Hath often still'd my brawling discontent. [*Exit Boy.*

Enter DUKE *disguised as before.*

I cry you mercy, sir; and well could wish
You had not found me here so musical:
Let me excuse me, and believe me so,
My mirth it much displeased, but pleased my woe.

DUKE

'Tis good; though music oft hath such a charm [27]
To make bad good, and good provoke to harm.
I pray you, tell me, hath any body inquired for me here to-day? much upon this time have
I promised here to meet.

MARIANA

You have not been inquired after: I have sat here all day.

Enter ISABELLA.

DUKE

I do constantly believe you. The time is come even now. I shall crave your forbearance a little: may be I will call upon you anon, for some advantage to yourself.

MARIANA

I am always bound to you. [*Exit.*

DUKE

Very well met, and well come.
What is the news from this good deputy?

ISABELLA

He hath a garden circummured with brick,
Whose western side is with a vineyard back'd;
And to that vineyard is a planched gate,
That makes his opening with this bigger key:
This other doth command a little door
Which from the vineyard to the garden leads;
There have I made my promise
Upon the heavy middle of the night
To call upon him.

DUKE

But shall you on your knowledge find this way?

ISABELLA

I have ta'en a due and wary note upon't:
With whispering and most guilty diligence,
In action all of precept, he did show me
The way twice o'er.

DUKE

Are there no other tokens
Between you 'greed concerning her observance?

ISABELLA

No, none, but only a repair i' the dark;
And that I have possess'd him my most stay
Can be but brief; for I have made him know

I have a servant comes with me along,
That stays upon me, whose persuasion is
I come about my brother.

DUKE
'Tis well borne up.
I have not yet made known to Mariana
A word of this. What, ho! within! come forth!

Re-enter MARIANA.

I pray you, be acquainted with this maid; 52
She comes to do you good.

ISABELLA
I do desire the like.

DUKE
Do you persuade yourself that I respect you?

MARIANA
Good friar, I know you do, and have found it.

DUKE
Take, then, this your companion by the hand,
Who hath a story ready for your ear.
I shall attend your leisure: but make haste;
The vaporous night approaches.

MARIANA
Will't please you walk aside?
[*Exeunt Mariana and Isabella.*

DUKE
O place and greatness! millions of false eyes 62
Are stuck upon thee: volumes of report
Run with these false and most contrarious quests
Upon thy doings: thousand escapes of wit
Make thee the father of their idle dreams
And rack thee in their fancies.

Re-enter MARIANA *and* ISABELLA.

Welcome, how agreed?

ISABELLA
She'll take the enterprise upon her, father,
If you advise it.

DUKE
It is not my consent,
But my entreaty too.

ISABELLA
Little have you to say
When you depart from him, but, soft and low,
'Remember now my brother.'

MARIANA
Fear me not. 76

DUKE
Nor, gentle daughter, fear you not at all.
He is your husband on a pre-contract:
To bring you thus together, 'tis no sin,
Sith that the justice of your title to him
Doth flourish the deceit. Come, let us go:
Our corn's to reap, for yet our tithe's to sow.
[*Exeunt.*

ACT FOUR SCENE TWO

A room in the prison.

Enter PROVOST *and* POMPEY.

PROVOST
Come hither, sirrah. Can you cut off a man's head?

POMPEY
If the man be a bachelor, sir, I can; but if he be a married man, he's his wife's head, and I can never cut off a woman's head.

PROVOST
Come, sir, leave me your snatches, and yield me a direct answer. To-morrow morning are to die Claudio and Barnardine. Here is in our prison a common executioner, who in his office lacks a helper: if you will take it on you to assist him, it shall redeem you from your gyves; if not, you shall have your full time of imprisonment and your deliverance with an unpitied whipping, for you have been a notorious bawd.

POMPEY
Sir, I have been an unlawful bawd time out of mind; but yet I will be content to be a lawful hangman. I would be glad to receive some instruction from my fellow partner.

PROVOST
What, ho! Abhorson! Where's Abhorson,
there? 18

Enter ABHORSON.

ABHORSON
Do you call, sir?

PROVOST
Sirrah, here's a fellow will help you to-morrow in your execution. If you think it meet, compound with him by the year, and let him abide here with you; if not, use him for the present and dismiss him. He cannot plead his estimation with you; he hath been a bawd.

ABHORSON
A bawd, sir? fie upon him! he will discredit our mystery. 27

PROVOST
Go to, sir; you weigh equally; a feather will turn the scale. [*Exit.*

POMPEY
Pray, sir, by your good favour,—for surely, sir, a good favour you have, but that you have a hanging look,—do you call, sir, your occupation a mystery?

ABHORSON
Ay, sir; a mystery.

POMPEY
Painting, sir, I have heard say, is a mystery; and your whores, sir, being members of my occupation, using

painting, do prove my occupation a mystery: but what mystery there should be in hanging, if I should be hanged, I cannot imagine.

ABHORSON

Sir, it is a mystery.

POMPEY

Proof?

ABHORSON

Every true man's apparel fits your thief: if it be too little for your thief, your true man thinks it big enough; if it be too big for your thief, your thief thinks it little enough: so every true man's apparel fits your thief. [28]

Re-enter PROVOST.

PROVOST

Are you agreed?

POMPEY

Sir, I will serve him; for I do find your hangman is a more penitent trade than your bawd; he doth oftener ask forgiveness.

PROVOST

You, sirrah, provide your block and your axe to-morrow four o'clock.

ABHORSON

Come on, bawd; I will instruct thee in my trade; follow.

POMPEY

I do desire to learn, sir: and I hope, if you have occasion to use me for your own turn, you shall find me yare; for truly, sir, for your kindness I owe you a good turn.

PROVOST

Call hither Barnardine and Claudio:
[*Exeunt Pompey and Abhorson.*
The one has my pity; not a jot the other,
Being a murderer, though he were my brother.

Enter CLAUDIO.

Look, here's the warrant, Claudio, for thy death:
'Tis now dead midnight, and by eight to-morrow
Thou must be made immortal. Where's Barnardine?

CLAUDIO

As fast lock'd up in sleep as guiltless labour
When it lies starkly in the traveller's bones:
He will not wake.

PROVOST

Who can do good on him?
Well, go, prepare yourself. [*Knocking within.*] But, hark, what noise?
Heaven give your spirits comfort! [*Exit Claudio.*] By and by.
I hope it is some pardon or reprieve
For the most gentle Claudio.

Enter DUKE *disguised as before.*

Welcome father.

DUKE

The best and wholesomest spirts of the night
Envelope you, good Provost! Who call'd here of late?

PROVOST

None, since the curfew rung.

DUKE

Not Isabel?

PROVOST

No.

DUKE

They will, then, ere't be long.

PROVOST

What comfort is for Claudio?

DUKE

There's some in hope.

PROVOST

It is a bitter deputy.

DUKE

Not so, not so; his life is parallel'd
Even with the stroke and line of his great justice:
He doth with holy abstinence subdue
That in himself which he spurs on his power
To qualify in others: were he meal'd with that
Which he corrects, then were he tyrannous;
But this being so, he's just. [*Knocking within.*
Now are they come. [*Exit Provost.*
This is a gentle provost: seldom when
The steeled gaoler is the friend of men.
[*Knocking within.*
How now! what noise? That spirit's possessed with haste
That wounds the unsisting postern with these strokes.

Re-enter PROVOST.

PROVOST

There he must stay until the officer
Arise to let him in: he is call'd up.

DUKE

Have you no countermand for Claudio yet,
But he must die to-morrow?

PROVOST

None, sir, none.

DUKE

As near the dawning, provost, as it is,
You shall hear more ere morning.

PROVOST

Happily
You something know; yet I believe there comes
No countermand; no such example have we:
Besides, upon the very siege of justice

Lord Angelo hath to the public ear
Profess'd the contrary.

Enter a MESSENGER.

This is his lordship's man.

DUKE

And here comes Claudio's pardon.

MESSENGER

[*Giving a paper.* My lord hath sent you this note; and by me this further charge, that you swerve not from the smallest article of it, neither in time, matter, or other circumstance. Good morrow; for, as I take it, it is almost day.

PROVOST

I shall obey him. [*Exit Messenger.*

DUKE

[*Aside*] This is his pardon, purchased by such sin 118
For which the pardoner himself is in.
Hence hath offence his quick celerity,
When it is borne in high authority:
When vice makes mercy, mercy's so extended,
That for the fault's love is the offender friended.
Now, sir, what news?

PROVOST

I told you. Lord Angelo, belike thinking me remiss in mine office, awakens me with this unwonted putting-on; methinks strangely, for he hath not used it before. 127

DUKE

Pray you, let's hear.

PROVOST

[*Reads*]

'Whatsoever you may hear to the contrary, let Claudio be executed by four of the clock; and in the afternoon Barnardine: for my better satisfaction, let me have Claudio's head sent me by five. Let this be duly performed; with a thought that more depends on it than we must yet deliver. Thus fail not to do your office, as you will answer it at your peril.' 135

What say you to this, sir?

DUKE

What is that Barnardine who is to be executed in the afternoon?

PROVOST

A Bohemian born, but here nursed up and bred; one that is a prisoner nine years old.

DUKE

How came it that the absent duke had not either delivered him to his liberty or executed him? I have heard it was ever his manner to do so. 143

PROVOST

His friends still wrought reprieves for him: and, indeed, his fact, till now in the government of Lord Angelo, came not to an undoubtful proof.

DUKE

It is now apparent?

PROVOST

Most manifest, and not denied by himself.

DUKE

Hath he born himself penitently in prison? How seems he to be touched?

PROVOST

A man that apprehends death no more dreadfully but as a drunken sleep; careless, reckless, and fearless of what's past, present, or to come; insensible of mortality, and desperately mortal.

DUKE

He wants advice.

PROVOST

He will hear none: he hath evermore had the liberty of the prison; give him leave to escape hence, he would not: drunk many times a day, if not many days entirely drunk. We have very oft awaked him, as if to carry him to execution, and showed him a seeming warrant for it: it hath not moved him at all. 161

DUKE

More of him anon. There is written in your brow, provost, honesty and constancy: if I read it not truly, my ancient skill beguiles me; but, in the boldness of my cunning, I will lay myself in hazard. Claudio, whom here you have warrant to execute, is no greater forfeit to the law than Angelo who hath sentenced him. To make you understand this in a manifested effect, I crave but four days' respite; for the which you are to do me both a present and a dangerous courtesy.

PROVOST

Pray, sir, in what?

DUKE

In the delaying death.

PROVOST

Alack, how may I do it, having the hour limited, and an express command, under penalty, to deliver his head in the view of Angelo? I may make my case as Claudio's, to cross this in the smallest. 177

DUKE

By the vow of mine order I warrant you, if my instructions may be your guide. Let this Barnardine be this morning executed, and his head born to Angelo.

PROVOST

Angelo hath seen them both, and will discover the favour.

DUKE

O, death's a great disguiser; and you may add to it. Shave the head, and tie the beard; and say it was the desire of the penitent to be so bared before his death: you know the course is common. If any thing fall to you upon this, more than thanks and good fortune, by the saint whom I profess, I will plead against it with my life.

PROVOST

Pardon me, good father; it is against my oath.

DUKE

Were you sworn to the duke, or to the deputy?

PROVOST

To him, and to his substitutes.

DUKE

You will think you have made no offence, if the duke avouch the justice of your dealing? 194

PROVOST

But what likelihood is in that?

DUKE

Not a resemblance, but a certainty. Yet since I see you fearful, that neither my coat, integrity, nor persuasion can with ease attempt you, I will go further than I meant, to pluck all fears out of you. Look you, sir, here is the hand and seal of the duke: you know the character, I doubt not; and the signet is not strange to you.

PROVOST

I know them both. 203

DUKE

The contents of this is the return of the duke: you shall anon over-read it at your pleasure; where you shall find, within these two days he will be here. This is a thing that Angelo knows not; for he this very day receives letters of strange tenor; perchance of the duke's death; perchance entering into some monastery; but, by chance, nothing of what is writ. Look, the unfolding star calls up the shepherd. Put not yourself into amazement how these things should be: all difficulties are but easy when they are known. Call your executioner, and off with Barnardine's head: I will give him a present shrift and advise him for a better place. Yet you are amazed; but this shall absolutely resolve you. Come away; it is almost clear dawn. [*Exeunt.*

ACT FOUR SCENE THREE

Another room in the same.

Enter POMPEY.

POMPEY

I am as well acquainted here as I was in our house of profession: one would think it were Mistress Overdone's own house, for here be many of her old customers. First, here's young Master Rash; he's in for a commodity of brown paper and old ginger, ninescore and seventeen pounds; of which he made five marks, ready money: marry, then ginger was not much in request, for the old women were all dead. Then is there here one Master Caper, at the suit of Master Three-pile the mercer, for some four suits of peach-coloured satin, which now peaches him a beggar. Then have we here young Dizy, and young Master Deep-vow, and Master Copperspur, and Master Starve-lackey the rapier and dagger man, and young Drop-heir that killed lusty Pudding, and Master Forthlight the tilter, and brave Master Shooty the great traveller, and wild Half-can that stabbed Pots, and, I think, forty more; all great doers in our trade, and are now 'for the Lord's sake.' 19

Enter ABHORSON.

ABHORSON

Sirrah, bring Barnardine hither.

POMPEY

Master Barnardine! you must rise and be hanged. Master Barnardine!

ABHORSON

What, ho, Barnardine!

BARNARDINE

[*Within*] A pox o' your throats! Who makes that noise there? What are you?

POMPEY

Your friends, sir; the hangman. You must be so good, sir, to rise and be put to death.

BARNARDINE

[*Within*] Away, you rogue, away! I am sleepy. 28

ABHORSON

Tell him he must awake, and that quickly too.

POMPEY

Pray, Master Barnardine, awake till you are executed, and sleep afterwards.

ABHORSON

Go in to him, and fetch him out.

POMPEY

He is coming, sir, he is coming; I hear his straw rustle.

ABHORSON

Is the axe upon the block, sirrah?

POMPEY

Very ready, sir. 35

Enter BARNARDINE.

BARNARDINE

How now, Abhorson? what's the news with you?

ABHORSON

Truly, sir, I would desire you to clap into your prayers; for, look you, the warrant's come.

BARNARDINE

You rogue, I have been drinking all night; I am not fitted for 't.

POMPEY

O, the better, sir; for he that drinks all night, and is hanged betimes in the morning, may sleep the sounder all the next day.

ABHORSON
Look you, sir; here comes your ghostly father: do we jest now, think you?

Enter DUKE *disguised as before.*

DUKE
Sir, induced by my charity, and hearing how hastily you are to depart, I am come to advise you, comfort you and pray with you.

BARNARDINE
Friar, not I: I have been drinking hard all night, and I will have more time to prepare me, or they shall beat out my brains with billets: I will not consent to die this day, that's certain.

DUKE
O, sir, you must: and therefore I beseech you 53
Look forward on the journey you shall go.

BARNARDINE
I swear I will not die to-day for any man's persuasion.

DUKE
But hear you.

BARNARDINE
Not a word: if you have anything to say to me, come to my ward; for thence will not I to-day. [*Exit.*

DUKE
Unfit to live or die: O gravel heart!
After him, fellows; bring him to the block.
[*Exeunt Abhorson and Pompey.*

Enter PROVOST.

PROVOST
Now, sir, how do you find the prisoner? 61

DUKE
A creature unprepared, unmeet for death;
And to transport him in the mind he is
Were damnable.

PROVOST
Here in the prison, father,
There died this morning of a cruel fever
One Ragozine, a most notorious pirate,
A man of Claudio's years; his beard and head
Just of his colour. What if we do omit
This reprobate till he were well inclined;
And satisfy the deputy with the visage
Of Ragozine, more like to Claudio? 72

DUKE
O, 'tis an accident that heaven provides!
Dispatch it presently; the hour draws on
Prefix'd by Angelo: see this be done,
And sent according to command; whiles I
Persuade this rude wretch willingly to die.

PROVOST
This shall be done, good father, presently.
But Barnardine must die this afternoon:
And how shall we continue Claudio,
To save me from the danger that might come
If he were known alive?

DUKE
Let this be done. 83
Put them in secret holds, both Barnardine and Claudio:
Ere twice the sun hath made his journal greeting
To the under generation, you shall find
Your safety manifested.

PROVOST
I am your free dependant.

DUKE
Quick, dispatch, and send the head to Angelo.
[*Exit Provost.*
Now will I write letters to Angelo,—
The provost, he shall bear them,—whose contents
Shall witness to him I am near at home,
And that, by great injunctions, I am bound
To enter publicly: him I'll desire
To meet me at the consecrated fount
A league below the city; and from thence,
By cold gradation and well-balanced form,
We shall proceed with Angelo.

Re-enter PROVOST.

PROVOST
Here is the head; I'll carry it myself.

DUKE
Convenient is it. Make a swift return;
For I would commune with you of such things
That want no ear but yours.

PROVOST
I'll make all speed. [*Exit.*

ISABELLA
[*Within*] Peace, ho, be here! 105

DUKE
The tongue of Isabel. She's come to know
If yet her brother's pardon be come hither:
But I will keep her ignorant of her good,
To make her heavenly comforts of despair,
When it is least expected.

Enter ISABELLA.

ISABELLA
Ho, by your leave!

DUKE
Good morning to you, fair and gracious daughter.

ISABELLA
The better, given me by so holy a man.
Hath yet the deputy sent my brother's pardon?

DUKE
He hath released him, Isabel, from the world:
His head is off and sent to Angelo. 116

ISABELLA
Nay, but it is not so.

DUKE

It is no other: show your wisdom, daughter,
In your close patience.

ISABELLA

O, I will to him and pluck out his eyes!

DUKE

You shall not be admitted to his sight.

ISABELLA

Unhappy Claudio! wretched Isabel!
Injurious world! most damned Angelo!

DUKE

This nor hurts him nor profits you a jot;
Forbear it therefore; give your cause to heaven.
Mark what I say, which you shall find 126
By every syllable a faithful verity:
The duke comes home to-morrow; nay, dry your eyes;
One of our convent, and his confessor,
Gives me this instance: already he hath carried
Notice to Escalus and Angelo,
Who do prepare to meet him at the gates,
There to give up their power. If you can, pace your wisdom
In that good path that I would wish it go,
And you shall have your bosom on this wretch,
Grace of the duke, revenge to your heart, 138
And general honour.

ISABELLA

I am directed by you.

DUKE

This letter, then, to Friar Peter give;
'Tis that he sent me of the duke's return:
Say, by this token, I desire his company
At Mariana's house to-night. Her cause and yours
I'll perfect him withal, and he shall bring you
Before the duke, and to the head of Angelo
Accuse him home and home. For my poor self,
I am combined by a sacred vow
And shall be absent. Wend you with this letter: 151
Command these fretting waters from your eyes
With a light heart; trust not my holy order,
If I pervert your course. Who's here?

Enter LUCIO.

LUCIO

Good even. Friar, where's the provost?

DUKE

Not within, sir.

LUCIO

O pretty Isabella, I am pale at mine heart to see thine eyes so red: thou must be patient. I am fain to dine and sup with water and bran; I dare not for my head fill my belly; one fruitful meal would set me to 't. But they say the duke will be here to-morrow. By my troth, Isabel, I loved thy brother: if the old fantastical duke of dark corners had been at home, he had lived.

[*Exit Isabella.*

DUKE

Sir, the duke is marvellous little beholding to your reports; but the best is, he lives not in them.

LUCIO

Friar, thou knowest not the duke so well as I do: he's a better woodman than thou takest him for. 167

DUKE

Well, you'll answer this one day. Fare ye well.

LUCIO

Nay, tarry; I'll go along with thee
I can tell thee pretty tales of the duke.

DUKE

You have told me too many of him already, sir, if they be true; if not true, none were enough.

LUCIO

I was once before him for getting a wench with child. 174

DUKE

Did you such a thing?

LUCIO

Yes, marry, did I: but I was fain to forswear it; they would else have married me to the rotten medlar.

DUKE

Sir, your company is fairer than honest. Rest you well.

LUCIO

By my troth, I'll go with thee to the lane's end: if bawdy talk offend you, we'll have very little of it. Nay, friar, I am a kind of burr; I shall stick. [*Exeunt.*

ACT FOUR SCENE FOUR

A room in ANGELO'S *house.*

Enter ANGELO *and* ESCALUS.

ESCALUS

Every letter he hath writ hath disvouched other.

ANGELO

In most uneven and distracted manner. His actions show much like to madness: pray heaven his wisdom be not tainted! And why meet him at the gates, and redeliver our authorities there? [29]

ESCALUS

I guess not.

ANGELO

And why should we proclaim it in an hour before his entering, that if any crave redress of injustice, they should exhibit their petitions in the street?

ESCALUS

He shows his reason for that: to have a dispatch of complaints, and to deliver us from devices hereafter, which shall then have no power to stand against us.

ANGELO

Well, I beseech you, let it be proclaimed betimes i' the morn; I'll call you at your house: give notice to such men of sort and suit as are to meet him. 20

ESCALUS

I shall, sir. Fare you well.

ANGELO

Good night. [*Exit Escalus.*
This deed unshapes me quite, makes me unpregnant
And dull to all proceedings. A deflower'd maid!
And by an eminent body that enforced
The law against it! But that her tender shame
Will not proclaim against her maiden loss,
How might she tongue me! Yet reason dares her no;
For my authority bears of a credent bulk, *30*
That no particular scandal once can touch 24
But it confounds the breather. He should have lived,
Save that riotous youth, with dangerous sense,
Might in the times to come have ta'en revenge,
By so receiving a dishonour'd life
With ransom of such shame. Would yet he had lived!
Alack, when once our grace we have forgot,
Nothing goes right: we would, and we would not.
[*Exit.*

ACT FOUR SCENE FIVE

Fields without the town.

Enter DUKE *in his own habit, and* FRIAR PETER.

DUKE

These letters at fit time deliver me
[*Giving letters.*
The provost knows our purpose and our plot.
The matter being afoot, keep your instruction,
And hold you ever to our special drift;
Though sometimes you do blench from this to that,
As cause doth minister. Go call at Flavius' house,
And tell him where I stay: give the like notice
To Valentinus, Rowland, and to Crassus,
And bid them bring the trumpets to the gate;
But send me Flavius first.

FRIAR PETER

It shall be speeded well. [*Exit.* 11

Enter VARRIUS.

DUKE

I thank thee, Varrius; thou hast made good haste:
Come, we will walk. There's other of our friends
Will greet us here anon, my gentle Varrius.
[*Exeunt.*

ACT FOUR SCENE SIX

Street near the city gate.

Enter ISABELLA *and* MARIANA.

ISABELLA

To speak so indirectly I am loath:
I would say the truth; but to accuse him so,
That is your part: yet I am advised to do it;
He says, to veil full purpose.

MARIANA

Be ruled by him.

ISABELLA

Besides, he tells me that, if peradventure
He speak against me on the adverse side,
I should not think it strange; for 'tis a physic
That's bitter to sweet end.

MARIANA

I would Friar Peter—

ISABELLA

O, peace! the friar is come.

Enter FRIAR PETER.

FRIAR PETER

Come, I have found you out a stand most fit, 12
Where you may have such vantage on the duke,
He shall not pass you. Twice have the trumpets sounded;
The generous and gravest citizens
Have hent the gates, and very near upon
The duke is entering: therefore, hence, away!
[*Exeunt.*

ACT FIVE SCENE ONE

The city gate.

MARIANA *veiled*, ISABELLA, *and* FRIAR PETER, *at their stand. Enter* DUKE, VARRIUS, Lords, ANGELO, ESCALUS, LUCIO, PROVOST, OFFICERS, *and* CITIZENS, *at several doors.*

DUKE

My very worthy cousin, fairly met!
Our old and faithful friend, we are glad to see you.

ANGELO, ESCALUS

Happy return be to your royal grace!

DUKE

Many and hearty thankings to you both.
We have made inquiry of you; and we hear

Such goodness of your justice, that our soul
Cannot but yield you forth to public thanks,
Forerunning more requital.

ANGELO
You make my bonds still greater.

DUKE
O, your desert speaks loud; and I should wrong it,
To lock it in the wards of covert bosom, 11
When it deserves, with characters of brass,
A forted residence 'gainst the tooth of time
And razure of oblivion. Give me your hand,
And let the subject see, to make them know
That outward courtesies would fain proclaim
Favours that keep within. Come, Escalus,
You must walk by us on our other hand;
And good supporters are you.

FRIAR PETER *and* ISABELLA *come forward.*

FRIAR PETER
Now is your time: speak loud and kneel before him.

ISABELLA
Justice, O royal duke! Vail your regard 21
Upon a wrong'd, I would fain have said, a maid!
O worthy prince, dishonour not your eye
By throwing it on any other object
Till you have heard me in my true complaint
And given me justice, justice, justice, justice!

DUKE
Relate your wrongs; in what? by whom? be brief.
Here is Lord Angelo shall give you justice:
Reveal yourself to him.

ISABELLA
O worthy duke,
You bid me seek redemption of the devil:
Hear me yourself; for that which I must speak
Must either punish me, not being believed, 33
Or wring redress from you. Hear me, O hear me, here!

ANGELO
My lord, her wits, I fear me, are not firm:
She hath been a suitor to me for her brother
Cut off by course of justice,—

ISABELLA
By course of justice!

ANGELO
And she will speak most bitterly and strange.

ISABELLA
Most strange, but yet most truly, will I speak:
That Angelo's forsworn; is it not strange?
That Angelo's a murderer; is 't not strange?
That Angelo is an adulterous thief, 44
An hypocrite, a virgin-violator;
Is it not strange and strange?

DUKE
Nay, it is ten times strange.

ISABELLA
It is not truer he is Angelo
Than this is all as true as it is strange:
Nay, it is ten times true; for truth is truth
To the end of reckoning.

DUKE
Away with her! Poor soul,
She speaks this in the infirmity of sense.

ISABELLA
O prince, I conjure thee, as thou believest
There is another comfort than this world,
That thou neglect me not, with that opinion 56
That I am touch'd with madness! Make not impossible
That which but seems unlike: 'tis not impossible
But one, the wicked'st caitiff on the ground,
May seem as shy, as grave, as just, as absolute
As Angelo; even so may Angelo,
In all his dressings, characts, titles, forms,
Be an arch-villain; believe it, royal prince:
If he be less, he's nothing; but he's more,
Had I more name for badness.

DUKE
By mine honesty,
If she be mad,—as I believe no other,— 68
Her madness hath the oddest frame of sense,
Such a dependency of thing on thing,
As e'er I heard in madness.

ISABELLA
O gracious duke,
Harp not on that, nor do not banish reason [31]
For inequality; but let your reason serve
To make the truth appear where it seems hid,
And hide the false seems true.

DUKE
Many that are not mad
Have, sure, more lack of reason. What would you say?

ISABELLA
I am the sister of one Claudio,
Condemn'd upon the act of fornication 81
To lose his head; condemn'd by Angelo:
I, in probation of a sisterhood,
Was sent to by my brother; one Lucio
As then the messenger,—

LUCIO
That's I, an't like your grace:
I came to her from Claudio, and desired her
To try her gracious fortune with Lord Angelo
For her poor brother's pardon.

ISABELLA
That's he indeed.

DUKE
You were not bid to speak.

LUCIO
No, my good lord;
Nor wish'd to hold my peace.

DUKE
I wish you now, then;
Pray you, take note of it: and when you have 95
A business for yourself, pray heaven you then
Be perfect.

LUCIO
I warrant your honour.

DUKE
The warrant's for yourself; take heed to't.

ISABELLA
This gentleman told somewhat of my tale,—

LUCIO
Right.

DUKE
It may be right; but you are i' the wrong
To speak before your time. Proceed.

ISABELLA
I went
To this pernicious caitiff deputy,—

DUKE
That's somewhat madly spoken.

ISABELLA
Pardon it;
The phrase is to the matter. 107

DUKE
Mended again. The matter; proceed.

ISABELLA
In brief, to set the needless process by,
How I persuaded, how I pray'd, and kneel'd,
How he refell'd me, and how I replied,—
For this was of much length,—the vile conclusion
I now begin with grief and shame to utter:
He would not, but by gift of my chaste body
To his concupiscible intemperate lust,
Release my brother; and, after much debatement,
My sisterly remorse confutes mine honour, 117
And I did yield to him: but the next morn betimes,
His purpose surfeiting, he sends a warrant
For my poor brother's head.

DUKE
This is most likely!

ISABELLA
O, that it were as like as it is true!

DUKE
By heaven, fond wretch, thou know'st not what thou speak'st,
Or else thou art suborn'd against his honour
In hateful practise. First, his integrity
Stands without blemish. Next, it imports no reason
That with such vehemency he should pursue
Faults proper to himself: if he had so offended,
He would have weigh'd thy brother by himself
And not have cut him off. Some one hath set you on:
Confess the truth, and say by whose advice
Thou camest here to complain.

ISABELLA
And is this all?
Then, O you blessed ministers above,
Keep me in patience, and with ripen'd time
Unfold the evil which is here wrap't up
In countenance! Heaven shield your grace from woe,
As I, thus wrong'd, hence unbelieved go!

DUKE
I know you'ld fain be gone. An officer! 141
To prison with her! Shall we thus permit
A blasting and a scandalous breath to fall
On him so near us? This needs must be a practise.
Who knew of your intent and coming hither?

ISABELLA
One that I would were here, Friar Lodowick.

DUKE
A ghostly father, belike. Who knows that Lodowick?

LUCIO
My lord, I know him; 'tis a meddling friar;
I do not like the man: had he been lay, my lord
For certain words he spake against your grace
In your retirement, I had swinged him soundly.

DUKE
Words against me! this is a good friar, belike! 152
And to set on this wretched woman here
Against our substitute! Let this friar be found.

LUCIO
But yesternight, my lord, she and that friar,
I saw them at the prison: a saucy friar,
A very scurvy fellow.

FRIAR PETER
Blessed be your royal grace!
I have stood by, my lord, and I have heard
Your royal ear abused. First, hath this woman
Most wrongfully accused your substitute, 161
Who is as free from touch or soil with her
As she from one ungot.

DUKE
We did believe no less.
Know you that Friar Lodowick that she speaks of?

FRIAR PETER
I know him for a man divine and holy;
Not scurvy, nor a temporary meddler,
As he's reported by this gentleman;
And, on my trust, a man that never yet
Did, as he vouches, misreport your grace.

LUCIO
My lord, most villanously; believe it.

FRIAR PETER
Well, he in time may come to clear himself; 172
But at this instant he is sick my lord,
Of a strange fever. Upon his mere request,
Being come to knowledge that there was complaint
Intended 'gainst Lord Angelo, came I hither,
To speak, as from his mouth, what he doth know
Is true and false; and what he with his oath
And all probation will make up full clear,
Whensoever he's convented. First, for this woman.
To justify this worthy nobleman,
So vulgarly and personally accused, 183
Her shall you hear disproved to her eyes,
Till she herself confess it.

DUKE
Good friar, let's hear it.
[Isabella is carried off guarded; and Marian comes forward.
Do you not smile at this, Lord Angelo?
O heaven, the vanity of wretched fools!
Give us some seats. Come, cousin Angelo;
In this I'll be impartial; be you judge
Of your own cause. Is this the witness, friar?
First let her show her face, and after speak.

MARIANA
Pardon, my lord; I will not show my face
Until my husband bid me. 194

DUKE
What, are you married?

MARIANA
No, my lord.

DUKE
Are you a maid?

MARIANA
No, my lord.

DUKE
A widow, then?

MARIANA
Neither, my lord.

DUKE
Why, you are nothing then: neither maid, widow, nor wife? 202

LUCIO
My lord, she may be a punk; for many of them are neither maid, widow, nor wife.

DUKE
Silence that fellow: I would he had some cause
To prattle for himself.

LUCIO
Well, my lord.

MARIANA
My lord, I do confess I ne'er was married;
And I confess besides I am no maid:
I have known my husband; yet my husband
Knows not that ever he knew me.

LUCIO
He was drunk then, my lord: it can be no better.

DUKE
For the benefit of silence, would thou wert so too! 214

LUCIO
Well, my lord.

DUKE
This is no witness for Lord Angelo.

MARIANA
Now I come to't my lord:
She that accuses him of fornication,
In self-same manner doth accuse my husband,
And charges him, my lord, with such a time
When I'll depose I had him in mine arms
With all the effect of love.

ANGELO
Charges she more than me?

MARIANA
Not that I know.

DUKE
No? you say your husband. 225

MARIANA
Why, just, my lord, and that is Angelo,
Who thinks he knows that he ne'er knew my body,
But knows he thinks that he knows Isabel's.

ANGELO
This is a strange abuse. Let's see thy face.

MARIANA
My husband bids me; now I will unmask.
[Unveiling.
This is that face, thou cruel Angelo,
Which once thou sworest was worth the looking on;
This is the hand which, with a vow'd contract,
Was fast belock'd in thine; this is the body
That took away the match from Isabel,
And did supply thee at thy garden-house
In her imagined person.

DUKE
Know you this woman?

LUCIO
Carnally, she says.

DUKE
Sirrah, no more!

LUCIO
Enough, my lord.

ANGELO
My lord, I must confess I know this woman:
And five years since there was some speech of marriage
Betwixt myself and her; which was broke off
Partly for that her promised proportions
Came short of composition, but in chief 246

For that her reputation was disvalued
In levity: since which time of five years
I never spake with her, saw her, nor heard from her,
Upon my faith and honour.

MARIANA
Noble prince,
As there comes light from heaven and words from breath,
As there is sense in truth and truth in virtue,
I am affianced this man's wife as strongly
As words could make up vows: and, my good lord,
But Tuesday night last gone in's garden-house
He knew me as a wife. As this is true,
Let me in safety raise me from my knees
Or else for ever be confixed here,
A marble monument!

ANGELO
I did but smile till now:
Now, good my lord, give me the scope of justice
My patience here is touch'd. I do perceive
These poor informal women are no more
But instruments of some more mightier member
That sets them on: let me have way, my lord,
To find this practice out.

DUKE
Ay, with my heart
And punish them to your height of pleasure.
Thou foolish friar, and thou pernicious woman,
Compact with her that's gone, think'st thou thy oaths,
Though they would swear down each particular saint,
Were testimonies against his worth and credit
That's seal'd in approbation? You, Lord Escalus,
Sit with my cousin; lend him your kind pains
To find out this abuse, whence 'tis derived.
There is another friar that set them on;
Let him be sent for.

FRIAR PETER
Would he were here, my lord! for he indeed
Hath set the women on to this complaint:
Your provost knows the place where he abides
And he may fetch him.

DUKE
Go do it instantly. [*Exit Provost.*
And you, my noble and well-warranted cousin,
Whom it concerns to hear this matter forth,
Do with your injuries as seems you best,
In any chastisement: I for a while will leave you;
But stir not you till you have well determined
Upon these slanderers.

ESCALUS
My lord, we'll do it throughly. [*Exit Duke.*
Signior Lucio, did not you say you knew that
Friar Lodowick to be a dishonest person?

LUCIO
'Cucullus non facit monachum:' honest in nothing but in his clothes; and one that hath spoke most villanous speeches of the duke.

ESCALUS
We shall entreat you to abide here till he come and enforce them against him: we shall find this friar a notable fellow.

LUCIO
As any in Vienna, on my word.

ESCALUS
Call that same Isabel here once again; I would speak with her. [*Exit an Attendant.*
Pray you, my lord, give me leave to question; you shall see how I'll handle her.

LUCIO
Not better than he, by her own report.

ESCALUS
Say you?

LUCIO
Marry, sir, I think, if you handled her privately, she would sooner confess: perchance, publicly, she'll be ashamed.

ESCALUS
I will go darkly to work with her.

LUCIO
That's the way; for women are light at midnight.

Re-enter Officers *with* ISABELLA; *and* PROVOST *with the* DUKE *in his friar's habit.*

ESCALUS
Come on, mistress: here's a gentlewoman denies all that you have said.

LUCIO
My lord, here comes the rascal I spoke of; here with the provost.

ESCALUS
In very good time: speak not you to him till we call upon you.

LUCIO
Mum.

ESCALUS
Come, sir: did you set these women on to slander Lord Angelo? they have confessed you did.

DUKE
'Tis false.

ESCALUS
How! know you where you are?

DUKE
Respect to your great place! and let the devil
Be sometime honour'd for his burning throne!
Where is the duke? 'tis he should hear me speak.

ESCALUS
The duke's in us; and we will hear you speak:
Look you speak justly.

DUKE
Boldly, at least. But, O, poor souls,
Come you to seek the lamb here of the fox?
Good night to your redress! Is the duke gone?
Then is your cause gone too. The duke's unjust,
Thus to retort your manifest appeal,
And put your trial in the villain's mouth
Which here you come to accuse.

LUCIO
This is the rascal; this is he I spoke of.

ESCALUS
Why, thou unreverend and unhallow'd friar,
Is't not enough thou hast suborn'd these women
To accuse this worthy man, but, in foul mouth
And in the witness of his proper ear, 340
To call him villain? and then to glance from him
To the duke himself, to tax him with injustice?
Take him hence; to the rack with him! We'll touse you
Joint by joint, but we will know his purpose.
What 'unjust'!

DUKE
Be not so hot; the duke
Dare no more stretch this finger of mine than he
Dare rack his own: his subject am I not,
Nor here provincial. My business in this state
Made me a looker on here in Vienna,
Where I have seen corruption boil and bubble
Till it o'er-run the stew; laws for all faults, 353
But faults so countenanced, that the strong statutes
Stand like the forfeits in a barber's shop, [32]
As much in mock as mark.

ESCALUS
Slander to the state! Away with him to prison!

ANGELO
What can you vouch against him, Signior Lucio?
Is this the man that you did tell us of?

LUCIO
'Tis he, my lord. Come hither, goodman baldpate: do you know me? 361

DUKE
I remember you, sir, by the sound of your voice: I met you at the prison, in the absence of the duke.

LUCIO
O, did you so? And do you remember what you said of the duke?

DUKE
Most notedly, sir.

LUCIO
Do you so, sir? And was the duke a fleshmonger, a fool, and a coward, as you then reported him to be?

DUKE
You must, sir, change persons with me, ere you make that my report: you, indeed, spoke so of him; and much more, much worse.

LUCIO
O thou damnable fellow! Did not I pluck thee by the nose for thy speeches?

DUKE
I protest I love the duke as I love myself.

ANGELO
Hark, how the villain would close now, after his treasonable abuses!

ESCALUS
Such a fellow is not to be talked withal. Away with him to prison! Where is the provost? Away with him to prison! lay bolts enough upon him: let him speak no more. Away with those giglots too, and with the other confederate companion!

DUKE
[*To Provost*] Stay, sir; stay awhile.

ANGELO
What, resists he? Help him, Lucio. 383

LUCIO
Come, sir; come, sir; come, sir; foh, sir! Why, you bald-pated, lying rascal, you must be hooded, must you? Show your knave's visage, with a pox to you! show your sheep-biting face, and be hanged an hour! Will't not off? [33]

[*Pulls off the friar's hood, and discovers the Duke.*

DUKE
Thou art the first knave that e'er madest a duke.
First, provost, let me bail these gentle three.
[*To Lucio*] Sneak not away, sir; for the friar and you
Must have a word anon. Lay hold on him.

LUCIO
This may prove worse than hanging.

DUKE
[*To Escalus*] What you have spoke I pardon: sit you down:
We'll borrow place of him. [*To Angelo*] Sir, by your leave.
Hast thou or word, or wit, or impudence,
That yet can do thee office? If thou hast,
Rely upon it till my tale be heard, 400
And hold no longer out.

ANGELO
O my dread lord,
I should be guiltier than my guiltiness,
To think I can be undiscernible,
When I perceive your grace, like power divine,
Hath look'd upon my passes. Then, good prince,
No longer session hold upon my shame,

But let my trial be mine own confession:
Immediate sentence then and sequent death
Is all the grace I beg.

DUKE

Come hither, Mariana.
Say, wast thou e'er contracted to this woman?

ANGELO

I was, my lord. 413

DUKE

Go take her hence, and marry her instantly.
Do you the office, friar; which consummate,
Return him here again. Go with him, provost.
[*Exeunt Angelo, Mariana, Friar Peter, and Provost.*

ESCALUS

My lord, I am more amazed at his dishonour
Than at the strangeness of it.

DUKE

Come hither, Isabel.
Your friar is now your prince: as I was then
Advertising and holy to your business,
Not changing heart with habit, I am still 421
Attorney'd at your service.

ISABELLA

O, give me pardon,
That I, your vassal, have employ'd and pain'd
Your unknown sovereignty!

DUKE

You are pardon'd, Isabel:
And now, dear maid, be you as free to us.
Your brother's death, I know, sits at your heart;
And you may marvel why I obscured myself,
Labouring to save his life, and would not rather
Make rash remonstrance of my hidden power
Than let him so be lost. O most kind maid,
It was the swift celerity of his death,
Which I did think with slower foot came on,
That brain'd my purpose. But, peace be with him! 435
That life is better life, past fearing death,
Than that which lives to fear: make it your comfort,
So happy is your brother.

ISABELLA

I do, my lord.

Re-enter ANGELO, MARIANA, FRIAR PETER, *and* PROVOST.

DUKE

For this new-married man approaching here,
Whose salt imagination yet hath wrong'd
Your well defended honour, you must pardon
For Mariana's sake: but as he adjudged your brother,—
Being criminal, in double violation
Of sacred chastity and of promise-breach 445
Thereon dependent, for your brother's life,—
The very mercy of the law cries out
Most audible, even from his proper tongue,
'An Angelo for Claudio, death for death!'
Haste still pays haste, and leisure answers leisure;
Like doth quit like, and MEASURE still FOR MEASURE.
Then, Angelo, thy fault's thus manifested;
Which, though thou wouldst deny, denies thee vantage.
We do condemn thee to the very block
Where Claudio stoop'd to death, and with like haste. 458
Away with him!

MARIANA

O my most gracious lord,
I hope you will not mock me with a husband.

DUKE

It is your husband mock'd you with a husband.
Consenting to the safeguard of your honour,
I thought your marriage fit; else imputation,
For that he knew you, might reproach your life
And choke your good to come; for his possessions,
Although by confiscation they are ours,
We do instate and widow you withal,
To buy you a better husband.

MARIANA

O my dear lord,
I crave no other, nor no better man. 471

DUKE

Never crave him; we are definitive.

MARIANA

Gentle my liege,— [*Kneeling.*

DUKE

You do but lose your labour.
Away with him to death! [*To Lucio*] Now, sir, to you.

MARIANA

O my good lord! Sweet Isabel, take my part;
Lend me your knees, and all my life to come
I'll lend you all my life to do you service.

DUKE

Against all sense you do importune her:
Should she kneel down in mercy of this fact,
Her brother's ghost his paved bed would break,
And take her hence in horror.

MARIANA

Isabel, 484
Sweet Isabel, do yet but kneel by me;
Hold up your hands, say nothing; I'll speak all.
They say, best men are moulded out of faults;
And, for the most, become much more the better
For being a little bad: so may my husband.
O Isabel, will you not lend a knee?

DUKE
He dies for Claudio's death.
ISABELLA
Most bounteous sir, [*Kneeling.*
Look, if it please you, on this man condemn'd,
As if my brother lived: I partly think
A due sincerity govern'd his deeds,
Till he did look on me: since it is so,
Let him not die. My brother had but justice,
In that he did the thing for which he died:
For Angelo,
His act did not o'ertake his bad intent,
And must be buried but as an intent
That perish'd by the way: thoughts are no subjects;
Intents but merely thoughts.
MARIANA
Merely, my lord.
DUKE
Your suit's unprofitable; stand up, I say.
I have bethought me of another fault.
Provost, how came it Claudio was beheaded
At an unusual hour?
PROVOST
It was commanded so.
DUKE
Had you a special warrant for the deed?
PROVOST
No, my good lord; it was by private message.
DUKE
For which I do discharge you of your office:
Give up your keys.
PROVOST
Pardon me, noble lord:
I thought it was a fault, but knew it not;
Yet did repent me, after more advice;
For testimony whereof, one in the prison,
That should by private order else have died,
I have reserved alive.
DUKE
What's he?
PROVOST
His name is Barnardine.
DUKE
I would thou hadst done so by Claudio.
Go fetch him hither; let me look upon him.
[*Exit Provost.*
ESCALUS
I am sorry, one so learned and so wise
As you, Lord Angelo, have still appear'd,
Should slip so grossly, both in the heat of blood.
And lack of temper'd judgment afterward.
ANGELO
I am sorry that such sorrow I procure:
And so deep sticks it in my penitent heart
That I crave death more willingly than mercy;
'Tis my deserving, and I do entreat it.

Re-enter PROVOST, *with* BARNARDINE, CLAUDIO *muffled, and* JULIET.

DUKE
Which is that Barnardine?
PROVOST
This, my lord.
DUKE
There was a friar told me of this man.
Sirrah, thou art said to have a stubborn soul.
That apprehends no further than this world,
And squarest thy life according. Thou'rt condemn'd:
But, for those earthly faults, I quit them all;
And pray thee take this mercy to provide
For better times to come. Friar, advise him;
I leave him to your hand. What muffled fellow's that?
PROVOST
This is another prisoner that I saved.
Who should have died when Claudio lost his head;
As like almost to Claudio as himself.
[*Unmuffles Claudio.*
DUKE
[*To Isabella*] If he be like your brother, for his sake
Is he pardon'd; and, for your lovely sake,
Give me your hand and say you will be mine. [34]
He is my brother too: but fitter time for that.
By this Lord Angelo perceives he's safe;
Methinks I see a quickening in his eye.
Well, Angelo, your evil quits you well:
Look that you love your wife; her worth worth yours.
I find an apt remission in myself;
And yet here's one in place I cannot pardon.
[*To Lucio*] You, sirrah, that knew me for a fool, a coward,
One all of luxury, an ass, a madman;
Wherein have I so deserved of you,
That you extol me thus?
LUCIO
Faith, my lord. I spoke it but according to the trick. If you will hang me for it, you may; but I had rather it would please you I might be whipt.
DUKE
Whipt first, sir, and hanged after.
Proclaim it, provost, round about the city.
Is any woman wrong'd by this lewd fellow,
As I have heard him swear himself there's one
Whom he begot with child, let her appear,
And he shall marry her: the nuptial finish'd,
Let him be whipt and hang'd.

LUCIO

I beseech your highness, do not marry me to a whore. Your highness said even now, I made you a duke: good my lord, do not recompense me in making me a cuckold.

DUKE

Upon mine honour, thou shalt marry her.
Thy slanders I forgive; and therewithal
Remit thy other forfeits. Take him to prison;
And see our pleasure herein executed.

LUCIO

Marrying a punk, my lord, is pressing to death, whipping, and hanging.

DUKE

Slandering a prince deserves it.
[*Exeunt Officers with Lucio.*
She, Claudio, that you wrong'd, look you restore.
Joy to you, Mariana! Love her, Angelo:
I have confess'd her and I know her virtue.
Thanks, good friend Escalus, for thy much goodness:
There's more behind that is more gratulate.
Thanks, provost, for thy care and secrecy:
We shill employ thee in a worthier place.
Forgive him, Angelo, that brought you home
The head of Ragozine for Claudio's:
The offence pardons itself. Dear Isabel,
I have a motion much imports your good;
Whereto if you'll a willing ear incline,
What's mine is yours and what is yours is mine.
So, bring us to our palace; where we'll show
What's yet behind, that's meet you all should know.
[*Exeunt.*

Notes

1. There is no gap in the Folios which is due to Theobald's plausible theory that the obscurity of the passage is due to some careless omission on the part of the printers. Various attempts have been made to explain the lines. *e.g.* "But that to your sufficiencies your worth is abled" (Johnson): "But your sufficiency as worth is able" (Farmer); Theobald supplied the missing words thus—

   "But that to your sufficiency you add
   Due diligency as your worth is able."

2. Hold therefore, Angelo; – the Duke probably says these words on tendering commission to Angelo.
3. There went but a pair of shears between us; i.e. – 'we are of one piece.'
4. Cp. St. Paul to the Romans – ix. 15, 18: "For He saith to Moses, I will have mercy *on whom I will* have mercy," and again, "Therefore hath He mercy *on whom He will* have mercy, and *whom He will* He hardeneth."
5. Morality; – the Folios misprint *'mortality.'*
6. Propagation; – Folio 1 reads *propogation,* corrected in Folio 2; *prorogation, procuration, preservation,* have been suggested by various editors, but the text as it stands is probably correct, though not altogether clear; ' *propagation'* = 'increase;' perhaps the word implies 'increase of interest,' and *'for propogation* = 'that she might continue to receive the interest, which was to be hers while she remained unmarried.'
7. To do in slander; – so the Folios; *'me'* and *'it'* have been suggested for *'in,'* but no change is necessary; *'do in'* = 'bring in, bring upon me.'
8. Some run from brakes of ice, and answer none; – the line as it stands in the Folios is obviously corrupt, and has occasioned much discussion. Shakespeare probably wrote *'brakes of vice;' brakes* = thickets, hence 'entanglements;' *'brakes of vice'* is antithetical to *'a fault alone,' cp. Henry VIII.* I. ii.

   "the rough brake
   That virtue must go through."

   The line therefore means 'some escape from whole thickets of sin, and pay no penalty.' Judging by the passage in *Henry VIII, through* for *from* would perhaps be an improvement.

9. An open room; – Schmidt, "public room;" perhaps it means 'open to sun, light, cheerful.'
10. Like man new made; – commentators are strongly tempted to refer the words to *'new made man,' i.e.* Adam; Holt White paraphrased thus:—"And you, Angelo, will breathe new life into Claudio, as the Creator animated Adam, by breathing into his nostrils the breath of life." Malone explains:—"You will then appear as tender-hearted and merciful as the first man was in his days of innocence, immediately after his creation." Schmidt and others, "like man redeemed and regenerated by divine grace." The lines are perhaps capable of this interpretation:—And mercy will breathe within your lips, even as Mercy (*i.e.* God) breathed within the lips of new made man.
11. "Dormiunt aliquando leges, moriuntur nunquam," is a well-known maxim in law (Holt White).
12. Where prayers cross, i. e. – where his prayer to possess Isabella crosses with hers, "Heaven keep your *honour* safe!"
13. The flaws of her own youth; – possibly Warburton's correction *"flames"* should be adopted; *cp.*

    'To flaming youth let virtue be as wax,
    And melt in her own fire.'
    —HAMLET. III. iv.

14. O injurious love – (Folios 'loue'); Hanmer's suggestion, *"law"* for *"loue,"* has been generally accepted; the law respited her 'a life whose very comfort' was 'a dying horror.'
15. Feared; – probably an error of *'feared,' i.e. 'seared,'* which, according to Collier, is the reading of Lord Ellesmere's copy of the first Folio.
16. That longing have been sick for; – Rowe suggested, "I've been sick for."
17. O perilous mouths; – the line is defective as it stands (?) *"O pernicious mouths"* (Walker), or *"these perilous"* (Seymour).

18. Prenzie; – the source of this strange word has baffled students; it seems identical with the Scottish *primsie,* 'demure, precise,' which in its turn is connected with *prim* (in Old French *prin, pren*): under any circumstances there is no reason why the word should be changed, as has been proposed, to 'princely,' the readers of the second Folio, or 'priestly,' 'pensive,' &c.
19. "The passage seems to us to imply, furred (that is, lined with lamb-skin fur inside, and trimmed with fox-skin fur outside) with both kinds of fur, to show that craft (fox-skin), being richer than innocency (lamb-skin), is used for decoration" (Clarke).
20. Good father friar ... 'good brother father;' – the joke, as Tyrwhitt pointed out, would be clearer in French, *'mon père frère' ... 'mon frère père.'*
21. From our faults, as faults from seeming, free! – So Folio 1, Folio 2 and Folio 3, *'Free from our faults,'* &c.; Hanmer corrects the latter part of the line, *'As from faults seeming free.'* As it stands in the text, it would seem to mean "Would that we were as free from faults, as our faults are from seeming (hypocrisy)." One feels inclined to hazard—

    'Free from our faults, as from false seeming, free!'

    (*Cp.* II. iv. 15, *'thy false seeming.'*)
22. Security enough to make fellowships accurst; – *cp. Prov.* xi. 15.
23. These lines are in all probability not Shakespeare's, but by another hand.
24. Grace to stand, and virtue go; i.e. – 'To have grace to stand firm, and virtue to go forward.'
25. How may likeness made in crimes, – &c.; these lines do not readily admit of interpretation, and some corruption has probably crept into the text; Malone suggested *wade* for *made, i.e.* "How may hypocrisy wade in crimes;" Hanmer, "that likeness shading crimes," &c. None of the suggestions seem very satisfactory. Perhaps *to draw* = *'to-draw,' i. e.* 'pull to pieces' (?)
26. This song appears in Beaumont and Fletcher's *Bloody Brother,* with the addition of the following stanza, assuredly not Shakespeare's, though found in the spurious edition of his poems, (1640)—

    "Hide, O hide those hills of snow
    Which thy frozen bosom bears,
    On whose tops the pinks that grow
    Are of those that April wears;
    But first set my poor heart free,
    Bound by those icy chains by thee."
27. "Though the music soothed my sorrows, it had no tendency to produce light merriment" (Johnson).
28. If it be too little—thief; – the Folios give this to *Clo.* (Pompey); Capell first transferred it to Abhorson, and he has been followed by most editors. Cowden Clarke defends the Folio arrangement; among other arguments he maintains that "the speech is much more in character with the clown's snip-snap style of chop-logic than with Abhorson's manner, which is remarkably curt and bluff."
29. Redeliver; – Folio 1, *'re-liuer;'* Folio 2, *'deliuer;'* Capell first suggested *'re-deliver.'*
30. bears of a credent bulk; – so Folios 1, 2, 3; many emendations have been proposed; Dyce's seems the most plausible—'bears so credent bulk;' *'credent bulk'* = 'weight of credit.'
31. Do not banish reason, For in-equality; – *i.e.* because of 'improbability,' 'in-congruity,' or, according to some, 'partiality.'
32. "These shops," according to Nares, "were places of great resort, for passing away time in an idle manner. By way of enforcing some kind of regularity, and perhaps at least as much to promote drinking, certain laws were usually hung up, the transgression of which was to be punished by specific *forfeitures.* It is not to be wondered, that laws of that nature were as often laughed at as obeyed."
33. Be hanged an hour – seems to have been a cant phrase, meaning little more than 'be hanged!'
34. Give me your hand; i.e. 'if you give me your hand.'

THE MERCHANT OF VENICE

THE MERCHANT OF VENICE

DRAMATIS PERSONAE

The DUKE OF VENICE. suitor to Portia.
The PRINCE OF MOROCCO, suitor to Portia.
The PRINCE OF ARRAGON, suitor to Portia.
ANTONIO, a merchant of Venice.
BASSANIO, his friend, suitor likewise to Portia.
SALANIO, friend to Antonio and Bassanio.
SALARINO, friend to Antonio and Bassanio.
GRATIANO, friend to Antonio and Bassanio.
SALERIO, friend to Antonio and Bassanio.
LORENZO, in love with Jessica.
SHYLOCK, a rich Jew. [1]
TUBAL, a Jew, his friend.
LAUNCELOT GOBBO, the clown, servant to Shylock.
OLD GOBBO, father to Launcelot.
LEONARDO, servant to Bassanio.
BALTHASAR, servant to Portia.
STEPHANO, servant to Portia.
PORTIA, a rich heiress.
NERISSA, her waiting-maid.
JESSICA, daughter to Shylock.
Magnificoes of Venice, Officers of the Court of Justice, Gaoler, Servants to Portia, and other Attendants.

SCENE: *Partly at Venice, and partly at Belmont, the seat of Portia, on the Continent.*

ACT ONE SCENE ONE

Venice. A street.

Enter ANTONIO, SALARINO, *and* SALANIO.

ANTONIO
In sooth, I know not why I am so sad:
It wearies me; you say it wearies you;
But how I caught it, found it, or came by it,
What stuff 'tis made of, whereof it is born,
I am to learn;
And such a want-wit sadness makes of me,
That I have much ado to know myself.

SALARINO
Your mind is tossing on the ocean;
There, where your argosies with portly sail,
Like signiors and rich burghers on the flood,
Or, as it were, the pageants of the sea,
Do overpeer the petty traffickers,
That curtsy to them, do them reverence,
As they fly by them with their woven wings.

SALANIO
Believe me, sir, had I such venture forth,
The better part of my affections would
Be with my hopes abroad. I should be still
Plucking the grass to know where sits the wind,
Peering in maps for ports and piers and roads;
And every object that might make me fear
Misfortune to my ventures, out of doubt
Would make me sad.

SALARINO
My wind cooling my broth
Would blow me to an ague, when I thought
What harm a wind too great at sea might do.

I should not see the sandy hour-glass run,
But I should think of shallows and of flats,
And see my wealthy Andrew dock'd in sand, [2]
Vailing her high-top lower than her ribs
To kiss her burial. Should I go to church
And see the holy edifice of stone,
And not bethink me straight of dangerous rocks,
Which touching but my gentle vessel's side,
Would scatter all her spices on the stream,
Enrobe the roaring waters with my silks,
And, in a word, but even now worth this,
And now worth nothing? Shall I have the thought
To think on this, and shall I lack the thought
That such a thing bechanced would make me sad?
But tell not me; I know, Antonio
Is sad to think upon his merchandise.

ANTONIO
Believe me, no: I thank my fortune for it,
My ventures are not in one bottom trusted,
Nor to one place; nor is my whole estate
Upon the fortune of this present year:
Therefore my merchandise makes me not sad.

SALARINO
Why, then you are in love.

ANTONIO
Fie, fie!

SALARINO
Not in love neither? Then let us say you are sad,
Because you are not merry: and 'twere as easy
For you to laugh and leap and say you are merry,
Because you are not sad. Now, by two-headed Janus,
Nature hath framed strange fellows in her time:
Some that will evermore peep through their eyes
And laugh like parrots at a bag-piper,
And other of such vinegar aspect
That they'll not show their teeth in way of smile,
Though Nestor swears the jest be laughable.

Enter BASSANIO, LORENZO, *and* GRATIANO.

SALANIO
Here comes Bassanio, your most noble kinsman,
Gratiano and Lorenzo. Fare ye well:
We leave you now with better company.

SALARINO
I would have stay'd till I had made you merry,
If worthier friends had not prevented me.

ANTONIO
Your worth is very dear in my regard.
I take it, your own business calls on you
And you embrace the occasion to depart.

SALARINO
Good morrow, my good lords.

BASSANIO
Good signiors both, when shall we laugh? say, when?
You grow exceeding strange: must it be so?

SALARINO
We'll make our leisures to attend on yours.
[*Exeunt Salarino and Salanio.*

LORENZO
My Lord Bassanio, since you have found Antonio,
We two will leave you: but at dinner-time,
I pray you, have in mind where we must meet.

BASSANIO
I will not fail you.

GRATIANO
You look not well, Signior Antonio;
You have too much respect upon the world:
They lose it that do buy it with much care:
Believe me, you are marvellously changed.

ANTONIO
I hold the world but as the world, Gratiano;
A stage where every man must play a part,
And mine a sad one.

GRATIANO
Let me play the fool:
With mirth and laughter let old wrinkles come,
And let my liver rather heat with wine
Than my heart cool with mortifying groans.
Why should a man, whose blood is warm within,
Sit like his grandsire cut in alabaster?
Sleep when he wakes and creep into the jaundice
By being peevish? I tell thee what, Antonio—
I love thee, and it is my love that speaks—
There are a sort of men whose visages
Do cream and mantle like a standing pond,
And do a wilful stillness entertain,
With purpose to be dress'd in an opinion
Of wisdom, gravity, profound conceit,
As who should say 'I am Sir Oracle,
And when I ope my lips let no dog bark!'
O my Antonio, I do know of these
That therefore only are reputed wise
For saying nothing; when, I am very sure,
If they should speak, would almost damn those ears
Which, hearing them, would call their brothers fools.
I'll tell thee more of this another time:
But fish not, with this melancholy bait,
For this fool gudgeon, this opinion.
Come, good Lorenzo. Fare ye well awhile:
I'll end my exhortation after dinner.

LORENZO
Well, we will leave you then till dinner-time:
I must be one of these same dumb wise men,
For Gratiano never lets me speak.

GRATIANO
Well, keep me company but two years more,
Thou shalt not know the sound of thine own tongue.
ANTONIO
Farewell: I'll grow a talker for this gear.
GRATIANO
Thanks, i' faith, for silence is only commendable
In a neat's tongue dried and a maid not vendible.
[*Exeunt Gratiano and Lorenzo.*
ANTONIO
Is that any thing new? [3]
BASSANIO
Gratiano speaks an infinite deal of nothing, more than any man in all Venice. His reasons are as two grains of wheat hid in two bushels of chaff: you shall seek all day ere you find them, and when you have them, they are not worth the search.
ANTONIO
Well, tell me now what lady is the same
To whom you swore a secret pilgrimage
That you to-day promised to tell me of?
BASSANIO
'Tis not unknown to you, Antonio,
How much I have disabled mine estate,
By something showing a more swelling port
Than my faint means would grant continuance:
Nor do I now make moan to be abridged
From such a noble rate; but my chief care
Is to come fairly off from the great debts
Wherein my time something too prodigal
Hath left me gaged. To you, Antonio,
I owe the most, in money and in love,
And from your love I have a warranty
To unburden all my plots and purposes
How to get clear of all the debts I owe.
ANTONIO
I pray you, good Bassanio, let me know it;
And if it stand, as you yourself still do,
Within the eye of honour, be assured,
My purse, my person, my extremest means,
Lie all unlock'd to your occasions.
BASSANIO
In my school-days, when I had lost one shaft,
I shot his fellow of the self-same flight
The self-same way with more advised watch,
To find the other forth, and by adventuring both
I oft found both: I urge this childhood proof,
Because what follows is pure innocence.
I owe you much, and, like a wilful youth,
That which I owe is lost; but if you please
To shoot another arrow that self way
Which you did shoot the first, I do not doubt,
As I will watch the aim, or to find both
Or bring your latter hazard back again
And thankfully rest debtor for the first.
ANTONIO
You know me well, and herein spend but time
To wind about my love with circumstance;
And out of doubt you do me now more wrong
In making question of my uttermost
Than if you had made waste of all I have:
Then do but say to me what I should do
That in your knowledge may by me be done,
And I am prest unto it: therefore, speak.
BASSANIO
In Belmont is a lady richly left;
And she is fair and, fairer than that word,
Of wondrous virtues: sometimes from her eyes
I did receive fair speechless messages:
Her name is Portia, nothing undervalued
To Cato's daughter, Brutus' Portia:
Nor is the wide world ignorant of her worth,
For the four winds blow in from every coast
Renowned suitors, and her sunny locks
Hang on her temples like a golden fleece;
Which makes her seat of Belmont Colchos' strand,
And many Jasons come in quest of her.
O my Antonio, had I but the means
To hold a rival place with one of them,
I have a mind presages me such thrift,
That I should questionless be fortunate!
ANTONIO
Thou know'st that all my fortunes are at sea;
Neither have I money nor commodity
To raise a present sum: therefore go forth;
Try what my credit can in Venice do:
That shall be rack'd, even to the uttermost,
To furnish thee to Belmont, to fair Portia.
Go, presently inquire, and so will I,
Where money is, and I no question make
To have it of my trust or for my sake. [*Exeunt.*

ACT ONE SCENE TWO

Belmont. A room in PORTIA'S *house.*

Enter PORTIA *and* NERISSA.

PORTIA
By my troth, Nerissa, my little body is aweary of this great world.
NERISSA
You would be, sweet madam, if your miseries were in the same abundance as your good fortunes are: and yet, for aught I see, they are as sick that surfeit with too much as they that starve with nothing. It is no mean happiness therefore, to be seated in the

mean: superfluity comes sooner by white hairs, but competency lives longer. 9

PORTIA

Good sentences and well pronounced.

NERISSA

They would be better, if well followed.

PORTIA

If to do were as easy as to know what were good to do, chapels had been churches and poor men's cottages princes' palaces. It is a good divine that follows his own instructions: I can easier teach twenty what were good to be done, than be one of the twenty to follow mine own teaching. The brain may devise laws for the blood, but a hot temper leaps o'er a cold decree: such a hare is madness the youth, to skip o'er the meshes of good counsel the cripple. But this reasoning is not in the fashion to choose me a husband. O me, the word 'choose!' I may neither choose whom I would nor refuse whom I dislike; so is the will of a living daughter curbed by the will of a dead father. Is it not hard, Nerissa, that I cannot choose one nor refuse none? 25

NERISSA

Your father was ever virtuous; and holy men at their death have good inspirations: therefore the lottery, that he hath devised in these three chests of gold, silver and lead, whereof who chooses his meaning chooses you, will, no doubt, never be chosen by any rightly but one who shall rightly love. But what warmth is there in your affection towards any of these princely suitors that are already come?

PORTIA

I pray thee, over-name them; and as thou namest them, I will describe them; and, according to my description, level at my affection.

NERISSA

First, there is the Neapolitan prince.

PORTIA

Ay, that's a colt indeed, for he doth nothing but talk of his horse; and he makes it a great appropriation to his own good parts, that he can shoe him himself. I am much afeard my lady his mother played false with a smith.

NERISSA

Then there is the Count Palatine. 42

PORTIA

He doth nothing but frown, as who should say 'If you will not have me, choose:' he hears merry tales and smiles not: I fear he will prove the weeping philosopher when he grows old, being so full of unmannerly sadness in his youth. I had rather be married to a death's-head with a bone in his mouth than to either of these. God defend me from these two!

NERISSA

How say you by the French lord, Monsieur Le Bon? 51

PORTIA

God made him, and therefore let him pass for a man. In truth, I know it is a sin to be a mocker: but, he! why, he hath a horse better than the Neapolitan's, a better bad habit of frowning than the Count Palatine; he is every man in no man; if a throstle sing, he falls straight a capering: he will fence with his own shadow: if I should marry him, I should marry twenty husbands. If he would despise me I would forgive him, for if he love me to madness, I shall never requite him. 61

NERISSA

What say you, then, to Falconbridge, the young baron of England?

PORTIA

You know I say nothing to him, for he understands not me, nor I him: he hath neither Latin, French, nor Italian, and you will come into the court and swear that I have a poor pennyworth in the English. He is a proper man's picture, but, alas, who can converse with a dumb-show? How oddly he is suited! I think he bought his doublet in Italy, his round hose in France, his bonnet in Germany and his behavior every where.

NERISSA

What think you of the Scottish lord, his neighbour? [4]

PORTIA

That he hath a neighbourly charity in him, for he borrowed a box of the ear of the Englishman and swore he would pay him again when he was able: I think the Frenchman became his surety and sealed under for another. [5]

NERISSA

How like you the young German, the Duke of Saxony's nephew? 81

PORTIA

Very vilely in the morning, when he is sober, and most vilely in the afternoon, when he is drunk: when he is best, he is a little worse than a man, and when he is worst, he is little better than a beast: and the worst fall that ever fell, I hope I shall make shift to go without him.

NERISSA

If he should offer to choose, and choose the right casket, you should refuse to perform your father's will, if you should refuse to accept him.

PORTIA

Therefore, for fear of the worst, I pray thee, set a deep glass of rhenish wine on the contrary casket, for if the devil be within and that temptation without, I know he will choose it. I will do any thing, Nerissa, ere I'll be married to a sponge.

NERISSA

You need not fear, lady, the having any of these lords: they have acquainted me with their determinations; which is, indeed, to return to their home and to trouble you with no more suit, unless you may be won by some other sort than your father's imposition depending on the caskets.

PORTIA

If I live to be as old as Sibylla, I will die as chaste as Diana, unless I be obtained by the manner of my father's will. I am glad this parcel of wooers are so reasonable, for there is not one among them but I dote on his very absence, and I pray God grant them a fair departure.

NERISSA

Do you not remember, lady, in your father's time, a Venetian, a scholar and a soldier, that came hither in company of the Marquis of Montferrat?

PORTIA

Yes, yes, it was Bassanio; as I think, he was so called.

NERISSA

True, madam: he, of all the men that ever my foolish eyes looked upon, was the best deserving a fair lady.

PORTIA

I remember him well, and I remember him worthy of thy praise.

Enter a Servingman.

How now! what news?

SERVINGMAN

The four strangers seek for you, madam, to take their leave: and there is a forerunner come from a fifth, the Prince of Morocco, who brings word the prince his master will be here to-night. [6]

PORTIA

If I could bid the fifth welcome with so good a heart as I can bid the other four farewell, I should be glad of his approach: if he have the condition of a saint and the complexion of a devil, I had rather he should shrive me than wive me.

Come, Nerissa. Sirrah, go before.

Whiles we shut the gates upon one wooer, another knocks at the door. [*Exeunt.*

ACT ONE SCENE THREE

Venice. A public place.

Enter BASSANIO *and* SHYLOCK.

SHYLOCK

Three thousand ducats; well.

BASSANIO

Ay, sir, for three months.

SHYLOCK

For three months; well.

BASSANIO

For the which, as I told you, Antonio shall be bound.

SHYLOCK

Antonio shall become bound; well.

BASSANIO

May you stead me? will you pleasure me? shall I know your answer?

SHYLOCK

Three thousand ducats for three months and Antonio bound.

BASSANIO

Your answer to that.

SHYLOCK

Antonio is a good man.

BASSANIO

Have you heard any imputation to the contrary?

SHYLOCK

Oh, no, no, no, no: my meaning in saying he is a good man is to have you understand me that he is sufficient. Yet his means are in supposition: he hath an argosy bound to Tripolis, another to the Indies; I understand, moreover, upon the Rialto, he hath a third at Mexico, a fourth for England, and other ventures he hath, squandered abroad. But ships are but boards, sailors but men: there be land-rats and water-rats, water-thieves and land-thieves, I mean pirates, and then there is the peril of waters, winds and rocks. The man is, notwithstanding, sufficient. Three thousand ducats; I think I may take his bond.

BASSANIO

Be assured you may.

SHYLOCK

I will be assured I may; and, that I may be assured, I will bethink me. May I speak with Antonio?

BASSANIO

If it please you to dine with us.

SHYLOCK

Yes, to smell pork; to eat of the habitation which your prophet the Nazarite conjured the devil into. I will buy with you, sell with you, talk with you, walk with you, and so following, but I will not eat with you, drink with you, nor pray with you. What news on the Rialto? Who is he comes here?

Enter ANTONIO.

BASSANIO

This is Signior Antonio.

SHYLOCK

[*Aside*] How like a fawning publican he looks!
I hate him for he is a Christian,
But more for that in low simplicity

He lends out money gratis and brings down
The rate of usance here with us in Venice.
If I can catch him once upon the hip,
I will feed fat the ancient grudge I bear him.
He hates our sacred nation, and he rails,
Even there where merchants most do congregate,
On me, my bargains and my well-won thrift,
Which he calls interest. Cursed be my tribe,
If I forgive him!

BASSANIO

Shylock, do you hear?

SHYLOCK

I am debating of my present store,
And, by the near guess of my memory,
I cannot instantly raise up the gross
Of full three thousand ducats. What of that
Tubal, a wealthy Hebrew of my tribe,
Will furnish me. But soft! how many months
Do you desire? [*To Antonio*] Rest you fair, good signior;
Your worship was the last man in our mouths.

ANTONIO

Shylock, although I neither lend nor borrow
By taking nor by giving of excess,
Yet, to supply the ripe wants of my friend,
I'll break a custom. Is he yet possess'd [7]
How much ye would?

SHYLOCK

Ay, ay, three thousand ducats.

ANTONIO

And for three months.

SHYLOCK

I had forgot; three months; you told me so.
Well then, your bond; and let me see; but hear you;
Methought you said you neither lend nor borrow
Upon advantage.

ANTONIO

I do never use it.

SHYLOCK

When Jacob grazed his uncle Laban's sheep— [8]
This Jacob from our holy Abram was,
As his wise mother wrought in his behalf,
The third possessor; ay, he was the third— [9]

ANTONIO

And what of him? did he take interest?

SHYLOCK

No, not take interest, not, as you would say,
Directly interest: mark what Jacob did.
When Laban and himself were compromised
That all the eanlings which were streak'd and pied
Should fall as Jacob's hire, the ewes, being rank,
In the end of autumn turned to the rams,
And, when the work of generation was
Between these woolly breeders in the act,
The skilful shepherd peel'd me certain wands
And, in the doing of the deed of kind,
He stuck them up before the fulsome ewes,
Who then conceiving did in eaning time
Fall parti-colour'd lambs, and those were Jacob's.
This was a way to thrive, and he was blest:
And thrift is blessing, if men steal it not.

ANTONIO

This was a venture, sir, that Jacob served for;
A thing not in his power to bring to pass,
But sway'd and fashion'd by the hand of heaven.
Was this inserted to make interest good?
Or is your gold and silver ewes and rams?

SHYLOCK

I cannot tell; I make it breed as fast:
But note me, signior.

ANTONIO

Mark you this, Bassanio,
The devil can cite Scripture for his purpose.
An evil soul producing holy witness
Is like a villain with a smiling cheek,
A goodly apple rotten at the heart:
O what a goodly outside falsehood hath!

SHYLOCK

Three thousand ducats; 'tis a good round sum.
Three months from twelve; then, let me see; the rate—

ANTONIO

Well, Shylock, shall we be beholding to you?

SHYLOCK

Signior Antonio, many a time and oft
In the Rialto you have rated me
About my moneys and my usances:
Still have I borne it with a patient shrug,
For sufferance is the badge of all our tribe.
You call me misbeliever, cut-throat dog,
And spit upon my Jewish gaberdine,
And all for use of that which is mine own.
Well then, it now appears you need my help:
Go to, then; you come to me, and you say
'Shylock, we would have moneys:' you say so;
You, that did void your rheum upon my beard
And foot me as you spurn a stranger cur
Over your threshold: moneys is your suit.
What should I say to you? Should I not say
'Hath a dog money? is it possible
A cur can lend three thousand ducats?' Or
Shall I bend low and in a bondman's key,
With bated breath and whispering humbleness,
Say this;
'Fair sir, you spit on me on Wednesday last;
You spurn'd me such a day; another time

You call'd me dog; and for these courtesies
I'll lend you thus much moneys'?
ANTONIO
I am as like to call thee so again,
To spit on thee again, to spurn thee too.
If thou wilt lend this money, lend it not
As to thy friends; for when did friendship take
A breed for barren metal of his friend? [10]
But lend it rather to thine enemy,
Who, if he break, thou mayst with better face
Exact the penalty.
SHYLOCK
Why, look you, how you storm!
I would be friends with you and have your love,
Forget the shames that you have stain'd me with
Supply your present wants and take no doit
Of usance for my moneys, and you'll not hear me:
This is kind I offer.
BASSANIO
This were kindness.
SHYLOCK
This kindness will I show.
Go with me to a notary, seal me there
Your single bond; and, in a merry sport,
If you repay me not on such a day,
In such a place, such sum or sums as are
Express'd in the condition, let the forfeit
Be nominated for an equal pound
Of your fair flesh, to be cut off and taken
In what part of your body pleaseth me.
ANTONIO
Content, i' faith: I'll seal to such a bond
And say there is much kindness in the Jew.
BASSANIO
You shall not seal to such a bond for me:
I'll rather dwell in my necessity.
ANTONIO
Why, fear not, man; I will not forfeit it:
Within these two months, that's a month before
This bond expires, I do expect return
Of thrice three times the value of this bond.
SHYLOCK
O father Abram, what these Christians are.
Whose own hard dealings teaches them suspect
The thoughts of others! Pray you, tell me this;
If he should break his day, what should I gain
By the exaction of the forfeiture?
A pound of man's flesh taken from a man
Is not so estimable, profitable neither,
As flesh of muttons, beefs, or goats. I say,
To buy his favour, I extend this friendship:
If he will take it, so; if not, adieu;
And, for my love, I pray you wrong me not.
ANTONIO
Yes, Shylock, I will seal unto this bond.
SHYLOCK
Then meet me forthwith at the notary's;
Give him direction for this merry bond,
And I will go and purse the ducats straight,
See to my house, left in the fearful guard
Of an unthrifty knave, and presently
I will be with you.
ANTONIO
Hie thee, gentle Jew. [*Exit Shylock.*
The Hebrew will turn Christian: he grows kind.
BASSANIO
I like not fair terms and a villain's mind.
ANTONIO
Come on: in this there can be no dismay;
My ships come home a month before the day.
[*Exeunt.*

ACT TWO SCENE ONE

Belmont. A room in PORTIA'S *house.*

Flourish of cornets. Enter the PRINCE OF MOROCCO *and his train*; PORTIA, NERISSA, *and others attending.* [11]

PRINCE OF MOROCCO
Mislike me not for my complexion,
The shadow'd livery of the burnish'd sun,
To whom I am a neighbour and near bred.
Bring me the fairest creature northward born,
Where Phoebus' fire scarce thaws the icicles,
And let us make incision for your love,
To prove whose blood is reddest, his or mine.
I tell thee, lady, this aspect of mine
Hath fear'd the valiant: by my love, I swear
The best-regarded virgins of our clime
Have loved it too: I would not change this hue,
Except to steal your thoughts, my gentle queen.
PORTIA
In terms of choice I am not solely led
By nice direction of a maiden's eyes;
Besides, the lottery of my destiny
Bars me the right of voluntary choosing:
But if my father had not scanted me
And hedged me by his wit, to yield myself
His wife who wins me by that means I told you
Yourself, renowned prince, then stood as fair
As any comer I have look'd on yet
For my affection.
PRINCE OF MOROCCO
Even for that I thank you:
Therefore, I pray you, lead me to the caskets

To try my fortune. By this scimitar
That slew the Sophy and a Persian prince [12]
That won three fields of Sultan Solyman,
I would outstare the sternest eyes that look,
Outbrave the heart most daring on the earth,
Pluck the young sucking cubs from the she-bear.
Yea, mock the lion when he roars for prey,
To win thee, lady. But, alas the while!
If Hercules and Lichas play at dice
Which is the better man, the greater throw
May turn by fortune from the weaker hand:
So is Alcides beaten by his page; [13]
And so may I, blind fortune leading me,
Miss that which one unworthier may attain,
And die with grieving.

PORTIA
You must take your chance,
And either not attempt to choose at all
Or swear before you choose, if you choose wrong
Never to speak to lady afterward
In way of marriage: therefore be advised.

PRINCE OF MOROCCO
Nor will not. Come, bring me unto my chance.

PORTIA
First, forward to the temple: after dinner
Your hazard shall be made.

PRINCE OF MOROCCO
Good fortune then!
To make me blest or cursed'st among men.

[*Cornets, and exeunt.*

ACT TWO SCENE TWO

Venice. A street.

Enter LAUNCELOT.

LAUNCELOT
Certainly my conscience will serve me to run from this Jew my master. The fiend is at mine elbow and tempts me saying to me 'Gobbo, Launcelot Gobbo, good Launcelot,' or 'good Gobbo,' or 'good Launcelot Gobbo, use your legs, take the start, run away.' My conscience says 'No; take heed, honest Launcelot; take heed, honest Gobbo,' or, as aforesaid, 'honest Launcelot Gobbo; do not run; scorn running with thy heels.' Well, the most courageous fiend bids me pack: 'Via!' says the fiend; 'away!' says the fiend; 'for the heavens, rouse up a brave mind,' says the fiend, 'and run.' Well, my conscience, hanging about the neck of my heart, says very wisely to me 'My honest friend Launcelot, being an honest man's son,' or rather an honest woman's son; for, indeed, my father did something smack, something grow to, he had a kind of taste; well, my conscience says 'Launcelot, budge not.' 'Budge,' says the fiend. 'Budge not,' says my conscience. 'Conscience,' say I, 'you counsel well;' 'Fiend,' say I, 'you counsel well:' to be ruled by my conscience, I should stay with the Jew my master, who, God bless the mark, is a kind of devil; and, to run away from the Jew, I should be ruled by the fiend, who, saving your reverence, is the devil himself. Certainly the Jew is the very devil incarnate; and, in my conscience, my conscience is but a kind of hard conscience, to offer to counsel me to stay with the Jew. The fiend gives the more friendly counsel: I will run, fiend; my heels are at your command; I will run.

Enter OLD GOBBO, *with a basket.*

OLD GOBBO
Master young man, you, I pray you, which is the way to master Jew's?

LAUNCELOT
[*Aside*] O heavens, this is my true-begotten father! who, being more than sand-blind, high-gravel blind, knows me not: I will try confusions with him.

OLD GOBBO
Master young gentleman, I pray you, which is the way to master Jew's?

LAUNCELOT
Turn up on your right hand at the next turning, but, at the next turning of all, on your left; marry, at the very next turning, turn of no hand, but turn down indirectly to the Jew's house.

OLD GOBBO
By God's sonties, 'twill be a hard way to hit. Can you tell me whether one Launcelot, that dwells with him, dwell with him or no?

LAUNCELOT
Talk you of young Master Launcelot? [*Aside*] Mark me now; now will I raise the waters. Talk you of young Master Launcelot?

OLD GOBBO
No master, sir, but a poor man's son: his father, though I say it, is an honest exceeding poor man, and, God be thanked, well to live.

LAUNCELOT
Well, let his father be what a' will, we talk of young Master Launcelot.

OLD GOBBO
Your worship's friend and Launcelot, sir.

LAUNCELOT
But I pray you, ergo, old man, ergo, I beseech you, talk you of young Master Launcelot?

OLD GOBBO
Of Launcelot, an't please your mastership.

LAUNCELOT
Ergo, Master Launcelot. Talk not of Master Launcelot, father; for the young gentleman, according

to Fates and Destinies and such odd sayings, the Sisters Three and such branches of learning, is indeed deceased, or, as you would say in plain terms, gone to heaven.

OLD GOBBO

Marry, God forbid! the boy was the very staff of my age, my very prop.

LAUNCELOT

Do I look like a cudgel or a hovel-post, a staff or a prop? Do you know me, father?

OLD GOBBO

Alack the day, I know you not, young gentleman; but, I pray you, tell me, is my boy, God rest his soul, alive or dead?

LAUNCELOT

Do you not know me, father?

OLD GOBBO

Alack, sir, I am sand-blind; I know you not.

LAUNCELOT

Nay, indeed, if you had your eyes, you might fail of the knowing me: it is a wise father that knows his own child. Well, old man, I will tell you news of your son: give me your blessing: truth will come to light; murder cannot be hid long; a man's son may, but at the length truth will out.

OLD GOBBO

Pray you, sir, stand up: I am sure you are not Launcelot, my boy.

LAUNCELOT

Pray you, let's have no more fooling about it, but give me your blessing: I am Launcelot, your boy that was, your son that is, your child that shall be.

OLD GOBBO

I cannot think you are my son. [14]

LAUNCELOT

I know not what I shall think of that: but I am Launcelot, the Jew's man, and I am sure Margery your wife is my mother.

OLD GOBBO

Her name is Margery, indeed: I'll be sworn, if thou be Launcelot, thou art mine own flesh and blood. Lord worshipped might he be! what a beard hast thou got! thou hast got more hair on thy chin than Dobbin my fill-horse has on his tail.

LAUNCELOT

It should seem, then, that Dobbin's tail grows backward: I am sure he had more hair of his tail than I have of my face when I last saw him.

OLD GOBBO

Lord, how art thou changed! How dost thou and thy master agree? I have brought him a present. How 'gree you now?

LAUNCELOT

Well, well: but, for mine own part, as I have set up my rest to run away, so I will not rest till I have run some ground. My master's a very Jew: give him a present! give him a halter: I am famished in his service; you may tell every finger I have with my ribs. Father, I am glad you are come: give me your present to one Master Bassanio, who, indeed, gives rare new liveries: if I serve not him, I will run as far as God has any ground. O rare fortune! here comes the man: to him, father; for I am a Jew, if I serve the Jew any longer.

Enter BASSANIO, *with* LEONARDO *and other followers.*

BASSANIO

You may do so; but let it be so hasted that supper be ready at the farthest by five of the clock. See these letters delivered; put the liveries to making, and desire Gratiano to come anon to my lodging.

[*Exit a Servant.*

LAUNCELOT

To him, father.

OLD GOBBO

God bless your worship!

BASSANIO

Gramercy! wouldst thou aught with me?

OLD GOBBO

Here's my son, sir, a poor boy,—

LAUNCELOT

Not a poor boy, sir, but the rich Jew's man; that would, sir, as my father shall specify—

OLD GOBBO

He hath a great infection, sir, as one would say, to serve,—

LAUNCELOT

Indeed, the short and the long is, I serve the Jew, and have a desire, as my father shall specify—

OLD GOBBO

His master and he, saving your worship's reverence, are scarce cater-cousins—

LAUNCELOT

To be brief, the very truth is that the Jew, having done me wrong, doth cause me, as my father, being, I hope, an old man, shall frutify unto you—

OLD GOBBO

I have here a dish of doves that I would bestow upon your worship, and my suit is—

LAUNCELOT

In very brief, the suit is impertinent to myself, as your worship shall know by this honest old man; and, though I say it, though old man, yet poor man, my father.

BASSANIO

One speak for both. What would you?

LAUNCELOT

Serve you, sir.

OLD GOBBO

That is the very defect of the matter, sir.

BASSANIO
I know thee well; thou hast obtain'd thy suit:
Shylock thy master spoke with me this day,
And hath preferr'd thee, if it be preferment
To leave a rich Jew's service, to become
The follower of so poor a gentleman.

LAUNCELOT
The old proverb is very well parted between my master Shylock and you, sir: you have the grace of God, sir, and he hath enough.

BASSANIO
Thou speak'st it well. Go, father, with thy son.
Take leave of thy old master and inquire
My lodging out. Give him a livery
More guarded than his fellows': see it done.

LAUNCELOT
Father, in. I cannot get a service, no; I have ne'er a tongue in my head. Well, if any man in Italy have a fairer table which doth offer to swear upon a book, I shall have good fortune. Go to, here's a simple line of life: here's a small trifle of wives: alas, fifteen wives is nothing; eleven widows and nine maids is a simple coming-in for one man: and then to 'scape drowning thrice, and to be in peril of my life with the edge of a feather-bed; here are simple scapes. Well, if Fortune be a woman, she's a good wench for this gear. Father, come; I'll take my leave of the Jew in the twinkling of an eye. [15] *[Exeunt Launcelot and Old Gobbo.*

BASSANIO
I pray thee, good Leonardo, think on this:
These things being bought and orderly bestow'd,
Return in haste, for I do feast to-night
My best-esteem'd acquaintance: hie thee, go.

LEONARDO
My best endeavours shall be done herein.

Enter GRATIANO.

GRATIANO
Where is your master?

LEONARDO
Yonder, sir, he walks. *[Exit.*

GRATIANO
Signior Bassanio!

BASSANIO
Gratiano!

GRATIANO
I have a suit to you.

BASSANIO
You have obtain'd it.

GRATIANO
You must not deny me: I must go with you to Belmont.

BASSANIO
Why, then you must. But hear thee, Gratiano;
Thou art too wild, too rude and bold of voice;
Parts that become thee happily enough
And in such eyes as ours appear not faults;
But where thou art not known, why, there they show
Something too liberal. Pray thee, take pain
To allay with some cold drops of modesty
Thy skipping spirit, lest through thy wild behaviour
I be misconstrued in the place I go to
And lose my hopes.

GRATIANO
Signior Bassanio, hear me:
If I do not put on a sober habit,
Talk with respect and swear but now and then,
Wear prayer-books in my pocket, look demurely,
Nay more, while grace is saying, hood mine eyes
Thus with my hat, and sigh and say 'amen,'
Use all the observance of civility,
Like one well studied in a sad ostent
To please his grandam, never trust me more.

BASSANIO
Well, we shall see your bearing.

GRATIANO
Nay, but I bar to-night: you shall not gauge me
By what we do to-night.

BASSANIO
No, that were pity:
I would entreat you rather to put on
Your boldest suit of mirth, for we have friends
That purpose merriment. But fare you well:
I have some business.

GRATIANO
And I must to Lorenzo and the rest:
But we will visit you at supper-time. *[Exeunt.*

ACT TWO SCENE THREE

The same. A room in SHYLOCK'S *house.*

Enter JESSICA *and* LAUNCELOT.

JESSICA
I am sorry thou wilt leave my father so:
Our house is hell, and thou, a merry devil,
Didst rob it of some taste of tediousness.
But fare thee well, there is a ducat for thee:
And, Launcelot, soon at supper shalt thou see
Lorenzo, who is thy new master's guest:
Give him this letter; do it secretly;
And so farewell: I would not have my father
See me in talk with thee.

LAUNCELOT
Adieu! tears exhibit my tongue. Most beautiful pagan, most sweet Jew! if a Christian did not play the knave and get thee, I am much deceived. But,

adieu: these foolish drops do something drown my manly spirit: adieu. 16

JESSICA

Farewell, good Launcelot. *[Exit Launcelot.*
Alack, what heinous sin is it in me
To be ashamed to be my father's child!
But though I am a daughter to his blood,
I am not to his manners. O Lorenzo,
If thou keep promise, I shall end this strife, 20
Become a Christian and thy loving wife. *[Exit.*

ACT TWO SCENE FOUR

The same. A street.

Enter GRATIANO, LORENZO, SALARINO, *and* SALANIO.

LORENZO

Nay, we will slink away in supper-time,
Disguise us at my lodging and return,
All in an hour.

GRATIANO

We have not made good preparation.

SALARINO

We have not spoke us yet of torch-bearers.

SALANIO

'Tis vile, unless it may be quaintly order'd,
And better in my mind not undertook.

LORENZO

'Tis now but four o'clock: we have two hours
To furnish us.

Enter LAUNCELOT, *with a letter.*

Friend Launcelot, what's the news?

LAUNCELOT

An' it shall please you to break up this, it shall seem to signify. 12

LORENZO

I know the hand: in faith, 'tis a fair hand;
And whiter than the paper it writ on
Is the fair hand that writ.

GRATIANO

Love-news, in faith.

LAUNCELOT

By your leave, sir.

LORENZO

Whither goest thou?

LAUNCELOT

Marry, sir, to bid my old master the
Jew to sup to-night with my new master the Christian.

LORENZO

Hold here, take this: tell gentle Jessica
I will not fail her; speak it privately. 21
Go, gentlemen, *[Exit Launcelot.*
Will you prepare you for this masque to-night? I am provided of a torch-bearer.

SALARINO

Ay, marry, I'll be gone about it straight.

SALANIO

And so will I.

LORENZO

Meet me and Gratiano
At Gratiano's lodging some hour hence.

SALARINO

'Tis good we do so. *[Exeunt Salarino and Salanio.*

GRATIANO

Was not that letter from fair Jessica?

LORENZO

I must needs tell thee all. She hath directed 32
How I shall take her from her father's house,
What gold and jewels she is furnish'd with,
What page's suit she hath in readiness.
If e'er the Jew her father come to heaven,
It will be for his gentle daughter's sake:
And never dare misfortune cross her foot,
Unless she do it under this excuse,
That she is issue to a faithless Jew.
Come, go with me; peruse this as thou goest:
Fair Jessica shall be my torch-bearer. *[Exeunt.*

ACT TWO SCENE FIVE

The same. Before SHYLOCK'S *house.*

Enter SHYLOCK *and* LAUNCELOT.

SHYLOCK

Well, thou shalt see, thy eyes shall be thy judge,
The difference of old Shylock and Bassanio:—
What, Jessica!—thou shalt not gormandise,
As thou hast done with me:—What, Jessica!—
And sleep and snore, and rend apparel out;—
Why, Jessica, I say!

LAUNCELOT

Why, Jessica!

SHYLOCK

Who bids thee call? I do not bid thee call.

LAUNCELOT

Your worship was wont to tell me that
I could do nothing without bidding.

Enter JESSICA.

JESSICA

Call you? what is your will? 11

SHYLOCK

I am bid forth to supper, Jessica:
There are my keys. But wherefore should I go?

I am not bid for love; they flatter me:
But yet I'll go in hate, to feed upon
The prodigal Christian. Jessica, my girl,
Look to my house. I am right loath to go:
There is some ill a-brewing towards my rest,
For I did dream of money-bags to-night.

LAUNCELOT

I beseech you, sir, go: my young master doth expect your reproach. 21

SHYLOCK

So do I his.

LAUNCELOT

And they have conspired together, I will not say you shall see a masque; but if you do, then it was not for nothing that my nose fell a-bleeding on Black-Monday last at six o'clock i' the morning, falling out that year on Ash-Wednesday was four year, in the afternoon. [17]

SHYLOCK

What, are there masques? Hear you me, Jessica:
Lock up my doors; and when you hear the drum
And the vile squealing of the wry-neck'd fife,
Clamber not you up to the casements then,
Nor thrust your head into the public street
To gaze on Christian fools with varnish'd faces,
But stop my house's ears, I mean my casements:
Let not the sound of shallow foppery enter
My sober house. By Jacob's staff, I swear, [18]
I have no mind of feasting forth to-night:
But I will go. Go you before me, sirrah;
Say I will come.

LAUNCELOT

I will go before, sir. Mistress, look out at window, for all this; 42
There will come a Christian boy,
Will be worth a Jewess' eye. [19] [*Exit.*

SHYLOCK

What says that fool of Hagar's offspring, ha?

JESSICA

His words were 'Farewell mistress;' nothing else.

SHYLOCK

The patch is kind enough, but a huge feeder;
Snail-slow in profit, and he sleeps by day
More than the wild-cat; drones hive not with me;
Therefore I part with him, and part with him
To one that I would have him help to waste 51
His borrow'd purse. Well, Jessica, go in:
Perhaps I will return immediately:
Do as I bid you; shut doors after you:
Fast bind, fast find;
A proverb never stale in thrifty mind. [*Exit.*

JESSICA

Farewell; and if my fortune be not crost,
I have a father, you a daughter, lost. [*Exit.*

ACT TWO SCENE SIX

The same.

Enter GRATIANO *and* SALARINO, *masqued.*

GRATIANO

This is the pent-house under, which Lorenzo
Desired us to make stand.

SALARINO

His hour is almost past.

GRATIANO

And it is marvel he out-dwells his hour,
For lovers ever run before the clock.

SALARINO

O, ten times faster Venus' pigeons fly
To seal love's bonds new-made, than they are wont
To keep obliged faith unforfeited!

GRATIANO

That ever holds: who riseth from a feast
With that keen appetite that he sits down?
Where is the horse that doth untread again 12
His tedious measures with the unbated fire
That he did pace them first? All things that are,
Are with more spirit chased than enjoy'd.
How like a younker or a prodigal
The scarfed bark puts from her native bay,
Hugg'd and embraced by the strumpet wind!
How like the prodigal doth she return,
With over-weather'd ribs and ragged sails,
Lean, rent and beggar'd by the strumpet wind!

SALARINO

Here comes Lorenzo: more of this hereafter. 22

Enter LORENZO.

LORENZO

Sweet friends, your patience for my long abode;
Not I, but my affairs, have made you wait:
When you shall please to play the thieves for wives,
I'll watch as long for you then. Approach;
Here dwells my father Jew. Ho! who's within?

Enter JESSICA, *above, in boy's clothes.*

JESSICA

Who are you? Tell me, for more certainty,
Albeit I'll swear that I do know your tongue.

LORENZO

Lorenzo and thy love.

JESSICA

Lorenzo, certain, and my love indeed,
For who love I so much? And now who knows
But you, Lorenzo, whether I am yours? 44

LORENZO

Heaven and thy thoughts are witness that thou art.

JESSICA
Here, catch this casket; it is worth the pains.
I am glad 'tis night, you do not look on me,
For I am much ashamed of my exchange:
But love is blind and lovers cannot see
The pretty follies that themselves commit;
For if they could, Cupid himself would blush
To see me thus transformed to a boy.
LORENZO
Descend, for you must be my torch-bearer.
JESSICA
What, must I hold a candle to my shames?
They in themselves, good sooth, are too too light.
Why, 'tis an office of discovery, love;
And I should be obscured.
LORENZO
So are you, sweet,
Even in the lovely garnish of a boy.
But come at once;
For the close night doth play the runaway,
And we are stay'd for at Bassanio's feast.
JESSICA
I will make fast the doors, and gild myself
With some more ducats, and be with you straight.
[*Exit above.*
GRATIANO
Now, by my hood, a Gentile and no Jew. [20]
LORENZO
Beshrew me but I love her heartily;
For she is wise, if I can judge of her,
And fair she is, if that mine eyes be true,
And true she is as she hath proved herself,
And therefore, like herself, wise, fair and true,
Shall she be placed in my constant soul.

Enter JESSICA, *below.*

What, art thou come? On, gentlemen; away!
Our masquing mates by this time for us stay.
[*Exit with Jessica and Salarino.*

Enter ANTONIO.

ANTONIO
Who's there?
GRATIANO
Signior Antonio!
ANTONIO
Fie, fie, Gratiano! where are all the rest?
'Tis nine o'clock: our friends all stay for you.
No masque to-night: the wind is come about;
Bassanio presently will go aboard:
I have sent twenty out to seek for you.
GRATIANO
I am glad on't: I desire no more delight
Than to be under sail and gone to-night.
[*Exeunt.*

ACT TWO SCENE SEVEN

Belmont. A room in PORTIA'S *house.*

Flourish of cornets. Enter PORTIA, *with the* PRINCE OF MOROCCO, *and their trains.*

PORTIA
Go draw aside the curtains and discover
The several caskets to this noble prince.
Now make your choice.
PRINCE OF MOROCCO
The first, of gold, who this inscription bears,
'Who chooseth me shall gain what many men desire;'
The second, silver, which this promise carries,
'Who chooseth me shall get as much as he deserves;'
This third, dull lead, with warning all as blunt,
'Who chooseth me must give and hazard all he hath.'
How shall I know if I do choose the right?
PORTIA
The one of them contains my picture, prince:
If you choose that, then I am yours withal.
PRINCE OF MOROCCO
Some god direct my judgement! Let me see;
I will survey the inscriptions back again.
What says this leaden casket?
'Who chooseth me must give and hazard all he hath.'
Must give: for what? for lead? hazard for lead?
This casket threatens. Men that hazard all
Do it in hope of fair advantages:
A golden mind stoops not to shows of dross;
I'll then nor give nor hazard aught for lead.
What says the silver with her virgin hue?
'Who chooseth me shall get as much as he deserves.'
As much as deserve! Pause there, Morocco,
And weigh thy value with an even hand
If thou be'st rated by thy estimation,
Thou dost deserve enough; and yet enough
May not extend so far as to the lady
And yet to be afeard of my deserving
Were but a weak disabling of myself.
As much as I deserve! Why, that's the lady:
I do in birth deserve her, and in fortunes,
In graces and in qualities of breeding;
But more than these, in love I do deserve.
What if I stray'd no further, but chose here?
Let's see once more this saying graved in gold;
'Who chooseth me shall gain what many men desire.'
Why, that's the lady; all the world desires her;
From the four corners of the earth they come,
To kiss this shrine, this mortal-breathing saint:
The Hyrcanian deserts and the vasty wilds [21]

Of wide Arabia are as thoroughfares now
For princes to come view fair Portia:
The watery kingdom, whose ambitious head
Spits in the face of heaven, is no bar
To stop the foreign spirits, but they come,
As o'er a brook, to see fair Portia.
One of these three contains her heavenly picture.
Is't like that lead contains her? 'Twere damnation
To think so base a thought: it were too gross
To rib her cerecloth in the obscure grave.
Or shall I think in silver she's immured,
Being ten times undervalued to tried gold? [22]
O sinful thought! Never so rich a gem
Was set in worse than gold. They have in England
A coin that bears the figure of an angel
Stamped in gold, but that's insculp'd upon;
But here an angel in a golden bed
Lies all within. Deliver me the key:
Here do I choose, and thrive I as I may!

PORTIA
There, take it, prince; and if my form lie there,
Then I am yours. [*He unlocks the golden casket.*

PRINCE OF MOROCCO
O hell! what have we here?
A carrion Death, within whose empty eye
There is a written scroll! I'll read the writing.
[*Reads*] All that glitters is not gold;
Often have you heard that told:
Many a man his life hath sold
But my outside to behold:
Gilded tombs do worms infold, [23]
Had you been as wise as bold,
Young in limbs, in judgement old,
Your answer had not been inscroll'd:
Fare you well; your suit is cold.
Cold, indeed; and labour lost:
Then, farewell, heat, and welcome, frost! [24]
Portia, adieu. I have too grieved a heart
To take a tedious leave: thus losers part.
[*Exit with his train. Flourish of cornets.*

PORTIA
A gentle riddance. Draw the curtains, go.
Let all of his complexion choose me so. [*Exeunt.*

ACT TWO SCENE EIGHT

Venice. A street.

Enter SALARINO *and* SALANIO.

SALARINO
Why, man, I saw Bassanio under sail:
With him is Gratiano gone along;
And in their ship I am sure Lorenzo is not.

SALANIO
The villain Jew with outcries raised the duke,
Who went with him to search Bassanio's ship.

SALARINO
He came too late, the ship was under sail:
But there the duke was given to understand
That in a gondola were seen together
Lorenzo and his amorous Jessica:
Besides, Antonio certified the duke
They were not with Bassanio in his ship.

SALANIO
I never heard a passion so confused,
So strange, outrageous, and so variable,
As the dog Jew did utter in the streets:
'My daughter! O my ducats! O my daughter!
Fled with a Christian! O my Christian ducats!
Justice! the law! my ducats, and my daughter!
A sealed bag, two sealed bags of ducats,
Of double ducats, stolen from me by my daughter!
And jewels, two stones, two rich and precious stones,
Stolen by my daughter! Justice! find the girl;
She hath the stones upon her, and the ducats.'

SALARINO
Why, all the boys in Venice follow him,
Crying, his stones, his daughter, and his ducats.

SALANIO
Let good Antonio look he keep his day,
Or he shall pay for this.

SALARINO
Marry, well remember'd.
I reason'd with a Frenchman yesterday,
Who told me, in the narrow seas that part
The French and English, there miscarried
A vessel of our country richly fraught:
I thought upon Antonio when he told me;
And wish'd in silence that it were not his.

SALANIO
You were best to tell Antonio what you hear;
Yet do not suddenly, for it may grieve him.

SALARINO
A kinder gentleman treads not the earth.
I saw Bassanio and Antonio part:
Bassanio told him he would make some speed
Of his return: he answer'd, 'Do not so;
Slubber not business for my sake, Bassanio,
But stay the very riping of the time;
And for the Jew's bond which he hath of me,
Let it not enter in your mind of love:
Be merry, and employ your chiefest thoughts
To courtship and such fair ostents of love
As shall conveniently become you there:'
And even there, his eye being big with tears,
Turning his face, he put his hand behind him,

And with affection wondrous sensible
He wrung Bassanio's hand; and so they parted.

SALANIO
I think he only loves the world for him.
I pray thee, let us go and find him out
And quicken his embraced heaviness
With some delight or other.

SALARINO
Do we so. [*Exeunt.*

ACT TWO SCENE NINE

Belmont. A room in PORTIA'S *house.*

Enter NERISSA *with a* Servitor.

NERISSA
Quick, quick, I pray thee; draw the curtain straight:
The Prince of Arragon hath ta'en his oath,
And comes to his election presently.

Flourish of cornets. Enter the PRINCE OF ARRAGON, PORTIA, *and their trains.*

PORTIA
Behold, there stand the caskets, noble prince:
If you choose that wherein I am contain'd,
Straight shall our nuptial rites be solemnized:
But if you fail, without more speech, my lord,
You must be gone from hence immediately.

PRINCE OF ARRAGON
I am enjoin'd by oath to observe three
First, never to unfold to any one
Which casket 'twas I chose; next, if I fail
Of the right casket never in my life
To woo a maid in way of marriage:
Lastly,
If I do fail in fortune of my choice,
Immediately to leave you and be gone.

PORTIA
To these injunctions every one doth swear
That comes to hazard for my worthless self.

PRINCE OF ARRAGON
And so have I address'd me. Fortune now
To my heart's hope! Gold; silver; and base lead.
'Who chooseth me must give and hazard all he hath.'
You shall look fairer, ere I give or hazard.
What says the golden chest? ha! let me see:
'Who chooseth me shall gain what many men desire.'
What many men desire! that 'many' may be meant
By the fool multitude, that choose by show,
Not learning more than the fond eye doth teach;
Which pries not to the interior, but, like the martlet,
Builds in the weather on the outward wall,
Even in the force and road of casualty.
I will not choose what many men desire,
Because I will not jump with common spirits
And rank me with the barbarous multitudes.
Why, then to thee, thou silver treasure-house;
Tell me once more what title thou dost bear:
'Who chooseth me shall get as much as he deserves:'
And well said too; for who shall go about
To cozen fortune and be honourable
Without the stamp of merit? Let none presume
To wear an undeserved dignity.
O, that estates, degrees and offices
Were not derived corruptly, and that clear honour
Were purchased by the merit of the wearer!
How many then should cover that stand bare!
How many be commanded that command!
How much low peasantry would then be glean'd
From the true seed of honour! and how much honour
Pick'd from the chaff and ruin of the times
To be new-varnish'd! Well, but to my choice:
'Who chooseth me shall get as much as he deserves.'
I will assume desert. Give me a key for this,
And instantly unlock my fortunes here.
[*He opens the silver casket.*

PORTIA
Too long a pause for that which you find there.

PRINCE OF ARRAGON
What's here? the portrait of a blinking idiot,
Presenting me a schedule! I will read it.
How much unlike art thou to Portia!
How much like my hopes and my deservings!
'Who chooseth me shall have as much as he deserves.'
Did I deserve no more than a fool's head?
Is that my prize? are my deserts no better?

PORTIA
To offend, and judge, are distinct offices
And of opposed natures.

PRINCE OF ARRAGON
What is here?
[*Reads*] The fire seven times tried this:
Seven times tried that judgement is,
That did never choose amiss.
Some there be that shadows kiss;
Such have but a shadow's bliss:
There be fools alive, I wis,
Silver'd o'er; and so was this.
Take what wife you will to bed,
I will ever be your head:
So be gone: you are sped.
Still more fool I shall appear
By the time I linger here:

With one fool's head I came to woo,
But I go away with two.
Sweet, adieu. I'll keep my oath,
Patiently to bear my wroth.
[*Exeunt Arragon and train.*

PORTIA
Thus hath the candle singed the moth.
O, these deliberate fools! when they do choose,
They have the wisdom by their wit to lose.

NERISSA
The ancient saying is no heresy,
Hanging and wiving goes by destiny.

PORTIA
Come, draw the curtain, Nerissa.

Enter a Servant.

SERVANT
Where is my lady?

PORTIA
Here: what would my lord?

SERVANT
Madam, there is alighted at your gate
A young Venetian, one that comes before
To signify the approaching of his lord;
From whom he bringeth sensible regrets,
To wit, besides commends and courteous breath,
Gifts of rich value. Yet I have not seen
So likely an ambassador of love:
A day in April never came so sweet,
To show how costly summer was at hand,
As this fore-spurrer comes before his lord.

PORTIA
No more, I pray thee: I am half afeard
Thou wilt say anon he is some kin to thee,
Thou spend'st such high-day wit in praising him.
Come, come, Nerissa; for I long to see
Quick Cupid's post that comes so mannerly.

NERISSA
Bassanio, lord Love, if thy will it be! [*Exeunt.*

ACT THREE SCENE ONE

Venice. A street.

Enter SALANIO *and* SALARINO.

SALANIO
Now, what news on the Rialto?

SALARINO
Why, yet it lives there unchecked that Antonio hath a ship of rich lading wrecked on the narrow seas; the Goodwins, I think they call the place; a very dangerous flat and fatal, where the carcasses of many a tall ship lie buried, as they say, if my gossip Report be an honest woman of her word.

SALANIO
I would she were as lying a gossip in that as ever knapped ginger or made her neighbours believe she wept for the death of a third husband. But it is true, without any slips of prolixity or crossing the plain highway of talk, that the good Antonio, the honest Antonio,—O that I had a title good enough to keep his name company!— [25]

SALARINO
Come, the full stop.

SALANIO
Ha! what sayest thou? Why, the end is, he hath lost a ship.

SALARINO
I would it might prove the end of his losses.

SALANIO
Let me say 'amen' betimes, lest the devil cross my prayer, for here he comes in the likeness of a Jew.

Enter SHYLOCK.

How, now, Shylock! what news among the merchants?

SHYLOCK
You knew, none so well, none so well as you, of my daughter's flight.

SALARINO
That's certain: I, for my part, knew the tailor that made the wings she flew withal.

SALANIO
And Shylock, for his own part, knew the bird was fledged; and then it is the complexion of them all to leave the dam.

SHYLOCK
She is damned for it.

SALARINO
That's certain, if the devil may be her judge.

SHYLOCK
My own flesh and blood to rebel!

SALANIO
Out upon it, old carrion! rebels it at these years?

SHYLOCK
I say, my daughter is my flesh and blood.

SALARINO
There is more difference between thy flesh and hers than between jet and ivory; more between your bloods than there is between red wine and rhenish. But tell us, do you hear whether Antonio have had any loss at sea or no?

SHYLOCK
There I have another bad match: a bankrupt, a prodigal, who dare scarce show his head on the Rialto; a beggar, that was used to come so smug upon the mart; let him look to his bond: he was wont to call me usurer; let him look to his bond: he was wont to lend money for a Christian courtesy; let him look to his bond.

SALARINO
Why, I am sure, if he forfeit, thou wilt not take his flesh: what's that good for?

SHYLOCK
To bait fish withal: if it will feed nothing else, it will feed my revenge. He hath disgraced me, and hindered me half a million; laughed at my losses, mocked at my gains, scorned my nation, thwarted my bargains, cooled my friends, heated mine enemies; and what's his reason? I am a Jew. Hath not a Jew eyes? hath not a Jew hands, organs, dimensions, senses, affections, passions? fed with the same food, hurt with the same weapons, subject to the same diseases, healed by the same means, warmed and cooled by the same winter and summer, as a Christian is? If you prick us, do we not bleed? if you tickle us, do we not laugh? if you poison us, do we not die? and if you wrong us, shall we not revenge? If we are like you in the rest, we will resemble you in that. If a Jew wrong a Christian, what is his humility? Revenge. If a Christian wrong a Jew, what should his sufferance be by Christian example? Why, revenge. The villany you teach me, I will execute, and it shall go hard but I will better the instruction. [26]

Enter a Servant.

SERVANT Gentlemen, my master Antonio is at his house and desires to speak with you both.

SALARINO
We have been up and down to seek him. 68

Enter TUBAL.

SALANIO
Here comes another of the tribe: a third cannot be matched, unless the devil himself turn Jew.

[*Exeunt Salanio, Salarino, and Servant.*

SHYLOCK
How now, Tubal! what news from Genoa? hast thou found my daughter?

TUBAL
I often came where I did hear of her, but cannot find her.

SHYLOCK
Why, there, there, there, there! a diamond gone, cost me two thousand ducats in Frankfort! The curse never fell upon our nation till now; I never felt it till now: two thousand ducats in that; and other precious, precious jewels. I would my daughter were dead at my

SHYLOCK The curse never fell upon our nation till now; I never felt it till now.

foot, and the jewels in her ear! would she were hearsed at my foot, and the ducats in her coffin! No news of them? Why, so: and I know not what's spent in the search: why, thou loss upon loss! the thief gone with so much, and so much to find the thief; and no satisfaction, no revenge: nor no ill luck stirring but what lights on my shoulders; no sighs but of my breathing; no tears but of my shedding. 87

TUBAL
Yes, other men have ill luck too: Antonio, as I heard in Genoa,—

SHYLOCK
What, what, what? ill luck, ill luck?

TUBAL
Hath an argosy cast away, coming from Tripolis.

SHYLOCK
I thank God, I thank God. Is't true, is't true?

TUBAL
I spoke with some of the sailors that escaped the wreck. 94

SHYLOCK
I thank thee, good Tubal: good news, good news! ha, ha! where? in Genoa?

TUBAL
Your daughter spent in Genoa, as I heard, in one night fourscore ducats.

SHYLOCK
Thou stickest a dagger in me: I shall never see my gold again: fourscore ducats at a sitting! fourscore ducats!

TUBAL
There came divers of Antonio's creditors in my company to Venice, that swear he cannot choose but break. 104

SHYLOCK
I am very glad of it: I'll plague him; I'll torture him: I am glad of it.

TUBAL
One of them showed me a ring that he had of your daughter for a monkey.

SHYLOCK
Out upon her! Thou torturest me, Tubal: it was my turquoise: I had it of Leah when I was a bachelor: I would not have given it for a wilderness of monkeys. [27]

TUBAL
But Antonio is certainly undone. 113

SHYLOCK
Nay, that's true, that's very true. Go, Tubal, fee me an officer; bespeak him a fortnight before. I will have the heart of him, if he forfeit; for, were he out of Venice, I can make what merchandise I will. Go, go, Tubal, and meet me at our synagogue; go, good Tubal; at our synagogue, Tubal. [*Exeunt.*

ACT THREE SCENE TWO

Belmont. A room in PORTIA'S *house.*

Enter BASSANIO, PORTIA, GRATIANO, NERISSA, *and* Attendants.

PORTIA
I pray you, tarry: pause a day or two
Before you hazard; for, in choosing wrong,
I lose your company; therefore forbear awhile.
There's something tells me, but it is not love,
I would not lose you; and you know yourself,
Hate counsels not in such a quality.
But lest you should not understand me well,—
And yet a maiden hath no tongue but thought,—
I would detain you here some month or two 10
Before you venture for me. I could teach you
How to choose right, but I am then forsworn;
So will I never be: so may you miss me;
But if you do you'll make me wish a sin,
That I had been forsworn. Beshrew your eyes,
They have o'erlook'd me and divided me;
One half of me is yours, the other half yours,
Mine own, I would say; but if mine, then yours,
And so all yours. O, these naughty times
Put bars between the owners and their rights!
And so, though yours, not yours. Prove it so.
Let fortune go to hell for it, not I. 22
I speak too long; but 'tis to peize the time,
To eke it and to draw it out in length,
To stay you from election.

BASSANIO
Let me choose;
For as I am, I live upon the rack.

PORTIA
Upon the rack, Bassanio! then confess
What treason there is mingled with your love.

BASSANIO
None but that ugly treason of mistrust,
Which makes me fear the enjoying of my love:
There may as well be amity and life 32
'Tween snow and fire, as treason and my love.

PORTIA
Ay, but I fear you speak upon the rack,
Where men enforced do speak anything.

BASSANIO
Promise me life, and I'll confess the truth.

PORTIA
Well, then, confess and live.

BASSANIO
'Confess' and 'love'
Had been the very sum of my confession:
O happy torment, when my torturer

Doth teach me answers for deliverance!
But let me to my fortune and the caskets.

PORTIA

Away, then! I am lock'd in one of them:
If you do love me, you will find me out.
Nerissa and the rest, stand all aloof.
Let music sound while he doth make his choice;
Then, if he lose, he makes a swan-like end,
Fading in music: that the comparison
May stand more proper, my eye shall be the stream
And watery death-bed for him. He may win;
And what is music then? Then music is
Even as the flourish when true subjects bow
To a new-crowned monarch; such it is
As are those dulcet sounds in break of day
That creep into the dreaming bridegroom's ear
And summon him to marriage. Now he goes,
With no less presence, but with much more love, [28]
Than young Alcides, when he did redeem
The virgin tribute paid by howling Troy
To the sea-monster: I stand for sacrifice;
The rest aloof are the Dardanian wives,
With bleared visages, come forth to view
The issue of the exploit. Go, Hercules!
Live thou, I live: with much much more dismay
I view the fight than thou that makest the fray.

Music, whilst BASSANIO *comments on the caskets to himself.*

SONG.

Tell me where is fancy bred,
Or in the heart or in the head?
How begot, how nourished?
Reply, reply.
It is engender'd in the eyes,
With gazing fed; and fancy dies
In the cradle where it lies.
Let us all ring fancy's knell:
I'll begin it,—Ding dong, bell.

ALL

Ding, dong, bell.

BASSANIO

So may the outward shows be least themselves:
The world is still deceived with ornament.
In law, what plea so tainted and corrupt,
But, being season'd with a gracious voice,
Obscures the show of evil? In religion,
What damned error, but some sober brow
Will bless it and approve it with a text,
Hiding the grossness with fair ornament?
There is no vice so simple but assumes
Some mark of virtue on his outward parts:
How many cowards, whose hearts are all as false
As stairs of sand, wear yet upon their chins
The beards of Hercules and frowning Mars,
Who, inward search'd, have livers white as milk;
And these assume but valour's excrement
To render them redoubted! Look on beauty,
And you shall see 'tis purchased by the weight;
Which therein works a miracle in nature,
Making them lightest that wear most of it:
So are those crisped snaky golden locks
Which make such wanton gambols with the wind,
Upon supposed fairness, often known
To be the dowry of a second head,
The skull that bred them in the sepulchre.
Thus ornament is but the guiled shore
To a most dangerous sea; the beauteous scarf
Veiling an Indian beauty; in a word, [29]
The seeming truth which cunning time puts on
To entrap the wisest. Therefore, thou gaudy gold,
Hard food for Midas, I will none of thee; [30]
Nor none of thee, thou pale and common drudge
'Tween man and man: but thou, thou meagre lead,
Which rather threatenest than dost promise aught,
Thy paleness moves me more than eloquence; [31]
And here choose I: joy be the consequence!

PORTIA

[*Aside*] How all the other passions fleet to air,
As doubtful thoughts, and rash-embraced despair,
And shuddering fear, and green-eyed jealousy!
O love,
Be moderate; allay thy ecstasy;
In measure rein thy joy; scant this excess. [32]
I feel too much thy blessing: make it less,
For fear I surfeit.

BASSANIO

What find I here? [*Opening the leaden casket.*
Fair Portia's counterfeit! What demi-god
Hath come so near creation? Move these eyes?
Or whether, riding on the balls of mine,
Seem they in motion? Here are sever'd lips,
Parted with sugar breath: so sweet a bar
Should sunder such sweet friends. Here in her hairs
The painter plays the spider and hath woven
A golden mesh to entrap the hearts of men
Faster than gnats in cobwebs: but her eyes,—
How could he see to do them? having made one,
Methinks it should have power to steal both his
And leave itself unfurnish'd. Yet look, how far
The substance of my praise doth wrong this shadow
In underprizing it, so far this shadow
Doth limp behind the substance. Here's the scroll,
The continent and summary of my fortune.
[*Reads*] You that choose not by the view,
Chance as fair and choose as true!

Since this fortune falls to you,
Be content and seek no new.
If you be well pleased with this
And hold your fortune for your bliss,
Turn you where your lady is
And claim her with a loving kiss.
A gentle scroll. Fair lady, by your leave;
I come by note, to give and to receive.
Like one of two contending in a prize,
That thinks he hath done well in people's eyes,
Hearing applause and universal shout,
Giddy in spirit, still gazing in a doubt
Whether those peals of praise be his or no;
So, thrice fair lady, stand I, even so;
As doubtful whether what I see be true,
Until confirm'd, sign'd, ratified by you.

PORTIA
You see me, Lord Bassanio, where I stand,
Such as I am: though for myself alone
I would not be ambitious in my wish,
To wish myself much better; yet, for you
I would be trebled twenty times myself;
A thousand times more fair, ten thousand times
More rich;
That only to stand high in your account,
I might in virtue, beauties, livings, friends,
Exceed account; but the full sum of me
Is sum of something, which, to term in gross,
Is an unlesson'd girl, unschool'd, unpractised;
Happy in this, she is not yet so old
But she may learn; happier than this,
She is not bred so dull but she can learn;
Happiest of all is that her gentle spirit
Commits itself to yours to be directed,
As from her lord, her governor, her king.
Myself and what is mine to you and yours
Is now converted: but now I was the lord
Of this fair mansion, master of my servants,
Queen o'er myself; and even now, but now,
This house, these servants and this same myself
Are yours, my lord: I give them with this ring;
Which when you part from, lose, or give away,
Let it presage the ruin of your love
And be my vantage to exclaim on you.

BASSANIO
Madam, you have bereft me of all words,
Only my blood speaks to you in my veins;
And there is such confusion in my powers,
As, after some oration fairly spoke
By a beloved prince, there doth appear
Among the buzzing pleased multitude;
Where every something, being blent together,
Turns to a wild of nothing, save of joy,
Express'd and not express'd. But when this ring
Parts from this finger, then parts life from hence:
O, then be bold to say Bassanio's dead!

NERISSA
My lord and lady, it is now our time,
That have stood by and seen our wishes prosper,
To cry, good joy: good joy, my lord and lady!

GRATIANO
My lord Bassanio and my gentle lady,
I wish you all the joy that you can wish;
For I am sure you can wish none from me:
And when your honours mean to solemnize
The bargain of your faith, I do beseech you,
Even at that time I may be married too.

BASSANIO
With all my heart, so thou canst get a wife.

GRATIANO
I thank your lordship, you have got me one.
My eyes, my lord, can look as swift as yours:
You saw the mistress, I beheld the maid;
You loved, I loved for intermission.
No more pertains to me, my lord, than you.
Your fortune stood upon the casket there,
And so did mine too, as the matter falls;
For wooing here until I sweat again,
And swearing till my very roof was dry
With oaths of love, at last, if promise last,
I got a promise of this fair one here
To have her love, provided that your fortune
Achieved her mistress.

PORTIA
Is this true, Nerissa?

NERISSA
Madam, it is, so you stand pleased withal.

BASSANIO
And do you, Gratiano, mean good faith?

GRATIANO
Yes, faith, my lord.

BASSANIO
Our feast shall be much honour'd in your marriage.

GRATIANO
We'll play with them the first boy for a thousand ducats.

NERISSA
What, and stake down?

GRATIANO
No; we shall ne'er win at that sport, and stake down.
But who comes here? Lorenzo and his infidel?
What, and my old Venetian friend Salerio?

Enter LORENZO, JESSICA, *and* SALERIO, *a Messenger from Venice.*

BASSANIO
Lorenzo and Salerio, welcome hither;

If that the youth of my new interest here
Have power to bid you welcome. By your leave,
I bid my friends and countrymen,
Sweet Portia, welcome.

PORTIA
So do I, my lord;
They are entirely welcome.

LORENZO
I thank your honour. For my part, my lord,
My purpose was not to have seen you here;
But meeting with Salerio by the way,
He did intreat me, past all saying nay,
To come with him along.

SALERIO
I did, my lord;
And I have reason for it. Signior Antonio
Commends him to you. [*Gives Bassanio a letter.*

BASSANIO
Ere I ope his letter,
I pray you, tell me how my good friend doth.

SALERIO
Not sick, my lord, unless it be in mind;
Nor well, unless in mind: his letter there
Will show you his estate.

GRATIANO
Nerissa, cheer yon stranger; bid her welcome.
Your hand, Salerio: what's the news from Venice?
How doth that royal merchant, good Antonio?
I know he will be glad of our success;
We are the Jasons, we have won the fleece.

SALERIO
I would you had won the fleece that he hath lost.

PORTIA
There are some shrewd contents in yon same paper,
That steals the colour from Bassanio's cheek:
Some dear friend dead; else nothing in the world
Could turn so much the constitution
Of any constant man. What, worse and worse!
With leave, Bassanio: I am half yourself,
And I must freely have the half of anything
That this same paper brings you.

BASSANIO
O sweet Portia,
Here are a few of the unpleasant'st words
That ever blotted paper! Gentle lady,
When I did first impart my love to you,
I freely told you, all the wealth I had
Ran in my veins, I was a gentleman;
And then I told you true: and yet, dear lady,
Rating myself at nothing, you shall see
How much I was a braggart. When I told you
My state was nothing, I should then have told you
That I was worse than nothing; for, indeed,
I have engaged myself to a dear friend,
Engaged my friend to his mere enemy,
To feed my means. Here is a letter, lady;
The paper as the body of my friend,
And every word in it a gaping wound,
Issuing life-blood. But is it true, Salerio?
Have all his ventures fail'd? What, not
one hit?
From Tripolis, from Mexico and England,
From Lisbon, Barbary and India?
And not one vessel 'scaped the dreadful touch
Of merchant-marring rocks?

SALERIO
Not one, my lord.
Besides, it should appear, that if he had
The present money to discharge the Jew,
He would not take it. Never did I know
A creature, that did bear the shape of man,
So keen and greedy to confound a man:
He plies the duke at morning and at night,
And doth impeach the freedom of the state,
If they deny him justice: twenty merchants,
The duke himself, and the magnificoes
Of greatest port, have all persuaded with him;
But none can drive him from the envious plea
Of forfeiture, of justice and his bond.

JESSICA
When I was with him I have heard him swear
To Tubal and to Chus, his countrymen,
That he would rather have Antonio's flesh
Than twenty times the value of the sum
That he did owe him: and I know, my lord.
If law, authority and power deny not,
It will go hard with poor Antonio.

PORTIA
Is it your dear friend that is thus in trouble?

BASSANIO
The dearest friend to me, the kindest man,
The best-condition'd and unwearied spirit
In doing courtesies, and one in whom
The ancient Roman honour more appears
Than any that draws breath in Italy.

PORTIA
What sum owes he the Jew?

BASSANIO
For me three thousand ducats.

PORTIA
What, no more?
Pay him six thousand, and deface the bond;
Double six thousand, and then treble that,
Before a friend of this description
Shall lose a hair through Bassanio's fault.
First go with me to church and call me wife,
And then away to Venice to your friend;
For never shall you lie by Portia's side

With an unquiet soul. You shall have gold
To pay the petty debt twenty times over:
When it is paid, bring your true friend along.
My maid Nerissa and myself meantime
Will live as maids and widows. Come, away!
For you shall hence upon your wedding-day:
Bid your friends welcome, show a merry cheer:
Since you are dear bought, I will love you dear.
But let me hear the letter of your friend.

BASSANIO

[*Reads*] Sweet Bassanio, my ships have all miscarried, my creditors grow cruel, my estate is very low, my bond to the Jew is forfeit; and since in paying it, it is impossible I should live, all debts are cleared between you and I, if I might but see you at my death. Notwithstanding, use your pleasure: if your love do not persuade you to come, let not my letter.

PORTIA

O love, dispatch all business, and be gone!

BASSANIO

Since I have your good leave to go away,
I will make haste: but, till I come again,
No bed shall e'er be guilty of my stay,
No rest be interposer 'twixt us twain.
[*Exeunt.*

ACT THREE SCENE THREE

Venice. A street.

Enter SHYLOCK, SALARINO, ANTONIO, *and* Gaoler.

SHYLOCK

Gaoler, look to him: tell not me of mercy;
This is the fool that lent out money gratis:
Gaoler, look to him.

ANTONIO

Hear me yet, good Shylock.

SHYLOCK

I'll have my bond; speak not against my bond:
I have sworn an oath that I will have my bond.
Thou call'dst me dog before thou hadst a cause;
But, since I am a dog, beware my fangs:
The duke shall grant me justice. I do wonder,
Thou naughty gaoler, that thou art so fond
To come abroad with him at his request.

ANTONIO

I pray thee, hear me speak.

SHYLOCK

I'll have my bond; I will not hear thee speak:
I'll have my bond; and therefore speak no more.
I'll not be made a soft and dull-eyed fool,
To shake the head, relent, and sigh, and yield
To Christian intercessors. Follow not;
I'll have no speaking: I will have my bond. [*Exit.*

SALARINO

It is the most impenetrable cur
That ever kept with men.

ANTONIO

Let him alone:
I'll follow him no more with bootless prayers.
He seeks my life; his reason well I know:
I oft deliver'd from his forfeitures
Many that have at times made moan to me;
Therefore he hates me.

SALARINO

I am sure the duke
Will never grant this forfeiture to hold.

ANTONIO

The duke cannot deny the course of law:
For the commodity that strangers have
With us in Venice, if it be denied,
Will much impeach the justice of his state;
Since that the trade and profit of the city
Consisteth of all nations. Therefore, go:
These griefs and losses have so bated me,
That I shall hardly spare a pound of flesh
To-morrow to my bloody creditor.
Well, gaoler, on. Pray God, Bassanio come
To see me pay his debt, and then I care not!
[*Exeunt.*

ACT THREE SCENE FOUR

Belmont. A room in PORTIA'S *house.*

Enter PORTIA, NERISSA, LORENZO, JESSICA, *and* BALTHASAR.

LORENZO

Madam, although I speak it in your presence,
You have a noble and a true conceit
Of god-like amity; which appears most strongly
In bearing thus the absence of your lord.
But if you knew to whom you show this honour,
How true a gentleman you send relief,
How dear a lover of my lord your husband,
I know you would be prouder of the work
Than customary bounty can enforce you.

PORTIA

I never did repent for doing good,
Nor shall not now: for in companions
That do converse and waste the time together,
Whose souls do bear an equal yoke of love,
There must be needs a like proportion
Of lineaments, of manners and of spirit;
Which makes me think that this Antonio,

Being the bosom lover of my lord,
Must needs be like my lord. If it be so,
How little is the cost I have bestow'd
In purchasing the semblance of my soul
From out the state of hellish misery!
This comes too near the praising of myself;
Therefore no more of it: hear other things.
Lorenzo, I commit into your hands
The husbandry and manage of my house
Until my lord's return: for mine own part,
I have toward heaven breathed a secret vow
To live in prayer and contemplation,
Only attended by Nerissa here,
Until her husband and my lord's return:
There is a monastery two miles off;
And there will we abide. I do desire you
Not to deny this imposition;
The which my love and some necessity
Now lays upon you.

LORENZO
Madam, with all my heart;
I shall obey you in all fair commands.

PORTIA
My people do already know my mind,
And will acknowledge you and Jessica
In place of Lord Bassanio and myself.
And so farewell, till we shall meet again.

LORENZO
Fair thoughts and happy hours attend on you!

JESSICA
I wish your ladyship all heart's content.

PORTIA
I thank you for your wish, and am well pleased
To wish it back on you: fare you well Jessica.
[*Exeunt Jessica and Lorenzo.*
Now, Balthasar,
As I have ever found thee honest-true,
So let me find thee still. Take this same letter,
And use thou all the endeavour of a man
In speed to Padua: see thou render this
Into my cousin's hand, Doctor Bellario;
And, look, what notes and garments he doth give thee,
Bring them, I pray thee, with imagined speed
Unto the tranect, to the common ferry
Which trades to Venice. Waste no time in words,
But get thee gone: I shall be there before thee.

BALTHASAR
Madam, I go with all convenient speed. [*Exit.*

PORTIA
Come on, Nerissa; I have work in hand
That you yet know not of: we'll see our husbands
Before they think of us.

NERISSA
Shall they see us?

PORTIA
They shall, Nerissa; but in such a habit,
That they shall think we are accomplished
With that we lack. I'll hold thee any wager,
When we are both accoutred like young men,
I'll prove the prettier fellow of the two,
And wear my dagger with the braver grace,
And speak between the change of man and boy
With a reed voice, and turn two mincing steps
Into a manly stride, and speak of frays
Like a fine bragging youth, and tell quaint lies,
How honourable ladies sought my love,
Which I denying, they fell sick and died;
I could not do withal; then I'll repent,
And wish, for all that, that I had not kill'd them;
And twenty of these puny lies I'll tell,
That men shall swear I have discontinued school
Above a twelvemonth. I have within my mind
A thousand raw tricks of these bragging Jacks,
Which I will practise.

NERISSA
Why, shall we turn to men?

PORTIA
Fie, what a question's that,
If thou wert near a lewd interpreter!
But come, I'll tell thee all my whole device
When I am in my coach, which stays for us
At the park gate; and therefore haste away,
For we must measure twenty miles to-day.
[*Exeunt.*

ACT THREE SCENE FIVE

The same. A garden.

Enter LAUNCELOT *and* JESSICA.

LAUNCELOT
Yes, truly; for, look you, the sins of the father are to be laid upon the children: therefore, I promise ye, I fear you. I was always plain with you, and so now I speak my agitation of the matter: therefore be of good cheer, for truly I think you are damned. There is but one hope in it that can do you any good; and that is but a kind of bastard hope neither.

JESSICA
And what hope is that, I pray thee?

LAUNCELOT
Marry, you may partly hope that your father got you not, that you are not the Jew's daughter.

JESSICA
That were a kind of bastard hope, indeed: so the sins of my mother should be visited upon me.

LAUNCELOT

Truly then I fear you are damned both by father and mother: thus when I shun Scylla, your father, I fall into Charybdis, your mother: well, you are gone both ways.

JESSICA

I shall be saved by my husband; he hath made me a Christian.

LAUNCELOT

Truly, the more to blame he: we were Christians enow before; e'en as many as could well live, one by another. This making Christians will raise the price of hogs: if we grow all to be pork-eaters, we shall not shortly have a rasher on the coals for money.

Enter LORENZO.

JESSICA

I'll tell my husband, Launcelot, what you say: here he comes.

LORENZO

I shall grow jealous of you shortly, Launcelot, if you thus get my wife into corners.

JESSICA

Nay, you need not fear us, Lorenzo: Launcelot and I are out. He tells me flatly, there is no mercy for me in heaven, because I am a Jew's daughter: and he says, you are no good member of the commonwealth, for in converting Jews to Christians, you raise the price of pork.

LORENZO

I shall answer that better to the commonwealth than you can the getting up of the negro's belly: the Moor is with child by you, Launcelot.

LAUNCELOT

It is much that the Moor should be more than reason: but if she be less than an honest woman, she is indeed more than I took her for.

LORENZO

How every fool can play upon the word! I think the best grace of wit will shortly turn into silence, and discourse grow commendable in none only but parrots. Go you! then bid them prepare for dinner.

LAUNCELOT

That is done, sir; they have all stomachs.

LORENZO

Goodly Lord, what a wit-snapper are you! then bid them prepare dinner.

LAUNCELOT

That is done too, sir; only 'cover' is the word.

LORENZO

Will you cover then, sir?

LAUNCELOT

Not so, sir, neither; I know my duty.

LORENZO

Yet more quarrelling with occasion! Wilt thou show the whole wealth of thy wit in an instant? I pray tree, understand a plain man in his plain meaning: go to thy fellows; bid them cover the table, serve in the meat, and we will come in to dinner.

LAUNCELOT

For the table, sir, it shall be served in; for the meat, sir, it shall be covered; for your coming in to dinner, sir, why, let it be as humours and conceits shall govern. [*Exit.*

LORENZO

O dear discretion, how his words are suited!
The fool hath planted in his memory
An army of good words; and I do know
A many fools, that stand in better place,
Garnish'd like him, that for a tricksy word
Defy the matter. How cheer'st thou, Jessica?
And now, good sweet, say thy opinion,
How dost thou like the Lord Bassanio's wife?

JESSICA

Past all expressing. It is very meet
The Lord Bassanio live an upright life;
For, having such a blessing in his lady,
He finds the joys of heaven here on earth;
And if on earth he do not mean it, then [33]
In reason he should never come to heaven.
Why, if two gods should play some heavenly match
And on the wager lay two earthly women,
And Portia one, there must be something else
Pawn'd with the other, for the poor rude world
Hath not her fellow.

LORENZO

Even such a husband
Hast thou of me as she is for a wife.

JESSICA

Nay, but ask my opinion too of that.

LORENZO

I will anon: first, let us go to dinner.

JESSICA

Nay, let me praise you while I have a stomach.

LORENZO

No, pray thee, let it serve for table-talk;
Then, howso'er thou speak'st, 'mong other things
I shall digest it.

JESSICA

Well, I'll set you forth. [*Exeunt.*

ACT FOUR SCENE ONE

Venice. A court of justice.

Enter the DUKE, *the Magnificoes,* ANTONIO, BASSANIO, GRATIANO, SALERIO, *and others.*

DUKE

What, is Antonio here?

ANTONIO
Ready, so please your grace.
DUKE
I am sorry for thee: thou art come to answer
A stony adversary, an inhuman wretch
Uncapable of pity, void and empty
From any dram of mercy.
ANTONIO
I have heard
Your grace hath ta'en great pains to qualify
His rigorous course; but since he stands obdurate
And that no lawful means can carry me
Out of his envy's reach, I do oppose
My patience to his fury, and am arm'd
To suffer, with a quietness of spirit,
The very tyranny and rage of his.
DUKE
Go one, and call the Jew into the court.
SALERIO
He is ready at the door: he comes, my lord.

Enter SHYLOCK.

DUKE
Make room, and let him stand before our face.
Shylock, the world thinks, and I think so too,
That thou but lead'st this fashion of thy malice
To the last hour of act; and then 'tis thought
Thou'lt show thy mercy and remorse more strange
Than is thy strange apparent cruelty;
And where thou now exact'st the penalty,
Which is a pound of this poor merchant's flesh,
Thou wilt not only loose the forfeiture,
But, touch'd with human gentleness and love,
Forgive a moiety of the principal;
Glancing an eye of pity on his losses,
That have of late so huddled on his back,
Enow to press a royal merchant down
And pluck commiseration of his state
From brassy bosoms and rough hearts of flint,
From stubborn Turks and Tartars, never train'd
To offices of tender courtesy.
We all expect a gentle answer, Jew.
SHYLOCK
I have possess'd your grace of what I purpose;
And by our holy Sabbath have I sworn [34]
To have the due and forfeit of my bond:
If you deny it, let the danger light
Upon your charter and your city's freedom.
You'll ask me, why I rather choose to have
A weight of carrion flesh than to receive
Three thousand ducats: I'll not answer that:
But, say, it is my humour: is it answer'd?
What if my house be troubled with a rat
And I be pleased to give ten thousand ducats
To have it baned? What, are you answer'd yet?
Some men there are love not a gaping pig;
Some, that are mad if they behold a cat;
And others, when the bagpipe sings i' the nose,
Cannot contain their urine: for affection,
Mistress of passion, sways it to the mood
Of what it likes or loathes. Now, for your answer:
As there is no firm reason to be render'd,
Why he cannot abide a gaping pig;
Why he, a harmless necessary cat;
Why he, a woollen bagpipe; but of force [35]
Must yield to such inevitable shame
As to offend, himself being offended;
So can I give no reason, nor I will not,
More than a lodged hate and a certain loathing
I bear Antonio, that I follow thus
A losing suit against him. Are you answer'd?
BASSANIO
This is no answer, thou unfeeling man,
To excuse the current of thy cruelty.
SHYLOCK
I am not bound to please thee with my answers.
BASSANIO
Do all men kill the things they do not love?
SHYLOCK
Hates any man the thing he would not kill?
BASSANIO
Every offence is not a hate at first.
SHYLOCK
What, wouldst thou have a serpent sting thee twice?
ANTONIO
I pray you, think you question with the Jew:
You may as well go stand upon the beach
And bid the main flood bate his usual height;
You may as well use question with the wolf
Why he hath made the ewe bleat for the lamb;
You may as well forbid the mountain pines
To wag their high tops and to make no noise,
When they are fretten with the gusts of heaven;
You may as well do anything most hard,
As seek to soften that— than which what's harder?—
His Jewish heart: therefore, I do beseech you,
Make no more offers, use no farther means,
But with all brief and plain conveniency
Let me have judgement and the Jew his will.
BASSANIO
For thy three thousand ducats here is six.
SHYLOCK
If every ducat in six thousand ducats
Were in six parts and every part a ducat,
I would not draw them; I would have my bond.
DUKE
How shalt thou hope for mercy, rendering none?

SHYLOCK
What judgement shall I dread, doing no wrong?
You have among you many a purchased slave,
Which, like your asses and your dogs and mules,
You use in abject and in slavish parts,
Because you bought them: shall I say to you,
Let them be free, marry them to your heirs?
Why sweat they under burthens? let their beds
Be made as soft as yours and let their palates
Be season'd with such viands? You will answer
'The slaves are ours:' so do I answer you:
The pound of flesh, which I demand of him,
Is dearly bought; 'tis mine and I will have it.
If you deny me, fie upon your law!
There is no force in the decrees of Venice.
I stand for judgement: answer; shall I have it?

DUKE
Upon my power I may dismiss this court,
Unless Bellario, a learned doctor,
Whom I have sent for to determine this,
Come here to-day.

SALERIO
My lord, here stays without
A messenger with letters from the doctor,
New come from Padua.

DUKE
Bring us the letter; call the messenger.

BASSANIO
Good cheer, Antonio! What, man, courage yet!
The Jew shall have my flesh, blood, bones and all,
Ere thou shalt loose for me one drop of blood.

ANTONIO
I am a tainted wether of the flock,
Meetest for death: the weakest kind of fruit
Drops earliest to the ground; and so let me:
You cannot better be employ'd, Bassanio,
Than to live still and write mine epitaph.

Enter NERISSA, *dressed like a lawyer's clerk.*

DUKE
Came you from Padua, from Bellario?

NERISSA
From both, my lord. Bellario greets your grace.
[*Presenting a letter.*

BASSANIO
Why dost thou whet thy knife so earnestly?

SHYLOCK
To cut the forfeiture from that bankrupt there.

GRATIANO
Not on thy sole, but on thy soul, harsh Jew,
Thou makest thy knife keen; but no metal can,
No, not the hangman's axe, bear half the keenness
Of thy sharp envy. Can no prayers pierce thee?

SHYLOCK
No, none that thou hast wit enough to make.

GRATIANO
O, be thou damn'd, inexecrable dog!
And for thy life let justice be accused.
Thou almost makest me waver in my faith
To hold opinion with Pythagoras,
That souls of animals infuse themselves
Into the trunks of men: thy currish spirit
Govern'd a wolf, who, hang'd for human slaughter,
Even from the gallows did his fell soul fleet,
And, whilst thou lay'st in thy unhallow'd dam,
Infus'd itself in thee; for thy desires
Are wolvish, bloody, starved and ravenous.

SHYLOCK
Till thou canst rail the seal from off my bond,
Thou but offend'st thy lungs to speak so loud:
Repair thy wit, good youth, or it will fall
To cureless ruin. I stand here for law.

DUKE
This letter from Bellario doth commend
A young and learned doctor to our court.
Where is he?

NERISSA
He attendeth here hard by,
To know your answer, whether you'll admit him.

DUKE
With all my heart. Some three or four of you
Go give him courteous conduct to this place.
Meantime the court shall hear Bellario's letter.

Clerk. [Reads] Your grace shall understand that at the receipt of your letter I am very sick: but in the instant that your messenger came, in loving visitation was with me a young doctor of Rome; his name is Balthasar. I acquainted him with the cause in controversy between the Jew and Antonio the merchant: we turned o'er many books together: he is furnished with my opinion; which, bettered with his own learning, the greatness whereof I cannot enough commend, comes with him, at my importunity, to fill up your grace's request in my stead. I beseech you, let his lack of years be no impediment to let him lack a reverend estimation; for I never knew so young a body with so old a head. I leave him to your gracious acceptance, whose trial shall better publish his commendation.

DUKE
You hear the learn'd Bellario, what he writes:
And here, I take it, is the doctor come.

Enter PORTIA, *dressed like a doctor of laws.*

Give me your hand. Come you from old Bellario?

PORTIA
I did, my lord.

DUKE
You are welcome: take your place.
Are you acquainted with the difference
That holds this present question in the court?

PORTIA
I am informed thoroughly of the cause.
Which is the merchant here, and which the Jew?

DUKE
Antonio and old Shylock, both stand forth.

PORTIA
Is your name Shylock?

SHYLOCK
Shylock is my name.

PORTIA
Of a strange nature is the suit you follow;
Yet in such rule that the Venetian law
Cannot impugn you as you do proceed.
You stand within his danger, do you not?

ANTONIO
Ay, so he says.

PORTIA
Do you confess the bond?

ANTONIO
I do.

PORTIA
Then must the Jew be merciful. [36]

SHYLOCK
On what compulsion must I? tell me that. [37]

PORTIA
The quality of mercy is not strain'd,
It droppeth as the gentle rain from heaven
Upon the place beneath: it is twice blest;
It blesseth him that gives and him that takes:
'Tis mightiest in the mightiest: it becomes
The throned monarch better than his crown;
His sceptre shows the force of temporal power,
The attribute to awe and majesty,
Wherein doth sit the dread and fear of kings;
But mercy is above this sceptred sway;
It is enthroned in the hearts of kings,
It is an attribute to God himself;
And earthly power doth then show likest God's
When mercy seasons justice. Therefore, Jew,
Though justice be thy plea, consider this,
That, in the course of justice, none of us
Should see salvation: we do pray for mercy;
And that same prayer doth teach us all to render
The deeds of mercy. I have spoke thus much
To mitigate the justice of thy plea;
Which if thou follow, this strict court of Venice
Must needs give sentence 'gainst the merchant there.

SHYLOCK
My deeds upon my head! I crave the law,
The penalty and forfeit of my bond.

PORTIA
Is he not able to discharge the money?

BASSANIO
Yes, here I tender it for him in the court;
Yea, twice the sum: if that will not suffice,
I will be bound to pay it ten times o'er,
On forfeit of my hands, my head, my heart:
If this will not suffice, it must appear
That malice bears down truth. And I beseech you,
Wrest once the law to your authority:
To do a great right, do a little wrong,
And curb this cruel devil of his will.

PORTIA
It must not be; there is no power in Venice
Can alter a decree established:
'Twill be recorded for a precedent,
And many an error by the same example
Will rush into the state: it cannot be.

SHYLOCK
A Daniel come to judgement! yea, a Daniel!
O wise young judge, how I do honour thee!

PORTIA
I pray you, let me look upon the bond.

SHYLOCK
Here 'tis, most reverend doctor, here it is.

PORTIA
Shylock, there's thrice thy money offer'd thee.

SHYLOCK
An oath, an oath, I have an oath in heaven:
Shall I lay perjury upon my soul?
No, not for Venice.

PORTIA
Why, this bond is forfeit;
And lawfully by this the Jew may claim
A pound of flesh, to be by him cut off
Nearest the merchant's heart. Be merciful:
Take thrice thy money; bid me tear the bond.

SHYLOCK
When it is paid according to the tenor.
It doth appear you are a worthy judge;
You know the law, your exposition
Hath been most sound: I charge you by the law,
Whereof you are a well-deserving pillar,
Proceed to judgement: by my soul I swear
There is no power in the tongue of man
To alter me: I stay here on my bond.

ANTONIO
Most heartily I do beseech the court
To give the judgement.

PORTIA
Why then, thus it is:
You must prepare your bosom for his knife.

SHYLOCK
O noble judge! O excellent young man!

PORTIA
For the intent and purpose of the law
Hath full relation to the penalty,
Which here appeareth due upon the bond.
SHYLOCK
'Tis very true: O wise and upright judge! 262
How much more elder art thou than thy looks!
PORTIA
Therefore lay bare your bosom.
SHYLOCK
Ay, his breast:
So says the bond: doth it not, noble judge?
'Nearest his heart:' those are the very words.
PORTIA
It is so. Are there balance here to weigh [38]
The flesh?
SHYLOCK
I have them ready.
PORTIA
Have by some surgeon, Shylock, on your charge,
To stop his wounds lest he do bleed to death.
SHYLOCK
Is it so nominated in the bond?
PORTIA
It is not so express'd: but what of that?
'Twere good you do so much for charity. 275
SHYLOCK
I cannot find it; 'tis not in the bond.
PORTIA
You, merchant, have you any thing to say?
ANTONIO
But little: I am arm'd and well prepared.
Give me your hand, Bassanio: fare you well!
Grieve not that I am fallen to this for you;
For herein Fortune shows herself more kind
Than is her custom: it is still her use
To let the wretched man outlive his wealth,
To view with hollow eye and wrinkled brow
An age of poverty; from which lingering penance
Of such misery doth she cut me off.
Commend me to your honourable wife:
Tell her the process of Antonio's end;
Say how I loved you, speak me fair in death;
And, when the tale is told, bid her be judge
Whether Bassanio had not once a love.
Repent but you that you shall lose your friend,
And he repents not that he pays your debt;
For if the Jew do cut but deep enough, 294
I'll pay it presently with all my heart.
BASSANIO
Antonio, I am married to a wife
Which is as dear to me as life itself;
But life itself, my wife, and all the world,
Are not with me esteem'd above thy life:
I would lose all, ay, sacrifice them all
Here to this devil, to deliver you.
PORTIA
Your wife would give you little thanks for that,
If she were by, to hear you make the offer.
GRATIANO
I have a wife, whom, I protest, I love:
I would she were in heaven, so she could 305
Entreat some power to change this currish Jew.
NERISSA
'Tis well you offer it behind her back;
The wish would make else an unquiet house.
SHYLOCK
These be the Christian husbands. I have a daughter;
Would any of the stock of Barrabas
Had been her husband rather than a Christian!
[*Aside.*
We trifle time: I pray thee, pursue sentence.
PORTIA
A pound of that same merchant's flesh is thine:
The court awards it, and the law doth give it.
SHYLOCK
Most rightful judge! 316
PORTIA
And you must cut this flesh from off his breast:
The law allows it, and the court awards it.
SHYLOCK
Most learned judge! A sentence! Come, prepare!
PORTIA
Tarry a little; there is something else.
This bond doth give thee here no jot of blood;
The words expressly are 'a pound of flesh:'
Take then thy bond, take thou thy pound of flesh;
But, in the cutting it, if thou dost shed
One drop of Christian blood, thy lands and goods 326
Are, by the laws of Venice, confiscate
Unto the state of Venice.
GRATIANO
O upright judge! Mark, Jew: O learned judge!
SHYLOCK
Is that the law?
PORTIA
Thyself shalt see the act:
For, as thou urgest justice, be assured
Thou shalt have justice, more than thou desirest.
GRATIANO
O learned judge! Mark, Jew: a learned judge!
SHYLOCK
I take this offer, then; pay the bond thrice
And let the Christian go.
BASSANIO
Here is the money.

PORTIA Take then thy bond.

PORTIA
Soft! 338
The Jew shall have all justice; soft! no haste:
He shall have nothing but the penalty.

GRATIANO
O Jew! an upright judge, a learned judge!

PORTIA
Therefore prepare thee to cut off the flesh.
Shed thou no blood, nor cut thou less nor more
But just a pound of flesh: if thou cut'st more
Or less than a just pound, be it but so much
As makes it light or heavy in the substance,
Or the division of the twentieth part
Of one poor scruple, nay, if the scale do turn
But in the estimation of a hair, 349
Thou diest and all thy goods are confiscate.

GRATIANO
A second Daniel, a Daniel, Jew!
Now, infidel, I have you on the hip.

PORTIA
Why doth the Jew pause? take thy forfeiture.

SHYLOCK
Give me my principal, and let me go.

BASSANIO
I have it ready for thee; here it is.

PORTIA
He hath refused it in the open court:
He shall have merely justice and his bond. 357

GRATIANO
A Daniel, still say I, a second Daniel!
I thank thee, Jew, for teaching me that word.

SHYLOCK
Shall I not have barely my principal?

PORTIA
Thou shalt have nothing but the forfeiture,
To be so taken at thy peril, Jew.

SHYLOCK
Why, then the devil give him good of it!

I'll stay no longer question.

PORTIA

Tarry, Jew:
The law hath yet another hold on you.
It is enacted in the laws of Venice,
If it be proved against an alien
That by direct or indirect attempts
He seek the life of any citizen,
The party 'gainst the which he doth contrive
Shall seize one half his goods; the other half
Comes to the privy coffer of the state;
And the offender's life lies in the mercy
Of the duke only, 'gainst all other voice.
In which predicament, I say, thou stand'st;
For it appears, by manifest proceeding,
That indirectly and directly too
Thou hast contrived against the very life
Of the defendant; and thou hast incurr'd
The danger formerly by me rehearsed.
Down therefore and beg mercy of the duke.

GRATIANO

Beg that thou mayst have leave to hang thyself:
And yet, thy wealth being forfeit to the state,
Thou hast not left the value of a cord;
Therefore thou must be hang'd at the state's charge.

DUKE

That thou shalt see the difference of our spirits,
I pardon thee thy life before thou ask it:
For half thy wealth, it is Antonio's;
The other half comes to the general state,
Which humbleness may drive unto a fine.

PORTIA

Ay, for the state, not for Antonio.

SHYLOCK

Nay, take my life and all; pardon not that:
You take my house when you do take the prop
That doth sustain my house; you take my life
When you do take the means whereby I live.

PORTIA

What mercy can you render him, Antonio?

GRATIANO

A halter gratis; nothing else, for God's sake.

ANTONIO

So please my lord the duke and all the court
To quit the fine for one half of his goods,
I am content; so he will let me have
The other half in use, to render it,
Upon his death, unto the gentleman
That lately stole his daughter:
Two things provided more, that, for this favour,
He presently become a Christian;
The other, that he do record a gift,
Here in the court, of all he dies possess'd,
Unto his son Lorenzo and his daughter.

DUKE

He shall do this, or else I do recant
The pardon that I late pronounced here.

PORTIA

Art thou contented, Jew? what dost thou say?

SHYLOCK

I am content.

PORTIA

Clerk, draw a deed of gift.

SHYLOCK

I pray you, give me leave to go from hence;
I am not well: send the deed after me,
And I will sign it.

DUKE

Get thee gone, but do it.

GRATIANO

In christening shalt thou have two godfathers:
Had I been judge, thou shouldst have had ten more,
To bring thee to the gallows, not the font.
[Exit Shylock.

DUKE

Sir, I entreat you home with me to dinner.

PORTIA

I humbly do desire your grace of pardon:
I must away this night toward Padua,
And it is meet I presently set forth.

DUKE

I am sorry that your leisure serves you not.
Antonio, gratify this gentleman,
For, in my mind, you are much bound to him.
[Exeunt Duke and his train.

BASSANIO

Most worthy gentleman, I and my friend
Have by your wisdom been this day acquitted
Of grievous penalties; in lieu whereof,
Three thousand ducats, due unto the Jew,
We freely cope your courteous pains withal.

ANTONIO

And stand indebted, over and above,
In love and service to you evermore.

PORTIA

He is well paid that is well satisfied;
And I, delivering you, am satisfied
And therein do account myself well paid:
My mind was never yet more mercenary.
I pray you, know me when we meet again:
I wish you well, and so I take my leave.

BASSANIO

Dear sir, of force I must attempt you further:
Take some remembrance of us, as a tribute,
Not as a fee: grant me two things, I pray you,
Not to deny me, and to pardon me.

PORTIA

You press me far, and therefore I will yield.

[*To Antonio*] Give me your gloves, I'll wear them for your sake;
[*To Bassanio*] And, for your love, I'll take this ring from you:
Do not draw back your hand; I'll take no more;
And you in love shall not deny me this.

BASSANIO
This ring, good sir, alas, it is a trifle!
I will not shame myself to give you this. 453

PORTIA
I will have nothing else but only this;
And now methinks I have a mind to it.

BASSANIO
There's more depends on this than on the value.
The dearest ring in Venice will I give you,
And find it out by proclamation:
Only for this, I pray you, pardon me.

PORTIA
I see, sir, you are liberal in offers:
You taught me first to beg; and now methinks
You teach me how a beggar should be answer'd.

BASSANIO
Good sir, this ring was given me by my wife; 463
And when she put it on, she made me vow
That I should neither sell nor give nor lose it.

PORTIA
That 'scuse serves many men to save their gifts.
An if your wife be not a mad-woman,
And know how well I have deserved the ring,
She would not hold out enemy for ever,
For giving it to me. Well, peace be with you!
[*Exeunt Portia and Nerissa.*

ANTONIO
My Lord Bassanio, let him have the ring:
Let his deservings and my love withal 472
Be valued 'gainst your wife's commandment.

BASSANIO
Go, Gratiano, run and overtake him;
Give him the ring, and bring him, if thou canst,
Unto Antonio's house: away! make haste.
[*Exit Gratiano.*
Come, you and I will thither presently;
And in the morning early will we both
Fly toward Belmont: come, Antonio. [*Exeunt.*

ACT FOUR SCENE TWO

The same. A street.

Enter PORTIA *and* NERISSA.

PORTIA
Inquire the Jew's house out, give him this deed.
And let him sign it: we'll away to-night
And be a day before our husbands home:
This deed will be well welcome to Lorenzo.

Enter GRATIANO.

GRATIANO
Fair sir, you are well o'erta'en:
My Lord Bassanio upon more advice
Hath sent you here this ring, and doth entreat
Your company at dinner.

PORTIA
That cannot be:
His ring I do accept most thankfully:
And so, I pray you, tell him: furthermore, 11
I pray you, show my youth old Shylock's house.

GRATIANO
That will I do.

NERISSA
Sir, I would speak with you.
[*Aside to Portia*] I'll see if I can get my husband's ring,
Which I did make him swear to keep for ever.

PORTIA
[*Aside to Nerissa*] Thou mayst, I warrant.
We shall have old swearing
That they did give the rings away to men;
But we'll outface them, and outswear them too.
[*Aloud*] Away! make haste: thou know'st where I will tarry.

NERISSA
Come, good sir, will you show me to this house?
[*Exeunt.*

ACT FIVE SCENE ONE

Belmont. Avenue to PORTIA'S *house.*

Enter LORENZO *and* JESSICA.

LORENZO
The moon shines bright: in such a night as this,
When the sweet wind did gently kiss the trees
And they did make no noise, in such a night
Troilus methinks mounted the Troyan walls [39]
And sigh'd his soul toward the Grecian tents,
Where Cressid lay that night.

JESSICA
In such a night
Did Thisbe fearfully o'ertrip the dew [40]
And saw the lion's shadow ere himself
And ran dismay'd away.

LORENZO
In such a night
Stood Dido with a willow in her hand 12
Upon the wild sea banks and waft her love
To come again to Carthage.

JESSICA
In such a night
Medea gather'd the enchanted herbs

That did renew old Aeson.

LORENZO

In such a night
Did Jessica steal from the wealthy Jew [41]
And with an unthrift love did run from Venice
As far as Belmont.

JESSICA

In such a night
Did young Lorenzo swear he loved her well,
Stealing her soul with many vows of faith
And ne'er a true one.

LORENZO

In such a night
Did pretty Jessica, like a little shrew,
Slander her love, and he forgave it her.

JESSICA

I would out-night you, did no body come;
But, hark, I hear the footing of a man.

Enter STEPHANO.

LORENZO

Who comes so fast in silence of the night?

STEPHANO

A friend.

LORENZO

A friend! what friend? your name, I pray you, friend?

STEPHANO

Stephano is my name; and I bring word
My mistress will before the break of day
Be here at Belmont: she doth stray about
By holy crosses, where she kneels and prays
For happy wedlock hours.

LORENZO

Who comes with her?

STEPHANO

None but a holy hermit and her maid.
I pray you, is my master yet return'd?

LORENZO

He is not, nor we have not heard from him.
But go we in, I pray thee, Jessica,
And ceremoniously let us prepare
Some welcome for the mistress of the house.

Enter LAUNCELOT.

LAUNCELOT

Sola, sola! wo ha, ho! sola, sola!

LORENZO

Who calls?

LAUNCELOT

Sola! did you see Master Lorenzo?
Master Lorenzo, sola, sola!

LORENZO

Leave hollaing, man: here.

LAUNCELOT

Sola! where? where?

LORENZO

Here.

LAUNCELOT

Tell him there's a post come from my master, with his horn full of good news: my master will be here ere morning. [*Exit.*

LORENZO

Sweet soul, let's in, and there expect their coming.
And yet no matter: why should we go in?
My friend Stephano, signify, I pray you,
Within the house, your mistress is at hand;
And bring your music forth into the air.
[*Exit Stephano.*
How sweet the moonlight sleeps upon this bank!
Here will we sit and let the sounds of music
Creep in our ears: soft stillness and the night
Become the touches of sweet harmony.
Sit, Jessica. Look how the floor of heaven
Is thick inlaid with patines of bright gold:
There's not the smallest orb which thou behold'st
But in his motion like an angel sings, [42]
Still quiring to the young-eyed cherubins;
Such harmony is in immortal souls;
But whilst this muddy vesture of decay
Doth grossly close it in, we cannot hear it. [43]

Enter Musicians.

Come, ho! and wake Diana with a hymn:
With sweetest touches pierce your mistress' ear,
And draw her home with music. [*Music.*

JESSICA

I am never merry when I hear sweet music.

LORENZO

The reason is, your spirits are attentive:
For do but note a wild and wanton herd,
Or race of youthful and unhandled colts,
Fetching mad bounds, bellowing and neighing loud,
Which is the hot condition of their blood;
If they but hear perchance a trumpet sound,
Or any air of music touch their ears,
You shall perceive them make a mutual stand,
Their savage eyes turn'd to a modest gaze
By the sweet power of music: therefore the poet
Did feign that Orpheus drew trees, stones and floods;
Since nought so stockish, hard and full of rage,
But music for the time doth change his nature.
The man that hath no music in himself,
Nor is not moved with concord of sweet sounds,
Is fit for treasons, stratagems and spoils;
The motions of his spirit are dull as night
And his affections dark as Erebus:
Let no such man be trusted. Mark the music.

Enter PORTIA *and* NERISSA.

PORTIA
That light we see is burning in my hall.
How far that little candle throws his beams! 99
So shines a good deed in a naughty world.

NERISSA
When the moon shone, we did not see the candle.

PORTIA
So doth the greater glory dim the less:
A substitute shines brightly as a king
Until the king be by, and then his state
Empties itself, as doth an inland brook
Into the main of waters. Music! hark!

NERISSA
It is your music, madam, of the house.

PORTIA
Nothing is good, I see, without respect:
Methinks it sounds much sweeter than by day.

NERISSA
Silence bestows that virtue on it, madam. 111

PORTIA
The crow doth sing as sweetly as the lark
When neither is attended, and I think
The nightingale, if she should sing by day,
When every goose is cackling, would be thought
No better a musician than the wren.
How many things by season season'd are
To their right praise and true perfection!
Peace, ho! the moon sleeps with Endymion
And would not be awaked. [*Music ceases.*

LORENZO
That is the voice, 121
Or I am much deceived, of Portia.

PORTIA
He knows me as the blind man knows the cuckoo,
By the bad voice.

LORENZO
Dear lady, welcome home.

PORTIA
We have been praying for our husbands' healths,
Which speed, we hope, the better for our words.
Are they return'd?

LORENZO
Madam, they are not yet;
But there is come a messenger before,
To signify their coming.

PORTIA
Go in, Nerissa;
Give order to my servants that they take
No note at all of our being absent hence; 135
Nor you, Lorenzo; Jessica, nor you.
[*A tucket sounds.*

LORENZO
Your husband is at hand; I hear his trumpet:
We are no tell-tales, madam; fear you not.

PORTIA
This night methinks is but the daylight sick;
It looks a little paler: 'tis a day,
Such as the day is when the sun is hid.

Enter BASSANIO, ANTONIO, GRATIANO, *and their followers.*

BASSANIO
We should hold day with the Antipodes,
If you would walk in absence of the sun.

PORTIA
Let me give light, but let me not be light;
For a light wife doth make a heavy husband,
And never be Bassanio so for me:
But God sort all! You are welcome home, my lord.

BASSANIO
I thank you, madam. Give welcome to my friend.
This is the man, this is Antonio,
To whom I am so infinitely bound.

PORTIA
You should in all sense be much bound to him.
For, as I hear, he was much bound for you.

ANTONIO
No more than I am well acquitted of.

PORTIA
Sir, you are very welcome to our house:
It must appear in other ways than words, 155
Therefore I scant this breathing courtesy.

GRATIANO
[*To Nerissa*] By yonder moon I swear you do me wrong;
In faith, I gave it to the judge's clerk:
Would he were gelt that had it, for my part,
Since you do take it, love, so much at heart.

PORTIA
A quarrel, ho, already! what's the matter?

GRATIANO
About a hoop of gold, a paltry ring
That she did give me, whose posy was
For all the world like cutler's poetry
Upon a knife, 'Love me, and leave me not.'

NERISSA
What talk you of the posy or the value?
You swore to me, when I did give it you,
That you would wear it till your hour of death
And that it should lie with you in your grave:
Though not for me, yet for your vehement oaths,
You should have been respective and have kept it.
Gave it a judge's clerk! no, God's my judge,
The clerk will ne'er wear hair on's face that had it.

GRATIANO
He will, an if he live to be a man.

NERISSA
Ay, if a woman live to be a man.

GRATIANO
Now, by this hand, I gave it to a youth,
A kind of boy, a little scrubbed boy,
No higher than thyself; the judge's clerk,
A prating boy, that begg'd it as a fee:
I could not for my heart deny it him.

PORTIA
You were to blame, I must be plain with you,
To part so slightly with your wife's first gift:
A thing stuck on with oaths upon your finger
And so riveted with faith unto your flesh.
I gave my love a ring and made him swear
Never to part with it; and here he stands;
I dare be sworn for him he would not leave it
Nor pluck it from his finger, for the wealth
That the world masters. Now, in faith, Gratiano,
You give your wife too unkind a cause of grief:
An 'twere to me, I should be mad at it.

BASSANIO
[*Aside*] Why, I were best to cut my left hand off
And swear I lost the ring defending it.

GRATIANO
My Lord Bassanio gave his ring away
Unto the judge that begg'd it and indeed
Deserved it too; and then the boy, his clerk,
That took some pains in writing, he begg'd mine;
And neither man nor master would take aught
But the two rings.

PORTIA
What ring gave you, my lord?
Not that, I hope, which you received of me.

BASSANIO
If I could add a lie unto a fault,
I would deny it; but you see my finger
Hath not the ring upon it; it is gone.

PORTIA
Even so void is your false heart of truth.
By heaven, I will ne'er come in your bed
Until I see the ring.

NERISSA
Nor I in yours
Till I again see mine. [44]

BASSANIO
Sweet Portia,
If you did know to whom I gave the ring,
If you did know for whom I gave the ring
And would conceive for what I gave the ring
And how unwillingly I left the ring,
When nought would be accepted but the ring,
You would abate the strength of your displeasure.

PORTIA
If you had known the virtue of the ring,
Or half her worthiness that gave the ring,
Or your own honour to contain the ring,
You would not then have parted with the ring.
What man is there so much unreasonable,
If you had pleased to have defended it
With any terms of zeal, wanted the modesty
To urge the thing held as a ceremony?
Nerissa teaches me what to believe:
I'll die for't but some woman had the ring.

BASSANIO
No, by my honour, madam, by my soul,
No woman had it, but a civil doctor,
Which did refuse three thousand ducats of me
And begg'd the ring; the which I did deny him
And suffer'd him to go displeased away;
Even he that did uphold the very life
Of my dear friend. What should I say, sweet lady?
I was enforced to send it after him;
I was beset with shame and courtesy;
My honour would not let ingratitude
So much besmear it. Pardon me, good lady;
For, by these blessed candles of the night,
Had you been there, I think you would have begg'd
The ring of me to give the worthy doctor.

PORTIA
Let not that doctor e'er come near my house:
Since he hath got the jewel that I loved,
And that which you did swear to keep for me,
I will become as liberal as you;
I'll not deny him any thing I have,
No, not my body nor my husband's bed:
Know him I shall, I am well sure of it:
Lie not a night from home; watch me like Argus:
If you do not, if I be left alone,
Now, by mine honour, which is yet mine own,
I'll have that doctor for my bedfellow.

NERISSA
And I his clerk; therefore be well advised
How you do leave me to mine own protection.

GRATIANO
Well, do you so: let not me take him, then;
For if I do, I'll mar the young clerk's pen.

ANTONIO
I am the unhappy subject of these quarrels.

PORTIA
Sir, grieve not you; you are welcome notwithstanding.

BASSANIO
Portia, forgive me this enforced wrong;
And, in the hearing of these many friends,
I swear to thee, even by thine own fair eyes,
Wherein I see myself—

PORTIA
Mark you but that!

In both my eyes he doubly sees himself;
In each eye, one: swear by your double self,
And there's an oath of credit.

BASSANIO
Nay, but hear me:
Pardon this fault, and by my soul I swear
I never more will break an oath with thee.

ANTONIO
I once did lend my body for his wealth;
Which, but for him that had your husband's ring, 272
Had quite miscarried: I dare be bound again,
My soul upon the forfeit, that your lord
Will never more break faith advisedly.

PORTIA
Then you shall be his surety. Give him this
And bid him keep it better than the other.

ANTONIO
Here, Lord Bassanio; swear to keep this ring.

BASSANIO
By heaven, it is the same I gave the doctor!

PORTIA
I had it of him: pardon me, Bassanio;
For, by this ring, the doctor lay with me. 281

NERISSA
And pardon me, my gentle Gratiano;
For that same scrubbed boy, the doctor's clerk,
In lieu of this last night did lie with me.

GRATIANO
Why, this is like the mending of highways
In summer, where the ways are fair enough:
What, are we cuckolds ere we have deserved it?

PORTIA
Speak not so grossly. You are all amazed:
Here is a letter; read it at your leisure;
It comes from Padua, from Bellario:
There you shall find that Portia was the doctor,
Nerissa there her clerk: Lorenzo here 292
Shall witness I set forth as soon as you
And even but now return'd; I have not yet
Enter'd my house. Antonio, you are welcome;
And I have better news in store for you
Than you expect: unseal this letter soon;
There you shall find three of your argosies
Are richly come to harbour suddenly:
You shall not know by what strange accident
I chanced on this letter.

ANTONIO
I am dumb.

BASSANIO
Were you the doctor and I knew you not? 303

GRATIANO
Were you the clerk that is to make me cuckold?

NERISSA
Ay, but the clerk that never means to do it,
Unless he live until he be a man.

BASSANIO
Sweet doctor, you shall be my bed-fellow:
When I am absent, then lie with my wife.

ANTONIO
Sweet lady, you have given me life and living;
For here I read for certain that my ships
Are safely come to road.

PORTIA
How now, Lorenzo!
My clerk hath some good comforts too for you.

NERISSA
Ay, and I'll give them him without a fee. 314
There do I give to you and Jessica,
From the rich Jew, a special deed of gift,
After his death, of all he dies possess'd of.

LORENZO
Fair ladies, you drop manna in the way
Of starved people.

PORTIA
It is almost morning,
And yet I am sure you are not satisfied
Of these events at full. Let us go in;
And charge us there upon inter'gatories,
And we will answer all things faithfully.

GRATIANO
Let it be so: the first inter'gatory 325
That my Nerissa shall be sworn on is,
Whether till the next night she had rather stay
Or go to bed now, being two hours to day:
But were the day come, I should wish it dark,
That I were couching with the doctor's clerk.
Well, while I live I'll fear no other thing.
So sore as keeping safe Nerissa's ring. [*Exeunt.*

Notes

1. The name *'Shylock'* may have been derived by Shakespeare from a pamphlet called *'Caleb Shillocke his prophecies, or the Jewes Prediction';* the Pepysion ballad on this subject belongs to the year 1607; to the same year belongs a prose piece printed at the end of a rare tract called *'A Jewes prophecie, or Newes from Rome of two mighty armies,'* &c. Its ultimate origin is unknown; it may have been an Italian name *Sciolocca.* According to Hunter, *Scialac* was the name of a Maronite of Mount Libanus, who was living in 1614.
2. Dock'd; – Rowe's emendation for 'docks,' the reading of the Quartos and Folios.
3. Is that any thing new? – The old editions read *'Is that any thing now,'* changed to *'new'* by Johnson. Rowe first suggested the interrogation.
4. The Scottish lord; in the first Folio 'Scottish' is changed to 'other.'

5. "Alluding to the constant assistance, or rather, constant promises of assistance, that the French gave the Scots in their quarrels with the English" (Warburton).
6. The four strangers; – allusion has been made to six strangers. An interesting oversight on the poet's part.
7. Is he yet possess'd How much ye would, – so read the second and third Quartos; the Folios read *'he would'*; the first Quarto *'are you resolv'd how much he would have'*: this is one of the important points in which the second Quarto is superior to the first.
8. Cp. – Genesis xxx.
9. The third, – *i.e.* 'reckoning Abraham himself as the first.'
10. A breed for barren metal; – the reading of the Folio *'a breed of'*; 'for' must be equivalent to 'in exchange for'; *'breed'* = 'interest money bred from the principal' (*cp.* Gr. TÓKOS).
11. The old stage direction ran as follows:—*'Enter Morochus a tawnie Moore all in white, and three or four followers accordingly, with Portia, Nerissa and their traine.'*
12. The Sophy, – *cp.* *"Sofi,* and *Sofito,* an ancient word signifying a wise man, learned and skillful in Magike Naturale. It has grown to be the common name of the Emperour of Persia" (Abraham Hartwell's translation of Minadoi's *History of the Wars between the Turks and the Persians*).

    The *'Sefii of Persia'* is mentioned in the German play *Der Jude von Venedig.*

13. Page; – Theobald's emendation for 'rage,' the reading of all the old editions.
14. Gobbo's 'you,' as a mark of respect, changes to 'thou,' after the recognition.
15. "Long and deep lines from the Mount of Venus (the ball of the thumb) towards the line of life, signifieth so many wives.

    . . . These lines visible and deep, so many wives the party shall have" (Saunder's *Chiromancie,* quoted by Halliwell).

16. Did; – the Quartos and first Folio read 'doe'; the reading 'did' was first given in the second Folio; if this is adopted, *'get'* = 'beget.'
17. Black-Monday, – *i.e.* Easter Monday, so called, because of a storm which occurred on April 14, 1360, being Easter Monday, when Edward III, was lying with his army before Paris, and when many of his men-at-arms died of cold (*Stowe*).
18. Jacob's staff; cp. – Gen. xxxii. and Heb. xi. 21. *'A Jacob's staff'* was generally used in the sense of 'a pilgrim's staff,' because St. James (or Jacob) was the patron saint of pilgrims.
19. A Jewess eye; – the Quartos and Folios read *'a Jewes eye,'* probably pronounced *Jewës;'* 'worth a Jew's eye' was a proverbial phrase: 'that worth was the price which the Jews paid for immunity from mutilation and death.' The reading *"Jewess"* seems very doubtful.
20. By my hood; – this phrase is found nowhere else in Shakespeare; according to Malone, Gratiano is in a masqued habit, to which it is probable that formerly, as at present, a large cape or hood was affixed.
21. The Hyrcanian deserts; – Shakespeare three times mentions the tigers of Hyrcania, 'the name given to a district of indefinite extent south of the Caspian,' where, according to Pliny, tigers were bred.
22. Undervalued – "in the beginning of Elizabeth's reign, gold was to silver in the proportion of 11 to 1; in the forty-third year of her reign it was in the proportion of 10 to 1" (Clarendon).
23. Tombs do; – Johnson's emendation for the old reading *'timber do.'*
24. Halliwell notes that this line is a paraphrastical inversion of the common old proverb: 'Farewell, frost,' which was used in the absence or departure of anything that was unwelcome or displeasing.
25. Knapped ginger; – perhaps *'to knap ginger'* is to 'nibble ginger'; old women were fond of this condiment: Cotgrave invariably gives *'knap'* as a synonym of *'gnaw'* or *'nibble.'*
26. Humility, – rightly explained by Schmidt as 'kindness, benevolence, humanity.'
27. The special value of the 'turquoise' was its supposed virtue in indicating the health of the wearer: it was said to brighten or fade as its wearer was well or ill, and to give warning of approaching danger.
28. More love; – because Hercules rescued Hesione not for love of the lady, but for the sake of the horses promised him by Laomedon.
29. Veiling an Indian beauty; – it has been pointed out that Montaigne in his Essay on 'Beauty' says: "The Indians describe it black and swarthy, with blabbered thick lips, with a broad and flat nose." If Shakespeare gives us a reminiscence of this, he must have read Montaigne in French, as Florio's translation was not published until 1603.
30. Hard food for Midas, – who prayed that everything he touched might turn to gold, and soon regretted his prayer.
31. Paleness; – as Bassanio uses 'pale' of silver a few lines before, Theobald, on Warburton's suggestion, proposed to read *'plainness'*; but *'pale'* is a regular epithet of lead, and there seems no reason for changing the reading here.
32. Rain, – the reading of the second Quarto, *'rein,'* is generally preferred.
33. And if on earth he do not mean it, then In reason; – the second Quarto *'it, it'*; the Folios *'it, it is.'*

    Various emendations have been suggested for *'mean,'* but no change is necessary *'mean'* = 'aim at.' A kind correspondent, Mr. S. W. Orson, calls attention to Herbert's use of the word in *'The Church Porch'* (E. Stock's reprint of the first edition) "Shoots higher much than he than *means* a tree" (p. 12), and "Scorns his first bed of dirt, and means the sky" (p. 163).

34. Our holy Sabbath; – so the first Quarto; the second reads *'Sabaoth'*; it is just possible that Shakespeare might have been misled by the expression, 'Lord God of Sabaoth,' which occurs in the New Testament. 'Sabbath' and 'Sabaoth' (i.e. 'hosts,' in the phrase 'Lord of hosts') were confused even by Sir Walter Scott, when in *Ivanhoe,* ch. x. he refers to "the gains of a week, aye the space between two Sabaoths." Similarly Spenser (F. Q. viii. 2):—

'But henceforth all shall rest eternally
With him that is the God of Sabaoth hight.'

Dr. Johnson treated the two words as identical in the first edition of his Dictionary.

35. Affection, Mistress of passion; – the Quartos and Folios read *'affection. Master of passion.'* The reading now generally adopted was first suggested by Thrilby; *'Maistres'* or *'mastres,'* the old spelling of *'mistress'* evidently produced the error. 'Affection,' when contrasted with 'passion,' seems to denote 'emotions produced through the senses by external objects.'
36. A wollen bag-pipe; – the reading of all the old editions; 'wawling,' 'swollen,' 'bollen,' have been variously suggested; *'woollen'* probably refers to the covering of the wind-bag.
37. Cp. – "Mercy is seasonable in the time of affliction, as clouds of rain in the time of drought," Ecclesiasticus, xxxv. 20.
38. Are there balance; balance – was frequently treated as a plural by Elizabethan writers, though this is the only instance in Shakespeare.
39. Troilus; – the image is from Chaucer's *Troilus and Cresseide:* "Upon the wallis fast eke would he walke" (Bk. v. 666).
40. Thisbe, – &c. Hunter (*New Illustrations,* i.) ingeniously suggests that the old Folio of Chaucer was lying open before Shakespeare when he wrote this dialogue, and that there he found Thisbe, Dido, and Medea, as well as Troilus. It is certainly striking that Thisbe, Dido, and Medea follow each other in the *'Legend of Good Women.'* Shakespeare has seemingly transferred to Dido what he found in Chaucer's *Legend* concerning Ariadne (*'And to the stronde barefote faste she went'—'And turne agayne, and on the stronde hire fyinde.'*) Chaucer's *Medea* directed Shakespeare's mind to Ovid, *Metam.* VII.
41. Jessica; – Medea, who stole away from her father Aeetes, with the golden fleece, suggests Jessica's own story to Lorenzo.
42. &c. "The corresponding passage in Plato is in his tenth book *De Republica,* where he speaks of the harmony of the Spheres, and represents a syren sitting on each of the eight orbs, and singing to each in its proper tone, while they are thus guided through the heavens, and consent in a diapason of perfect harmony, the Fates themselves chanting to this celestial music" (Du Bois, *The Wreath,* p. 60, quoted by Furness). The Platonic doctrine is, however, blended with reminiscences of Job xxxviii. 7, "The morning stars sang together."
43. Close it in; – Quarto 1 and Folios read *'in it,'* which some editors have taken as equivalent to *'close-in-it.'*
44. A similar repetition of the word *'love'* at the end of ten consecutive lines is found in *'The Fayre Mayde of the Exchange'* (1607); *cp. Edward III.* Act II. sc. i., where *'the sun'* ends eight consecutive lines.

PERICLES-PRINCE OF TYRE

PERICLES-PRINCE OF TYRE

DRAMATIS PERSONAE

ANTIOCHUS, king of Antioch.
PERICLES prince of Tyre.
HELICANUS, lord of Tyre.
ESCANES, lord of Tyre.
SIMONIDES, king of Pentapolis.
CLEON governor of Tarsus.
LYSIMACHUS, governor of Mytilene.
CERIMON, a lord of Ephesus.
THALIARD, a lord of Antioch.
PHILEMON, servant to Cerimon.
LEONINE, servant to Dionyza.
Marshal.
A Pandar.
BOULT, his servant.
The Daughter of Antiochus.
DIONYZA, wife to Cleon.
THAISA, daughter to Simonides.
MARINA, daughter to Pericles and Thaisa.
LYCHORIDA, nurse to Marina.
A Bawd.
Lords, Knights, Gentlemen, Sailors, Pirates, Fishermen, and Messengers.
DIANA, as Chorus
GOWER, as Chorus.

SCENE: *Dispersedly in various countries.*

ACT ONE

Enter GOWER.

Before the palace of Antioch.

To sing a song that old was sung,
From ashes ancient Gower is come;
Assuming man's infirmities,
To glad your ear, and please your eyes.
It hath been sung at festivals,
On ember-eves and holy-ales;
And lords and ladies in their lives
Have read it for restoratives:
The purchase is to make men glorious;
Et bonum quo antiquius, eo melius.
If you, born in these latter times,
When wit 's more ripe, accept my rhymes,
And that to hear an old man sing
May to your wishes pleasure bring,
I life would wish, and that I might
Waste it for you, like taper-light.
This Antioch, then, Antiochus the Great
Built up, this city, for his chiefest seat;
The fairest in all Syria,
I tell you what mine authors say:
This king unto him took a fere,
Who died and left a female heir,
So buxom, so blithe, and full of face,
As heaven had lent her all his grace;
With whom the father liking took,
And her to incest did provoke:
Bad child; worse father! To entice his own
To evil should be done by none:
But custom what they did begin

Was with long use account no sin.
The beauty of this sinful dame
Made many princes thither frame,
To seek her as a bed-fellow,
In marriage-pleasures play-fellow:
Which to prevent he made a law,
To keep her still, and men in awe,
That whoso ask'd her for his wife,
His riddle told not, lost his life:
So for her many a wight did die,
As yon grim looks do testify.
What now ensues, to the judgement of your eye
I give, my cause who best can justify. [*Exit.*

ACT ONE SCENE ONE

Antioch. A room in the palace.

Enter ANTIOCHUS, PRINCE PERICLES, *and followers.*

ANTIOCHUS
Young prince of Tyre, you have at large received
The danger of the task you undertake.

PERICLES
I have, Antiochus, and, with a soul
Embolden'd with the glory of her praise,
Think death no hazard in this enterprise.

ANTIOCHUS
Bring in our daughter, clothed like a bride,
For the embracements even of Jove himself;
At whose conception, till Lucina reign'd,
Nature this dowry gave, to glad her presence,
The senate-house of planets all did sit,
To knit in her their best perfections.

Music. Enter the Daughter of Antiochus.

PERICLES
See where she comes, apparell'd like the spring,
Graces her subjects, and her thoughts the king
Of every virtue gives renown to men!
Her face the book of praises, where is read
Nothing but curious pleasures, as from thence
Sorrow were ever razed and testy wrath
Could never be her mild companion.
You gods that made me man, and sway in love,
That have inflamed desire in my breast
To taste the fruit of yon celestial tree,
Or die in the adventure, be my helps,
As I am son and servant to your will,
To compass such a boundless happiness! [1]

ANTIOCHUS
Prince Pericles,—

PERICLES
That would be son to great Antiochus.

ANTIOCHUS
Before thee stands this fair Hesperides,
With golden fruit, but dangerous to be touch'd;
For death-like dragons here affright thee hard: [2]
Her face, like heaven, enticeth thee to view
Her countless glory, which desert must gain;
And which, without desert, because thine eye
Presumes to reach, all thy whole heap must die.
Yon sometimes famous princes, like thyself,
Drawn by report, adventurous by desire,
Tell thee, with speechless tongues and semblance pale,
That without covering, save yon field of stars,
Here they stand martyrs, slain in Cupid's wars;
And with dead cheeks advise thee to desist
For going on death's net, whom none resist.

PERICLES
Antiochus, I thank thee, who hath taught
My frail mortality to know itself,
And by those fearful objects to prepare
This body, like to them, to what I must;
For death remember'd should be like a mirror,
Who tells us life's but breath, to trust it error.
I'll make my will then, and, as sick men do
Who know the world, see heaven, but, feeling woe,
Gripe not at earthly joys as erst they did;
So I bequeath a happy peace to you
And all good men, as every prince should do;
My riches to the earth from whence they came;
But my unspotted fire of love to you.
[*To the Daughter of Antiochus.*
Thus ready for the way of life or death,
I wait the sharpest blow, Antiochus. [3]

ANTIOCHUS
Scorning advice, read the conclusion, then:
Which read and not expounded, 'tis decreed,
As these before thee thou thyself shalt bleed.

DAUGHTER
Of all say'd yet, mayst thou prove prosperous! [4]
Of all say'd yet, I wish thee happiness!

PERICLES
Like a bold champion, I assume the lists,
Nor ask advice of any other thought
But faithfulness and courage.

He reads the riddle.

I am no viper, yet I feed
On mother's flesh which did me breed.
I sought a husband, in which labour
I found that kindness in a father:
He 's father, son, and husband mild;
I mother, wife, and yet his child.

ANTIOCHUS Before thee stands this fair Hesperides.

How they may be, and yet in two,
As you will live, resolve it you.
Sharp physic is the last: but, O you powers
That give heaven countless eyes to view men's acts,
Why cloud they not their sights perpetually,
If this be true, which makes me pale to read it?
Fair glass of light, I loved you, and could still,
[*Takes hold of the hand of the Princess.*
Were not this glorious casket stored with ill:
But I must tell you, now my thoughts revolt
For he 's no man on whom perfections wait
That, knowing sin within, will touch the gate.
You are a fair viol, and your sense the strings;
Who, finger'd to make man his lawful music,
Would draw heaven down, and all the gods, to hearken;
But being play'd upon before your time,
Hell only danceth at so harsh a chime.
Good sooth, I care not for you.

ANTIOCHUS
Prince Pericles, touch not, upon thy life.
For that 's an article within our law,
As dangerous as the rest. Your time 's expired:
Either expound now, or receive your sentence.

PERICLES
Great king,
Few love to hear the sins they love to act;
'Twould braid yourself too near for me to tell it.
Who has a book of all that monarchs do,
He 's more secure to keep it shut than shown:
For vice repeated is like the wandering wind.
Blows dust in other's eyes, to spread itself;
And yet the end of all is bought thus dear,
The breath is gone, and the sore eyes see clear:
To stop the air would hurt them. The blind mole casts
Copp'd hills towards heaven, to tell the earth is throng'd
By man's oppression; and the poor worm doth die for't.
Kings are earth's gods; in vice their law's their will;
And if Jove stray, who dares say Jove doth ill?
It is enough you know; and it is fit,
What being more known grows worse, to smother it.
All love the womb that their first being bred,
Then give my tongue like leave to love my head.

ANTIOCHUS
[*Aside*] Heaven, that I had thy head! he has found the meaning:
But I will gloze with him.—Young prince of Tyre,
Though by the tenour of our strict edict,
Your exposition misinterpreting,
We might proceed to cancel of your days; [5]
Yet hope, succeeding from so fair a tree
As your fair self, doth tune us otherwise:
Forty days longer we do respite you;
If by which time our secret be undone,
This mercy shows we 'll joy in such a son:
And until then your entertain shall be
As doth befit our honour and your worth.
[*Exeunt all but Pericles.*

PERICLES
How courtesy would seem to cover sin,
When what is done is like an hypocrite,
The which is good in nothing but in sight!
If it be true that I interpret false,
Then were it certain you were not so bad
As with foul incest to abuse your soul;
Where now you're both a father and a son,
By your untimely claspings with your child, [6]
Which pleasure fits an husband, not a father;
And she an eater of her mother's flesh,
By the defiling of her parent's bed;
And both like serpents are, who though they feed
On sweetest flowers, yet they poison breed.
Antioch, farewell! for wisdom sees, those men
Blush not in actions blacker than the night, [7]
Will shun no course to keep them from the light.
One sin, I know, another doth provoke;
Murder's as near to lust as flame to smoke:
Poison and treason are the hands of sin,
Ay, and the targets, to put off the shame:
Then, lest my lie be cropp'd to keep you clear,
By flight I'll shun the danger which I fear. [*Exit.*

Re-enter ANTIOCHUS.

ANTIOCHUS
He hath found the meaning, for which we mean
To have his head.
He must not live to trumpet forth my infamy,
Nor tell the world Antiochus doth sin
In such a loathed manner;
And therefore instantly this prince must die;
For by his fall my honour must keep high.
Who attends us there?

Enter THALIARD.

THALIARD
Doth your highness call?

ANTIOCHUS
Thaliard,
You are of our chamber, and our mind partakes
Her private actions to your secrecy;
And for your faithfulness we will advance you.
Thaliard, behold, here 's poison, and here 's gold;
We hate the prince of Tyre, and thou must kill him:
It fits thee not to ask the reason why,
Because we bid it. Say, is it done?

THALIARD
My lord,
'Tis done.

ANTIOCHUS
Enough.

Enter a Messenger.

Let your breath cool yourself, telling your haste.

MESSENGER
My lord, prince Pericles is fled. [*Exit.*

ANTIOCHUS
As thou
Wilt live, fly after: and like an arrow shot
From a well-experienced archer hits the mark
His eye doth level at, so thou ne'er return
Unless thou say 'Prince Pericles is dead.'

THALIARD
My lord,
If I can get him within my pistol's length,

I'll make him sure enough: so, farewell to your highness.

ANTIOCHUS

Thaliard, adieu! [*Exit Thaliard*] Till Pericles be dead,
My heart can lend no succour to my head. [*Exit.*

ACT ONE SCENE TWO

Tyre. A room in the palace.

Enter PERICLES.

PERICLES

[*To Lords without*] Let none disturb us.—Why should this change of thoughts, [8]
The sad companion, dull-eyed melancholy,
Be my so used a guest as not an hour, [9]
In the day's glorious walk, or peaceful night,
The tomb where grief should sleep, can breed me quiet?
Here pleasures court mine eyes, and mine eyes shun them,
And danger, which I fear'd, is at Antioch,
Whose arm seems far too short to hit me here: [10]
Yet neither pleasure's art can joy my spirits,
Nor yet the other's distance comfort me. 13
Then it is thus: the passions of the mind,
That have their first conception by mis-dread,
Have after-nourishment and life by care;
And what was first but fear what might be done,
Grows elder now and cares it be not done.
And so with me: the great Antiochus,
'Gainst whom I am too little to contend,
Since he 's so great can make his will his act,
Will think me speaking, though I swear to silence;
Nor boots it me to say I honour him. 23
If he suspect I may dishonour him:
And what may make him blush in being known,
He 'll stop the course by which it might be known;
With hostile forces he 'll o'erspread the land,
And with the ostent of war will look so huge,
Amazement shall drive courage from the state;
Our men be vanquish'd ere they do resist,
And subjects punish'd that ne'er thought offence:
Which care of them, not pity of myself, 32
Who am no more but as the tops of trees, [11]
Which fence the roots they grow by and defend them,
Makes both my body pine and soul to languish,
And punish that before that he would punish.

Enter HELICANUS, *with other* LORDS.

FIRST LORD

Joy and all comfort in your sacred breast!

SECOND LORD

And keep your mind, till you return to us,
Peaceful and comfortable!

HELICANUS

Peace, peace, and give experience tongue.
They do abuse the king that flatter him:
For flattery is the bellows blows up sin;
The thing the which is flatter'd, but a spark, 44
To which that blast gives heat and stronger glowing; [12]
Whereas reproof, obedient and in order,
Fits kings, as they are men, for they may err.
When Signior Sooth here does proclaim a peace,
He flatters you, makes war upon your life.
Prince, pardon me, or strike me, if you please;
I cannot be much lower than my knees.

PERICLES

All leave us else; but let your cares o'erlook
What shipping and what lading 's in our haven,
And then return to us. [*Exeunt Lords.*
Helicanus, thou 56
Hast moved us: what seest thou in our looks?

HELICANUS

An angry brow, dread lord.

PERICLES

If there be such a dart in princes' frowns,
How durst thy tongue move anger to our face?

HELICANUS

How dare the plants look up to heaven, from whence [13]
They have their nourishment?

PERICLES

Thou know'st I have power
To take thy life from thee.

HELICANUS

[*Kneeling*] I have ground the axe myself;
Do you but strike the blow.

PERICLES

Rise, prithee, rise.
Sit down: thou art no flatterer: 69
I thank thee for it; and heaven forbid
That kings should let their ears hear their faults hid!
Fit counsellor and servant for a prince,
Who by thy wisdom makest a prince thy servant,
What wouldst thou have me do?

HELICANUS

To bear with patience
Such griefs as you yourself do lay upon yourself.

PERICLES

Thou speak'st like a physician, Helicanus,
That minister'st a potion unto me
That thou wouldst tremble to receive thyself.
Attend me, then: I went to Antioch, 81

Where as thou know'st, against the face of death,
I sought the purchase of a glorious beauty.
From whence an issue I might propagate,
Are arms to princes, and bring joys to subjects.
Her face was to mine eye beyond all wonder;
The rest—hark in thine ear—as black as incest:
Which by my knowledge found, the sinful father
Seem'd not to strike, but smooth: but thou know'st this,
'Tis time to fear when tyrants seem to kiss.
Which fear so grew in me, I hither fled,
Under the covering of a careful night,
Who seem'd my good protector; and, being here,
Bethought me what was past, what might succeed.
I knew him tyrannous; and tyrants' fears
Decrease not, but grow faster than the years:
And should he doubt it, as no doubt he doth, [14]
That I should open to the listening air
How many worthy princes' bloods were shed,
To keep his bed of blackness unlaid ope,
To lop that doubt, he 'll fill this land with arms,
And make pretence of wrong that I have done him;
When all, for mine, if I may call offence,
Must feel war's blow, who spares not innocence: [15]
Which love to all, of which thyself art one,
Who now reprovest me for it,— [16]

HELICANUS
Alas, sir!

PERICLES
Drew sleep out of mine eyes, blood from my cheeks,
Musings into my mind, with thousand doubts
How I might stop this tempest ere it came;
And finding little comfort to relieve them,
I thought it princely charity to grieve them.

HELICANUS
Well, my lord, since you have given me leave to speak.
Freely will I speak. Antiochus you fear,
And justly too, I think, you fear the tyrant,
Who either by public war or private treason
Will take away your life.
Therefore, my lord, go travel for a while,
Till that his rage and anger be forgot,
Or till the Destinies do cut his thread of life.
Your rule direct to any; if to me.
Day serves not light more faithful than I'll be.

PERICLES
I do not doubt thy faith;
But should he wrong my liberties in my absence?

HELICANUS
We 'll mingle our bloods together in the earth,
From whence we had our being and our birth.

PERICLES
Tyre, I now look from thee then, and to Tarsus
Intend my travel, where I'll hear from thee;
And by whose letters I'll dispose myself.
The care I had and have of subjects' good
On thee I lay, whose wisdom's strength can bear it.
I'll take thy word for faith, not ask thine oath:
Who shuns not to break one will sure crack both:
But in our orbs we 'll live so round and safe,
That time of both this truth shall ne'er convince,
Thou show'dst a subject's shine, I a true prince.

[*Exeunt.*

ACT ONE SCENE THREE

Tyre. An ante-chamber in the palace.

Enter THALIARD.

THALIARD
So, this is Tyre, and this the court. Here must I kill King Pericles; and if I do it not, I am sure to be hanged at home: 'tis dangerous. Well, I perceive he was a wise fellow, and had good discretion, that, being bid to ask what he would of the king, desired he might know none of his secrets: now do I see he had some reason for't; for if a king bid a man be a villain, he's bound by the indenture of his oath to be one. Hush! here come the lords of Tyre. [17]

Enter HELICANUS *and* ESCANES, *with other* Lords *of Tyre.*

HELICANUS
You shall not need, my fellow peers of Tyre,
Further to question me of your king's departure:
His seal'd commission, left in trust with me,
Doth speak sufficiently he's gone to travel.

THALIARD
[*Aside*] How! the king gone!

HELICANUS
If further yet you will be satisfied,
Why, as it were unlicensed of your loves,
He would depart, I'll give some light unto you.
Being at Antioch—

THALIARD
[*Aside*] What from Antioch?

HELICANUS
Royal Antiochus—on what cause I know not—
Took some displeasure at him; at least he judged so:
And doubting lest that he had err'd or sinn'd,
To show his sorrow, he 'ld correct himself;
So puts himself unto the shipman's toil,
With whom each minute threatens life or death.

THALIARD
[*Aside*] Well, I perceive
I shall not be hang'd now, although I would;

But since he's gone, the king's seas must please: [18]
He 'scaped the land, to perish at the sea.
I'll present myself. Peace to the lords of Tyre!

HELICANUS
Lord Thaliard from Antiochus is welcome.

THALIARD
From him I come
With message unto princely Pericles;
But since my landing I have understood
Your lord has betook himself to unknown travels,
My message must return from whence it came.

HELICANUS
We have no reason to desire it,
Commended to our master, not to us:
Yet, ere you shall depart, this we desire,
As friends to Antioch, we may feast in Tyre.
[*Exeunt.*

ACT ONE SCENE FOUR

Tarsus. A room in the Governor's house.

Enter CLEON, *the governor of Tarsus, with* DIONYZA, *and others.*

CLEON
My Dionyza, shall we rest us here,
And by relating tales of others' griefs,
See if 'twill teach us to forget our own?

DIONYZA
That were to blow at fire in hope to quench it;
For who digs hills because they do aspire
Throws down one mountain to cast up a higher.
O my distressed lord, even such our griefs are;
Here they're but felt, and seen with mischief's eyes, [19]
But like to groves, being topp'd, they higher rise.

CLEON
O Dionyza,
Who wanteth food, and will not say he wants it,
Or can conceal his hunger till he famish?
Our tongues and sorrows do sound deep [20]
Our woes into the air; our eyes do weep,
Till tongues fetch breath that may proclaim them louder; [21]
That, if heaven slumber while their creatures want,
They may awake their helps to comfort them.
I'll then discourse our woes, felt several years,
And wanting breath to speak help me with tears.

DIONYZA
I'll do my best, sir.

CLEON
This Tarsus, o'er which I have the government,
A city on whom plenty held full hand,
For riches strew'd herself even in the streets;
Whose towers bore heads so high they kiss'd the clouds,
And strangers ne'er beheld but wondered at;
Whose men and dames so jetted and adorn'd,
Like one another's glass to trim them by:
Their tables were stored full, to glad the sight,
And not so much to feed on as delight;
All poverty was scorn'd, and pride so great,
The name of help grew odious to repeat.

DIONYZA
O, 'tis too true.

CLEON
But see what heaven can do! By this our change,
These mouths, who but of late, earth, sea, and air,
Were all too little to content and please,
Although they gave their creatures in abundance,
As houses are defiled for want of use,
They are now starved for want of exercise:
Those palates who, not yet two summers younger, [22]
Must have inventions to delight the taste,
Would now be glad of bread, and beg for it:
Those mothers who, to nousle up their babes,
Thought nought too curious, are ready now
To eat those little darlings whom they loved.
So sharp are hunger's teeth, that man and wife
Draw lots who first shall die to lengthen life:
Here stands a lord, and there a lady weeping;
Here many sink, yet those which see them fall
Have scarce strength left to give them burial.
Is not this true?

DIONYZA
Our cheeks and hollow eyes do witness it.

CLEON
O, let those cities that of plenty's cup
And her prosperities so largely taste,
With their superfluous riots, hear these tears!
The misery of Tarsus may be theirs.

Enter a Lord.

LORD
Where's the lord governor?

CLEON
Here.
Speak out thy sorrows which thou bring'st in haste,
For comfort is too far for us to expect.

LORD
We have descried, upon our neighbouring shore,
A portly sail of ships make hitherward.

CLEON
I thought as much.
One sorrow never comes but brings an heir,
That may succeed as his inheritor;

And so in ours: some neighbouring nation,
Taking advantage of our misery,
Hath stuff'd these hollow vessels with their power,
To beat us down, the which are down already;
And make a conquest of unhappy me, [23]
Whereas no glory's got to overcome.

LORD
That's the least fear; for, by the semblance
Of their white flags display'd, they bring us peace,
And come to us as favourers, not as foes.

CLEON
Thou speak'st like him's untutor'd to repeat: [24]
Who makes the fairest show means most deceit.
But bring they what they will and what they can,
What need we fear?
The ground's the lowest, and we are half way there.
Go tell their general we attend him here,
To know for what he comes, and whence he comes,
And what he craves.

LORD
I go, my lord. [*Exit.*

CLEON
Welcome is peace, if he on peace consist;
If wars, we are unable to resist.

Enter PERICLES *with* Attendants.

PERICLES
Lord governor, for so we hear you are,
Let not our ships and number of our men
Be like a beacon fired to amaze your eyes.
We have heard your miseries as far as Tyre,
And seen the desolation of your streets:
Nor come we to add sorrow to your tears,
But to relieve them of their heavy load;
And these our ships, you happily may think
Are like the Trojan horse was stuff'd within
With bloody veins, expecting overthrow,
Are stored with corn to make your needy bread,
And give them life whom hunger starved half dead.

ALL
The gods of Greece protect you!
And we 'll pray for you.

PERICLES
Arise, I pray you, rise:
We do not look for reverence, but to love,
And harbourage for ourself, our ships, and men.

CLEON
The which when any shall not gratify,
Or pay you with unthankfulness in thought,
Be it our wives, our children, or ourselves,
The curse of heaven and men succeed their evils!
Till when,—the which I hope shall ne'er be seen,—
Your grace is welcome to our town and us.

PERICLES
Which welcome we 'll accept; feast here awhile,
Until our stars that frown lend us a smile.
[*Exeunt.*

ACT TWO

Enter GOWER.

GOWER
Here have you seen a mighty king
His child, I wis, to incest bring;
A better prince and benign lord,
That will prove awful both in deed and word.
Be quiet then as men should be,
Till he hath pass'd necessity.
I'll show you those in troubles reign,
Losing a mite, a mountain gain.
The good in conversation,
To whom I give my benison,
Is still at Tarsus, where each man
Thinks all is writ he speken can;
And, to remember what he does,
Build his statue to make him glorious:
But tidings to the contrary
Are brought your eyes; what need speak I?

DUMB SHOW.

Enter at one door PERICLES *talking with* CLEON; *all the train with them. Enter at another door a* Gentleman, *with a letter to* PERICLES; PERICLES *shows the letter to* CLEON; *gives the* Messenger *a reward, and knights him. Exit* PERICLES *at one door, and* CLEON *at another.*

Good Helicane, that stay'd at home,
Not to eat honey like a drone
From others' labours; for though he strive [25]
To killen bad, keep good alive;
And to fulfil his prince' desire,
Sends word of all that haps in Tyre: [26]
How Thaliard came full bent with sin
And had intent to murder him;
And that in Tarsus was not best
Longer for him to make his rest.
He, doing so, put forth to seas,
Where when men been, there's seldom ease;
For now the wind begins to blow;
Thunder above and deeps below
Make such unquiet, that the ship
Should house him safe is wreck'd and split;
And he, good prince, having all lost,
By waves from coast to coast is tost:
All perishen of man, of pelf,
Ne aught escapen but himself;

Till fortune, tired with doing bad,
Threw him ashore, to give him glad:
And here he comes. What shall be next,
Pardon old Gower,—this longs the text.

[*Exit.*

ACT TWO SCENE ONE

Pentapolis. An open place by the sea-side.

Enter PERICLES, *wet.*

PERICLES

Yet cease your ire, you angry stars of heaven!
Wind, rain, and thunder, remember, earthly man
Is but a substance that must yield to you;
And I, as fits my nature, do obey you:
Alas, the sea hath cast me on the rocks,
Wash'd me from shore to shore, and left me breath
Nothing to think on but ensuing death:
Let it suffice the greatness of your powers
To have bereft a prince of all his fortunes;
And having thrown him from your watery grave,
Here to have death in peace is all he 'll crave.

Enter three Fishermen.

FIRST FISHERMEN

What, ho, Pilch!

SECOND FISHERMEN

Ha, come and bring away the nets!

FIRST FISHERMEN

What, Patch-breech, I say!

THIRD FISHERMEN

What say you, master?

FIRST FISHERMEN

Look how thou stirrest now! come away, or I'll fetch thee with a wanion.

THIRD FISHERMEN

'Faith, master, I am thinking of the poor men that were cast away before us even now.

FIRST FISHERMEN

Alas, poor souls, it grieved my heart to hear what pitiful cries they made to us to help them, when, well-a-day, we could scarce help ourselves.

THIRD FISHERMEN

Nay, master, said not I as much when I saw the porpus how he bounced and tumbled? they say they're half fish, half flesh: a plague on them, they ne'er come but I look to be washed. Master, I marvel how the fishes live in the sea.

FIRST FISHERMEN

Why, as men do a-land; the great ones eat up the little ones: I can compare our rich misers to nothing so fitly as to a whale; a' plays and tumbles, driving the poor fry before him, and at last devours them all at a mouthful: such whales have I heard on o' the land, who never leave gaping till they've swallowed the whole parish, church, steeple, bells, and all.

PERICLES

[*Aside*] A pretty moral.

THIRD FISHERMEN

But, master, if I had been the sexton, I would have been that day in the belfry.

SECOND FISHERMEN

Why, man?

THIRD FISHERMEN

Because he should have swallowed me too: and when I had been in his belly, I would have kept such a jangling of the bells, that he should never have left, till he cast bells, steeple, church, and parish up again. But if the good King Simonides were of my mind,—

PERICLES

[*Aside*] Simonides!

THIRD FISHERMEN

We would purge the land of these drones, that rob the bee of her honey.

PERICLES

[*Aside*] How from the finny subject of the sea [27]
These fishers tell the infirmities of men;
And from their watery empire recollect
All that may men approve or men detect!
Peace be at your labour, honest fishermen.

SECOND FISHERMEN

Honest! good fellow, what's that? If it be a day fits you, search out of the calendar, and nobody look after it. [28]

PERICLES

May see the sea hath cast upon your coast. [29]

SECOND FISHERMEN

What a drunken knave was the sea to cast thee in our way!

PERICLES

A man whom both the waters and the wind.
In that vast tennis-court, have made the ball For them to play upon, entreats you pity him;
He asks of you, that never used to beg.

FIRST FISHERMEN

No, friend, cannot you beg? Here's them in our country of Greece gets more with begging than we can do with working.

SECOND FISHERMEN

Canst thou catch any fishes, then?

PERICLES

I never practised it.

SECOND FISHERMEN

Nay, then thou wilt starve, sure; for here's nothing to be got now-a-days, unless thou canst fish for't.

PERICLES
What I have been I have forgot to know;
But what I am, want teaches me to think on:
A man throng'd up with cold: my veins are chill,
And have no more of life than may suffice
To give my tongue that heat to ask your help;
Which if you shall refuse, when I am dead,
For that I am a man, pray see me buried.

FIRST FISHERMAN
Die quoth-a? Now gods forbid! I have a gown here; come, put it on; keep thee warm. Now, afore me, a handsome fellow! Come, thou shalt go home, and we 'll have flesh for holidays, fish for fasting-days, and moreo'er puddings and flap-jacks, and thou shalt be welcome.

PERICLES
I thank you, sir.

SECOND FISHERMAN
Hark you, my friend; you said you could not beg.

PERICLES
I did but crave.

SECOND FISHERMAN
But crave! Then I'll turn craver too, and so I shall 'scape whipping.

PERICLES
Why, are all your beggars whipped, then?

SECOND FISHERMAN
O, not all, my friend, not all; for if all your beggars were whipped, I would wish no better office than to be beadle. But, master, I'll go draw up the net.
[*Exit with Third Fisherman.*

PERICLES
[*Aside*] How well this honest mirth becomes their labour!

FIRST FISHERMAN
Hark you, sir, do you know where ye are?

PERICLES
Not well.

FIRST FISHERMAN
Why, I'll tell you: this is called Pentapolis, and our king the good Simonides.

PERICLES
The good King Simonides, do you call him?

FIRST FISHERMAN
Ay, sir; and he deserves so to be called for his peaceable reign and good government.

PERICLES
He is a happy king, since he gains from his subjects the name of good by his government. How far is his court distant from this shore?

FIRST FISHERMAN
Marry, sir, half a day's journey: and I'll tell you, he hath a fair daughter, and to-morrow is her birth-day; and there are princes and knights come from all parts of the world to just and tourney for her love.

PERICLES
Were my fortunes equal to my desires, I could wish to make one there.

FIRST FISHERMAN
O, sir, things must be as they may; and what a man cannot get, he may lawfully deal for—his wife's soul.

Re-enter Second *and* Third Fishermen, *drawing up a net.*

SECOND FISHERMAN
Help, master, help! here's a fish hangs in the net, like a poor man's right in the law; 'twill hardly come out. Ha! bots on't, 'tis come at last, and 'tis turned to a rusty armour.

PERICLES
An armour, friends! I pray you, let me see it.
Thanks, fortune, yet, that, after all my crosses,
Thou givest me somewhat to repair myself;
And though it was mine own, part of my heritage,
Which my dead father did bequeath to me,
With this strict charge, even as he left his life.
'Keep it, my Pericles; it hath been a shield
'Twixt me and death;'—and pointed to this brace;—
'For that it saved me, keep it; in like necessity—
The which the gods protect thee from!—may defend thee.'
It kept where I kept, I so dearly loved it;
Till the rough seas, that spare not any man,
Took it in rage, though calm'd have given't again:
I thank thee for't: my shipwreck now's no ill,
Since I have here my father's gift in 's will.

FIRST FISHERMAN
What mean you, sir?

PERICLES
To beg of you, kind friends, this coat of worth,
For it was sometime target to a king;
I know it by this mark. He loved me dearly,
And for his sake I wish the having of it;
And that you 'ld guide me to your sovereign's court,
Where with it I may appear a gentleman;
And if that ever my low fortune's better,
I'll pay your bounties; till then rest your debtor.

FIRST FISHERMAN
Why, wilt thou tourney for the lady?

PERICLES
I'll show the virtue I have borne in arms.

FIRST FISHERMAN
Why, do 'e take it, and the gods give thee good on't!

SECOND FISHERMAN
Ay, but hark you, my friend; 'twas we that made up this garment through the rough seams of the waters: there

are certain condolements, certain vails. I hope, sir, if you thrive, you'll remember from whence you had it.

PERICLES

Believe 't, I will.
By your furtherance I am clothed in steel;
And, spite of all the rapture of the sea,
This jewel holds his building on my arm:
Unto thy value I will mount myself
Upon a courser, whose delightful steps
Shall make the gazer joy to see him tread.
Only, my friend, I yet am unprovided
Of a pair of bases.

SECOND FISHERMAN

We 'll sure provide: thou shalt have my best gown to make thee a pair; and I'll bring thee to the court myself.

PERICLES

Then honour be but a goal to my will,
This day I'll rise, or else add ill to ill. [*Exeunt.*

ACT TWO SCENE TWO

The same. A public way or platform leading to the lists. A pavilion by the side of it for the reception of King, Princess, Lords, &c.

Enter SIMONIDES, THAISA, Lords, *and* Attendants.

SIMONIDES

Are the knights ready to begin the triumph?

FIRST LORD

They are, my liege;
And stay your coming to present themselves.

SIMONIDES

Return them, we are ready; and our daughter,
In honour of whose birth these triumphs are,
Sits here, like beauty's child, whom nature gat
For men to see, and seeing wonder at.
[*Exit a Lord.*

THAISA

It pleaseth you, my royal father, to express
My commendations great, whose merit's less.

SIMONIDES

It's fit it should be so; for princes are
A model, which heaven makes like to itself:
As jewels lose their glory if neglected,
So princes their renowns if not respected.
'Tis now your honour, daughter, to explain
The labour of each knight in his device.

THAISA

Which, to preserve mine honour, I'll perform.

Enter a Knight; *he passes over, and his* Squire *presents his shield to the* Princess.

SIMONIDES

Who is the first that doth prefer himself?

THAISA

A knight of Sparta, my renowned father;
And the device he bears upon his shield
Is a black Ethiope reaching at the sun:
The word, 'Lux tua vita mihi.'

SIMONIDES

He loves you well that holds his life of you.
[*The Second Knight passes over.*
Who is the second that presents himself?

THAISA

A prince of Macedon, my royal father;
And the device he bears upon his shield
Is an arm'd knight that's conquer'd by a lady;
The motto thus, in Spanish, 'Piu por dulzura que por fuerza.' [*The Third Knight passes over.*

SIMONIDES

And what's the third?

THAISA

The third of Antioch;
And his device, a wreath of chivalry;
The word, 'Me pompae provexit apex.'
[*The Fourth Knight passes over.*

SIMONIDES

What is the fourth?

THAISA

A burning torch that's turned upside down;
The word, 'Quod me alit, me extinguit.'

SIMONIDES

Which shows that beauty hath his power and will,
Which can as well inflame as it can kill.
[*The Fifth Knight passes over.*

THAISA

The fifth, an hand environed with clouds,
Holding out gold that's by the touchstone tried;
The motto thus, 'sic spectanda fides.'
[*The Sixth Knight, Pericles, passes over.*

SIMONIDES

And what's
The sixth and last, the which the knight himself
With such a graceful courtesy deliver'd?

THAISA

He seems to be a stranger; but his present is
A wither'd branch, that's only green at top;
The motto, 'In hac spe vivo.'

SIMONIDES

A pretty moral;
From the dejected state wherein he is,
He hopes by you his fortunes yet may flourish.

FIRST LORD
He had need mean better than his outward show
Can any way speak in his just commend;
For by his rusty outside he appears
To have practised more the whipstock than the lance.
SECOND LORD
He well may be a stranger, for he comes
To an honour'd triumph strangely furnished.
THIRD LORD
And on set purpose let his armour rust
Until this day, to scour it in the dust.
SIMONIDES
Opinion's but a fool, that makes us scan
The outward habit by the inward man.
But stay, the knights are coming: we will withdraw
Into the gallery. [*Exeunt.*
[*Great shouts within, and all cry* 'The mean knight!'

ACT TWO SCENE THREE

The same. A hall of state: a banquet prepared.
Enter SIMONIDES, THAISA, Lords, Attendants, *and* Knights, *from tilting.*

SIMONIDES
Knights,
To say you're welcome were superfluous.
To place upon the volume of your deeds,
As in a title-page, your worth in arms,
Were more than you expect, or more than's fit,
Since every worth in show commends itself.
Prepare for mirth, for mirth becomes a feast:
You are princes and my guests.
THAISA
But you, my knight and guest;
To whom this wreath of victory I give,
And crown you king of this day's happiness.
PERICLES
'Tis more by fortune, lady, than by merit.
SIMONIDES
Call it by what you will, the day is yours;
And here, I hope, is none that envies it.
In framing an artist, art hath thus decreed,
To make some good, but others to exceed;
And you are her labour'd scholar. Come, queen o' the feast,—
For, daughter, so you are,—here take your place:
Marshal the rest, as they deserve their grace. [31]
KNIGHTS
We are honour'd much by good Simonides.
SIMONIDES
Your presence glads our days; honour we love;
For who hates honour hates the gods above.
MARSHAL
Sir, yonder is your place.
PERICLES
Some other is more fit.
FIRST KNIGHT
Contend not, sir; for we are gentlemen
That neither in our hearts nor outward eyes
Envy the great nor do the low despise.
PERICLES
You are right courteous knights.
SIMONIDES
Sit, sir, sit.
PERICLES
By Jove, I wonder, that is king of thoughts,
These cates resist me, she but thought upon. [32]
THAISA
By Juno, that is queen of marriage,
All viands that I eat do seem unsavoury.
Wishing him my meat. Sure, he 's a gallant gentleman.
SIMONIDES
He 's but a country gentleman;
Has done no more than other knights have done;
Has broken a staff or so; so let it pass.
THAISA
To me he seems like diamond to glass.
PERICLES
Yon king's to me like to my father's picture,
Which tells me in that glory once he was;
Had princes sit, like stars, about his throne,
And he the sun, for them to reverence;
None that beheld him, but, like lesser lights,
Did vail their crowns to his supremacy:
Where now his son's like a glow-worm in the night,
The which hath fire in darkness, none in light:
Whereby I see that Time's the king of men,
He's both their parent, and he is their grave,
And gives them what he will, not what they crave.
SIMONIDES
What, are you merry, knights?
KNIGHTS
Who can be other in this royal presence?
SIMONIDES
Here, with a cup that's stored unto the brim,— [33]
As you do love, fill to your mistress' lips,—
We drink this health to you.
KNIGHTS
We thank your grace.
SIMONIDES
Yet pause awhile:
Yon knight doth sit too melancholy,

As if the entertainment in our court
Had not a show might countervail his worth.
Note it not you, Thaisa?
THAISA
What is it
To me, my father?
SIMONIDES
O, attend, my daughter:
Princes in this should live like gods above,
Who freely give to every one that comes 67
To honour them:
And princes not doing so are like to gnats,
Which make a sound, but kill'd are wonder'd at. [34]
Therefore to make his entrance more sweet,
Here, say we drink this standing-bowl of wine to him.
THAISA
Alas, my father, it befits not me
Unto a stranger knight to be so bold:
He may my proffer take for an offence,
Since men take women's gifts for impudence.
SIMONIDES
How! 77
Do as I bid you, or you 'll move me else.
THAISA
[*Aside*] Now, by the gods, he could not please me better.
SIMONIDES
And furthermore tell him, we desire to know of him,
Of whence he is, his name and parentage.
THAISA
The king my father, sir, has drunk to you.
PERICLES
I thank him.
THAISA
Wishing it so much blood unto your life.
PERICLES
I thank both him and you, and pledge him freely.
THAISA
And further he desires to know of you,
Of whence you are, your name and parentage.
PERICLES
A gentleman of Tyre; my name, Pericles; 89
My education been in arts and arms;
Who, looking for adventures in the world,
Was by the rough seas reft of ships and men,
And after shipwreck driven upon this shore.
THAISA
He thanks your grace; names himself Pericles,
A gentleman of Tyre,
Who only by misfortune of the seas
Bereft of ships and men, cast on this shore.
SIMONIDES
Now, by the gods, I pity his misfortune, 98
And will awake him from his melancholy.
Come, gentlemen, we sit too long on trifles,
And waste the time, which looks for other revels.
Even in your armours, as you are address'd,
Will very well become a soldier's dance.
I will not have excuse, with saying this
Loud music is too harsh for ladies' heads,
Since they love men in arms as well as beds.
[*The Knights dance.*
So, this was well ask'd, 'twas so well perform'd. 107
Come, sir;
Here is a lady that wants breathing too:
And I have heard, you knights of Tyre
Are excellent in making ladies trip;
And that their measures are as excellent.
PERICLES
In those that practise them they are, my lord.
SIMONIDES
O, that's as much as you would be denied
Of your fair courtesy.
[*The Knights and Ladies dance.*
Unclasp, unclasp:
Thanks, gentlemen, to all; all have done well.
[*To Pericles*] But you the best. Pages and lights, to conduct
These knights unto their several lodgings!
[*To Pericles*] Yours, sir, 121
We have given order to be next our own.
PERICLES
I am at your grace's pleasure.
SIMONIDES
Princes, it is too late to talk of love;
And that's the mark I know you level at:
Therefore each one betake him to his rest;
To-morrow all for speeding do their best.
[*Exeunt.*

ACT TWO SCENE FOUR

Tyre. A room in the Governor's house.
Enter HELICANUS *and* ESCANES.

HELICANUS
No, Escanes, know this of me,
Antiochus from incest lived not free:
For which, the most high gods not minding longer
To withhold the vengeance that they had in store,
Due to this heinous capital offence,
Even in the height and pride of all his glory,
When he was seated in a chariot
Of an inestimable value, and his daughter with him,
A fire from heaven came and shrivell'd up
Their bodies, even to loathing; for they so stunk, 11

That all those eyes adored them ere their fall
Scorn now their hand should give them burial.
ESCANES
'Twas very strange.
HELICANUS
And yet but justice; for though
This king were great, his greatness was no guard
To bar heaven's shaft, but sin had his reward.
ESCANES
'Tis very true.

Enter two or three Lords.

FIRST LORD
See, not a man in private conference
Or council has respect with him but he.
SECOND LORD
It shall no longer grieve without reproof.
THIRD LORD
And cursed be he that will not second it. 22
FIRST LORD
Follow me, then. Lord Helicane, a word.
HELICANUS
With me? and welcome: happy day, my lords.
FIRST LORD
Know that our griefs are risen to the top,
And now at length they overflow their banks.
HELICANUS
Your griefs! for what? wrong not your prince you love.
FIRST LORD
Wrong not yourself, then, noble Helicane;
But if the prince do live, let us salute him,
Or know what ground's made happy by his breath.
If in the world he live, we 'll seek him out;
If in his grave he rest, we 'll find him there;
And be resolved he lives to govern us,
Or dead, give's cause to mourn his funeral,
And leave us to our free election.
SECOND LORD
Whose death indeed 's the strongest in our censure:
And knowing this kingdom is without a head,—
Like goodly buildings left without a roof
Soon fall to ruin,—your noble self,
That best know how to rule and how to reign,
We thus submit unto,—our sovereign.
ALL
Live, noble Helicane! 43
HELICANUS
For honour's cause, forbear your suffrages: [35]
If that you love Prince Pericles, forbear.
Take I your wish, I leap into the seas,
Where 's hourly trouble for a minute's ease.
A twelve month longer, let me entreat you to
Forbear the absence of your king;
If in which time expired, he not return,
I shall with aged patience bear your yoke.
But if I cannot win you to this love,
Go search like nobles, like noble subjects, 53
And in your search spend your adventurous worth;
Whom if you find, and win unto return,
You shall like diamonds sit about his crown.
FIRST LORD
To wisdom he's a fool that will not yield;
And since Lord Helicane enjoineth us,
We with our travels will endeavour us.
HELICANUS
Then you love us, we you, and we 'll clasp hands:
When peers thus knit, a kingdom ever stands.
[*Exeunt.*

ACT TWO SCENE FIVE

Pentapolis. A room in the palace.

Enter SIMONIDES, *reading a letter, at one door: the* Knights *meet him.*

FIRST KNIGHT
Good morrow to the good Simonides.
SIMONIDES
Knights, from my daughter this I let you know,
That for this twelvemonth she 'll not undertake
A married life.
Her reason to herself is only known,
Which yet from her by no means can I get.
SECOND KNIGHT
May we not get access to her, my lord?
SIMONIDES
'Faith, by no means; she has so strictly tied
Her to her chamber, that 'tis impossible.
One twelve moons more she'll wear Diana's livery; 11
This by the eye of Cynthia hath she vow'd,
And on her virgin honour will not break it.
THIRD KNIGHT
Loath to bid farewell, we take our leaves.
[*Exeunt Knights.*
SIMONIDES
So,
They are well dispatch'd; now to my daughter's letter:
She tells me here, she 'll wed the stranger knight,
Or never more to view nor day nor light.
'Tis well, mistress; your choice agrees with mine;
I like that well: nay, how absolute she 's in 't,
Not minding whether I dislike or no! 21
Well, I do commend her choice;
And will no longer have it be delay'd.
Soft! here he comes: I must dissemble it.

Enter PERICLES.

PERICLES
All fortune to the good Simonides!
SIMONIDES
To you as much, sir! I am beholding to you
For your sweet music this last night: I do
Protest my ears were never better fed
With such delightful pleasing harmony.
PERICLES
It is your grace's pleasure to commend;
Not my desert.
SIMONIDES
Sir, you are music's master.
PERICLES
The worst of all her scholars, my good lord.
SIMONIDES
Let me ask you one thing:
What do you think of my daughter, sir?
PERICLES
A most virtuous princess.
SIMONIDES
And she is fair too, is she not?
PERICLES
As a fair day in summer, wondrous fair.
SIMONIDES
Sir, my daughter thinks very well of you;
Ay, so well, that you must be her master,
And she will be your scholar: therefore look to it.
PERICLES
I am unworthy for her schoolmaster.
SIMONIDES
She thinks not so; peruse this writing else.
PERICLES
[*Aside*] What's here?
A letter, that she loves the knight of Tyre!
'Tis the king's subtlety to have my life.
O, seek not to entrap me, gracious lord,
A stranger and distressed gentleman,
That never aim'd so high to love your daughter,
But bent all offices to honour her.
SIMONIDES
Thou hast bewitch'd my daughter, and thou art
A villain.
PERICLES
By the gods, I have not:
Never did thought of mine levy offence;
Nor never did my actions yet commence
A deed might gain her love or your displeasure.
SIMONIDES
Traitor, thou liest.
PERICLES
Traitor!
SIMONIDES
Ay, traitor.
PERICLES
Even in his throat—unless it be the king—
That calls me traitor, I return the lie.
SIMONIDES
[*Aside*] Now, by the gods, I do applaud his courage.
PERICLES
My actions are as noble as my thoughts,
That never relish'd of a base descent.
I came unto your court for honour's cause,
And not to be a rebel to her state;
And he that otherwise accounts of me,
This sword shall prove he's honour's enemy.
SIMONIDES
No?
Here comes my daughter, she can witness it.

Enter THAISA.

PERICLES
Then, as you are as virtuous as fair,
Resolve your angry father, if my tongue
Did e're solicit, or my hand subscribe
To any syllable that made love to you.
THAISA
Why, sir, say if you had,
Who takes offence at that would make me glad?
SIMONIDES
Yea, mistress, are you so peremptory?
[*Aside*] I am glad on't with all my heart.—
I'll tame you; I'll bring you in subjection.
Will you, not having my consent,
Bestow your love and your affections
Upon a stranger? [*Aside*] who, for aught I know,
May be, nor can I think the contrary,
As great in blood as I myself.—
Therefore hear you, mistress; either frame
Your will to mine,—and you, sir, hear you,
Either be ruled by me, or I will make you—
Man and wife:
Nay, come, your hands and lips must seal it too:
And being join'd, I'll thus your hopes destroy;
And for a further grief,—God give you joy!—
What, are you both pleased?
THAISA
Yes, if you love me, sir.
PERICLES
Even as my life, my blood that fosters it.
SIMONIDES
What, are you both agreed?
BOTH
Yes, if it please your majesty.
SIMONIDES
It pleaseth me so well, that I will see you wed;
And then with what haste you can get you to bed.
[*Exeunt.*

ACT THREE

Enter GOWER.

GOWER

Now sleep yslaked hath the rout;
No din but snores the house about,
Made louder by the o'er-fed breast
Of this most pompous marriage-feast.
The cat, with eyne of burning coal,
Now couches fore the mouse's hole;
And crickets sing at the oven's mouth,
E'er the blither for their drouth.
Hymen hath brought the bride to bed.
Where, by the loss of maidenhead,
A babe is moulded. Be attent,
And time that is so briefly spent
With your fine fancies quaintly eche:
What's dumb in show I'll plain with speech.

DUMB SHOW.

Enter, PERICLES *and* SIMONIDES, *at one door, with* Attendants; a Messenger *meets them, kneels, and gives* PERICLES *a letter*: PERICLES *shows it* SIMONIDES; *the* Lords *kneel to him. Then enter* THAISA *with child, with* LYCHORIDA *a nurse. The* KING *shows her the letter; she rejoices: she and* PERICLES *takes leave of her father, and depart with* LYCHORIDA *and their* Attendants. *Then exeunt* SIMONIDES *and the rest.*

By many a dern and painful perch
Of Pericles the careful search,
By the four opposing coigns
Which the world together joins,
Is made with all due diligence
That horse and sail and high expense
Can stead the quest. At last from Tyre,
Fame answering the most strange inquire,
To the court of King Simonides
Are letters brought, the tenor these:
Antiochus and his daughter dead;
The men of Tyrus on the head
Of Helicanus would set on
The crown of Tyre, but he will none:
The mutiny he there hastes t' oppress;
Says to 'em, if King Pericles
Come not home in twice six moons,
He, obedient to their dooms,
Will take the crown. The sum of this,
Brought hither to Pentapolis,
Y-ravished the regions round, [36]
And every one with claps can sound,
'Our heir-apparent is a king!
Who dream'd, who thought of such a thing?'
Brief, he must hence depart to Tyre:
His queen with child makes her desire—
Which who shall cross?—along to go:
Omit we all their dole and woe:
Lychorida, her nurse, she takes,
And so to sea. Their vessel shakes
On Neptune's billow; half the flood
Hath their keel cut: but fortune's mood
Varies again; the grisled north
Disgorges such a tempest forth,
That, as a duck for life that dives,
So up and down the poor ship drives:
The lady shrieks, and well-a-near
Does fall in travail with her fear:
And what ensues in this fell storm
Shall for itself itself perform.
I nill relate, action may
Conveniently the rest convey;
Which might not what by me is told.
In your imagination hold
This stage the ship, upon whose deck
The sea-tost Pericles appears to speak. [*Exit.*

ACT THREE SCENE ONE

Enter PERICLES, *on shipboard.*

PERICLES

Thou god of this great vast, rebuke these surges,
Which wash both heaven and hell; and thou that hast
Upon the winds command, bind them in brass,
Having call'd them from the deep! O, still
Thy deafening, dreadful thunders; gently quench
Thy nimble, sulphurous flashes! O, how, Lychorida,
How does my queen? Thou stormest venomously; [37]
Wilt thou spit all thyself? The seaman's whistle
Is as a whisper in the ears of death,
Unheard. Lychorida!—Lucina, O
Divinest patroness, and midwife gentle
To those that cry by night, convey thy deity
Aboard our dancing boat; make swift the pangs
Of my queen's travails! [38]

Enter LYCHORIDA, *with an Infant.*

Now, Lychorida!

LYCHORIDA

Here is a thing too young for such a place,
Who, if it had conceit, would die, as I
Am like to do: take in your arms this piece
Of your dead queen.

PERICLES

How, how, Lychorida!

LYCHORIDA
Patience, good sir; do not assist the storm.
Here's all that is left living of your queen,
A little daughter: for the sake of it,
Be manly, and take comfort.
PERICLES
O you gods!
Why do you make us love your goodly gifts,
And snatch them straight away? We here below
Recall not what we give, and therein may
Use honour with you. [39]
LYCHORIDA
Patience, good sir,
Even for this charge.
PERICLES
Now, mild may be thy life!
For a more blustrous birth had never babe:
Quiet and gentle thy conditions! for
Thou art the rudeliest welcome to this world
That ever was prince's child. Happy what follows! 39
Thou hast as chiding a nativity
As fire, air, water, earth, and heaven can make,
To herald thee from the womb: even at the first
Thy loss is more than can thy portage quit,
With all thou canst find here. Now, the good gods
Throw their best eyes upon't!

Enter two Sailors.

FIRST SAILOR
What courage, sir? God save you!
PERICLES
Courage enough: I do not fear the flaw;
It hath done to me the worst. Yet, for the love 48
Of this poor infant, this fresh-new sea-farer,
I would it would be quiet.
FIRST SAILOR
Slack the bolins there! Thou wilt not, wilt thou? Blow, and split thyself.
SECOND SAILOR
But sea-room, an the brine and cloudy billow kiss the moon, I care not.
FIRST SAILOR
Sir, your queen must overboard: the sea works high, the wind is loud, and will not lie till the ship be cleared of the dead.
PERICLES
That's your superstition. 58
FIRST SAILOR
Pardon us, sir; with us at sea it hath been still observed; and we are strong in custom. Therefore briefly yield her; for she must overboard straight.
PERICLES
As you think meet. Most wretched queen!
LYCHORIDA
Here she lies, sir.
PERICLES
A terrible childbed hast thou had, my dear;
No light, no fire: the unfriendly elements
Forgot thee utterly; nor have I time 66
To give thee hallow'd to thy grave, but straight
Must cast thee, scarcely coffin'd, in the ooze;
Where, for a monument upon thy bones,
And e'er-remaining lamps, the belching whale [40]
And humming water must o'erwhelm thy corpse,
Lying with simple shells. O Lychorida,
Bid Nestor bring me spices, ink and paper,
My casket and my jewels; and bid Nicander
Bring me the satin coffer: lay the babe
Upon the pillow: hie thee, whiles I say 77
A priestly farewell to her: suddenly, woman.
[*Exit Lychorida.*
SECOND SAILOR
Sir, we have a chest beneath the hatches, caulked and bitumed ready.
PERICLES
I thank thee. Mariner, say what coast is this?
SECOND SAILOR
We are near Tarsus.
PERICLES
Thither, gentle mariner.
Alter thy course for Tyre. When canst thou reach it?
SECOND SAILOR
By break of day, if the wind cease.
PERICLES
O, make for Tarsus!
There will I visit Cleon, for the babe 87
Cannot hold out to Tyrus: there I'll leave it
At careful nursing. Go thy ways, good mariner:
I'll bring the body presently. [*Exeunt.*

ACT THREE SCENE TWO

Ephesus. A room in Cerimon's house.

Enter CERIMON, *with a Servant, and some Persons who have been shipwrecked.*

CERIMON
Philemon, ho!

Enter PHILEMON.

PHILEMON
Doth my lord call?
CERIMON
Get fire and meat for these poor men:
'T has been a turbulent and stormy night.

SERVANT
I have been in many; but such a night as this,
Till now, I ne'er endured.
CERIMON
Your master will be dead ere you return;
There's nothing can be minister'd to nature
That can recover him. [*To Philemon*] Give this to the 'pothecary,
And tell me how it works.
[*Exeunt all but Cerimon.*

Enter two Gentlemen.

FIRST GENTLEMAN
Good morrow. 12
SECOND GENTLEMAN
Good morrow to your lordship.
CERIMON
Gentlemen,
Why do you stir so early?
FIRST GENTLEMAN
Sir,
Our lodgings, standing bleak upon the sea,
Shook as the earth did quake;
The very principals did seem to rend,
And all-to topple: pure surprise and fear [41]
Made me to quit the house.
SECOND GENTLEMAN
That is the cause we trouble you so early;
'Tis not our husbandry.
CERIMON
O, you say well. 24
FIRST GENTLEMAN
But I much marvel that your lordship, having
Rich tire about you, should at these early hours [42]
Shake off the golden slumber of repose.
'Tis most strange,
Nature should be so conversant with pain,
Being thereto not compell'd.
CERIMON
I hold it ever,
Virtue and cunning were endowments greater
Than nobleness and riches: careless heirs
May the two latter darken and expend;
But immortality attends the former, 35
Making a man a god. 'Tis known, I ever
Have studied physic, through which secret art,
By turning o'er authorities, I have,
Together with my practise, made familiar
To me and to my aid the blest infusions
That dwell in vegetives, in metals, stones;
And I can speak of the disturbances
That nature works, and of her cures; which doth give me
A more content in course of true delight
Than to be thirsty after tottering honour, 46
Or tie my treasure up in silken bags, [43]
To please the fool and death. [44]
SECOND GENTLEMAN
Your honour has through Ephesus pour'd forth
Your charity, and hundreds call themselves
Your creatures, who by you have been restored:
And not your knowledge, your personal pain, but even
Your purse, still open, hath built Lord Cerimon
Such strong renown as time shall ne'er decay. [45]

Enter two or three Servants *with a chest.*

FIRST SERVANT
So; lift there.
CERIMON
What is that?
FIRST SERVANT
Sir, even now
Did the sea toss upon our shore this chest: 59
'Tis of some wreck.
CERIMON
Set 't down, let's look upon't.
SECOND GENTLEMAN
'Tis like a coffin, sir.
CERIMON
Whate'er it be,
'Tis wondrous heavy. Wrench it open straight:
If the sea's stomach be o'ercharged with gold,
'Tis a good constraint of fortune it belches upon us.
SECOND GENTLEMAN
'Tis so, my lord.
CERIMON
How close 'tis caulk'd and bitumed!
Did the sea cast it up?
FIRST SERVANT
I never saw so huge a billow, sir,
As toss'd it upon shore.
CERIMON
Wrench it open;
Soft! it smells most sweetly in my sense. 74
SECOND GENTLEMAN
A delicate odour.
CERIMON
As ever hit my nostril. So, up with it.
O you most potent gods! what's here? a corse!
FIRST GENTLEMAN
Most strange!
CERIMON
Shrouded in cloth of state; balm'd and entreasured
With full bags of spices! A passport too!
Apollo, perfect me in the characters!
[*Reads from a scroll.*

CERIMON This queen will live: nature awakes—

'Here I give to understand,
If e'er this coffin drive a-land,
I, King Pericles, have lost
This queen, worth all our mundane cost.
Who finds her, give her burying;
She was the daughter of a king:
Besides this treasure for a fee,
The gods requite his charity!'
If thou livest, Pericles, thou hast a heart
That even cracks for woe! This chanced to-night.

SECOND GENTLEMAN
Most likely, sir.

CERIMON
Nay, certainly to-night;
For look how fresh she looks! They were too rough
That threw her in the sea. Make a fire within:
Fetch hither all my boxes in my closet.

[*Exit a Servant.*

Death may usurp on nature many hours,
And yet the fire of life kindle again
The o'erpress'd spirits. I heard of an Egyptian
That had nine hours lien dead,
Who was by good appliance recovered.

Re-enter a Servant, *with boxes, napkins, and fire.*

Well said, well said; the fire and cloths.
The rough and woeful music that we have,
Cause it to sound, beseech you.
The viol once more: how thou stirr'st, thou block!
The music there!—I pray you, give her air.
Gentlemen.
This queen will live: nature awakes; a warmth
Breathes out of her: she hath not been entranced
Above five hours: see how she gins to blow
Into life's flower again!

FIRST GENTLEMAN
The heavens,
Through you, increase our wonder and set up
Your fame forever.

CERIMON
She is alive; behold,
Her eyelids, cases to those heavenly jewels
Which Pericles hath lost,
Begin to part their fringes of bright gold;
The diamonds of a most praised water
Do appear, to make the world twice rich. Live,

And make us weep to hear your fate, fair creature,
Rare as you seem to be. [*She moves.*

THAISA
O dear Diana,
Where am I? Where's my lord? What world is this?

SECOND GENTLEMAN
Is not this strange?

FIRST GENTLEMAN
Most rare.

CERIMON
Hush, my gentle neighbours!
Lend me your hands; to the next chamber bear her.
Get linen: now this matter must be look'd to,
For her relapse is mortal. Come, come;
And Aesculapius guide us!
[*Exeunt, carrying her away.*

ACT THREE SCENE THREE

Tarsus. A room in Cleon's house.

Enter PERICLES, CLEON, DIONYZA, *and* LYCHORIDA *with* MARINA *in her arms.*

PERICLES
Most honour'd Cleon, I must needs be gone;
My twelve months are expired, and Tyrus stands
In a litigious peace. You, and your lady,
Take from my heart all thankfulness! The gods
Make up the rest upon you!

CLEON
Your shafts of fortune, though they hurt you mortally,
Yet glance full wanderingly on us. [46]

DIONYZA
O your sweet queen!
That the strict fates had pleased you had brought her hither,
To have bless'd mine eyes with her!

PERICLES
We cannot but obey
The powers above us. Could I rage and roar
As doth the sea she lies in, yet the end
Must be as 'tis. My gentle babe Marina, whom,
For she was born at sea, I have named so, here
I charge your charity withal, leaving her
The infant of your care; beseeching you
To give her princely training, that she may be
Manner'd as she is born.

CLEON
Fear not, my lord, but think
Your grace, that fed my country with your corn,
For which the people's prayers still fall upon you,
Must in your child be thought on. If neglection
Should therein make me vile, the common body,
By you relieved, would force me to my duty:
But if to that my nature need a spur,
The gods revenge it upon me and mine,
To the end of generation!

PERICLES
I believe you;
Your honour and your goodness teach me to 't,
Without your vows. Till she be married, madam,
By bright Diana, whom we honour, all
Unscissar'd shall this hair of mine remain, [47]
Though I show ill in 't. So I take my leave. [48]
Good madam, make me blessed in your care
In bringing up my child.

DIONYZA
I have one myself,
Who shall not be more dear to my respect
Than yours, my lord.

PERICLES
Madam, my thanks and prayers.

CLEON
We 'll bring your grace e'en to the edge o' the shore,
Then give you up to the mask'd Neptune and
The gentlest winds of heaven.

PERICLES
I will embrace
Your offer. Come, dearest madam. O, no tears,
Lychorida, no tears:
Look to your little mistress, on whose grace
You may depend hereafter. Come, my lord.
[*Exeunt.*

ACT THREE SCENE FOUR

Ephesus. A room in Cerimon's house.

Enter CERIMON *and* THAISA.

CERIMON
Madam, this letter, and some certain jewels,
Lay with you in your coffer: which are now
At your command. Know you the character?

THAISA
It is my lord's.
That I was shipp'd at sea, I well remember,
Even on my eaning time; but whether there
Deliver'd, by the holy gods,
I cannot rightly say. But since King Pericles,
My wedded lord, I ne'er shall see again,
A vestal livery will I take me to,
And never more have joy.

CERIMON
Madam, if this you purpose as ye speak,
Diana's temple is not distant far,

Where you may abide till your date expire.
Moreover, if you please, a niece of mine
Shall there attend you.

THAISA

My recompense is thanks, that's all;
Yet my good will is great, though the gift small.

[*Exeunt.*

ACT FOUR

Enter GOWER.

GOWER

Imagine Pericles arrived at Tyre,
Welcomed and settled to his own desire.
His woeful queen we leave at Ephesus,
Unto Diana there a votaress.
Now to Marina bend your mind,
Whom our fast-growing scene must find
At Tarsus, and by Cleon train'd
In music, letters; who hath gain'd
Of education all the grace,
Which makes her both the heart and place
Of general wonder. But, alack,
That monster envy, oft the wrack
Of earned praise, Marina's life
Seeks to take off by treason's knife.
And in this kind hath our Cleon
One daughter, and a wench full grown,
Even ripe for marriage-rite; this maid [49]
Hight Philoten: and it is said
For certain in our story, she
Would ever with Marina be:
Be't when she weaved the sleided silk
With fingers long, small, white as milk;
Or when she would with sharp needle wound
The cambric, which she made more sound
By hurting it; or when to the lute
She sung, and made the night-bird mute, [50]
That still records with moan; or when
She would with rich and constant pen
Vail to her mistress Dian; still
This Philoten contends in skill
With absolute Marina: so
With the dove of Paphos might the crow
Vie feathers white. Marina gets
All praises, which are paid as debts,
And not as given. This so darks
In Philoten all graceful marks,
That Cleon's wife, with envy rare,
A present murderer does prepare
For good Marina, that her daughter
Might stand peerless by this slaughter.
The sooner her vile thoughts to stead,
Lychorida, our nurse, is dead:
And cursed Dionyza hath
The pregnant instrument of wrath
Prest for this blow. The unborn event
I do commend to your content:
Only I carry winged time
Post on the lame feet of my rhyme;
Which never could I so convey,
Unless your thoughts went on my way.
Dionyza does appear,
With Leonine, a murderer.

[*Exit.*

ACT FOUR SCENE ONE

Tarsus. An open place near the sea-shore.

Enter DIONYZA *and* LEONINE.

DIONYZA

Thy oath remember; thou hast sworn to do 't:
'Tis but a blow, which never shall be known.
Thou canst not do a thing in the world so soon,
To yield thee so much profit. Let not conscience,
Which is but cold, inflaming love i' thy bosom, [51]
Inflame too nicely; nor let pity, which
Even women have cast off, melt thee, but be
A soldier to thy purpose.

LEONINE

I will do 't; but yet she is a goodly creature.

DIONYZA

The fitter, then, the gods should have her. Here she comes weeping for her only mistress' death. Thou art resolved? [52]

LEONINE

I am resolved.

Enter MARINA, *with a basket of flowers.*

MARINA

No, I will rob Tellus of her weed,
To strew thy green with flowers: the yellows, blues,
The purple violets, and marigolds,
Shall as a carpet hang upon thy grave,
While summer-days do last. Ay me! poor maid,
Born in a tempest, when my mother died,
This world to me is like a lasting storm,
Whirring me from my friends.

DIONYZA

How now, Marina! why do you keep alone?
How chance my daughter is not with you? Do not
Consume your blood with sorrowing: you have
A nurse of me. Lord, how your favour's changed
With this unprofitable woe!
Come, give me your flowers, ere the sea mar it.

MARINA To strew thy green with flowers.

Walk with Leonine; the air is quick there,
And it pierces and sharpens the stomach. Come,
Leonine, take her by the arm, walk with her.

MARINA
No, I pray you;
I'll not bereave you of your servant.

DIONYZA
Come, come;
I love the king your father, and yourself,
With more than foreign heart. We every day
Expect him here: when he shall come and find
Our paragon to all reports thus blasted,
He will repent the breadth of his great voyage;
Blame both my lord and me, that we have taken
No care to your best courses. Go, I pray you,
Walk, and be cheerful once again; reserve
That excellent complexion, which did steal
The eyes of young and old. Care not for me;
I can go home alone.

MARINA
Well, I will go;
But yet I have no desire to it.

DIONYZA
Come, come, I know 'tis good for you.
Walk half an hour, Leonine, at the least:
Remember what I have said.

LEONINE
I warrant you, madam.

DIONYZA
I'll leave you, my sweet lady, for a while:
Pray, walk softly, do not heat your blood:
What! I must have a care of you.

MARINA
My thanks, sweet madam.
[*Exit Dionyza.*
Is this wind westerly that blows?

LEONINE
South-west.

MARINA
When I was born, the wind was north.

LEONINE
Was't so?

MARINA
My father, as nurse said, did never fear,

But cried 'Good seaman!' to the sailors, galling
His kingly hands, haling ropes;
And, clasping to the mast, endured a sea
That almost burst the deck.

LEONINE
When was this?

MARINA
When I was born:
Never was waves nor wind more violent;
And from the ladder-tackle washes off
A canvas-climber. 'Ha!' says one, 'wilt out?'
And with a dropping industry they skip
From stem to stern: the boatswain whistles, and [53]
The master calls, and trebles their confusion.

LEONINE
Come, say your prayers.

MARINA
What mean you?

LEONINE
If you require a little space for prayer,
I grant it: pray; but be not tedious,
For the gods are quick of ear, and I am sworn
To do my work with haste.

MARINA
Why will you kill me?

LEONINE
To satisfy my lady.

MARINA
Why would she have me kill'd?
Now, as I can remember, by my troth,
I never did her hurt in all my life:
I never spake bad word, nor did ill turn
To any living creature: believe me, la,
I never kill'd a mouse, nor hurt a fly:
I trod upon a worm against my will,
But I wept for it. How have I offended,
Wherein my death might yield her any profit,
Or my life imply her any danger?

LEONINE
My commission
Is not to reason of the deed, but do it.

MARINA
You will not do't for all the world, I hope.
You are well favour'd, and your looks foreshow
You have a gentle heart. I saw you lately,
When you caught hurt in parting two that fought:
Good sooth, it show'd well in you: do so now:
Your lady seeks my life; come you between,
And save poor me, the weaker.

LEONINE
I am sworn,
And will dispatch. [*He seizes her.*

Enter Pirates.

FIRST PIRATE
Hold, villain! [*Leonine runs away.*

SECOND PIRATE
A prize! a prize!

THIRD PIRATE
Half-part, mates, half-part.
Come, let's have her aboard suddenly.
[*Exeunt Pirates with Marina.*

Re-enter LEONINE.

LEONINE
These roguing thieves serve the great pirate Valdes; [54]
And they have seized Marina. Let her go:
There's no hope she will return. I'll swear she's dead,
And thrown into the sea. But I'll see further:
Perhaps they will but please themselves upon her,
Not carry her aboard. If she remain,
Whom they have ravish'd must by me be slain.
[*Exit.*

ACT FOUR SCENE TWO

Mytilene. A room in a brothel.

Enter PANDAR, BAWD, *and* BOULT.

PANDAR
Boult!

BOULT
Sir?

PANDAR
Search the market narrowly; Mytilene is full of gallants. We lost too much money this mart by being too wenchless.

BAWD
We were never so much out of creatures. We have but poor three, and they can do no more than they can do; and they with continual action are even as good as rotten.

PANDAR
Therefore let's have fresh ones, whate'er we pay for them. If there be not a conscience to be used in every trade, we shall never prosper.

BAWD
Thou sayest true: 'tis not our bringing up of poor bastards,—as, I think, I have brought up some eleven—

BOULT
Ay, to eleven; and brought them down again. But shall I search the market?

BAWD
What else, man? The stuff we have, a strong wind will blow it to pieces, they are so pitifully sodden.

PANDAR

Thou sayest true; they 're too unwholesome, o' conscience. The poor Transylvanian is dead, that lay with the little baggage.

BOULT

Ay, she quickly pooped him; she made him roast-meat for worms. But I'll go search the market.

[*Exit.*

PANDAR

Three or four thousand chequins were as pretty a proportion to live quietly, and so give over.

BAWD

Why to give over, I pray you? is it a shame to get when we are old?

PANDAR

O, our credit comes not in like the commodity, nor the commodity wages not with the danger: therefore, if in our youths we could pick up some pretty estate, 'twere not amiss to keep our door hatched. Besides, the sore terms we stand upon with the gods will be strong with us for giving over.

BAWD

Come, other sorts offend as well as we.

PANDAR

As well as we! ay, and better too; we offend worse. Neither is our profession any trade; it's no calling. But here comes Boult.

Re-enter BOULT, *with the* Pirates *and* MARINA.

BOULT

[*To Marina*] Come your ways. My masters, you say she 's a virgin?

FIRST PIRATE

O, sir, we doubt it not.

BOULT

Master, I have gone through for this piece, you see: if you like her, so; if not, I have lost my earnest.

BAWD

Boult, has she any qualities?

BOULT

She has a good face, speaks well, and has excellent good clothes: there's no further necessity of qualities can make her be refused.

BAWD

What's her price, Boult?

BOULT

I cannot be bated one doit of a thousand pieces.

PANDAR

Well, follow me, my masters, you shall have your money presently. Wife, take her in; instruct her what she has to do, that she may not be raw in her entertainment.

[*Exeunt Pandar and Pirates.*

BAWD

Boult, take you the marks of her, the colour of her hair, complexion, height, age, with warrant of her virginity; and cry 'He that will give most shall have her first.' Such a maidenhead were no cheap thing, if men were as they have been. Get this done as I command you.

BOULT

Performance shall follow. [*Exit.*

MARINA

Alack that Leonine was so slack, so slow!
He should have struck, not spoke; or that these pirates,
Not enough barbarous, had not o'erboard thrown me
For to seek my mother!

BAWD

Why lament you, pretty one?

MARINA

That I am pretty.

BAWD

Come, the gods have done their part in you.

MARINA

I accuse them not.

BAWD

You are light into my hands, where you are like to live.

MARINA

The more my fault
To scape his hands where I was like to die.

BAWD

Ay, and you shall live in pleasure.

MARINA

No.

BAWD

Yes, indeed shall you, and taste gentlemen of all fashions: you shall fare well; you shall have the difference of all complexions. What! do you stop your ears?

MARINA

Are you a woman?

BAWD

What would you have me be, an I be not a woman?

MARINA

An honest woman, or not a woman.

BAWD

Marry, whip thee, gosling: I think I shall have something to do with you. Come, you're a young foolish sapling, and must be bowed as I would have you.

MARINA

The gods defend me!

BAWD

If it please the gods to defend you by men, then men must comfort you, men must feed you, men must stir you up. Boult's returned.

Re-enter BOULT.

Now, sir, hast thou cried her through the market?

BOULT

I have cried her almost to the number of her hairs; I have drawn her picture with my voice.

BAWD

And I prithee tell me, how dost thou find the inclination of the people, especially of the younger sort?

BOULT

'Faith, they listened to me as they would have hearkened to their father's testament. There was a Spaniard's mouth so watered, that he went to bed to her very description.

BAWD

We shall have him here to-morrow with his best ruff on.

BOULT

To-night, to-night. But, mistress, do you know the French knight that cowers i' the hams?

BAWD

Who, Monsieur Veroles?

BOULT

Ay, he: he offered to cut a caper at the proclamation; but he made a groan at it, and swore he would see her to-morrow.

BAWD

Well, well; as for him, he brought his disease hither: here he does but repair it. I know he will come in our shadow, to scatter his crowns in the sun.

BOULT

Well, if we had of every nation a traveller, we should lodge them with this sign.

BAWD

[*To Marina*] Pray you, come hither awhile. You have fortunes coming upon you. Mark me: you must seem to do that fearfully which you commit willingly, despise profit where you have most gain. To weep that you live as ye do makes pity in your lovers: seldom but that pity begets you a good opinion, and that opinion a mere profit.

MARINA

I understand you not.

BOULT

O, take her home, mistress, take her home: these blushes of hers must be quenched with some present practise.

BAWD

Thou sayest true, i' faith so they must; for your bride goes to that with shame which is her way to go with warrant.

BOULT

'Faith, some do, and some do not. But, mistress, if I have bargained for the joint,—

BAWD

Thou mayst cut a morsel off the spit.

BOULT

I may so.

BAWD

Who should deny it? Come, young one, I like the manner of your garments well.

BOULT

Ay, by my faith, they shall not be changed yet.

BAWD

Boult, spend thou that in the town: report what a sojourner we have; you 'll lose nothing by custom. When nature flamed this piece, she meant thee a good turn; therefore say what a paragon she is, and thou hast the harvest out of thine own report.

BOULT

I warrant you, mistress, thunder shall not so awake the beds of eels as my giving out her beauty stir up the lewdly-inclined, I'll bring home some to-night.

BAWD

Come your ways; follow me.

MARINA

If fires be hot, knives sharp, or waters deep,
Untied I still my virgin knot will keep.
Diana, aid my purpose!

BAWD

What have we to do with Diana? Pray you, will you go with us? [*Exeunt.*

ACT FOUR SCENE THREE

Tarsus. A room in Cleon's house.

Enter CLEON *and* DIONYZA.

DIONYZA

Why, are you foolish? Can it be undone?

CLEON

O Dionyza, such a piece of slaughter
The sun and moon ne'er look'd upon!

DIONYZA

I think
You 'll turn a child again.

CLEON

Were I chief lord of all this spacious world,
I 'ld give it to undo the deed. O lady,
Much less in blood than virtue, yet a princess
To equal any single crown o' the earth
I' the justice of compare! O villain Leonine!
Whom thou hast poison'd too:
If thou hadst drunk to him, 't had been a kindness
Becoming well thy fact: what canst thou say
When noble Pericles shall demand his child?

DIONYZA
That she is dead. Nurses are not the fates,
To foster it, nor ever to preserve.
She died at night; I'll say so. Who can cross it?
Unless you play the pious innocent, [55]
And for an honest attribute cry out
'She died by foul play.'

CLEON
O, go to. Well, well,
Of all the faults beneath the heavens, the gods
Do like this worst.

DIONYZA
Be one of those that think
The petty wrens of Tarsus will fly hence,
And open this to Pericles. I do shame
To think of what a noble strain you are,
And of how coward a spirit.

CLEON
To such proceeding
Who ever but his approbation added,
Though not his prime consent, he did not flow
From honourable sources.

DIONYZA
Be it so, then:
Yet none does know, but you, how she came dead,
Nor none can know, Leonine being gone.
She did disdain my child, and stood between
Her and her fortunes: none would look on her,
But cast their gazes on Marina's face;
Whilst ours was blurted at and held a malkin
Not worth the time of day. It pierced me through;
And though you call my course unnatural,
You not your child well loving, yet I find
It greets me as an enterprise of kindness
Perform'd to your sole daughter.

CLEON
Heavens forgive it!

DIONYZA
And as for Pericles,
What should he say? We wept after her hearse,
And yet we mourn: her monument
Is almost finish'd, and her epitaphs
In glittering golden characters express
A general praise to her, and care in us
At whose expense 'tis done.

CLEON
Thou art like the harpy,
Which, to betray, dost, with thine angel's face, [56]
Seize with thine eagle's talons. [57]

DIONYZA
You are like one that superstitiously
Doth swear to the gods that winter kills the flies:
But yet I know you 'll do as I advise. [*Exeunt.*

ACT FOUR SCENE FOUR

Enter GOWER, *before the monument of* MARINA *at Tarsus.*

GOWER
Thus time we waste, and longest leagues make short;
Sail seas in cockles, have an wish but for't;
Making, to take your imagination,
From bourn to bourn, region to region.
By you being pardon'd, we commit no crime
To use one language in each several clime
Where our scenes seem to live. I do beseech you
To learn of me, who stand i' the gaps to teach you,
The stages of our story. Pericles
Is now again thwarting the wayward seas,
Attended on by many a lord and knight.
To see his daughter, all his life's delight.
Old Escanes, whom Helicanus late [58]
Advanced in time to great and high estate,
Is left to govern. Bear you it in mind,
Old Helicanus goes along behind.
Well-sailing ships and bounteous winds have brought
This king to Tarsus,—think his pilot thought; [59]
So with his steerage shall your thoughts grow on,—
To fetch his daughter home, who first is gone.
Like motes and shadows see them move awhile;
Your ears unto your eyes I'll reconcile.

DUMB SHOW.

Enter PERICLES, *at one door, with all his train;* CLEON *and* DIONYZA, *at the other.* CLEON *shows* PERICLES *the tomb; whereat* PERICLES *makes lamentation, puts on sackcloth, and in a mighty passion departs. Then exeunt* CLEON *and* DIONYZA.

See how belief may suffer by foul show!
This borrow'd passion stands for true old woe;
And Pericles, in sorrow all devour'd,
With sighs shot through, and biggest tears o'ershower'd,
Leaves Tarsus and again embarks. He swears
Never to wash his face, nor cut his hairs:
He puts on sackcloth, and to sea. He bears
A tempest, which his mortal vessel tears,
And yet he rides it out. Now please you wit.
The epitaph is for Marina writ
By wicked Dionyza.
[*Reads the inscription on Marina's monument.*
'The fairest, sweet'st, and best lies here,
Who wither'd in her spring of year.
She was of Tyrus the king's daughter,
On whom foul death hath made this slaughter;

Marina was she call'd; and at her birth,
Thetis, being proud, swallow'd some part o' the earth:
Therefore the earth, fearing to be o'erflow'd,
Hath Thetis' birth-child on the heavens bestow'd:
Wherefore she does, and swears she 'll never stint,
Make raging battery upon shores of flint.'
No visor does become black villany
So well as soft and tender flattery.
Let Pericles believe his daughter's dead,
And bear his courses to be ordered
By Lady Fortune; while our scene must play
His daughter's woe and heavy well-a-day
In her unholy service. Patience, then,
And think you now are all in Mytilene. [*Exit.*

ACT FOUR SCENE FIVE

Mytilene. A street before the brothel.

Enter, from the brothel, two Gentlemen.

FIRST GENTLEMAN
Did you ever hear the like?

SECOND GENTLEMAN
No, nor never shall do in such a place as this, she being once gone.

FIRST GENTLEMAN
But to have divinity preached there! did you ever dream of such a thing?

SECOND GENTLEMAN
No, no. Come, I am for no more bawdy-houses: shall 's go hear the vestals sing?

FIRST GENTLEMAN
I'll do any thing now that is virtuous; but I am out of the road of rutting for ever. [*Exeunt.*

ACT FOUR SCENE SIX

The same. A room in the brothel.

Enter PANDAR, BAWD, *and* BOULT.

PANDAR
Well, I had rather than twice the worth of her she had ne'er come here.

BAWD
Fie, fie upon her! she's able to freeze the god Priapus, and undo a whole generation. We must either get her ravished, or be rid of her. When she should do for clients her fitment, and do me the kindness of our profession, she has me her quirks, her reasons, her master reasons, her prayers, her knees; that she would make a puritan of the devil, if he should cheapen a kiss of her.

BOULT
'Faith, I must ravish her, or she 'll disfurnish us of all our cavaliers, and make our swearers priests.

PANDAR
Now, the pox upon her green-sickness for me!

BAWD
'Faith, there's no way to be rid on't but by the way to the pox. Here comes the Lord Lysimachus disguised.

BOULT
We should have both lord and lown, if the peevish baggage would but give way to customers.

Enter LYSIMACHUS.

LYSIMACHUS
How now! How a dozen of virginities?

BAWD
Now, the gods to bless your honour!

BOULT
I am glad to see your honour in good health.

LYSIMACHUS
You may so; 'tis the better for you that your resorters stand upon sound legs. How now! wholesome iniquity have you that a man may deal withal, and defy the surgeon?

BAWD
We have here one, sir, if she would—but there never came her like in Mytilene.

LYSIMACHUS
If she 'ld do the deed of darkness, thou wouldst say.

BAWD
Your honour knows what 'tis to say well enough.

LYSIMACHUS
Well, call forth, call forth.

BOULT
For flesh and blood, sir, white and red, you shall see a rose; and she were a rose indeed, if she had but—

LYSIMACHUS
What, prithee?

BOULT
O, sir, I can be modest.

LYSIMACHUS
That dignifies the renown of a bawd, no less than it gives a good report to a number to be chaste. [*Exit Boult.*

BAWD
Here comes that which grows to the stalk; never plucked yet, I can assure you.

Re-enter BOULT *with* MARINA.

Is she not a fair creature?

LYSIMACHUS
'Faith, she would serve after a long voyage at sea. Well, there's for you: leave us.

BAWD

I beseech your honour, give me leave: a word, and I'll have done presently.

LYSIMACHUS

I beseech you, do.

BAWD

[*To Marina*] First, I would have you note, this is an honourable man.

MARINA

I desire to find him so, that I may worthily note him.

BAWD

Next, he's the governor of this country, and a man whom I am bound to.

MARINA

If he govern the country, you are bound to him indeed; but how honourable he is in that, I know not. 51

BAWD

Pray you, without any more virginal fencing, will you use him kindly? He will line your apron with gold.

MARINA

What he will do graciously, I will thankfully receive.

LYSIMACHUS

Ha' you done?

BAWD

My lord, she's not paced yet: you must take some pains to work her to your manage. Come, we will leave his honour and her together. Go thy ways. [*Exeunt Bawd, Pandar, and Boult.*

LYSIMACHUS

Now, pretty one, how long have you been at this trade?

MARINA

What trade, sir?

LYSIMACHUS

Why, I cannot name't but I shall offend.

MARINA

I cannot be offended with my trade. Please you to name it.

LYSIMACHUS

How long have you been of this profession?

MARINA

E'er since I can remember.

LYSIMACHUS

Did you go to 't so young? Were you a gamester at five or at seven? 68

MARINA

Earlier too, sir, if now I be one.

LYSIMACHUS

Why, the house you dwell in proclaims you to be a creature of sale.

MARINA

Do you know this house to be a place of such resort, and will come into 't? I hear say you are of honourable parts, and are the governor of this place.

LYSIMACHUS

Why, hath your principal made known unto you who I am? 76

MARINA

Who is my principal?

LYSIMACHUS

Why, your herb-woman; she that sets seeds and roots of shame and iniquity. O, you have heard something of my power, and so stand aloof for more serious wooing. But I protest to thee, pretty one, my authority shall not see thee, or else look friendly upon thee. Come, bring me to some private place: come, come.

MARINA

If you were born to honour, show it now;
If put upon you, make the judgment good
That thought you worthy of it.

LYSIMACHUS

How 's this? how 's this? Some more; be sage.

MARINA

For me,
That am a maid, though most ungentle fortune
Have placed me in this sty, where, since I came,
Diseases have been sold dearer than physic,
O, that the gods
Would set me free from this unhallow'd place,
Though they did change me to the meanest bird
That flies i' the purer air!

LYSIMACHUS

I did not think
Thou couldst have spoke so well; ne'er dream'd thou couldst. 99
Had I brought hither a corrupted mind,
Thy speech had alter'd it. Hold, here's gold for thee:
Persever in that clear way thou goest,
And the gods strengthen thee!

MARINA

The good gods preserve you!

LYSIMACHUS

For me, be you thoughten
That I came with no ill intent; for to me
The very doors and windows savour vilely.
Fare thee well. Thou art a piece of virtue, and
I doubt not but thy training hath been noble.
Hold, here's more gold for thee. 110
A curse upon him, die he like a thief,
That robs thee of thy goodness! If thou dost
Hear from me, it shall be for thy good.

Re-enter BOULT.

BOULT

I beseech your honour, one piece for me.

LYSIMACHUS

Avaunt, thou damned door-keeper!

Your house, but for this virgin that doth prop it,
Would sink and overwhelm you. Away! [*Exit.*

BOULT

How 's this? We must take another course with you. If your peevish chastity, which is not worth a breakfast in the cheapest country under the cope, shall undo a whole household, let me be gelded like a spaniel. Come your ways.

MARINA

Whither would you have me?

BOULT

I must have your maidenhead taken off, or the common hangman shall execute it. Come your ways. We 'll have no more gentlemen driven away. Come your ways, I say.

Re-enter Bawd.

BAWD

How now! what's the matter?

BOULT

Worse and worse, mistress; she has here spoken holy words to the Lord Lysimachus.

BAWD

O abominable!

BOULT

She makes our profession as it were to stink afore the face of the gods.

BAWD

Marry, hang her up for ever!

BOULT

The nobleman would have dealt with her like a nobleman, and she sent him away as cold as a snowball; saying his prayers too.

BAWD

Boult, take her away; use her at thy pleasure: crack the glass of her virginity, and make the rest malleable.

BOULT

An if she were a thornier piece of ground than she is, she shall be ploughed.

MARINA

Hark, hark, you gods!

BAWD

She conjures: away with her! Would she had never come within my doors! Marry, hang you! She's born to undo us. Will you not go the way of women-kind? Marry, come up, my dish of chastity with rosemary and bays! [*Exit.*

BOULT

Come, mistress; come your ways with me.

MARINA

Whither wilt thou have me?

BOULT

To take from you the jewel you hold so dear.

MARINA

Prithee, tell me one thing first.

BOULT

Come now, your one thing.

MARINA

What canst thou wish thine enemy to be?

BOULT

Why, I could wish him to be my master, or rather, my mistress.

MARINA

Neither of these are so bad as thou art,
Since they do better thee in their command.
Thou hold'st a place, for which the pained'st fiend
Of hell would not in reputation change:
Thou art the damned doorkeeper to every
Coistrel that comes inquiring for his Tib;
To the choleric fisting of every rogue
Thy ear is liable; thy food is such
As hath been belch'd on by infected lungs.

BOULT

What would you have me do? go to the wars, would you? where a man may serve seven years for the loss of a leg, and have not money enough in the end to buy him a wooden one?

MARINA

Do any thing but this thou doest. Empty
Old receptacles, or common shores, of filth;
Serve by indenture to the common hangman:
Any of these ways are yet better than this;
For what thou professest, a baboon, could he speak,
Would own a name too dear. O, that the gods
Would safely deliver me from this place!
Here, here's gold for thee.
If that thy master would gain by thee,
Proclaim that I can sing, weave, sew, and dance,
With other virtues, which I'll keep from boast;
And I will undertake all these to teach.
I doubt not but this populous city will
Yield many scholars.

BOULT

But can you teach all this you speak of?

MARINA

Prove that I cannot, take me home again,
And prostitute me to the basest groom
That doth frequent your house.

BOULT

Well, I will see what I can do for thee: if I can place thee, I will.

MARINA

But amongst honest women.

BOULT

'Faith, my acquaintance lies little amongst them. But since my master and mistress have bought you, there's no going but by their consent: therefore I will make them acquainted with your purpose, and I doubt not but I shall find them tractable enough. Come, I'll do for thee what I can; come your ways. [*Exeunt.*

ACT FIVE

Enter GOWER.

GOWER
Marina thus the brothel 'scapes, and chances
Into an honest house, our story says.
She sings like one immortal, and she dances
As goddess-like to her admired lays;
Deep clerks she dumbs; and with her needle composes
Nature's own shape, of bud, bird, branch, or berry,
That even her art sisters the natural roses;
Her inkle, silk, twin with the rubied cherry:
That pupils lacks she none of noble race, 9
Who pour their bounty on her; and her gain
She gives the cursed bawd. Here we her place;
And to her father turn our thoughts again,
Where we left him, on the sea. We there him lost;
Whence, driven before the winds, he is arrived
Here where his daughter dwells; and on this coast
Suppose him now at anchor. The city strived
God Neptune's annual feast to keep: from whence
Lysimachus our Tyrian ship espies,
His banners sable, trimm'd with rich expense;
And to him in his barge with fervor hies. 20
In your supposing once more put your sight
Of heavy Pericles; think this his bark:
Where what is done in action, more, if might,
Shall be discover'd; please you, sit and hark.
[*Exit.*

ACT FIVE SCENE ONE

On board Pericles' ship, off Mytilene. A close pavilion on deck, with a curtain before it; Pericles within it, reclined on a couch. A barge lying beside the Tyrian vessel.

Enter two Sailors, *one belonging to the Tyrian vessel, the other to the barge; to them* HELICANUS.

TYRIAN SAILOR
[*To the Sailor of Mytilene*] Where is lord Helicanus? he can resolve you.
O, here he is.
Sir, there's a barge put off from Mytilene,
And in it is Lysimachus the governor,
Who craves to come aboard. What is your will?

HELICANUS
That he have his. Call up some gentlemen.

TYRIAN SAILOR
Ho, gentlemen! my lord calls.

Enter two or three Gentlemen.

FIRST GENTLEMAN
Doth your lordship call?

HELICANUS
Gentlemen, there's some of worth would come aboard;
I pray ye, greet them fairly. 12
[*The Gentlemen and the two Sailors descend, and go on board the barge.*

Enter, from thence, LYSIMACHUS *and* Lords; *with the* Gentlemen *and the two* Sailors.

TYRIAN SAILOR
Sir,
This is the man that can, in aught you would,
Resolve you.

LYSIMACHUS
Hail, reverend sir! the gods preserve you!

HELICANUS
And you, sir, to outlive the age I am.
And die as I would do.

LYSIMACHUS
You wish me well.
Being on shore, honouring of Neptune's triumphs,
Seeing this goodly vessel ride before us,
I made to it, to know of whence you are.

HELICANUS
First, what is your place? 23

LYSIMACHUS
I am the governor of this place you lie before.

HELICANUS
Sir,
Our vessel is of Tyre, in it the king;
A man who for this three months hath not spoken
To any one, nor taken sustenance
But to prorogue his grief.

LYSIMACHUS
Upon what ground is his distemperature?

HELICANUS
'Twould be too tedious to repeat;
But the main grief springs from the loss
Of a beloved daughter and a wife. 34

LYSIMACHUS
May we not see him?

HELICANUS
You may;
But bootless is your sight: he will not speak
To any.

LYSIMACHUS
Yet let me obtain my wish.

HELICANUS
Behold him. [*Pericles discovered.*] This was a goodly person,
Till the disaster that, one mortal night,
Drove him to this.
LYSIMACHUS
Sir king, all hail! the gods preserve you!
Hail, royal sir! 45
HELICANUS
It is in vain; he will not speak to you.
FIRST LORD
Sir,
We have a maid in Mytilene, I durst wager,
Would win some words of him.
LYSIMACHUS
'Tis well bethought.
She questionless with her sweet harmony
And other chosen attractions, would allure,
And make a battery through his deafen'd parts, [61]
Which now are midway stopp'd:
She is all happy as the fairest of all,
And, with her fellow maids is now upon 57
The leafy shelter that abuts against
The island's side.
[*Whispers a Lord, who goes off in the barge of Lysimachus.*
HELICANUS
Sure, all 's effectless; yet nothing we 'll omit
That bears recovery's name. But, since your kindness
We have stretch'd thus far, let us beseech you
That for our gold we may provision have,
Wherein we are not destitute for want,
But weary for the staleness.
LYSIMACHUS
O, sir, a courtesy
Which if we should deny, the most just gods
For every graff would send a caterpillar, 69
And so afflict our province. Yet once more
Let me entreat to know at large the cause
Of your king's sorrow.
HELICANUS
Sit, sir, I will recount it to you:
But, see, I am prevented.

Re-enter, from the barge, Lord, *with* MARINA, *and a young* Lady.

LYSIMACHUS
O, here is
The lady that I sent for. Welcome, fair one!
Is't not a goodly presence?
HELICANUS
She's a gallant lady.
LYSIMACHUS
She's such a one, that, were I well assured
Came of a gentle kind and noble stock,
I 'ld wish no better choice, and think me rarely wed. 82
Fair one, all goodness that consists in bounty
Expect even here, where is a kingly patient:
If that thy prosperous and artificial feat [62]
Can draw him but to answer thee in aught,
Thy sacred physic shall receive such pay
As thy desires can wish.
MARINA
Sir, I will use
My utmost skill in his recovery,
Provided
That, none but I and my companion maid
Be suffer'd to come near him.
LYSIMACHUS
Come, let us leave her;
And the gods make her prosperous! 95
[*Marina sings.*
LYSIMACHUS
Mark'd he your music?
MARINA
No, nor look'd on us.
LYSIMACHUS
See, she will speak to him.
MARINA
Hail, sir! my lord, lend ear.
PERICLES
Hum, ha!
MARINA
I am a maid,
My lord, that ne'er before invited eyes,
But have been gazed on like a comet: she speaks,
My lord, that, may be, hath endured a grief
Might equal yours, if both were justly weigh'd.
Though wayward fortune did malign my state,
My derivation was from ancestors 107
Who stood equivalent with mighty kings:
But time hath rooted out my parentage,
And to the world and awkward casualties
Bound me in servitude. [*Aside*] I will desist;
But there is something glows upon my cheek,
And whispers in mine ear, 'Go not till he speak.'
PERICLES
My fortunes—parentage—good parentage—
To equal mine!—was it not thus? what say you?
MARINA
I said, my lord, if you did know my parentage, 117
You would not do me violence.
PERICLES
I do think so. Pray you, turn your eyes upon me.

You are like something that—What country-woman?
Here of these shores?

MARINA

No, nor of any shores:
Yet I was mortally brought forth, and am
No other than I appear.

PERICLES

I am great with woe, and shall deliver weeping.
My dearest wife was like this maid, and such a one
My daughter might have been: my queen's square brows;
Her stature to an inch; as wand-like straight;
As silver-voiced; her eyes as jewel-like 130
And cased as richly; in pace another Juno;
Who starves the ears she feeds, and makes them hungry,
The more she gives them speech. Where do you live?

MARINA

Where I am but a stranger: from the deck
You may discern the place.

PERICLES

Where were you bred?
And how achieved you these endowments, which
You make more rich to owe?

MARINA

If I should tell my history, it would seem
Like lies disdain'd in the reporting.

PERICLES

Prithee, speak: 142
Falseness cannot come from thee; for thou look'st
Modest as Justice, and thou seem'st a palace
For the crown'd Truth to dwell in: I will believe thee,
And make my senses credit thy relation
To points that seem impossible; for thou look'st
Like one I loved indeed. What were thy friends?
Didst thou not say, when I did push thee back—
Which was when I perceived thee—that thou camest
From good descending?

MARINA

So indeed I did.

PERICLES

Report thy parentage. I think thou said'st 153
Thou hadst been toss'd from wrong to injury,
And that thou thought'st thy griefs might equal mine,
If both were open'd.

MARINA

Some such thing
I said, and said no more but what my thoughts
Did warrant me was likely.

PERICLES

Tell thy story;
If thine consider'd prove the thousandth part
Of my endurance, thou art a man, and I
Have suffer'd like a girl: yet thou dost look
Like Patience gazing on kings' graves, and smiling
Extremity out of act. What were thy friends?
How lost thou them? Thy name, my most kind virgin? 168
Recount, I do beseech thee: come, sit by me.

MARINA

My name is Marina.

PERICLES

O, I am mock'd,
And thou by some incensed god sent hither
To make the world to laugh at me.

MARINA

Patience, good sir,
Or here I'll cease.

PERICLES

Nay, I'll be patient.
Thou little know'st how thou dost startle me,
To call thyself Marina.

MARINA

The name
Was given me by one that had some power,
My father, and a king.

PERICLES

How! a king's daughter? 182
And call'd Marina?

MARINA

You said you would believe me;
But, not to be a troubler of your peace,
I will end here.

PERICLES

But are you flesh and blood?
Have you a working pulse? and are no fairy?
Motion! Well; speak on. Where were you born?
And wherefore call'd Marina?

MARINA

Call'd Marina
For I was born at sea.

PERICLES

At sea! what mother?

MARINA

My mother was the daughter of a king;
Who died the minute I was born, 195
As my good nurse Lychorida hath oft
Deliver'd weeping.

PERICLES

O, stop there a little!
[*Aside*] This is the rarest dream that e'er dull sleep
Did mock sad fools withal: this cannot be:
My daughter's buried. Well: where were you bred?
I'll hear you more, to the bottom of your story,
And never interrupt you.

MARINA
You scorn: believe me, 'twere best I did give o'er.
PERICLES
I will believe you by the syllable
Of what you shall deliver. Yet, give me leave:
How came you in these parts? where were you bred?
MARINA
The king my father did in Tarsus leave me;
Till cruel Cleon, with his wicked wife,
Did seek to murder me: and having woo'd
A villain to attempt it, who having drawn to do't,
A crew of pirates came and rescued me;
Brought me to Mytilene. But, good sir,
Whither will you have me? Why do you weep? It may be,
You think me an impostor: no, good faith;
I am the daughter to King Pericles,
If good King Pericles be.
PERICLES
Ho, Helicanus!
HELICANUS
Calls my lord?
PERICLES
Thou art a grave and noble counsellor,
Most wise in general: tell me, if thou canst,
What this maid is, or what is like to be,
That thus hath made me weep?
HELICANUS
I know not; but
Here is the regent, sir, of Mytilene
Speaks nobly of her.
LYSIMACHUS
She would never tell
Her parentage; being demanded that,
She would sit still and weep.
PERICLES
O Helicanus, strike me, honour'd sir;
Give me a gash, put me to present pain;
Lest this great sea of joys rushing upon me
O'erbear the shores of my mortality,
And drown me with their sweetness. O, come hither,
Thou that beget'st him that did thee beget;
Thou that wast born at sea, buried at Tarsus,
And found at sea again! O Helicanus,
Down on thy knees, thank the holy gods as loud
As thunder threatens us: this is Marina.
What was thy mother's name? tell me but that,
For truth can never be confirm'd enough,
Though doubts did ever sleep.
MARINA
First, sir, I pray,
What is your title?
PERICLES
I am Pericles of Tyre: but tell me now
My drown'd queen's name, as in the rest you said
Thou hast been godlike perfect,
The heir of kingdoms and another like [63]
To Pericles thy father.
MARINA
Is it no more to be your daughter than
To say my mother's name was Thaisa?
Thaisa was my mother, who did end
The minute I began.
PERICLES
Now, blessing on thee! rise; thou art my child.
Give me fresh garments. Mine own, Helicanus;
She is not dead at Tarsus, as she should have been,
By savage Cleon: she shall tell thee all;
When thou shalt kneel, and justify in knowledge
She is thy very princess. Who is this?
HELICANUS
Sir, 'tis the governor of Mytilene,
Who, hearing of your melancholy state,
Did come to see you.
PERICLES
I embrace you.
Give me my robes. I am wild in my beholding.
O heavens bless my girl! But, hark, what music?
Tell Helicanus, my Marina, tell him
O'er, point by point, for yet he seems to doubt,
How sure you are my daughter. But, what music?
HELICANUS
My lord, I hear none.
PERICLES
None!
The music of the spheres! List, my Marina.
LYSIMACHUS
It is not good to cross him; give him way.
PERICLES
Rarest sounds! Do ye not hear?
LYSIMACHUS
My lord, I hear. [*Music.*
PERICLES
Most heavenly music!
It nips me unto listening, and thick slumber [64]
Hangs upon mine eyes: let me rest. [*Sleeps.*
LYSIMACHUS
A pillow for his head:
So, leave him all. Well, my companion friends,
If this but answer to my just belief,
I'll well remember you.
[*Exeunt all but Pericles.*

DIANA *appears to* PERICLES *as in a vision.*

DIANA
My temple stands in Ephesus: hie thee thither,
And do upon mine altar sacrifice.

There, when my maiden priests are met together,
Before the people all,
Reveal how thou at sea didst lose thy wife:
To mourn thy crosses, with thy daughter's, call
And give them repetition to the life. [65]
Or perform my bidding, or thou livest in woe;
Do it, and happy; by my silver bow!
Awake, and tell thy dream. [*Disappears.*

PERICLES
Celestial Dian, goddess argentine,
I will obey thee. Helicanus!

Re-enter HELICANUS, LYSIMACHUS, *and* MARINA.

HELICANUS
Sir?

PERICLES
My purpose was for Tarsus, there to strike
The inhospitable Cleon; but I am
For other service first: toward Ephesus
Turn our blown sails; eftsoons I'll tell thee why.
[*To Lysimachus*] Shall we refresh us, sir, upon your shore,
And give you gold for such provision
As our intents will need?

LYSIMACHUS
Sir,
With all my heart; and, when you come ashore,
I have another suit.

PERICLES
You shall prevail,
Were it to woo my daughter; for it seems
You have been noble towards her.

LYSIMACHUS
Sir, lend me your arm.

PERICLES
Come, my Marina. [*Exeunt.*

ACT FIVE SCENE TWO

Enter GOWER, *before the temple of* DIANA *at Ephesus.*

GOWER
Now our sands are almost run;
More a little, and then dumb.
This, my last boon, give me,
For such kindness must relieve me,
That you aptly will suppose
What pageantry, what feats, what shows,
What minstrelsy, and pretty din,
The regent made in Mytilene
To greet the king. So he thrived,
That he is promised to be wived
To fair Marina; but in no wise
Till he had done his sacrifice,
As Dian bade: whereto being bound,
The interim, pray you, all confound.
In feather'd briefness sails are fill'd,
And wishes fall out as they're will'd.
At Ephesus, the temple see,
Our king and all his company.
That he can hither come so soon,
Is by your fancy's thankful doom. [*Exit.*

ACT FIVE SCENE THREE

The temple of Diana at Ephesus; THAISA *standing near the altar, as high priestess; a number of Virgins on each side;* CERIMON *and other Inhabitants of Ephesus attending.*

Enter PERICLES, *with his train;* LYSIMACHUS, HELICANUS, MARINA, *and a* Lady.

PERICLES
Hail, Dian! to perform thy just command,
I here confess myself the king of Tyre;
Who, frighted from my country, did wed
At Pentapolis the fair Thaisa.
At sea in childbed died she, but brought forth
A maid-child call'd Marina; who, O goddess,
Wears yet thy silver livery. She at Tarsus
Was nursed with Cleon; who at fourteen years
He sought to murder: but her better stars
Brought her to Mytilene; 'gainst whose shore
Riding, her fortunes brought the maid aboard us,
Where, by her own most clear remembrance, she
Made known herself my daughter.

THAISA
Voice and favour!
You are, you are—O royal Pericles! [*Faints.*

PERICLES
What means the nun? she dies! help, gentlemen!

CERIMON
Noble sir,
If you have told Diana's altar true,
This is your wife.

PERICLES
Reverend appearer, no;
I threw her overboard with these very arms.

CERIMON
Upon this coast, I warrant you.

PERICLES
'Tis most certain.

CERIMON
Look to the lady; O, she's but o'erjoy'd.

Early in blustering morn this lady was
Thrown upon this shore. I oped the coffin,
Found there rich jewels; recover'd her, and placed her
Here in Diana's temple.

PERICLES
May we see them?

CERIMON
Great sir, they shall be brought you to my house,
Whither I invite you. Look, Thaisa is Recovered.

THAISA
O, let me look!
If he be none of mine, my sanctity
Will to my sense bend no licentious ear, 35
But curb it, spite of seeing. O, my lord,
Are you not Pericles? Like him you spake,
Like him you are: did you not name a tempest,
A birth, and death?

PERICLES
The voice of dead Thaisa!

THAISA
That Thaisa am I, supposed dead
And drown'd.

PERICLES
Immortal Dian!

THAISA
Now I know you better.
When we with tears parted Pentapolis,
The king my father gave you such a ring.
[*Shows a ring.*

PERICLES
This, this: no more, you gods! your present kindness 48
Makes my past miseries sports: you shall do well,
That on the touching of her lips I may
Melt and no more be seen. O, come, be buried
A second time within these arms.

MARINA
My heart
Leaps to be gone into my mother's bosom.
[*Kneels to Thaisa.*

PERICLES
Look, who kneels here! Flesh of thy flesh, Thaisa;
Thy burden at the sea, and call'd Marina
For she was yielded there.

THAISA
Blest, and mine own!

HELICANUS
Hail, madam, and my queen!

THAISA
I know you not.

PERICLES
You have heard me say, when I did fly from Tyre, 62
I left behind an ancient substitute:
Can you remember what I call'd the man?
I have named him oft.

THAISA
'Twas Helicanus then.

PERICLES
Still confirmation:
Embrace him, dear Thaisa; this is he.
Now do I long to hear how you were found;
How possibly preserved; and who to thank,
Besides the gods, for this great miracle.

THAISA
Lord Cerimon, my lord; this man,
Through whom the gods have shown their power; that can 74
From first to last resolve you.

PERICLES
Reverend sir,
The gods can have no mortal officer
More like a god than you. Will you deliver
How this dead queen re-lives?

CERIMON
I will, my lord.
Beseech you, first go with me to my house,
Where shall be shown you all was found with her;
How she came placed here in the temple;
No needful thing omitted.

PERICLES
Pure Dian, bless thee for thy vision! I
Will offer night-oblations to thee. Thaisa, 86
This prince, the fair-betrothed of your daughter,
Shall marry her at Pentapolis. And now,
This ornament
Makes me look dismal will I clip to form;
And what this fourteen years no razor touch'd,
To grace thy marriage-day, I'll beautify.

THAISA
Lord Cerimon hath letters of good credit, sir,
My father's dead.

PERICLES
Heavens make a star of him! Yet there, my queen,
We 'll celebrate their nuptials, and ourselves
Will in that kingdom spend our following days:
Our son and daughter shall in Tyrus reign.
Lord Cerimon, we do our longing stay
To hear the rest untold: sir, lead's the way.
[*Exeunt.*

Enter GOWER.

GOWER
In Antiochus and his daughter you have heard
Of monstrous lust the due and just reward:
In Pericles, his queen and daughter, seen,
Although assail'd with fortune fierce and keen,

Virtue preserved from fell destruction's blast,
Led on by heaven, and crown'd with joy at last: 107
In Helicanus may you well descry
A figure of truth, of faith, of loyalty:
In reverend Cerimon there well appears
The worth that learned charity aye wears:
For wicked Cleon and his wife, when fame
Had spread their cursed deed, and honour'd name
Of Pericles, to rage the city turn,
That him and his they in his palace burn;
The gods for murder seemed so content
To punish them; although not done, but meant. 118
So, on your patience evermore attending,
New joy wait on you! Here our play has ending.
[*Exit.*

Notes

1. Boundless; – Rowe's emendation of Quartos; Folios 3, 4, *'bondlesse.'*
2. Death-like dragons here affright; – Daniel conjectured *'death, like dragons, here affrights'*; S. Walker conjectured *'affront'*; Hudson conjectured *'affronts.'*
3. The arrangement of the text, confused in Quartos and Folios, was first made by Malone.
4. Of all 'say'd yet; – Mason conjectured *'In all, save that'*; Mitford conjectured *'O false! and yet.'*
5. Cancel of; – Malone's emendation; Folios 3, 4, *'cancel off'*; Quartos 1, 2, 3, 4, 6, *'counsell of'*; Quarto 5, *'counsel of.'*
6. Untimely; – Wilkins, in the Novel, writes *'uncomely,'* which may, perhaps, give the correct reading of the line.
7. Blush, i.e. who blush; – the omission of the pronoun, personal or relative, is characteristic of the non-Shakespearian portions of the play.
8. Change of thoughts, i.e. – perturbation of thought; Steevens conjectured *'charge of thoughts?'*; Mason conjectured *'change of thoughts?'*; Singer (ed. 2), *'charge our thoughts?'*; Staunton conjectured *'change our thoughts?'*; Bailey conjectured *'child of thought'*; Daniel conjectured *'cast of thought.'*
9. Be my so used a guest as; – Dyce's emendation; Quarto 1, *'By me so used a guest, as'*; Malone (1780), *'By me's so us'd a guest, as'*; Jackson conjectured *'Be by me so us'd a guest?'*
10. Arm; – so Folio 4; Dyce reads *'aim.'*
11. Who am; – Farmer conjectured; Quartos, Folios 3, 4, *'Who once'*; Malone (1780), *'Who owe'*; (1790), *'Who wants.'*
12. Blast; – Mason conjectured; Quartos, Folios 3, 4, *'spark'*; Malone (1790), *'breath'*; Steevens conjectured *'wind.'*
13. Plants; – so Quarto 1; Malone's emendation of Quartos and Folios, *'planets.'*
14. Doubt it; – Steevens conjectured; Quartos 1, 2, 3, *'doo't'*; Quartos 4, 5, 6, and Folios, *'thinke.'*
15. Spares; – So Quarto 1; Quartos 2-6, and Folios 3, 4, *'feares'* and *'fears.'*
16. Reprovest; – Malone, *'reprov'st'*; Quartos 1, 2, 3, *'reprou'dst'*; Quartos 4, 5, 6, *'reprovedst'*; Folios 3, 4, *'reproved'st.'*
17. "I will therefore commend the poet Philipides, who, being demanded by King Lysimachus what favour he might do unto him, for that he loved him, made him answer to the king, that your Majesty would never impart unto me any of your secrets."—Barnabie Riche's *Soldier's Wish to Briton's Welfare.*
18. But since he's gone, the king's seas must please; – Mason conjectured *'But since he is gone, the king, seas must please'*; Percy conjectured *'But since he's gone, the king it sure must please'*; Collier (ed. 2), *'But since he is gone the king's ease must please'*; Perring conjectured *'But since he's gone, the king this news must please'*; Dyce conjectured *'But since he's gone the king's ears it must please.'*
19. Mischief's eyes; – Steevens, *'mistful eyes'*; Anonymous conjecture (1814), *'mischief-size'*; Singer (ed. 2), *'mistie eyes'*; S. Walker conjectured *'misery's eyes'*; Kinnear conjectured *'weakness' eyes'*; Mr. T. Tyler's suggestion, *'not seen with mischief's eyes,' i.e.* 'not seen with the eyes of despair,' seems to be the most ingenious correction of the line, if any change is necessary.
20. Our tongues and sorrows do sound deep Our woes; – Hudson reads *'Our tongues do sound our sorrows and deep woes':—*; *'sorrows do'*; Cartwright conjectured *'sobbings do'*; Bailey conjectured *'bosoms too'*; Anonymous conjecture, *'sorrowing bosoms do.'*
21. Tongues; – Quartos 1, 2, 3, *'toungs'*; Steevens conjectured *'lungs.'*
22. Yet two summers younger; – Mason conjectured; Quarto 1, *'yet too sauers younger'*; Folios 3, 4, *'yet to savers younger.'*
23. Of unhappy me; – Malone (1780), *'of unhappy men'*; Steevens conjectured *'of unhappy we'*; Jackson conjectured *'O unhappy me.'*
24. Him's, i.e. him who is; – Malone's reading; Quarto 1, *'himnes'*; Quarto 2, 3, Folio 3, *'hymnes'*; Quartos 4, 5, *'hymnes'*; Quarto 6, *'hywmes'*; Folio 4, *'hymns'*; Steevens conjectured *'him who is.'*
25. For though; – Steevens, *'forth'*; Singer (ed. 2), *'for thy'*; Nicholson conjectured *'for-though'*; Kinnear conjectured *'for through.'*
26. Sends word; – Steevens conjectured; Quartos 1-5 read *'Sau'd one'*; Quarto 6, Folios 3, 4, *'Sav'd one.'*
27. Finny; – Steevens conjectured (from Wilkins' novel); Quartos, Folios 3, 4, *'fenny.'*
28. Search; – Steevens conjectured *'scratch it'*; Singer (ed. 2), *'scratch't'*; Staunton, *'scratch'*; Anonymous conjecture, *'steal it'*; Hudson, *'steal't.'*
29. May see the sea hath cast upon your coast; – so Quartos; Folios 3, 4, *'Y' may see the sea hath cast me upon your coast'*; Malone (1780), *'You may see the sea hath cast me on your coast'*; Steevens, adopted by Malone (1790), *'Nay, see, the sea hath cast upon your coast—.'*
30. Entertain; – Steevens conjectured *'explain'*; Anonymous conjecture, *'entreat'*; Anonymous conjecture, *'emblazon'*; Schmidt conjectured *'interpret.'*
31. Marshal; – Malone's emendation; Quartos, Folio 3, *'Martiall'*; Folio 4, *'Martial.'*

32. Resist; – Collier conjectured *'distaste.'*
——; *'he not';* so Quartos 2-6, Folios 3, 4; Malone, *'she not';* Malone conjectured *'he now';* Steevens conjectured *'be not';* Mason conjectured *'she but';* Dyce conjectured *'he but.'*
33. Stored; – Steevens conjectured; Quartos 1, 2, 3, 6, *'stur'd';* Folios 3, 4, *'stirr'd';* Mason conjectured *'stow'd.'*
34. Kill'd are wonder'd at; – Daniel, *'still ne'er wondered at';* Anonymous conjecture, *'kill'd are scorned at';* Kinnear, *'little are wonder'd at.'*
35. For honour's cause; – Dyce's reading; Quartos, Folios 3, 4, *'Try honours cause';* Steevens conjectured *'Try honour's course';* Jackson conjectured *'Cry, honour's cause!';* Anonymous conjecture *'By honour's cause.'*
36. Y-ravished; – Steevens conjectured; Quarto 1, *'Iranyshed';* Quarto 2, *'Irany shed';* the rest, *'Irony shed.'*
37. Thou stormest venomously; Wilt; – Dyce's reading; Quartos, Folios 3, 4, *'then storme venomously, Wilt';* Malone, *'Thou storm, venomously, Wilt';* Steevens, *'Thou, storm, thou! venomously Wilt';* Collier, *'Thou storm, venomously Wilt.'*
38. Travails; – Folio 3, *'travels';* Dyce, *'travail.'*
39. Use honour with you; – Steevens reads *'Vie honour with yourselves';* Mason conjectured *'Vie honour with you.'*
40. Aye-remaining lamps; – Malone's conjecture; Quartos 1, 2, 3, *'ayre remayning lampes';* Quartos 4, 5, 6, *'ayre remaining lampes';* Folio 3, *'ayre remaining lamps';* Folio 4, *'air remaining lamps';* Jackson conjectured *'area-manesing,'* &c.
41. All-to topple; – Singer (ed. 2), *'al-to topple';* Quartos, Folios 3, 4, *'all to topple';* Dyce, *'all to-topple.'*
42. Rich tire; – Steevens conjectured *'Such towers';* Quartos 1, 2, 3, *'Rich tire';* the rest, *'Rich attire';* Jackson conjectured *'Rich Tyre';* Collier (ed. 2), *'Rich 'tire.'*
43. Treasure; – Steevens' emendation for *'pleasures'* and *'pleasure'* of Quartos, Folios 3, 4.
44. Steevens explained the words as an allusion to an old print exhibiting *Death* in the act of plundering a miser of his bags, and the *Fool* standing behind, and grinning at the process.
45. Time shall never….; – so Quartos 1, 2, 3; Quartos 4, 5, 6, Folios 3, 4, *'never shall decay';* Malone, *'time shall never—';* Dyce, *'time shall never raze';* Staunton, *'time shall ne'er decay';* Anonymous conjecture, *'time shall never end.'*
46. Wanderingly; – Quartos, Folios 3, 4, *'wondringly';* Schmidt conjectured *'woundingly.'*
47. Unscissar'd shall this hair; – Steevens' emendation; Quartos 1–4, *'unsisterd … heyre';* Quarto 5, *'unsisterd shall his heyres';* Quarto 6, *'unsisterd … heire';* Folios 3, 4, *'unsister'd … heir.'*
48. Show ill; – Quartos and Folios read *'show will';* the correction was made independently by Malone and Dyce; this and the previous emendations are confirmed by the corresponding passage in the Novel.
49. Marriage rite; – Collier's reading; Percy conjectured *'marriage rites';* Quartos, Folios 3, 4, *'marriage sight';* Steevens conjecture, adopted by Malone, *'marriage fight';* Steevens conjectured *'marriage night.'*
50. Night-bird; – Malone's emendation of Quartos, Folios 3, 4, *'night-bed.'*
51. Inflaming love i' thy bosom; – Knight's emendation of Quarto 1, *'in flaming, thy love bosome,'* &c.
52. Only mistress' death; – Malone (1790), *'old mistress' death';* Percy conjectured *'old nurse's death';* &c. &c.
53. Stem to stern; – Malone's emendation; Quartos, *'sterne to sterne';* Folios 3, 4, *'stern to stern.'*
54. The great pirate Valdes; – "perhaps there is here a scornful allusion to Don Pedro de Valdes, a Spanish admiral taken by Drake in 1588" (Malone).
55. Pious; – Mason conjecture and Wilkins' novel, adopted by Collier; Quartos 1, 2, 3, *'impious';* the rest omit the word.
56. Dost, with thine angel's face, Seize; – Malone conjectured *'dost wear thine angel's face; Seize;* Steevens, *'doth wear an angel's face, Seize';* Hudson (1881), *'doth use an angel's face, Then seize.'*
57. Talons; – Rowe's emendation of Quartos, Folios 3, 4, *'talents.'*
58. The arrangement of the lines is according to Hudson's edition (1881).
59. His pilot thought; – Steevens conjectured *'his pilot wrought';* Mason conjectured *'this pilot-thought';* Quartos 1, 2, 3, *'this Pilot thought';* the rest, *'this Pilate thought.'*
60. Scene must play; – Malone's emendation (1790); Quartos, Folios 3, 4 read *'Steare must play';* Steevens conjecture, adopted by Malone (1780), *'tears must play';* Malone conjectured *'stage must play';* Steevens, *'scenes display.'*
61. Deafen'd; – Malone's emendation; Quarto 1, *'defend';* the rest, *'defended.'*
62. Prosperous and artificial feat; i.e. 'gracefully and skilfully performed'; – Mason conjectured *'prosperous aritifice and fate';* Steevens, *'prosperous-artificial feat':*
——; *'feat';* Percy conjecture, adopted by Steevens, Quartos, Folios 3, 4, *'fate.'*
63. The passage is so corrupt that the Cambridge editors found themselves obliged to leave it as it stands in the Quartos and Folios.
64. Rips; – Collier conjectured *'raps.'*
65. Life; – Charlemont conjectured, adopted by Malone; Quartos, Folios 3, 4, *'like.'*

CYMBELINE

CYMBELINE

DRAMATIS PERSONAE

CYMBELINE, king of Britain.
CLOTEN, son to the Queen by a former husband.
POSTHUMUS LEONATUS, a gentleman, husband to Imogen.
BELARIUS, a banished lord, disguised under the name of Morgan.
GUIDERIUS, son to Cymbeline, disguised under the names of Polydore and Cadwal, supposed son to Morgan.
ARVIRAGUS, son to Cymbeline, disguised under the names of Polydore and Cadwal, supposed son to Morgan.
PHILARIO, friend to Posthumus, Italian.
JACHIMO, friend to Philario, Italian.
CAIUS LUCIUS, general of the Roman forces.
PISANIO, servant to Posthumus.
CORNELIUS, a physician.
A Roman Captain.
Two British Captains.
A Frenchman, friend to Philario.
Two Lords of Cymbeline's court.
Two Gentlemen of the same.
Two Gaolers.
Queen, wife to Cymbeline.
IMOGEN, daughter to Cymbeline by a former queen.
HELEN, a lady attending on Imogen.
Lords, Ladies, Roman Senators, Tribunes, a Soothsayer, a Dutchman, a Spaniard, Musicians, Officers, Captains, Soldiers, Messengers, and other attendants.
Apparitions.

SCENE: *Britain; Rome.*

ACT ONE SCENE ONE

Britain. The garden of Cymbeline's palace.

Enter two Gentlemen.

FIRST GENTLEMAN
You do not meet a man but frowns: our bloods
No more obey the heavens than our courtiers
Still seem as does the king. [1]

SECOND GENTLEMAN
But what's the matter?

FIRST GENTLEMAN
His daughter, and the heir of 's kingdom, whom
He purposed to his wife's sole son—a widow
That late he married—hath referr'd herself
Unto a poor but worthy gentleman: she's wedded;
Her husband banish'd; she imprison'd: all
Is outward sorrow; though I think the king
Be touch'd at very heart.

SECOND GENTLEMAN
None but the king?

FIRST GENTLEMAN
He that hath lost her too; so is the queen,
That most desired the match; but not a courtier,
Although they wear their faces to the bent
Of the king's look's, hath a heart that is not
Glad at the thing they scowl at.

SECOND GENTLEMAN
And why so?

FIRST GENTLEMAN
He that hath miss'd the princess is a thing
Too bad for bad report: and he that hath her—
I mean, that married her, alack, good man!
And therefore banish'd—is a creature such
As, to seek through the regions of the earth
For one his like, there would be something failing
In him that should compare. I do not think
So fair an outward and such stuff within
Endows a man but he.

SECOND GENTLEMAN
You speak him far.

FIRST GENTLEMAN
I do extend him, sir, within himself,
Crush him together rather than unfold
His measure duly.

SECOND GENTLEMAN
What's his name and birth?

FIRST GENTLEMAN
I cannot delve him to the root: his father
Was called Sicilius, who did join his honour
Against the Romans with Cassibelan,
But had his titles by Tenantius whom
He served with glory and admired success,
So gain'd the sur-addition Leonatus;
And had, besides this gentleman in question,
Two other sons, who in the wars o' the time
Died with their swords in hand; for which their father,
Then old and fond of issue, took such sorrow
That he quit being, and his gentle lady,
Big of this gentleman our theme, deceased
As he was born. The king he takes the babe
To his protection, calls him Posthumus Leonatus,
Breeds him and makes him of his bed-chamber,
Puts to him all the learnings that his time
Could make him the receiver of; which he took,
As we do air, fast as 'twas minister'd,
And in's spring became a harvest, lived in court—
Which rare it is to do—most praised, most loved,
A sample to the youngest, to the more mature
A glass that feated them, and to the graver
A child that guided dotards; to his mistress,
For whom he now is banish'd, her own price
Proclaims how she esteem'd him and his virtue;
By her election may be truly read
What kind of man he is.

SECOND GENTLEMAN
I honour him
Even out of your report. But, pray you, tell me,
Is she sole child to the king?

FIRST GENTLEMEN
His only child.
He had two sons: if this be worth your hearing,
Mark it: the eldest of them at three years old,
I' the swathing-clothes the other, from their nursery
Were stol'n, and to this hour no guess in knowledge
Which way they went.

SECOND GENTLEMAN
How long is this ago?

FIRST GENTLEMAN
Some twenty years.

SECOND GENTLEMAN
That a king's children should be so convey'd,
So slackly guarded, and the search so slow,
That could not trace them!

FIRST GENTLEMAN
Howsoe'er 'tis strange,
Or that the negligence may well be laugh'd at,
Yet is it true, sir.

SECOND GENTLEMAN
I do well believe you.

FIRST GENTLEMAN
We must forbear: here comes the gentleman,
The queen, and princess. [*Exeunt.*

Enter the QUEEN, POSTHUMUS LEONATUS, *and* IMOGEN.

QUEEN
No, be assured you shall not find me, daughter,
After the slander of most stepmothers,
Evil-eyed unto you: you're my prisoner, but
Your gaoler shall deliver you the keys
That lock up your restraint. For you, Posthumus,
So soon as I can win the offended king,
I will be known your advocate: marry, yet
The fire of rage is in him, and 'twere good
You lean'd unto his sentence with what patience
Your wisdom may inform you.

POSTHUMUS LEONATUS
Please your highness,
I will from hence to-day.

QUEEN
You know the peril.
I'll fetch a turn about the garden, pitying
The pangs of barr'd affections, though the king
Hath charged you should not speak together. [*Exit.*

IMOGEN
O
Dissembling courtesy! How fine this tyrant
Can tickle where she wounds! My dearest husband,
I something fear my father's wrath; but nothing—
Always reserved my holy duty—what
His rage can do on me: you must be gone;
And I shall here abide the hourly shot
Of angry eyes, not comforted to live,

But that there is this jewel in the world
That I may see again.

POSTHUMUS LEONATUS
My queen! my mistress!
O lady, weep no more, lest I give cause
To be suspected of more tenderness
Than doth become a man. I will remain
The loyal'st husband that did e'er plight troth:
My residence in Rome at one Philario's,
Who to my father was a friend, to me
Known but by letter: thither write, my queen,
And with mine eyes I'll drink the words you send,
Though ink be made of gall.

Re-enter QUEEN.

QUEEN
Be brief, I pray you:
If the king come, I shall incur I know not
How much of his displeasure. [*Aside*] Yet I'll move him
To walk this way: I never do him wrong,
But he does buy my injuries, to be friends;
Pays dear for my offences. [*Exit.*

POSTHUMUS LEONATUS
Should we be taking leave
As long a term as yet we have to live,
The loathness to depart would grow. Adieu!

IMOGEN
Nay, stay a little:
Were you but riding forth to air yourself,
Such parting were too petty. Look here, love;
This diamond was my mother's: take it, heart;
But keep it till you woo another wife,
When Imogen is dead.

POSTHUMUS LEONATUS
How, how! another?
You gentle gods, give me but this I have,
And sear up my embracements from a next
With bonds of death! [*Putting on the ring.*]
Remain, remain thou here
While sense can keep it on. And, sweetest, fairest,
As I my poor self did exchange for you,
To your so infinite loss, so in our trifles
I still win of you: for my sake wear this;
It is a manacle of love; I'll place it
Upon this fairest prisoner.
[*Putting a bracelet upon her arm.*

IMOGEN
O the gods!
When shall we see again?

Enter CYMBELINE *and* Lords.

POSTHUMUS LEONATUS
Alack, the king!

CYMBELINE
Thou basest thing, avoid! hence, from my sight!
If after this command thou fraught the court
With thy unworthiness, thou diest: away!
Thou'rt poison to my blood.

POSTHUMUS LEONATUS
The gods protect you!
And bless the good remainders of the court!
I am gone. [*Exit.*

IMOGEN
There cannot be a pinch in death
More sharp than this is.

CYMBELINE
O disloyal thing,
That should'st repair my youth, thou heap'st
A year's age on me. [2]

IMOGEN
I beseech you, sir,
Harm not yourself with your vexation:
I am senseless of your wrath; a touch more rare
Subdues all pangs, all fears.

CYMBELINE
Past grace? obedience?

IMOGEN
Past hope, and in despair; that way, past grace.

CYMBELINE
That mightst have had the sole son of my queen!

IMOGEN
O blest, that I might not! I chose an eagle,
And did avoid a puttock.

CYMBELINE
Thou took'st a beggar; wouldst have made my throne
A seat for baseness.

IMOGEN
No; I rather added
A lustre to it.

CYMBELINE
O thou vile one!

IMOGEN
Sir,
It is your fault that I have loved Posthumus:
You bred him as my playfellow, and he is
A man worth any woman, overbuys me
Almost the sum he pays.

CYMBELINE
What, art thou mad?

IMOGEN
Almost, sir: heaven restore me! Would I were
A neat-herd's daughter, and my Leonatus
Our neighbour shepherd's son!

CYMBELINE
Thou foolish thing!

Re-enter QUEEN.

They were again together: you have done
Not after our command. Away with her,
And pen her up.

QUEEN
Beseech your patience. Peace,
Dear lady daughter, peace! Sweet sovereign,
Leave us to ourselves; and make yourself some comfort
Out of your best advice.

CYMBELINE
Nay, let her languish
A drop of blood a day; and, being aged,
Die of this folly! [*Exeunt Cymbeline and Lords.*

QUEEN
Fie! you must give way.

Enter PISANIO.

Here is your servant. How now, sir! What news?

PISANIO
My lord your son drew on my master.

QUEEN
Ha! 199
No harm, I trust, is done?

PISANIO
There might have been,
But that my master rather play'd than fought
And had no help of anger: they were parted
By gentlemen at hand.

QUEEN
I am very glad on't.

IMOGEN
Your son's my father's friend; he takes his part.
To draw upon an exile! O brave sir!
I would they were in Afric both together;
Myself by with a needle, that I might prick
The goer-back. Why came you from your master?

PISANIO
On his command: he would not suffer me 211
To bring him to the haven; left these notes
Of what commands I should be subject to,
When 't pleased you to employ me.

QUEEN
This hath been
Your faithful servant: I dare lay mine honour
He will remain so.

PISANIO
I humbly thank your highness.

QUEEN
Pray, walk awhile.

IMOGEN
About some half-hour hence,
I pray you, speak with me: you shall at least
Go see my lord aboard: for this time leave me.
[*Exeunt.*

ACT ONE SCENE TWO

The same. A public place.

Enter CLOTEN *and two* Lords.

FIRST LORD
Sir, I would advise you to shift a shirt; the violence of action hath made you reek as a sacrifice: where air comes out, air comes in: there's none abroad so wholesome as that you vent.

CLOTEN
If my shirt were bloody, then to shift it. Have I hurt him?

SECOND LORD
[*Aside*] No, 'faith; not so much as his patience. 7

FIRST LORD
Hurt him! his body's a passable carcass, if he be not hurt: it is a throughfare for steel, if it be not hurt.

SECOND LORD
[*Aside*] His steel was in debt; it went o' the backside the town.

CLOTEN
The villain would not stand me.

SECOND LORD
[*Aside*] No; but he fled forward still, toward your face.

FIRST LORD
Stand you! You have land enough of your own: but he added to your having; gave you some ground. 16

SECOND LORD
[*Aside*] As many inches as you have oceans. Puppies!

CLOTEN
I would they had not come between us.

SECOND LORD
[*Aside*] So would I, till you had measured how long a fool you were upon the ground.

CLOTEN
And that she should love this fellow and refuse me!

SECOND LORD
[*Aside*] If it be a sin to make a true election, she is damned. 23

FIRST LORD
Sir, as I told you always, her beauty and her brain go not together: she's a good sign, but I have seen small reflection of her wit.

SECOND LORD
[*Aside*] She shines not upon fools, lest the reflection should hurt her.

CLOTEN
Come, I'll to my chamber. Would there had been some hurt done!

SECOND LORD
[*Aside*] I wish not so; unless it had been the fall of an ass, which is no great hurt.

CLOTEN
You'll go with us?
FIRST LORD
I'll attend your lordship.
CLOTEN
Nay, come, let's go together.
SECOND LORD
Well, my lord. [*Exeunt.*

ACT ONE SCENE THREE

A room in Cymbeline's palace.
Enter IMOGEN *and* PISANIO.

IMOGEN
I would thou grew'st unto the shores o' the haven,
And question'dst every sail: if he should write,
And I not have it, 'twere a paper lost,
As offer'd mercy is. What was the last
That he spake to thee?
PISANIO
It was his queen, his queen!
IMOGEN
Then waved his handkerchief?
PISANIO
And kiss'd it, madam.
IMOGEN
Senseless linen! happier therein than I!
And that was all?
PISANIO
No, madam; for so long
As he could make me with this eye or ear [3]
Distinguish him from others, he did keep
The deck, with glove, or hat, or handkerchief,
Still waving, as the fits and stirs of 's mind
Could best express how slow his soul sail'd on,
How swift his ship.
IMOGEN
Thou shouldst have made him
As little as a crow, or less, ere left
To after-eye him.
PISANIO
Madam, so I did.
IMOGEN
I would have broke mine eye-strings; crack'd them, but
To look upon him, till the diminution
Of space had pointed him sharp as my needle,
Nay, follow'd him, till he had melted from
The smallness of a gnat to air, and then
Have turn'd mine eye and wept. But, good Pisanio,
When shall we hear from him?
PISANIO
Be assured, madam,
With his next vantage.
IMOGEN
I did not take my leave of him, but had
Most pretty things to say: ere I could tell him
How I would think on him at certain hours
Such thoughts and such, or I could make him swear
The shes of Italy should not betray
Mine interest and his honour, or have charged him,
At the sixth hour of morn, at noon, at midnight,
To encounter me with orisons, for then
I am in heaven for him; or ere I could
Give him that parting kiss which I had set
Betwixt two charming words, comes in my father
And like the tyrannous breathing of the north
Shakes all our buds from growing.

Enter a Lady.

LADY
The queen, madam,
Desires your highness' company.
IMOGEN
Those things I bid you do, get them dispatch'd.
I will attend the queen.
PISANIO
Madam, I shall. [*Exeunt.*

ACT ONE SCENE FOUR

Rome. Philario's house.
Enter PHILARIO, IACHIMO, *a* Frenchman, *a* Dutchman, *and a* Spaniard.

IACHIMO
Believe it, sir, I have seen him in Britain: he was then of a crescent note, expected to prove so worthy as since he hath been allowed the name of; but I could then have looked on him without the help of admiration, though the catalogue of his endowments had been tabled by his side and I to peruse him by items.
PHILARIO
You speak of him when he was less furnished than now he is with that which makes him both without and within.
FRENCHMAN
I have seen him in France: we had very many there could behold the sun with as firm eye as he.
IACHIMO
This matter of marrying his king's daughter, wherein he must be weighed rather by her value than his own, words him, I doubt not, a great deal from the matter.
FRENCHMAN
And then his banishment.

IACHIMO

Ay, and the approbation of those that weep this lamentable divorce under her colours are wonderfully to extend him; be it but to fortify her judgment, which else an easy battery might lay flat, for taking a beggar without less quality. But how comes it he is to sojourn with you? How creeps acquaintance? [4]

PHILARIO

His father and I were soldiers together; to whom I have been often bound for no less than my life.

Here comes the Briton: let him be so entertained amongst you as suits, with gentlemen of your knowing, to a stranger of his quality.

Enter POSTHUMUS.

I beseech you all, be better known to this gentleman; whom I commend to you as a noble friend of mine: how worthy he is I will leave to appear hereafter, rather than story him in his own hearing.

FRENCHMAN

Sir, we have known together in Orleans.

POSTHUMUS LEONATUS

Since when I have been debtor to you for courtesies, which I will be ever to pay and yet pay still.

FRENCHMAN

Sir, you o'er-rate my poor kindness: I was glad I did atone my countryman and you; it had been pity you should have been put together with so mortal a purpose as then each bore, upon importance of so slight and trivial a nature.

POSTHUMUS LEONATUS

By your pardon, sir, I was then a young traveller; rather shunned to go even with what I heard than in my every action to be guided by others' experiences: but upon my mended judgment—if I offend not to say it is mended—my quarrel was not altogether slight.

FRENCHMAN

'Faith, yes, to be put to the arbitrement of swords, and by such two that would by all likelihood have confounded one the other, or have fallen both.

IACHIMO

Can we, with manners, ask what was the difference?

FRENCHMAN

Safely, I think: 'twas a contention in public, which may, without contradiction, suffer the report.

It was much like an argument that fell out last night, where each of us fell in praise of our country mistresses; this gentleman at that time vouching—and upon warrant of bloody affirmation—his to be more fair, virtuous, wise, chaste, constant-qualified and less attemptable than any the rarest of our ladies in France.

IACHIMO

That lady is not now living, or this gentleman's opinion by this worn out.

POSTHUMUS LEONATUS

She holds her virtue still and I my mind.

IACHIMO

You must not so far prefer her 'fore ours of Italy.

POSTHUMUS LEONATUS

Being so far provoked as I was in France, I would abate her nothing, though I profess myself her adorer, not her friend.

IACHIMO

As fair and as good—a kind of hand-in-hand comparison—had been something too fair and too good for any lady in Britain. If she went before others I have seen, as that diamond of yours outlustres many I have beheld, I could not but believe she excelled many: but I have not seen the most precious diamond that is, nor you the lady. [5]

POSTHUMUS LEONATUS

I praised her as I rated her: so do I my stone.

IACHIMO

What do you esteem it at?

POSTHUMUS LEONATUS

More than the world enjoys.

IACHIMO

Either your unparagoned mistress is dead, or she's outprized by a trifle.

POSTHUMUS LEONATUS

You are mistaken: the one may be sold, or given, if there were wealth enough for the purchase, or merit for the gift: the other is not a thing for sale, and only the gift of the gods.

IACHIMO

Which the gods have given you?

POSTHUMUS LEONATUS

Which, by their graces, I will keep.

IACHIMO

You may wear her in title yours: but, you know, strange fowl light upon neighbouring ponds. Your ring may be stolen too: so your brace of unprizable estimations; the one is but frail and the other casual; a cunning thief, or a that way accomplished courtier, would hazard the winning both of first and last.

POSTHUMUS LEONATUS

Your Italy contains none so accomplished a courtier to convince the honour of my mistress, if, in the holding or loss of that, you term her frail. I do nothing doubt you have store of thieves; notwithstanding, I fear not my ring.

PHILARIO

Let us leave here, gentlemen.

POSTHUMUS LEONATUS

Sir, with all my heart. This worthy signior, I thank him, makes no stranger of me; we are familiar at first.

IACHIMO

With five times so much conversation, I should get ground of your fair mistress, make her go back, even to the yielding, had I admittance and opportunity to friend.

POSTHUMUS LEONATUS

No, no.

IACHIMO

I dare thereupon pawn the moiety of my estate to your ring; which, in my opinion, o'ervalues it something: but I make my wager rather against your confidence than her reputation: and, to bar your offence herein too, I durst attempt it against any lady in the world. [6]

POSTHUMUS LEONATUS

You are a great deal abused in too bold a persuasion; and I doubt not you sustain what you're worthy of by your attempt.

IACHIMO

What's that?

POSTHUMUS LEONATUS

A repulse: though your attempt, as you call it, deserve more; a punishment too.

PHILARIO

Gentlemen, enough of this: it came in too suddenly; let it die as it was born, and, I pray you, be better acquainted.

IACHIMO

Would I had put my estate and my neighbour's on the approbation of what I have spoke!

POSTHUMUS LEONATUS

What lady would you choose to assail?

IACHIMO

Yours; whom in constancy you think stands so safe.

I will lay you ten thousand ducats to your ring, that, commend me to the court where your lady is, with no more advantage than the opportunity of a second conference, and I will bring from thence that honour of hers which you imagine so reserved.

POSTHUMUS LEONATUS

I will wage against your gold, gold to it: my ring
I hold dear as my finger; 'tis part of it.

IACHIMO

You are afraid, and therein the wiser. If you buy ladies' flesh at a million a dram, you cannot preserve it from tainting: but I see you have some religion in you, that you fear. [7]

POSTHUMUS LEONATUS

This is but a custom in your tongue; you bear a graver purpose, I hope.

IACHIMO

I am the master of my speeches, and would undergo what's spoken, I swear.

POSTHUMUS LEONATUS

Will you? I shall but lend my diamond till your return: let there be covenants drawn between's: my mistress exceeds in goodness the hugeness of your unworthy thinking: I dare you to this match: here's my ring.

PHILARIO

I will have it no lay.

IACHIMO

By the gods, it is one. If I bring you no sufficient testimony that I have enjoyed the dearest bodily part of your mistress, my ten thousand ducats are yours; so is your diamond too: if I come off, and leave her in such honour as you have trust in, she your jewel, this your jewel, and my gold are yours: provided I have your commendation for my more free entertainment.

POSTHUMUS LEONATUS

I embrace these conditions; let us have articles betwixt us. Only, thus far you shall answer: if you make your voyage upon her and give me directly to understand you have prevailed, I am no further your enemy; she is not worth our debate: if she remain unseduced, you not making it appear otherwise, for your ill opinion and the assault you have made to her chastity you shall answer me with your sword.

IACHIMO

Your hand; a covenant: we will have these things set down by lawful counsel, and straight away for Britain, lest the bargain should catch cold and starve: I will fetch my gold and have our two wagers recorded.

POSTHUMUS LEONATUS

Agreed. *[Exeunt Posthumus and Iachimo.*

FRENCHMAN

Will this hold, think you?

PHILARIO

Signior Iachimo will not from it.
Pray, let us follow 'em. *[Exeunt.*

ACT ONE SCENE FIVE

Britain. A room in Cymbeline's palace.

Enter QUEEN, Ladies, *and* CORNELIUS.

QUEEN

Whiles yet the dew's on ground, gather those flowers;
Make haste: who has the note of them?

FIRST LADY

I, madam.

QUEEN

Dispatch. *[Exeunt Ladies.*
Now, master doctor, have you brought those drugs?

CORNELIUS

Pleaseth your highness, ay: here they are, madam:
[Presenting a small box.
But I beseech your grace, without offence,—

My conscience bids me ask—wherefore you have
Commanded of me those most poisonous compounds,
Which are the movers of a languishing death;
But though slow, deadly?

QUEEN
I wonder, doctor,
Thou ask'st me such a question. Have I not been
Thy pupil long? Hast thou not learn'd me how
To make perfumes? distil? preserve? yea, so
That our great king himself doth woo me oft
For my confections? Having thus far proceeded,—
Unless thou think'st me devilish—is't not meet
That I did amplify my judgment in
Other conclusions? I will try the forces
Of these thy compounds on such creatures as
We count not worth the hanging, but none human,
To try the vigour of them and apply
Allayments to their act, and by them gather
Their several virtues and effects.

CORNELIUS
Your highness
Shall from this practice but make hard your heart:
Besides, the seeing these effects will be
Both noisome and infectious.

QUEEN
O, content thee.

Enter PISANIO.

[*Aside*] Here comes a flattering rascal; upon him
Will I first work: he's for his master,
An enemy to my son. How now, Pisanio!
Doctor, your service for this time is ended;
Take your own way.

CORNELIUS
[*Aside*] I do suspect you, madam;
But you shall do no harm.

QUEEN
[*To Pisanio*] Hark thee, a word.

CORNELIUS
[*Aside*] I do not like her. She doth think she has
Strange lingering poisons: I do know her spirit,
And will not trust one of her malice with
A drug of such damn'd nature. Those she has
Will stupefy and dull the sense awhile;
Which first, perchance, she'll prove on cats and dogs,
Then afterward up higher: but there is
No danger in what show of death it makes,
More than the locking-up the spirits a time,
To be more fresh, reviving. She is fool'd
With a most false effect; and I the truer,
So to be false with her.

QUEEN
No further service, doctor,
Until I send for thee.

CORNELIUS
I humbly take my leave. [*Exit.*

QUEEN
Weeps she still, say'st thou? Dost thou think in time
She will not quench and let instructions enter
Where folly now possesses? Do thou work:
When thou shalt bring me word she loves my son,
I'll tell thee on the instant thou art then
As great as is thy master, greater, for
His fortunes all lie speechless and his name
Is at last gasp: return he cannot, nor
Continue where he is: to shift his being
Is to exchange one misery with another,
And every day that comes comes to decay
A day's work in him. What shalt thou expect,
To be depender on a thing that leans,
Who cannot be new built, nor has no friends,
So much as but to prop him? [*The Queen drops the box: Pisanio takes it up.*] Thou takest up
Thou know'st not what; but take it for thy labour:
It is a thing I made, which hath the king
Five times redeem'd from death: I do not know
What is more cordial. Nay, I prithee, take it;
It is an earnest of a further good
That I mean to thee. Tell thy mistress how
The case stands with her; do't as from thyself.
Think what a chance thou changest on, but think [8]
Thou hast thy mistress still, to boot, my son,
Who shall take notice of thee: I'll move the king
To any shape of thy preferment such
As thou'lt desire; and then myself, I chiefly,
That set thee on to this desert, am bound
To load thy merit richly. Call my women:
Think on my words. [*Exit Pisanio.*
A sly and constant knave,
Not to be shaked; the agent for his master
And the remembrancer of her to hold
The hand-fast to her lord. I have given him that
Which, if he take, shall quite unpeople her
Of liegers for her sweet, and which she after,
Except she bend her humour, shall be assured
To taste of too.

Re-enter PISANIO *and* Ladies.

So, so: well done, well done:
The violets, cowslips, and the primroses,
Bear to my closet. Fare thee well, Pisanio;
Think on my words. [*Exeunt Queen and Ladies.*

PISANIO
And shall do:

But when to my good lord I prove untrue,
I'll choke myself: there's all I'll do for you. [*Exit.*

ACT ONE SCENE SIX

The same. Another room in the palace.

Enter IMOGEN.

IMOGEN
A father cruel, and a step-dame false;
A foolish suitor to a wedded lady,
That hath her husband banish'd;—O, that husband!
My supreme crown of grief! and those repeated
Vexations of it! Had I been thief-stol'n,
As my two brothers, happy! but most miserable
Is the desire that's glorious: blest be those,
How mean soe'er, that have their honest wills,
Which seasons comfort. Who may this be? Fie!

Enter PISANIO *and* IACHIMO.

PISANIO
Madam, a noble gentleman of Rome,
Comes from my lord with letters.
IACHIMO
Change you, madam? 12
The worthy Leonatus is in safety
And greets your highness dearly.
[*Presents a letter.*
IMOGEN
Thanks, good sir:
You're kindly welcome.
IACHIMO
[*Aside*] All of her that is out of door most rich!
If she be furnish'd with a mind so rare,
She is alone the Arabian bird, and I
Have lost the wager. Boldness be my friend!
Arm me, audacity, from head to foot!
Or, like the Parthian, I shall flying fight; 22
Rather, directly fly.
IMOGEN
[*Reads*] 'He is one of the noblest note, to whose kindnesses I am most infinitely tied. Reflect upon him accordingly, as you value your trust— [9] LEONATUS.'
So far I read aloud:
But even the very middle of my heart
Is warm'd by the rest, and takes it thankfully.
You are as welcome, worthy sir, as I
Have words to bid you, and shall find it so 31
In all that I can do.
IACHIMO
Thanks, fairest lady.
What, are men mad? Hath nature given them eyes
To see this vaulted arch, and the rich crop
Of sea and land, which can distinguish 'twixt
The fiery orbs above and the twinn'd stones
Upon the number'd beach? and can we not [10]
Partition make with spectacles so precious
'Twixt fair and foul?
IMOGEN
What makes your admiration?
IACHIMO
It cannot be i' the eye, for apes and monkeys
'Twixt two such shes would chatter this way and 44
Contemn with mows the other; nor i' the judgment,
For idiots in this case of favour would
Be wisely definite; nor i' the appetite;
Sluttery to such neat excellence opposed
Should make desire vomit emptiness, [11]
Not so allured to feed.
IMOGEN
What is the matter, trow?
IACHIMO
The cloyed will,
That satiate yet unsatisfied desire, that tub
Both fill'd and running, ravening first the lamb
Longs after for the garbage.
IMOGEN
What, dear sir, 56
Thus raps you? Are you well?
IACHIMO
Thanks, madam; well. [*To Pisanio.*
Beseech you, sir, desire
My man's abode where I did leave him: he
Is strange and peevish.
PISANIO
I was going, sir,
To give him welcome. [*Exit.*
IMOGEN
Continues well my lord? His health, beseech you?
IACHIMO
Well, madam.
IMOGEN
Is he disposed to mirth? I hope he is.
IACHIMO
Exceeding pleasant; none a stranger there
So merry and so gamesome: he is call'd 68
The Briton reveller.
IMOGEN
When he was here,
He did incline to sadness, and oft-times
Not knowing why.
IACHIMO
I never saw him sad.
There is a Frenchman his companion, one
An eminent monsieur, that, it seems, much loves
A Gallian girl at home; he furnaces

The thick sighs from him, whiles the jolly Briton—
Your lord, I mean—laughs from's free lungs, cries 'O,
Can my sides hold, to think that man, who knows
By history, report, or his own proof, 81
What woman is, yea, what she cannot choose
But must be, will his free hours languish for
Assured bondage?'

IMOGEN
Will my lord say so?

IACHIMO
Ay, madam, with his eyes in flood with laughter:
It is a recreation to be by
And hear him mock the Frenchman. But, heavens know,
Some men are much to blame.

IMOGEN
Not he, I hope.

IACHIMO
Not he: but yet heaven's bounty towards him might
Be used more thankfully. In himself, 'tis much;
In you, which I account his beyond all talents,
Whilst I am bound to wonder, I am bound 95
To pity too.

IMOGEN
What do you pity, sir?

IACHIMO
Two creatures heartily.

IMOGEN
Am I one, sir?
You look on me: what wreck discern you in me
Deserves your pity?

IACHIMO
Lamentable! What,
To hide me from the radiant sun and solace
I' the dungeon by a snuff?

IMOGEN
I pray you, sir,
Deliver with more openness your answers
To my demands. Why do you pity me?

IACHIMO
That others do— 107
I was about to say—enjoy your—But
It is an office of the gods to venge it,
Not mine to speak on 't.

IMOGEN
You do seem to know
Something of me, or what concerns me: pray you,—
Since doubting things go ill often hurts more
Than to be sure they do; for certainties
Either are past remedies, or, timely knowing,
The remedy then born—discover to me
What both you spur and stop.

IACHIMO
Had I this cheek 118
To bathe my lips upon; this hand, whose touch,
Whose every touch, would force the feeler's soul
To the oath of loyalty; this object, which
Takes prisoner the wild motion of mine eye,
Fixing it only here; should I, damn'd then,
Slaver with lips as common as the stairs
That mount the capitol; join gripes with hands
Made hard with hourly falsehood—falsehood, as
With labour; then by-peeping in an eye
Base and unlustrous as the smoky light [12]
That's fed with stinking tallow; it were fit
That all the plagues of hell should at one time
Encounter such revolt.

IMOGEN
My lord, I fear,
Has forgot Britain.

IACHIMO
And himself. Not I,
Inclined to this intelligence, pronounce
The beggary of his change; but 'tis your graces
That from my mutest conscience to my tongue
Charms this report out.

IMOGEN
Let me hear no more.

IACHIMO
O dearest soul! your cause doth strike my heart
With pity, that doth make me sick. A lady
So fair, and fasten'd to an empery, 143
Would make the great'st king double,—to be partner'd
With tomboys hired with that self-exhibition
Which your own coffers yield! with diseased ventures
That play with all infirmities for gold
Which rottenness can lend nature! such boil'd stuff
As well might poison poison! Be revenged;
Or she that bore you was no queen, and you
Recoil from your great stock.

IMOGEN
Revenged!
How should I be revenged? If this be true,—
As I have such a heart that both mine ears
Must not in haste abuse—if it be true,
How should I be revenged?

IACHIMO
Should he make me
Live, like Diana's priest, betwixt cold sheets,
Whiles he is vaulting variable ramps,
In your despite, upon your purse? Revenge it.
I dedicate myself to your sweet pleasure,
More noble than that runagate to your bed,
And will continue fast to your affection,
Still close as sure.

IMOGEN
What, ho, Pisanio!

IACHIMO
Let me my service tender on your lips.

IMOGEN
Away! I do condemn mine ears that have
So long attended thee. If thou wert honourable,
Thou wouldst have told this tale for virtue, not
For such an end thou seek'st,—as base as strange
Thou wrong'st a gentleman, who is as far
From thy report as thou from honour, and
Solicit'st here a lady that disdains
Thee and the devil alike. What ho, Pisanio!
The king my father shall be made acquainted
Of thy assault: if he shall think it fit,
A saucy stranger in his court to mart
As in a Romish stew and to expound
His beastly mind to us, he hath a court
He little cares for and a daughter who
He not respects at all. What, ho, Pisanio!

IACHIMO
O happy Leonatus! I may say:
The credit that thy lady hath of thee
Deserves thy trust, and thy most perfect goodness
Her assured credit. Blessed live you long!
A lady to the worthiest sir that ever
Country call'd his! and you his mistress, only
For the most worthiest fit! Give me your pardon.
I have spoke this, to know if your affiance
Were deeply rooted; and shall make your lord,
That which he is, new o'er: and he is one
The truest manner'd; such a holy witch
That he enchants societies into him;
Half all men's hearts are his.

IMOGEN
You make amends.

IACHIMO
He sits 'mongst men like a descended god:
He hath a kind of honour sets him off,
More than a mortal seeming. Be not angry,
Most mighty princess, that I have adventured
To try your taking of a false report; which hath
Honour'd with confirmation your great judgment
In the election of a sir so rare,
Which you know cannot err: the love I bear him
Made me to fan you thus, but the gods made you,
Unlike all others, chaffless. Pray, your pardon.

IMOGEN
All's well, sir: take my power i' the court for yours.

IACHIMO
My humble thanks. I had almost forgot
To entreat your grace but in a small request,
And yet of moment to, for it concerns
Your lord; myself and other noble friends,
Are partners in the business.

IMOGEN
Pray, what is't?

IACHIMO
Some dozen Romans of us and your lord—
The best feather of our wing—have mingled sums
To buy a present for the emperor;
Which I, the factor for the rest, have done
In France: 'tis plate of rare device, and jewels
Of rich and exquisite form; their values great;
And I am something curious, being strange,
To have them in safe stowage: may it please you
To take them in protection?

IMOGEN
Willingly;
And pawn mine honour for their safety: since
My lord hath interest in them, I will keep them
In my bedchamber.

IACHIMO
They are in a trunk,
Attended by my men: I will make bold
To send them to you, only for this night;
I must aboard to-morrow.

IMOGEN
O, no, no.

IACHIMO
Yes, I beseech; or I shall short my word
By lengthening my return. From Gallia
I cross'd the seas on purpose and on promise
To see your grace.

IMOGEN
I thank you for your pains:
But not away to-morrow!

IACHIMO
O, I must, madam:
Therefore I shall beseech you, if you please
To greet your lord with writing, do't to-night:
I have outstood my time; which is material
To the tender of our present.

IMOGEN
I will write.
Send your trunk to me; it shall safe be kept,
And truly yielded you. You're very welcome.

[*Exeunt.*

ACT TWO SCENE ONE

Britain. Before Cymbeline's palace.

Enter CLOTEN *and two* Lords.

CLOTEN
Was there ever man had such luck! when I kissed the jack, upon an up-cast to be hit away! I had a hundred pound on't: and then a whoreson jackanapes must take me up for swearing; as if I borrowed mine oaths of him and might not spend them at my pleasure.

FIRST LORD
What got he by that? You have broke his pate with your bowl.
SECOND LORD
[*Aside*] If his wit had been like him that broke it, it would have run all out.
CLOTEN
When a gentleman is disposed to swear, it is not for any standers-by to curtail his oaths, ha?
SECOND LORD
No, my lord; [*Aside*] nor crop the ears of them.
CLOTEN
Whoreson dog! I give him satisfaction? Would he had been one of my rank!
SECOND LORD
[*Aside*] To have smelt like a fool.
CLOTEN
I am not vexed more at any thing in the earth: a pox on't! I had rather not be so noble as I am; they dare not fight with me, because of the queen my mother: every Jack-slave hath his bellyful of fighting, and I must go up and down like a cock that nobody can match.
SECOND LORD
[*Aside*] You are cock and capon too; and you crow, cock, with your comb on.
CLOTEN
Sayest thou?
SECOND LORD
It is not fit your lordship should undertake every companion that you give offence to.
CLOTEN
No, I know that: but it is fit I should commit offence to my inferiors.
SECOND LORD
Ay, it is fit for your lordship only.
CLOTEN
Why, so I say.
FIRST LORD
Did you hear of a stranger that's come to court to-night?
CLOTEN
A stranger, and I not know on't?
SECOND LORD
[*Aside*] He's a strange fellow himself, and knows it not.
FIRST LORD
There's an Italian come; and, 'tis thought, one of Leonatus' friends.
CLOTEN
Leonatus! a banished rascal; and he's another, whatsoever he be. Who told you of this stranger?
FIRST LORD
One of your lordship's pages.
CLOTEN
Is it fit I went to look upon him? is there no derogation in't?
SECOND LORD
You cannot derogate, my lord.
CLOTEN
Not easily, I think.
SECOND LORD
[*Aside*] You are a fool granted; therefore your issues, being foolish, do not derogate.
CLOTEN
Come, I'll go see this Italian: what I have lost to-day at bowls I'll win to-night of him. Come, go.
SECOND LORD
I'll attend your lordship. [*Exeunt Cloten and First Lord.*
That such a crafty devil as is his mother
Should yield the world this ass! a woman that
Bears all down with her brain; and this her son
Cannot take two from twenty, for his heart,
And leave eighteen. Alas, poor princess,
Thou divine Imogen, what thou endurest,
Betwixt a father by thy step-dame govern'd,
A mother hourly coining plots, a wooer
More hateful than the foul expulsion is
Of thy dear husband, than that horrid act
Of the divorce he'ld make! The heavens hold firm
The walls of thy dear honour, keep unshak'd
That temple, thy fair mind, that thou mayst stand,
To enjoy thy banish'd lord and this great land!
[*Exit.*

ACT TWO SCENE TWO

Imogen's bedchamber in Cymbeline's palace: a trunk in one corner of it.
IMOGEN *in bed, reading; a* Lady *attending.*
IMOGEN
Who's there? my woman Helen?
LADY
Please you, madam.
IMOGEN
What hour is it?
LADY
Almost midnight, madam.
IMOGEN
I have read three hours then: mine eyes are weak:
Fold down the leaf where I have left: to bed:
Take not away the taper, leave it burning;
And if thou canst awake by four o' the clock,
I prithee, call me. Sleep hath seized me wholly
[*Exit Lady.*
To your protection I commend me, gods.
From fairies and the tempters of the night
Guard me, beseech ye.
[*Sleeps. Iachimo comes from the trunk.*

IACHIMO
The crickets sing, and man's o'er-labour'd sense
Repairs itself by rest. Our Tarquin thus
Did softly press the rushes, ere he waken'd
The chastity he wounded. Cytherea,
How bravely thou becomest thy bed, fresh lily,
And whiter than the sheets! That I might touch!
But kiss; one kiss! Rubies unparagon'd,
How dearly they do't! 'Tis her breathing that
Perfumes the chamber thus: the flame o' the taper
Bows toward her, and would under-peep her lids,
To see the enclosed lights, now canopied 23
Under these windows, white and azure laced
With blue of heaven's own tinct. But my design,
To note the chamber: I will write all down:
Such and such pictures; there the window; such
The adornment of her bed; the arras; figures,
Why, such and such; and the contents o' the story.
Ah, but some natural notes about her body,
Above ten thousand meaner moveables
Would testify, to enrich mine inventory. 32
O sleep, thou ape of death, lie dull upon her!
And be her sense but as a monument,
Thus in a chapel lying! Come off, come off:
[*Taking off her bracelet.*
As slippery as the Gordian knot was hard!
'Tis mine; and this will witness outwardly,
As strongly as the conscience does within,
To the madding of her lord. On her left breast
A mole cinque-spotted, like the crimson drops
I' the bottom of a cowslip: here's a voucher,
Stronger than ever law could make: this secret
Will force him think I have pick'd the lock and ta'en
The treasure of her honour. No more. To what end?
Why should I write this down, that's riveted,
Screw'd to my memory? She hath been reading late
The tale of Tereus; here the leaf 's turn'd down
Where Philomel gave up. I have enough:
To the trunk again, and shut the spring of it.
Swift, swift, you dragons of the night, that dawning
May bare the raven's eye! I lodge in fear; [13]
Though this a heavenly angel, hell is here. 52
[*Clock strikes.*
One, two, three: time, time!
[*Goes into the trunk. The scene closes.*

ACT TWO SCENE THREE

An ante-chamber adjoining Imogen's apartments.

Enter CLOTEN *and* Lords.

FIRST LORD
Your lordship is the most patient man in loss, the most coldest that ever turned up ace.

CLOTEN
It would make any man cold to lose.

FIRST LORD
But not every man patient after the noble temper of your lordship. You are most hot and furious when you win.

CLOTEN
Winning will put any man into courage. If I could get this foolish Imogen, I should have gold enough. It's almost morning, is't not?

FIRST LORD
Day, my lord. 10

CLOTEN
I would this music would come: I am advised to give her music o' mornings; they say it will penetrate.

Enter Musicians.

Come on; tune: if you can penetrate her with your fingering, so; we'll try with tongue too: if none will do, let her remain; but I'll never give o'er. First, a very excellent good-conceited thing; after, a wonderful sweet air, with admirable rich words to it: and then let her consider. 18

SONG.

Hark, hark! the lark at heaven's gate sings,
And Phoebus 'gins arise,
His steeds to water at those springs
On chaliced flowers that lies;
And winking Mary-buds begin
To ope their golden eyes:
With every thing that pretty is, [14]
My lady sweet, arise:
Arise, arise. 27

CLOTEN
So, get you gone. If this penetrate, I will consider your music the better: if it do not, it is a vice in her ears, which horse-hairs and calves'-guts, nor the voice of unpaved eunuch to boot, can never amend. [15]
[*Exeunt Musicians.*

SECOND LORD
Here comes the king.

CLOTEN
I am glad I was up so late; for that's the reason I was up so early: he cannot choose but take this service I have done fatherly.

Enter CYMBELINE *and* QUEEN.

Good morrow to your majesty and to my gracious mother. 37

CYMBELINE
Attend you here the door of our stern daughter?
Will she not forth?

CLOTEN
I have assailed her with music, but she vouchsafes no notice.

CYMBELINE
The exile of her minion is too new;
She hath not yet forgot him: some more time
Must wear the print of his remembrance out,
And then she's yours.
QUEEN
You are most bound to the king,
Who lets go by no vantages that may 47
Prefer you to his daughter. Frame yourself
To orderly soliciting, and be friended [16]
With aptness of the season; make denials
Increase your services; so seem as if
You were inspired to do those duties which
You tender to her; that you in all obey her,
Save when command to your dismission tends,
And therein you are senseless.
CLOTEN
Senseless! not so.

Enter a Messenger.

MESSENGER
So like you, sir, ambassadors from Rome;
The one is Caius Lucius.
CYMBELINE
A worthy fellow, 59
Albeit he comes on angry purpose now;
But that's no fault of his: we must receive him
According to the honour of his sender;
And towards himself, his goodness forespent on us,
We must extend our notice. Our dear son,
When you have given good morning to your mistress,
Attend the queen and us; we shall have need
To employ you towards this Roman. Come, our queen. [*Exeunt all but Cloten.*
CLOTEN
If she be up, I'll speak with her; if not,
Let her lie still and dream. [*Knocks*] By your leave, ho! 72
I know her women are about her: what
If I do line one of their hands? 'Tis gold
Which buys admittance; oft it doth; yea, and makes
Diana's rangers false themselves, yield up
Their deer to the stand o' the stealer; and 'tis gold
Which makes the true man kill'd and saves the thief;
Nay, sometime hangs both thief and true man: what
Can it not do and undo? I will make
One of her women lawyer to me, for
I yet not understand the case myself. 82
[*Knocks*] By your leave.

Enter a Lady

LADY
Who's there that knocks?
CLOTEN
A gentleman.
LADY
No more?
CLOTEN
Yes, and a gentlewoman's son.
LADY
That's more
Than some, whose tailors are as dear as yours,
Can justly boast of. What's your lordship's pleasure?
CLOTEN
Your lady's person: is she ready?
LADY
Ay,
To keep her chamber.
CLOTEN
There is gold for you;
Sell me your good report.
LADY
How! my good name? or to report of you
What I shall think is good?—The princess!

Enter IMOGEN.

CLOTEN
Good morrow, fairest: sister, your sweet hand. [*Exit Lady.*
IMOGEN
Good morrow, sir. You lay out too much pains
For purchasing but trouble: the thanks I give
Is telling you that I am poor of thanks
And scarce can spare them.
CLOTEN
Still, I swear I love you.
IMOGEN
If you but said so, 'twere as deep with me:
If you swear still, your recompense is still
That I regard it not.
CLOTEN
This is no answer.
IMOGEN
But that you shall not say I yield being silent,
I would not speak. I pray you, spare me: 'faith, 109
I shall unfold equal discourtesy
To your best kindness: one of your great knowing
Should learn, being taught, forbearance.
CLOTEN
To leave you in your madness, 'twere my sin:
I will not.
IMOGEN
Fools are not mad folks. [17]
CLOTEN
Do you call me fool?
IMOGEN
As I am mad, I do:

If you'll be patient, I'll no more be mad;
That cures us both. I am much sorry, sir,
You put me to forget a lady's manners, 120
By being so verbal: and learn now, for all,
That I, which know my heart, do here pronounce,
By the very truth of it, I care not for you,
And am so near the lack of charity—
To accuse myself—I hate you; which I had rather
You felt than make't my boast.

CLOTEN
You sin against
Obedience, which you owe your father. For
The contract you pretend with that base wretch,
One bred of alms and foster'd with cold dishes,
With scraps o' the court, it is no contract, none:
And though it be allow'd in meaner parties—
Yet who than he more mean?—to knit their souls,
On whom there is no more dependency
But brats and beggary, in self-figured knot;
Yet you are curb'd from that enlargement by
The consequence o' the crown, and must not soil
The precious note of it with a base slave.
A hilding for a livery, a squire's cloth,
A pantler, not so eminent.

IMOGEN
Profane fellow!
Wert thou the son of Jupiter and no more 142
But what thou art besides, thou wert too base
To be his groom: thou wert dignified enough,
Even to the point of envy, if 'twere made
Comparative for your virtues, to be styled
The under-hangman of his kingdom, and hated
For being preferred so well.

CLOTEN
The south-fog rot him!

IMOGEN
He never can meet more mischance than come
To be but named of thee. His meanest garment,
That ever hath but clipp'd his body, is dearer
In my respect than all the hairs above thee,
Were they all made such men. How now, Pisanio!

Enter PISANIO.

CLOTEN
'His garment!' Now the devil—

IMOGEN
To Dorothy my woman hie thee presently—

CLOTEN
'His garment!'

IMOGEN
I am sprited with a fool,
Frighted, and anger'd worse: go bid my woman
Search for a jewel that too casually
Hath left mine arm: it was thy master's: 'shrew me,
If I would lose it for a revenue
Of any king's in Europe. I do think
I saw't this morning: confident I am 164
Last night 'twas on mine arm; I kiss'd it:
I hope it be not gone to tell my lord
That I kiss aught but he.

PISANIO
'Twill not be lost.

IMOGEN
I hope so: go and search. [*Exit Pisanio.*

CLOTEN
You have abused me:
'His meanest garment!'

IMOGEN
Ay, I said so, sir:
If you will make't an action, call witness to't.

CLOTEN
I will inform your father.

IMOGEN
Your mother too:
She's my good lady, and will conceive, I hope,
But the worst of me. So, I leave you, sir.
To the worst of discontent. [*Exit.*

CLOTEN
I'll be revenged: 179
'His meanest garment!' Well. [*Exit.*

ACT TWO SCENE FOUR

Rome. Philario's house.

Enter POSTHUMUS *and* PHILARIO.

POSTHUMUS LEONATUS
Fear it not, sir: I would I were so sure
To win the king as I am bold her honour
Will remain hers.

PHILARIO
What means do you make to him?

POSTHUMUS LEONATUS
Not any, but abide the change of time,
Quake in the present winter's state and wish
That warmer days would come: in these sear'd hopes,
I barely gratify your love; they failing,
I must die much your debtor.

PHILARIO
Your very goodness and your company
O'erpays all I can do. By this, your king 12
Hath heard of great Augustus: Caius Lucius
Will do's commission throughly: and I think
He'll grant the tribute, send the arrearages,
Or look upon our Romans, whose remembrance
Is yet fresh in their grief.

POSTHUMUS LEONATUS
I do believe,

Statist though I am none, nor like to be,
That this will prove a war; and you shall hear
The legions now in Gallia sooner landed
In our not-fearing Britain than have tidings
Of any penny tribute paid. Our countrymen
Are men more order'd than when Julius Caesar
Smiled at their lack of skill, but found their courage
Worthy his frowning at: their discipline,
Now mingled with their courages, will make known
To their approvers they are people such
That mend upon the world.

Enter IACHIMO.

PHILARIO
See! Iachimo!

POSTHUMUS LEONATUS
The swiftest harts have posted you by land;
And winds of all the comers kiss'd your sails,
To make your vessel nimble.

PHILARIO
Welcome, sir.

POSTHUMUS LEONATUS
I hope the briefness of your answer made 35
The speediness of your return.

IACHIMO
Your lady
Is one of the fairest that I have look'd upon.

POSTHUMUS LEONATUS
And therewithal the best; or let her beauty
Look through a casement to allure false hearts
And be false with them.

IACHIMO
Here are letters for you.

POSTHUMUS LEONATUS
Their tenor good, I trust.

IACHIMO
'Tis very like.

PHILARIO
Was Caius Lucius in the Britain court
When you were there?

IACHIMO
He was expected then,
But not approach'd.

POSTHUMUS LEONATUS
All is well yet. 49
Sparkles this stone as it was wont? or is't not
Too dull for your good wearing?

IACHIMO
If I had lost it,
I should have lost the worth of it in gold.
I'll make a journey twice as far, to enjoy
A second night of such sweet shortness which
Was mine in Britain, for the ring is won.

POSTHUMUS LEONATUS
The stone's too hard to come by.

IACHIMO
Not a whit,
Your-lady being so easy.

POSTHUMUS LEONATUS
Make not, sir,
Your loss your sport: I hope you know that we
Must not continue friends.

IACHIMO
Good sir, we must,
If you keep covenant. Had I not brought 64
The knowledge of your mistress home, I grant
We were to question further: but I now
Profess myself the winner of her honour,
Together with your ring; and not the wronger
Of her or you, having proceeded but
By both your wills.

POSTHUMUS LEONATUS
If you can make't apparent
That you have tasted her in bed, my hand
And ring is yours; if not, the foul opinion
You had of her pure honour gains or loses 74
Your sword or mine, or masterless leaves both
To who shall find them.

IACHIMO
Sir, my circumstances,
Being so near the truth as I will make them,
Must first induce you to believe: whose strength
I will confirm with oath; which, I doubt not,
You'll give me leave to spare, when you shall find
You need it not.

POSTHUMUS LEONATUS
Proceed.

IACHIMO
First, her bedchamber,—
Where, I confess, I slept not, but profess
Had that was well worth watching—it was hang'd
With tapesty of silk and silver; the story
Proud Cleopatra, when she met her Roman, 88
And Cydnus swell'd above the banks, or for
The press of boats or pride: a piece of work
So bravely done, so rich, that it did strive
In workmanship and value; which I wonder'd
Could be so rarely and exactly wrought,
Since the true life on't was—

POSTHUMUS LEONATUS
This is true;
And this you might have heard of here, by me,
Or by some other.

IACHIMO
More particulars
Must justify my knowledge.

POSTHUMUS LEONATUS
So they must,
Or do your honour injury.

IACHIMO
The chimney 102
Is south the chamber, and the chimney-piece
Chaste Dian bathing: never saw I figures
So likely to report themselves: the cutter
Was as another nature, dumb; outwent her,
Motion and breath left out.
POSTHUMUS LEONATUS
This is a thing
Which you might for relation likewise reap,
Being, as it is, much spoke of.
IACHIMO
The roof o' the chamber
With golden cherubins is fretted: her andirons—
I had forgot them—were two winking Cupids
Of silver, each on one foot standing, nicely 114
Depending on their brands.
POSTHUMUS LEONATUS
This is her honour!
Let it be granted you have seen all this—and praise
Be given to your remembrance—the description
Of what is in her chamber nothing saves
The wager you have laid.
IACHIMO
Then, if you can, [*Showing the bracelet.*
Be pale: I beg but leave to air this jewel; see!
And now 'tis up again: it must be married
To that your diamond; I'll keep them.
POSTHUMUS LEONATUS
Jove!
Once more let me behold it: is it that
Which I left with her?
IACHIMO
Sir—I thank her—that: 128
She stripp'd it from her arm; I see her yet;
Her pretty action did outsell her gift,
And yet enrich'd it too: she gave it me, and said
She prized it once.
POSTHUMUS LEONATUS
May be she pluck'd it off
To send it me.
IACHIMO
She writes so to you, doth she?
POSTHUMUS LEONATUS
O, no, no, no! 'tis true. Here, take this too;
[*Gives the ring.*
It is a basilisk unto mine eye,
Kills me to look on't. Let there be no honour
Where there is beauty; truth, where semblance; love,
Where there's another man: the vows of
women 141
Of no more bondage be, to where they are made,
Than they are to their virtues; which is nothing.
O, above measure false!
PHILARIO
Have patience, sir,
And take your ring again; 'tis not yet won:
It may be probable she lost it; or
Who knows if one of her women, being corrupted,
Hath stol'n it from her?
POSTHUMUS LEONATUS
Very true;
And so, I hope, he came by't. Back my ring:
Render to me some corporal sign about her,
More evident than this; for this was stolen.
IACHIMO
By Jupiter, I had it from her arm.
POSTHUMUS LEONATUS
Hark you, he swears; by Jupiter he swears.
'Tis true:— nay, keep the ring—'tis true: I am sure
She would not lose it: her attendants are
All sworn and honourable:—they induced to
steal it!
And by a stranger!—No, he hath enjoy'd her:
The cognizance of her incontinency
Is this: she hath bought the name of whore thus
dearly.
There, take thy hire; and all the fiends of hell
Divide themselves between you!
PHILARIO
Sir, be patient: 166
This is not strong enough to be believed
Of one persuaded well of—
POSTHUMUS LEONATUS
Never talk on't;
She hath been colted by him.
IACHIMO
If you seek
For further satisfying, under her breast—
Worthy the pressing—lies a mole, right proud
Of that most delicate lodging: by my life,
I kiss'd it; and it gave me present hunger.
To feed again, though full. You do remember
This stain upon her?
POSTHUMUS LEONATUS
Ay, and it doth confirm
Another stain, as big as hell can hold, 179
Were there no more but it.
IACHIMO
Will you hear more?
POSTHUMUS LEONATUS
Spare your arithmetic: never count the turns;
Once, and a million!
IACHIMO
I'll be sworn—
POSTHUMUS LEONATUS
No swearing.
If you will swear you have not done't, you lie;

And I will kill thee, if thou dost deny
Thou'st made me cuckold.

IACHIMO
I'll deny nothing.

POSTHUMUS LEONATUS
O, that I had her here, to tear her limb-meal!
I will go there and do't, i' the court, before
Her father. I'll do something— [*Exit.*

PHILARIO
Quite besides
The government of patience! You have won:
Let's follow him, and pervert the present wrath
He hath against himself.

IACHIMO
With an my heart. [*Exeunt.*

ACT TWO SCENE FIVE

Another room in Philario's house.

Enter POSTHUMUS.

POSTHUMUS LEONATUS
Is there no way for men to be but women
Must be half-workers? We are all bastards;
And that most venerable man which I
Did call my father, was I know not where
When I was stamp'd; some coiner with his tools
Made me a counterfeit: yet my mother seem'd
The Dian of that time: so doth my wife
The nonpareil of this. O, vengeance, vengeance!
Me of my lawful pleasure she restrain'd
And pray'd me oft forbearance; did it with
A pudency so rosy the sweet view on't
Might well have warm'd old Saturn; that I thought her
As chaste as unsunn'd snow. O, all the devils!
This yellow Iachimo, in an hour,—wast not?—
Or less,—at first?—perchance he spoke not, but,
Like a full-acorn'd boar, a German one,
Cried 'O!' and mounted; found no opposition
But what he look'd for should oppose and she
Should from encounter guard. Could I find out
The woman's part in me! For there's no motion
That tends to vice in man, but I affirm
It is the woman's part: be it lying, note it,
The woman's; flattering, hers; deceiving, hers;
Lust and rank thoughts, hers, hers; revenges, hers;
Ambitions, covetings, change of prides, disdain,
Nice longing, slanders, mutability,
All faults that may be named, nay that hell knows,
Why, hers, in part or all; but rather, all;
For even to vice
They are not constant, but are changing still
One vice, but of a minute old, for one
Not half so old as that. I'll write against them,
Detest them, curse them: yet 'tis greater skill
In a true hate, to pray they have their will:
The very devils cannot plague them better. [*Exit.*

ACT THREE SCENE ONE

Britain. A hall in Cymbeline's palace.

Enter in state, CYMBELINE, QUEEN , CLOTEN, *and* Lords *at one door, and at another*, CAIUS LUCIUS *and* Attendants.

CYMBELINE
Now say, what would Augustus Caesar with us?

CAIUS LUCIUS
When Julius Caesar, whose remembrance yet
Lives in men's eyes and will to ears and tongues
Be theme and hearing ever, was in this Britain
And conquer'd it, Cassibelan, thine uncle,—
Famous in Caesar's praises, no whit less
Than in his feats deserving it—for him
And his succession granted Rome a tribute,
Yearly three thousand pounds, which by these lately
Is left untender'd.

QUEEN
And, to kill the marvel,
Shall be so ever.

CLOTEN
There be many Caesars,
Ere such another Julius. Britain is
A world by itself; and we will nothing pay
For wearing our own noses.

QUEEN
That opportunity
Which then they had to take from 's, to resume
We have again. Remember, sir, my liege,
The kings your ancestors, together with
The natural bravery of your isle, which stands
As Neptune's park, ribbed and paled in
With rocks unscaleable and roaring waters, [18]
With sands that will not bear your enemies' boats,
But suck them up to the topmast. A kind of conquest
Caesar made here; but made not here his brag
Of 'Came' and 'saw' and 'overcame:' with shame—
The first that ever touch'd him—he was carried
From off our coast, twice beaten; and his shipping—
Poor ignorant baubles!—on our terrible seas,
Like egg-shells moved upon their surges, crack'd
As easily 'gainst our rocks: for joy whereof
The famed Cassibelan, who was once at point—
O giglot fortune!—to master Caesar's sword,
Made Lud's town with rejoicing fires bright
And Britons strut with courage.

CLOTEN

Come, there's no more tribute to be paid: our kingdom is stronger than it was at that time; and, as I said, there is no moe such Caesars: other of them may have crook'd noses, but to owe such straight arms, none.

CYMBELINE

Son, let your mother end.

CLOTEN

We have yet many among us can gripe as hard as Cassibelan: I do not say I am one; but I have a hand. Why tribute? why should we pay tribute? If Caesar can hide the sun from us with a blanket, or put the moon in his pocket, we will pay him tribute for light; else, sir, no more tribute, pray you now.

CYMBELINE

You must know,
Till the injurious Romans did extort
This tribute from us, we were free:
Caesar's ambition,
Which swell'd so much that it did almost stretch
The sides o' the world, against all colour here
Did put the yoke upon 's; which to shake off
Becomes a warlike people, whom we reckon
Ourselves to be.

CLOTEN and LORDS

We do. [19]

CYMBELINE

Say, then, to Caesar,
Our ancestor was that Mulmutius which
Ordain'd our laws, whose use the sword of Caesar
Hath too much mangled; whose repair and franchise
Shall, by the power we hold, be our good deed,
Though Rome be therefore angry: Mulmutius made our laws,
Who was the first of Britain which did put
His brows within a golden crown and call'd
Himself a king.

CAIUS LUCIUS

I am sorry, Cymbeline,
That I am to pronounce Augustus Caesar—
Caesar, that hath more kings his servants than
Thyself domestic officers—thine enemy:
Receive it from me, then: war and confusion
In Caesar's name pronounce I 'gainst thee: look
For fury not to be resisted. Thus defied,
I thank thee for myself.

CYMBELINE

Thou art welcome, Caius.
Thy Caesar knighted me; my youth I spent
Much under him; of him I gather'd honour;
Which he to seek of me again, perforce,
Behoves me keep at utterance. I am perfect
That the Pannonians and Dalmatians for
Their liberties are now in arms; a precedent
Which not to read would show the Britons cold:
So Caesar shall not find them.

CAIUS LUCIUS

Let proof speak.

CLOTEN

His majesty bids you welcome. Make pastime with us a day or two, or longer: if you seek us afterwards in other terms, you shall find us in our salt-water girdle: if you beat us out of it, it is yours; if you fall in the adventure, our crows shall fare the better for you; and there's an end.

CAIUS LUCIUS

So, sir.

CYMBELINE

I know your master's pleasure and he mine:
All the remain is 'Welcome!' [*Exeunt.*

ACT THREE SCENE TWO

Another room in the palace.

Enter PISANIO, *with a letter.*

PISANIO

How! of adultery? Wherefore write you not
What monster's her accuser? Leonatus!
O master! what a strange infection
Is fall'n into thy ear! What false Italian,
As poisonous-tongued as handed, hath prevail'd
On thy too ready hearing? Disloyal! No:
She's punish'd for her truth, and undergoes,
More goddess-like than wife-like, such assaults
As would take in some virtue. O my master!
Thy mind to her is now as low as were
Thy fortunes. How! that I should murder her?
Upon the love and truth and vows which I
Have made to thy command? I, her? her blood?
If it be so to do good service, never
Let me be counted serviceable. How look I,
That I should seem to lack humanity
So much as this fact comes to? [*Reading*] 'Do't: the letter
That I have sent her, by her own command
Shall give thee opportunity.' O damn'd paper!
Black as the ink that's on thee! Senseless bauble,
Art thou a feodary for this act, and look'st
So virgin-like without? Lo, here she comes.
I am ignorant in what I am commanded.

Enter IMOGEN.

IMOGEN

How now, Pisanio!

PISANIO

Madam, here is a letter from my lord.

IMOGEN
Who? thy lord? that is my lord, Leonatus!
O, learn'd indeed were that astronomer
That knew the stars as I his characters;
He'ld lay the future open. You good gods,
Let what is here contain'd relish of love, 32
Of my lord's health, of his content, yet not
That we two are asunder; let that grieve him:
Some griefs are med'cinable; that is one of them,
For it doth physic love: of his content,
All but in that! Good wax, thy leave. Blest be
You bees that make these locks of counsel! Lovers
And men in dangerous bonds pray not alike:
Though forfeiters you cast in prison, yet
You clasp young Cupid's tables. Good news, gods! 42

[*Reads*] 'Justice, and your father's wrath, should he take me in his dominion, could not be so cruel to me, as you O, the dearest of creatures, would even renew me with your eyes. Take notice that I am in Cambria, at Milford-Haven: what your own love will out of this advise you, follow. So he wishes you all happiness, that remains loyal to his vow, and your, increasing in love,

LEONATUS POSTHUMUS.

O, for a horse with wings! Hear'st thou, Pisanio?
He is at Milford-Haven: read, and tell me
How far 'tis thither. If one of mean affairs
May plod it in a week, why may not I
Glide thither in a day? Then, true Pisanio,—
Who long'st, like me, to see thy lord; who long'st,—
O, let me bate,—but not like me—yet long'st,
But in a fainter kind:—O, not like me;
For mine's beyond beyond—say, and speak thick;
Love's counsellor should fill the bores of hearing,
To the smothering of the sense—how far it is
To this same blessed Milford: and by the way
Tell me how Wales was made so happy as
To inherit such a haven: but first of all,
How we may steal from hence, and for the gap
That we shall make in time, from our hence-going
And our return, to excuse: but first, how get hence:
Why should excuse be born or e'er begot?
We'll talk of that hereafter. Prithee, speak,
How many score of miles may we well ride
'Twixt hour and hour?

PISANIO
One score 'twixt sun and sun,
Madam, 's enough for you: [*Aside*] and too much too. 73

IMOGEN
Why, one that rode to's execution, man,
Could never go so slow: I have heard of riding wagers,
Where horses have been nimbler than the sands
That run i' the clock's behalf. But this is foolery:
Go bid my woman feign a sickness; say
She'll home to her father: and provide me presently
A riding-suit, no costlier than would fit
A franklin's housewife.

PISANIO
Madam, you're best consider.

IMOGEN
I see before me, man: nor here, nor here, 84
Nor what ensues, but have a fog in them,
That I cannot look through. Away, I prithee;
Do as I bid thee: there's no more to say;
Accessible is none but Milford way. [*Exeunt.*

ACT THREE SCENE THREE

Wales: a mountainous country with a cave.

Enter, from the cave, BELARIUS; GUIDERIUS, *and* ARVIRAGUS *following.*

BELARIUS
A goodly day not to keep house, with such
Whose roof's as low as ours! Stoop, boys; this gate [20]
Instructs you how to adore the heavens and bows you
To a morning's holy office: the gates of monarchs
Are arch'd so high that giants may jet through
And keep their impious turbans on, without [21]
Good morrow to the sun. Hail, thou fair heaven!
We house i' the rock, yet use thee not so hardly
As prouder livers do.

GUIDERIUS
Hail, heaven!

ARVIRAGUS
Hail, heaven!

BELARIUS
Now for our mountain sport: up to yond hill; 13
Your legs are young; I'll tread these flats. Consider,
When you above perceive me like a crow,
That it is place which lessens and sets off:
And you may then revolve what tales I have told you
Of courts, of princes, of the tricks in war:
This service is not service, so being done.
But being so allow'd: to apprehend thus,
Draws us a profit from all things we see;
And often, to our comfort, shall we find
The sharded beetle in a safer hold 23
Than is the full-wing'd eagle. O, this life
Is nobler than attending for a check,
Richer than doing nothing for a bauble, [22]
Prouder than rustling in unpaid-for silk:
Such gain the cap of him that makes 'em fine,
Yet keeps his book uncross'd: no life to ours.

GUIDERIUS
Out of your proof you speak: we, poor unfledged,
Have never wing'd from view o' the nest, nor know not
What air's from home. Haply this life is best,
If quiet life be best; sweeter to you
That have a sharper known; well corresponding
With your stiff age: but unto us it is
A cell of ignorance; travelling a-bed;
A prison for a debtor, that not dares [23]
To stride a limit.

ARVIRAGUS
What should we speak of
When we are old as you? when we shall hear
The rain and wind beat dark December, how,
In this our pinching cave, shall we discourse
The freezing hours away? We have seen nothing;
We are beastly, subtle as the fox for prey,
Like warlike as the wolf for what we eat;
Our valour is to chase what flies; our cage
We make a quire, as doth the prison'd bird,
And sing our bondage freely.

BELARIUS
How you speak!
Did you but know the city's usuries
And felt them knowingly; the art o' the court,
As hard to leave as keep; whose top to climb
Is certain falling, or so slippery that
The fear's as bad as falling; the toil o' the war,
A pain that only seems to seek out danger
I' the name of fame and honour; which dies i' the search,
And hath as oft a slanderous epitaph
As record of fair act; nay, many times,
Doth ill deserve by doing well; what's worse,
Must court'sy at the censure:—O boys, this story
The world may read in me: my body's mark'd
With Roman swords, and my report was once
First with the best of note: Cymbeline loved me,
And when a soldier was the theme, my name
Was not far off: then was I as a tree
Whose boughs did bend with fruit: but in one night,
A storm or robbery, call it what you will,
Shook down my mellow hangings, nay, my leaves,
And left me bare to weather.

GUIDERIUS
Uncertain favour!

BELARIUS
My fault being nothing—as I have told you oft—
But that two villains, whose false oaths prevail'd
Before my perfect honour, swore to Cymbeline
I was confederate with the Romans: so
Follow'd my banishment, and this twenty years
This rock and these demesnes have been my world;
Where I have lived at honest freedom, paid
More pious debts to heaven than in all
The fore-end of my time. But up to the mountains!
This is not hunters' language: he that strikes
The venison first shall be the lord o' the feast;
To him the other two shall minister;
And we will fear no poison, which attends
In place of greater state. I'll meet you in the valleys.
[*Exeunt Guiderius and Arviragus.*
How hard it is to hide the sparks of nature!
These boys know little they are sons to the king;
Nor Cymbeline dreams that they are alive.
They think they are mine; and though train'd up thus meanly
I' the cave wherein they bow, their thoughts do hit [24]
The roofs of palaces, and nature prompts them
In simple and low things to prince it much
Beyond the trick of others. This Polydore,
The heir of Cymbeline and Britain, who
The king his father call'd Guiderius,—Jove!
When on my three-foot stool I sit and tell
The warlike feats I have done, his spirits fly out
Into my story: say 'Thus, mine enemy fell,
And thus I set my foot on 's neck;' even then
The princely blood flows in his cheek, he sweats,
Strains his young nerves and puts himself in posture
That acts my words. The younger brother, Cadwal,
Once Arviragus, in as like a figure,
Strikes life into my speech and shows much more
His own conceiving.—Hark, the game is roused!—
O Cymbeline! heaven and my conscience knows
Thou didst unjustly banish me: whereon,
At three and two years old, I stole these babes;
Thinking to bar thee of succession, as
Thou reft'st me of my lands. Euriphile,
Thou wast their nurse; they took thee for their mother,
And every day do honour to her grave:
Myself, Belarius, that am Morgan call'd,
They take for natural father. The game is up. [*Exit.*

ACT THREE SCENE FOUR

Country near Milford-Haven.

Enter PISANIO *and* IMOGEN.

IMOGEN
Thou told'st me, when we came from horse, the place
Was near at hand: ne'er long'd my mother so
To see me first, as I have now. Pisanio! man!
Where is Posthumus? What is in thy mind,

That makes thee stare thus? Wherefore breaks that sigh
From the inward of thee? One, but painted thus,
Would be interpreted a thing perplex'd
Beyond self-explication: put thyself
Into a haviour of less fear, ere wildness
Vanquish my staider senses. What's the matter?
Why tender'st thou that paper to me, with
A look untender? If't be summer news,
Smile to't before; if winterly, thou need'st
But keep that countenance still. My husband's hand!
That drug-damn'd Italy hath out-craftied him,
And he's at some hard point. Speak, man: thy tongue
May take off some extremity, which to read
Would be even mortal to me.

PISANIO
Please you, read;
And you shall find me, wretched man, a thing
The most disdain'd of fortune.

IMOGEN
[*Reads*] 'Thy mistress, Pisanio, hath played the strumpet in my bed; the testimonies whereof lie bleeding in me. I speak not out of weak surmises, but from proof as strong as my grief and as certain as I expect my revenge. That part thou, Pisanio, must act for me, if thy faith be not tainted with the breach of hers. Let thine own hands take away her life: I shall give thee opportunity at Milford-Haven. She hath my letter for the purpose: where, if thou fear to strike and to make me certain it is done, thou art the pandar to her dishonour and equally to me disloyal.'

PISANIO
What shall I need to draw my sword? the paper
Hath cut her throat already. No, 'tis slander,
Whose edge is sharper than the sword, whose tongue
Outvenoms all the worms of Nile, whose breath
Rides on the posting winds and doth belie
All corners of the world: kings, queens and states,
Maids, matrons, nay, the secrets of the grave
This viperous slander enters. What cheer, madam?

IMOGEN
False to his bed! What is it to be false?
To lie in watch there and to think on him?
To weep 'twixt clock and clock? if sleep charge nature,
To break it with a fearful dream of him
And cry myself awake? that's false to's bed, is it?

PISANIO
Alas, good lady!

IMOGEN
I false! Thy conscience witness: Iachimo,
Thou didst accuse him of incontinency;
Thou then look'dst like a villain; now methinks
Thy favour's good enough. Some jay of Italy
Whose mother was her painting, hath betray'd him: [25]
Poor I am stale, a garment out of fashion;
And, for I am richer than to hang by the walls,
I must be ripp'd:—to pieces with me!—O
Men's vows are women's traitors! All good seeming,
By thy revolt, O husband, shall be thought
Put on for villany; not born where't grows,
But worn a bait for ladies.

PISANIO
Good madam, hear me.

IMOGEN
True honest men being heard, like false Aeneas,
Were in his time thought false, and Sinon's weeping
Did scandal many a holy tear, took pity
From most true wretchedness: so thou, Posthumus,
Wilt lay the leaven on all proper men;
Goodly and gallant shall be false and perjured
From thy great fail. Come, fellow, be thou honest:
Do thou thy master's bidding: when thou see'st him,
A little witness my obedience: look!
I draw the sword myself: take it, and hit
The innocent mansion of my love, my heart:
Fear not; 'tis empty of all things but grief:
Thy master is not there, who was indeed
The riches of it: do his bidding; strike.
Thou mayst be valiant in a better cause;
But now thou seem'st a coward.

PISANIO
Hence, vile instrument!
Thou shalt not damn my hand.

IMOGEN
Why, I must die;
And if I do not by thy hand, thou art
No servant of thy master's. Against self-slaughter
There is a prohibition so divine
That cravens my weak hand. Come, here's my heart.
Something's afore't. Soft, soft! we'll no defence; [26]
Obedient as the scabbard. What is here?
The scriptures of the loyal Leonatus,
All turn'd to heresy? Away, away,
Corrupters of my faith! you shall no more
Be stomachers to my heart. Thus may poor fools
Believe false teachers: though those that are betray'd
Do feel the treason sharply, yet the traitor
Stands in worse case of woe.
And thou, Posthumus, thou that didst set up
My disobedience 'gainst the king my father
And make me put into contempt the suits
Of princely fellows, shalt hereafter find
It is no act of common passage, but

A strain of rareness: and I grieve myself
To think, when thou shalt be disedged by her
That now thou tirest on, how the memory
Will then be pang'd by me. Prithee, dispatch:
The lamb entreats the butcher: where's thy knife?
Thou art too slow to do thy master's bidding,
When I desire it too.

PISANIO
O gracious lady,
Since I received command to do this business
I have not slept one wink.

IMOGEN
Do't, and to bed then.

PISANIO
I'll wake mine eye-balls blind first. [27]

IMOGEN
Wherefore then
Didst undertake it? Why hast thou abused
So many miles with a pretence? this place?
Mine action and thine own? our horses' labour?
The time inviting thee? the perturb'd court,
For my being absent? whereunto I never
Purpose return. Why hast thou gone so far,
To be unbent when thou hast ta'en thy stand,
The elected deer before thee?

PISANIO
But to win time
To lose so bad employment; in the which
I have consider'd of a course. Good lady,
Hear me with patience.

IMOGEN
Talk thy tongue weary; speak:
I have heard I am a strumpet; and mine ear,
Therein false struck, can take no greater wound,
Nor tent to bottom that. But speak.

PISANIO
Then, madam,
I thought you would not back again.

IMOGEN
Most like;
Bringing me here to kill me.

PISANIO
Not so, neither:
But if I were as wise as honest, then
My purpose would prove well. It cannot be
But that my master is abused:
Some villain, ay, and singular in his art,
Hath done you both this cursed injury.

IMOGEN
Some Roman courtezan.

PISANIO
No, on my life.
I'll give but notice you are dead and send him
Some bloody sign of it; for 'tis commanded
I should do so: you shall be miss'd at court,
And that will well confirm it.

IMOGEN
Why good fellow,
What shall I do the while? where bide? how live?
Or in my life what comfort, when I am
Dead to my husband?

PISANIO
If you'll back to the court—

IMOGEN
No court, no father; nor no more ado
With that harsh, noble, simple nothing, [28]
That Cloten, whose love-suit hath been to me
As fearful as a siege.

PISANIO
If not at court,
Then not in Britain must you bide.

IMOGEN
Where then? [29]
Hath Britain all the sun that shines? Day, night,
Are they not but in Britain? I' the world's volume
Our Britain seems as of it, but not in 't;
In a great pool a swan's nest: prithee, think
There's livers out of Britain.

PISANIO
I am most glad
You think of other place. The ambassador,
Lucius the Roman, comes to Milford-Haven
To-morrow: now, if you could wear a mind
Dark as your fortune is, and but disguise
That which, to appear itself, must not yet be
But by self-danger, you should tread a course
Pretty and full of view; yea, haply, near
The residence of Posthumus; so nigh at least
That though his actions were not visible, yet
Report should render him hourly to your ear
As truly as he moves.

IMOGEN
O, for such means!
Though peril to my modesty, not death on't,
I would adventure.

PISANIO
Well, then, here's the point:
You must forget to be a woman; change
Command into obedience: fear and niceness—
The handmaids of all women, or, more truly,
Woman its pretty self—into a waggish courage:
Ready in gibes, quick-answer'd, saucy and
As quarrelous as the weasel; nay, you must
Forget that rarest treasure of your cheek,
Exposing it—but, O, the harder heart!
Alack, no remedy!—to the greedy touch

Of common-kissing Titan, and forget
Your laboursome and dainty trims, wherein
You made great Juno angry.

IMOGEN
Nay, be brief:
I see into thy end, and am almost
A man already.

PISANIO
First, make yourself but like one. 199
Fore-thinking this, I have already fit—
'Tis in my cloak-bag—doublet, hat, hose, all
That answer to them: would you in their serving,
And with what imitation you can borrow
From youth of such a season, 'fore noble Lucius
Present yourself, desire his service, tell him
Wherein you're happy,—which you'll make him know, 30
If that his head have ear in music,—doubtless
With joy he will embrace you, for he's honourable
And doubling that, most holy. Your means abroad. 211
You have me, rich; and I will never fail
Beginning nor supplyment.

IMOGEN
Thou art all the comfort
The gods will diet me with. Prithee, away:
There's more to be consider'd; but we'll even
All that good time will give us: this attempt
I am soldier to, and will abide it with
A prince's courage. Away, I prithee.

PISANIO
Well, madam, we must take a short farewell,
Lest, being miss'd, I be suspected of
Your carriage from the court. My noble mistress, 223
Here is a box; I had it from the queen:
What's in't is precious; if you are sick at sea,
Or stomach-qualm'd at land, a dram of this
Will drive away distemper. To some shade,
And fit you to your manhood. May the gods
Direct you to the best!

IMOGEN
Amen: I thank thee. [*Exeunt, severally.*

ACT THREE SCENE FIVE

A room in Cymbeline's palace.

Enter CYMBELINE, QUEEN, CLOTEN, LUCIUS, Lords, *and* Attendants.

CYMBELINE
Thus far; and so farewell.

CAIUS LUCIUS
Thanks, royal sir.
My emperor hath wrote, I must from hence;
And am right sorry that I must report ye
My master's enemy.

CYMBELINE
Our subjects, sir,
Will not endure his yoke; and for ourself
To show less sovereignty than they, must needs
Appear unkinglike.

CAIUS LUCIUS
So, sir; I desire of you
A conduct over-land to Milford-Haven.
Madam, all joy befal your grace!

QUEEN
And you!

CYMBELINE
My lords, you are appointed for that office; 14
The due of honour in no point omit.
So farewell, noble Lucius.

CAIUS LUCIUS
Your hand, my lord.

CLOTEN
Receive it friendly; but from this time forth
I wear it as your enemy.

CAIUS LUCIUS
Sir, the event
Is yet to name the winner: fare you well.

CYMBELINE
Leave not the worthy Lucius, good my lords,
Till he have cross'd the Severn. Happiness! [*Exeunt Lucius and Lords.*

QUEEN
He goes hence frowning: but it honours us
That we have given him cause.

CLOTEN
'Tis all the better;
Your valiant Britons have their wishes in it.

CYMBELINE
Lucius hath wrote already to the emperor
How it goes here. It fits us therefore ripely
Our chariots and our horsemen be in readiness:
The powers that he already hath in Gallia
Will soon be drawn to head, from whence he moves
His war for Britain.

QUEEN
'Tis not sleepy business;
But must be look'd to speedily and strongly.

CYMBELINE
Our expectation that it would be thus
Hath made us forward. But, my gentle queen,
Where is our daughter? She hath not appear'd 38
Before the Roman, nor to us hath tender'd
The duty of the day: she looks us like
A thing more made of malice than of duty:
We have noted it. Call her before us; for
We have been too slight in sufferance.
[*Exit an Attendant.*

QUEEN
Royal sir,
Since the exile of Posthumus, most retired
Hath her life been; the cure whereof, my lord,
'Tis time must do. Beseech your majesty,
Forbear sharp speeches to her: she's a lady
So tender of rebukes that words are strokes
And strokes death to her.

Re-enter Attendant.

CYMBELINE
Where is she, sir? How
Can her contempt be answer'd?
ATTENDANT
Please you, sir,
Her chambers are all lock'd; and there's no answer
That will be given to the loudest noise we make. [31]
QUEEN
My lord, when last I went to visit her,
She pray'd me to excuse her keeping close,
Whereto constrain'd by her infirmity,
She should that duty leave unpaid to you,
Which daily she was bound to proffer: this
She wish'd me to make known; but our great court
Made me to blame in memory.
CYMBELINE
Her doors lock'd?
Not seen of late? Grant, heavens, that which I fear
Prove false! [*Exit.*
QUEEN
Son, I say, follow the king.
CLOTEN
That man of hers, Pisanio, her old servant,
I have not seen these two days.
QUEEN
Go, look after. [*Exit Cloten.*
Pisanio, thou that stand'st so for Posthumus!
He hath a drug of mine; I pray his absence
Proceed by swallowing that, for he believes
It is a thing most precious. But for her,
Where is she gone? Haply, despair hath seized her,
Or, wing'd with fervour of her love, she's flown
To her desired Posthumus: gone she is
To death or to dishonour; and my end
Can make good use of either: she being down,
I have the placing of the British crown.

Re-enter CLOTEN.

How now, my son!
CLOTEN
'Tis certain she is fled.
Go in and cheer the king: he rages; none
Dare come about him.
QUEEN
[*Aside*] All the better: may
This night forestall him of the coming day! [*Exit.*
CLOTEN
I love and hate her: for she's fair and royal,
And that she hath all courtly parts more exquisite
Than lady, ladies, woman; from every one [32]
The best she hath, and she, of all compounded,
Outsells them all; I love her therefore: but
Disdaining me and throwing favours on
The low Posthumus slanders so her judgement
That what's else rare is choked; and in that point
I will conclude to hate her, nay, indeed,
To be revenged upon her. For when fools
Shall—

Enter PISANIO.

Who is here? What, are you packing, sirrah?
Come hither: ah, you precious pander! Villain,
Where is thy lady? In a word; or else
Thou art straightway with the fiends.
PISANIO
O, my good lord!
CLOTEN
Where is thy lady? or, by Jupiter,—
I will not ask again. Close villain,
I'll have this secret from thy heart, or rip
Thy heart to find it. Is she with Posthumus?
From whose so many weights of baseness cannot
A dram of worth be drawn.
PISANIO
Alas, my lord,
How can she be with him? When was she miss'd?
He is in Rome.
CLOTEN
Where is she, sir? Come nearer;
No further halting: satisfy me home
What is become of her.
PISANIO
O, my all-worthy lord!
CLOTEN
All-worthy villain!
Discover where thy mistress is at once,
At the next word: no more of 'worthy lord!'
Speak, or thy silence on the instant is
Thy condemnation and thy death.
PISANIO
Then, sir,
This paper is the history of my knowledge
Touching her flight. [*Presenting a letter.*
CLOTEN
Let's see't. I will pursue her
Even to Augustus' throne.

PISANIO
[*Aside*] Or this, or perish.
She's far enough; and what he learns by this
May prove his travel, not her danger.

CLOTEN
Hum!

PISANIO
[*Aside*] I'll write to my lord she's dead. O Imogen,
Safe mayst thou wander, safe return again!

CLOTEN
Sirrah, is this letter true?

PISANIO
Sir, as I think.

CLOTEN
It is Posthumus' hand; I know't. Sirrah, if thou wouldst not be a villain, but do me true service, undergo those employments wherein I should have cause to use thee with a serious industry, that is, what villany soe'er I bid thee do, to perform it directly and truly, I would think thee an honest man: thou shouldst neither want my means for thy relief nor my voice for thy preferment.

PISANIO
Well, my good lord.

CLOTEN
Wilt thou serve me? for since patiently and constantly thou hast stuck to the bare fortune of that beggar Posthumus, thou canst not, in the course of gratitude, but be a diligent follower of mine: wilt thou serve me?

PISANIO
Sir, I will.

CLOTEN
Give me thy hand; here's my purse. Hast any of thy late master's garments in thy possession?

PISANIO
I have, my lord, at my lodging, the same suit he wore when he took leave of my lady and mistress.

CLOTEN
The first service thou dost me, fetch that suit hither: let it be thy service; go.

PISANIO
I shall, my lord. [*Exit.*

CLOTEN
Meet thee at Milford-Haven!—I forgot to ask him one thing; I'll remember't anon:—even there, thou villain Posthumus, will I kill thee. I would these garments were come. She said upon a time— the bitterness of it I now belch from my heart—that she held the very garment of Posthumus in more respect than my noble and natural person together with the adornment of my qualities. With that suit upon my back, will I ravish her: first kill him, and in her eyes; there shall she see my valour, which will then be a torment to her contempt. He on the ground, my speech of insultment ended on his dead body, and when my lust hath dined,—which, as I say, to vex her I will execute in the clothes that she so praised,—to the court I'll knock her back, foot her home again. She hath despised me rejoicingly, and I'll be merry in my revenge.

Re-enter PISANIO, *with the clothes.*

Be those the garments?

PISANIO
Ay, my noble lord.

CLOTEN
How long is't since she went to Milford-Haven?

PISANIO
She can scarce be there yet.

CLOTEN
Bring this apparel to my chamber; that is the second thing that I have commanded thee: the third is, that thou wilt be a voluntary mute to my design. Be but duteous, and true preferment shall tender itself to thee. My revenge is now at Milford: would I had wings to follow it! Come, and be true. [*Exit.*

PISANIO
Thou bid'st me to my loss: for true to thee
Were to prove false, which I will never be,
To him that is most true. To Milford go,
And find not her whom thou pursuest. Flow, flow,
You heavenly blessings, on her! This fool's speed
Be cross'd with slowness; labour be his meed! [*Exit.*

ACT THREE SCENE SIX

Wales. Before the cave of Belarius.

Enter IMOGEN, *in boy's clothes.*

IMOGEN
I see a man's life is a tedious one:
I have tired myself, and for two nights together
Have made the ground my bed. I should be sick,
But that my resolution helps me. Milford,
When from the mountain-top Pisanio show'd thee,
Thou wast within a ken: O Jove! I think
Foundations fly the wretched; such, I mean,
Where they should be relieved. Two beggars told me
I could not miss my way: will poor folks lie,
That have afflictions on them, knowing 'tis
A punishment or trial? Yes; no wonder,
When rich ones scarce tell true. To lapse in fulness
Is sorer than to lie for need, and falsehood
Is worse in kings than beggars. My dear lord!
Thou art one o' the false ones. Now I think on thee,
My hunger's gone; but even before, I was
At point to sink for food. But what is this?

Here is a path to't: 'tis some savage hold:
I were best not to call; I dare not call: yet famine,
Ere clean it o'erthrow nature, makes it valiant,
Plenty and peace breeds cowards: hardness ever
Of hardiness is mother. Ho! who's here?
If any thing that's civil, speak; if savage,
Take or lend. Ho! No answer? Then I'll enter.
Best draw my sword: and if mine enemy
But fear the sword like me, he'll scarcely look on't.
Such a foe, good heavens! [*Exit, to the cave.*

Enter BELARIUS, GUIDERIUS, *and* ARVIRAGUS.

BELARIUS
You, Polydote, have proved best woodman and
Are master of the feast: Cadwal and I
Will play the cook and servant; 'tis our match:
The sweat of industry would dry and die,
But for the end it works to. Come; our stomachs
Will make what's homely savoury: weariness
Can snore upon the flint, when resty sloth
Finds the down pillow hard. Now peace be here,
Poor house, that keep'st thyself!

GUIDERIUS
I am thoroughly weary.

ARVIRAGUS
I am weak with toil, yet strong in appetite.

GUIDERIUS
There is cold meat i' the cave; we'll browse on that,
Whilst what we have kill'd be cook'd.

BELARIUS
[*Looking into the cave*] Stay; not in.
But that it eats our victuals, I should think
Here were a fairy.

GUIDERIUS
What's the matter, sir?

BELARIUS
By Jupiter, an angel! or, if not,
An earthly paragon! Behold divineness
No elder than a boy!

Re-enter IMOGEN.

IMOGEN
Good masters, harm me not:
Before I enter'd here, I call'd; and thought
To have begg'd or bought what I have took: good troth,
I have stol'n nought, nor would not, though I had found
Gold strew'd i' the floor. Here's money for my meat:
I would have left it on the board so soon
As I had made my meal, and parted
With prayers for the provider.

GUIDERIUS
Money, youth?

ARVIRAGUS
All gold and silver rather turn to dirt!
As 'tis no better reckon'd, but of those
Who worship dirty gods.

IMOGEN
I see you're angry:
Know, if you kill me for my fault, I should
Have died had I not made it.

BELARIUS
Whither bound?

IMOGEN
To Milford-Haven.

BELARIUS
What's your name? 67

IMOGEN
Fidele, sir. I have a kinsman who
Is bound for Italy; he embark'd at Milford;
To whom being going, almost spent with hunger,
I am fall'n in this offence.

BELARIUS
Prithee, fair youth,
Think us no churls, nor measure our good minds
By this rude place we live in. Well encounter'd!
'Tis almost night: you shall have better cheer
Ere you depart; and thanks to stay and eat it.
Boys, bid him welcome.

GUIDERIUS
Were you a woman, youth,
I should woo hard but be your groom. In honesty, 80
I bid for you as I'ld buy. [33]

ARVIRAGUS
I'll make't my comfort
He is a man; I'll love him as my brother:
And such a welcome as I'ld give to him
After long absence, such is yours: most welcome!
Be sprightly, for you fall 'mongst friends.

IMOGEN
'Mongst friends,
If brothers. [*Aside*] Would it had been so, that they
Had been my father's sons! then had my prize
Been less, and so more equal ballasting
To thee, Posthumus.

BELARIUS
He wrings at some distress.

GUIDERIUS
Would I could free't!

ARVIRAGUS
Or I, whate'er it be, 94
What pain it cost, what danger. Gods!

BELARIUS
Hark, boys! [*Whispering.*

IMOGEN
Great men,
That had a court no bigger than this cave,
That did attend themselves and had the virtue
Which their own conscience seal'd them—laying by
That nothing-gift of differing multitudes—
Could not out-peer these twain. Pardon me, gods!
I'ld change my sex to be companion with them,
Since Leonatus's false.

BELARIUS
It shall be so.
Boys, we'll go dress our hunt. Fair youth, come in: 108
Discourse is heavy, fasting; when we have supp'd,
We'll mannerly demand thee of thy story,
So far as thou wilt speak it.

GUIDERIUS
Pray, draw near.

ARVIRAGUS
The night to the owl and morn to the lark less welcome.

IMOGEN
Thanks, sir.

ARVIRAGUS
I pray, draw near. [*Exeunt.*

ACT THREE SCENE SEVEN

Rome. A public place.

Enter two Senators *and* Tribunes.

FIRST SENATOR
This is the tenor of the emperor's writ:
That since the common men are now in action
'Gainst the Pannonians and Dalmatians,
And that the legions now in Gallia are
Full weak to undertake our wars against
The fall'n-off Britons, that we do incite
The gentry to this business. He creates
Lucius proconsul: and to you the tribunes,
For this immediate levy, he commands [34]
His absolute commission. Long live Caesar!

FIRST TRIBUNE
Is Lucius general of the forces?

SECOND SENATOR
Ay.

FIRST TRIBUNE
Remaining now in Gallia?

FIRST SENATOR
With those legions
Which I have spoke of, whereunto your levy
Must be supplyant: the words of your commission
Will tie you to the numbers and the time
Of their dispatch.

FIRST TRIBUNE
We will discharge our duty. [*Exeunt.*

ACT FOUR SCENE ONE

Wales: near the cave of Belarius.

Enter CLOTEN.

CLOTEN
I am near to the place where they should meet, if Pisanio have mapped it truly. How fit his garments serve me! Why should his mistress, who was made by him that made the tailor, not be fit too? the rather—saving reverence of the word—for 'tis said a woman's fitness comes by fits. Therein I must play the workman. I dare speak it to myself—for it is not vain-glory for a man and his glass to confer in his own chamber—I mean, the lines of my body are as well drawn as his; no less young, more strong, not beneath him in fortunes, beyond him in the advantage of the time, above him in birth, alike conversant in general services, and more remarkable in single oppositions: yet this imperceiverant thing loves him in my despite. What mortality is! Posthumus, thy head, which now is growing upon thy shoulders, shall within this hour be off; thy mistress enforced; thy garments cut to pieces before thy face: and all this done, spurn her home to her father; who may haply be a little angry for my so rough usage; but my mother, having power of his testiness, shall turn all into my commendations. My horse is tied up safe: out, sword, and to a sore purpose! Fortune, put them into my hand! This is the very description of their meeting-place; and the fellow dares not deceive me. [*Exit.*

ACT FOUR SCENE TWO

Before the cave of Belarius.

Enter, from the cave, BELARIUS, GUIDERIUS, ARVIRAGUS, *and* IMOGEN.

BELARIUS
[*To Imogen*] You are not well: remain here in the cave;
We'll come to you after hunting.

ARVIRAGUS
[*To Imogen*] Brother, stay here:
Are we not brothers?

IMOGEN
So man and man should be;
But clay and clay differs in dignity,
Whose dust is both alike. I am very sick.

GUIDERIUS
Go you to hunting; I'll abide with him.
IMOGEN
So sick I am not, yet I am not well;
But not so citizen a wanton as
To seem to die ere sick: so please you, leave me;
Stick to your journal course: the breach of custom 14
Is breach of all. I am ill, but your being by me
Cannot amend me; society is no comfort
To one not sociable: I am not very sick,
Since I can reason of it. Pray you, trust me here:
I'll rob none but myself; and let me die,
Stealing so poorly.
GUIDERIUS
I love thee; I have spoke it:
How much the quantity, the weight as much,
As I do love my father.
BELARIUS
What! how! how!
ARVIRAGUS
If it be sin to say so, I yoke me
In my good brother's fault: I know not why
I love this youth; and I have heard you say,
Love's reason's without reason: the bier at door,
And a demand who is't shall die, I'ld say
'My father, not this youth.'
BELARIUS
[*Aside*] O noble strain!
O worthiness of nature! breed of greatness!
Cowards father cowards and base things sire base:
Nature hath meal and bran, contempt and grace.
I'm not their father; yet who this should be,
Doth miracle itself, loved before me.
'Tis the ninth hour o' the morn.
ARVIRAGUS
Brother, farewell. 38
IMOGEN
I wish ye sport.
ARVIRAGUS
You health. So please you, sir.
IMOGEN
[*Aside*] These are kind creatures. Gods, what lies
I have heard!
Our courtiers say all's savage but at court:
Experience, O, thou disprovest report!
The imperious seas breed monsters, for the dish
Poor tributary rivers as sweet fish.
I am sick still; heart-sick. Pisanio,
I'll now taste of thy drug. [*Swallows some.*
GUIDERIUS
I could not stir him:
He said he was gentle, but unfortunate;
Dishonestly afflicted, but yet honest. 51
ARVIRAGUS
Thus did he answer me: yet said, hereafter
I might know more.
BELARIUS
To the field, to the field!
We'll leave you for this time: go in and rest.
ARVIRAGUS
We'll not be long away.
BELARIUS
Pray, be not sick,
For you must be our housewife.
IMOGEN
Well or ill,
I am bound to you.
BELARIUS
And shalt be ever. [*Exit Imogen, to the cave.*
This youth, how'er distress'd, appears he hath had
Good ancestors.
ARVIRAGUS
How angel-like he sings!
GUIDERIUS
But his neat cookery! he cut our roots
In characters,
And sauced our broths, as Juno had been sick
And he her dieter.
ARVIRAGUS
Nobly he yokes 69
A smiling with a sigh, as if the sigh
Was that it was, for not being such a smile;
The smile mocking the sigh, that it would fly
From so divine a temple, to commix
With winds that sailors rail at.
GUIDERIUS
I do note
That grief and patience, rooted in him both,
Mingle their spurs together.
ARVIRAGUS
Grow, patience!
And let the stinking elder, grief, untwine
His perishing root with the increasing vine!
BELARIUS
It is great morning. Come, away!—
Who's there?

Enter CLOTEN.

CLOTEN
I cannot find those runagates; that villain
Hath mock'd me. I am faint.
BELARIUS
'Those runagates!'
Means he not us? I partly know him: 'tis
Cloten, the son o' the queen. I fear some ambush.
I saw him not these many years, and yet
I know 'tis he. We are held as outlaws: hence!

GUIDERIUS
He is but one: you and my brother search
What companies are near: pray you, away;
Let me alone with him. [*Exeunt Belarius and Arviragus.*

CLOTEN
Soft! What are you 93
That fly me thus? some villain mountaineers?
I have heard of such. What slave art thou?

GUIDERIUS
A thing
More slavish did I ne'er than answering
A slave without a knock.

CLOTEN
Thou art a robber,
A law-breaker, a villain: yield thee, thief.

GUIDERIUS
To who? to thee? What art thou? Have not I
An arm as big as thine? a heart as big?
Thy words, I grant, are bigger, for I wear not
My dagger in my mouth. Say what thou art
Why I should yield to thee?

CLOTEN
Thou villain base, 106
Know'st me not by my clothes?

GUIDERIUS
No, nor thy tailor, rascal,
Who is thy grandfather: he made those clothes,
Which, as it seems, make thee.

CLOTEN
Thou precious varlet,
My tailor made them not.

GUIDERIUS
Hence, then, and thank
The man that gave them thee. Thou art some fool;
I am loath to beat thee.

CLOTEN
Thou injurious thief,
Hear but my name, and tremble.

GUIDERIUS
What's thy name?

CLOTEN
Cloten, thou villain.

GUIDERIUS
Cloten, thou double villain, be thy name,
I cannot tremble at it: were it Toad, or
Adder, Spider, 122
'Twould move me sooner.

CLOTEN
To thy further fear,
Nay, to thy mere confusion, thou shalt know
I am son to the queen.

GUIDERIUS
I am sorry for 't; not seeming
So worthy as thy birth.

CLOTEN
Art not afeard?

GUIDERIUS
Those that I reverence those I fear, the wise:
At fools I laugh, not fear them.

CLOTEN
Die the death:
When I have slain thee with my proper hand,
I'll follow those that even now fled hence,
And on the gates of Lud's-town set your heads:
Yield, rustic mountaineer. 136
[*Exeunt, fighting.*

Re-enter BELARIUS *and* ARVIRAGUS.

BELARIUS
No companies abroad?

ARVIRAGUS
None in the world: you did mistake him, sure.

BELARIUS
I cannot tell: long is it since I saw him,
But time hath nothing blurr'd those lines of favour
Which then he wore; the snatches in his voice,
And burst of speaking, were as his: I am absolute
'Twas very Cloten.

ARVIRAGUS
In this place we left them:
I wish my brother make good time with him,
You say he is so fell.

BELARIUS
Being scarce made up,
I mean, to man, he had not apprehension 148
Of roaring terrors; for the effect of judgement
Is oft the cause of fear. But, see, thy brother.

Re-enter GUIDERIUS, *with* CLOTEN'S *head.*

GUIDERIUS
This Cloten was a fool, an empty purse;
There was no money in't: not Hercules
Could have knock'd out his brains, for he had none:
Yet I not doing this, the fool had borne
My head as I do his.

BELARIUS
What hast thou done?

GUIDERIUS
I am perfect what: cut off one Cloten's head,
Son to the queen, after his own report;
Who call'd me traitor, mountaineer, and swore
With his own single hand he'ld take us in
Displace our heads where — thank the gods!—they grow,
And set them on Lud's-town.

BELARIUS
We are all undone.

GUIDERIUS
Why, worthy father, what have we to lose,
But that he swore to take, our lives? The law

Protects not us: then why should we be tender
To let an arrogant piece of flesh threat us,
Play judge and executioner all himself,
For we do fear the law? What company
Discover you abroad?

BELARIUS
No single soul 172
Can we set eye on; but in all safe reason
He must have some attendants. Though his humour [35]
Was nothing but mutation, ay, and that
From one bad thing to worse; not frenzy, not
Absolute madness could so far have raved
To bring him here alone; although perhaps
It may be heard at court that such as we
Cave here, hunt here, are outlaws, and in time
May make some stronger head; the which he hearing—
As it is like him—might break out, and swear
He'ld fetch us in; yet is't not probable 185
To come alone, either he so undertaking,
Or they so suffering: then on good ground we fear,
If we do fear this body hath a tail
More perilous than the head.

ARVIRAGUS
Let ordinance
Come as the gods foresay it: howsoe'er,
My brother hath done well.

BELARIUS
I had no mind
To hunt this day: the boy Fidele's sickness
Did make my way long forth.

GUIDERIUS
With his own sword,
Which he did wave against my throat, I have ta'en 198
His head from him: I'll throw't into the creek
Behind our rock; and let it to the sea,
And tell the fishes he's the queen's son, Cloten:
That's all I reck. [*Exit.*

BELARIUS
I fear 'twill be revenged:
Would, Polydote, thou hadst not done't! though valour
Becomes thee well enough.

ARVIRAGUS
Would I had done't
So the revenge alone pursued me! Polydore,
I love thee brotherly, but envy much
Thou hast robb'd me of this deed: I would revenges,
That possible strength might meet, would seek us through 212
And put us to our answer.

BELARIUS
Well, 'tis done:
We'll hunt no more to-day, nor seek for danger
Where's there no profit. I prithee, to our rock;
You and Fidele play the cooks: I'll stay
Till hasty Polydote return, and bring him
To dinner presently.

ARVIRAGUS
Poor sick Fidele!
I'll weringly to him: to gain his colour
I'ld let a parish of such Clotens blood, [36]
And praise myself for charity. [*Exit.*

BELARIUS
O thou goddess, 224
Thou divine Nature, how thyself thou blazon'st
In these two princely boys! They are as gentle
As zephyrs blowing below the violet,
Not wagging his sweet head; and yet as rough,
Their royal blood enchafed, as the rudest wind,
That by the top doth take the mountain pine,
And make him stoop to the vale. 'Tis wonder
That an invisible instinct should frame them
To royalty unlearn'd, honour untaught,
Civility not seen from other, valour
That wildly grows in them, but yields a crop
As if it had been sow'd. Yet still it's strange
What Cloten's being here to us portends,
Or what his death will bring us.

Re-enter GUIDERIUS.

GUIDERIUS
Where's my brother?
I have sent Cloten's clotpoll down the stream,
In embassy to his mother: his body's hostage
For his return. [*Solemn music.*

BELARIUS
My ingenious instrument!
Hark, Polydore, it sounds! But what occasion
Hath Cadwal now to give it motion? Hark!

GUIDERIUS
Is he at home?

BELARIUS
He went hence even now.

GUIDERIUS
What does he mean? since death of my dear'st mother 249
It did not speak before. All solemn things
Should answer solemn accidents. The matter?
Triumphs for nothing and lamenting toys
Is jollity for apes and grief for boys.
Is Cadwal mad?

BELARIUS
Look, here he comes,
And brings the dire occasion in his arms
Of what we blame him for.

Re-enter ARVIRAGUS, *with* IMOGEN, *as dead, bearing her in his arms.*

ARVIRAGUS
The bird is dead.
That we have made so much on. I had rather
Have skipp'd from sixteen years of age to sixty,
To have turn'd my leaping-time into a crutch,
Than have seen this.

GUIDERIUS
O sweetest, fairest lily! 263
My brother wears thee not the one half so well
As when thou grew'st thyself.

BELARIUS
O melancholy!
Who ever yet could sound thy bottom? find
The ooze, to show what coast thy sluggish crare
Might easiliest harbour in? Thou blessed thing!
Jove knows what man thou might'st have made; but I,
Thou diedst, a most rare boy, of melancholy.
How found you him?

ARVIRAGUS
Stark, as you see:
Thus smiling, as some fly hid tickled slumber,
Not as death's dart, being laugh'd at; his right cheek 277
Reposing on a cushion.

GUIDERIUS
Where?

ARVIRAGUS
O' the floor;
His arms thus leagued: I thought he slept, and put
My clouted brogues from off my feet, whose rudeness
Answer'd my steps too loud.

GUIDERIUS
Why, he but sleeps:
If he be gone, he'll make his grave a bed;
With female fairies will his tomb be haunted,
And worms will not come to thee.

ARVIRAGUS
With fairest flowers
Whilst summer lasts and I live here, Fidele,
I'll sweeten thy sad grave: thou shalt not lack
The flower that's like thy face, pale primrose, nor 292

ARVIRAGUS The bird is dead. That we have made so much on.

The azured harebell, like thy veins, no, nor
The leaf of eglantine, whom not to slander, [37]
Out-sweeten'd not thy breath: the ruddock would,
With charitable bill,—O bill, sore-shaming
Those rich-left heirs that let their fathers lie
Without a monument!—bring thee all this;
Yea, and furr'd moss besides, when flowers are none,
To winter-ground thy corse.

GUIDERIUS
Prithee, have done;
And do not play in wench-like words with that
Which is so serious. Let us bury him,
And not protract with admiration what
Is now due debt. To the grave!

ARVIRAGUS
Say, where shall's lay him?

GUIDERIUS
By good Euriphile, our mother.

ARVIRAGUS
Be't so:
And let us, Polydore, though now our voices
Have got the mannish crack, sing him to the ground,
As once our mother; use like note and words,
Save that Euriphile must be Fidele.

GUIDERIUS
Cadwal,
I cannot sing: I'll weep, and word it with thee;
For notes of sorrow out of tune are worse
Than priests and fanes that lie.

ARVIRAGUS
We'll speak it, then.

BELARIUS
Great griefs, I see, medicine the less; for Cloten
Is quite forgot. He was a queen's son, boys;
And though he came our enemy, remember
He was paid for that: though mean and mighty, rotting
Together, have one dust, yet reverence,
That angel of the world, doth make distinction
Of place 'tween high and low. Our foe was princely;
And though you took his life, as being our foe,
Yet bury him as a prince.

GUIDERIUS
Pray you, fetch him hither.
Thersites' body is as good as Ajax',
When neither are alive.

ARVIRAGUS
If you'll go fetch him,
We'll say our song the whilst. Brother, begin.
[*Exit Belarius.*

GUIDERIUS
Nay, Cadwal, we must lay his head to the east;
My father hath a reason for't.

ARVIRAGUS
'Tis true.

GUIDERIUS
Come on then, and remove him.

ARVIRAGUS
So. Begin.

SONG.

GUIDERIUS
Fear no more the heat o' the sun,
Nor the furious winter's rages;
Thou thy worldly task hast done,
Home art gone, and ta'en thy wages:
Golden lads and girls all must,
As chimney-sweepers, come to dust.

ARVIRAGUS
Fear no more the frown o' the great;
Thou art past the tyrant's stroke;
Care no more to clothe and eat;
To thee the reed is as the oak:
The sceptre, learning, physic, must
All follow this, and come to dust.

GUIDERIUS
Fear no more the lightning-flash,

ARVIRAGUS
Nor the all-dreaded thunder-stone;

GUIDERIUS
Fear not slander, censure rash;

ARVIRAGUS
Thou hast finish'd joy and moan:

GUIDERIUS and ARVIRAGUS
All lovers young, all lovers must
Consign to thee, and come to dust.

GUIDERIUS
No exorciser harm thee!

ARVIRAGUS
Nor no witchcraft charm thee!

GUIDERIUS
Ghost unlaid forbear thee!

ARVIRAGUS
Nothing ill come near thee!

GUIDERIUS and ARVIRAGUS
Quiet consummation have;
And renowned be thy grave!

Re-enter BELARIUS, *with the body of* CLOTEN.

GUIDERIUS
We have done our obsequies: come, lay him down.

BELARIUS
Here's a few flowers; but 'bout midnight, more:
The herbs that have on them cold dew o' the night
Are strewings fitt'st for graves. Upon their faces.

You were as flowers, now wither'd: even so
These herblets shall, which we upon you strew.
Come on, away: apart upon our knees.
The ground that gave them first has them again:
Their pleasures here are past, so is their pain.
[*Exeunt Belarius, Guiderius, and Arviragus.*

IMOGEN
[*Awaking*] Yes, sir, to Milford-Haven; which is the way?—
I thank you.—By yond bush?—Pray, how far thither?
'Ods pittikins! can it be six mile yet?—
I have gone all night. 'Faith, I'll lie down and sleep.
But, soft! no bedfellow!—O gods and goddesses!
[*Seeing the body of Cloten.*
These flowers are like the pleasures of the world;
This bloody man, the care on't. I hope I dream;
For so I thought I was a cave-keeper,
And cook to honest creatures: but 'tis not so;
'Twas but a bolt of nothing, shot at nothing,
Which the brain makes of fumes: our very eyes
Are sometimes like our judgments, blind. Good faith,
I tremble stiff with fear: but if there be
Yet left in heaven as small a drop of pity
As a wren's eye, fear'd gods, a part of it!
The dream's here still: even when I wake, it is
Without me, as within me; not imagined, felt.
A headless man! The garments of Posthumus!
I know the shape of's leg: this is his hand;
His foot Mercurial; his Martial thigh;
The brawns of Hercules: but his Jovial face—
Murder in heaven?—How!—'Tis gone. Pisanio,
All curses madded Hecuba gave the Greeks,
And mine to boot, be darted on thee! Thou,
Conspired with that irregulous devil, Cloten,
Hast here cut off my lord. To write and read
Be henceforth treacherous! Damn'd Pisanio
Hath with his forged letters,—damn'd Pisanio—
From this most bravest vessel of the world
Struck the main-top! O Posthumus! alas,
Where is thy head? where's that? Ay me! where's that?
Pisanio might have kill'd thee at the heart,
And left this head on. How should this be? Pisanio?
'Tis he and Cloten: malice and lucre in them
Have laid this woe here. O, 'tis pregnant, pregnant!
The drug he gave me, which he said was precious
And cordial to me, have I not found it
Murderous to the senses? That confirms it home:
This is Pisanio's deed, and Cloten's: O!
Give colour to my pale cheek with thy blood,
That we the horrider may seem to those
Which chance to find us: O, my lord, my lord!
[*Falls on the body.*

Enter LUCIUS, *a* Captain *and other* Officers, *and a* Soothsayer.

CAPTAIN
To them the legions garrison'd in Gallia,
After your will, have cross'd the sea, attending
You here at Milford-Haven with your ships:
They are in readiness.

CAIUS LUCIUS
But what from Rome?

CAPTAIN
The senate hath stirr'd up the confiners
And gentlemen of Italy, most willing spirits,
That promise noble service: and they come
Under the conduct of bold Iachimo,
Syenna's brother.

CAIUS LUCIUS
When expect you them?

CAPTAIN
With the next benefit o' the wind.

CAIUS LUCIUS
This forwardness
Makes our hopes fair. Command our present numbers
Be muster'd; bid the captains look to't. Now, sir,
What have you dream'd of late of this war's purpose?

SOOTHSAYER
Last night the very gods show'd me a vision—
I fast and pray'd for their intelligence—thus:
I saw Jove's bird, the Roman eagle, wing'd
From the spongy south to this part of the west,
There vanish'd in the sunbeams: which portends—
Unless my sins abuse my divination—
Success to the Roman host.

CAIUS LUCIUS
Dream often so,
And never false. Soft, ho! what trunk is here
Without his top? The ruin speaks that sometime
It was a worthy building. How! a page!
Or dead, or sleeping on him? But dead rather;
For nature doth abhor to make his bed
With the defunct, or sleep upon the dead.
Let's see the boy's face.

CAPTAIN
He's alive, my lord.

CAIUS LUCIUS
He'll then instruct us of this body. Young one,
Inform us of thy fortunes, for it seems
They crave to be demanded. Who is this
Thou makest thy bloody pillow? Or who was he
That, otherwise than noble nature did,
Hath alter'd that good picture? What's thy interest
In this sad wreck? How came it? Who is it?
What art thou?

IMOGEN
I am nothing: or if not,
Nothing to be were better. This was my master,
A very valiant Briton and a good,
That here by mountaineers lies slain. Alas!
There is no more such masters: I may wander
From east to occident, cry out for service,
Try many, all good, serve truly, never
Find such another master.

CAIUS LUCIUS
'Lack, good youth!
Thou movest no less with thy complaining than
Thy master in bleeding: say his name, good friend.

IMOGEN
Richard du Champ. [*Aside*] If I do lie and do
No harm by it, though the gods hear, I hope
They'll pardon it.—Say you, sir?

CAIUS LUCIUS
Thy name?

IMOGEN
Fidele, sir.

CAIUS LUCIUS
Thou dost approve thyself the very same:
Thy name well fits thy faith, thy faith thy name.
Wilt take thy chance with me? I will not say
Thou shalt be so well master'd, but, be sure,
No less beloved. The Roman emperor's letters,
Sent by a consul to me, should not sooner
Than thine own worth prefer thee: go with me.

IMOGEN
I'll follow, sir. But first, an't please the gods,
I'll hide my master from the flies, as deep
As these poor pickaxes can dig; and when
With wild wood-leaves and weeds I ha' strew'd his grave,
And on it said a century of prayers,
Such as I can, twice o'er, I'll weep and sigh;
And leaving so his service, follow you,
So please you entertain me.

CAIUS LUCIUS
Ay, good youth;
And rather father thee than master thee.
My friends,
The boy hath taught us manly duties: let us
Find out the prettiest daisied plot we can,
And make him with our pikes and partisans
A grave: come, arm him. Boy, he is preferr'd
By thee to us, and he shall be interr'd
As soldiers can. Be cheerful; wipe thine eyes:
Some falls are means the happier to arise. [*Exeunt.*

ACT FOUR SCENE THREE

A room in Cymbeline's palace.

Enter CYMBELINE, Lords, PISANIO, *and* Attendants.

CYMBELINE
Again; and bring me word how 'tis with her. [*Exit an Attendant.*
A fever with the absence of her son,
A madness, of which her life's in danger.
Heavens,
How deeply you at once do touch me! Imogen,
The great part of my comfort, gone; my queen
Upon a desperate bed, and in a time
When fearful wars point at me; her son gone,
So needful for this present: it strikes me, past
The hope of comfort. But for thee, fellow,
Who needs must know of her departure and
Dost seem so ignorant, we'll enforce it from thee
By a sharp torture.

PISANIO
Sir, my life is yours;
I humbly set it at your will; but, for my mistress,
I nothing know where she remains, why gone,
Nor when she purposes return. Beseech your highness,
Hold me your loyal servant.

FIRST LORD
Good my liege,
The day that she was missing he was here:
I dare be bound he's true and shall perform
All parts of his subjection loyally. For Cloten,
There wants no diligence in seeking him,
And will, no doubt, be found.

CYMBELINE
The time is troublesome. [*To Pisanio*] We'll slip you for a season; but our jealousy
Does yet depend.

FIRST LORD
So please your majesty,
The Roman legions, all from Gallia drawn,
Are landed on your coast, with a supply
Of Roman gentlemen, by the senate sent.

CYMBELINE
Now for the counsel of my son and queen!
I am amazed with matter.

FIRST LORD
Good my liege,
Your preparation can affront no less
Than what you hear of: come more, for more you're ready:
The want is but to put those powers in motion
That long to move.

CYMBELINE
I thank you. Let's withdraw;
And meet the time as it seeks us. We fear not
What can from Italy annoy us; but
We grieve at chances here. Away!
[*Exeunt all but Pisanio.*

PISANIO
I heard no letter from my master since 38
I wrote him Imogen was slain: 'tis strange:
Nor hear I from my mistress who did promise
To yield me often tidings: neither know I
What is betid to Cloten; but remain 49
Perplex'd in all. The heavens still must work.
Wherein I am false I am honest; not true, to be true.
These present wars shall find I love my country,
Even to the note o' the king, or I'll fall in them.
All other doubts, by time let them be clear'd:
Fortune brings in some boats that are not steer'd. [*Exit.*

ACT FOUR SCENE FOUR

Wales: before the cave of Belarius.
Enter BELARIUS, GUIDERIUS, *and* ARVIRAGUS .

GUIDERIUS
The noise is round about us.

BELARIUS
Let us from it.

ARVIRAGUS
What pleasure, sir, find we in life, to lock it
From action and adventure?

GUIDERIUS
Nay, what hope
Have we in hiding us? This way, the Romans
Must or for Britons slay us, or receive us
For barbarous and unnatural revolts
During their use, and slay us after.

BELARIUS
Sons,
We'll higher to the mountains; there secure us.
To the king's party there's no going: newness
Of Cloten's death—we being not known, not muster'd 13
Among the bands—may drive us to a render
Where we have lived, and so extort from's that
Which we have done, whose answer would be death
Drawn on with torture.

GUIDERIUS
This is, sir, a doubt
In such a time nothing becoming you,
Nor satisfying us.

ARVIRAGUS
It is not likely
That when they hear the Roman horses neigh,
Behold their quarter'd fires, have both their eyes
And ears so cloy'd importantly as now,
That they will waste their time upon our note,
To know from whence we are.

BELARIUS
O, I am known 27
Of many in the army: many years,
Though Cloten then but young, you see, not wore him
From my remembrance. And, besides, the king
Hath not deserved my service nor your loves;
Who find in my exile the want of breeding,
The certainty of this hard life; aye hopeless
To have the courtesy your cradle promised,
But to be still hot summer's tanlings and
The shrinking slaves of winter.

GUIDERIUS
Than be so 38
Better to cease to be. Pray, sir, to the army:
I and my brother are not known; yourself
So out of thought, and thereto so o'ergrown,
Cannot be question'd.

ARVIRAGUS
By this sun that shines,
I'll thither: what thing is it that I never
Did see man die! scarce ever look'd on blood,
But that of coward hares, hot goats, and venison!
Never bestrid a horse, save one that had
A rider like myself, who ne'er wore rowel
Nor iron on his heel! I am ashamed 49
To look upon the holy sun, to have
The benefit of his blest beams, remaining
So long a poor unknown.

GUIDERIUS
By heavens, I'll go:
If you will bless me, sir, and give me leave,
I'll take the better care, but if you will not,
The hazard therefore due fall on me by
The hands of Romans!

ARVIRAGUS
So say I: amen.

BELARIUS
No reason I, since of your lives you set
So slight a valuation, should reserve
My crack'd one to more care. Have with you, boys! 62
If in your country wars you chance to die,
That is my bed too, lads, an there I'll lie:
Lead, lead. [*Aside*] The time seems long; their blood thinks scorn,
Till it fly out and show them princes born. [*Exeunt.*

ACT FIVE SCENE ONE

Britain. The Roman camp.

Enter POSTHUMUS, *with a bloody handkerchief.*

POSTHUMUS LEONATUS

Yea, bloody cloth, I'll keep thee, for I wish'd
Thou shouldst be colour'd thus. You married ones,
If each of you should take this course, how many
Must murder wives much better than themselves
For wrying but a little! O Pisanio!
Every good servant does not all commands:
No bond but to do just ones. God! if you
Should have ta'en vengeance on my faults, I never
Had lived to put on this: so had you saved
The noble Imogen to repent, and struck
Me, wretch more worth your vengeance. But, alack,
You snatch some hence for little faults; that's love,
To have them fall no more: you some permit
To second ills with ills, each elder worse,
And make them dread it, to the doers' thrift. [39]
But Imogen is your own: do your best wills,
And make me blest to obey! I am brought hither
Among the Italian gentry, and to fight
Against my lady's kingdom: 'tis enough
That, Britain, I have kill'd thy mistress; peace!
I'll give no wound to thee. Therefore, good heavens,
Hear patiently my purpose: I'll disrobe me
Of these Italian weeds and suit myself
As does a Briton peasant: so I'll fight
Against the part I come with; so I'll die
For thee, O Imogen, even for whom my life
Is every breath a death; and thus, unknown,
Pitied nor hated, to the face of peril
Myself I'll dedicate. Let me make men know
More valour in me than my habits show.
Gods, put the strength o' the Leonati in me!
To shame the guise o' the world, I will begin
The fashion, less without and more within. [*Exit.*

ACT FIVE SCENE TWO

Field of battle between the British and Roman camps.

Enter, from one side, LUCIUS, IACHIMO, *and the* Roman Army: *from the other side, the* British Army;

POSTHUMUS LEONATUS Yea, bloody cloth, I'll keep thee, for I wish'd

LEONATUS POSTHUMUS following, like a poor soldier. They march over and go out. Then enter again, in skirmish, IACHIMO and POSTHUMUS: he vanquisheth and disarmeth IACHIMO, and then leaves him.

IACHIMO
The heaviness and guilt within my bosom
Takes off my manhood: I have belied a lady,
The princess of this country, and the air on't
Revengingly enfeebles me; or could this carl,
A very drudge of nature's, have subdued me
In my profession? Knighthoods and honours, borne
As I wear mine, are titles but of scorn.
If that thy gentry, Britain, go before
This lout as he exceeds our lords, the odds
Is that we scarce are men and you are gods.
[*Exit.*

The battle continues; the Britons fly; CYMBELINE is taken: then enter, to his rescue, BELARIUS, GUIDERIUS, and ARVIRAGUS.

BELARIUS
Stand, stand! We have the advantage of the ground;
The lane is guarded: nothing routs us but
The villany of our fears.
GUIDERIUS
Stand, stand, and fight!
ARVIRAGUS
Stand, stand, and fight!

Re-enter POSTHUMUS, and seconds the Britons: they rescue CYMBELINE, and exeunt. Then re-enter LUCIUS, and IACHIMO, with IMOGEN.

CAIUS LUCIUS
Away, boy, from the troops, and save thyself;
For friends kill friends, and the disorder's such
As war were hoodwink'd.
IACHIMO
'Tis their fresh supplies.
CAIUS LUCIUS
It is a day turn'd strangely: or betimes
Let's re-inforce, or fly.
[*Exeunt.*

ACT FIVE SCENE THREE

Another part of the field.

Enter POSTHUMUS and a British Lord.

LORD
Camest thou from where they made the stand?
POSTHUMUS LEONATUS
I did.
Though you, it seems, come from the fliers.
LORD
I did.
POSTHUMUS LEONATUS
No blame be to you, sir; for all was lost,
But that the heavens fought: the king himself
Of his wings destitute, the army broken,
And but the backs of Britons seen, all flying
Through a straight lane; the enemy full-hearted,
Lolling the tongue with slaughtering, having work
More plentiful than tools to do't, struck down
Some mortally, some slightly touch'd, some falling
Merely through fear; that the strait pass was damm'd
With dead men hurt behind, and cowards living
To die with lengthen'd shame.
LORD
Where was this lane?
POSTHUMUS LEONATUS
Close by the battle, ditch'd, and wall'd with turf;
Which gave advantage to an ancient soldier,
An honest one, I warrant; who deserved
So long a breeding as his white beard came to,
In doing this for's country: athwart the lane,
He, with two striplings—lads more like to run
The country base than to commit such slaughter;
With faces fit for masks, or rather fairer
Than those for preservation cased, or shame,—
Made good the passage; cried to those that fled,
'Our Britain's harts die flying, not our men:
To darkness fleet souls that fly backwards. Stand;
Or we are Romans and will give you that [40]
Like beasts which you shun beastly, and may save,
But to look back in frown: stand, stand.'
These three,
Three thousand confident, in act as many—
For three performers are the file when all
The rest do nothing—with this word 'Stand, stand,'
Accommodated by the place, more charming
With their own nobleness, which could have turn'd
A distaff to a lance, gilded pale looks,
Part shame, part spirit renew'd; that some, turn'd coward
But by example—O, a sin in war,
Damn'd in the first beginners!—gan to look
The way that they did, and to grin like lions
Upon the pikes o' the hunters. Then began
A stop i' the chaser, a retire, anon
A rout, confusion thick; forthwith they fly
Chickens, the way which they stoop'd eagles; slaves,
The strides they victors made: and now our cowards, [41]
Like fragments in hard voyages, became
The life o' the need: having found the backdoor open

Of the unguarded hearts, heavens, how they wound!
Some slain before; some dying; some their friends
O'er borne i' the former wave: ten, chased by one,
Are now each one the slaughter-man of twenty:
Those that would die or ere resist are grown
The mortal bugs o' the field.

LORD
This was strange chance:
A narrow lane, an old man, and two boys.

POSTHUMUS LEONATUS
Nay, do not wonder at it: you are made 42
Rather to wonder at the things you hear
Than to work any. Will you rhyme upon't,
And vent it for a mockery? Here is one:
'Two boys, an old man twice a boy, a lane,
Preserved the Britons, was the Romans' bane.'

LORD
Nay, be not angry, sir.

POSTHUMUS LEONATUS
'Lack, to what end?
Who dares not stand his foe, I'll be his friend;
For if he'll do as he is made to do, 71
I know he'll quickly fly my friendship too.
You have put me into rhyme.

LORD
Farewell; you're angry.

POSTHUMUS LEONATUS
Still going? [*Exit Lord.*] This is a lord! O noble misery,
To be i' the field, and ask 'what news?' of me!
To-day how many would have given their honours
To have saved their carcases! took heel to do't,
And yet died too! I, in mine own woe charm'd,
Could not find death where I did hear him groan,
Nor feel him where he struck: being an ugly monster, 82
'Tis strange he hides him in fresh cups, soft beds,
Sweet words; or hath more ministers than we
That draw his knives i' the war. Well, I will find him:
For being now a favourer to the Briton,
No more a Briton, I have resumed again
The part I came in: fight I will no more,
But yield to me to the veriest hind that shall
Once touch my shoulder. Great the slaughter is
Here made by the Roman; great the answer be
Britons must take. For me, my ransom's death; 93
On either side I come to spend my breath;
Which neither here I'll keep nor bear again,
But end it by some means for Imogen.

Enter two British Captains *and* Soldiers.

FIRST CAPTAIN
Great Jupiter be praised! Lucius is taken.
'Tis thought the old man and his sons were angels.

SECOND CAPTAIN
There was a fourth man, in a silly habit,
That gave the affront with them.

FIRST CAPTAIN
So 'tis reported:
But none of 'em can be found. Stand! who's there?

POSTHUMUS LEONATUS
A Roman,
Who had not now been drooping here, if seconds 105
Had answer'd him.

SECOND CAPTAIN
Lay hands on him; a dog!
A leg of Rome shall not return to tell
What crows have peck'd them here. He brags his service
As if he were of note: bring him to the king.

Enter CYMBELINE, BELARIUS, GUIDERIUS, ARVIRAGUS, PISANIO, Soldiers, Attendants, *and* Roman Captives. *The* Captains *present* POSTHUMUS *to* CYMBELINE, *who delivers him over to a* Gaoler: *then exeunt omnes.*

ACT FIVE SCENE FOUR

A British prison.

Enter POSTHUMUS *and two* Gaolers.

FIRST GAOLER
You shall not now be stol'n, you have locks upon you;
So graze as you find pasture.

SECOND GAOLER
Ay, or a stomach. [*Exeunt Gaolers.*

POSTHUMUS LEONATUS
Most welcome, bondage! for thou art a way,
I think, to liberty: yet am I better
Than one that's sick o' the gout; since he had rather
Groan so in perpetuity than be cured
By the sure physician, death, who is the key
To unbar these locks. My conscience, thou art fetter'd
More than my shanks and wrists: you good gods, give me
The penitent instrument to pick that bolt, 13
Then, free for ever! Is't enough I am sorry?
So children temporal fathers do appease;
Gods are more full of mercy. Must I repent?
I cannot do it better than in gyves,
Desired more than constrain'd: to satisfy,
If of my freedom 'tis the main part, take
No stricter render of me than my all.
I know you are more clement than vile men,

Who of their broken debtors take a third,
A sixth, a tenth, letting them thrive again
On their abatement: that's not my desire:
For Imogen's dear life take mine; and though
'Tis not so dear, yet 'tis a life; you coin'd it:
'Tween man and man they weigh not every stamp;
Though light, take pieces for the figure's sake:
You rather mine, being yours: and so, great powers,
If you will take this audit, take this life,
And cancel these cold bonds. O Imogen!
I'll speak to thee in silence. [*Sleeps.*

Solemn music. Enter, as in an apparition, SICILIUS LEONATUS, *father to Posthumus, an old man, attired like a warrior; leading in his hand an ancient matron, his wife, and mother to Posthumus, with music before them: then, after other music, follow the two young* LEONATI, *brothers to Posthumus, with wounds as they died in the wars. They circle* POSTHUMUS *round, as he lies sleeping.*

SICILIUS LEONATUS
No more, thou thunder-master, show
Thy spite on mortal flies:
With Mars fall out, with Juno chide,
That thy adulteries
Rates and revenges.
Hath my poor boy done aught but well,
Whose face I never saw?
I died whilst in the womb he stay'd
Attending nature's law:
Whose father then, as men report
Thou orphans' father art,
Thou shouldst have been, and shielded him
From this earth-vexing smart.

MOTHER
Lucina lent not me her aid,
But took me in my throes;
That from me was Posthumus ript,
Came crying 'mongst his foes,
A thing of pity!

SICILIUS LEONATUS
Great nature, like his ancestry,
Moulded the stuff so fair,
That he deserved the praise o' the world,
As great Sicilius' heir.

FIRST BROTHER
When once he was mature for man,
In Britain where was he
That could stand up his parallel;
Or fruitful object be
In eye of Imogen, that best
Could deem his dignity?

MOTHER
With marriage wherefore was he mock'd,
To be exiled, and thrown
From Leonati seat, and cast
From her his dearest one,
Sweet Imogen?

SICILIUS LEONATUS
Why did you suffer Iachimo,
Slight thing of Italy,
To taint his nobler heart and brain
With needless jealosy:
And to become the geck and scorn
O' th' other's villany?

SECOND BROTHER
For this from stiller seats we came,
Our parents and us twain,
That striking in our country's cause
Fell bravely and were slain,
Our fealty and Tenantius' right
With honour to maintain.

FIRST BROTHER
Like hardiment Posthumus hath
To Cymbeline perform'd:
Then, Jupiter, thou king of gods,
Why hast thou thus adjourn'd
The graces for his merits due,
Being all to dolours turn'd?

SICILIUS LEONATUS
Thy crystal window ope; look out;
No longer exercise
Upon a valiant race thy harsh
And potent injuries.

MOTHER
Since, Jupiter, our son is good,
Take off his miseries.

SICILIUS LEONATUS
Peep through thy marble mansion; help;
Or we poor ghosts will cry
To the shining synod of the rest
Against thy deity.

BOTH BROTHER
Help, Jupiter; or we appeal,
And from thy justice fly.

JUPITER *descends in thunder and lightning, sitting upon an eagle: he throws a thunderbolt. The Ghosts fall on their knees.*

JUPITER
No more, you petty spirits of region low,
Offend our hearing; hush! How dare you ghosts
Accuse the thunder, whose bolt, you know,
Sky-planted batters all rebelling coasts?
Poor shadows of Elysium, hence, and rest
Upon your never-withering banks of flowers:
Be not with mortal accidents oppress;
No care of yours it is; you know 'tis ours.
Whom best I love I cross; to make my gift,
The more delay'd, delighted. Be content;

Your low-laid son our godhead will uplift:
His comforts thrive, his trials well are spent.
Our Jovial star reign'd at his birth, and in
Our temple was he married. Rise, and fade.
He shall be lord of lady Imogen,
And happier much by his affliction made.
This tablet lay upon his breast, wherein
Our pleasure his full fortune doth confine:
And so, away: no further with your din
Express impatience, lest you stir up mine.
Mount, eagle, to my palace crystalline. [*Ascends.*

SICILIUS LEONATUS
He came in thunder; his celestial breath
Was sulphurous to smell: the holy eagle
Stoop'd as to foot us: his ascension is
More sweet than our blest fields: his royal bird
Prunes the immortal wing and cloys his beak,
As when his god is pleased.

ALL
Thanks, Jupiter!

SICILIUS LEONATUS
The marble pavement closes, he is enter'd
His radiant root. Away! and, to be blest,
Let us with care perform his great behest.
[*The Ghost vanish.*

POSTHUMUS LEONATUS
[*Waking*] Sleep, thou hast been a grandsire, and begot
A father to me; and thou hast created
A mother and two brothers: but, O scorn!
Gone! they went hence so soon as they were born:
And so I am awake. Poor wretches that depend
On greatness' favour dream as I have done,
Wake and find nothing. But, alas, I swerve:
Many dream not to find, neither deserve,
And yet are steep'd in favours: so am I,
That have this golden chance and know not why.
What fairies haunt this ground? A book? O rare one!
Be not, as is our fangled world, a garment
Nobler than that it covers: let thy effects
So follow, to be most unlike our courtiers,
As good as promise.

[*Reads*] 'When as a lion's whelp shall, to himself unknown, without seeking find, and be embraced by a piece of tender air; and when from a stately cedar shall be lopped branches, which, being dead many years, shall after revive, be jointed to the old stock and freshly grow; then shall Posthumus end his miseries, Britain be fortunate and flourish in peace and plenty.'

'Tis still a dream, or else such stuff as madmen
Tongue and brain not; either both or nothing;
Or senseless speaking or a speaking such
As sense cannot untie. Be what it is,
The action of my life is like it, which
I'll keep, if but for sympathy.

Re-enter Gaolers.

FIRST GAOLER
Come, sir, are you ready for death?

POSTHUMUS LEONATUS
Over-roasted rather; ready long ago.

FIRST GAOLER
Hanging is the word, sir: if you be ready for that, you are well cooked.

POSTHUMUS LEONATUS
So, if I prove a good repast to the spectators, the dish pays the shot.

FIRST GAOLER
A heavy reckoning for you, sir. But the comfort is, you shall be called to no more payments, fear no more tavern-bills; which are often the sadness of parting, as the procuring of mirth: you come in flint for want of meat, depart reeling with too much drink; sorry that you have paid too much, and sorry that you are paid too much; purse and brain both empty; the brain the heavier for being too light, the purse too light, being drawn of heaviness: of this contradiction you shall now be quit. O, the charity of a penny cord! It sums up thousands in a trice: you have no true debitor and creditor but it; of what's past, is, and to come, the discharge: your neck, sir, is pen, book and counters; so the acquittance follows.

POSTHUMUS LEONATUS
I am merrier to die than thou art to live.

FIRST GAOLER
Indeed, sir, he that sleeps feels not the tooth-ache: but a man that were to sleep your sleep, and a hangman to help him to bed, I think he would change places with his officer; for, look you, sir, you know not which way you shall go.

POSTHUMUS LEONATUS
Yes, indeed do I, fellow.

FIRST GAOLER
Your death has eyes in 's head then; I have not seen him so pictured: you must either be directed by some that take upon them to know, or do take upon yourself that which I am sure you do not know, or jump the after inquiry on your own peril: and how you shall speed in your journey's end, I think you'll never return to tell one.

POSTHUMUS LEONATUS
I tell thee, fellow, there are none want eyes to direct them the way I am going, but such as wink and will not use them.

FIRST GAOLER
What an infinite mock is this, that a man should have the best use of eyes to see the way of blindness! I am sure hangin's the way of winking.

Enter a Messenger.

MESSENGER

Knock off his manacles; bring your prisoner to the king. 198

POSTHUMUS LEONATUS

Thou bring'st good news; I am called to be made free.

FIRST GAOLER

I'll be hang'd then.

POSTHUMUS LEONATUS

Thou shalt be then freer than a gaoler; no bolts for the dead. [*Exeunt all but the First Gaoler.*

FIRST GAOLER

Unless a man would marry a gallows and beget young gibbets, I never saw one so prone. Yet, on my conscience, there are verier knaves desire to live, for all he be a Roman: and there be some of them too that die against their wills; so should I, if I were one. I would we were all of one mind, and one mind good; O, there were desolation of gaolers and gallowses! I speak against my present profit, but my wish hath a preferment in 't. [*Exit.*

ACT FIVE SCENE FIVE

Cymbeline's tent.

Enter CYMBELINE, BELARIUS, GUIDERIUS, ARVIRAGUS, PISANIO, Lords, Officers, *and* Attendants.

CYMBELINE

Stand by my side, you whom the gods have made
Preservers of my throne. Woe is my heart
That the poor soldier that so richly fought,
Whose rags shamed gilded arms, whose naked breast
Stepp'd before targes of proof, cannot be found:
He shall be happy that can find him, if
Our grace can make him so.

BELARIUS

I never saw
Such noble fury in so poor a thing;
Such precious deeds in one that promises nought
But beggary and poor looks.

CYMBELINE

No tidings of him? 13

PISANIO

He hath been search'd among the dead and living,
But no trace of him.

CYMBELINE

To my grief, I am
The heir of his reward; [*To Belarius, Guiderius, and Arviragus*] which I will add
To you, the liver, heart and brain of Britain,
By whom I grant she lives. 'Tis now the time
To ask of whence you are. Report it.

BELARIUS

Sir,
In Cambria are we born, and gentlemen:
Further to boast were neither true nor modest,
Unless I add, we are honest.

CYMBELINE

Bow your knees.
Arise my knights o' the battle; I create you 28
Companions to our person and will fit you
With dignities becoming your estates.

Enter CORNELIUS *and* Ladies.

There's business in these faces. Why so sadly
Greet you our victory? you look like Romans,
And not o' the court of Britain.

CORNELIUS

Hail, great king!
To sour your happiness, I must report
The queen is dead.

CYMBELINE

Who worse than a physician
Would this report become? But I consider,
By medicine life may be prolong'd, yet death
Will seize the doctor too. How ended she?

CORNELIUS

With horror, madly dying, like her life,
Which, being cruel to the world, concluded
Most cruel to herself. What she confess'd
I will report, so please you: these her women
Can trip me, if I err; who with wet cheeks
Were present when she finish'd.

CYMBELINE

Prithee, say.

CORNELIUS

First, she confess'd she never loved you, only
Affected greatness got by you, not you:
Married your royalty, was wife to your place;
Abhorr'd your person.

CYMBELINE

She alone knew this; 52
And, but she spoke it dying, I would not
Believe her lips in opening it. Proceed.

CORNELIUS

Your daughter, whom she bore in hand to love
With such integrity, she did confess
Was as a scorpion to her sight; whose life,
But that her flight prevented it, she had 58
Ta'en off by poison.

CYMBELINE

O most delicate fiend!
Who is't can read a woman? Is there more?

CORNELIUS
More, sir, and worse. She did confess she had
For you a mortal mineral; which, being took,
Should by the minute feed on life and lingering
By inches waste you: in which time she purposed,
By watching, weeping, tendance, kissing, to
O'ercome you with her show, and in time [43]
When she had fitted you with her craft, to work
Her son into the adoption of the crown:
But, failing of her end by his strange absence,
Grew shameless-desperate; open'd, in despite
Of heaven and men, her purposes; repented
The evils she hatch'd were not effected; so 73
Despairing died.
CYMBELINE
Heard you all this, her women?
FIRST LADY
We did, so please your highness.
CYMBELINE
Mine eyes
Were not in fault, for she was beautiful;
Mine ears, that heard her flattery; nor my heart,
That thought her like her seeming; it had been vicious
To have mistrusted her: yet, O my daughter!
That it was folly in me, thou mayst say,
And prove it in thy feeling. Heaven mend all!

Enter LUCIUS, IACHIMO, *the* Soothsayer, *and other* Roman Prisoners, *guarded*; POSTHUMUS *behind, and* IMOGEN.

Thou comest not, Caius, now for tribute; that
The Britons have razed out, though with the loss 86
Of many a bold one; whose kinsmen have made suit
That their good souls may be appeased with slaughter
Of you their captives, which ourself have granted:
So think of your estate.
CAIUS LUCIUS
Consider, sir, the chance of war: the day
Was yours by accident; had it gone with us,
We should not, when the blood was cool, have threaten'd
Our prisoners with the sword. But since the gods
Will have it thus, that nothing but our lives
May be call'd ransom, let it come: sufficeth 98
A Roman with a Roman's heart can suffer:
Augustus lives to think on't: and so much
For my peculiar care. This one thing only
I will entreat; my boy, a Briton born,
Let him be ransom'd: never master had
A page so kind, so duteous, diligent,
So tender over his occasions, true,
So feat, so nurse-like: let his virtue join
With my request, which I'll make bold your highness
Cannot deny; he hath done no Briton harm,
Though he have served a Roman: save him, sir,
And spare no blood beside.
CYMBELINE
I have surely seen him:
His favour is familiar to me. Boy,
Thou hast look'd thyself into my grace,
And art mine own. I know not why, wherefore,
To say 'live, boy:' ne'er thank thy master; live:
And ask of Cymbeline what boon thou wilt,
Fitting my bounty and thy state, I'll give it;
Yea, though thou do demand a prisoner,
The noblest ta'en.
IMOGEN
I humbly thank your highness. 120
CAIUS LUCIUS
I do not bid thee beg my life, good lad;
And yet I know thou wilt.
IMOGEN
No, no: alack,
There's other work in hand: I see a thing
Bitter to me as death: your life, good master,
Must shuffle for itself.
CAIUS LUCIUS
The boy disdains me,
He leaves me, scorns me: briefly die their joys
That place them on the truth of girls and boys.
Why stands he so perplex'd?
CYMBELINE
What wouldst thou, boy?
I love thee more and more: think more and more
What's best to ask. Know'st him thou look'st on? speak, 134
Wilt have him live? Is he thy kin? thy friend?
IMOGEN
He is a Roman; no more kin to me
Than I to your highness; who, being born your vassal,
Am something nearer.
CYMBELINE
Wherefore eyest him so?
IMOGEN
I'll tell you, sir, in private, if you please
To give me hearing.
CYMBELINE
Ay, with all my heart,
And lend my best attention. What's thy name?
IMOGEN
Fidele, sir.
CYMBELINE
Thou'rt my good youth, my page;
I'll be thy master: walk with me; speak freely.
[Cymbeline *and* Imogen *converse apart.*
BELARIUS
Is not this boy revived from death?

ARVIRAGUS
One sand another 149
Not more resembles that sweet rosy lad
Who died, and was Fidele. What think you?
GUIDERIUS
The same dead thing alive.
BELARIUS
Peace, peace! see further: he eyes us not; forbear;
Creatures may be alike: were 't he, I am sure
He would have spoke to us.
GUIDERIUS
But we saw him dead.
BELARIUS
Be silent; let's see further.
PISANIO
[*Aside*] It is my mistress:
Since she is living, let the time run on
To good or bad.
[*Cymbeline and Imogen come forward.*
CYMBELINE
Come, stand thou by our side;
Make thy demand aloud. [*To* Iachimo] Sir, step you forth; 163
Give answer to this boy, and do it freely;
Or, by our greatness and the grace of it,
Which is our honour, bitter torture shall
Winnow the truth from falsehood. On, speak to him.
IMOGEN
My boon is, that this gentleman may render
Of whom he had this ring.
POSTHUMUS LEONATUS
[*Aside*] What's that to him?
CYMBELINE
That diamond upon your finger, say
How came it yours?
IACHIMO
Thou'lt torture me to leave unspoken that
Which, to be spoke, would torture thee.
CYMBELINE
How! me? 176
IACHIMO
I am glad to be constrain'd to utter that
Which torments me to conceal. By villany
I got this ring: 'twas Leonatus' jewel;
Whom thou didst banish; and—which more may grieve thee,
As it doth me—a nobler sir ne'er lived
'Twixt sky and ground. Wilt thou hear more, my lord?
CYMBELINE
All that belongs to this.
IACHIMO
That paragon, thy daughter,—
For whom my heart drops blood, and my false spirits
Quail to remember—Give me leave; I faint.
CYMBELINE
My daughter! what of her? Renew thy strength: 189
I had rather thou shouldst live while nature will
Than die ere I hear more: strive, man, and speak.
IACHIMO
Upon a time,—unhappy was the clock
That struck the hour!—it was in Rome,—accursed
The mansion where!—'twas at a feast, — O, would
Our viands had been poison'd, or at least
Those which I heaved to head!—the good Posthumus—
What should I say? he was too good to be
Where ill men were; and was the best of all
Amongst the rarest of good ones,—sitting sadly,
Hearing us praise our loves of Italy 201
For beauty that made barren the swell'd boast
Of him that best could speak, for feature, laming
The shrine of Venus, or straight-pight Minerva.
Postures beyond brief nature, for condition,
A shop of all the qualities that man
Loves woman for, besides that hook of wiving,
Fairness which strikes the eye—
CYMBELINE
I stand on fire:
Come to the matter.
IACHIMO
All too soon I shall,
Unless thou wouldst grieve quickly. This Posthumus, 213
Most like a noble lord in love and one
That had a royal lover, took his hint;
And, not dispraising whom we praised,— therein
He was as calm as virtue—he began
His mistress' picture; which by his tongue being made,
And then a mind put in't, either our brags
Were crack'd of kitchen-trulls, or his description
Proved us unspeaking sots.
CYMBELINE
Nay, nay, to the purpose.
IACHIMO
Your daughter's chastity—there it begins.
He spake of her, as Dian had hot dreams, 225
And she alone were cold: whereat I, wretch,
Made scruple of his praise; and wager'd with him
Pieces of gold 'gainst this which then he wore
Upon his honour'd finger, to attain
In suit the place of's bed and win this ring
By hers and mine adultery. He, true knight,
No lesser of her honour confident
Than I did truly find her, stakes this ring;
And would so, had it been a carbuncle 234
Of Phoebus' wheel, and might so safely, had it
Been all the worth of's car. Away to Britain

Post I in this design: well may you, sir,
Remember me at court; where I was taught
Of your chaste daughter the wide difference
'Twixt amorous and villanous. Being thus quench'd
Of hope, not longing, mine Italian brain
'Gan in your duller Britain operate
Most vilely; for my vantage, excellent:
And, to be brief, my practice so prevail'd,
That I return'd with simular proof enough
To make the noble Leonatus mad,
By wounding his belief in her renown
With tokens thus, and thus; averring notes
Of chamber-hanging, pictures, this her bracelet,—
O cunning, how I got it!—nay, some marks
Of secret on her person, that he could not
But think her bond of chastity quite crack'd,
I having ta'en the forfeit. Whereupon—
Methinks, I see him now—

POSTHUMUS LEONATUS
[*Advancing*] Ay, so thou dost,
Italian fiend! Ay, me, most credulous fool,
Egregious murderer, thief, any thing
That's due to all the villains past, in being,
To come! O, give me cord, or knife, or poison,
Some upright justicer! Thou, king, send out
For torturers ingenious: it is I
That all the abhorred things o' the earth amend
By being worse than they. I am Posthumus,
That kill'd thy daughter:—villain-like, I lie—
That caused a lesser villain than myself,
A sacrilegious thief, to do't: the temple
Of virtue was she; yea, and she herself.
Spit, and throw stones, cast mire upon me, set
The dogs o' the street to bay me: every villain
Be call'd Posthumus Leonatus; and
Be villany less than 'twas! O Imogen!
My queen, my life, my wife! O Imogen,
Imogen, Imogen!

IMOGEN
Peace, my lord; hear, hear—

POSTHUMUS LEONATUS
Shall's have a play of this? Thou scornful page,
There lie thy part. [*Striking her: she falls.*

PISANIO
O, gentlemen, help!
Mine and your mistress! O, my lord Posthumus!
You ne'er kill'd Imogen till now. Help, help!
Mine honour'd lady!

CYMBELINE
Does the world go round?

POSTHUMUS LEONATUS
How come these staggers on me?

PISANIO
Wake, my mistress!

CYMBELINE
If this be so, the gods do mean to strike me
To death with mortal joy.

PISANIO
How fares thy mistress?

IMOGEN
O, get thee from my sight;
Thou gavest me poison: dangerous fellow, hence!
Breathe not where princes are.

CYMBELINE
The tune of Imogen!

PISANIO
Lady,
The gods throw stones of sulphur on me, if
That box I gave you was not thought by me
A precious thing: I had it from the queen.

CYMBELINE
New matter still?

IMOGEN
It poison'd me.

CORNELIUS
O gods!
I left out one thing which the queen confess'd.
Which must approve thee honest: 'If Pisanio
Have,' said she, 'given his mistress that confection
Which I gave him for cordial, she is served
As I would serve a rat.'

CYMBELINE
What's this, Cornelius?

CORNELIUS
The queen, sir, very oft importuned me
To temper poisons for her, still pretending
The satisfaction of her knowledge only
In killing creatures vile, as cats and dogs,
Of no esteem: I, dreading that her purpose
Was of more danger, did compound for her
A certain stuff, which, being ta'en, would cease
The present power of life, but in short time
All offices of nature should again
Do their due functions. Have you ta'en of it?

IMOGEN
Most like I did, for I was dead.

BELARIUS
My boys,
There was our error.

GUIDERIUS
This is, sure, Fidele.

IMOGEN
Why did you throw your wedded lady from you?
Think that you are upon a rock; and now
Throw me again. [44] [*Embracing him.*

POSTHUMUS LEONATUS
Hang there like a fruit, my soul,
Till the tree die!

CYMBELINE
How now, my flesh, my child!
What, makest thou me a dullard in this act?
Wilt thou not speak to me?
IMOGEN
[*Kneeling*] Your blessing, sir.
BELARIUS
[*To Guiderius and Arviragus*] Though you did love this youth, I blame ye not;
You had a motive for't.
CYMBELINE
My tears that fall
Prove holy water on thee! Imogen,
Thy mother's dead.
IMOGEN
I am sorry for't, my lord. 334
CYMBELINE
O, she was nought; and long of her it was
That we meet here so strangely: but her son
Is gone, we know not how nor where.
PISANIO
My lord,
Now fear is from me, I'll speak troth. Lord Cloten,
Upon my lady's missing, came to me
With his sword drawn; foam'd at the mouth, and swore,
If I discover'd not which way she was gone,
It was my instant death. By accident,
I had a feigned letter of my master's
Then in my pocket; which directed him 346
To seek her on the mountains near to Milford;
Where, in a frenzy, in my master's garments,
Which he enforced from me, away he posts
With unchaste purpose and with oath to violate
My lady's honour: what became of him
I further know not.
GUIDERIUS
Let me end the story:
I slew him there.
CYMBELINE
Marry, the gods forfend!
I would not thy good deeds should from my lips
Pluck a bard sentence: prithee, valiant youth,
Deny't again.
GUIDERIUS
I have spoke it, and I did it. 359
CYMBELINE
He was a prince.
GUIDERIUS
A most incivil one: the wrongs he did me
Were nothing prince-like; for he did provoke me
With language that would make me spurn the sea,
If it could so roar to me: I cut off's head;
And am right glad he is not standing here
To tell this tale of mine.
CYMBELINE
I am sorry for thee:
By thine own tongue thou art condemn'd, and must
Endure our law: thou'rt dead.
IMOGEN
That headless man
I thought had been my lord.
CYMBELINE
Bind the offender, 372
And take him from our presence.
BELARIUS
Stay, sir king:
This man is better than the man he slew,
As well descended as thyself; and hath
More of thee merited than a band of Clotens
Had ever scar for. [*To the Guard*] Let his arms alone; [45]
They were not born for bondage.
CYMBELINE
Why, old soldier,
Wilt thou undo the worth thou art unpaid for,
By tasting of our wrath? How of descent
As good as we?
ARVIRAGUS
In that he spake too far.
CYMBELINE
And thou shalt die for't.
BELARIUS
We will die all three: 387
But I will prove that two on's are as good
As I have given out him. My sons, I must,
For mine own part, unfold a dangerous speech,
Though, haply, well for you.
ARVIRAGUS
Your danger's ours.
GUIDERIUS
And our good his.
BELARIUS
Have at it then, by leave.
Thou hadst, great king, a subject who
Was call'd Belarius.
CYMBELINE
What of him? he is
A banish'd traitor.
BELARIUS
He it is that hath
Assumed this age; indeed a banish'd man;
I know not how a traitor.
CYMBELINE
Take him hence: 402
The whole world shall not save him.
BELARIUS
Not too hot:

First pay me for the nursing of thy sons;
And let it be confiscate all, so soon
As I have received it.

CYMBELINE
Nursing of my sons!

BELARIUS
I am too blunt and saucy: here's my knee:
Ere I arise, I will prefer my sons;
Then spare not the old father. Mighty sir,
These two young gentlemen, that call me father
And think they are my sons, are none of mine;
They are the issue of your loins, my liege,
And blood of your begetting.

CYMBELINE
How! my issue!

BELARIUS
So sure as you your father's. I, old Morgan,
Am that Belarius whom you sometime banish'd:
Your pleasure was my mere offence, my punishment
Itself, and all my treason; that I suffer'd
Was all the harm I did. These gentle princes—
For such and so they are—these twenty years
Have I train'd up: those arts they have as I
Could put into them; my breeding was, sir, as
Your highness knows. Their nurse, Euriphile,
Whom for the theft I wedded, stole these children
Upon my banishment: I moved her to't,
Having received the punishment before,
For that which I did then: beaten for loyalty
Excited me to treason: their dear loss,
The more of you 'twas felt, the more it shaped
Unto my end of stealing them. But, gracious sir,
Here are your sons again; and I must lose
Two of the sweet'st companions in the world.
The benediction of these covering heavens
Fall on their heads like dew! for they are worthy
To inlay heaven with stars.

CYMBELINE
Thou weep'st, and speak'st.
The service that you three have done is more
Unlike than this thou tell'st. I lost my children:
If these be they, I know not how to wish
A pair of worthier sons.

BELARIUS
Be pleased awhile.
This gentleman, whom I call Polydore,
Most worthy prince, as yours, is true Guiderius:
This gentleman, my Cadwal, Arviragus,
Your younger princely son; he, sir, was lapp'd
In a most curious mantle, wrought by the hand
Of his queen mother, which for more probation
I can with ease produce.

CYMBELINE
Guiderius had
Upon his neck a mole, a sanguine star;
It was a mark of wonder.

BELARIUS
This is he;
Who hath upon him still that natural stamp:
It was wise nature's end in the donation,
To be his evidence now.

CYMBELINE
O, what, am I
A mother to the birth of three? Ne'er mother
Rejoiced deliverance more. Blest pray you be,
That, after this strange starting from your orbs,
You may reign in them now! O Imogen,
Thou hast lost by this a kingdom.

IMOGEN
No, my lord;
I have got two worlds by 't. O my gentle brothers,
Have we thus met? O, never say hereafter
But I am truest speaker: you call'd me brother,
When I was but your sister; I you brothers,
When ye were so indeed. [46]

CYMBELINE
Did e'er meet?

ARVIRAGUS
Ay, my good lord.

GUIDERIUS
And at first meeting loved;
Continued so, until we thought he died.

CORNELIUS
By the queen's dram she swallow'd.

CYMBELINE
O rare instinct!
When shall I hear all through? This fierce abridgement [47]
Hath to it circumstantial branches, which
Distinction should be rich in. Where? how lived you? [48]
And when came you to serve our Roman captive?
How parted with your brothers? how first met them?
Why fled you from the court? and whither? These,
And your three motives to the battle, with
I know not how much more, should be demanded;
And all the other by-dependencies,
From chance to chance: but nor the time nor place
Will serve our long inter'gatories. See, [49]
Posthumus anchors upon Imogen,
And she, like harmless lightning, throws her eye
On him, her brother, me, her master, hitting
Each object with a joy: the counterchange
Is severally in all. Let's quit this ground,
And smoke the temple with our sacrifices.
[*To Belarius*] Thou art my brother; so we'll hold thee ever.

IMOGEN
You are my father too, and did relieve me,
To see this gracious season.
CYMBELINE
All o'erjoy'd,
Save these in bonds: let them be joyful too,
For they shall taste our comfort.
IMOGEN
My good master,
I will yet do you service.
CAIUS LUCIUS
Happy be you!
CYMBELINE
The forlorn soldier, that so nobly fought,
He would have well becomed this place, and graced
The thankings of a king.
POSTHUMUS LEONATUS
I am, sir,
The soldier that did company these three
In poor beseeming; 'twas a fitment for
The purpose I then follow'd. That I was he,
Speak, Iachimo: I had you down and might
Have made you finish.
IACHIMO
[*Kneeling*] I am down again:
But now my heavy conscience sinks my knee,
As then your force did. Take that life, beseech you,
Which I so often owe: but your ring first;
And here the bracelet of the truest princess
That ever swore her faith.
POSTHUMUS LEONATUS
Kneel not to me:
The power that I have on you is to spare you;
The malice towards you to forgive you: live,
And deal with others better.
CYMBELINE
Nobly doom'd!
We'll learn our freeness of a son-in-law;
Pardon's the word to all.
ARVIRAGUS
You holp us, sir,
As you did mean indeed to be our brother;
Joy'd are we that you are.
POSTHUMUS LEONATUS
Your servant, princes. Good my lord of Rome,
Call forth your soothsayer: as I slept, me-thought
Great Jupiter, upon his eagle back'd,
Appear'd to me, with other spritely shows
Of mine own kindred: when I waked, I found
This label on my bosom; whose containing
Is so from sense in hardness, that I can
Make no collection of it: let him show
His skill in the construction.
CAIUS LUCIUS
Philarmonus!
SOOTHSAYER
Here, my good lord.
CAIUS LUCIUS
Read, and declare the meaning.
SOOTHSAYER
[*Reads*] 'When as a lion's whelp shall, to himself unknown, without seeking find, and be embraced by a piece of tender air; and when from a stately cedar shall be lopped branches, which, being dead many years, shall after revive, be jointed to the old stock, and freshly grow; then shall Posthumus end his miseries, Britain be fortunate and flourish in peace and plenty.'
Thou, Leonatus, art the lion's whelp;
The fit and apt construction of thy name,
Being Leonatus, doth import so much.
[*To Cymbeline*] The piece of tender air, thy virtuous daughter,
Which we call 'mollis aer;' and 'mollis aer'
We term it 'mulier:' which 'mulier' I divine
Is this most constant wife; who, even now,
Answering the letter of the oracle,
Unknown to you, unsought, were clipp'd about
With this most tender air.
CYMBELINE
This hath some seeming.
SOOTHSAYER
The lofty cedar, royal Cymbeline,
Personates thee: and thy lopp'd branches point
Thy two sons forth; who, by Belarius stol'n,
For many years thought dead, are now revived,
To the majestic cedar join'd, whose issue
Promises Britain peace and plenty.
CYMBELINE
Well;
My peace we will begin. And, Caius Lucius,
Although the victor, we submit to Caesar,
And to the Roman empire; promising
To pay our wonted tribute, from the which
We were dissuaded by our wicked queen;
Whom heavens, in justice, both on her and hers,
Have laid most heavy hand.
SOOTHSAYER
The fingers of the powers above do tune
The harmony of this peace. The vision
Which I made known to Lucius, ere the stroke
Of this yet scarce-cold battle, at this instant
Is full accomplish'd; for the Roman eagle,
From south to west on wing soaring aloft,
Lessen'd herself, and in the beams o' the sun
So vanish'd: which foreshow'd our princely eagle,
The imperial Caesar, should again unite
His favour with the radiant Cymbeline,
Which shines here in the west.
CYMBELINE
Laud we the gods;

And let our crooked smokes climb to their nostrils
From our blest altars. Publish we this peace
To all our subjects. Set we forward: let
A Roman and a British ensign wave
Friendly together: so through Lud's-town march:
And in the temple of great Jupiter
Our peace we'll ratify; seal it with feasts.
Set on there! Never was a war did cease,
Ere bloody hands were wash'd, with such a peace.
[*Exeunt.*

Notes

1. Does the king; – Tyrwhitt's conjecture; Folios. *'do's the Kings'*; Hanmer, *'do the kings.'*
2. A year's age; – this reading seems weak; one expects some stronger expression. Warburton, adopted by Theobald, *'a yare* [*i.e.* speedy] *age'*; Hanmer, *'many A year's age'*; Nicholson, *'more than Thy years' age'*; &c., &c.
3. Make me with this eye or ear; – Folios, *'his'* for *'this.'*
4. Are wonderfully to; – Warburton conjectured *'aids wonderfully to'*; Capell conjectured *'are wonderful to'*; Eccles, *'and wonderfully do.'*
5. Could not but; – Malone's emendation of Folios, *'could not.'*
6. Herein too; – so Folios 3, 4; Folios 1, 2, *'heerin to'*; Grant White, *'hereinto'*; Anon. conjecture, *'hereunto'*; Vaughan conjectured *'herein, so.'*
7. Afraid; – Warburton's emendation, adopted by Theobald; Folios, *'a Friend'*; Becket conjectured *'affied'*; Jackson conjectured *'affianc'd'*; Collier MS., *'afeard'*; Ingleby conjectured *'her friend.'*
8. Chance thou changest on; – so Folios, Rowe reads *'chance thou chancest on'*; Theobald, *'change thou chancest on.'*
9. Trust—; – Boswell's readings, Folios, *'trust'*; Hanmer, *'truest'*; Rann, *'truest'*; Thirlby conjectured *'trusty.'*
10. Number'd; – (?) 'rich in numbers'; Theobald, *'unnumber'd'*; Warburton, *'humbl'd'*; Farmer conjectured *'umber'd'*; Jackson conjectured *'member'd'*; Theobald's excellent emendation has much to commend it.
11. Desire vomit emptiness; – Johnson explained these difficult words as follows:—"*Desire,* when it approached *sluttery,* and considered it in comparison with *such neat* excellence, would not only be *not so allured to feed,* but seized with a fit of loathing, would *vomit emptiness,* would feel the convulsions of disgust, though being unfed, it had no object." Pope, *'desire vomit ev'n emptiness'*; Capell, *'desire vomit to emptiness'*; Hudson, *'desire vomit from emptiness.'*
12. Unlustrous; – Rowe's emendation of Folios, *'illustrious'*; Ingleby, *'illlustrous.'*
13. Bare the raven's eye; – Theobald's conjecture, adopted by Steevens; Folios, *'beare the Rauens eye.'*
14. With every thing that pretty is; – Hanmer (unnecessarily, for the sake of the rhyme), *'With all the things that pretty bin'*; Warburton, *'With everything that pretty bin.'*
15. Vice; – Rowe's emendation of Folios, *'voyce.'*
16. Soliciting; – the reading of Collier (ed. 2); Folio 1 reads *'solicity'*; Folios 2, 3, 4, *'solicits'*; Pope, *'solicits.'*
17. Are not; – Warburton's conjecture, adopted by Theobald, *'cure not'*; but no change is necessary.
18. Rocks; – Seward conjecture, adopted by Hanmer; Folios, *'Oakes.'*
19. We do; – these words are part of Cymbeline's speech in Folios; Collier MS. assigns them to Cloten, and the arrangement has been generally adopted.
20. Stoop; – Hanmer's emendation of Folios, *'Sleepe.'*
21. Turbans; – Folio 1, *'Turbonds'*; Folios 2, 3, 4, *'Turbands.'*
22. Bauble; – Rowe's emendation of Folios, *'Babe'*; Hanmer, *'bribe'*; the latter suggestion has been accepted by many modern editors; Brae, *'badge,' i.e.* decoration, ribbon.
23. Prison for; – Pope's emendation of Folio 1, *'Prison, or'*; Folios 2, 3, 4, *'Prison or'*; Anon. conjecture, and Vaughan conjecture, *'prison of.'*
24. I' the cave wherein they bow; – Warburton's emendation; Folios, *'I' th' Cave, whereon the Bowe'*; Rowe, *'I' th' cave, where on the bow'*; Pope, *'Here in the cave, wherein'*; Theobald, *'I' th' cave, there, on the brow,'* &c.
25. Whose mother was her painting, i.e. – 'who owed her beauty to her painted face'; or, perhaps 'whose painted face was the sum of her woman-like qualities': according to others, 'whose mother aided and abetted her daughter in her trade.'
26. Afore't; – Rowe's emendation of Folios, *'a-foot.'*
27. I'll wake mine eye-balls blind first; – Hanmer's emendation; Folios read *'I'll wake mine eye-balles first'*; Rowe, *'I'll break mine eye-balls first'*; Johnson conjecture, adopted by Ingleby, *'I'll wake mine eye-balls out first'*; Collier MS., *'I'll crack mine eye-balls first.'*
28. Vaughan proposed *'With that harsh noble—noble simply in nothing'*; Spence, *'trash noble'* (*i.e.* base coin); Elze, *'that ignoble,'* &c.
29. Where then? – perhaps these words should be assigned to Pisanio.
30. Which you'll make him know; – Hanmer's reading; Folios read *'Which will make him know'*; Theobald, *'Which will make him so.'*
31. Loud'st of noise; – Capell's emendation; Folios 1, 2, *'lowd of noise'*; Rowe, *'loudest noise.'*
32. Possibly, as explained by Johnson, these words are to be explained as meaning, 'than any lady, than all ladies, than all womankind'; Hanmer, *'than any lady, winning from each one.'*
33. Perhaps should read, with Hanmer, *'I'd bid'*; *i.e.* 'I'd bid for you and make up my mind to have you.'
34. Commends; – Warburton's emendation, adopted by Theobald; Folios, *'commands'* (perhaps = 'commands to be given').
35. Humour; – Theobald's emendation of Folios, *'honor.'*
36. Parish; – Hanmer, *'marish'*; Garrick's version, *'river'*; Becket conjectured *'parage.'*
37. The ruddock, – &c.; the kindly service of the Robin Redbreast is often referred to in Elizabethan literature, *e.g.*

   "Covering with moss the dead's unclosed eye,
   The little redbreast teacheth charitie."
   Drayton, *The Owl.*

   It is worth while nothing that the story of *The Babes in the Wood* was dramatised as early as 1600 in Yarrington's *Two Lamentable Tragedies.*

38. I heard no letter, i.e. – (?) 'I've not had a line'; Hanmer reads *'I've had';* Capell, *'I have had';* Mason conjecture, and Warburton conjecture, adopted by Collier (ed. 2), *'I had.'*
39. Dread it, to the doers' thrift; – perhaps this means that the guilty benefit by their dread, for their dread makes them repent, and repentance brings them salvation. Theobald suggested *'dreaded … thrift';* but the text, though somewhat difficult, may be correct.
40. That, i.e. – 'that death.'
41. They; – Theobald's correction of Folios, *'the'; i.e.* 'retracing as slaves the strides they made as victors.'
42. Nay, do not wonder; – Theobald reads *'Nay, do but wonder';* Staunton conjectured *'Ay, do but wonder';* "Posthumus first bids him not wonder, then tells him in another mode of reproach that wonder was all he was made for" (Johnson).
43. And in time; – so Folios 1; Folios 2, 3, 4, *'yes and in time';* S. Walker conjectured *'and in due time,'* &c.
44. The stage-direction was first inserted by Hanmer, and explains the meaning of the lines, and gets rid of a long series of unnecessary emendations.
45. Scar; – *'had ever s. for,' i.e.* had ever received a scar for; Folios 1, 2, *'scarre';* Collier conjectured *'sense';* Singer (ed. 2), *'score';* Bailey conjectured *'soar.'*
46. When ye; – Rowe's emendation of Folios, *'When we';* Capell, *'When you.'*
47. Fierce, – disordered; (?) vehement, rapid; Collier conjectured *'forc'd';* Bailey conjectured *'brief.'*
48. Distinction should be rich in, i.e. – "Ought to be rendered distinct by a liberal amplitude of narrative" (Steevens).
49. Our long inter'gatories; – Tyrwhitt conjecture, adopted by Malone; Folios, *'our long Interrogatories.'*

THE WINTER'S TALE

THE WINTER'S TALE

DRAMATIS PERSONAE

LEONTES, king of Sicilia.
MAMILLIUS, young prince of Sicilia.
CAMILLO, Lords of Sicilia.
ANTIGONUS, Lords of Sicilia.
CLEOMENES, Lords of Sicilia.
DION, Lords of Sicilia.
POLIXENES, King of Bohemia.
FLORIZEL, Prince of Bohemia.
ARCHIDAMUS, a Lord of Bohemia.
Old Shepherd, reputed father of Perdita.
Clown, his son.
AUTOLYCUS, a rogue.
A Mariner.
A Gaoler.
HERMIONE, queen to Leontes.
PERDITA, daughter to Leontes and Hermione.
PAULINA, wife to Antigonus.
EMILIA, a lady attending on Hermione.
MOPSA, Shepherdesses.
DORCAS, Shepherdesses.
Other Lords and Gentlemen, Ladies, Officers, and Servants, Shepherds, and Shepherdesses.
Time, as Chorus.

SCENE: *Sicilia, and Bohemia.*

ACT ONE SCENE ONE

Antechamber in LEONTES' *palace.*

Enter CAMILLO *and* ARCHIDAMUS.

ARCHIDAMUS
If you shall chance, Camillo, to visit Bohemia, on the like occasion whereon my services are now on foot, you shall see, as I have said, great difference betwixt our Bohemia and your Sicilia.

CAMILLO
I think, this coming summer, the King of Sicilia means to pay Bohemia the visitation which he justly owes him.

ARCHIDAMUS
Wherein our entertainment shall shame us we will be justified in our loves; for indeed— 9

CAMILLO
Beseech you,—

ARCHIDAMUS
Verily, I speak it in the freedom of my knowledge: we cannot with such magnificence—in so rare—I know not what to say. We will give you sleepy drinks, that your senses, unintelligent of our insufficience, may, though they cannot praise us, as little accuse us.

CAMILLO
You pay a great deal too dear for what's given
freely. 17

ARCHIDAMUS
Believe me, I speak as my understanding instructs me and as mine honesty puts it to utterance.

CAMILLO
Sicilia cannot show himself over-kind to Bohemia. They were trained together in their childhoods; and there rooted betwixt them then such an affection, which cannot choose but branch now. Since their more mature dignities and royal necessities made separation of their society, their encounters, though

not personal, have been royally attorneyed with interchange of gifts, letters, loving embassies; that they have seemed to be together, though absent, shook hands, as over a vast, and embraced, as it were, from the ends of opposed winds. The heavens continue their loves!

ARCHIDAMUS

I think there is not in the world either malice or matter to alter it. You have an unspeakable comfort of your young prince Mamillius: it is a gentleman of the greatest promise that ever came into my note.

CAMILLO

I very well agree with you in the hopes of him: it is a gallant child; one that indeed physics the subject, makes old hearts fresh: they that went on crutches ere he was born desire yet their life to see him a man.

ARCHIDAMUS

Would they else be content to die?

CAMILLO

Yes; if there were no other excuse why they should desire to live.

ARCHIDAMUS

If the king had no son, they would desire to live on crutches till he had one.

[*Exeunt.*

ACT ONE SCENE TWO

A room of state in the same.

Enter LEONTES, HERMIONE, MAMILLIUS, POLIXENES, CAMILLO, *and* Attendants.

POLIXENES

Nine changes of the watery star hath been
The shepherd's note since we have left our throne
Without a burthen: time as long again
Would be fill'd up, my brother, with our thanks;
And yet we should, for perpetuity,
Go hence in debt: and therefore, like a cipher,
Yet standing in rich place, I multiply
With one 'We thank you' many thousands moe
That go before it.

LEONTES

Stay your thanks a while;
And pay them when you part.

POLIXENES

Sir, that's to-morrow.
I am question'd by my fears, of what may chance
Or breed upon our absence; that may blow
No sneaping winds at home, to make us say
'This is put forth too truly:' besides, I have stay'd
To tire your royalty.

LEONTES

We are tougher, brother,
Than you can put us to't.

POLIXENES

No longer stay.

LEONTES

One seven-night longer.

POLIXENES

Very sooth, to-morrow.

LEONTES

We'll part the time between's then; and in that
I'll no gainsaying.

POLIXENES

Press me not, beseech you, so.
There is no tongue that moves, none, none i' the world,
So soon as yours could win me: so it should now,
Were there necessity in your request, although
'Twere needful I denied it. My affairs
Do even drag me homeward: which to hinder
Were in your love a whip to me; my stay
To you a charge and trouble: to save both,
Farewell, our brother.

LEONTES

Tongue-tied our queen? speak you.

HERMIONE

I had thought, sir, to have held my peace until
You had drawn oaths from him not to stay. You, sir,
Charge him too coldly. Tell him, you are sure
All in Bohemia's well: this satisfaction
The by-gone day proclaim'd: say this to him,
He's beat from his best ward.

LEONTES

Well said, Hermione.

HERMIONE

To tell, he longs to see his son, were strong:
But let him say so then, and let him go;
But let him swear so, and he shall not stay,
We'll thwack him hence with distaffs.
Yet of your royal presence I'll adventure
The borrow of a week. When at Bohemia
You take my lord, I'll give him my commission
To let him there a month behind the gest
Prefix'd for's parting: yet, good deed, Leontes,
I love thee not a jar o' the clock behind
What lady-she her lord. You'll stay? [1]

POLIXENES

No, madam.

HERMIONE

Nay, but you will?

POLIXENES

I may not, verily.

HERMIONE

Verily!

You put me off with limber vows; but I,
Though you would seek to unsphere the stars with oaths,
Should yet say 'Sir, no going.' Verily,
You shall not go: a lady's 'Verily's 62
As potent as a lord's. Will you go yet?
Force me to keep you as a prisoner,
Not like a guest; so you shall pay your fees
When you depart, and save your thanks. How say you?
My prisoner? or my guest? by your dread 'Verily,'
One of them you shall be.

POLIXENES
Your guest, then, madam:
To be your prisoner should import offending;
Which is for me less easy to commit
Than you to punish.

HERMIONE
Not your gaoler, then,
But your kind hostess. Come, I'll question you
Of my lord's tricks and yours when you were boys: 77
You were pretty lordings then?

POLIXENES
We were, fair queen,
Two lads that thought there was no more behind
But such a day to-morrow as to-day,
And to be boy eternal.

HERMIONE
Was not my lord
The verier wag o' the two?

POLIXENES
We were as twinn'd lambs that did frisk i' the sun,
And bleat the one at the other: what we changed
Was innocence for innocence; we knew not 86
The doctrine of ill-doing, nor dream'd [2]
That any did. Had we pursued that life,
And our weak spirits ne'er been higher rear'd
With stronger blood, we should have answer'd heaven
Boldly 'not guilty;' the imposition clear'd
Hereditary ours.

HERMIONE
By this we gather
You have tripp'd since.

POLIXENES
O my most sacred lady!
Temptations have since then been born to's for
In those unfledged days was my wife a girl;
Your precious self had then not cross'd the eyes
Of my young play-fellow.

HERMIONE
Grace to boot! 100
Of this make no conclusion, lest you say
Your queen and I are devils: yet go on;
The offences we have made you do we'll answer,
If you first sinn'd with us and that with us
You did continue fault and that you slipp'd not
With any but with us.

LEONTES
Is he won yet?

HERMIONE
He'll stay, my lord.

LEONTES
At my request he would not.
Hermione, my dearest, thou never spokest
To better purpose.

HERMIONE
Never?

LEONTES
Never, but once.

HERMIONE
What! have I twice said well? when was't before? 115
I prithee tell me; cram's with praise, and make's
As fat as tame things: one good deed dying tongueless
Slaughters a thousand waiting upon that.
Our praises are our wages: you may ride's
With one soft kiss a thousand furlongs ere
With spur we beat an acre. But to the goal:
My last good deed was to entreat his stay:
What was my first? it has an elder sister,
Or I mistake you: O, would her name were Grace!
But once before I spoke to the purpose: when?
Nay, let me have't; I long.

LEONTES
Why, that was when 127
Three crabbed months had sour'd themselves to death,
Ere I could make thee open thy white hand
And clap thyself my love: then didst thou utter
'I am yours forever.'

HERMIONE
'Tis grace indeed.
Why, lo you now, I have spoke to the purpose twice:
The one for ever earn'd a royal husband;
The other for some while a friend.

LEONTES
[*Aside*] Too hot, too hot!
To mingle friendship far is mingling bloods.
I have tremor cordis on me: my heart dances;
But not for joy; not joy. This entertainment
May a free face put on, derive a liberty
From heartiness, from bounty, fertile bosom,
And well become the agent; 't may, I grant;
But to be paddling palms and pinching fingers,
As now they are, and making practised smiles,
As in a looking-glass, and then to sigh, as 'twere
The mort o' the deer; O, that is entertainment

My bosom likes not, nor my brows! Mamillius,
Art thou my boy?

MAMILLIUS
Ay, my good lord.

LEONTES
I' fecks!
Why, that's my bawcock. What, hast smutch'd thy nose?
They say it is a copy out of mine. Come, captain,
We must be neat; not neat, but cleanly, captain:
And yet the steer, the heifer and the calf
Are all call'd neat.—Still virginalling
Upon his palm!—How now, you wanton calf!
Art thou my calf?

MAMILLIUS
Yes, if you will, my lord.

LEONTES
Thou want'st a rough pash and the shoots that I have,
To be full like me: yet they say we are
Almost as like as eggs; women say so,
That will say any thing: but were they false
As o'er-dyed blacks, as wind, as waters, false [3]
As dice are to be wish'd by one that fixes
No bourn 'twixt his and mine, yet were it true
To say this boy were like me. Come, sir page,
Look on me with your welkin eye: sweet villain!
Most dear'st! my collop! Can thy dam?—may't be?—
Affection! thy intention stabs the centre:
Thou dost make possible things not so held,
Communicatest with dreams;—how can this be?—
With what's unreal thou coactive art,
And fellow'st nothing: then 'tis very credent
Thou mayst co-join with something; and thou dost,
And that beyond commission, and I find it,
And that to the infection of my brains
And hardening of my brows.

POLIXENES
What means Sicilia?

HERMIONE
He something seems unsettled.

POLIXENES
How, my lord!
What cheer? how is't with you, best brother?

HERMIONE
You look
As if you held a brow of much distraction:
Are you moved, my lord?

LEONTES
No, in good earnest.
How sometimes nature will betray its folly
Its tenderness, and make itself a pastime
To harder bosoms! Looking on the lines
Of my boy's face, methoughts I did recoil [4]
Twenty-three years, and saw myself unbreech'd,
In my green velvet coat, my dagger muzzled,
Lest it should bite its master, and so prove,
As ornaments oft do, too dangerous:
How like, methought, I then was to this kernel,
This squash, this gentleman. Mine honest friend,
Will you take eggs for money?

MAMILLIUS
No, my lord, I'll fight.

LEONTES
You will! why, happy man be's dole! My brother,
Are you so fond of your young prince as we
Do seem to be of ours?

POLIXENES
If at home, sir,
He's all my exercise, my mirth, my matter,
Now my sworn friend and then mine enemy,
My parasite, my soldier, statesman, all:
He makes a July's day short as December,
And with his varying childness cures in me
Thoughts that would thick my blood.

LEONTES
So stands this squire
Officed with me: we two will walk, my lord,
And leave you to your graver steps. Hermione,
How thou lovest us, show in our brother's welcome;
Let what is dear in Sicily be cheap:
Next to thyself and my young rover, he's
Apparent to my heart.

HERMIONE
If you would seek us,
We are yours i' the garden: shall's attend you there?

LEONTES
To your own bents dispose you: you'll be found,
Be you beneath the sky. [*Aside*] I am angling now,
Though you perceive me not how I give line.
Go to, go to!
How she holds up the neb, the bill to him!
And arms her with the boldness of a wife
To her allowing husband!
[*Exeunt Polixenes, Hermione, and Attendants.*
Gone already!
Inch-thick, knee-deep, o'er head and ears a fork'd one!
Go, play, boy, play: thy mother plays, and I
Play too, but so disgraced a part, whose issue
Will hiss me to my grave: contempt and clamour
Will be my knell. Go, play, boy, play. There have been,
Or I am much deceived, cuckolds ere now;

And many a man there is, even at this present,
Now while I speak this, holds his wife by the arm,
That little thinks she has been sluiced in's absence
And his pond fish'd by his next neighbour, by
Sir Smile, his neighbour: nay, there's comfort in't
Whiles other men have gates and those gates open'd,
As mine, against their will. Should all despair
That have revolted wives, the tenth of mankind
Would hang themselves. Physic for't there is none;
It is a bawdy planet, that will strike
Where 'tis predominant; and 'tis powerful, think it,
From east, west, north and south: be it concluded,
No barricado for a berry; know't;
It will let in and out the enemy
With bag and baggage: many thousand on's
Have the disease, and feel't not. How now, boy!

MAMILLIUS
I am like you, they say.

LEONTES
Why that's some comfort. What, Camillo there?

CAMILLO
Ay, my good lord.

LEONTES
Go play, Mamillius; thou'rt an honest man.
[*Exit Mamillius.*
Camillo, this great sir will yet stay longer.

CAMILLO
You had much ado to make his anchor hold:
When you cast out, it still came home.

LEONTES
Didst note it?

CAMILLO
He would not stay at your petitions; made
His business more material.

LEONTES
Didst perceive it?
[*Aside*] They're here with me already, whispering, rounding
'Sicilia is a so-forth:' 'tis far gone,
When I shall gust it last. How came't, Camillo
That he did stay?

CAMILLO
At the good queen's entreaty.

LEONTES
At the queen's be't: 'good' should be pertinent;
But, so it is, it is not. Was this taken
By any understanding pate but thine?
For thy conceit is soaking, will draw in
More than the common blocks: not noted, is't,
But of the finer natures? by some severals
Of head-piece extraordinary? lower messes
Perchance are to this business purblind? say.

CAMILLO
Business, my lord! I think most understand
Bohemia stays here longer.

LEONTES
Ha!

CAMILLO
Stays here longer.

LEONTES
Ay, but why?

CAMILLO
To satisfy your highness and the entreaties
Of our most gracious mistress.

LEONTES
Satisfy!
The entreaties of your mistress! satisfy!
Let that suffice. I have trusted thee, Camillo
With all the nearest things to my heart, as well
My chamber-councils, wherein, priest-like, thou
Hast cleansed my bosom, I from thee departed
Thy penitent reform'd: but we have been
Deceived in thy integrity, deceived
In that which seems so.

CAMILLO
Be it forbid, my lord!

LEONTES
To bide upon't, thou art not honest, or,
If thou inclinest that way, thou art a coward,
Which hoxes honesty behind, restraining
From course required; or else thou must be counted
A servant grafted in my serious trust
And therein negligent; or else a fool
That seest a game play'd home, the rich stake drawn,
And takest it all for jest.

CAMILLO
My gracious lord,
I may be negligent, foolish and fearful;
In every one of these no man is free,
But that his negligence, his folly, fear,
Among the infinite doings of the world,
Sometime puts forth. In your affairs, my lord,
If ever I were wilful-negligent,
It was my folly; if industriously
I play'd the fool, it was my negligence,
Not weighing well the end; if ever fearful
To do a thing, where I the issue doubted,
Whereof the execution did cry out
Against the non-performance, 'twas a fear
Which oft infects the wisest: these, my lord,
Are such allow'd infirmities that honesty
Is never free of. But, beseech your grace,
Be plainer with me; let me know my trespass
By its own visage: if I then deny it,
'Tis none of mine.

LEONTES
Ha' not you seen, Camillo,—
But that's past doubt, you have, or your eye-glass
Is thicker than a cuckold's horn,—or heard,—
For to a vision so apparent rumour
Cannot be mute,—or thought,—for cogitation
Resides not in that man that does not think,—
My wife is slippery? If thou wilt confess,
Or else be impudently negative,
To have nor eyes nor ears nor thought, then say
My wife's a hobby-horse, deserves a name
As rank as any flax-wench that puts to
Before her troth-plight: say't and justify't.

CAMILLO
I would not be a stander-by to hear
My sovereign mistress clouded so, without
My present vengeance taken: 'shrew my heart,
You never spoke what did become you less
Than this; which to reiterate were sin
As deep as that, though true. [5]

LEONTES
Is whispering nothing?
Is leaning cheek to cheek? is meeting noses?
Kissing with inside lip? stopping the career
Of laughing with a sigh?—a note infallible
Of breaking honesty—horsing foot on foot?
Skulking in corners? wishing clocks more swift?
Hours, minutes? noon, midnight? and all eyes
Blind with the pin and web but theirs, theirs only,
That would unseen be wicked? is this nothing?
Why, then the world and all that's in't is nothing;
The covering sky is nothing; Bohemia nothing;
My wife is nothing; nor nothing have these nothings,
If this be nothing.

CAMILLO
Good my lord, be cured
Of this diseased opinion, and betimes;
For 'tis most dangerous.

LEONTES
Say it be, 'tis true.

CAMILLO
No, no, my lord.

LEONTES
It is; you lie, you lie:
I say thou liest, Camillo, and I hate thee,
Pronounce thee a gross lout, a mindless slave,
Or else a hovering temporizer, that
Canst with thine eyes at once see good and evil,
Inclining to them both: were my wife's liver
Infected as her life, she would not live
The running of one glass.

CAMILLO
Who does infect her?

LEONTES
Why, he that wears her like her medal, hanging
About his neck, Bohemia: who, if I
Had servants true about me, that bare eyes
To see alike mine honour as their profits,
Their own particular thrifts, they would do that
Which should undo more doing: ay, and thou,
His cupbearer,—whom I from meaner form
Have bench'd and rear'd to worship, who mayst see
Plainly as heaven sees earth and earth sees heaven,
How I am galled,—mightst bespice a cup,
To give mine enemy a lasting wink;
Which draught to me were cordial.

CAMILLO
Sir, my lord,
I could do this, and that with no rash potion,
But with a lingering dram that should not work
Maliciously like poison: but I cannot
Believe this crack to be in my dread mistress,
So sovereignly being honourable.
I have loved thee,—

LEONTES
Make that thy question, and go rot!
Dost think I am so muddy, so unsettled,
To appoint myself in this vexation, sully
The purity and whiteness of my sheets,
Which to preserve is sleep, which being spotted
Is goads, thorns, nettles, tails of wasps,
Give scandal to the blood o' the prince my son,
Who I do think is mine and love as mine,
Without ripe moving to't? Would I do this?
Could man so blench?

CAMILLO
I must believe you, sir:
I do; and will fetch off Bohemia for't;
Provided that, when he's removed, your highness
Will take again your queen as yours at first,
Even for your son's sake; and thereby for sealing
The injury of tongues in courts and kingdoms
Known and allied to yours.

LEONTES
Thou dost advise me
Even so as I mine own course have set down:
I'll give no blemish to her honour, none.

CAMILLO
My lord,
Go then; and with a countenance as clear
As friendship wears at feasts, keep with Bohemia
And with your queen. I am his cupbearer:
If from me he have wholesome beverage,
Account me not your servant.

LEONTES
This is all:

Do't and thou hast the one half of my heart;
Do't not, thou split'st thine own.

CAMILLO
I'll do't, my lord.

LEONTES
I will seem friendly, as thou hast advised me.
[*Exit*.

CAMILLO
O miserable lady! But, for me,
What case stand I in? I must be the poisoner
Of good Polixenes; and my ground to do't
Is the obedience to a master, one
Who in rebellion with himself will have
All that are his so too. To do this deed,
Promotion follows. If I could find example
Of thousands that had struck anointed kings
And flourish'd after, I'ld not do't; but since
Nor brass nor stone nor parchment bears not one,
Let villany itself forswear't. I must
Forsake the court: to do't, or no, is certain
To me a break-neck. Happy star, reign now?
Here comes Bohemia.

Re-enter POLIXENES.

POLIXENES
This is strange: methinks
My favour here begins to warp. Not speak?
Good day, Camillo.

CAMILLO
Hail, most royal sir!

POLIXENES
What is the news i' the court?

CAMILLO
None rare, my lord.

POLIXENES
The king hath on him such a countenance
As he had lost some province and a region
Loved as he loves himself: even now I met him
With customary compliments; when he,
Wafting his eyes to the contrary and falling
A lip of much contempt, speeds from me and
So leaves me to consider what is breeding
That changeth thus his manners.

CAMILLO
I dare not know, my lord.

POLIXENES
How! dare not! do not. Do you know and dare not?
Be intelligent to me: 'tis thereabouts;
For, to yourself, what you do know, you must,
And cannot say, you dare not. Good Camillo,
Your changed complexions are to me a mirror
Which shows me mine changed too; for I must be
A party in this alteration, finding
Myself thus alter'd with 't.

CAMILLO
There is a sickness
Which puts some of us in distemper, but
I cannot name the disease; and it is caught
Of you that yet are well.

POLIXENES
How! caught of me!
Make me not sighted like the basilisk:
I have look'd on thousands, who have sped the better
By my regard, but kill'd none so. Camillo,—
As you are certainly a gentleman, thereto
Clerk-like experienced, which no less adorns
Our gentry than our parents' noble names,
In whose success we are gentle,—I beseech you,
If you know aught which does behove my knowledge
Thereof to be inform'd, imprison't not
In ignorant concealment.

CAMILLO
I may not answer.

POLIXENES
A sickness caught of me, and yet I well!
I must be answer'd. Dost thou hear, Camillo,
I conjure thee, by all the parts of man
Which honour does acknowledge, whereof the least
Is not this suit of mine, that thou declare
What incidency thou dost guess of harm
Is creeping toward me; how far off, how near;
Which may be prevented, if to be;
If not, how best to bear it.

CAMILLO
Sir, I will tell you;
Since I am charged in honour and by him
That I think honourable; therefore mark my counsel,
Which must be even as swiftly follow'd as
I mean to utter it, or both yourself and me
Cry lost, and so good night!

POLIXENES
On, good Camillo.

CAMILLO
I am appointed him to murder you.

POLIXENES
By whom, Camillo?

CAMILLO
By the king.

POLIXENES
For what?

CAMILLO
He thinks, nay, with all confidence he swears,
As he had seen't or been an instrument
To vice you to't, that you have touch'd his queen
Forbiddenly.

POLIXENES
O, then my best blood turn
To an infected jelly and my name
Be yoked with his that did betray the Best!
Turn then my freshest reputation to
A savour that may strike the dullest nostril
Where I arrive, and my approach be shunn'd,
Nay, hated too, worse than the great'st infection
That e'er was heard or read!
CAMILLO
Swear his thought over
By each particular star in heaven and
By all their influences, you may as well
Forbid the sea for to obey the moon
As or by oath remove or counsel shake
The fabric of his folly, whose foundation
Is piled upon his faith and will continue
The standing of his body.
POLIXENES
How should this grow?
CAMILLO
I know not: but I am sure 'tis safer to
Avoid what's grown than question how 'tis born.
If therefore you dare trust my honesty,
That lies enclosed in this trunk which you
Shall bear along unpawn'd, away to-night!
Your followers I will whisper to the business,
And will by twos and threes at several posterns
Clear them o' the city. For myself, I'll put
My fortunes to your service, which are here
By this discovery lost. Be not uncertain;
For, by the honour of my parents, I
Have utter'd truth: which if you seek to prove,
I dare not stand by; nor shall you be safer
Than one condemn'd by the king's own mouth, thereon
His execution sworn.
POLIXENES
I do believe thee:
I saw his heart in 's face. Give me thy hand:
Be pilot to me and thy places shall
Still neighbour mine. My ships are ready and
My people did expect my hence departure
Two days ago. This jealousy
Is for a precious creature: as she's rare
Must it be great, and as his person's mighty,
Must it be violent, and as he does conceive
He is dishonour'd by a man which ever
Profess'd to him, why, his revenges must
In that be made more bitter. Fear o'ershades me:
Good expedition be my friend, and comfort
The gracious queen, part of his theme, but nothing
Of his ill-ta'en suspicion! Come, Camillo;
I will respect thee as a father if
Thou bear'st my life off hence: let us avoid.
CAMILLO
It is in mine authority to command
The keys of all the posterns: please your highness
To take the urgent hour. Come, sir, away.
[*Exeunt.*

ACT TWO SCENE ONE

A room in LEONTES' *palace.*

Enter HERMIONE, MAMILLIUS, *and* Ladies.

HERMIONE
Take the boy to you: he so troubles me,
'Tis past enduring.
FIRST LADY
Come, my gracious lord,
Shall I be your playfellow?
MAMILLIUS
No, I'll none of you.
FIRST LADY
Why, my sweet lord?
MAMILLIUS
You'll kiss me hard and speak to me as if
I were a baby still. I love you better.
SECOND LADY
And why so, my lord?
MAMILLIUS
Not for because
Your brows are blacker; yet black brows, they say,
Become some women best, so that there be not
Too much hair there, but in a semicircle
Or a half-moon made with a pen.
SECOND LADY
Who taught you this? [6]
MAMILLIUS
I learnt it out of women's faces. Pray now
What colour are your eyebrows?
FIRST LADY
Blue, my lord.
MAMILLIUS
Nay, that's a mock: I have seen a lady's nose
That has been blue, but not her eyebrows.
FIRST LADY
Hark ye;
The queen your mother rounds apace: we shall
Present our services to a fine new prince
One of these days; and then you'ld wanton with us,
If we would have you.
SECOND LADY
She is spread of late
Into a goodly bulk: good time encounter her!

HERMIONE
What wisdom stirs amongst you? Come, sir, now 29
I am for you again: pray you, sit by us,
And tell 's a tale.

MAMILLIUS
Merry or sad shall't be?

HERMIONE
As merry as you will.

MAMILLIUS
A sad tale's best for winter: I have one [7]
Of sprites and goblins.

HERMIONE
Let's have that, good sir.
Come on, sit down: come on, and do your best
To fright me with your sprites; you're powerful at it.

MAMILLIUS
There was a man—

HERMIONE
Nay, come, sit down; then on.

MAMILLIUS
Dwelt by a churchyard: I will tell it softly; 41
Yond crickets shall not hear it.

HERMIONE
Come on, then,
And give't me in mine ear.

Enter LEONTES, *with* ANTIGONUS, Lords *and* others.

LEONTES
Was he met there? his train? Camillo with him?

FIRST LORD
Behind the tuft of pines I met them; never
Saw I men scour so on their way: I eyed them
Even to their ships.

LEONTES
How blest am I
In my just censure, in my true opinion!
Alack, for lesser knowledge! how accursed
In being so blest! There may be in the cup [8]
A spider steep'd, and one may drink, depart,
And yet partake no venom, for his knowledge
Is not infected: but if one present
The abhorr'd ingredient to his eye, make known
How he hath drunk, he cracks his gorge, his sides,
With violent hefts. I have drunk, and seen the spider.
Camillo was his help in this, his pander:
There is a plot against my life, my crown;
All's true that is mistrusted: that false villain
Whom I employ'd was pre-employ'd by him:
He has discover'd my design, and I 63
Remain a pinch'd thing; yea, a very trick
For them to play at will. How came the posterns
So easily open?

FIRST LORD
By his great authority;
Which often hath no less prevail'd than so
On your command.

LEONTES
I know't too well.
Give me the boy: I am glad you did not nurse him:
Though he does bear some signs of me, yet you
Have too much blood in him.

HERMIONE
What is this? sport?

LEONTES
Bear the boy hence; he shall not come about her;
Away with him! and let her sport herself 76
With that she's big with; for 'tis Polixenes
Has made thee swell thus.

HERMIONE
But I'ld say he had not,
And I'll be sworn you would believe my saying,
Howe'er you lean to the nayward.

LEONTES
You, my lords,
Look on her, mark her well; be but about
To say 'she is a goodly lady,' and
The justice of your hearts will thereto add
'Tis pity she's not honest, honourable:'
Praise her but for this her without-door form,
Which on my faith deserves high speech, and straight 89
The shrug, the hum or ha, these petty brands
That calumny doth use—O, I am out—
That mercy does, for calumny will sear
Virtue itself: these shrugs, these hums and ha's,
When you have said 'she's goodly,' come between
Ere you can say 'she's honest:' but be 't known,
From him that has most cause to grieve it should be,
She's an adulteress.

HERMIONE
Should a villain say so,
The most replenish'd villain in the world,
He were as much more villain: you, my lord
Do but mistake. 101

LEONTES
You have mistook, my lady,
Polixenes for Leontes: O thou thing!
Which I'll not call a creature of thy place,
Lest barbarism, making me the precedent,
Should a like language use to all degrees
And mannerly distinguishment leave out
Betwixt the prince and beggar: I have said
She's an adulteress; I have said with whom:
More. she's a traitor and Camillo is
A federary with her, and one that knows 111
What she should shame to know herself

But with her most vile principal, that she's
A bed-swerver, even as bad as those
That vulgars give bold'st titles, ay, and privy
To this their late escape.

HERMIONE
No, by my life.
Privy to none of this. How will this grieve you,
When you shall come to clearer knowledge that
You thus have publish'd me! Gentle my lord,
You scarce can right me throughly then to say
You did mistake.

LEONTES
No; if I mistake 123
In those foundations which I build upon,
The centre is not big enough to bear
A school-boy's top. Away with her! to prison!
He who shall speak for her is afar off guilty
But that he speaks.

HERMIONE
There's some ill planet reigns:
I must be patient till the heavens look
With an aspect more favourable. Good my lords,
I am not prone to weeping, as our sex
Commonly are; the want of which vain dew
Perchance shall dry your pities: but I have
That honourable grief lodged here which burns
Worse than tears drown: beseech you all, my lords,
With thoughts so qualified as your charities
Shall best instruct you, measure me; and so
The king's will be perform'd!

LEONTES
Shall I be heard?

HERMIONE
Who is't that goes with me? Beseech your highness,
My women may be with me; for you see
My plight requires it. Do not weep, good fools;
There is no cause: when you shall know your mistress
Has deserved prison, then abound in tears 145
As I come out: this action I now go on
Is for my better grace. Adieu, my lord:
I never wish'd to see you sorry; now
I trust I shall. My women, come; you have leave.

LEONTES
Go, do our bidding; hence!
[*Exit Queen, guarded; with Ladies.*

FIRST LORD
Beseech your highness, call the queen again.

ANTIGONUS
Be certain what you do, sir, lest your justice
Prove violence; in the which three great ones suffer,
Yourself, your queen, your son.

FIRST LORD
For her, my lord,
I dare my life lay down and will do't, sir,
Please you to accept it, that the queen is spotless
I' the eyes of heaven and to you; I mean,
In this which you accuse her.

ANTIGONUS
If it prove
She's otherwise, I'll keep my stables where [9]
I lodge my wife; I'll go in couples with her;
Than when I feel and see her no farther trust her;
For every inch of woman in the world,
Ay, every dram of woman's flesh is false,
If she be.

LEONTES
Hold your peaces.

FIRST LORD
Good my lord,—

ANTIGONUS
It is for you we speak, not for ourselves: 168
You are abused and by some putter-on
That will be damn'd for't; would I knew the villain,
I would land-damn him. Be she honour-flaw'd, [10]
I have three daughters; the eldest is eleven;
The second and the third, nine, and some five;
If this prove true, they'll pay for't: by mine honour,
I'll geld 'em all; fourteen they shall not see,
To bring false generations: they are co-heirs;
And I had rather glib myself than they
Should not produce fair issue.

LEONTES
Cease; no more.
You smell this business with a sense as cold
As is a dead man's nose: but I do see't and feel't
As you feel doing thus; and see withal [11]
The instruments that feel.

ANTIGONUS
If it be so,
We need no grave to bury honesty:
There's not a grain of it the face to sweeten
Of the whole dungy earth.

LEONTES
What! lack I credit?

FIRST LORD
I had rather you did lack than I, my lord,
Upon this ground; and more it would content me 192
To have her honour true than your suspicion,
Be blamed for't how you might.

LEONTES
Why, what need we
Commune with you of this, but rather follow
Our forceful instigation? Our prerogative
Calls not your counsels, but our natural goodness
Imparts this; which if you, or stupified
Or seeming so in skill, cannot or will not

Relish a truth like us, inform yourselves
We need no more of your advice: the matter,
The loss, the gain, the ordering on't, is all
Properly ours.

ANTIGONUS
And I wish, my liege,
You had only in your silent judgement tried it,
Without more overture.

LEONTES
How could that be?
Either thou art most ignorant by age,
Or thou wert born a fool. Camillo's flight,
Added to their familiarity,
Which was as gross as ever touch'd conjecture,
That lack'd sight only, nought for approbation
But only seeing, all other circumstances
Made up to the deed, doth push on this proceeding:
Yet, for a greater confirmation,
For in an act of this importance 'twere
Most piteous to be wild, I have dispatch'd in post
To sacred Delphos, to Apollo's temple,
Cleomenes and Dion, whom you know
Of stuff'd sufficiency: now from the oracle
They will bring all; whose spiritual counsel had,
Shall stop or spur me. Have I done well?

FIRST LORD
Well done, my lord.

LEONTES
Though I am satisfied and need no more
Than what I know, yet shall the oracle
Give rest to the minds of others, such as he
Whose ignorant credulity will not
Come up to the truth. So have we thought it good
From our free person she should be confined,
Lest that the treachery of the two fled hence
Be left her to perform. Come, follow us;
We are to speak in public; for this business
Will raise us all.

ANTIGONUS
[*Aside*] To laughter, as I take it,
If the good truth were known. [*Exeunt.*

ACT TWO SCENE TWO

A prison.

Enter PAULINA, *a* Gentleman, *and* Attendants.

PAULINA
The keeper of the prison, call to him;
Let him have knowledge who I am. [*Exit Gentleman.*
Good lady,
No court in Europe is too good for thee;
What dost thou then in prison?

Re-enter Gentleman, *with the* Gaoler.

Now, good sir,
You know me, do you not?

GAOLER
For a worthy lady
And one whom much I honour.

PAULINA
Pray you then,
Conduct me to the queen.

GAOLER
I may not, madam:
To the contrary I have express commandment.

PAULINA
Here's ado,
To lock up honesty and honour from
The access of gentle visitors! Is't lawful, pray you,
To see her women? any of them? Emilia?

GAOLER
So please you, madam,
To put apart these your attendants, I
Shall bring Emilia forth.

PAULINA
I pray now, call her.
Withdraw yourselves.
[*Exeunt Gentleman and Attendants.*

GAOLER
And, madam,
I must be present at your conference.

PAULINA
Well, be't so, prithee. [*Exit Gaoler.*
Here's such ado to make no stain a stain
As passes colouring.

Re-enter Gaoler, *with* EMILIA.

Dear gentlewoman,
How fares our gracious lady?

EMILIA
As well as one so great and so forlorn
May hold together: on her frights and griefs,
Which never tender lady hath borne greater,
She is something before her time deliver'd.

PAULINA
A boy?

EMILIA
A daughter, and a goodly babe,
Lusty and like to live: the queen receives
Much comfort in't; says 'My poor prisoner,
I am innocent as you.'

PAULINA
I dare be sworn:
These dangerous unsafe lunes i' the king, beshrew them!
He must be told on't, and he shall: the office
Becomes a woman best; I'll take't upon me:

If I prove honey-mouth'd let my tongue blister
And never to my red-look'd anger be
The trumpet any more. Pray you, Emilia,
Commend my best obedience to the queen:
If she dares trust me with her little babe,
I'll show't the king and undertake to be
Her advocate to the loud'st. We do not know
How he may soften at the sight o' the child:
The silence often of pure innocence
Persuades when speaking fails.

EMILIA
Most worthy madam,
Your honour and your goodness is so evident
That your free undertaking cannot miss
A thriving issue: there is no lady living
So meet for this great errand. Please your ladyship
To visit the next room, I'll presently
Acquaint the queen of your most noble offer;
Who but to-day hammer'd of this design,
But durst not tempt a minister of honour, 62
Lest she should be denied.

PAULINA
Tell her, Emilia.
I'll use that tongue I have: if wit flow from't
As boldness from my bosom, let 't not be doubted
I shall do good.

EMILIA
Now be you blest for it!
I'll to the queen: please you, come something nearer.

GAOLER
Madam, if't please the queen to send the babe,
I know not what I shall incur to pass it,
Having no warrant.

PAULINA
You need not fear it, sir:
This child was prisoner to the womb and is
By law and process of great nature thence 75
Freed and enfranchised, not a party to
The anger of the king nor guilty of,
If any be, the trespass of the queen.

GAOLER
I do believe it.

PAULINA
Do not you fear: upon mine honour, I
Will stand betwixt you and danger. [*Exeunt.*

ACT TWO SCENE THREE

A room in LEONTES' *palace.*
Enter LEONTES, ANTIGONUS, Lords, *and* Servants.

LEONTES
Nor night nor day no rest: it is but weakness
To bear the matter thus; mere weakness. If
The cause were not in being,—part o' the cause,
She the adulteress; for the harlot king
Is quite beyond mine arm, out of the blank
And level of my brain, plot-proof; but she
I can hook to me; say that she were gone,
Given to the fire, a moiety of my rest
Might come to me again. Who's there?

FIRST SERVANT
My lord?

LEONTES
How does the boy?

FIRST SERVANT
He took good rest to-night; 12
'Tis hoped his sickness is discharged.

LEONTES
To see his nobleness!
Conceiving the dishonour of his mother,
He straight declined, droop'd, took it deeply,
Fasten'd and fix'd the shame on't in himself,
Threw off his spirit, his appetite, his sleep,
And downright languish'd. Leave me solely: go,
See how he fares. [*Exit Servant*] Fie, fie! no thought of him:
The very thought of my revenges that way
Recoil upon me: in himself too mighty, 23
And in his parties, his alliance; let him be
Until a time may serve: for present vengeance,
Take it on her. Camillo and Polixenes
Laugh at me, make their pastime at my sorrow:
They should not laugh if I could reach them, nor
Shall she within my power.

Enter PAULINA, *with a child.*

FIRST LORD
You must not enter.

PAULINA
Nay, rather, good my lords, be second to me:
Fear you his tyrannous passion more, alas,
Than the queen's life? a gracious innocent soul,
More free than he is jealous.

ANTIGONUS
That's enough. 35

SECOND SERVANT
Madam, he hath not slept tonight; commanded
None should come at him.

PAULINA
Not so hot, good sir:
I come to bring him sleep. 'Tis such as you,
That creep like shadows by him and do sigh
At each his needless heavings, such as you
Nourish the cause of his awaking: I
Do come with words as medicinal as true,
Honest as either, to purge him of that humour
That presses him from sleep.

LEONTES
What noise there, ho?
PAULINA
No noise, my lord; but needful conference
About some gossips for your highness.
LEONTES
How!
Away with that audacious lady! Antigonus,
I charged thee that she should not come about me:
I knew she would.
ANTIGONUS
I told her so, my lord,
On your displeasure's peril and on mine,
She should not visit you.
LEONTES
What, canst not rule her?
PAULINA
From all dishonesty he can: in this,
Unless he take the course that you have done,
Commit me for committing honour, trust it,
He shall not rule me.
ANTIGONUS
La you now, you hear:
When she will take the rein I let her run;
But she'll not stumble.
PAULINA
Good my liege, I come;
And, I beseech you, hear me, who profess
Myself your loyal servant, your physician,
Your most obedient counsellor, yet that dare
Less appear so in comforting your evils,
Than such as most seem yours: I say, I come
From your good queen.
LEONTES
Good queen!
PAULINA
Good queen, my lord,
Good queen; I say good queen;
And would by combat make her good, so were I
A man, the worst about you.
LEONTES
Force her hence.
PAULINA
Let him that makes but trifles of his eyes
First hand me: on mine own accord I'll off;
But first I'll do my errand. The good queen,
For she is good, hath brought you forth a daughter;
Here 'tis; commends it to your blessing.
[*Laying down the child.*
LEONTES
Out!
A mankind witch! Hence with her, out o' door:
A most intelligencing bawd!
PAULINA
Not so:
I am as ignorant in that as you
In so entitling me, and no less honest
Than you are mad; which is enough, I'll warrant,
As this world goes, to pass for honest.
LEONTES
Traitors!
Will you not push her out? Give her the bastard.
Thou dotard! thou art woman-tired, unroosted
By thy dame Partlet here. Take up the bastard;
Take't up, I say; give't to thy crone.
PAULINA
For ever
Unvenerable be thy hands, if thou
Takest up the princess by that forced baseness
Which he has put upon't!
LEONTES
He dreads his wife.
PAULINA
So I would you did; then 'twere past all doubt
You'ld call your children yours.
LEONTES
A nest of traitors!
ANTIGONUS
I am none, by this good light.
PAULINA
Nor I, nor any
But one that's here, and that's himself, for he
The sacred honour of himself, his queen's,
His hopeful son's, his babe's, betrays to slander,
Whose sting is sharper than the sword's; and will not—
For, as the case now stands, it is a curse
He cannot be compell'd to't—once remove
The root of his opinion, which is rotten
As ever oak or stone was sound.
LEONTES
A callet
Of boundless tongue, who late hath beat her husband
And now baits me! This brat is none of mine;
It is the issue of Polixenes:
Hence with it, and together with the dam
Commit them to the fire!
PAULINA
It is yours;
And, might we lay the old proverb to your charge,
So like you, 'tis the worse. Behold, my lords,
Although the print be little, the whole matter
And copy of the father, eye, nose, lip,
The trick of's frown, his forehead, nay, the valley,
The pretty dimples of his chin and cheek,
His smiles,

The very mould and frame of hand, nail, finger:
And thou, good goddess Nature, which hast made it
So like to him that got it, if thou hast
The ordering of the mind too, 'mongst all colours
No yellow in't, lest she suspect, as he does,
Her children not her husband's!

LEONTES
A gross hag!
And, lozel, thou art worthy to be hang'd,
That wilt not stay her tongue.

ANTIGONUS
Hang all the husbands
That cannot do that feat, you'll leave yourself
Hardly one subject.

LEONTES
Once more, take her hence.

PAULINA
A most unworthy and unnatural lord
Can do no more.

LEONTES
I'll ha' thee burnt.

PAULINA
I care not:
It is an heretic that makes the fire,
Not she which burns in't. I'll not call you tyrant;
But this most cruel usage of your queen,
Not able to produce more accusation
Than your own weak-hinged fancy, something savours
Of tyranny and will ignoble make you,
Yea, scandalous to the world.

LEONTES
On your allegiance,
Out of the chamber with her! Were I a tyrant,
Where were her life? she durst not call me so,
If she did know me one. Away with her!

PAULINA
I pray you, do not push me; I'll be gone.
Look to your babe, my lord; 'tis yours: Jove send her
A better guiding spirit! What needs these hands?
You, that are thus so tender o'er his follies,
Will never do him good, not one of you.
So, so: farewell; we are gone. [*Exit.*

LEONTES
Thou, traitor, hast set on thy wife to this.
My child? away with't! Even thou, that hast
A heart so tender o'er it, take it hence
And see it instantly consumed with fire;
Even thou and none but thou. Take it up straight:
Within this hour bring me word 'tis done,
And by good testimony, or I'll seize thy life,
With what thou else call'st thine. If thou refuse
And wilt encounter with my wrath, say so;
The bastard brains with these my proper hands
Shall I dash out. Go, take it to the fire;
For thou set'st on thy wife.

ANTIGONUS
I did not, sir;
These lords, my noble fellows, if they please,
Can clear me in't.

LORDS
We can: my royal liege,
He is not guilty of her coming hither.

LEONTES
You're liars all.

FIRST LORD
Beseech your highness, give us better credit:
We have always truly served you, and beseech you
So to esteem of us, and on our knees we beg,
As recompense of our dear services
Past and to come, that you do change this purpose,
Which being so horrible, so bloody, must
Lead on to some foul issue: we all kneel.

LEONTES
I am a feather for each wind that blows:
Shall I live on to see this bastard kneel
And call me father? better burn it now
Than curse it then. But be it; let it live.
It shall not neither. You, sir, come you hither;
You that have been so tenderly officious
With Lady Margery, your midwife there,
To save this bastard's life,—for 'tis a bastard,
So sure as this beard's grey,—what will you adventure
To save this brat's life?

ANTIGONUS
Any thing, my lord,
That my ability may undergo
And nobleness impose: at least thus much:
I'll pawn the little blood which I have left
To save the innocent: any thing possible.

LEONTES
It shall be possible. Swear by this sword
Thou wilt perform my bidding.

ANTIGONUS
I will, my lord.

LEONTES
Mark and perform it, see'st thou! for the fail
Of any point in't shall not only be
Death to thyself but to thy lewd-tongued wife,
Whom for this time we pardon. We enjoin thee,
As thou art liege-man to us, that thou carry
This female bastard hence and that thou bear it
To some remote and desert place quite out
Of our dominions, and that there thou leave it,
Without more mercy, to its own protection [12]
And favour of the climate. As by strange fortune
It came to us, I do in justice charge thee,
On thy soul's peril and thy body's torture,

That thou commend it strangely to some place
Where chance may nurse or end it. Take it up.

ANTIGONUS
I swear to do this, though a present death
Had been more merciful. Come on, poor babe:
Some powerful spirit instruct the kites and ravens
To be thy nurses! Wolves and bears, they say
Casting their savageness aside have done
Like offices of pity. Sir, be prosperous
In more than this deed does require! And blessing
Against this cruelty fight on thy side,
Poor thing, condemn'd to loss!
[*Exit with the child.*

LEONTES
No, I'll not rear
Another's issue.

Enter a Servant.

SERVANT
Please your highness, posts
From those you sent to the oracle are come
An hour since: Cleomenes and Dion,
Being well arrived from Delphos, are both landed,
Hasting to the court.

FIRST LORD
So please you, sir, their speed
Hath been beyond account.

LEONTES
Twenty three days
They have been absent: 'tis good speed; foretells
The great Apollo suddenly will have
The truth of this appear. Prepare you, lords;
Summon a session, that we may arraign
Our most disloyal lady, for, as she hath
Been publicly accused, so shall she have
A just and open trial. While she lives
My heart will be a burthen to me. Leave me,
And think upon my bidding. [*Exeunt.*

ACT THREE SCENE ONE

A sea-port in Sicilia.

Enter CLEOMENES *and* DION.

CLEOMENES
The climate's delicate, the air most sweet,
Fertile the isle, the temple much surpassing
The common praise it bears.

DION
I shall report,
For most it caught me, the celestial habits,
Methinks I so should term them, and the reverence
Of the grave wearers. O, the sacrifice!
How ceremonious, solemn and unearthly
It was i' the offering!

CLEOMENES
But of all, the burst
And the ear-deafening voice o' the oracle,
Kin to Jove's thunder, so surprised my sense.
That I was nothing.

DION
If the event o' the journey
Prove as successful to the queen,—O be't so!—
As it hath been to us rare, pleasant, speedy,
The time is worth the use on't.

CLEOMENES
Great Apollo
Turn all to the best! These proclamations,
So forcing faults upon Hermione,
I little like.

DION
The violent carriage of it
Will clear or end the business: when the oracle,
Thus by Apollo's great divine seal'd up,
Shall the contents discover, something rare
Even then will rush to knowledge. Go: fresh horses!
And gracious be the issue! [*Exeunt.*

ACT THREE SCENE TWO

A court of Justice.

Enter LEONTES, Lords, *and* Officers.

LEONTES
This sessions, to our great grief we pronounce,
Even pushes 'gainst our heart: the party tried
The daughter of a king, our wife, and one
Of us too much beloved. Let us be clear'd
Of being tyrannous, since we so openly
Proceed in justice, which shall have due course,
Even to the guilt or the purgation.
Produce the prisoner.

OFFICER
It is his highness' pleasure that the queen
Appear in person here in court. Silence!

Enter HERMIONE *guarded*; PAULINA *and* Ladies *attending*.

LEONTES
Read the indictment.

OFFICER
[*Reads*] Hermione, queen to the worthy
Leontes, king of Sicilia, thou art here accused and arraigned of high treason, in committing adultery with Polixenes, king of Bohemia, and conspiring with Camillo

HERMIONE I doubt not, then, but innocence shall make false accusation blush.

to take away the life of our sovereign lord the king, thy royal husband: the pretence whereof being by circumstances partly laid open, thou, Hermione, contrary to the faith and allegiance of a true subject, didst counsel and aid them, for their better safety, to fly away by night.

HERMIONE

Since what I am to say must be but that
Which contradicts my accusation and
The testimony on my part no other
But what comes from myself, it shall scarce boot me
To say 'not guilty:' mine integrity
Being counted falsehood, shall, as I express it,
Be so received. But thus: if powers divine
Behold our human actions, as they do,
I doubt not then but innocence shall make
False accusation blush and tyranny
Tremble at patience. You, my lord, best know,
Who least will seem to do so, my past life
Hath been as continent, as chaste, as true,
As I am now unhappy; which is more
Than history can pattern, though devised
And play'd to take spectators. For behold me
A fellow of the royal bed, which owe
A moiety of the throne, a great king's daughter,
The mother to a hopeful prince, here standing
To prate and talk for life and honour 'fore
Who please to come and hear. For life, I prize it
As I weigh grief, which I would spare: for honour,
'Tis a derivative from me to mine,
And only that I stand for. I appeal
To your own conscience, sir, before Polixenes
Came to your court, how I was in your grace,
How merited to be so; since he came,
With what encounter so uncurrent I
Have strain'd to appear thus: if one jot beyond
The bound of honour, or in act or will
That way inclining, harden'd be the hearts
Of all that hear me, and my near'st of kin
Cry fie upon my grave!

LEONTES

I ne'er heard yet
That any of these bolder vices wanted
Less impudence to gainsay what they did
Than to perform it first.

HERMIONE
That's true enough;
Through 'tis a saying, sir, not due to me.
LEONTES
You will not own it.
HERMIONE
More than mistress of
Which comes to me in name of fault, I must not
At all acknowledge. For Polixenes,
With whom I am accused, I do confess
I loved him as in honour he required,
With such a kind of love as might become
A lady like me, with a love even such,
So and no other, as yourself commanded:
Which not to have done I think had been in me
Both disobedience and ingratitude
To you and toward your friend, whose love had spoke,
Even since it could speak, from an infant, freely
That it was yours. Now, for conspiracy,
I know not how it tastes; though it be dish'd
For me to try how: all I know of it
Is that Camillo was an honest man;
And why he left your court, the gods themselves,
Wotting no more than I, are ignorant.
LEONTES
You knew of his departure, as you know
What you have underta'en to do in's absence.
HERMIONE
Sir,
You speak a language that I understand not:
My life stands in the level of your dreams,
Which I'll lay down.
LEONTES
Your actions are my dreams;
You had a bastard by Polixenes,
And I but dream'd it. As you were past all shame,—
Those of your fact are so—so past all truth:
Which to deny concerns more than avails; for as
Thy brat hath been cast out, like to itself,
No father owning it,—which is, indeed,
More criminal in thee than it,—so thou
Shalt feel our justice, in whose easiest passage
Look for no less than death.
HERMIONE
Sir, spare your threats:
The bug which you would fright me with I seek.
To me can life be no commodity:
The crown and comfort of my life, your favour,
I do give lost; for I do feel it gone,
But know not how it went. My second joy
And first-fruits of my body, from his presence
I am barr'd, like one infectious. My third comfort,
Starr'd most unluckily, is from my breast,
The innocent milk in its most innocent mouth,
Haled out to murder: myself on every post
Proclaim'd a strumpet: with immodest hatred
The child-bed privilege denied, which 'longs
To women of all fashion; lastly, hurried
Here to this place, i' the open air, before
I have got strength of limit. Now, my liege,
Tell me what blessings I have here alive,
That I should fear to die? Therefore proceed.
But yet hear this; mistake me not; no life,
I prize it not a straw, but for mine honour,
Which I would free, if I shall be condemn'd
Upon surmises, all proofs sleeping else
But what your jealousies awake, I tell you
'Tis rigor and not law. Your honours all,
I do refer me to the oracle:
Apollo be my judge!
FIRST LORD
This your request
Is altogether just: therefore bring forth,
And in Apollo's name, his oracle.
[*Exeunt certain Officers.*
HERMIONE
The Emperor of Russia was my father:
O that he were alive, and here beholding
His daughter's trial! that he did but see
The flatness of my misery, yet with eyes
Of pity, not revenge!

Re-enter Officers, *with* CLEOMENES *and* DION.

OFFICER
You here shall swear upon this sword of justice,
That you, Cleomenes and Dion, have
Been both at Delphos, and from thence have brought
The seal'd-up oracle, by the hand deliver'd
Of great Apollo's priest and that since then
You have not dared to break the holy seal
Nor read the secrets in't.
CLEOMENES DION
All this we swear.
LEONTES
Break up the seals and read.
OFFICER
[*Reads*] Hermione is chaste; Polixenes blameless; Camillo a true subject; Leontes a jealous tyrant; his innocent babe truly begotten; and the king shall live without an heir, if that which is lost be not found.
LORDS
Now blessed be the great Apollo!
HERMIONE
Praised!

LEONTES
Hast thou read truth?
OFFICER
Ay, my lord; even so
As it is here set down. 149
LEONTES
There is no truth at all i' the oracle:
The sessions shall proceed: this is mere falsehood.

Enter Servant.

SERVANT
My lord the king, the king!
LEONTES
What is the business?
SERVANT
O sir, I shall be hated to report it!
The prince your son, with mere conceit and fear
Of the queen's speed, is gone.
LEONTES
How! gone!
SERVANT
Is dead.
LEONTES
Apollo's angry; and the heavens themselves
Do strike at my injustice. [*Hermione swoons.*
How now there!
PAULINA
This news is mortal to the queen: look down
And see what death is doing.
LEONTES
Take her hence: 164
Her heart is but o'ercharged; she will recover:
I have too much believed mine own suspicion:
Beseech you, tenderly apply to her
Some remedies for life.
[*Exeunt Paulina and Ladies, with Hermione.*
Apollo, pardon
My great profaneness 'gainst thine oracle!
I'll reconcile me to Polixenes,
New woo my queen, recall the good Camillo,
Whom I proclaim a man of truth, of mercy;
For, being transported by my jealousies
To bloody thoughts and to revenge, I chose
Camillo for the minister to poison
My friend Polixenes: which had been done,
But that the good mind of Camillo tardied
My swift command, though I with death and with
Reward did threaten and encourage him,
Not doing 't and being done: he, most humane
And fill'd with honour, to my kingly guest
Unclasp'd my practice, quit his fortunes here,
Which you knew great, and to the hazard
Of all incertainties himself commended, 185
No richer than his honour: how he glisters
Thorough my rust! and how his piety
Does my deeds make the blacker!

Re-enter PAULINA.

PAULINA
Woe the while!
O, cut my lace, lest my heart, cracking it,
Break too!
FIRST LORD
What fit is this, good lady?
PAULINA
What studied torments, tyrant, hast for me?
What wheels? racks? fires? what flaying? boiling?
In leads or oils? what old or newer torture
Must I receive, whose every word deserves
To taste of thy most worst? Thy tyranny 197
Together working with thy jealousies,
Fancies too weak for boys, too green and idle
For girls of nine, O, think what they have done
And then run mad indeed, stark mad! for all
Thy by-gone fooleries were but spices of it.
That thou betray'dst Polixenes, 'twas nothing;
That did but show thee, of a fool, inconstant
And damnable ingrateful: nor was't much,
Thou wouldst have poison'd good Camillo's honour,
To have him kill a king; poor trespasses, 207
More monstrous standing by: whereof I reckon
The casting forth to crows thy baby-daughter
To be or none or little; though a devil
Would have shed water out of fire ere done't:
Nor is't directly laid to thee, the death
Of the young prince, whose honourable thoughts,
Thoughts high for one so tender, cleft the heart
That could conceive a gross and foolish sire
Blemish'd his gracious dam: this is not, no,
Laid to thy answer: but the last,—O lords,
When have I said, cry 'woe!'—the queen, the queen,
The sweet'st, dear'st creature's dead, and vengeance for't
Not dropp'd down yet.
FIRST LORD
The higher powers forbid!
PAULINA
I say she's dead; I'll swear't. If word nor oath
Prevail not, go and see: if you can bring
Tincture or lustre in her lip, her eye,
Heat outwardly or breath within, I'll serve you
As I would do the gods. But, O thou tyrant!
Do not repent these things, for they are heavier
Than all thy woes can stir: therefore betake thee 230
To nothing but despair. A thousand knees
Ten thousand years together, naked, fasting,
Upon a barren mountain, and still winter

In storm perpetual, could not move the gods
To look that way thou wert.

LEONTES
Go on, go on:
Thou canst not speak too much; I have deserved
All tongues to talk their bitterest.

FIRST LORD
Say no more:
Howe'er the business goes, you have made fault
I' the boldness of your speech.

PAULINA
I am sorry for't:
All faults I make, when I shall come to know them, 244
I do repent. Alas! I have show'd too much
The rashness of a woman: he is touch'd
To the noble heart. What's gone and what's past help
Should be past grief: do not receive affliction
At my petition; I beseech you, rather
Let me be punish'd, that have minded you
Of what you should forget. Now, good my liege
Sir, royal sir, forgive a foolish woman:
The love I bore your queen—lo, fool again!—
I'll speak of her no more, nor of your children;
I'll not remember you of my own lord, 256
Who is lost too: take your patience to you,
And I'll say nothing.

LEONTES
Thou didst speak but well
When most the truth; which I receive much better
Than to be pitied of thee. Prithee, bring me
To the dead bodies of my queen and son:
One grave shall be for both: upon them shall
The causes of their death appear, unto
Our shame perpetual. Once a day I'll visit
The chapel where they lie, and tears shed there
Shall be my recreation: so long as nature 267
Will bear up with this exercise, so long
I daily vow to use it. Come and lead me
Unto these sorrows. [*Exeunt.*

ACT THREE SCENE THREE

Bohemia. A desert country near the sea.

Enter ANTIGONUS *with a Child, and a* Mariner.

ANTIGONUS
Thou art perfect then, our ship hath touch'd upon
The deserts of Bohemia?

MARINER
Ay, my lord: and fear
We have landed in ill time: the skies look grimly
And threaten present blusters. In my conscience,
The heavens with that we have in hand are angry
And frown upon 's.

ANTIGONUS
Their sacred wills be done! Go, get aboard;
Look to thy bark: I'll not be long before
I call upon thee.

MARINER
Make your best haste, and go not 11
Too far i' the land: 'tis like to be loud weather;
Besides, this place is famous for the creatures
Of prey that keep upon't.

ANTIGONUS
Go thou away:
I'll follow instantly.

MARINER
I am glad at heart
To be so rid o' the business. [*Exit.*

ANTIGONUS
Come, poor babe:
I have heard, but not believed, the spirits o' the dead
May walk again: if such thing be, thy mother
Appear'd to me last night, for ne'er was dream
So like a waking. To me comes a creature,
Sometimes her head on one side, some another;
I never saw a vessel of like sorrow, 25
So fill'd and so becoming: in pure white robes,
Like very sanctity, she did approach
My cabin where I lay; thrice bow'd before me,
And gasping to begin some speech, her eyes
Became two spouts: the fury spent, anon
Did this break-from her: 'Good Antigonus,'
Since fate, against thy better disposition,
Hath made thy person for the thrower-out
Of my poor babe, according to thine oath, 34
Places remote enough are in Bohemia,
There weep and leave it crying; and, for the babe
Is counted lost for ever, Perdita,
I prithee, call't. For this ungentle business,
Put on thee by my lord, thou ne'er shalt see
Thy wife Paulina more.' And so, with shrieks
She melted into air. Affrighted much,
I did in time collect myself and thought
This was so and no slumber. Dreams are toys:
Yet for this once, yea, superstitiously, 44
I will be squared by this. I do believe
Hermione hath suffer'd death, and that
Apollo would, this being indeed the issue
Of King Polixenes, it should here be laid,
Either for life or death, upon the earth
Of its right father. Blossom, speed thee well!
There lie, and there thy character: there these;
Which may, if fortune please, both breed thee, pretty,

And still rest thine. The storm begins: poor wretch,
That for thy mother's fault art thus exposed
To loss and what may follow! Weep I cannot,
But my heart bleeds; and most accursed am I
To be by oath enjoin'd to this. Farewell!
The day frowns more and more: thou'rt like to have
A lullaby too rough: I never saw
The heavens so dim by day. A savage clamour!
Well may I get aboard! This is the chase:
I am gone for ever. [*Exit, pursued by a bear.*

Enter a Shepherd.

SHEPHERD
I would there were no age between sixteen and three-and-twenty, or that youth would sleep out the rest; for there is nothing in the between but getting wenches with child, wronging the ancientry, stealing, fighting—Hark you now! Would any but these boiled brains of nineteen and two-and-twenty hunt this weather? They have scared away two of my best sheep, which I fear the wolf will sooner find than the master: if any where I have them, 'tis by the seaside, browsing of ivy. Good luck, an't be thy will! what have we here? Mercy on 's, a barne; a very pretty barne! A boy or a child, I wonder? A pretty one; a very pretty one: sure, some 'scape: though I am not bookish, yet I can read waiting-gentlewoman in the 'scape. This has been some stair-work, some trunk-work, some behind-door-work: they were warmer that got this than the poor thing is here. I'll take it up for pity: yet I'll tarry till my son come; he hallooed but even now. Whoa, ho, hoa!

Enter Clown.

CLOWN
Hilloa, loa!

SHEPHERD
What, art so near? If thou'lt see a thing to talk on when thou art dead and rotten, come hither. What ailest thou, man?

CLOWN
I have seen two such sights, by sea and by land! but I am not to say it is a sea, for it is now the sky: betwixt the firmament and it you cannot thrust a bodkin's point.

SHEPHERD
Why, boy, how is it?

CLOWN
I would you did but see how it chafes, how it rages, how it takes up the shore! but that's not to the point. O, the most piteous cry of the poor souls! sometimes to see 'em, and not to see 'em; now the ship boring the moon with her main-mast, and anon swallowed with yest and froth, as you'ld thrust a cork into a hogshead. And then for the land-service, to see how the bear tore out his shoulder-bone; how he cried to me for help and said his name was Antigonus, a nobleman. But to make an end of the ship, to see how the sea flap-dragoned it; but, first, how the poor souls roared, and the sea mocked them; and how the poor gentleman roared and the bear mocked him, both roaring louder than the sea or weather.

SHEPHERD
Name of mercy, when was this, boy?

CLOWN
Now, now: I have not winked since I saw these sights: the men are not yet cold under water, nor the bear half dined on the gentleman: he's at it now.

SHEPHERD
Would I had been by, to have helped the old man!

CLOWN
I would you had been by the ship side, to have helped her: there your charity would have lacked footing.

SHEPHERD
Heavy matters! heavy matters! but look thee here, boy. Now bless thyself: thou mettest with things dying, I with things newborn. Here's a sight for thee: look thee, a bearing-cloth for a squire's child! look thee here; take up, take up, boy; open't. So, let's see: it was told me I should be rich by the fairies. This is some changeling: open't. What's within, boy?

CLOWN
You're a made old man: if the sins of your youth are forgiven you, you're well to live. Gold! all gold! [13]

SHEPHERD
This is fairy gold, boy, and 'twill prove so: up with't, keep it close: home, home, the next way. We are lucky, boy; and to be so still requires nothing but secrecy. Let my sheep go: come, good boy, the next way home.

CLOWN
Go you the next way with your findings. I'll go see if the bear be gone from the gentleman and how much he hath eaten: they are never curst but when they are hungry: if there be any of him left, I'll bury it.

SHEPHERD
That's a good deed. If thou mayest discern by that which is left of him what he is, fetch me to the sight of him.

CLOWN
Marry, will I; and you shall help to put him i' the ground.

SHEPHERD
'Tis a lucky day, boy, and we'll do good deeds on't.
[*Exeunt.*

ACT FOUR SCENE ONE

Enter TIME, *the* Chorus.

TIME

I, that please some, try all, both joy and terror
Of good and bad, that makes and unfolds error,
Now take upon me, in the name of Time,
To use my wings. Impute it not a crime
To me or my swift passage, that I slide
O'er sixteen years and leave the growth untried
Of that wide gap, since it is in my power
To o'erthrow law and in one self-born hour
To plant and o'erwhelm custom. Let me pass
The same I am, ere ancient'st order was
Or what is now received: I witness to
The times that brought them in; so shall I do
To the freshest things now reigning and make stale
The glistering of this present, as my tale
Now seems to it. Your patience this allowing, [14]
I turn my glass and give my scene such growing
As you had slept between: Leontes leaving,
The effects of his fond jealousies so grieving
That he shuts up himself, imagine me,
Gentle spectators, that I now may be
In fair Bohemia; and remember well,
I mentioned a son o' the king's, which Florizel
I now name to you; and with speed so pace
To speak of Perdita, now grown in grace
Equal with wondering: what of her ensues
I list not prophesy; but let Time's news
Be known when 'tis brought forth. A shepherd's daughter,
And what to her adheres, which follows after,
Is the argument of Time. Of this allow,
If ever you have spent time worse ere now;
If never, yet that Time himself doth say
He wishes earnestly you never may. [*Exit.*

ACT FOUR SCENE TWO

Bohemia. The palace of POLIXENES.

Enter POLIXENES *and* CAMILLO.

POLIXENES

I pray thee, good Camillo, be no more importunate: 'tis a sickness denying thee any thing; a death to grant this.

CAMILLO

It is fifteen years since I saw my country:
though. [15]

I have for the most part been aired abroad, I desire to lay my bones there. Besides, the penitent king, my master, hath sent for me; to whose feeling sorrows I might be some allay, or I o'erween to think so, which is another spur to my departure. 9

POLIXENES

As thou lovest me, Camillo, wipe not out the rest of thy services by leaving me now: the need I have of thee thine own goodness hath made; better not to have had thee than thus to want thee: thou, having made me businesses which none without thee can sufficiently manage, must either stay to execute them thyself or take away with thee the very services thou hast done; which if I have not enough considered, as too much I cannot, to be more thankful to thee shall be my study, and my profit therein the heaping friendships. Of that fatal country, Sicilia, prithee speak no more; whose very naming punishes me with the remembrance of that penitent, as thou callest him, and reconciled king, my brother; whose loss of his most precious queen and children are even now to be afresh lamented. Say to me, when sawest thou the Prince Florizel, my son? Kings are no less unhappy, their issue not being gracious, than they are in losing them when they have approved their virtues.

CAMILLO

Sir, it is three days since I saw the prince. What his happier affairs may be, are to me unknown: but I have missingly noted, he is of late much retired from court and is less frequent to his princely exercises than formerly he hath appeared.

POLIXENES

I have considered so much, Camillo, and with some care; so far that I have eyes under my service which look upon his removedness; from whom I have this intelligence, that he is seldom from the house of a most homely shepherd; a man, they say, that from very nothing, and beyond the imagination of his neighbours, is grown into an unspeakable estate.

CAMILLO

I have heard, sir, of such a man, who hath a daughter of most rare note: the report of her is extended more than can be thought to begin from such a cottage. 43

POLIXENES

That's likewise part of my intelligence; but, I fear, the angle that plucks our son thither. Thou shalt accompany us to the place; where we will, not appearing what we are, have some question with the shepherd; from whose simplicity I think it not uneasy to get the cause of my son's resort thither. Prithee, be my present partner in this business, and lay aside the thoughts of Sicilia.

CAMILLO

I willingly obey your command. 52

POLIXENES

My best Camillo! We must disguise ourselves.

[*Exeunt.*

ACT FOUR SCENE THREE

A road near the Shepherd's cottage.

Enter AUTOLYCUS, *singing.*

AUTOLYCUS

When daffodils begin to peer,
With heigh! the doxy over the dale,
Why, then comes in the sweet o' the year;
For the red blood reigns in the winter's pale.
The white sheet bleaching on the hedge,
With heigh! the sweet birds, O, how they sing!
Doth set my pugging tooth on edge;
For a quart of ale is a dish for a king.
The lark, that tirra-lyra chants,
With heigh! with heigh! the thrush and the jay,
Are summer songs for me and my aunts,
While we lie tumbling in the hay.

I have served Prince Florizel and in my time wore three-pile; but now I am out of service:

But shall I go mourn for that, my dear?
The pale moon shines by night:
And when I wander here and there,
I then do most go right.
If tinkers may have leave to live,
And bear the sow-skin budget,
Then my account I well may give,
And in the stocks avouch it.

My traffic is sheets; when the kite builds, look to lesser linen. My father named me Autolycus; who being, as I am, littered under Mercury, was likewise a snapper-up of unconsidered trifles. With die and drab I purchased this caparison, and my revenue is the silly cheat. Gallows and knock are too powerful on the highway: beating and hanging are terrors to me: for the life to come, I sleep out the thought of it. A prize! a prize! [16]

Enter Clown.

CLOWN

Let me see: every 'leven wether tods; every tod yields pound and odd shilling; fifteen hundred shorn. what comes the wool to?

AUTOLYCUS

[*Aside*] If the springe hold, the cock's mine.

CLOWN

I cannot do't without counters. Let me see; what am I to buy for our sheep-shearing feast? Three pound of sugar, five pound of currants, rice,—what will this sister of mine do with rice? But my father hath made her mistress of the feast, and she lays it on. She hath made me four and twenty nosegays for the shearers, three-man-song-men all, and very good ones; but they are most of them means and bases; but one puritan amongst them, and he sings psalms to horn-pipes. I must have saffron to colour the warden pies; mace; dates?—none, that's out of my note; nutmegs, seven; a race or two of ginger, but that I may beg; four pound of prunes, and as many of raisins o' the sun.

AUTOLYCUS

O that ever I was born! [*Grovelling on the ground.*

CLOWN

I' the name of me— [17]

AUTOLYCUS

O, help me, help me! pluck but off these rags; and then, death, death!

CLOWN

Alack, poor soul! thou hast need of more rags to lay on thee, rather than have these off.

AUTOLYCUS

O sir, the loathsomeness of them offends me more than the stripes I have received, which are mighty ones and millions.

CLOWN

Alas, poor man! a million of beating may come to a great matter.

AUTOLYCUS

I am robbed, sir, and beaten; my money and apparel ta'en from me, and these detestable things put upon me.

CLOWN

What, by a horseman, or a footman?

AUTOLYCUS

A footman, sweet sir, a footman.

CLOWN

Indeed, he should be a footman by the garments he has left with thee: if this be a horseman's coat, it hath seen very hot service. Lend me thy hand, I'll help thee: come, lend me thy hand.

AUTOLYCUS

O, good sir, tenderly, O!

CLOWN

Alas, poor soul!

AUTOLYCUS

O, good sir, softly, good sir! I fear, sir, my shoulder-blade is out.

CLOWN

How now! canst stand?

AUTOLYCUS

[*Picking his pocket*] Softly, dear sir; good sir, softly. You ha' done me a charitable office

CLOWN

Dost lack any money? I have a little money for thee.

AUTOLYCUS

No, good sweet sir; no I beseech you, sir: I have a kinsman not past three quarters of a mile hence, unto whom I was going; I shall there have money, or anything I want: offer me no money, I pray you; that kills my heart.

CLOWN
What manner of fellow was he that robbed you? 82

AUTOLYCUS
A fellow, sir, that I have known to go about with troll-my-dames: I knew him once a servant of the prince: I cannot tell, good sir, for which of his virtues it was, but he was certainly whipped out of the court.

CLOWN
His vices, you would say; there's no virtue whipped out of the court: they cherish it to make it stay there; and yet it will no more but abide. 90

AUTOLYCUS
Vices, I would say, sir. I know this man well: he hath been since an ape-bearer; then a process-server, a bailiff; then he compassed a motion of the Prodigal Son, and married a tinker's wife within a mile where my land and living lies; and, having flown over many knavish professions, he settled only in rogue: some call him Autolycus.

CLOWN
Out upon him! prig, for my life, prig: he haunts wakes, fairs and bear-baitings.

AUTOLYCUS
Very true, sir; he, sir, he; that's the rogue that put me into this apparel. 101

CLOWN
Not a more cowardly rogue in all Bohemia: if you had but looked big and spit at him, he'ld have run.

AUTOLYCUS
I must confess to you, sir, I am no fighter: I am false of heart that way; and that he knew, I warrant him.

CLOWN
How do you now?

AUTOLYCUS
Sweet sir, much better than I was; I can stand and walk: I will even take my leave of you, and pace softly towards my kinsman's.

CLOWN
Shall I bring thee on the way?

AUTOLYCUS
No, good-faced sir; no, sweet sir.

CLOWN
Then fare thee well: I must go buy spices for our sheep-shearing.

AUTOLYCUS
Prosper you, sweet sir! [*Exit Clown.*
Your purse is not hot enough to purchase your spice. I'll be with you at your sheep-shearing too: if I make not this cheat bring out another and the shearers prove sheep, let me be unrolled and my name put in the book of virtue! 119
[*Sings*] Jog on, jog on, the foot-path way,
And merrily hent the stile-a:
A merry heart goes all the day,
Your sad tires in a mile-a. [*Exit.*

ACT FOUR SCENE FOUR

The Shepherd's *cottage.*

Enter FLORIZEL *and* PERDITA.

FLORIZEL
These your unusual weeds to each part of you
Do give a life: no shepherdess, but Flora
Peering in April's front. This your sheep-shearing
Is as a meeting of the petty gods,
And you the queen on't.

PERDITA
Sir, my gracious lord,
To chide at your extremes it not becomes me:
O, pardon, that I name them! Your high self,
The gracious mark o' the land, you have obscured
With a swain's wearing, and me, poor lowly maid,
Most goddess-like prank'd up: but that our feasts 11
In every mess have folly and the feeders
Digest it with a custom, I should blush
To see you so attired, sworn, I think,
To show myself a glass.

FLORIZEL
I bless the time
When my good falcon made her flight across
Thy father's ground.

PERDITA
Now Jove afford you cause!
To me the difference forges dread; your greatness
Hath not been used to fear. Even now I tremble
To think your father, by some accident,
Should pass this way as you did: O, the Fates!
How would he look, to see his work so noble
Vilely bound up? What would he say? Or how
Should I, in these my borrow'd flaunts, behold
The sternness of his presence?

FLORIZEL
Apprehend
Nothing but jollity. The gods themselves,
Humbling their deities to love, have taken
The shapes of beasts upon them: Jupiter
Became a bull, and bellow'd; the green Neptune
A ram, and bleated; and the fire-robed god,
Golden Apollo, a poor humble swain, 34
As I seem now. Their transformations
Were never for a piece of beauty rarer,
Nor in a way so chaste, since my desires
Run not before mine honour, nor my lusts
Burn hotter than my faith.

PERDITA
O, but, sir,
Your resolution cannot hold, when 'tis
Opposed, as it must be, by the power of the king:
One of these two must be necessities,
Which then will speak, that you must change this purpose,
Or I my life.

FLORIZEL
Thou dearest Perdita,
With these forced thoughts, I prithee, darken not
The mirth o' the feast. Or I'll be thine, my fair,
Or not my father's. For I cannot be
Mine own, nor any thing to any, if
I be not thine. To this I am most constant,
Though destiny say no. Be merry, gentle;
Strangle such thoughts as these with any thing
That you behold the while. Your guests are coming:
Lift up your countenance, as it were the day
Of celebration of that nuptial which
We two have sworn shall come.

PERDITA
'O lady Fortune,
Stand you auspicious!

FLORIZEL
See, your guests approach:
Address yourself to entertain them sprightly,
And let's be red with mirth.

Enter Shepherd, Clown, MOPSA, DORCAS, *and others, with* POLIXENES *and* CAMILLO *disguised.*

SHEPHERD
Fie, daughter! when my old wife lived, upon
This day she was both pantler, butler, cook,
Both dame and servant; welcomed all, served all;
Would sing her song and dance her turn; now here,
At upper end o' the table, now i' the middle;
On his shoulder, and his; her face o' fire
With labour and the thing she took to quench it,
She would to each one sip. You are retired,
As if you were a feasted one and not
The hostess of the meeting: pray you, bid
These unknown friends to's welcome; for it is
A way to make us better friends, more known.
Come, quench your blushes and present yourself
That which you are, mistress o' the feast: come on,
And bid us welcome to your sheep-shearing,
As your good flock shall prosper.

PERDITA
[*To Polixenes*] Sir, welcome:
It is my father's will I should take on me
The hostess-ship o' the day. [*To Camillo*]
You're welcome, sir.
Give me those flowers there, Dorcas. Reverend sirs,
For you there's rosemary and rue; these keep
Seeming and savour all the winter long:
Grace and remembrance be to you both,
And welcome to our shearing!

POLIXENES
Shepherdess,
A fair one are you—well you fit our ages
With flowers of winter.

PERDITA
Sir, the year growing ancient,
Not yet on summer's death, nor on the birth
Of trembling winter, the fairest flowers o' the season
Are our carnations and streak'd gillyvors,
Which some call nature's bastards: of that kind
Our rustic garden's barren; and I care not
To get slips of them.

POLIXENES
Wherefore, gentle maiden,
Do you neglect them?

PERDITA
For I have heard it said
There is an art which in their piedness shares
With great creating nature.

POLIXENES
Say there be;
Yet nature is made better by no mean
But nature makes that mean: so, over that art
Which you say adds to nature, is an art
That nature makes. You see, sweet maid, we marry
A gentler scion to the wildest stock,
And make conceive a bark of baser kind
By bud of nobler race: this is an art
Which does mend nature, change it rather, but
The art itself is nature.

PERDITA
So it is.

POLIXENES
Then make your garden rich in gillyvors,
And do not call them bastards.

PERDITA
I'll not put
The dibble in earth to set one slip of them;
No more than were I painted I would wish
This youth should say 'twere well and only therefore
Desire to breed by me. Here's flowers for you;
Hot lavender, mints, savoury, marjoram;
The marigold, that goes to bed wi' the sun
And with him rises weeping: these are flowers
Of middle summer, and I think they are given
To men of middle age. You're very welcome.

CAMILLO
I should leave grazing, were I of your flock,
And only live by gazing.

PERDITA For you there's rosemary and rue; . . . grace and remembrance be to you both.

PERDITA
Out, alas! 130
You'ld be so lean, that blasts of January
Would blow you through and through. Now, my fair'st friend,
I would I had some flowers o' the spring that might
Become your time of day; and yours, and yours,
That wear upon your virgin branches yet
Your maidenheads growing: O Proserpina,
For the flowers now, that frighted thou let'st fall
From Dis's waggon! daffodils,
That come before the swallow dares, and take
The winds of March with beauty; violets dim,
But sweeter than the lids of Juno's eyes 144
Or Cytherea's breath; pale primroses
That die unmarried, ere they can behold
Bight Phoebus in his strength—a malady
Most incident to maids; bold oxlips and
The crown imperial; lilies of all kinds,
The flower-de-luce being one! O, these I lack,
To make you garlands of, and my sweet friend,
To strew him o'er and o'er!

FLORIZEL
What, like a corse?

PERDITA
No, like a bank for love to lie and play on; 154
Not like a corse; or if, not to be buried,
But quick and in mine arms. Come, take your flowers:
Methinks I play as I have seen them do
In Whitsun pastorals: sure this robe of mine
Does change my disposition.

FLORIZEL
What you do
Still betters what is done. When you speak, sweet
I'ld have you do it ever: when you sing,
I'ld have you buy and sell so, so give alms,
Pray so; and, for the ordering your affairs,
To sing them too: when you do dance, I wish you 166
A wave o' the sea, that you might ever do
Nothing but that; move still, still so,
And own no other function: each your doing,
So singular in each particular,
Crowns what you are doing in the present deed,
That all your acts are queens.

PERDITA
O Doricles,
Your praises are too large: but that your youth,
And the true blood which peepeth fairly through't,
Do plainly give you out an unstain'd shepherd,
With wisdom I might fear, my Doricles,
You woo'd me the false way.
FLORIZEL
I think you have
As little skill to fear as I have purpose
To put you to't. But come; our dance, I pray:
Your hand, my Perdita: so turtles pair,
That never mean to part.
PERDITA
I'll swear for 'em.
POLIXENES
This is the prettiest low-born lass that ever
Ran on the green-sward: nothing she does or seems
But smacks of something greater than herself,
Too noble for this place.
CAMILLO
He tells her something
That makes her blood look out: good sooth, she is
The queen of curds and cream.
CLOWN
Come on, strike up!
DORCAS
Mopsa must be your mistress: marry, garlic,
To mend her kissing with!
MOPSA
Now, in good time!
CLOWN
Not a word, a word; we stand upon our manners.
Come, strike up!
[*Music. Here a dance of Shepherds and Shepherdesses.*
POLIXENES
Pray, good shepherd, what fair swain is this
Which dances with your daughter?
SHEPHERD
They call him Doricles; and boasts himself
To have a worthy feeding: but I have it
Upon his own report and I believe it;
He looks like sooth. He says he loves my daughter:
I think so too; for never gazed the moon
Upon the water as he'll stand and read
As 'twere my daughter's eyes: and, to be plain.
I think there is not half a kiss to choose
Who loves another best.
POLIXENES
She dances featly.
SHEPHERD
So she does any thing; though I report it,
That should be silent: if young Doricles
Do light upon her, she shall bring him that
Which he not dreams of.

Enter Servant.

SERVANT
O master, if you did but hear the pedlar at the door, you would never dance again after a tabor and pipe; no, the bagpipe could not move you: he sings several tunes faster than you'll tell money; he utters them as he had eaten ballads and all men's ears grew to his tunes.
CLOWN
He could never come better; he shall come in. I love a ballad but even too well, if it be doleful matter merrily set down, or a very pleasant thing indeed and sung lamentably.
SERVANT
He hath songs for man or woman, of all sizes; no milliner can so fit his customers with gloves: he has the prettiest love-songs for maids; so without bawdry, which is strange; with such delicate burthens of dildos and fadings, 'jump her and thump her;' and where some stretch-mouthed rascal would, as it were mean mischief and break a foul gap into the matter, he makes the maid to answer 'Whoop, do me no harm, good man;' puts him off, slights him, with
'Whoop, do me no harm, good man.'
POLIXENES
This is a brave fellow.
CLOWN
Believe me, thou talkest of an admirable conceited fellow. Has he any unbraided wares?
SERVANT
He hath ribbons of all the colours i' the rainbow; points more than all the lawyers in Bohemia can learnedly handle, though they come to him by the gross: inkles, caddisses, cambrics, lawns: why, he sings 'em over as they were gods or goddesses; you would think a smock were a she-angel, he so chants to the sleeve-hand and the work about the square on't.
CLOWN
Prithee bring him in; and let him approach singing.
PERDITA
Forewarn him that he use no scurrilous words in 's tunes. [*Exit Servant.*
CLOWN
You have of these pedlars, that have more in them than you'ld think, sister.
PERDITA
Ay, good brother, or go about to think.

Enter AUTOLYCUS, *singing.*

AUTOLYCUS
Lawn as white as driven snow;
Cyprus black as e'er was crow;

Gloves as sweet as damask roses;
Masks for faces and for noses;
Bugle bracelet, necklace amber,
Perfume for a lady's chamber;
Golden quoifs and stomachers,
For my lads to give their dears:
Pins and poking-sticks of steel,
What maids lack from head to heel:
Come buy of me, come; come buy, come buy;
Buy lads, or else your lasses cry: 261
Come buy.

CLOWN

If I were not in love with Mopsa, thou shouldst take no money of me; but being enthralled as I am, it will also be the bondage of certain ribbons and gloves.

MOPSA

I was promised them against the feast; but they come not too late now.

DORCAS

He hath promised you more than that, or there be liars. 269

MOPSA

He hath paid you all he promised you; may be, he has paid you more, which will shame you to give him again. 242

CLOWN

Is there no manners left among maids? will they wear their plackets where they should bear their faces? Is there not milking-time, when you are going to bed, or kiln-hole, to whistle off these secrets, but you must be tittle-tattling before all our guests? 'tis well they are whispering: clamour your tongues, and not a word more. [18]

MOPSA

I have done. Come, you promised me a tawdry-lace and a pair of sweet gloves.

CLOWN

Have I not told thee how I was cozened by the way and lost all my money?

AUTOLYCUS

And indeed, sir, there are cozeners abroad; therefore it behoves men to be wary.

CLOWN

Fear not thou, man, thou shalt lose nothing here.

AUTOLYCUS

I hope so, sir; for I have about me many parcels of charge. 287

CLOWN

What hast here? ballads?

MOPSA

Pray now, buy some: I love a ballad in print o' life, for then we are sure they are true.

AUTOLYCUS

Here's one to a very doleful tune, how a usurer's wife was brought to bed of twenty money-bags at a burthen and how she longed to eat adders' heads and toads carbonadoed.

MOPSA

Is it true, think you?

AUTOLYCUS

Very true, and but a month old. 296

DORCAS

Bless me from marrying a usurer!

AUTOLYCUS

Here's the midwife's name to't, one Mistress Tale-porter, and five or six honest wives that were present. Why should I carry lies abroad?

MOPSA

Pray you now, buy it.

CLOWN

Come on, lay it by: and let's first see moe ballads; we'll buy the other things anon.

AUTOLYCUS

Here's another ballad of a fish, that appeared upon the coast on Wednesday the fourscore of April, forty thousand fathom above water, and sung this ballad against the hard hearts of maids: it was thought she was a woman and was turned into a cold fish for she would not exchange flesh with one that loved her; the ballad is very pitiful and as true. [19]

DORCAS

Is it true too, think you?

AUTOLYCUS

Five justices' hand at it, and witnesses more than my pack will hold.

CLOWN

Lay it by too: another. 314

AUTOLYCUS

This is a merry ballad, but a very pretty one.

MOPSA

Let's have some merry ones.

AUTOLYCUS

Why, this is a passing merry one and goes to the tune of 'Two maids wooing a man:' there's scarce a maid westward but she sings it; 'tis in request, I can tell you.

MOPSA

We can both sing it: if thou'lt bear a part, thou shalt hear; 'tis in three parts. 321

DORCAS

We had the tune on't a month ago.

AUTOLYCUS

I can bear my part; you must know 'tis my occupation; have at it with you.

SONG.

A. Get you hence, for I must go
Where it fits not you to know.
D. Whither? M. O. Whither? D. Whiter?
M. It becomes thy oath full well,
Thou to me thy secrets tell.

AUTOLYCUS This is a passing merry one, and goes to the tune of "*Two maids wooing a man.*"

D. Me too, let me go thither.
M. Or thou goest to the grange or mill.
D. If to either, thou dost ill. 332
A. Neither. D. What, neither? A. Neither.
D. Thou hast sworn my love to be.
M. Thou hast sworn it more to me:
Then whither goest? say, whither?

CLOWN

We'll have this song out anon by ourselves: my father and the gentlemen are in sad talk, and we'll not trouble them. Come, bring away thy pack after me. Wenches, I'll buy for you both. Pedlar, let's have the first choice. Follow me, girls.

[*Exit with Dorcas and Mopsa.*

AUTOLYCUS

And you shall pay well for 'em. [*Follows singing.*
Will you buy any tape,
Or lace for your cape,
My dainty duck, my dear-a?
Any silk, any thread,
Any toys for your head,
Of the new'st and finest, finest wear-a?
Come to the pedlar;
Money's a medler, 350
That doth utter all men's ware-a. [*Exit.*

Re-enter Servant.

SERVANT

Master, there is three carters, three shepherds, three neat-herds, three swine-herds, that have made themselves all men of hair, they call themselves Saltiers, and they have a dance which the wenches say is a gallimaufry of gambols, because they are not in't; but they themselves are o' the mind, if it be not too rough for some that know little but bowling, it will please plentifully. 359

SHEPHERD

Away! we'll none on 't: here has been too much homely foolery already. I know, sir, we weary you.

POLIXENES

You weary those that refresh us: pray, let's see these four threes of herdsmen.

SERVANT

One three of them, by their own report, sir, hath danced before the king; and not the worst of the three but jumps twelve foot and a half by the squier.

SHEPHERD
Leave your prating: since these good men are pleased, let them come in; but quickly now.

SERVANT
Why, they stay at door, sir. *[Exit.*
Here a dance of twelve Satyrs.

POLIXENES
O, father, you'll know more of that hereafter.
[To Camillo] Is it not too far gone? 'Tis time to part them.
He's simple and tells much. *[To Florizel.*
How now, fair shepherd!
Your heart is full of something that does take
Your mind from feasting. Sooth, when I was young
And handed love as you do, I was wont
To load my she with knacks: I would have ransack'd
The pedlar's silken treasury and have pour'd it
To her acceptance; you have let him go
And nothing marted with him. If your lass
Interpretation should abuse and call this
Your lack of love or bounty, you were straited
For a reply, at least if you make a care
Of happy holding her.

FLORIZEL
Old sir, I know
She prizes not such trifles as these are:
The gifts she looks from me are pack'd and lock'd
Up in my heart; which I have given already,
But not deliver'd. O, hear me breathe my life
Before this ancient sir, who, it should seem,
Hath sometime loved! I take thy hand, this hand,
As soft as dove's down and as white as it
Or Ethiopian's tooth, or the fann'd snow that's bolted
By the northern blasts twice o'er.

POLIXENES
What follows this?
How prettily the young swain seems to wash
The hand was fair before! I have put you out:
But to your protestation; let me hear
What you profess.

FLORIZEL
Do, and be witness to 't.

POLIXENES
And this my neighbour too?

FLORIZEL
And he, and more
Than he, and men, the earth, the heavens, and all:
That, were I crown'd the most imperial monarch,
Thereof most worthy, were I the fairest youth
That ever made eye swerve, had force and knowledge
More than was ever man's, I would not prize them
Without her love; for her employ them all;
Commend them and condemn them to her service
Or to their own perdition.

POLIXENES
Fairly offer'd.

CAMILLO
This shows a sound affection.

SHEPHERD
But, my daughter,
Say you the like to him?

PERDITA
I cannot speak
So well, nothing so well; no, nor mean better:
By the pattern of mine own thoughts I cut out
The purity of his.

SHEPHERD
Take hands, a bargain!
And, friends unknown, you shall bear witness to 't:
I give my daughter to him, and will make
Her portion equal his.

FLORIZEL
O, that must be
I' the virtue of your daughter: one being dead,
I shall have more than you can dream of yet;
Enough then for your wonder. But, come on,
Contract us 'fore these witnesses.

SHEPHERD
Come, your hand;
And, daughter, yours.

POLIXENES
Soft, swain, awhile, beseech you;
Have you a father?

FLORIZEL
I have: but what of him?

POLIXENES
Knows he of this?

FLORIZEL
He neither does nor shall.

POLIXENES
Methinks a father
Is at the nuptial of his son a guest
That best becomes the table. Pray you once more,
Is not your father grown incapable
Of reasonable affairs? is he not stupid
With age and altering rheums? can he speak? hear?
Know man from man? dispute his own estate?
Lies he not bed-rid? and again does nothing
But what he did being childish?

FLORIZEL
No, good sir;
He has his health and ampler strength indeed
Than most have of his age.

POLIXENES
By my white beard,
You offer him, if this be so, a wrong
Something unfilial: reason my son

Should choose himself a wife, but as good reason
The father, all whose joy is nothing else
But fair posterity, should hold some counsel
In such a business.

FLORIZEL
I yield all this;
But for some other reasons, my grave sir,
Which 'tis not fit you know, I not acquaint
My father of this business.

POLIXENES
Let him know't.

FLORIZEL
He shall not.

POLIXENES
Prithee, let him.

FLORIZEL
No, he must not.

SHEPHERD
Let him, my son: he shall not need to grieve
At knowing of thy choice.

FLORIZEL
Come, come, he must not.
Mark our contract.

POLIXENES
Mark your divorce, young sir, [*Discovering himself.*
Whom son I dare not call; thou art too base
To be acknowledged: thou a sceptre's heir,
That thus affect'st a sheep-hook! Thou old traitor,
I am sorry that by hanging thee I can
But shorten thy life one week. And thou, fresh piece
Of excellent witchcraft, who of force must know
The royal fool thou copest with,—

SHEPHERD
O, my heart!

POLIXENES
I'll have thy beauty scratch'd with briers, and made
More homely than thy state. For thee, fond boy,
If I may ever know thou dost but sigh
That thou no more shalt see this knack, as never
I mean thou shalt, we'll bar thee from succession;
Not hold thee of our blood, no, not our kin,
Far than Deucalion off: mark thou my words: [20]
Follow us to the court. Thou churl, for this time,
Though full of our displeasure, yet we free thee
From the dead blow of it. And you, enchantment,—
Worthy enough a herdsman; yea, him too,
That makes himself, but for our honour therein,
Unworthy thee,—if ever henceforth thou
These rural latches to his entrance open,
Or hoop his body more with thy embraces,
I will devise a death as cruel for thee
As thou art tender to't. [*Exit.*

PERDITA
Even here undone!
I was not much afeard; for once or twice
I was about to speak and tell him plainly,
The selfsame sun that shines upon his court
Hides not his visage from our cottage but
Looks on alike. Will't please you, sir, be gone?
I told you what would come of this: beseech you,
Of your own state take care: this dream of mine,—
Being now awake, I'll queen it no inch farther,
But milk my ewes and weep.

CAMILLO
Why, how now, father!
Speak ere thou diest.

SHEPHERD
I cannot speak, nor think
Nor dare to know that which I know. O sir!
You have undone a man of fourscore three,
That thought to fill his grave in quiet, yea,
To die upon the bed my father died,
To lie close by his honest bones: but now
Some hangman must put on my shroud and lay me
Where no priest shovels in dust. O cursed wretch,
That knew'st this was the prince, and wouldst adventure
To mingle faith with him! Undone! undone!
If I might die within this hour, I have lived
To die when I desire. [*Exit.*

FLORIZEL
Why look you so upon me?
I am but sorry, not afeard; delay'd,
But nothing alter'd: what I was, I am;
More straining on for plucking back, not following
My leash unwillingly.

CAMILLO
Gracious my lord,
You know your father's temper: at this time
He will allow no speech, which I do guess
You do not purpose to him; and as hardly
Will he endure your sight as yet, I fear:
Then, till the fury of his highness settle,
Come not before him.

FLORIZEL
I not purpose it.
I think, Camillo?

CAMILLO
Even he, my lord.

PERDITA
How often have I told you 'twould be thus!
How often said, my dignity would last
But till 'twere known!

FLORIZEL
It cannot fail but by
The violation of my faith; and then
Let nature crush the sides o' the earth together
And mar the seeds within! Lift up thy looks:

From my succession wipe me, father; I 541
Am heir to my affection.

CAMILLO
Be advised.

FLORIZEL
I am, and by my fancy: if my reason
Will thereto be obedient, I have reason;
If not, my senses, better pleased with madness,
Do bid it welcome.

CAMILLO
This is desperate, sir.

FLORIZEL
So call it: but it does fulfil my vow;
I needs must think it honesty. Camillo,
Not for Bohemia, nor the pomp that may
Be thereat glean'd, for all the sun sees or 552
The close earth wombs or the profound seas hide
In unknown fathoms, will I break my oath
To this my fair beloved: therefore, I pray you,
As you have ever been my father's honour'd friend,
When he shall miss me,—as, in faith, I mean not
To see him any more,—cast your good counsels
Upon his passion; let myself and fortune
Tug for the time to come. This you may know
And so deliver, I am put to sea
With her whom here I cannot hold on shore;
And most opportune to our need I have 563
A vessel rides fast by, but not prepared
For this design. What course I mean to hold
Shall nothing benefit your knowledge, nor
Concern me the reporting.

CAMILLO
O my lord!
I would your spirit were easier for advice,
Or stronger for your need.

FLORIZEL
Hark, Perdita [*Drawing her aside.*
I'll hear you by and by.

CAMILLO
He's irremoveable,
Resolved for flight. Now were I happy, if
His going I could frame to serve my turn,
Save him from danger, do him love and honour,
Purchase the sight again of dear Sicilia 577
And that unhappy king, my master, whom
I so much thirst to see.

FLORIZEL
Now, good Camillo;
I am so fraught with curious business that
I leave out ceremony.

CAMILLO
Sir, I think
You have heard of my poor services, i' the love
That I have borne your father?

FLORIZEL
Very nobly
Have you deserved: it is my father's music
To speak your deeds, not little of his care
To have them recompensed as thought on.

CAMILLO
Well, my lord,
If you may please to think I love the king 591
And through him what is nearest to him, which is
Your gracious self, embrace but my direction:
If your more ponderous and settled project
May suffer alteration, on mine honour,
I'll point you where you shall have such receiving
As shall become your highness; where you may
Enjoy your mistress, from the whom, I see,
There's no disjunction to be made, but by—
As heavens forefend!—your ruin; marry her,
And, with my best endeavours in your absence,
Your discontenting father strive to qualify
And bring him up to liking.

FLORIZEL
How, Camillo,
May this, almost a miracle, be done?
That I may call thee something more than man
And after that trust to thee.

CAMILLO
Have you thought on
A place whereto you'll go?

FLORIZEL
Not any yet:
But as the unthought-on accident is guilty
To what we wildly do, so we profess
Ourselves to be the slaves of chance and flies
Of every wind that blows.

CAMILLO
Then list to me: 615
This follows, if you will not change your purpose
But undergo this flight, make for Sicilia,
And there present yourself and your fair princess,
For so I see she must be, 'fore Leontes:
She shall be habited as it becomes
The partner of your bed. Methinks I see
Leontes opening his free arms and weeping
His welcomes forth; asks thee the son forgiveness,
As 'twere i' the father's person; kisses the
hands 625
Of your fresh princess; o'er and o'er divides him
'Twixt his unkindness and his kindness; the one
He chides to hell and bids the other grow
Faster than thought or time.

FLORIZEL
Worthy Camillo,
What colour for my visitation shall I
Hold up before him?

CAMILLO
Sent by the king your father
To greet him and to give him comforts. Sir,
The manner of your bearing towards him, with
What you as from your father shall deliver,
Things known betwixt us three, I'll write you
down: 638
The which shall point you forth at every sitting
What you must say; that he shall not perceive
But that you have your father's bosom there
And speak his very heart.

FLORIZEL
I am bound to you:
There is some sap in this.

CAMILLO
A course more promising
Than a wild dedication of yourselves
To unpath'd waters, undream'd shores, most
certain
To miseries enough; no hope to help you,
But as you shake off one to take another;
Nothing so certain as your anchors, who 651
Do their best office, if they can but stay you
Where you'll be loath to be: besides you know
Prosperity's the very bond of love,
Whose fresh complexion and whose heart together
Affliction alters.

PERDITA
One of these is true:
I think affliction may subdue the cheek,
But not take in the mind.

CAMILLO
Yea, say you so?
There shall not at your father's house these seven
years
Be born another such.

FLORIZEL
My good Camillo,
She is as forward of her breeding as 665
She is i' the rear our birth. [21]

CAMILLO
I cannot say 'tis pity
She lacks instructions, for she seems a mistress
To most that teach.

PERDITA
Your pardon, sir; for this
I'll blush you thanks.

FLORIZEL
My prettiest Perdita!
But O, the thorns we stand upon! Camillo,
Preserver of my father, now of me,
The medicine of our house, how shall we do?
We are not furnish'd like Bohemia's son,
Nor shall appear in Sicilia. [22]

CAMILLO
My lord,
Fear none of this: I think you know my
fortunes 680
Do all lie there: it shall be so my care
To have you royally appointed as if
The scene you play were mine. For instance, sir,
That you may know you shall not want, one word.
[*They talk aside.*

Re-enter AUTOLYCUS.

AUTOLYCUS
Ha, ha! what a fool Honesty is! and Trust, his sworn brother, a very simple gentleman! I have sold all my trumpery; not a counterfeit stone, not a ribbon, glass, pomander, brooch, table-book, ballad, knife, tape, glove, shoe-tie, bracelet, horn-ring, to keep my pack from fasting: they throng who should buy first, as if my trinkets had been hallowed and brought a benediction to the buyer: by which means I saw whose purse was best in picture; and what I saw, to my good use I remembered. My clown, who wants but something to be a reasonable man, grew so in love with the wenches' song, that he would not stir his pettitoes till he had both tune and words; which so drew the rest of the herd to me that all their other senses stuck in ears: you might have pinched a placket, it was senseless; 'twas nothing to geld a codpiece of a purse; I could have filed keys off that hung in chains: no hearing, no feeling, but my sir's song, and admiring the nothing of it. So that in this time of lethargy I picked and cut most of their festival purses; and had not the old man come in with a whoo-bub against his daughter and the king's son and scared my choughs from the chaff, I had not left a purse alive in the whole army. 708
[*Camillo, Florizel, and Perdita come forward.*

CAMILLO
Nay, but my letters, by this means being there
So soon as you arrive, shall clear that doubt.

FLORIZEL
And those that you'll procure from King Leontes—

CAMILLO
Shall satisfy your father.

PERDITA
Happy be you!
All that you speak shows fair.

CAMILLO
Who have we here? [*Seeing Autolycus.*
We'll make an instrument of this, omit
Nothing may give us aid.

AUTOLYCUS
If they have overheard me now, why,
hanging. 719

CAMILLO

How now, good fellow! why shakest thou so? Fear not, man; here's no harm intended to thee.

AUTOLYCUS

I am a poor fellow, sir.

CAMILLO

Why, be so still; here's nobody will steal that from thee: yet for the outside of thy poverty we must make an exchange; therefore discase thee instantly,—thou must think there's a necessity in't,—and change garments with this gentleman: though the pennyworth on his side be the worst, yet hold thee, there's some boot. 728

AUTOLYCUS

I am a poor fellow, sir. [*Aside*] I know ye well enough.

CAMILLO

Nay, prithee, dispatch: the gentleman is half flayed already.

AUTOLYCUS

Are you in earnest, sir? [*Aside*] I smell the trick on't.

FLORIZEL

Dispatch, I prithee.

AUTOLYCUS

Indeed, I have had earnest; but I cannot with conscience take it.

CAMILLO

Unbuckle, unbuckle. 737

[*Florizel and Autolycus exchange garments.*

Fortunate mistress,—let my prophecy
Come home to ye!—you must retire yourself
Into some covert: take your sweetheart's hat
And pluck it o'er your brows, muffle your face,
Dismantle you, and, as you can, disliken
The truth of your own seeming; that you may—
For I do fear eyes over—to shipboard
Get undescried.

PERDITA

I see the play so lies
That I must bear a part.

CAMILLO

No remedy. 748
Have you done there?

FLORIZEL

Should I now meet my father,
He would not call me son.

CAMILLO

Nay, you shall have no hat. [*Giving it to Perdita.*
Come, lady, come. Farewell, my friend.

AUTOLYCUS

Adieu, sir.

FLORIZEL

O Perdita, what have we twain forgot!
Pray you, a word.

CAMILLO

[*Aside*] What I do next, shall be to tell the king
Of this escape and whither they are bound;
Wherein my hope is I shall so prevail
To force him after: in whose company
I shall review Sicilia, for whose sight
I have a woman's longing.

FLORIZEL

Fortune speed us!
Thus we set on, Camillo, to the sea-side. 764

CAMILLO

The swifter speed the better.

[*Exeunt Florizel, Perdita, and Camillo.*

AUTOLYCUS

I understand the business, I hear it: to have an open ear, a quick eye, and a nimble hand, is necessary for a cut-purse; a good nose is requisite also, to smell out work for the other senses. I see this is the time that the unjust man doth thrive. What an exchange had this been without boot! What a boot is here with this exchange! Sure the gods do this year connive at us, and we may do any thing extempore. The prince himself is about a piece of iniquity, stealing away from his father with his clog at his heels: if I thought it were a piece of honesty to acquaint the king withal, I would not do't: I hold it the more knavery to conceal it; and therein am I constant to my profession.

Re-enter Clown *and* Shepherd.

Aside, aside; here is more matter for a hot brain: every lane's end, every shop, church, session, hanging, yields a careful man work.

CLOWN

See, see; what a man you are now!
There is no other way but to tell the king she's a changeling and none of your flesh and blood.

SHEPHERD

Nay, but hear me.

CLOWN

Nay, but hear me.

SHEPHERD

Go to, then.

CLOWN

She being none of your flesh and blood, your flesh and blood has not offended the king; and so your flesh and blood is not to be punished by him. Show those things you found about her, those secret things, all but what she has with her: this being done, let the law go whistle: I warrant you.

SHEPHERD

I will tell the king all, every word, yea, and his son's pranks too; who, I may say, is no honest man, neither to his father nor to me, to go about to make me the king's brother-in-law. 797

CLOWN
Indeed, brother-in-law was the farthest off you could have been to him and then your blood had been the dearer by I know how much an ounce.

AUTOLYCUS
[*Aside*] Very wisely, puppies!

SHEPHERD
Well, let us to the king: there is that in this fardel will make him scratch his beard.

AUTOLYCUS
[*Aside*] I know not what impediment this complaint may be to the flight of my master.

CLOWN
Pray heartily he be at palace. [23]

AUTOLYCUS
[*Aside*] Though I am not naturally honest, I am so sometimes by chance: let me pocket up my pedlar's excrement. [*Takes off his false beard.*] How now, rustics! whither are you bound?

SHEPHERD
To the palace, an it like your worship.

AUTOLYCUS
Your affairs there, what, with whom, the condition of that fardel, the place of your dwelling, your names, your ages, of what having, breeding, and any thing that is fitting to be known, discover.

CLOWN
We are but plain fellows, sir.

AUTOLYCUS
A lie; you are rough and hairy. Let me have no lying: it becomes none but tradesmen, and they often give us soldiers the lie: but we pay them for it with stamped coin, not stabbing steel; therefore they do not give us the lie.

CLOWN
Your worship had like to have given us one, if you had not taken yourself with the manner.

SHEPHERD
Are you a courtier, an't like you, sir?

AUTOLYCUS
Whether it like me or no, I am a courtier. Seest thou not the air of the court in these enfoldings? hath not my gait in it the measure of the court? receives not thy nose court-odour from me? reflect I not on thy baseness court-contempt? Thinkest thou, for that I insinuate, or toaze from thee thy business, I am therefore no courtier? I am courtier cap-a-pe; and one that will either push on or pluck back thy business there: whereupon I command thee to open thy affair.

SHEPHERD
My business, sir, is to the king.

AUTOLYCUS
What advocate hast thou to him?

SHEPHERD
I know not, an't like you.

CLOWN
Advocate's the court-word for a pheasant: say you have none.

SHEPHERD
None, sir; I have no pheasant, cock nor hen.

AUTOLYCUS
How blessed are we that are not simple men!
Yet nature might have made me as these are,
Therefore I will not disdain.

CLOWN
This cannot be but a great courtier.

SHEPHERD
His garments are rich, but he wears them not handsomely.

CLOWN
He seems to be the more noble in being fantastical: a great man, I'll warrant; I know by the picking on's teeth.

AUTOLYCUS
The fardel there? what's i' the fardel?
Wherefore that box?

SHEPHERD
Sir, there lies such secrets in this fardel and box, which none must know but the king; and which he shall know within this hour, if I may come to the speech of him.

AUTOLYCUS
Age, thou hast lost thy labour.

SHEPHERD
Why, sir?

AUTOLYCUS
The king is not at the palace; he is gone aboard a new ship to purge melancholy and air himself: for, if thou beest capable of things serious, thou must know the king is full of grief.

SHEPHERD
So 'tis said, sir; about his son, that should have married a shepherd's daughter.

AUTOLYCUS
If that shepherd be not in hand-fast, let him fly: the curses he shall have, the tortures he shall feel, will break the back of man, the heart of monster.

CLOWN
Think you so, sir?

AUTOLYCUS
Not he alone shall suffer what wit can make heavy and vengeance bitter; but those that are germane to him, though removed fifty times, shall all come under the hangman: which though it be great pity, yet it is necessary. An old sheep-whistling rogue, a ram-tender, to offer to have his daughter come into grace! Some say he shall be stoned; but that death is too soft for him, say I: draw our throne into a sheep-cote! all deaths are too few, the sharpest too easy.

CLOWN

Has the old man e'er a son, sir, do you hear, an't like you, sir? 876

AUTOLYCUS

He has a son, who shall be flayed alive; then 'nointed over with honey, set on the head of a wasp's nest; then stand till he be three quarters and a dram dead; then recovered again with aqua-vitae or some other hot infusion; then, raw as he is, and in the hottest day prognostication proclaims, shall he be set against a brick-wall, the sun looking with a southward eye upon him, where he is to behold him with flies blown to death. But what talk we of these traitorly rascals, whose miseries are to be smiled at, their offences being so capital? Tell me, for you seem to be honest plain men, what you have to the king: being something gently considered, I'll bring you where he is aboard, tender your persons to his presence, whisper him in your behalfs; and if it be in man besides the king to effect your suits, here is man shall do it.

CLOWN

He seems to be of great authority: close with him, give him gold; and though authority be a stubborn bear, yet he is oft led by the nose with gold: show the inside of your purse to the outside of his hand, and no more ado. Remember 'stoned,' and 'flayed alive.'

SHEPHERD

An't please you, sir, to undertake the business for us, here is that gold I have: I'll make it as much more and leave this young man in pawn till I bring it you.

AUTOLYCUS

After I have done what I promised?

SHEPHERD

Ay, sir. 902

AUTOLYCUS

Well, give me the moiety. Are you a party in this business?

CLOWN

In some sort, sir: but though my case be a pitiful one, I hope I shall not be flayed out of it.

AUTOLYCUS

O, that's the case of the shepherd's son: hang him, he'll be made an example.

CLOWN

Comfort, good comfort! We must to the king and show our strange sights: he must know 'tis none of your daughter nor my sister; we are gone else. Sir, I will give you as much as this old man does when the business is performed, and remain, as he says, your pawn till it be brought you.

AUTOLYCUS

I will trust you. Walk before toward the sea-side; go on the right hand: I will but look upon the hedge and follow you.

CLOWN

We are blest in this man, as I may say, even blest.

SHEPHERD

Let's before as he bids us: he was provided to do us good. [*Exeunt Shepherd and Clown.*

AUTOLYCUS

If I had a mind to be honest, I see Fortune would not suffer me: she drops booties in my mouth. I am courted now with a double occasion, gold and a means to do the prince my master good; which who knows how that may turn back to my advancement? I will bring these two moles, these blind ones, aboard him: if he think it fit to shore them again and that the complaint they have to the king concerns him nothing, let him call me rogue for being so far officious; for I am proof against that title and what shame else belongs to't. To him will I present them: there may be matter in it. [*Exit.*

ACT FIVE SCENE ONE

A room in LEONTES' *palace.*

Enter LEONTES, CLEOMENES, DION, PAULINA, *and Servants.*

CLEOMENES

Sir, you have done enough, and have perform'd
A saint-like sorrow: no fault could you make,
Which you have not redeem'd; indeed, paid down
More penitence than done trespass: at the last,
Do as the heavens have done, forget your evil;
With them forgive yourself.

LEONTES

Whilst I remember
Her and her virtues, I cannot forget
My blemishes in them, and so still think of
The wrong I did myself; which was so much,
That heirless it hath made my kingdom and
Destroy'd the sweet'st companion that e'er man
Bred his hopes out of.

PAULINA

True, too true, my lord:
If, one by one, you wedded all the world,
Or from the all that are took something good,
To make a perfect woman, she you kill'd
Would be unparallel'd.

LEONTES

I think so. Kill'd!
She I kill'd! I did so: but thou strikest me
Sorely, to say I did; it is as bitter
Upon thy tongue as in my thought: now, good now,
Say so but seldom.

CLEOMENES

Not at all, good lady: 24

You might have spoken a thousand things that would
Have done the time more benefit and graced
Your kindness better.

PAULINA
You are one of those
Would have him wed again.

DION
If you would not so,
You pity not the state, nor the remembrance
Of his most sovereign name; consider little
What dangers, by his highness' fail of issue,
May drop upon his kingdom and devour
Incertain lookers on. What were more holy
Than to rejoice the former queen is well? 37
What holier than, for royalty's repair,
For present comfort and for future good,
To bless the bed of majesty again
With a sweet fellow to't?

PAULINA
There is none worthy,
Respecting her that's gone. Besides, the gods
Will have fulfill'd their secret purposes;
For has not the divine Apollo said,
Is't not the tenour of his oracle,
That King Leontes shall not have an heir
Till his lost child be found? which that it shall,
Is all as monstrous to our human reason 49
As my Antigonus to break his grave
And come again to me; who, on my life,
Did perish with the infant. 'Tis your counsel
My lord should to the heavens be contrary,
Oppose against their wills. [*To Leontes.*
Care not for issue;
The crown will find an heir: great Alexander
Left his to the worthiest; so his successor
Was like to be the best.

LEONTES
Good Paulina,
Who hast the memory of Hermione, 60
I know, in honour, O, that ever I
Had squared me to thy counsel! then, even now,
I might have look'd upon my queen's full eyes,
Have taken treasure from her lips—

PAULINA
And left them
More rich for what they yielded.

LEONTES
Thou speak'st truth.
No more such wives; therefore, no wife: one worse,
And better used, would make her sainted spirit
Again possess her corpse, and on this stage,
Where we're offenders now, appear soul-vex'd,
And begin, 'Why to me?'

PAULINA
Had she such power, 73
She had just cause.

LEONTES
She had; and would incense me
To murder her I married.

PAULINA
I should so.
Were I the ghost that walk'd, I'ld bid you mark
Her eye, and tell me for what dull part in't
You chose her; then I'ld shriek, that even your ears
Should rift to hear me; and the words that follow'd
Should be 'Remember mine.'

LEONTES
Stars, stars,
And all eyes else dead coals! Fear thou no wife;
I'll have no wife, Paulina.

PAULINA
Will you swear
Never to marry but by my free leave? 88

LEONTES
Never, Paulina; so be blest my spirit!

PAULINA
Then, good my lords, bear witness to his oath.

CLEOMENES
You tempt him over-much.

PAULINA
Unless another,
As like Hermione as is her picture,
Affront his eye.

CLEOMENES
Good madam,—

PAULINA
I have done.
Yet, if my lord will marry,—if you will, sir,
No remedy, but you will,—give me the office
To choose you a queen: she shall not be so young
As was your former; but she shall be such
As, walk'd your first queen's ghost, it should take joy 102
To see her in your arms.

LEONTES
My true Paulina,
We shall not marry till thou bid'st us.

PAULINA
That
Shall be when your first queen's again in breath;
Never till then.

Enter a Gentleman.

GENTLEMAN
One that gives out himself Prince Florizel,
Son of Polixenes, with his princess, she

The fairest I have yet beheld, desires access
To your high presence.

LEONTES
What with him? he comes not
Like to his father's greatness: his approach,
So out of circumstance and sudden, tells us
'Tis not a visitation framed, but forced
By need and accident. What train?

GENTLEMAN
But few,
And those but mean.

LEONTES
His princess, say you, with him?

GENTLEMAN
Ay, the most peerless piece of earth, I think,
That e'er the sun shone bright on.

PAULINA
O Hermione,
As every present time doth boast itself
Above a better gone, so must thy grave
Give way to what's seen now! Sir, you yourself
Have said and writ so, but your writing now
Is colder than that theme, 'She had not been,
Nor was not to be equall'd;'—thus your verse
Flow'd with her beauty once: 'tis shrewdly ebb'd,
To say you have seen a better.

GENTLEMAN
Pardon, madam:
The one I have almost forgot,—your pardon,—
The other, when she has obtain'd your eye,
Will have your tongue too. This is a creature,
Would she begin a sect, might quench the zeal
Of all professors else, make proselytes
Of who she but bid follow.

PAULINA
How! not women?

GENTLEMAN
Women will love her, that she is a woman
More worth than any man; men, that she is
The rarest of all women.

LEONTES
Go, Cleomenes;
Yourself, assisted with your honour'd friends,
Bring them to our embracement. Still, 'tis strange
[*Exeunt. Cleomenes and others.*
He thus should steal upon us.

PAULINA
Had our prince,
Jewel of children, seen this hour, he had pair'd
Well with this lord: there was not full a month
Between their births.

LEONTES
Prithee, no more; cease; thou know'st
He dies to me again when talk'd of: sure,
When I shall see this gentleman, thy speeches
Will bring me to consider that which may
Unfurnish me of reason. They are come.

Re-enter CLEOMENES *and others, with* FLORIZEL *and* PERDITA.

Your mother was most true to wedlock, prince;
For she did print your royal father off,
Conceiving you: were I but twenty one,
Your father's image is so hit in you,
His very air, that I should call you brother,
As I did him, and speak of something wildly
By us perform'd before. Most dearly welcome!
And your fair princess,—goddess!—O, alas!
I lost a couple, that 'twixt heaven and earth
Might thus have stood begetting wonder as
You, gracious couple, do: and then I lost—
All mine own folly—the society,
Amity too, of your brave father, whom,
Though bearing misery, I desire my life
Once more to look on him.

FLORIZEL
By his command
Have I here touch'd Sicilia and from him
Give you all greetings that a king, at friend,
Can send his brother: and, but infirmity
Which waits upon worn times hath something seized
His wish'd ability, he had himself
The lands and waters 'twixt your throne and his
Measured to look upon you; whom he loves—
He bade me say so—more than all the sceptres
And those that bear them living.

LEONTES
O my brother,
Good gentleman! the wrongs I have done thee stir
Afresh within me, and these thy offices,
So rarely kind, are as interpreters
Of my behind-hand slackness. Welcome hither,
As is the spring to the earth. And hath he too
Exposed this paragon to the fearful usage,
At least ungentle, of the dreadful Neptune,
To greet a man not worth her pains, much less
The adventure of her person?

FLORIZEL
Good my lord,
She came from Libya.

LEONTES
Where the warlike Smalus,
That noble honour'd lord, is fear'd and loved?

FLORIZEL
Most royal sir, from thence; from him, whose daughter
His tears proclaim'd his, parting with her:
thence,
A prosperous south-wind friendly, we have cross'd,

To execute the charge my father gave me
For visiting your highness: my best train
I have from your Sicilian shores dismiss'd;
Who for Bohemia bend, to signify
Not only my success in Libya, sir,
But my arrival and my wife's in safety
Here where we are.

LEONTES
The blessed gods
Purge all infection from our air whilst you
Do climate here! You have a holy father,
A graceful gentleman; against whose person,
So sacred as it is, I have done sin:
For which the heavens, taking angry note,
Have left me issueless; and your father's blest,
As he from heaven merits it, with you
Worthy his goodness. What might I have been,
Might I a son and daughter now have look'd on,
Such goodly things as you!

Enter a Lord.

LORD
Most noble sir,
That which I shall report will bear no credit,
Were not the proof so nigh. Please you, great sir, 219
Bohemia greets you from himself by me;
Desires you to attach his son, who has—
His dignity and duty both cast off—
Fled from his father, from his hopes, and with
A shepherd's daughter.

LEONTES
Where's Bohemia? speak.

LORD
Here in your city; I now came from him:
I speak amazedly; and it becomes
My marvel and my message. To your court
Whiles he was hastening, in the chase, it seems,
Of this fair couple, meets he on the way 230
The father of this seeming lady and
Her brother, having both their country quitted
With this young prince.

FLORIZEL
Camillo has betray'd me;
Whose honour and whose honesty till now
Endured all weathers.

LORD
Lay't so to his charge:
He's with the king your father.

LEONTES
Who? Camillo?

LORD
Camillo, sir; I spake with him; who now
Has these poor men in question. Never saw I
Wretches so quake: they kneel, they kiss the earth:
Forswear themselves as often as they speak:
Bohemia stops his ears, and threatens them
With divers deaths in death.

PERDITA
O my poor father!
The heaven spies upon us, will not have
Our contract celebrated.

LEONTES
You are married?

FLORIZEL
We are not, sir, nor are we like to be;
The stars, I see, will kiss the valleys first:
The odds for high and low's alike.

LEONTES
My lord,
Is this the daughter of a king?

FLORIZEL
She is,
When once she is my wife.

LEONTES
That 'once,' I see by your good father's speed, 257
Will come on very slowly. I am sorry,
Most sorry, you have broken from his liking
Where you were tied in duty, and as sorry
Your choice is not so rich in worth as beauty,
That you might well enjoy her.

FLORIZEL
Dear, look up:
Though Fortune, visible an enemy,
Should chase us with my father, power no jot
Hath she to change our loves. Beseech you, sir,
Remember since you owed no more to time
Than I do now: with thought of such affections,
Step forth mine advocate; at your request
My father will grant precious things as trifles.

LEONTES
Would he do so, I'ld beg your precious mistress,
Which he counts but a trifle.

PAULINA
Sir, my liege,
Your eye hath too much youth in't: not a month
'Fore your queen died, she was more worth such gazes
Than what you look on now.

LEONTES
I thought of her,
Even in these looks I made. [*To Florizel.*
But your petition
Is yet unanswer'd. I will to your father:
Your honour not o'erthrown by your desires,
I am friend to them and you: upon which errand
I now go toward him; therefore follow me
And mark what way I make: come, good my lord.
[*Exeunt.*

ACT FIVE SCENE TWO

Before LEONTES' *palace.*

Enter AUTOLYCUS *and a* Gentleman.

AUTOLYCUS

Beseech you, sir, were you present at this relation?

FIRST GENTLEMAN

I was by at the opening of the fardel, heard the old shepherd deliver the manner how he found it: whereupon, after a little amazedness, we were all commanded out of the chamber; only this methought I heard the shepherd say, he found the child.

AUTOLYCUS

I would most gladly know the issue of it. 7

FIRST GENTLEMAN

I make a broken delivery of the business; but the changes I perceived in the king and Camillo were very notes of admiration: they seemed almost, with staring on one another, to tear the cases of their eyes; there was speech in their dumbness, language in their very gesture; they looked as they had heard of a world ransomed, or one destroyed: a notable passion of wonder appeared in them; but the wisest beholder, that knew no more but seeing, could not say if the importance were joy or sorrow; but in the extremity of the one, it must needs be.

Enter another Gentleman.

Here comes a gentleman that haply knows more.
The news, Rogero?

SECOND GENTLEMAN

Nothing but bonfires: the oracle is fulfilled; the king's daughter is found: such a deal of wonder is broken out within this hour that ballad-makers cannot be able to express it.

Enter a third Gentleman.

Here comes the Lady Paulina's steward: he can deliver you more. How goes it now, sir? this news which is called true is so like an old tale, that the verity of it is in strong suspicion: has the king found his heir?

THIRD GENTLEMAN

Most true, if ever truth were pregnant by circumstance: that which you hear you'll swear you see, there is such unity in the proofs. The matter of Queen Hermione's, her jewel about the neck of it, the letters of Antigonus found with it which they know to be his character, the majesty of the creature in resemblance of the mother, the affection of nobleness which nature shows above her breeding, and many other evidences proclaim her with all certainty to be the king's daughter. Did you see the meeting of the two kings?

SECOND GENTLEMAN

No.

THIRD GENTLEMAN

Then have you lost a sight, which was to be seen, cannot be spoken of. There might you have beheld one joy crown another, so and in such manner that it seemed sorrow wept to take leave of them, for their joy waded in tears. There was casting up of eyes, holding up of hands, with countenances of such distraction that they were to be known by garment, not by favour. Our king, being ready to leap out of himself for joy of his found daughter, as if that joy were now become a loss, cries 'O, thy mother, thy mother!' then asks Bohemia forgiveness; then embraces his son-in-law; then again worries he his daughter with clipping her; now he thanks the old shepherd, which stands by like a weather-bitten conduit of many kings' reigns. I never heard of such another encounter, which lames report to follow it and undoes description to do it. 24

SECOND GENTLEMAN

What, pray you, became of Antigonus, that carried hence the child?

THIRD GENTLEMAN

Like an old tale still, which will have matter to rehearse, though credit be asleep and not an ear open. He was torn to pieces with a bear: this avouches the shepherd's son; who has not only his innocence, which seems much, to justify him, but a handkerchief and rings of his that Paulina knows.

FIRST GENTLEMAN

What became of his bark and his followers?

THIRD GENTLEMAN

Wrecked the same instant of their master's death and in the view of the shepherd: so that all the instruments which aided to expose the child were even then lost when it was found. But O, the noble combat that 'twixt joy and sorrow was fought in Paulina! She had one eye declined for the loss of her husband, another elevated that the oracle was fulfilled: she lifted the princess from the earth, and so locks her in embracing, as if she would pin her to her heart that she might no more be in danger of losing.

FIRST GENTLEMAN

The dignity of this act was worth the audience of kings and princes; for by such was it acted.

THIRD GENTLEMAN

One of the prettiest touches of all and that which angled for mine eyes, caught the water though not the fish, was when, at the relation of the queen's death, with the manner how she came to't bravely confessed and lamented by the king, how attentiveness wounded his daughter; till, from one sign of dolour to another, she did, with an 'Alas,' I would fain say, bleed tears, for I am sure my heart wept blood. Who was most marble there changed colour; some swooned, all sorrowed: if all the world could have seen 't, the woe had been universal. 86

FIRST GENTLEMAN

Are they returned to the court?

THIRD GENTLEMAN

No: the princess hearing of her mother's statue, which is in the keeping of Paulina,—a piece many years in doing and now newly performed by that rare Italian master, Julio Romano, who, had he himself eternity and could put breath into his work, would beguile Nature of her custom, so perfectly he is her ape: he so near to Hermione hath done Hermione that they say one would speak to her and stand in hope of answer: thither with all greediness of affection are they gone, and there they intend to sup. [25]

SECOND GENTLEMAN

I thought she had some great matter there in hand; for she hath privately twice or thrice a day, ever since the death of Hermione, visited that removed house. Shall we thither and with our company piece the rejoicing?

FIRST GENTLEMAN

Who would be thence that has the benefit of access? every wink of an eye some new grace will be born: our absence makes us unthrifty to our knowledge. Let's along. [*Exeunt Gentlemen.*

AUTOLYCUS

Now, had I not the dash of my former life in me, would preferment drop on my head. I brought the old man and his son aboard the prince; told him I heard them talk of a fardel and I know not what: but he at that time, over-fond of the shepherd's daughter, so he then took her to be, who began to be much seasick, and himself little better, extremity of weather continuing, this mystery remained undiscovered. But 'tis all one to me; for had I been the finder out of this secret, it would not have relished among my other discredits.

Enter Shepherd *and* Clown.

Here come those I have done good to against my will, and already appearing in the blossoms of their fortune.

SHEPHERD

Come, boy; I am past moe children, but thy sons and daughters will be all gentlemen born.

CLOWN

You are well met, sir. You denied to fight with me this other day, because I was no gentleman born. See you these clothes? say you see them not and think me still no gentleman born: you were best say these robes are not gentlemen born: give me the lie, do, and try whether I am not now a gentleman born.

AUTOLYCUS

I know you are now, sir, a gentleman born.

CLOWN

Ay, and have been so any time these four hours.

SHEPHERD

And so have I, boy.

CLOWN

So you have: but I was a gentleman born before my father; for the king's son took me by the hand, and called me brother; and then the two kings called my father brother; and then the prince my brother and the princess my sister called my father father; and so we wept, and there was the first gentleman-like tears that ever we shed.

SHEPHERD

We may live, son, to shed many more.

CLOWN

Ay; or else 'twere hard luck, being in so preposterous estate as we are.

AUTOLYCUS

I humbly beseech you, sir, to pardon me all the faults I have committed to your worship and to give me your good report to the prince my master.

SHEPHERD

Prithee, son, do; for we must be gentle, now we are gentlemen.

CLOWN

Thou wilt amend thy life?

AUTOLYCUS

Ay, an it like your good worship.

CLOWN

Give me thy hand: I will swear to the prince thou art as honest a true fellow as any is in Bohemia.

SHEPHERD

You may say it, but not swear it.

CLOWN

Not swear it, now I am a gentleman? Let boors and franklins say it, I'll swear it.

SHEPHERD

How if it be false, son?

CLOWN

If it be ne'er so false, a true gentleman may swear it in the behalf of his friend: and I'll swear to the prince thou art a tall fellow of thy hands and that thou wilt not be drunk; but I know thou art no tall fellow of thy hands and that thou wilt be drunk: but I'll swear it, and I would thou wouldst be a tall fellow of thy hands.

AUTOLYCUS

I will prove so, sir, to my power.

CLOWN

Ay, by any means prove a tall fellow: if I do not wonder how thou darest venture to be drunk, not being a tall fellow, trust me not. Hark! the kings and the princes, our kindred, are going to see the queen's picture. Come, follow us: we'll be thy good masters.

[*Exeunt.*

ACT FIVE SCENE THREE

A chapel in PAULINA'S *house.*

Enter LEONTES, POLIXENES, FLORIZEL, PERDITA, CAMILLO, PAULINA, Lords, *and* Attendants.

LEONTES
O grave and good Paulina, the great comfort
That I have had of thee!
PAULINA
What, sovereign sir,
I did not well I meant well. All my services
You have paid home: but that you have vouchsafed,
With your crown'd brother and these your contracted
Heirs of your kingdoms, my poor house to visit,
It is a surplus of your grace, which never
My life may last to answer.
LEONTES
O Paulina,
We honour you with trouble: but we came
To see the statue of our queen: your gallery
Have we pass'd through, not without much content
In many singularities; but we saw not
That which my daughter came to look upon,
The statue of her mother.
PAULINA
As she lived peerless,
So her dead likeness, I do well believe,
Excels whatever yet you look'd upon
Or hand of man hath done; therefore I keep it
Lonely, apart. But here it is: prepare
To see the life as lively mock'd as ever
Still sleep mock'd death: behold, and say 'tis well.
[*Paulina draws a curtain, and discovers Hermione standing like a statue.*
I like your silence, it the more shows off 25
Your wonder: but yet speak; first, you, my liege,
Comes it not something near?
LEONTES
Her natural posture!
Chide me, dear stone, that I may say indeed
Thou art Hermione; or rather, thou art she
In thy not chiding, for she was as tender
As infancy and grace. But yet, Paulina,
Hermione was not so much wrinkled, nothing
So aged as this seems.
POLIXENES
O, not by much.
PAULINA
So much the more our carver's excellence; 36
Which lets go by some sixteen years and makes her
As she lived now.
LEONTES
As now she might have done,
So much to my good comfort, as it is
Now piercing to my soul. O, thus she stood,
Even with such life of majesty, warm life,
As now it coldly stands, when first I woo'd her!
I am ashamed: does not the stone rebuke me
For being more stone than it? O royal piece,
There's magic in thy majesty, which has
My evils conjured to remembrance and 47
From thy admiring daughter took the spirits,
Standing like stone with thee.
PERDITA
And give me leave,
And do not say 'tis superstition, that
I kneel and then implore her blessing. Lady,
Dear queen, that ended when I but began,
Give me that hand of yours to kiss.
PAULINA
O, patience!
The statue is but newly fix'd, the colour's
Not dry.
CAMILLO
My lord, your sorrow was too sore laid on,
Which sixteen winters cannot blow away, 59
So many summers dry: scarce any joy
Did ever so long live; no sorrow
But kill'd itself much sooner.
POLIXENES
Dear my brother,
Let him that was the cause of this have power
To take off so much grief from you as he
Will piece up in himself.
PAULINA
Indeed, my lord,
If I had thought the sight of my poor image
Would thus have wrought you,—for the stone is mine—
I'ld not have show'd it.
LEONTES
Do not draw the curtain.
PAULINA
No longer shall you gaze on't, lest your fancy 73
May think anon it moves.
LEONTES
Let be, let be.
Would I were dead, but that, methinks, already—
What was he that did make it? See, my lord,
Would you not deem it breathed? and that those veins
Did verily bear blood?
POLIXENES
Masterly done.
The very life seems warm upon her lip.

LEONTES
The fixture of her eye has motion in't,
As we are mock'd with art.
PAULINA
I'll draw the curtain:
My lord's almost so far transported that
He'll think anon it lives.
LEONTES
O sweet Paulina, 88
Make me to think so twenty years together!
No settled senses of the world can match
The pleasure of that madness. Let 't alone.
PAULINA
I am sorry, sir, I have thus far stirr'd you: but
I could afflict you farther.
LEONTES
Do, Paulina;
For this affliction has a taste as sweet
As any cordial comfort. Still, methinks,
There is an air comes from her: what fine chisel
Could ever yet cut breath? Let no man mock me,
For I will kiss her.
PAULINA
Good my lord, forbear: 99
The ruddiness upon her lip is wet;
You'll mar it if you kiss it, stain your own
With oily painting. Shall I draw the curtain?
LEONTES
No, not these twenty years.
PERDITA
So long could I
Stand by, a looker on.
PAULINA
Either forbear,
Quit presently the chapel, or resolve you
For more amazement. If you can behold it,
I'll make the statue move indeed, descend
And take you by the hand: but then you'll think—
Which I protest against—I am assisted 112
By wicked powers.
LEONTES
What you can make her do,
I am content to look on: what to speak,
I am content to hear; for 'tis as easy
To make her speak as move.
PAULINA
It is required
You do awake your faith. Then all stand still;
On: those that think it is unlawful business
I am about, let them depart.
LEONTES
Proceed:
No foot shall stir.
PAULINA
Music, awake her; strike! [*Music.*
'Tis time; descend; be stone no more; approach; 125
Strike all that look upon with marvel. Come,
I'll fill your grave up: stir, nay, come away,
Bequeath to death your numbness, for from him
Dear life redeems you. You perceive she stirs:
[*Hermione comes down.*
Start not; her actions shall be holy as
You hear my spell is lawful: do not shun her
Until you see her die again; for then
You kill her double. Nay, present your hand:
When she was young you woo'd her; now in age
Is she become the suitor?
LEONTES
O, she's warm!
If this be magic, let it be an art
Lawful as eating.
POLIXENES
She embraces him.
CAMILLO
She hangs about his neck:
If she pertain to life let her speak too.
POLIXENES
Ay, and make't manifest where she has lived,
Or how stolen from the dead.
PAULINA
That she is living,
Were it but told you, should be hooted at
Like an old tale: but it appears she lives,
Though yet she speak not. Mark a little while.
Please you to interpose, fair madam: kneel
And pray your mother's blessing. Turn, good lady; 150
Our Perdita is found.
HERMIONE
You gods, look down
And from your sacred vials pour your graces
Upon my daughter's head! Tell me, mine own,
Where hast thou been preserved? where lived? how found
Thy father's court? for thou shalt hear that I,
Knowing by Paulina that the oracle
Gave hope thou wast in being, have preserved
Myself to see the issue.
PAULINA
There's time enough for that;
Lest they desire upon this push to trouble
Your joys with like relation. Go together, 163
You precious winners all; your exultation
Partake to every one. I, an old turtle,
Will wing me to some wither'd bough and there
My mate, that's never to be found again,
Lament till I am lost.

LEONTES
O, peace, Paulina!
Thou shouldst a husband take by my consent,
As I by thine a wife: this is a match,
And made between's by vows. Thou hast found mine;
But how, is to be question'd; for I saw her,
As I thought, dead, and have in vain said many
A prayer upon her grave. I'll not seek far—
For him, I partly know his mind—to find thee
An honourable husband. Come, Camillo,
And take her by the hand, whose worth and honesty
Is richly noted and here justified
By us, a pair of kings. Let's from this place.
What! look upon my brother: both your pardons,
That e'er I put between your holy looks
My ill suspicion. This is your son-in-law
And son unto the king, who, heavens directing,
Is troth-plight to your daughter. Good Paulina,
Lead us from hence, where we may leisurely
Each one demand an answer to his part
Perform'd in this wide gap of time since first
We were dissever'd: hastily lead away. [*Exeunt.*

Notes

1. What lady she her lord; – 'she' has been variously interpreted; Collier and Dyce proposed 'should,' destroying the beauty of the line; Schmidt makes the phrase 'lady she' = 'a woman that is a lady,' taking 'she' 'woman'; others print 'lady-she'; perhaps the word may be best explained as the pleonastic pronoun so common in popular poetry; the rhythm seems to favour this latter view.
2. The doctrine of ill-doing, nor dream'd; – so Folio 1; the later Folios, *'no nor dream'd'*; Spedding, *'neither dream'd'*; perhaps *'doctrine'* should be read as a tri-syllable; a harsh line would, however, result; and the reading of the later Folios has much to commend it.
3. False As o'er-dyed blacks; – Folios 1, 2, 3, *'o're dy'd'*; the words have been variously interpreted to mean 'fabrics dyed over with some other colour,' or, 'dyed too much'; Steevens saw in the phrase an allusion to the fact that black will receive no other hue without discovering itself through it; the passage may simply contain the idea, 'the blacker the garb, the less sincere the mourning.'
4. Methoughts; – so the Folios in this and other places; this erroneous form was probably due to *'methinks'*; it is noteworthy that the correct *'methought'* occurs a few lines below.
5. That, i.e. – 'that of which you accuse her.'
6. Who taught you this? – Rowe's emendation of the reading of Folio 1, *'taught 'this'* (with an apostrophe before *'this,'* indicating an elision); the later Folios, *'taught this.'*
7. A sad tale's best for winter, – hence the title of the play.
8. There may be in the cup A spider, – &c.; it was formerly believed that spiders were venomous.
9. I'll keep my stables where I lodge my wife; i.e. – 'I'll degrade my wife's chamber into a stable or dog kennel.'
10. I would land-damn him; – so the Folios; *'land-damm,' 'laudanum,' 'lamback,'* (*i.e.* 'ebat'), *'half-damn,' 'live-damn,' 'landan* (*lantan, rantan*),' *'lant-dam,'* are among the various emendations proposed; Schmidt suggests *'I would—Lord, damn him!'* In all probability the reading of the Folios should not be departed from, and it seems likely that Antigonus, having in the previous phrase used the word *'damn'd,'* here uses 'land-damn,' as a sort of grim quibble for *'landan,'*—a Gloucestershire word still in use "to express the punishment meted out to slanderers and adulterers by rustics traversing from house to house along the country side, blowing trumpets and beating drums or pans and kettles; when an audience was assembled the delinquents' names were proclaimed, and they were said to be landanned" (*cp.* Halliwell's *Dictionary of Archaic Words,* and *Notes and Queries* iii.): *landan, lantan, rantan,* were variants of the same word, which was probably imitative in its origin.
11. As you feel doing thus, – probably = my doing thus to you (*i.e.* touching him, or perhaps pulling his beard); *'the instruments that feel'* = my fingers.
12. To it own protection, – so Folios 1, 2; Folios 3, 4, *'its;'* the old possessive form 'it,' still in use in Lancashire, occurs again in this play (III. ii.); there are some dozen instances elsewhere: *'it own,'* may be regarded as a sort of idiomatic compound, the combination helping to maintain the archaism; *'its'* (Folio, *it 's*) *own,'* to be found in Act I. ii. 266 is said to be the only instance of its use in Shakespeare.
13. You're a made old man; – Theobald's emendation of the Folio reading *'mad,'* confirmed by a passage in Shakespeare's original:—"The goodman desired her to be quiet … if she could hold her peace they were made for ever."
14. To it, i.e. – 'the present.'
15. It is fifteen years since, – &c.; changed by Hanmer to *'sixteen,'* the number intended by Shakespeare.
16. When the kite builds, look to lesser linen; – alluding to this bird's habit of carrying off small linen garments hung out to dry; Autolycus preferred more substantial prey.
17. I' the name of me —; – probably, as has been suggested, the Clown's exclamation of *'Mercy'* is interrupted by Autolycus.
18. Clamour your tongues; – Hanmer's emendation *'charm'* has been generally adopted, but *'clamour'* is almost certainly correct (Taylor, the Water-Poet, wrote *'Clamour the promulgation of your tongues'*); *'clamour'* or rather *'clammer,'* is probably radically identical with *'clamber,'* the Scandinavian original of which *'klambra'* = 'to pinch closely together, to clamp.'
19. Another ballad of a fish; cp. e.g. – "A strange report of a monstrous fish that appeared in the form of a woman from her waist upward, seen in the sea"; entered in the Stationers' Registers in 1604.
20. Far than Deucalion off; 'far' – = 'farther'; the Folios all correctly read *'farre,' i.e.* the old form of the comparative of *'far.'*
21. I – *the rear o' her birth'*; Folios 1, 2, 3, *"our birth'*; Rowe first emended the line as in the text, though in his second edition he read *'o' our'* for *'o' her.'*

22. Appear, i.e. – appear so (like Bohemia's son).
23. At palace; – Folio 1, *'at 'Pallace;'* probably the apostrophe indicates "the omission of the article or its absorption in rapid pronunciation."
24. Weather-bitten conduit; – changed to *'weather-beaten'* in Folio 3; but *'weather-bitten'* is undoubtedly the correct form (*cp.* Skeat's *Etymological Dictionary*): *conduits* were frequently in the form of human figures.
25. That rare Italian master; – Giulio Pippi, known as 'Giulio Romano,' was born in 1492, and died in 1546; his fame as a painter was widespread; Shakespeare, taking him as 'a type of artistic excellence,' makes him a sculptor; it must, however, be remembered that the statue was a 'painted picture.' Much has been made of this reference by the advocates of Shakespeare's alleged Italian Journeys (*cp.* Elze's *Essays on Shakespeare*).

THE TEMPEST

THE TEMPEST

DRAMATIS PERSONAE

ALONSO, King of Naples.
SEBASTIAN, his brother.
PROSPERO, the right Duke of Milan.
ANTONIO, his brother, the usurping Duke of Milan.
FERDINAND, son to the King of Naples.
GONZALO, an honest old Counsellor.
ADRIAN, Lord.
FRANCISCO, Lord.
CALIBAN, a savage and deformed Slave.
TRINCULO, a Jester.
STEPHANO, a drunken Butler.
Master of a Ship.
Boatswain.
Mariners.
MIRANDA, daughter to Prospero.
ARIEL, an airy Spirit.
IRIS, presented by Spirits.
CERES, presented by Spirits.
JUNO, presented by Spirits.
Nymphs, presented by Spirits.
Reapers, presented by Spirits.
Other Spirits attending on Prospero.

SCENE—*A Ship at Sea: an island.*

ACT ONE SCENE ONE

On a ship at sea: a tempestuous noise of thunder and lightning heard.

Enter a Ship-Master *and* a Boatswain.

MASTER
Boatswain!

BOATSWAIN
Here, master: what cheer?

MASTER
Good, speak to the mariners: fall to't, yarely, or we run ourselves aground: bestir, bestir. [*Exit.*

Enter Mariners.

BOATSWAIN
Heigh, my hearts! cheerly, cheerly, my hearts! yare, yare! Take in the topsail. Tend to the master's whistle. Blow, till thou burst thy wind, if room enough!

Enter ALONSO, SEBASTIAN, ANTONIO, FERDINAND, GONZALO, *and others.*

ALONSO
Good boatswain, have care. Where's the master? Play the men. 9

BOATSWAIN
I pray now, keep below.

ANTONIO
Where is the master, boatswain?

BOATSWAIN
Do you not hear him? You mar our labour: keep your cabins: you do assist the storm.

GONZALO
Nay, good, be patient.

BOATSWAIN
When the sea is. Hence! What cares these roarers for the name of king? To cabin: silence! trouble us not.

GONZALO
Good, yet remember whom thou hast aboard. 17

BOATSWAIN
None that I more love than myself. You are a counsellor; if you can command these elements to silence, and work the peace of the present, we will not hand a rope more; use your authority: if you cannot, give thanks you have lived so long, and make yourself ready in your cabin for the mischance of the hour, if it so hap. Cheerly, good hearts! Out of our way, I say. [*Exit.*

GONZALO
I have great comfort from this fellow: methinks he hath no drowning mark upon him; his complexion is perfect gallows. Stand fast, good Fate, to his hanging: make the rope of his destiny our cable, for our own doth little advantage. If he be not born to be hanged, our case is miserable. [*Exeunt*

Re-enter Boatswain.

BOATSWAIN
Down with the topmast! yare! lower, lower! Bring her to try with main-course. [*A cry within.*
A plague upon this howling! they are louder than the weather or our office.

Re-enter SEBASTIAN, ANTONIO, *and* GONZALO.

Yet again! what do you here? Shall we give o'er and drown? Have you a mind to sink?

SEBASTIAN
A pox o' your throat, you bawling, blasphemous, incharitable dog!

BOATSWAIN
Work you then.

ANTONIO
Hang, cur! hang, you whoreson, insolent noisemaker! We are less afraid to be drowned than thou art.

GONZALO
I'll warrant him for drowning; though the ship were no stronger than a nutshell and as leaky as an unstaunched wench.

BOATSWAIN
Lay her a-hold, a-hold! set her two courses off to sea again: lay her off.

Enter Mariners *wet.*

MARINERS
All lost! to prayers, to prayers! all lost!

BOATSWAIN
What, must our mouths be cold?

GONZALO
The king and prince at prayers! let's assist them.
For our case is as theirs.

SEBASTIAN
I'm out of patience.

ANTONIO
We are merely cheated of our lives by drunkards:
This wide-chapp'd rascal—would thou mightst lie drowning
The washing of ten tides!

GONZALO
He'll be hang'd yet,
Though every drop of water swear against it
And gape at widest to glut him.
[A confused noise within: Mercy on us!—'We split, we split!'—'Farewell my wife and children!'—
'Farewell, brother!'—'We split, we split, we split!']

ANTONIO
Let's all sink with the king.

SEBASTIAN
Let's take leave of him. [*Exeunt Antonio and Sebastian.*

GONZALO
Now would I give a thousand furlongs of sea for an acre of barren ground, long heath, brown furze, any thing. The wills above be done! but I would fain die a dry death. [1] [*Exeunt.*

ACT ONE SCENE TWO

The island. Before PROSPERO'S *cell.*

Enter PROSPERO *and* MIRANDA.

MIRANDA
If by your art, my dearest father, you have
Put the wild waters in this roar, allay them.
The sky, it seems, would pour down stinking pitch,
But that the sea, mounting to the welkin's cheek.
Dashes the fire out. O, I have suffer'd
With those that I saw suffer: a brave vessel,
Who had, no doubt, some noble creature in her,
Dash'd all to pieces. O, the cry did knock
Against my very heart. Poor souls, they perish'd.
Had I been any god of power, I would
Have sunk the sea within the earth or ere
It should the good ship so have swallow'd and
The fraughting souls within her.

PROSPERO
Be collected:
No more amazement: tell your piteous heart
There's no harm done.

MIRANDA
O, woe the day!

PROSPERO
No harm.
I have done nothing but in care of thee,
Of thee, my dear one, thee, my daughter, who
Art ignorant of what thou art, nought knowing
Of whence I am, nor that I am more better

Than Prospero, master of a full poor cell, 23
And thy no greater father.

MIRANDA
More to know
Did never meddle with my thoughts.

PROSPERO
'Tis time
I should inform thee farther. Lend thy hand,
And pluck my magic garment from me. So:
[*Lays down his mantle.*
Lie there, my art. Wipe thou thine eyes; have comfort.
The direful spectacle of the wreck, which touch'd
The very virtue of compassion in thee,
I have with such provision in mine art
So safely ordered that there is no soul—
No, not so much perdition as an hair 35
Betid to any creature in the vessel
Which thou heard'st cry, which thou saw'st sink. Sit down;
For thou must now know farther.

MIRANDA
You have often
Begun to tell me what I am, but stopp'd
And left me to a bootless inquisition,
Concluding 'Stay: not yet.'

PROSPERO
The hour's now come;
The very minute bids thee ope thine ear;
Obey and be attentive. Canst thou remember
A time before we came unto this cell?
I do not think thou canst, for then thou wast not 49
Out three years old.

MIRANDA
Certainly, sir, I can.

PROSPERO
By what? by any other house or person?
Of any thing the image tell me that
Hath kept with thy remembrance.

MIRANDA
'Tis far off
And rather like a dream than an assurance
That my remembrance warrants. Had I not
Four or five women once that tended me?

PROSPERO
Thou hadst, and more, Miranda. But how is it
That this lives in thy mind? What seest thou else
In the dark backward and abysm of time? 61
If thou remember'st aught ere thou camest here,
How thou camest here thou mayst.

MIRANDA
But that I do not.

PROSPERO
Twelve year since, Miranda, twelve year since,
Thy father was the Duke of Milan and
A prince of power.

MIRANDA
Sir, are not you my father?

PROSPERO
Thy mother was a piece of virtue, and
She said thou wast my daughter; and thy father
Was Duke of Milan; and thou his only heir
And princess no worse issued.

MIRANDA
O the heavens!
What foul play had we, that we came from thence? 75
Or blessed was't we did?

PROSPERO
Both, both, my girl:
By foul play, as thou say'st, were we heaved thence,
But blessedly holp hither.

MIRANDA
O, my heart bleeds
To think o' the teen that I have turn'd you to,
Which is from my remembrance! Please you, farther.

PROSPERO
My brother and thy uncle, call'd Antonio—
I pray thee, mark me—that a brother should
Be so perfidious!—he whom next thyself
Of all the world I loved and to him put
The manage of my state; as at that time 87
Through all the signories it was the first
And Prospero the prime duke, being so reputed
In dignity, and for the liberal arts
Without a parallel; those being all my study,
The government I cast upon my brother
And to my state grew stranger, being transported
And rapt in secret studies. Thy false uncle—
Dost thou attend me?

MIRANDA
Sir, most heedfully.

PROSPERO
Being once perfected how to grant suits,
How to deny them, who to advance and who 98
To trash for over-topping, new created
The creatures that were mine, I say, or changed 'em,
Or else new form'd 'em; having both the key
Of officer and office, set all hearts i' the state
To what tune pleased his ear; that now he was
The ivy which had hid my princely trunk,
And suck'd my verdure out on't. Thou attend'st not.

MIRANDA
O, good sir, I do.

PROSPERO
I pray thee, mark me.
I, thus neglecting worldly ends, all dedicated
To closeness and the bettering of my mind 109

With that which, but by being so retired,
O'er-prized all popular rate, in my false brother
Awaked an evil nature; and my trust,
Like a good parent, did beget of him
A falsehood in its contrary as great
As my trust was; which had indeed no limit,
A confidence sans bound. He being thus lorded,
Not only with what my revenue yielded,
But what my power might else exact, like one
Who having into truth, by telling of it, [2]
Made such a sinner of his memory, 120
To credit his own lie, he did believe
He was indeed the duke; out o' the substitution,
And executing the outward face of royalty,
With all prerogative: hence his ambition growing—
Dost thou hear?

MIRANDA
Your tale, sir, would cure deafness.

PROSPERO
To have no screen between this part he play'd
And him he play'd it for, he needs will be
Absolute Milan. Me, poor man, my library
Was dukedom large enough: of temporal royalties 131
He thinks me now incapable; confederates—
So dry he was for sway—wi' the King of Naples
To give him annual tribute, do him homage,
Subject his coronet to his crown and bend
The dukedom yet unbow'd—alas, poor Milan!—
To most ignoble stooping.

MIRANDA
O the heavens!

PROSPERO
Mark his condition and the event; then tell me
If this might be a brother.

MIRANDA
I should sin
To think but nobly of my grandmother:
Good wombs have borne bad sons.

PROSPERO
Now the condition. 144
This King of Naples, being an enemy
To me inveterate, hearkens my brother's suit;
Which was, that he, in lieu o' the premises
Of homage and I know not how much tribute,
Should presently extirpate me and mine
Out of the dukedom and confer fair Milan
With all the honours on my brother: whereon,
A treacherous army levied, one midnight
Fated to the purpose did Antonio open
The gates of Milan, and, i' the dead of darkness, 155
The ministers for the purpose hurried thence
Me and thy crying self.

MIRANDA
Alack, for pity!
I, not remembering how I cried out then,
Will cry it o'er again: it is a hint
That wrings mine eyes to't.

PROSPERO
Hear a little further
And then I'll bring thee to the present business
Which now's upon's; without the which this story
Were most impertinent.

MIRANDA
Wherefore did they not
That hour destroy us?

PROSPERO
Well demanded, wench:
My tale provokes that question. Dear, they durst not, 170
So dear the love my people bore me, nor set
A mark so bloody on the business, but
With colours fairer painted their foul ends.
In few, they hurried us aboard a bark,
Bore us some leagues to sea; where they prepared
A rotten carcass of a boat, not rigg'd,
Nor tackle, sail, nor mast; the very rats
Instinctively have quit it: there they hoist us,
To cry to the sea that roar'd to us, to sigh
To the winds whose pity, sighing back again,
Did us but loving wrong.

MIRANDA
Alack, what trouble 182
Was I then to you!

PROSPERO
O, a cherubin
Thou wast that did preserve me. Thou didst smile,
Infused with a fortitude from heaven,
When I have deck'd the sea with drops full salt,
Under my burthen groan'd; which raised in me
An undergoing stomach, to bear up
Against what should ensue.

MIRANDA
How came we ashore?

PROSPERO
By Providence divine.
Some food we had and some fresh water that
A noble Neapolitan, Gonzalo, 195
Out of his charity, who being then appointed
Master of this design, did give us, with
Rich garments, linens, stuffs and necessaries,
Which since have steaded much; so, of his gentleness,
Knowing I loved my books, he furnish'd me
From mine own library with volumes that
I prize above my dukedom.

MIRANDA
Would I might
But ever see that man!
PROSPERO
Now I arise: [3] [*Resumes his mantle.*
Sit still, and hear the last of our sea-sorrow.
Here in this island we arrived; and here 208
Have I, thy schoolmaster, made thee more profit
Than other princesses can that have more time
For vainer hours and tutors not so careful.
MIRANDA
Heavens thank you for't! And now, I pray you, sir,
For still 'tis beating in my mind, your reason
For raising this sea-storm?
PROSPERO
Know thus far forth.
By accident most strange, bountiful Fortune,
Now my dear lady, hath mine enemies
Brought to this shore; and by my prescience
I find my zenith doth depend upon 219
A most auspicious star, whose influence
If now I court not but omit, my fortunes
Will ever after droop. Here cease more questions:
Thou art inclined to sleep; 'tis a good dulness,
And give it way: I know thou canst not choose.
[*Miranda sleeps.*
Come away, servant, come. I am ready now.
Approach, my Ariel, come.

Enter ARIEL.

ARIEL
All hail, great master! grave sir, hail! I come
To answer thy best pleasure; be't to fly, 228
To swim, to dive into the fire, to ride
On the curl'd clouds, to thy strong bidding task
Ariel and all his quality.
PROSPERO
Hast thou, spirit,
Perform'd to point the tempest that I bade thee?
ARIEL
To every article.
I boarded the king's ship; now on the beak,
Now in the waist, the deck, in every cabin,
I flamed amazement: sometime I'ld divide,
And burn in many places; on the topmast,
The yards and bowsprit, would I flame distinctly,
Then meet and join. Jove's lightnings, the precursors 241
O' the dreadful thunder-claps, more momentary
And sight-outrunning were not; the fire and cracks
Of sulphurous roaring the most mighty Neptune
Seem to besiege and make his bold waves tremble,
Yea, his dread trident shake.
PROSPERO
My brave spirit!
Who was so firm, so constant, that this coil
Would not infect his reason?
ARIEL
Not a soul
But felt a fever of the mad and play'd
Some tricks of desperation. All but mariners
Plunged in the foaming brine and quit the vessel, 255
Then all afire with me: the king's son, Ferdinand,
With hair up-staring,—then like reeds, not hair,—
Was the first man that leap'd; cried, 'Hell is empty,
And all the devils are here.'
PROSPERO
Why, that's my spirit!
But was not this nigh shore?
ARIEL
Close by, my master.
PROSPERO
But are they, Ariel, safe?
ARIEL
Not a hair perish'd;
On their sustaining garments not a blemish,
But fresher than before: and, as thou badest me,
In troops I have dispersed them 'bout the isle.
The king's son have I landed by himself; 269
Whom I left cooling of the air with sighs
In an odd angle of the isle and sitting,
His arms in this sad knot.
PROSPERO
Of the king's ship
The mariners say how thou hast disposed
And all the rest o' the fleet.
ARIEL
Safely in harbour
Is the king's ship; in the deep nook, where once
Thou call'dst me up at midnight to fetch dew
From the still-vex'd Bermoothes, there she's hid:
The mariners all under hatches stow'd; 280
Who, with a charm join'd to their suffer'd labour,
I have left asleep: and for the rest o' the fleet
Which I dispersed, they all have met again
And are upon the Mediterranean flote,
Bound sadly home for Naples,
Supposing that they saw the king's ship wreck'd
And his great person perish.
PROSPERO
Ariel, thy charge
Exactly is perform'd: but there's more work.
What is the time o' the day?
ARIEL
Past the mid season.

PROSPERO
At least two glasses. The time 'twixt six and now
Must by us both be spent most preciously.
ARIEL
Is there more toil? Since thou dost give me pains,
Let me remember thee what thou hast promised
Which is not yet perform'd me.
PROSPERO
How now? moody?
What is't thou canst demand?
ARIEL
My liberty.
PROSPERO
Before the time be out? no more!
ARIEL
I prithee,
Remember I have done thee worthy service;
Told thee no lies, made thee no mistakings, served
Without or grudge or grumblings: thou didst promise
To bate me a full year.
PROSPERO
Dost thou forget
From what a torment I did free thee?
ARIEL
No.
PROSPERO
Thou dost, and think'st it much to tread the ooze
Of the salt deep,
To run upon the sharp wind of the north,
To do me business in the veins o' the earth
When it is baked with frost.
ARIEL
I do not, sir.
PROSPERO
Thou liest, malignant thing! Hast thou forgot
The foul witch Sycorax, who with age and envy
Was grown into a hoop? hast thou forgot her?
ARIEL
No, sir.
PROSPERO
Thou hast. Where was she born? speak; tell me.
ARIEL
Sir, in Argier.
PROSPERO
O, was she so? I must
Once in a month recount what thou hast been,
Which thou forget'st. This damn'd witch Sycorax,
For mischiefs manifold and sorceries terrible
To enter human hearing, from Argier,
Thou know'st, was banish'd: for one thing she did [4]
They would not take her life. Is not this true?
ARIEL
Ay, sir.
PROSPERO
This blue-eyed hag was hither brought with child
And there was left by the sailors. Thou, my slave,
As thou report'st thyself, wast then her servant;
And, for thou wast a spirit too delicate
To act her earthly and abhorr'd commands,
Refusing her grand hests, she did confine thee,
By help of her more potent ministers
And in her most unmitigable rage,
Into a cloven pine; within which rift
Imprison'd thou didst painfully remain
A dozen years; within which space she died
And left thee there; where thou didst vent thy groans
As fast as mill-wheels strike. Then was this island—
Save for the son that she did litter here,
A freckled whelp hag-born—not honour'd with
A human shape.
ARIEL
Yes, Caliban her son.
PROSPERO
Dull thing, I say so; he, that Caliban
Whom now I keep in service. Thou best know'st
What torment I did find thee in; thy groans
Did make wolves howl and penetrate the breasts
Of ever angry bears: it was a torment
To lay upon the damn'd, which Sycorax
Could not again undo: it was mine art,
When I arrived and heard thee, that made gape
The pine and let thee out.
ARIEL
I thank thee, master.
PROSPERO
If thou more murmur'st, I will rend an oak
And peg thee in his knotty entrails till
Thou hast howl'd away twelve winters.
ARIEL
Pardon, master;
I will be correspondent to command
And do my spiriting gently.
PROSPERO
Do so, and after two days
I will discharge thee.
ARIEL
That's my noble master!
What shall I do? say what; what shall I do?
PROSPERO
Go make thyself like a nymph o' the sea: be subject
To no sight but thine and mine, invisible
To every eyeball else. Go take this shape

And hither come in't: go, hence with diligence!
[*Exit Ariel.*
Awake, dear heart, awake! thou hast slept well, Awake!

MIRANDA
The strangeness of your story put
Heaviness in me.

PROSPERO
Shake it off. Come on;
We'll visit Caliban my slave, who never
Yields us kind answer.

MIRANDA
'Tis a villain, sir,
I do not love to look on.

PROSPERO
But, as 'tis, 384
We cannot miss him: he does make our fire,
Fetch in our wood and serves in offices
That profit us. What, ho! slave! Caliban!
Thou earth, thou! speak.

CALIBAN
[*Within*] There's wood enough within.

PROSPERO
Come forth, I say! there's other business for thee:
Come, thou tortoise! when?

Re-enter ARIEL *like a water-nymph.*

Fine apparition! My quaint Ariel,
Hark in thine ear.

ARIEL
My lord, it shall be done. [*Exit.*

PROSPERO
Thou poisonous slave, got by the devil himself
Upon thy wicked dam, come forth! 396

Enter CALIBAN.

CALIBAN
As wicked dew as e'er my mother brush'd
With raven's feather from unwholesome fen
Drop on you both! a south-west blow on ye
And blister you all o'er!

PROSPERO
For this, be sure, to-night thou shalt have cramps,
Side-stitches that shall pen thy breath up; urchins
Shall, for that vast of night that they may work,
All exercise on thee; thou shalt be pinch'd
As thick as honeycomb, each pinch more stinging
Than bees that made 'em.

CALIBAN
I must eat my dinner. 407
This island's mine, by Sycorax my mother,
Which thou takest from me. When thou camest first,
Thou strokedst me and madest much of me, wouldst give me
Water with berries in't, and teach me how
To name the bigger light, and how the less,
That burn by day and night: and then I loved thee
And show'd thee all the qualities o' the isle,
The fresh springs, brine-pits, barren place and fertile:
Cursed be I that did so! All the charms
Of Sycorax, toads, beetles, bats, light on you!
For I am all the subjects that you have, 420
Which first was mine own king: and here you sty me
In this hard rock, whiles you do keep from me
The rest o' the island.

PROSPERO
Thou most lying slave,
Whom stripes may move, not kindness! I have used thee,
Filth as thou art, with human care, and lodged thee
In mine own cell, till thou didst seek to violate
The honour of my child.

CALIBAN
O ho, O ho! would't had been done!
Thou didst prevent me; I had peopled else
This isle with Calibans.

PROSPERO
Abhorred slave,
Which any print of goodness wilt not take,
Being capable of all ill! I pitied thee,
Took pains to make thee speak, taught thee each hour
One thing or other: when thou didst not, savage,
Know thine own meaning, but wouldst gabble like
A thing most brutish, I endow'd thy purposes
With words that made them known. But thy vile race,
Though thou didst learn, had that in't which good natures
Could not abide to be with; therefore wast thou
Deservedly confined into this rock 446
Who hadst deserved more than a prison.

CALIBAN
You taught me language; and my profit on't
Is, I know how to curse. The red plague rid you
For learning me your language!

PROSPERO
Hag-seed, hence!
Fetch us in fuel; and be quick, thou'rt best,
To answer other business. Shrug'st thou, malice?
If thou neglect'st or dost unwillingly
What I command, I'll rack thee with old cramps,
Fill all thy bones with aches, make thee roar
That beasts shall tremble at thy din.

CALIBAN
No, pray thee.
[*Aside*] I must obey: his art is of such power,
It would control my dam's god, Setebos,
And make a vassal of him.

PROSPERO
So, slave; hence! [*Exit Caliban.*

Re-enter ARIEL, *invisible, playing and singing;* FERDINAND *following.*

ARIEL'S song.
Come unto these yellow sands,
And then take hands:
Courtsied when you have and kiss'd
The wild waves whist,[5]
Foot it featly here and there; 467
And, sweet sprites, the burthen bear.
Burthen [*Dispersedly*]. Hark, hark! Bow-wow.
The watch-dogs bark:
Bow-wow

ARIEL
Hark, hark! I hear
The strain of strutting chanticleer
Cry, Cock-a-diddle-dow.

FERDINAND
Where should this music be? i' the air or the earth?
It sounds no more: and, sure it waits upon
Some god o' the island. Sitting on a bank,
Weeping again the king my father's wreck,
This music crept by me upon the waters,
Allaying both their fury and my passion
With its sweet air: thence I have follow'd it,
Or it hath drawn me rather. But 'tis gone.
No, it begins again.

ARIEL *sings.*
Full fathom five thy father lies;
Of his bones are coral made;
Those are pearls that were his eyes:
Nothing of him that doth fade
But doth suffer a sea-change 488
Into something rich and strange.
Sea-nymphs hourly ring his knell:
Burthen. Ding-dong

ARIEL
Hark! now I hear them,—Ding-dong, bell.

FERDINAND
The ditty does remember my drown'd father.
This is no mortal business, nor no sound
That the earth owes. I hear it now above me.

PROSPERO
The fringed curtains of thine eye advance
And say what thou seest yond.

MIRANDA
What is't? a spirit?
Lord, how it looks about! Believe me, sir,
It carries a brave form. But 'tis a spirit.

PROSPERO
No, wench; it eats and sleeps and hath such senses
As we have, such. This gallant which thou seest
Was in the wreck; and, but he's something stain'd
With grief that's beauty's canker, thou mightst call him
A goodly person: he hath lost his fellows
And strays about to find 'em.

MIRANDA
I might call him
A thing divine, for nothing natural
I ever saw so noble.

PROSPERO
[*Aside*] It goes on, I see,
As my soul prompts it. Spirit, fine spirit! I'll free thee 513
Within two days for this.

FERDINAND
Most sure, the goddess
On whom these airs attend! Vouchsafe my prayer
May know if you remain upon this island;
And that you will some good instruction give
How I may bear me here: my prime request,
Which I do last pronounce, is, O you wonder!
If you be maid or no?

MIRANDA
No wonder, sir;
But certainly a maid.

FERDINAND
My language! heavens!
I am the best of them that speak this speech,
Were I but where 'tis spoken.

PROSPERO
How? the best? 527
What wert thou, if the King of Naples heard thee?

FERDINAND
A single thing, as I am now, that wonders
To hear thee speak of Naples. He does hear me:
And that he does I weep: myself am Naples,
Who with mine eyes, never since at ebb, beheld
The king my father wreck'd.

MIRANDA
Alack, for mercy!

FERDINAND
Yes, faith, and all his lords; the Duke of Milan
And his brave son being twain.

PROSPERO
[*Aside*] The Duke of Milan
And his more braver daughter could control thee,
If now 'twere fit to do't. At the first sight 539
They have changed eyes. Delicate Ariel,
I'll set thee free for this. [*To Ferdinand*] A word, good sir;
I fear you have done yourself some wrong: a word.

MIRANDA
Why speaks my father so ungently? This
Is the third man that e'er I saw, the first

That e'er I sigh'd for: pity move my father
To be inclined my way!

FERDINAND
O, if a virgin,
And your affection not gone forth, I'll make you
The queen of Naples.

PROSPERO
Soft, sir! one word more.
[*Aside*] They are both in either's powers; but this swift business
I must uneasy make, lest too light winning
Make the prize light. [*To Ferdinand*] One word more; I charge thee
That thou attend me: thou dost here usurp
The name thou owest not; and hast put thyself
Upon this island as a spy, to win it
From me, the lord on't.

FERDINAND
No, as I am a man.

MIRANDA
There's nothing ill can dwell in such a temple:
If the ill spirit have so fair a house,
Good things will strive to dwell with't.

PROSPERO
Follow me.
Speak not you for him; he's a traitor. Come;
I'll manacle thy neck and feet together:
Sea-water shalt thou drink; thy food shall be
The fresh-brook muscles, wither'd roots and husks
Wherein the acorn cradled. Follow.

FERDINAND
No;
I will resist such entertainment till
Mine enemy has more power.
[*Draws, and is charmed from moving.*

MIRANDA
O dear father,
Make not too rash a trial of him, for
He's gentle and not fearful.

PROSPERO
What? I say,
My foot my tutor? Put thy sword up, traitor;
Who makest a show but darest not strike, thy conscience
Is so possess'd with guilt: come from thy ward,
For I can here disarm thee with this stick
And make thy weapon drop.

MIRANDA
Beseech you, father.

PROSPERO
Hence! hang not on my garments.

MIRANDA
Sir, have pity;
I'll be his surety.

PROSPERO
Silence! one word more
Shall make me chide thee, if not hate thee. What!
An advocate for an imposter! hush!
Thou think'st there is no more such shapes as he,
Having seen but him and Caliban: foolish wench!
To the most of men this is a Caliban
And they to him are angels.

MIRANDA
My affections
Are then most humble; I have no ambition
To see a goodlier man.

PROSPERO
Come on; obey:
Thy nerves are in their infancy again
And have no vigour in them.

FERDINAND
So they are;
My spirits, as in a dream, are all bound up.
My father's loss, the weakness which I feel,
The wreck of all my friends, nor this man's threats,
To whom I am subdued, are but light to me,
Might I but through my prison once a day
Behold this maid: all corners else o' the earth
Let liberty make use of; space enough
Have I in such a prison.

PROSPERO
[*Aside*] It works. [*To Ferdinand*] Come on.
Thou hast done well, fine Ariel! [*To Ferdinand*] Follow me.
[*To Ariel*] Hark what thou else shalt do me.

MIRANDA
Be of comfort;
My father's of a better nature, sir,
Than he appears by speech: this is unwonted
Which now came from him.

PROSPERO
Thou shalt be as free
As mountain winds: but then exactly do
All points of my command.

ARIEL
To the syllable.

PROSPERO
Come, follow. Speak not for him. [*Exeunt.*

ACT TWO SCENE ONE

Another part of the island.

Enter ALONSO, SEBASTIAN, ANTONIO, GONZALO, ADRIAN, FRANCISCO, *and others.*

GONZALO
Beseech you, sir, be merry; you have cause,
So have we all, of joy; for our escape

Is much beyond our loss. Our hint of woe
Is common; every day some sailor's wife,
The masters of some merchant and the merchant [6]
Have just our theme of woe; but for the miracle,
I mean our preservation, few in millions
Can speak like us: then wisely, good sir, weigh
Our sorrow with our comfort,

ALONSO

Prithee, peace.

SEBASTIAN

He receives comfort like cold porridge.

ANTONIO

The visitor will not give him o'er so. 13

SEBASTIAN

Look, he's winding up the watch of his wit; by and by it will strike.

GONZALO

Sir,—

SEBASTIAN

One: tell.

GONZALO

When every grief is entertain'd that's offer'd,
Comes to the entertainer—

SEBASTIAN

A dollar.

GONZALO

Dolour comes to him, indeed: you have spoken truer than you purposed. 22

SEBASTIAN

You have taken it wiselier than I meant you should.

GONZALO

Therefore, my lord,—

ANTONIO

Fie, what a spendthrift is he of his tongue!

ALONSO

I prithee, spare.

GONZALO

Well, I have done: but yet,—

SEBASTIAN

He will be talking.

ANTONIO

Which, of he or Adrian, for a good wager, first begins to crow? [7] 31

SEBASTIAN

The old cock.

ANTONIO

The cockerel.

SEBASTIAN

Done. The wager?

ANTONIO

A laughter.

SEBASTIAN

A match!

ADRIAN

Though this island seem to be desert,—

SEBASTIAN

Ha, ha, ha! So, you're paid. [8]

ADRIAN

Uninhabitable and almost inaccessible,—

SEBASTIAN

Yet,—

ADRIAN

Yet,—

ANTONIO

He could not miss't. 41

ADRIAN

It must needs be of subtle, tender and delicate temperance.

ANTONIO

Temperance was a delicate wench.

SEBASTIAN

Ay, and a subtle; as he most learnedly delivered.

ADRIAN

The air breathes upon us here most sweetly.

SEBASTIAN

As if it had lungs and rotten ones.

ANTONIO

Or as 'twere perfumed by a fen.

GONZALO

Here is every thing advantageous to life.

ANTONIO

True; save means to live. 50

SEBASTIAN

Of that there's none, or little.

GONZALO

How lush and lusty the grass looks! how green!

ANTONIO

The ground indeed is tawny.

SEBASTIAN

With an eye of green in't.

ANTONIO

He misses not much.

SEBASTIAN

No; he doth but mistake the truth totally.

GONZALO

But the rarity of it is,—which is indeed almost beyond credit,—

SEBASTIAN

As many vouched rarities are. 59

GONZALO

That our garments, being, as they were, drenched in the sea, hold notwithstanding their freshness and glosses, being rather new-dyed than stained with salt water.

ANTONIO

If but one of his pockets could speak, would it not say he lies?

SEBASTIAN
Ay, or very falsely pocket up his report.
GONZALO
Methinks our garments are now as fresh as when we put them on first in Afric, at the marriage of the king's fair daughter Claribel to the King of Tunis. 69
SEBASTIAN
'Twas a sweet marriage, and we prosper well in our return.
ADRIAN
Tunis was never graced before with such a paragon to their queen.
GONZALO
Not since widow Dido's time.
ANTONIO
Widow! a pox o' that! How came that widow in? widow Dido!
SEBASTIAN
What if he had said 'widower Aeneas' too? Good Lord, how you take it! 78
ADRIAN
'Widow Dido' said you? you make me study of that: she was of Carthage, not of Tunis.
GONZALO
This Tunis, sir, was Carthage.
ADRIAN
Carthage?
GONZALO
I assure you, Carthage.
SEBASTIAN
His word is more than the miraculous harp; he hath raised the wall and houses too.
ANTONIO
What impossible matter will he make easy next?
SEBASTIAN
I think he will carry this island home in his pocket and give it his son for an apple. 88
ANTONIO
And, sowing the kernels of it in the sea, bring forth more islands.
GONZALO
Ay.
ANTONIO
Why, in good time.
GONZALO
Sir, we were talking that our garments seem now as fresh as when we were at Tunis at the marriage of your daughter, who is now queen.
ANTONIO
And the rarest that e'er came there.
SEBASTIAN
Bate, I beseech you, widow Dido. 97
ANTONIO
O, widow Dido! ay, widow Dido.
GONZALO
Is not, sir, my doublet as fresh as the first day I wore it? I mean, in a sort.
ANTONIO
That sort was well fished for.
GONZALO
When I wore it at your daughter's marriage?
ALONSO
You cram these words into mine ears against
The stomach of my sense. Would I had never
Married my daughter there! for, coming thence,
My son is lost and, in my rate, she too,
Who is so far from Italy removed 107
I ne'er again shall see her. O thou mine heir
Of Naples and of Milan, what strange fish
Hath made his meal on thee?
FRANCISCO
Sir, he may live:
I saw him beat the surges under him,
And ride upon their backs; he trod the water,
Whose enmity he flung aside, and breasted
The surge most swoln that met him; his bold head
'Bove the contentious waves he kept, and oar'd
Himself with his good arms in lusty stroke
To the shore, that o'er his wave-worn basis bow'd,
As stooping to relieve him: I not doubt 119
He came alive to land.
ALONSO
No, no, he's gone.
SEBASTIAN
Sir, you may thank yourself for this great loss,
That would not bless our Europe with your daughter,
But rather lose her to an African;
Where she at least is banish'd from your eye,
Who hath cause to wet the grief on't. [9]
ALONSO
Prithee, peace.
SEBASTIAN
You were kneel'd to and importuned otherwise
By all of us, and the fair soul herself
Weigh'd between loathness and obedience, at
Which end o' the beam should bow. We have lost your son, [10]
I fear, for ever: Milan and Naples have 133
Moe widows in them of this business' making
Than we bring men to comfort them:
The fault's your own.
ALONSO
So is the dear'st o' the loss.
GONZALO
My lord Sebastian,
The truth you speak doth lack some gentleness
And time to speak it in: you rub the sore,
When you should bring the plaster.

SEBASTIAN
Very well.
ANTONIO
And most chirurgeonly. 143
GONZALO
It is foul weather in us all, good sir,
When you are cloudy.
SEBASTIAN
Foul weather?
ANTONIO
Very foul.
GONZALO
Had I plantation of this isle, my lord,—
ANTONIO
He'ld sow't with nettle-seed.
SEBASTIAN
Or docks, or mallows.
GONZALO
And were the king on't, what would I do?
SEBASTIAN
'Scape being drunk for want of wine.
GONZALO
I' the commonwealth I would by contraries
Execute all things; for no kind of traffic
Would I admit; no name of magistrate; 155
Letters should not be known; riches, poverty,
And use of service, none; contract, succession,
Bourn, bound of land, tilth, vineyard, none;
No use of metal, corn, or wine, or oil;
No occupation; all men idle, all;
And women too, but innocent and pure;
No sovereignty;—
SEBASTIAN
Yet he would be king on't.
ANTONIO
The latter end of his commonwealth forgets the beginning.
GONZALO
All things in common nature should produce 166
Without sweat or endeavour: treason, felony,
Sword, pike, knife, gun, or need of any engine,
Would I not have; but nature should bring forth,
Of it own kind, all foison, all abundance,
To feed my innocent people.
SEBASTIAN
No marrying 'mong his subjects?
ANTONIO
None, man; all idle: whores and knaves.
GONZALO.
I would with such perfection govern, Sir,
To excel the golden age.
SEBASTIAN
God save his majesty!
ANTONIO
Long live Gonzalo!
GONZALO
And,—do you mark me, sir?
ALONSO
Prithee, no more: thou dost talk nothing to me. 179
GONZALO
I do well believe your highness; and did it to minister occasion to these gentlemen, who are of such sensible and nimble lungs that they always use to laugh at nothing.
ANTONIO
'Twas you we laughed at.
GONZALO
Who in this kind of merry fooling am nothing to you: so you may continue and laugh at nothing still.
ANTONIO
What a blow was there given! 186
SEBASTIAN
An it had not fallen flat-long.
GONZALO
You are gentlemen of brave mettle; you would lift the moon out of her sphere, if she would continue in it five weeks without changing.

Enter ARIEL, *invisible, playing solemn music.*

SEBASTIAN
We would so, and then go a bat-fowling.
ANTONIO
Nay, good my lord, be not angry.
GONZALO
No, I warrant you; I will not adventure my discretion so weakly. Will you laugh me asleep, for I am very heavy?
ANTONIO
Go sleep, and hear us. 196
[*All sleep except Alonso, Sebastian, and Antonio.*
ALONSO
What, all so soon asleep! I wish mine eyes
Would with themselves, shut up my thoughts: I find
They are inclined to do so.
SEBASTIAN
Please you, sir,
Do not omit the heavy offer of it:
It seldom visits sorrow; when it doth,
It is a comforter.
ANTONIO
We two, my lord,
Will guard your person while you take your rest,
And watch your safety.
ALONSO
Thank you. Wondrous heavy.
[*Alonso sleeps. Exit Ariel.*
SEBASTIAN
What a strange drowsiness possesses them! 208
ANTONIO
It is the quality o' the climate.

SEBASTIAN
Why
Doth it not then our eyelids sink? I find not
Myself disposed to sleep.
ANTONIO
Nor I; my spirits are nimble.
They fell together all, as by consent;
They dropp'd, as by a thunder-stroke. What might,
Worthy Sebastian? O, what might?—No more:—
And yet methinks I see it in thy face,
What thou shouldst be: the occasion speaks thee, and
My strong imagination sees a crown
Dropping upon thy head.
SEBASTIAN
What, art thou waking?
ANTONIO
Do you not hear me speak?
SEBASTIAN
I do; and surely
It is a sleepy language and thou speak'st
Out of thy sleep. What is it thou didst say?
This is a strange repose, to be asleep
With eyes wide open; standing, speaking, moving,
And yet so fast asleep.
ANTONIO
Noble Sebastian,
Thou let'st thy fortune sleep—die, rather; wink'st
Whiles thou art waking.
SEBASTIAN
Thou dost snore distinctly;
There's meaning in thy snores.
ANTONIO
I am more serious than my custom: you
Must be so too, if heed me; which to do
Trebles thee o'er.
SEBASTIAN
Well, I am standing water.
ANTONIO
I'll teach you how to flow.
SEBASTIAN
Do so: to ebb
Hereditary sloth instructs me.
ANTONIO
O,
If you but knew how you the purpose cherish
Whiles thus you mock it! how, in stripping it,
You more invest it! Ebbing men, indeed,
Most often do so near the bottom run
By their own fear or sloth.
SEBASTIAN
Prithee, say on;
The setting of thine eye and cheek proclaim
A matter from thee, and a birth indeed
Which throes thee much to yield.
ANTONIO
Thus, sir:
Although this lord of weak remembrance, this,
Who shall be of as little memory
When he is earth'd, hath here almost persuaded,—
For he's a spirit of persuasion, only
Professes to persuade,—the king his son's alive,
'Tis as impossible that he's undrown'd
And he that sleeps here swims.
SEBASTIAN
I have no hope
That he's undrown'd.
ANTONIO
O, out of that 'no hope'
What great hope have you! no hope that way is
Another way so high a hope that even
Ambition cannot pierce a wink beyond,
But doubt discovery there. Will you grant with me [11]
That Ferdinand is drown'd?
SEBASTIAN
He's gone.
ANTONIO
Then, tell me,
Who's the next heir of Naples?
SEBASTIAN
Claribel.
ANTONIO
She that is queen of Tunis; she that dwells
Ten leagues beyond man's life; she that from Naples
Can have no note, unless the sun were post—
The man i' the moon's too slow—till new-born chins
Be rough and razorable; she that—from whom? [12]
We all were sea-swallow'd, though some cast again,
And by that destiny to perform an act
Whereof what's past is prologue, what to come
In yours and my discharge.
SEBASTIAN
What stuff is this! how say you?
'Tis true, my brother's daughter's queen of Tunis;
So is she heir of Naples: 'twixt which regions
There is some space.
ANTONIO
A space whose every cubit
Seems to cry out, 'How shall that Claribel
Measure us back to Naples? Keep in Tunis,
And let Sebastian wake.' Say, this were death
That now hath seized them; why, they were no worse

Than now they are. There be that can rule Naples
As well as he that sleeps; lords that can prate
As amply and unnecessarily
As this Gonzalo; I myself could make
A chough of as deep chat. O, that you bore
The mind that I do! what a sleep were this
For your advancement! Do you understand me?

SEBASTIAN
Methinks I do.

ANTONIO
And how does your content
Tender your own good fortune?

SEBASTIAN
I remember 308
You did supplant your brother Prospero.

ANTONIO
True:
And look how well my garments sit upon me;
Much feater than before: my brother's servants
Were then my fellows; now they are my men.

SEBASTIAN
But, for your conscience?

ANTONIO
Ay, sir; where lies that? if 'twere a kibe,
'Twould put me to my slipper: but I feel not
This deity in my bosom: twenty consciences,
That stand 'twixt me and Milan, candied be they[13]
And melt ere they molest! Here lies your brother, 321
No better than the earth he lies upon,
If he were that which now he's like, that's dead;
Whom I, with this obedient steel, three inches of it,
Can lay to bed for ever; whiles you, doing thus,
To the perpetual wink for aye might put
This ancient morsel, this Sir Prudence, who
Should not upbraid our course. For all the rest,
They'll take suggestion as a cat laps milk;
They'll tell the clock to any business that 331
We say befits the hour.

SEBASTIAN
Thy case, dear friend,
Shall be my precedent; as thou got'st Milan,
I'll come by Naples. Draw thy sword: one stroke
Shall free thee from the tribute which thou payest;
And I the king shall love thee.

ANTONIO
Draw together;
And when I rear my hand, do you the like,
To fall it on Gonzalo.

SEBASTIAN
O, but one word. [*They talk apart.*

Re-enter ARIEL, *invisible.*

ARIEL
My master through his art foresees the danger
That you, his friend, are in; and sends me forth—
For else his project dies—to keep them living.
[*Sings in Gonzalo's ear.*
While you here do snoring lie, 345
Open-eyed conspiracy
His time doth take.
If of life you keep a care,
Shake off slumber, and beware:
Awake, awake!

ANTONIO
Then let us both be sudden.

GONZALO
Now, good angels
Preserve the king. [*They wake.*

ALONSO
Why, how now? ho, awake! Why are you drawn?
Wherefore this ghastly looking?

GONZALO
What's the matter?

SEBASTIAN
Whiles we stood here securing your repose, 357
Even now, we heard a hollow burst of bellowing
Like bulls, or rather lions: did't not wake you?
It struck mine ear most terribly.

ALONSO
I heard nothing.

ANTONIO
O, 'twas a din to fright a monster's ear,
To make an earthquake! sure, it was the roar
Of a whole herd of lions.

ALONSO
Heard you this, Gonzalo?

GONZALO
Upon mine honour, sir, I heard a humming,
And that a strange one too, which did awake me:
I shaked you, sir, and cried: as mine eyes open'd, 368
I saw their weapons drawn: there was a noise,
That's verily. 'Tis best we stand upon our guard,
Or that we quit this place: let's draw our weapons.

ALONSO
Lead off this ground; and let's make further search
For my poor son.

GONZALO
Heavens keep him from these beasts!
For he is, sure, i' the island.

ALONSO
Lead away.

ARIEL
Prospero my lord shall know what I have done:
So, king, go safely on to seek thy son. [*Exeunt.*

ACT TWO SCENE TWO

Another part of the island.

Enter CALIBAN *with a burden of wood. A noise of thunder heard.*

CALIBAN

All the infections that the sun sucks up
From bogs, fens, flats, on Prosper fall and make him
By inch-meal a disease! His spirits hear me
And yet I needs must curse. But they'll nor pinch,
Fright me with urchin-shows, pitch me i' the mire,
Nor lead me, like a firebrand, in the dark
Out of my way, unless he bid 'em; but
For every trifle are they set upon me;
Sometime like apes that mow and chatter at me.
And after bite me, then like hedgehogs which
Lie tumbling in my barefoot way and mount
Their pricks at my footfall; sometime am I
All wound with adders who with cloven longues
Do hiss me into madness.

Enter TRINCULO.

Lo, now, lo!
Here comes a spirit of his, and to torment me
For bringing wood in slowly. I'll fall flat;
Perchance he will not mind me.

TRINCULO

Here's neither bush nor shrub, to bear off any weather at all, and another storm brewing; I hear it sing i' the wind: yond same black cloud, yond huge one, looks like a foul bombard that would shed his liquor. If it should thunder as it did before, I know not where to hide my head: yond same cloud cannot choose but fall by pailfuls. What have we here? a man or a fish? dead or alive? A fish: he smells like a fish; a very ancient and fish-like smell; a kind of not of the newest Poor-John. A strange fish! Were I in England now, as once I was, and had but this fish painted, not a holiday fool there but would give a piece of silver: there would this monster make a man; any strange beast there makes a man: when they will not give a doit to relieve a lame beggar, they will lay out ten to see a dead Indian. Legged like a man! and his fins like arms! Warm o' my troth! I do now let loose my opinions; hold it no longer: this is no fish, but an islander, that hath lately suffered by a thunderbolt. [Thunder.] Alas, the storm is come again! my best way is to creep under his gaberdine; there is no other shelter hereabouts: misery acquaints a man with strange bed-fellows. I will here shroud till the dregs of the storm be past.

Enter STEPHANO, *singing: a bottle in his hand.*

STEPHANO

I shall no more to sea, to sea,
Here shall I die ashore—

This is a very scurvy tune to sing at a man's funeral: well, here's my comfort. *Drinks.* [*Sings.*

The master, the swabber, the boatswain and I,
The gunner and his mate
Loved Mall, Meg and Marian and Margery,
But none of us cared for Kate; 51
For she had a tongue with a tang,
Would cry to a sailor, Go hang!
She loved not the savour of tar nor of pitch,
Yet a tailor might scratch her where'er she did itch:
Then to sea, boys, and let her go hang!

This is a scurvy tune too: but here's my comfort. [*Drinks.*

CALIBAN

Do not torment me: Oh!

STEPHANO

What's the matter? Have we devils here? Do you put tricks upon's with savages and men of Ind, ha? I have not 'scaped drowning to be afeard now of your four legs; for it hath been said, As proper a man as ever went on four legs cannot make him give ground; and it shall be said so again while Stephano breathes at nostrils.

CALIBAN

The spirit torments me; Oh!

STEPHANO

This is some monster of the isle with four legs, who hath got, as I take it, an ague. Where the devil should he learn our language? I will give him some relief, if it be but for that. If I can recover him and keep him tame and get to Naples with him, he's a present for any emperor that ever trod on neat's -leather.

CALIBAN

Do not torment me, prithee; I'll bring my wood home faster.

STEPHANO

He's in his fit now and does not talk after the wisest. He shall taste of my bottle: if he have never drunk wine afore, it will go near to remove his fit. If I can recover him and keep him tame, I will not take too much for him; he shall pay for him that hath him, and that soundly. [14]

CALIBAN

Thou dost me yet but little hurt; thou wilt anon, I know it by thy trembling: now Prosper works upon thee.

STEPHANO

Come on your ways; open your mouth; here is that which will give language to you, cat: open your mouth;

this will shake your shaking, I can tell you, and that soundly: you cannot tell who's your friend: open your chaps again.

TRINCULO

I should know that voice: it should be—but he is drowned; and these are devils: O defend me!

STEPHANO

Four legs and two voices: a most delicate monster! His forward voice now is to speak well of his friend; his backward voice is to utter foul speeches and to detract. If all the wine in my bottle will recover him, I will help his ague. Come. Amen! I will pour some in thy other mouth.

TRINCULO

Stephano!

STEPHANO

Doth thy other mouth call me? Mercy, mercy! This is a devil, and no monster: I will leave him; I have no long spoon.

TRINCULO

Stephano! If thou beest Stephano, touch me and speak to me: for I am Trinculo—be not afeard—thy good friend Trinculo.

STEPHANO

If thou beest Trinculo, come forth: I'll pull thee by the lesser legs: if any be Trinculo's legs, these are they. Thou art very Trinculo indeed! How camest thou to be the siege of this moon-calf? can he vent Trinculos?

TRINCULO

I took him to be killed with a thunder-stroke. But art thou not drowned, Stephano? I hope now thou art not drowned. Is the storm overblown? I hid me under the dead moon-calf's gaberdine for fear of the storm. And art thou living, Stephano? O Stephano, two Neapolitans 'scaped!

STEPHANO

Prithee, do not turn me about; my stomach is not constant.

CALIBAN

[*Aside*] These be fine things, an if they be not sprites.
That's a brave god and bears celestial liquor.
I will kneel to him.

STEPHANO

How didst thou 'scape? How camest thou hither? swear by this bottle how thou camest hither. I escaped upon a butt of sack which the sailors heaved o'erboard, by this bottle! which I made of the bark of a tree with mine own hands since I was cast ashore.

CALIBAN

I'll swear upon that bottle to be thy true subject; for the liquor is not earthly.

STEPHANO

Here; swear then how thou escapedst.

TRINCULO

Swum ashore. man, like a duck: I can swim like a duck, I'll be sworn.

STEPHANO

Here, kiss the book. Though thou canst swim like a duck, thou art made like a goose.

TRINCULO

O Stephano, hast any more of this?

STEPHANO

The whole butt, man: my cellar is in a rock by the sea-side where my wine is hid. How now, moon-calf! how does thine ague?

CALIBAN

Hast thou not dropp'd from heaven?

STEPHANO

Out o' the moon, I do assure thee: I was the man i' the moon when time was.

CALIBAN

I have seen thee in her and I do adore thee:
My mistress show'd me thee and thy dog and thy bush.

STEPHANO

Come, swear to that; kiss the book: I will furnish it anon with new contents: swear.

TRINCULO

By this good light, this is a very shallow monster! I afeard of him! A very weak monster! The man i' the moon! A most poor credulous monster! Well drawn, monster, in good sooth!

CALIBAN

I'll show thee every fertile inch o' th' island;
And I will kiss thy foot: I prithee, be my god.

TRINCULO

By this light, a most perfidious and drunken monster! when 's god's asleep, he'll rob his bottle.

CALIBAN

I'll kiss thy foot; I'll swear myself thy subject.

STEPHANO

Come on then; down, and swear.

TRINCULO

I shall laugh myself to death at this puppy-headed monster. A most scurvy monster! I could find in my heart to beat him,—

STEPHANO

Come, kiss.

TRINCULO

But that the poor monster's in drink: an abominable monster!

CALIBAN

I'll show thee the best springs; I'll pluck thee berries;
I'll fish for thee and get thee wood enough.
A plague upon the tyrant that I serve!
I'll bear him no more sticks, but follow thee,
Thou wondrous man.

TRINCULO
A most ridiculous monster, to make a wonder of a Poor drunkard!

CALIBAN
I prithee, let me bring thee where crabs grow;
And I with my long nails will dig thee pignuts;
Show thee a jay's nest and instruct thee how
To snare the nimble marmoset; I'll bring thee
To clustering filberts and sometimes I'll get thee
Young scamels from the rock. Wilt thou go with me? [15]

STEPHANO
I prithee now, lead the way without any more talking. Trinculo, the king and all our company else being drowned, we will inherit here: here; bear my bottle: fellow Trinculo, we'll fill him by and by again.

CALIBAN
[*Sings drunkenly*] Farewell' master; farewell, farewell!

TRINCULO
A howling monster; a drunken monster!

CALIBAN
No more dams I'll make for fish;
Nor fetch in firing
At requiring;
Nor scrape trencher, nor wash dish:
'Ban, 'Ban, Cacaliban
Has a new master: get a new man.
Freedom, hey-day! hey-day, freedom! freedom, hey-day, freedom!

STEPHANO
O brave monster! Lead the way. [*Exeunt.*

ACT THREE SCENE ONE

Before PROSPERO'S *cell.*

Enter FERDINAND, *bearing a log.*

FERDINAND
There be some sports are painful, and their labour
Delight in them sets off: some kinds of baseness
Are nobly undergone and most poor matters
Point to rich ends. This my mean task
Would be as heavy to me as odious, but
The mistress which I serve quickens what's dead
And makes my labours pleasures: O, she is
Ten times more gentle than her father's crabbed,
And he's composed of harshness. I must remove
Some thousands of these logs and pile them up,
Upon a sore injunction: my sweet mistress
Weeps when she sees me work, and says, such baseness
Had never like executor. I forget:
But these sweet thoughts do even refresh my labours,
Most busy lest, when I do it. [16]

Enter MIRANDA; *and* PROSPERO *at a distance, unseen.*

MIRANDA
Alas, now, pray you,
Work not so hard: I would the lightning had
Burnt up those logs that you are enjoin'd to pile!
Pray, set it down and rest you: when this burns,
'Twill weep for having wearied you. My father
Is hard at study; pray now, rest yourself;
He's safe for these three hours.

FERDINAND
O most dear mistress,
The sun will set before I shall discharge
What I must strive to do.

MIRANDA
If you'll sit down,
I'll bear your logs the while: pray, give me that;
I'll carry it to the pile.

FERDINAND
No, precious creature;
I had rather crack my sinews, break my back,
Than you should such dishonour undergo,
While I sit lazy by.

MIRANDA
It would become me
As well as it does you: and I should do it
With much more ease; for my good will is to it,
And yours it is against.

PROSPERO
Poor worm, thou art infected!
This visitation shows it.

MIRANDA
You look wearily.

FERDINAND
No, noble mistress; 'tis fresh morning with me
When you are by at night. I do beseech you—
Chiefly that I might set it in my prayers—
What is your name?

MIRANDA
Miranda.—O my father,
I have broke your hest to say so!

FERDINAND
Admired Miranda!
Indeed the top of admiration! worth
What's dearest to the world! Full many a lady
I have eyed with best regard and many a time
The harmony of their tongues hath into bondage
Brought my too diligent ear: for several virtues
Have I liked several women; never any

MIRANDA I believe thee; for I think thou never wast where grace was said.

With so fun soul, but some defect in her
Did quarrel with the noblest grace she owed
And put it to the foil: but you, O you,
So perfect and so peerless, are created
Of every creature's best!

MIRANDA

I do not know
One of my sex; no woman's face remember,
Save, from my glass, mine own; nor have
I seen 64
More that I may call men than you, good friend,
And my dear father: how features are abroad
I am skilless of; but, by my modesty,
The jewel in my dower, I would not wish
Any companion in the world but you,
Nor can imagination form a shape,
Besides yourself, to like of. But I prattle
Something too wildly and my father's precepts
I therein do forget.

FERDINAND

I am in my condition
A prince, Miranda; I do think, a king; 75
I would, not so!—and would no more endure
This wooden slavery than to suffer
The flesh-fly blow my mouth. Hear my soul speak:
The very instant that I saw you, did
My heart fly to your service: there resides,
To make me slave to it; and for your sake
Am I this patient log-man.

MIRANDA

Do you love me?

FERDINAND

O heaven, O earth, bear witness to this sound
And crown what I profess with kind event
If I speak true! if hollowly, invert 86
What best is boded me to mischief! I
Beyond all limit of what else i' the world
Do love, prize, honour you.

MIRANDA

I am a fool
To weep at what I am glad of.

PROSPERO

Fair encounter
Of two most rare affections! Heavens rain grace
On that which breeds between 'em!

FERDINAND

Wherefore weep you?

MIRANDA

At mine unworthiness that dare not offer
What I desire to give, and much less take
What I shall die to want. But this is trifling;
And all the more it seeks to hide itself, 99
The bigger bulk it shows. Hence, bashful cunning!
And prompt me, plain and holy innocence!
I am your wife, it you will marry me,
If not, I'll die your maid: to be your fellow
You may deny me; but I'll be your servant,
Whether you will or no.

FERDINAND

My mistress, dearest;
And I thus humble ever.

MIRANDA

My husband, then?

FERDINAND

Ay, with a heart as willing
As bondage e'er of freedom: here's my hand.

MIRANDA

And mine, with my heart in't: and now farewell 111
Till half an hour hence.

FERDINAND

A thousand thousand!

[*Exeunt Ferdinand and Miranda severally.*

PROSPERO

So glad of this as they I cannot be,
Who are surprised withal: but my rejoicing
At nothing can be more. I'll to my book,
For yet ere supper-time must I perform
Much business appertaining. [*Exit.*

CALIBAN How does thy honour? Let me lick thy shoe.

ACT THREE SCENE TWO

Another part of the island.

Enter CALIBAN, STEPHANO, *and* TRINCULO.

STEPHANO

Tell not me; when the butt is out, we will drink water; not a drop before: therefore bear up, and board 'em. Servant-monster, drink to me.

TRINCULO

Servant-monster! the folly of this island! They say there's but five upon this isle: we are three of them; if th' other two be brained like us, the state totters.

STEPHANO

Drink, servant-monster, when I bid thee: thy eyes are almost set in thy head.

TRINCULO

Where should they be set else? he were a brave monster indeed, if they were set in his tail.

STEPHANO

My man-monster hath drown'd his tongue in sack: for my part, the sea cannot drown me; I swam, ere I could recover the shore, five and thirty leagues off and on. By this light, thou shalt be my lieutenant, monster, or my standard.

TRINCULO

Your lieutenant, if you list; he's no standard.

STEPHANO

We'll not run, Monsieur Monster.

TRINCULO

Nor go neither; but you'll lie like dogs and yet say nothing neither.

STEPHANO

Moon-calf, speak once in thy life, if thou beest a good moon-calf.

CALIBAN

How does thy honour? Let me lick thy shoe.

I'll not serve him; he's not valiant.

TRINCULO

Thou liest, most ignorant monster: I am in case to justle a constable. Why, thou deboshed fish, thou, was there ever man a coward that hath drunk so much sack as I to-day? Wilt thou tell a monstrous lie, being but half a fish and half a monster?

CALIBAN
Lo, how he mocks me! wilt thou let him, my lord?
TRINCULO
'Lord' quoth he! That a monster should be such a natural!
CALIBAN
Lo, lo, again! bite him to death, I prithee.
STEPHANO
Trinculo, keep a good tongue in your head: if you prove a mutineer,—the next tree! The poor monster's my subject and he shall not suffer indignity.
CALIBAN
I thank my noble lord. Wilt thou be pleased to hearken once again to the suit I made to thee?
STEPHANO
Marry, will I: kneel and repeat it; I will stand, and so shall Trinculo.

Enter ARIEL, *invisible.*

CALIBAN
As I told thee before, I am subject to a tyrant, a sorcerer, that by his cunning hath cheated me of the island. 41
ARIEL
Thou liest.
CALIBAN
Thou liest, thou jesting monkey, thou: I would my valiant master would destroy thee! I do not lie.
STEPHANO
Trinculo, if you trouble him any more in's tale, by this hand, I will supplant some of your teeth.
TRINCULO
Why, I said nothing.
STEPHANO
Mum, then, and no more. Proceed.
CALIBAN
I say, by sorcery he got this isle; 49
From me he got it. If thy greatness will
Revenge it on him,—for I know thou darest,
But this thing dare not,—
STEPHANO
That's most certain.
CALIBAN
Thou shalt be lord of it and I'll serve thee.
STEPHANO
How now shall this be compassed?
Canst thou bring me to the party?
CALIBAN
Yea, yea, my lord: I'll yield him thee asleep,
Where thou mayst knock a nail into his head.
ARIEL
Thou liest; thou canst not. 59
CALIBAN
What a pied ninny's this! Thou scurvy patch!
I do beseech thy greatness, give him blows
And take his bottle from him: when that's gone
He shall drink nought but brine; for I'll not show him
Where the quick freshes are.
STEPHANO
Trinculo, run into no further danger: interrupt the monster one word further, and, by this hand, I'll turn my mercy out o' doors and make a stock-fish of thee.
TRINCULO
Why, what did I? I did nothing. I'll go farther off. 69
STEPHANO
Didst thou not say he lied?
ARIEL
Thou liest.
STEPHANO
Do I so? take thou that. [*Beats Trinculo*]
As you like this, give me the lie another time.
TRINCULO
I did not give the lie. Out o' your wits and hearing too? A pox o' your bottle! this can sack and drinking do. A murrain on your monster, and the devil take your fingers!
CALIBAN
Ha, ha, ha! 78
STEPHANO
Now, forward with your tale. Prithee, stand farther off.
CALIBAN
Beat him enough: after a little time I'll beat him too.
STEPHANO
Stand farther. Come, proceed.
CALIBAN
Why, as I told thee, 'tis a custom with him,
I' th' afternoon to sleep: there thou mayst brain him,
Having first seized his books, or with a log
Batter his skull, or paunch him with a stake,
Or cut his wezand with thy knife. Remember
First to possess his books; for without them
He's but a sot, as I am, nor hath not
One spirit to command: they all do hate him
As rootedly as I. Burn but his books.
He has brave utensils,—for so he calls them,—
Which when he has a house, he'll deck withal.
And that most deeply to consider is
The beauty of his daughter; he himself
Calls her a nonpareil: I never saw a woman,
But only Sycorax my dam and she;
But she as far surpasseth Sycorax 98
As great'st does least.
STEPHANO
Is it so brave a lass?
CALIBAN
Ay, lord; she will become thy bed, I warrant.
And bring thee forth brave brood.

STEPHANO
Monster, I will kill this man: his daughter and I will be king and queen—save our graces!—and Trinculo and thyself shall be viceroys. Dost thou like the plot, Trinculo?

TRINCULO
Excellent.

STEPHANO
Give me thy hand: I am sorry I beat thee; but, while thou livest, keep a good tongue in thy head.

CALIBAN
Within this half hour will he be asleep: Wilt thou destroy him then?

STEPHANO
Ay, on mine honour.

ARIEL
This will I tell my master.

CALIBAN
Thou makest me merry; I am full of pleasure:
Let us be jocund: will you troll the catch
You taught me but while-ere?

STEPHANO
At thy request, monster, I will do reason, any reason. Come on, Trinculo, let us sing. [*Sings.*
Flout 'em and scout 'em
And scout 'em and flout 'em;
Thought is free.

CALIBAN
That's not the tune.
[*Ariel plays the tune on a tabor and pipe.*

STEPHANO
What is this same?

TRINCULO
This is the tune of our catch, played by the picture of Nobody.

STEPHANO
If thou beest a man, show thyself in thy likeness: if thou beest a devil, take't as thou list.

TRINCULO
O, forgive me my sins!

STEPHANO
He that dies pays all debts: I defy thee. Mercy upon us!

CALIBAN
Art thou afeard?

STEPHANO
No, monster, not I.

CALIBAN
Be not afeard; the isle is full of noises.
Sounds and sweet airs, that give delight and hurt not.
Sometimes a thousand twangling instruments
Will hum about mine ears, and sometimes voices
That, if I then had waked after long sleep,
Will make me sleep again: and then, in dreaming,
The clouds methought would open and show riches
Ready to drop upon me, that, when I waked,
I cried to dream again.

STEPHANO
This will prove a brave kingdom to me, where I shall have my music for nothing.

CALIBAN
When Prospero is destroyed.

STEPHANO
That shall be by and by: I remember the story.

TRINCULO
The sound is going away; let's follow it, and after do our work.

STEPHANO
Lead, monster; we'll follow. I would I could see this taborer; he lays it on.

TRINCULO
Wilt come? I'll follow, Stephano.
[*Exeunt.*

ACT THREE SCENE THREE

Another part of the island.

Enter ALONSO, SEBASTIAN, ANTONIO, GONZALO, ADRIAN, FRANCISCO, *and others.*

GONZALO
By'r lakin, I can go no further, sir;
My old bones ache: here's a maze trod indeed
Through forth-rights and meanders! By your patience,
I needs must rest me.

ALONSO
Old lord, I cannot blame thee,
Who am myself attach'd with weariness,
To the dulling of my spirits: sit down, and rest,
Even here I will put off my hope and keep it
No longer for my flatterer: he is drown'd
Whom thus we stray to find, and the sea mocks
Our frustrate search on land. Well, let him go.

ANTONIO
[*Aside to Sebastian*] I am right glad that he's so out of hope.
Do not, for one repulse, forego the purpose
That you resolved to effect.

SEBASTIAN
[*Aside to Antonio*] The next advantage will we take throughly.

ANTONIO
[*Aside to Sebastian*] Let it be to-night;
For, now they are oppress'd with travel, they

Will not, nor cannot, use such vigilance
As when they are fresh.

SEBASTIAN
[*Aside to Antonio*] I say, to-night: no more. [*Solemn and strange music.*

ALONSO
What harmony is this. My good friends, hark!

GONZALO
Marvellous sweet music!

Enter PROSPERO *above, invisible. Enter several strange Shapes, bringing in a banquet; they dance about it with gentle actions of salutation; and, inviting the King, &c., to eat, they depart.*

ALONSO
Give us kind keepers, heavens! What were these? 27

SEBASTIAN
A living drollery. Now I will believe
That there are unicorns, that in Arabia
There is one tree, the phoenix' throne, one phoenix
At this hour reigning there.

ANTONIO
I'll believe both;
And what does else want credit, come to me,
And I'll be sworn 'tis true; travellers ne'er did lie,
Though fools at home condemn 'em.

GONZALO
If in Naples
I should report this now, would they believe me?
If I should say, I saw such islanders—
For, certes, these are people of the island— 39
Who, though they are of monstrous shape, yet, note,
Their manners are more gentle-kind than of
Our human generation you shall find
Many, nay, almost any.

PROSPERO
[*Aside*] Honest lord,
Thou hast said well; for some of you there present
Are worse than devils.

ALONSO
I cannot too much muse
Such shapes, such gesture and such sound, expressing,
Although they want the use of tongue, a kind
Of excellent dumb discourse.

PROSPERO
[*Aside*] Praise in departing. [17]

FRANCISCO
They vanish'd strangely.

SEBASTIAN
No matter, since 53
They have left their viands behind; for we have stomachs.
Will't please you taste of what is here?

ALONSO
Not I.

GONZALO
Faith, sir, you need not fear. When we were boys,
Who would believe that there were mountaineers
Dew-lapp'd like bulls, whose throats had hanging at 'em
Wallets of flesh? or that there were such men
Whose heads stood in their breasts? which now we find
Each putter-out of five for one will bring us
Good warrant of.

ALONSO
I will stand to and feed,
Although my last: no matter, since I feel 68
The best is past. Brother, my lord the duke,
Stand to and do as we.

Thunder and lightning. Enter ARIEL, *like a harpy, claps his wings upon the table; and, with a quaint device, the banquet vanishes.*

ARIEL
You are three men of sin, whom Destiny,
That hath to instrument this lower world
And what is in't, the never-surfeited sea
Hath caused to belch up you: and on this island
Where man doth not inhabit; you 'mongst men
Being most unfit to live. I have made you mad;
And even with such-like valour men hang and drown
Their proper selves.
[*Alonso, Sebastian &c. draw their swords.*
You fools! I and my fellows 79
Are ministers of Fate: the elements,
Of whom your swords are temper'd, may as well
Wound the loud winds, or with bemock'd-at stabs
Kill the still-closing waters, as diminish
One dowle that's in my plume: my fellow-ministers
Are like invulnerable. If you could hurt,
Your swords are now too massy for your strengths
And will not be uplifted. But remember—
For that's my business to you—that you three
From Milan did supplant good Prospero; 89
Exposed unto the sea, which hath requit it,
Him and his innocent child: for which foul deed
The powers, delaying, not forgetting, have
Incensed the seas and shores, yea, all the creatures,
Against your peace. Thee of thy son, Alonso,
They have bereft; and do pronounce by me
Lingering perdition, worse than any death
Can be at once, shall step by step attend
You and your ways; whose wraths to guard you from—
Which here, in this most desolate isle, else falls
Upon your heads—is nothing but heart-sorrow
And a clear life ensuing. 101

He vanishes in thunder; then, to soft music, enter the Shapes again, and dance, with mocks and mows, and carrying out the table.

PROSPERO
Bravely the figure of this harpy hast thou
Perform'd, my Ariel; a grace it had, devouring:
Of my instruction hast thou nothing bated
In what thou hadst to say: so, with good life
And observation strange, my meaner ministers
Their several kinds have done. My high charms work
And these mine enemies are all knit up
In their distractions; they now are in my power;
And in these fits I leave them, while I visit
Young Ferdinand, whom they suppose is drown'd,
And his and mine loved darling. [*Exit above.*

GONZALO
I' the name of something holy, sir, why stand you
In this strange stare?

ALONSO
O, it is monstrous, monstrous!
Methought the billows spoke and told me of it;
The winds did sing it to me, and the thunder,
That deep and dreadful organ-pipe, pronounced
The name of Prosper: it did bass my trespass.
Therefore my son i' the ooze is bedded, and
I'll seek him deeper than e'er plummet sounded
And with him there lie mudded. [*Exit.*

SEBASTIAN
But one fiend at a time,
I'll fight their legions o'er.

ANTONIO
I'll be thy second. [*Exeunt Sebastian and Antonio.*

GONZALO
All three of them are desperate: their great guilt,
Like poison given to work a great time after,
Now 'gins to bite the spirits. I do beseech you
That are of suppler joints, follow them swiftly
And hinder them from what this ecstasy
May now provoke them to.

ADRIAN
Follow, I pray you. [*Exeunt.*

ACT FOUR SCENE ONE

Before PROSPERO'S *cell.*

Enter PROSPERO, FERDINAND, *and* MIRANDA.

PROSPERO
If I have too austerely punish'd you,
Your compensation makes amends, for I
Have given you here a third of mine own life,
Or that for which I live; who once again
I tender to thy hand: all thy vexations
Were but my trials of thy love, and thou
Hast strangely stood the test: here, afore Heaven,
I ratify this my rich gift. O Ferdinand,
Do not smile at me that I boast her off,
For thou shalt find she will outstrip all praise
And make it halt behind her.

FERDINAND
I do believe it
Against an oracle.

PROSPERO
Then, as my gift and thine own acquisition
Worthily purchased, take my daughter: but
If thou dost break her virgin-knot before
All sanctimonious ceremonies may
With full and holy rite be minister'd,
No sweet aspersion shall the heavens let fall
To make this contract grow; but barren hate,
Sour-eyed disdain and discord shall bestrew
The union of your bed with weeds so loathly
That you shall hate it both: therefore take heed,
As Hymen's lamps shall light you.

FERDINAND
As I hope
For quiet days, fair issue and long life,
With such love as 'tis now, the murkiest den,
The most opportune place, the strong'st suggestion
Our worser genius can, shall never melt
Mine honour into lust, to take away
The edge of that day's celebration
When I shall think, or Phoebus' steeds are founder'd,
Or Night kept chain'd below.

PROSPERO
Fairly spoke.
Sit then and talk with her; she is thine own.
What, Ariel! my industrious servant, Ariel!

Enter ARIEL.

ARIEL
What would my potent master? here I am.

PROSPERO
Thou and thy meaner fellows your last service
Did worthily perform; and I must use you
In such another trick. Go bring the rabble,
O'er whom I give thee power, here to this place:
Incite them to quick motion; for I must
Bestow upon the eyes of this young couple
Some vanity of mine art: it is my promise,
And they expect it from me.

ARIEL
Presently!

PROSPERO
Ay, with a twink.
ARIEL
Before you can say 'come' and 'go,'
And breathe twice and cry 'so, so,'
Each one, tripping on his toe,
Will be here with mop and mow.
Do you love me, master? no?
PROSPERO
Dearly, my delicate Ariel. Do not approach
Till thou dost hear me call.
ARIEL
Well, I conceive. [*Exit.* 57
PROSPERO
Look thou be true; do not give dalliance
Too much the rein: the strongest oaths are straw
To the fire i' the blood: be more abstemious,
Or else, good night your vow!
FERDINAND
I warrant you, sir;
The white cold virgin snow upon my heart
Abates the ardour of my liver.
PROSPERO
Well.
Now come, my Ariel! bring a corollary,
Rather than want a spirit: appear, and pertly!
No tongue! all eyes! be silent. [*Soft music.*

Enter IRIS.

IRIS
Ceres, most bounteous lady, thy rich leas 69
Of wheat, rye, barley, vetches, oats and pease;
Thy turfy mountains, where live nibbling sheep,
And flat meads thatch'd with stover, them to keep;
Thy banks with pioned and twilled brims, [18]
Which spongy April at thy hest betrims,
To make cold nymphs chaste crowns; and thy broom-groves,
Whose shadow the dismissed bachelor loves,
Being lass-lorn; thy pole-clipt vineyard;
And thy sea-marge, sterile and rocky-hard,
Where thou thyself dost air;—the queen o' the sky, 81
Whose watery arch and messenger am I,
Bids thee leave these, and with her sovereign grace,
Here on this grass-plot, in this very place,
To come and sport: her peacocks fly amain:
Approach, rich Ceres, her to entertain.

Enter CERES.

CERES
Hail, many-colour'd messenger, that ne'er
Dost disobey the wife of Jupiter;
Who with thy saffron wings upon my flowers
Diffusest honey-drops, refreshing showers,
And with each end of thy blue bow dost crown 92
My bosky acres and my unshrubb'd down,
Rich scarf to my proud earth; why hath thy queen
Summon'd me hither, to this short-grass'd green?
IRIS
A contract of true love to celebrate;
And some donation freely to estate
On the blest lovers.
CERES
Tell me, heavenly bow,
If Venus or her son, as thou dost know,
Do now attend the queen? Since they did plot
The means that dusky Dis my daughter got,
Her and her blind boy's scandal'd company
I have forsworn. 104
IRIS
Of her society
Be not afraid: I met her deity
Cutting the clouds towards Paphos and her son
Dove-drawn with her. Here thought they to have done
Some wanton charm upon this man and maid,
Whose vows are, that no bed-right shall be paid
Till Hymen's torch be lighted: but vain;
Mars's hot minion is return'd again;
Her waspish-headed son has broke his arrows,
Swears he will shoot no more but play with sparrows 116
And be a boy right out.
CERES
High'st queen of state,
Great Juno, comes: I know her by her gait.

Enter JUNO.

JUNO
How does my bounteous sister? Go with me
To bless this twain, that they may prosperous be
And honour'd in their issue. [*They sing*:
JUNO
Honour, riches, marriage-blessing,
Long continuance, and increasing,
Hourly joys be still upon you!
Juno sings her blessings upon you. 126
CERES
Earth's increase, foison plenty, [19]
Barns and garners never empty,
Vines and clustering bunches growing,
Plants with goodly burthen bowing;
Spring come to you at the farthest
In the very end of harvest!

Scarcity and want shall shun you;
Ceres' blessing so is on you.

FERDINAND
This is a most majestic vision, and
Harmonious charmingly. May I be bold
To think these spirits?

PROSPERO
Spirits, which by mine art 138
I have from their confines call'd to enact
My present fancies.

FERDINAND
Let me live here ever;
So rare a wonder'd father and a wife
Makes this place Paradise.

[Juno and Ceres whisper, and send Iris on employment.

PROSPERO
Sweet, now, silence!
Juno and Ceres whisper seriously;
There's something else to do: hush, and be mute,
Or else our spell is marr'd.

IRIS
You nymphs, call'd Naiads, of the windring brooks,
With your sedged crowns and ever-harmless looks, 150
Leave your crisp channels and on this green land
Answer your summons; Juno does command:
Come, temperate nymphs, and help to celebrate
A contract of true love; be not too late.

Enter certain Nymphs.

You sunburnt sicklemen, of August weary,
Come hither from the furrow and be merry:
Make holiday; your rye-straw hats put on
And these fresh nymphs encounter every one
In country footing.

Enter certain Reapers, properly habited: they join with the Nymphs in a graceful dance; towards the end whereof PROSPERO *starts suddenly, and speaks; after which, to a strange, hollow, and confused noise, they heavily vanish.*

PROSPERO
[*Aside.*] I had forgot that foul conspiracy
Of the beast Caliban and his confederates 161
Against my life: the minute of their plot
Is almost come. [*To the Spirits.*] Well done! avoid; no more!

FERDINAND
This is strange: your father's in some passion
That works him strongly.

MIRANDA
Never till this day
Saw I him touch'd with anger so distemper'd

PROSPERO
You do look, my son, in a moved sort,
As if you were dismay'd: be cheerful, sir. [20]
Our revels now are ended. These our actors
As I foretold you, were all spirits and
Are melted into air, into thin air: 173
And, like the baseless fabric of this vision,
The cloud-capp'd towers, the gorgeous palaces,
The solemn temples, the great globe itself,
Yea, all which it inherit, shall dissolve
And, like this insubstantial pageant faded,
Leave not a rack behind. We are such stuff
As dreams are made on, and our little life
Is rounded with a sleep. Sir, I am vex'd;
Bear with my weakness; my old brain is troubled:
Be not disturb'd with my infirmity: 183
If you be pleased, retire into my cell
And there repose; a turn or two I'll walk,
To still my beating mind.

FERDINAND, MIRANDA
We wish your peace. *[Exeunt.*

PROSPERO
Come with a though. I thank thee, Ariel: come.

Enter ARIEL.

ARIEL
Thy thoughts I cleave to. What's thy pleasure?

PROSPERO
Spirit,
We must prepare to meet with Caliban.

ARIEL
Ay, my commander: when I presented Ceres,
I thought to have told thee of it, but I fear'd
Lest I might anger thee.

PROSPERO
Say again, where didst thou leave these varlets? 196

ARIEL
I told you, sir, they were red-hot with drinking;
So full of valour that they smote the air
For breathing in their faces; beat the ground
For kissing of their feet; yet always bending
Towards their project. Then I beat my tabor;
At which, like unback'd colts, they prick'd their ears,
Advanced their eyelids, lifted up their noses
As they smelt music: so I charm'd their ears
That calf-like they my lowing follow'd through
Tooth'd briers, sharp furzes, pricking goss and thorns, 207
Which enter'd their frail shins: at last I left them
I' the filthy-mantled pool beyond your cell,
There dancing up to the chins, that the foul lake
O'erstunk their feet.

PROSPERO
This was well done, my bird.
Thy shape invisible retain thou still:
The trumpery in my house, go bring it hither,
For stale to catch these thieves.

ARIEL
I go, I go. [*Exit.*

PROSPERO
A devil, a born devil, on whose nature
Nurture can never stick; on whom my pains,
Humanely taken, all, all lost, quite lost;
And as with age his body uglier grows,
So his mind cankers. I will plague them all,
Even to roaring.

Re-enter ARIEL, *loaden with glistering apparel, &c.*

Come, hang them on this line. [21]

PROSPERO *and* ARIEL *remain, invisible.*
Enter CALIBAN, STEPHANO,
and TRINCULO, *all wet.*

CALIBAN
Pray you, tread softly, that the blind mole may not
Hear a foot fall: we now are near his cell.

STEPHANO
Monster, your fairy, which you say is a harmless fairy, has done little better than played the Jack with us.

TRINCULO
Monster, I do smell all horse-piss; at which my nose is in great indignation.

STEPHANO
So is mine. Do you hear, monster? If I should take a displeasure against you, look you,—

TRINCULO
Thou wert but a lost monster.

CALIBAN
Good my lord, give me thy favour still.
Be patient, for the prize I'll bring thee to
Shall hoodwink this mischance: therefore speak softly.
All's hush'd as midnight yet.

TRINCULO
Ay, but to lose our bottles in the pool,—

STEPHANO
There is not only disgrace and dishonour in that, monster, but an infinite loss.

TRINCULO
That's more to me than my wetting: yet this is your harmless fairy, monster.

STEPHANO
I will fetch off my bottle, though I be o'er ears for my labour.

CALIBAN
Prithee, my king, be quiet. See'st thou here,
This is the mouth o' the cell: no noise, and enter.
Do that good mischief which may make this island
Thine own for ever, and I, thy Caliban,
For aye thy foot-licker.

STEPHANO
Give me thy hand. I do begin to have bloody thoughts.

TRINCULO
O king Stephano! O peer! O worthy Stephano! look what a wardrobe here is for thee! [22]

CALIBAN
Let it alone, thou fool; it is but trash.

TRINCULO
O, ho, monster! we know what belongs to a frippery. O king Stephano!

STEPHANO
Put off that gown, Trinculo; by this hand, I'll have that gown.

TRINCULO
Thy grace shall have it.

CALIBAN
The dropsy drown this fool! what do you mean
To dote thus on such luggage? Let's alone [23]
And do the murder first: if he awake,
From toe to crown he'll fill our skins with pinches,
Make us strange stuff.

STEPHANO
Be you quiet, monster. Mistress line, is not this my jerkin? Now is the jerkin under the line: now, jerkin, you are like to lose your hair and prove a bald jerkin. [24]

TRINCULO
Do, do: we steal by line and level, an't like your grace.

STEPHANO
I thank thee for that jest; here's a garment for't: wit shall not go unrewarded while I am king of this country. 'Steal by line and level' is an excellent pass of pate; there's another garment for't.

TRINCULO
Monster, come, put some lime upon your fingers, and sway with the rest.

CALIBAN
I will have none on't: we shall lose our time,
And all be turn'd to barnacles, or to apes
With foreheads villanous low,

STEPHANO
Monster, lay to your fingers: help to bear this away where my hogshead of wine is, or I'll turn you out of my kingdom: go to, carry this.

TRINCULO
And this.

PROSPERO Let them be hunted soundly.

STEPHANO
Ay, and this.

A noise of hunters heard. Enter divers Spirits, in shape of dogs and hounds , and hunt them about, PROSPERO *and* ARIEL *setting them on.*

PROSPERO
Hey, Mountain, hey!
ARIEL
Silver! there it goes, Silver!
PROSPERO
Fury, Fury! there, Tyrant, there! hark! hark!
[*Caliban, Stephano, and Trinculo are driven out.*
Go charge my goblins that they grind their joints
With dry convulsions, shorten up their sinews
With aged cramps, and more pinch-spotted make them
Than pard or cat o' mountain.
ARIEL
Hark, they roar!
PROSPERO
Let them be hunted soundly. At this hour
Lie at my mercy all mine enemies:
Shortly shall all my labours end, and thou
Shalt have the air at freedom: for a little
Follow, and do me service. [*Exeunt.*

ACT FIVE SCENE ONE

Before PROSPERO'S *cell.*

Enter PROSPERO *in his magic robes, and* ARIEL.

PROSPERO
Now does my project gather to a head:
My charms crack not; my spirits obey; and time
Goes upright with his carriage. How's the day?
ARIEL
On the sixth hour; at which time, my lord,
You said our work should cease.
PROSPERO
I did say so,
When first I raised the tempest. Say, my spirit,
How fares the king and's followers?

ARIEL
Confined together
In the same fashion as you gave in charge,
Just as you left them; all prisoners, sir,
In the line-grove which weather-fends your cell;
They cannot budge till your release. The king,
His brother and yours, abide all three distracted
And the remainder mourning over them,
Brimful of sorrow and dismay; but chiefly
Him that you term'd, sir, 'The good old lord, Gonzalo;'
His tears run down his beard, like winter's drops
From eaves of reeds. Your charm so strongly works 'em
That if you now beheld them, your affections
Would become tender.

PROSPERO
Dost thou think so, spirit?

ARIEL
Mine would, sir, were I human.

PROSPERO
And mine shall.
Hast thou, which art but air, a touch, a feeling
Of their afflictions, and shall not myself,
One of their kind, that relish all as sharply, [25]
Passion as they, be kindlier moved than thou art?
Though with their high wrongs I am struck to the quick,
Yet with my nobler reason 'gainist my fury
Do I take part: the rarer action is
In virtue than in vengeance: they being penitent,
The sole drift of my purpose doth extend
Not a frown further. Go release them, Ariel:
My charms I'll break, their senses I'll restore,
And they shall be themselves.

ARIEL
I'll fetch them, sir. [*Exit.*

PROSPERO
Ye elves of hills, brooks, standing lakes and groves,
And ye that on the sands with printless foot
Do chase the ebbing Neptune and do fly him
When he comes back; you demi-puppets that
By moonshine do the green sour ringlets make,
Whereof the ewe not bites, and you whose pastime
Is to make midnight mushrooms, that rejoice
To hear the solemn curfew; by whose aid,
Weak masters though ye be, I have bedimm'd
The noontide sun, call'd forth the mutinous winds,
And 'twixt the green sea and the azured vault
Set roaring war: to the dread rattling thunder
Have I given fire and rifted Jove's stout oak
With his own bolt; the strong-based promontory
Have I made shake and by the spurs pluck'd up
The pine and cedar: graves at my command
Have waked their sleepers, oped, and let 'em forth
By my so potent art. But this rough magic
I here abjure, and, when I have required
Some heavenly music, which even now I do,
To work mine end upon their senses that
This airy charm is for, I'll break my staff,
Bury it certain fathoms in the earth,
And deeper than did ever plummet sound
I'll drown my book. [*Solemn music.*

Re-enter ARIEL *before: then* ALONSO, *with a frantic gesture, attended by* GONZALO; SEBASTIAN *and* ANTONIO *in like manner, attended by* ADRIAN *and* FRANCISCO: *they all enter the circle which* PROSPERO *had made, and there stand charmed; which* PROSPERO *observing, speaks:*

A solemn air and the best comforter
To an unsettled fancy cure thy brains,
Now useless, boil'd within thy skull! There stand,
For you are spell-stopp'd.
Holy Gonzalo, honourable man,
Mine eyes, even sociable to the show of thine,
Fall fellowly drops. The charm dissolves apace,
And as the morning steals upon the night,
Melting the darkness, so their rising senses
Begin to chase the ignorant fumes that mantle
Their clearer reason. O good Gonzalo,
My true preserver, and a loyal sir
To him you follow'st! I will pay thy graces
Home both in word and deed. Most cruelly
Didst thou, Alonso, use me and my daughter:
Thy brother was a furtherer in the act.
Thou art pinch'd for't now, Sebastian. Flesh and blood,
You, brother mine, that entertain'd ambition,
Expell'd remorse and nature; who, with Sebastian,
Whose inward pinches therefore are most strong,
Would here have kill'd your king; I do forgive thee,
Unnatural though thou art. Their understanding
Begins to swell, and the approaching tide
Will shortly fill the reasonable shore
That now lies foul and muddy. Not one of them
That yet looks on me, or would know me: Ariel,
Fetch me the hat and rapier in my cell:
I will discase me, and myself present
As I was sometime Milan: quickly, spirit;
Thou shalt ere long be free.

ARIEL *sings and helps to attire him.*

Where the bee sucks, there suck I:
In a cowslip's bell I lie;
There I couch when owls do cry.
On the bat's back I do fly
After summer merrily.
Merrily, merrily shall I live now
Under the blossom that hangs on the bough.

PROSPERO
Why, that's my dainty Ariel! I shall miss thee:
But yet thou shalt have freedom: so, so, so.
To the king's ship, invisible as thou art:
There shalt thou find the mariners asleep
Under the hatches; the master and the boatswain
Being awake, enforce them to this place,
And presently, I prithee.
ARIEL
I drink the air before me, and return
Or ere your pulse twice beat. [*Exit.*
GONZALO
All torment, trouble, wonder and amazement
Inhabits here: some heavenly power guide us
Out of this fearful country!
PROSPERO
Behold, sir king,
The wronged Duke of Milan, Prospero:
For more assurance that a living prince
Does now speak to thee, I embrace thy body;
And to thee and thy company I bid
A hearty welcome.
ALONSO
Whether thou be'st he or no,
Or some enchanted trifle to abuse me,
As late I have been, I not know: thy pulse
Beats as of flesh and blood; and, since I saw thee,
The affliction of my mind amends, with which,
I fear, a madness held me: this must crave,
An if this be at all, a most strange story.
Thy dukedom I resign and do entreat
Thou pardon me my wrongs. But how should Prospero
Be living and be here?
PROSPERO
First, noble friend,
Let me embrace thine age, whose honour cannot
Be measured or confined.
GONZALO
Whether this be
Or be not, I'll not swear.
PROSPERO
You do yet taste
Some subtilties o' the isle, that will not let you
Believe things certain. Welcome, my friends all!
[*Aside to Sebastian and Antonio*] But you, my brace of lords, were I so minded,
I here could pluck his highness' frown upon you
And justify you traitors: at this time
I will tell no tales,
SEBASTIAN
[*Aside*] The devil speaks in him.
PROSPERO
No.
For you, most wicked sir, whom to call brother
Would even infect my mouth, I do forgive
Thy rankest fault; all of them; and require
My dukedom of thee, which perforce, I know,
Thou must restore.
ALONSO
If thou be'st Prospero,
Give us particulars of thy preservation;
How thou hast met us here, who three hours since
Were wreck'd upon this shore; where I have lost—
How sharp the point of this remembrance is!—
My dear son Ferdinand.
PROSPERO
I am woe for't, sir.
ALONSO
Irreparable is the loss, and patience
Says it is past her cure.
PROSPERO
I rather think
You have not sought her help, of whose soft grace
For the like loss I have her sovereign aid
And rest myself content.
ALONSO
You the like loss!
PROSPERO
As great to me as late; and, supportable
To make the dear loss, have I means much weaker
Than you may call to comfort you, for I
Have lost my daughter.
ALONSO
A daughter?
O heavens, that they were living both in Naples,
The king and queen there! that they were,
I wish
Myself were mudded in that oozy bed
Where my son lies. When did you lose your daughter?
PROSPERO
In this last tempest. I perceive, these lords
At this encounter do so much admire
That they devour their reason and scarce think
Their eyes do offices of truth, their words
Are natural breath: but, howsoe'er you have
Been justled from your senses, know for certain
That I am Prospero and that very duke
Which was thrust forth of Milan, who most strangely
Upon this shore, where you were wreck'd, was landed,
To be the lord on't. No more yet of this;
For 'tis a chronicle of day by day,
Not a relation for a breakfast nor
Befitting this first meeting. Welcome, sir;
This cell's my court: here have I few attendants
And subjects none abroad: pray you, look in.

My dukedom since you have given me again,
I will requite you with as good a thing;
At least bring forth a wonder, to content ye
As much as me my dukedom.

Here Prospero discovers FERDINAND *and* MIRANDA *playing at chess.*

MIRANDA
Sweet lord, you play me false.

FERDINAND
No, my dear'st love,
I would not for the world.

MIRANDA
Yes, for a score of kingdoms you should wrangle,
And I would call it fair play.

ALONSO
If this prove
A vision of the Island, one dear son
Shall I twice lose.

SEBASTIAN
A most high miracle!

FERDINAND
Though the seas threaten, they are merciful;
I have cursed them without cause. [*Kneels.*

ALONSO
Now all the blessings
Of a glad father compass thee about! 208
Arise, and say how thou camest here.

MIRANDA
O, wonder!
How many goodly creatures are there here!
How beauteous mankind is! O brave new world,
That has such people in't!

PROSPERO
'Tis new to thee.

ALONSO
What is this maid with whom thou wast at play?
Your eld'st acquaintance cannot be three hours:
Is she the goddess that hath sever'd us,
And brought us thus together?

FERDINAND
Sir, she is mortal;
But by immortal Providence she's mine:
I chose her when I could not ask my father
For his advice, nor thought I had one. She
Is daughter to this famous Duke of Milan
Of whom so often I have heard renown,
But never saw before; of whom I have
Received a second life; and second father
This lady makes him to me.

ALONSO
I am hers:
But, O, how oddly will it sound that I
Must ask my child forgiveness!

PROSPERO
There, sir, stop:
Let us not burthen our remembrance with
A heaviness that's gone.

GONZALO
I have inly wept 234
Or should have spoke ere this. Look down, you gods
And on this couple drop a blessed crown!
For it is you that have chalk'd forth the way
Which brought us hither.

ALONSO
I say, Amen, Gonzalo!

GONZALO
Was Milan thrust from Milan, that his issue
Should become kings of Naples? O, rejoice
Beyond a common joy, and set it down
With gold on lasting pillars: In one voyage
Did Claribel her husband find at Tunis
And Ferdinand, her brother, found a wife
Where he himself was lost, Prospero his dukedom
In a poor isle and all of us ourselves
When no man was his own.

ALONSO
[*To Ferdinand and Miranda*] Give me your hands:
Let grief and sorrow still embrace his heart
That doth not wish you joy!

GONZALO
Be it so! Amen!

Re-enter ARIEL, *with the* Master *and* Boatswain *amazedly following.*

O, look, sir, look, sir! here is more of us:
I prophesied, if a gallows were on land,
This fellow could not drown. Now, blasphemy,
That swear'st grace o'erboard, not an oath on shore?
Hast thou no mouth by land? What is the news? 257

BOATSWAIN
The best news is, that we have safely found
Our king and company; the next, our ship—
Which, but three glasses since, we gave out split—
Is tight and yare and bravely rigg'd as when
We first put out to sea.

ARIEL
[*Aside to Prospero*] Sir, all this service
Have I done since I went.

PROSPERO
[*Aside to Ariel*] My tricksy spirit!

ALONSO
These are not natural events; they strengthen
From strange to stranger. Say, how came you hither?

BOATSWAIN
If I did think, sir, I were well awake, I'ld strive to tell you. We were dead of sleep, And—how we know not—all clapp'd under hatches; 270

Where but even now with strange and several noises
Of roaring, shrieking, howling, jingling chains,
And more diversity of sounds, all horrible,
We were awaked; straightway, at liberty;
Where we, in all her trim, freshly beheld
Our royal, good and gallant ship, our master
Capering to eye her: on a trice, so please you,
Even in a dream, were we divided from them
And were brought moping hither.

ARIEL
[*Aside to Prospero*] Was't well done?

PROSPERO
[*Aside to Ariel*] Bravely, my diligence. Thou shalt be free.

ALONSO
This is as strange a maze as e'er men trod;
And there is in this business more than nature
Was ever conduct of: some oracle
Must rectify our knowledge.

PROSPERO
Sir, my liege,
Do not infest your mind with beating on
The strangeness of this business; at pick'd leisure
Which shall be shortly, single I'll resolve you,
Which to you shall seem probable, of every
These happen'd accidents; till when, be cheerful
And think of each thing well. [*Aside to Ariel*] Come hither, spirit:
Set Caliban and his companions free;
Untie the spell. [*Exit Ariel.*] How fares my gracious sir?
There are yet missing of your company
Some few odd lads that you remember not.

Re-enter ARIEL, *driving in* CALIBAN, STEPHANO *and* TRINCULO, *in their stolen apparel.*

STEPHANO
Every man shift for all the rest, and let no man take care for himself; for all is but fortune. Coragio, bully-monster, coragio!

TRINCULO
If these be true spies which I wear in my head, here's a goodly sight.

CALIBAN
O Setebos, these be brave spirits indeed!
How fine my master is! I am afraid
He will chastise me.

SEBASTIAN
Ha, ha!
What things are these, my lord Antonio?
Will money buy 'em?

ANTONIO
Very like; one of them Is a plain fish, and, no doubt, marketable.

PROSPERO
Mark but the badges of these men, my lords,
Then say if they be true. This mis-shapen knave,
His mother was a witch, and one so strong
That could control the moon, make flows and ebbs,
And deal in her command without her power.
These three have robb'd me; and this demi-devil—
For he's a bastard one—had plotted with them
To take my life. Two of these fellows you
Must know and own; this thing of darkness I
Acknowledge mine.

CALIBAN
I shall be pinch'd to death.

ALONSO
Is not this Stephano, my drunken butler?

SEBASTIAN
He is drunk now: where had he wine?

ALONSO
And Trinculo is reeling ripe: where should they
Find this grand liquor that hath gilded 'em?
How camest thou in this pickle?

TRINCULO
I have been in such a pickle since I saw you last that, I fear me, will never out of my bones: I shall not fear fly-blowing.

SEBASTIAN
Why, how now, Stephano!

STEPHANO
O, touch me not; I am not Stephano, but a cramp.

PROSPERO
You'ld be king o' the isle, sirrah?

STEPHANO
I should have been a sore one then.

ALONSO
This is a strange thing as e'er I look'd on.
[*Pointing to Caliban.*

PROSPERO
He is as disproportion'd in his manners
As in his shape. Go, sirrah, to my cell;
Take with you your companions; as you look
To have my pardon, trim it handsomely.

CALIBAN
Ay, that I will; and I'll be wise hereafter
And seek for grace. What a thrice-double ass
Was I, to take this drunkard for a god
And worship this dull fool!

PROSPERO
Go to; away!

ALONSO
Hence, and bestow your luggage where you found it.

SEBASTIAN
Or stole it, rather. [*Exeunt Caliban, Stephano, and Trinculo.*

PROSPERO

Sir, I invite your highness and your train
To my poor cell, where you shall take your rest
For this one night; which, part of it, I'll waste
With such discourse as, I not doubt, shall make it
Go quick away; the story of my life
And the particular accidents gone by
Since I came to this isle: and in the morn
I'll bring you to your ship and so to Naples,
Where I have hope to see the nuptial
Of these our dear-beloved solemnized; [26]
And thence retire me to my Milan, where
Every third thought shall be my grave.

ALONSO

I long
To hear the story of your life, which must
Take the ear strangely.

PROSPERO

I'll deliver all;
And promise you calm seas, auspicious gales
And sail so expeditious that shall catch
Your royal fleet far off. [*Aside to Ariel*] My Ariel, chick,
That is thy charge: then to the elements
Be free, and fare thou well! Please you, draw near.

[*Exeunt.*

EPILOGUE.

SPOKEN BY PROSPERO.

Now my charms are all o'erthrown,
And what strength I have's mine own,
Which is most faint: now, 'tis true,
I must be here confined by you,
Or sent to Naples. Let me not,
Since I have my dukedom got
And pardon'd the deceiver, dwell
In this bare island by your spell;
But release me from my bands
With the help of your good hands:
Gentle breath of yours my sails
Must fill, or else my project fails,
Which was to please. Now I want
Spirits to enforce, art to enchant,
And my ending is despair,
Unless I be relieved by prayer,
Which pierces so that it assaults
Mercy itself and frees all faults.
As you from crimes would pardon'd be,
Let your indulgence set me free.

Notes

1. Long heath, brown furze; – so the Folios; Hanmer's emendation has been generally accepted:—'ling, heath, broom, furze.'
2. Who having into truth; – 'into,' used in the sense of 'unto,' and so emended in most editions; the sentence though very involved is intelligible without any alteration; 'into truth' depends upon 'a sinner'; and 'it' refers vaguely to 'his own lie'; 'to credit' = 'as to credit.'
3. Now I arise; – probably derived from astrology; 'now my star is in the ascendent;' it should be noted that the stage direction 'Resumes his mantle' is not in the Folios.
4. For one thing she did; – Shakespeare does not tell us what he refers to here; perhaps he merely added the point in order to account for her preservation, or the incident may have been mentioned in his original.
5. Kiss'd the wild waves; – so the Folios, *i.e.*, 'Kissed the wild waves into silence;' often printed with a comma after 'kissed.'
6. The masters of some merchant; – *i.e.*, 'the owners of some merchantman;' Steevens suggested 'mistress' (old spelling 'maistres'); the Cambridge editors 'master's' (*i.e.*, 'master's wife').
7. Which, of he or Adrian; – 'he' for 'him,' used somewhat substantively, probably owing to the use of the word in the previous sentence, 'he will be talking.'
8. The Folios read: 'Seb. *Ha, ha, ha!* Ant. *So you're paid.'* Theobald gives the whole line to Sebastian; and his reading is adopted by the Camb. edition. Possibly a better emendation is the transposition of the prefixes to the speeches; the point of the quibble is no doubt the old proverb 'let them laugh that win.' Capell ingeniously suggested that the Folio reading should stand with the slight change of 'you've paid' for 'you're paid.'
9. Who hath cause; – the antecedent of 'who' is most probably 'she'; some make the relative refer to 'eye,' *i.e.* 'which hath cause to weep.'
10. Should bow; – so Folios; seemingly unnecessary corrections have been made. *e.g.* 'she'd bow;' 'which end the beam should bow;' the omission of the pronoun 'it' or 'she' before 'should' can easily be paralleled in Shakespeare.
11. But doubt – *discovery there; i.e.* 'Cannot but doubt that anything can be discovered there.'
12. She that from whom; – the unnecessary 'that' is perhaps intentionally repeated, owing to the previous repetition of 'she that.'
13. Candied; – generally explained as 'sugared over, and so insensible;' perhaps a better interpretation is 'made sweet as sugar,' as in the phrase 'the candied tongue.' Is Antonio possibly playing on 'candied' and 'candid' (a word not yet fully naturalised in the language, but probably familiar)?
14. I will not take too much for him; i.e. – 'I will take as much as I can possibly get.'
15. Scamels; – not found elsewhere in Shakespeare. Many emendations have been made; staniel (a species of hawk) has been adopted by some editors; the word occurs probably in *Twelfth Night* (II. v.), though the editions read 'stallion.' 'Scamel' is evidently the name of a rock-breeding bird; Mr. Wright has pointed out that, according to Stevenson's "Birds of Norfolk," "the female Bar-tailed Godwit is called a 'Scamell' by the gunners of Blakeney."
16. Most busy lest, when I do it; – so the first Folio. Various readings have been suggested; Pope, 'least busy when

I do it'; Theobald, 'most busie-less when I do it'; Holt, 'most busiest, when I do it'; Spedding 'most busiest when idlest,' &c., &c. It seems likely that the reading of the second, third, and fourth Folios throws light on the real meaning of the line:—'most busy least, when I do it;' *i.e.,* 'most busy when I indulge my thoughts, least busy when I am actually at work.' A comma after 'busy' instead of after 'least' would simplify this reading, but it is possible to understand it as punctuated in the Folios; Shakespeare probably wished to make the superlatives as antithetical as possible; perhaps we should read 'labour' for 'labours.'

17. Praise in departing; – a proverbial expression; "stay your praises till you see how your entertainment will end."
18. Pioned and twilled; – various emendations have been suggested for these difficult words of the Folio:—'peonied and lilied,' 'tulip'd,' 'tilled,' &c. It is noted that 'piony' is an old spelling of 'peony,' and that the flower was formerly spoken of as 'the mayden piony' and 'virgin peonie.' In all probability the meaning of the words has not yet been discovered; they are evidently technical terms of horticulture. (*Cp.* Glossary.)
19. Mr. Wright suggests that 'earths' should be read as a dissyllable, 'earthes'; the second, third, and fourth Folios read *'and'* before 'foison.'
20. &c. In *The Tragedy of Darius,* by William Alexander, afterwards Earl of Sterling, published in the year 1603, occurs the following passage, which, according to Steevens, may have been the original of Shakespeare's Speech:

"Let greatnesse of her glascie sceptre vaunt:
Not scepters, no, but reeds, soone brus'd, soone broken
And let this worldlie pomp our wits inchant.
All fades, and scarcelie leaues behind a token.
Those golden pallaces, those gorgeous halles
With fourniture superfluouslie faire:
Those statelie courts, those sky-encountering walles
Evanish all like vapours in the aire."

21. The Folios read 'hang on them.'
22. O King Stephano! O Peer! – an allusion to the old song, often referred to in Elizabethan literature, "Take thy old cloak about thee":—

"King Stephen was a worthy peere,
His breeches cost him but a crowne,
He held them sixpence all too deere;
Therefore he called the taylor Lowne."

The ballad is printed in Percy's Reliques; Shakespeare quotes it also in Othello, II. iii. 92.

23. Let's alone; – some verb of motion must be understood, *i.e.,* 'let us go alone' (leaving Trinculo behind); 'alone' is possibly an error of the Folios for 'along,' as suggested by Theobald.
24. "An allusion to what often happens to people who pass the line. The violent fevers which they contract in that hot climate make them lose their hair."—STEEVENS.
25. The first and second Folios place a comma after 'sharply,' making 'passion' a verb; the comma is omitted in the third and fourth Folios.
26. The line is to be read, according to the Folios, "to see our dear belov'd solémnizéd."

SONNETS

TO THE ONLIE BEGETTER OF
THESE UNSUING SONNETS
MR. W. H. ALL HAPPINESSE
AND THAT ETERNITIE
PROMISED BY
OUR EVER-LIVING POET
WISHETH
THE WELL-WISHING
ADVENTURER IN
SETTING
FORTH

T.T.

1

FROM fairest creatures we desire increase,
That thereby beauty's rose might never die,
But as the riper should by time decease,
His tender heir might bear his memory:
But thou, contracted to thine own bright eyes,
Feed'st thy light'st flame with self-substantial fuel,
Making a famine where abundance lies,
Thyself thy foe, to thy sweet self too cruel.
Thou that art now the world's fresh ornament
And only herald to the gaudy spring,
Within thine own bud buriest thy content
And, tender churl, makest waste in niggarding.
  Pity the world, or else this glutton be,
  To eat the world's due, by the grave and thee.

2

When forty winters shall beseige thy brow,
And dig deep trenches in thy beauty's field,
Thy youth's proud livery, so gazed on now,
Will be a tatter'd weed, of small worth held:
Then being ask'd where all thy beauty lies,
Where all the treasure of thy lusty days,
To say, within thine own deep-sunken eyes,
Were an all-eating shame and thriftless praise.
How much more praise deserved thy beauty's use,
If thou couldst answer 'This fair child of mine
Shall sum my count and make my old excuse,'
Proving his beauty by succession thine!
  This were to be new made when thou art old,
  And see thy blood warm when thou feel'st it cold.

3

Look in thy glass, and tell the face thou viewest
Now is the time that face should form another;
Whose fresh repair if now thou not renewest,
Thou dost beguile the world, unbless some mother.
For where is she so fair whose unear'd womb

Thou that art now the world's fresh ornament.

Disdains the tillage of thy husbandry?
Or who is he so fond will be the tomb
Of his self-love, to stop posterity?
Thou art thy mother's glass, and she in thee
Calls back the lovely April of her prime:
So thou through windows of thine age shall see
Despite of wrinkles this thy golden time.
  But if thou live, remember'd not to be,
  Die single, and thine image dies with thee.

4

Unthrifty loveliness, why dost thou spend
Upon thyself thy beauty's legacy?
Nature's bequest gives nothing but doth lend,
And being frank she lends to those are free.
Then, beauteous niggard, why dost thou abuse
The bounteous largess given thee to give?
Profitless usurer, why dost thou use
So great a sum of sums, yet canst not live?
For having traffic with thyself alone,
Thou of thyself thy sweet self dost deceive.
Then how, when nature calls thee to be gone,
What acceptable audit canst thou leave?
  Thy unused beauty must be tomb'd with thee,
  Which, used, lives th' executor to be.

5

Those hours, that with gentle work did frame
The lovely gaze where every eye doth dwell,
Will play the tyrants to the very same
And that unfair which fairly doth excel;
For never-resting time leads summer on
To hideous winter and confounds him there;
Sap check with frost and lusty leaves quite gone,
Beauty o'ersnow'd and bareness every where:
Then, were not summer's distillation left,
A liquid prisoner pent in walls of glass,
Beauty's effect with beauty were bereft,
Nor it nor no remembrance what it was:
  But flowers distill'd, though they with winter meet,
  Leese but their show; their substance still lives sweet.

6

Then let not winter's ragged hand deface
In thee thy summer, ere thou be distill'd:
Make sweet some vial; treasure thou some place
With beauty's treasure, ere it be self-kill'd.
That use is not forbidden usury,
Which happies those that pay the willing loan;
That's for thyself to breed another thee,

Or ten times happier, be it ten for one;
Ten times thyself were happier than thou art,
If ten of thine ten times refigured thee:
Then what could death do, if thou shouldst depart,
Leaving thee living in posterity?
Be not self-will'd, for thou art much too fair
To be death's conquest and make worms thine heir.

7

Lo! in the orient when the gracious light
Lifts up his burning head, each under eye
Doth homage to his new-appearing sight,
Serving with looks his sacred majesty;
And having climb'd the steep-up heavenly hill,
Resembling strong youth in his middle age,
Yet mortal looks adore his beauty still,
Attending on his golden pilgrimage;
But when from highmost pitch, with weary car,
Like feeble age, he reeleth from the day,
The eyes, 'fore duteous, now converted are
From his low tract and look another way:
So thou, thyself out-going in thy noon,
Unlook'd on diest, unless thou get a son.

8

Music to hear, why hear'st thou music sadly?
Sweets with sweets war not, joy delights in joy.
Why lovest thou that which thou receivest not gladly,
Or else receivest with pleasure thine annoy?
If the true concord of well-tuned sounds,
By unions married, do offend thine ear,
They do but sweetly chide thee, who confounds
In singleness the parts that thou shouldst bear.
Mark how one string, sweet husband to another,
Strikes each in each by mutual ordering,
Resembling sire and child and happy mother
Who all in one, one pleasing note do sing:
Whose speechless song, being many, seeming one,
Sings this to thee: 'thou single wilt prove none.'

9

Is it for fear to wet a widow's eye
That thou consumest thyself in single life?
Ah! if thou issueless shalt hap to die.
The world will wail thee, like a makeless wife;
The world will be thy widow and still weep
That thou no form of thee hast left behind,
When every private widow well may keep
By children's eyes her husband's shape in mind.
Look, what an unthrift in the world doth spend
Shifts but his place, for still the world enjoys it;
But beauty's waste hath in the world an end,
And kept unused, the user so destroys it.
No love toward others in that bosom sits
That on himself such murderous shame commits.

10

For shame! deny that thou bear'st love to any,
Who for thyself art so unprovident.
Grant, if thou wilt, thou art beloved of many,
But that thou none lovest is most evident;
For thou art so possess'd with murderous hate
That 'gainst thyself thou stick'st not to conspire.
Seeking that beauteous roof to ruinate
Which to repair should be thy chief desire.
O, change thy thought, that I may change my mind!
Shall hate be fairer lodged than gentle love?
Be, as thy presence is, gracious and kind,
Or to thyself at least kind-hearted prove:
Make thee another self, for love of me,
That beauty still may live in thine or thee.

11

As fast as thou shalt wane, so fast thou growest
In one of thine, from that which thou departest;
And that fresh blood which youngly thou bestowest
Thou mayst call thine when thou from youth convertest.
Herein lives wisdom, beauty and increase:
Without this, folly, age and cold decay:
If all were minded so, the times should cease
And threescore year would make the world away.
Let those whom Nature hath not made for store,
Harsh, featureless and rude, barrenly perish:
Look, whom she best endow'd she gave the more;
Which bounteous gift thou shouldst in bounty cherish:
She carved thee for her seal, and meant thereby
Thou shouldst print more, not let that copy die.

12

When I do count the clock that tells the time,
And see the brave day sunk in hideous night;
When I behold the violet past prime,
And sable curls all silver'd o'er with white;
When lofty trees I see barren of leaves
Which erst from heat did canopy the herd,
And summer's green all girded up in sheaves

Borne on the bier with white and bristly beard,
Then of thy beauty do I question make,
That thou among the wastes of time must go,
Since sweets and beauties do themselves forsake
And die as fast as they see others grow;
And nothing 'gainst Time's scythe can make defence
Save breed, to brave him when he takes thee hence.

13

O, that you were yourself! but, love, you are
No longer yours than you yourself here live:
Against this coming end you should prepare,
And your sweet semblance to some other give. [1]
So should that beauty which you hold in lease
Find no determination: then you were
Yourself again after yourself's decease,
When your sweet issue your sweet form should bear.
Who lets so fair a house fall to decay,
Which husbandry in honour might uphold
Against the stormy gusts of winter's day
And barren rage of death's eternal cold?
O, none but unthrifts! Dear my love, you know
You had a father: let your son say so.

14

Not from the stars do I my judgment pluck;
And yet methinks I have astronomy,
But not to tell of good or evil luck,
Of plagues, of dearths, or seasons' quality;
Nor can I fortune to brief minutes tell,
Pointing to each his thunder, rain and wind,
Or say with princes if it shall go well,
By oft predict that I in heaven find:
But from thine eyes my knowledge I derive,
And, constant stars, in them I read such art
As truth and beauty shall together thrive,
If from thyself to store thou wouldst convert;
Or else of thee this I prognosticate:
Thy end is truth's and beauty's doom and date.

15

When I consider every thing that grows
Holds in perfection but a little moment,
That this huge stage presenteth nought but shows
Whereon the stars in secret influence comment;
When I perceive that men as plants increase,
Cheered and check even by the self-same sky,
Vaunt in their youthful sap, at height decrease,
And wear their brave state out of memory;
Then the conceit of this inconstant stay
Sets you most rich in youth before my sight,
Where wasteful Time debateth with Decay,
To change your day of youth to sullied night;
And all in war with Time for love of you,
As he takes from you, I engraft you new.

16

But wherefore do not you a mightier way
Make war upon this bloody tyrant, Time?
And fortify yourself in your decay
With means more blessed than my barren rhyme?
Now stand you on the top of happy hours,
And many maiden gardens yet unset
With virtuous wish would bear your living flowers,
Much liker than your painted counterfeit:
So should the lines of life that life repair,
Which this, Time's pencil, or my pupil pen, [2]
Neither in inward worth nor outward fair,
Can make you live yourself in eyes of men.
To give away yourself keeps yourself still,
And you must live, drawn by your own sweet skill.

17

Who will believe my verse in time to come,
If it were fill'd with your most high deserts?
Though yet, heaven knows, it is but as a tomb
Which hides your life and shows not half your parts.
If I could write the beauty of your eyes
And in fresh numbers number all your graces,
The age to come would say 'This poet lies;
Such heavenly touches ne'er touch'd earthly faces.'
So should my papers yellow'd with their age
Be scorn'd like old men of less truth than tongue,
And your true rights be term'd a poet's rage
And stretched metre of an antique song:
But were some child of yours alive that time,
You should live twice; in it and in my rhyme.

18

Shall I compare thee to a summer's day?
Thou art more lovely and more temperate:
Rough winds do shake the darling buds of May,
And summer's lease hath all too short a date:
Sometime too hot the eye of heaven shines,
And often is his gold complexion dimm'd;
And every fair from fair sometime declines,
By chance or nature's changing course untrimm'd;
But thy eternal summer shall not fade

Nor lose possession of that fair thou owest;
Nor shall Death brag thou wander'st in his shade,
When in eternal lines to time thou growest:
  So long as men can breathe or eyes can see,
  So long lives this and this gives life to thee.

19

Devouring Time, blunt thou the lion's paws,
And make the earth devour her own sweet brood;
Pluck the keen teeth from the fierce tiger's jaws,
And burn the long-lived phoenix in her blood;
Make glad and sorry seasons as thou fleets, [3]
And do whate'er thou wilt, swift-footed Time,
To the wide world and all her fading sweets;
But I forbid thee one most heinous crime:
O, carve not with thy hours my love's fair brow,
Nor draw no lines there with thine antique pen;
Him in thy course untainted do allow
For beauty's pattern to succeeding men.
  Yet, do thy worst, old Time: despite thy wrong,
  My love shall in my verse ever live young.

20

A woman's face with Nature's own hand painted
Hast thou, the master-mistress of my passion;
A woman's gentle heart, but not acquainted
With shifting change, as is false women's fashion;
An eye more bright than theirs, less false in rolling,
Gilding the object whereupon it gazeth;
A man in hue, all 'hues' in his controlling, [4]
Much steals men's eyes and women's souls amazeth.
And for a woman wert thou first created;
Till Nature, as she wrought thee, fell a-doting,
And by addition me of thee defeated,
By adding one thing to my purpose nothing.
  But since she prick'd thee out for women's pleasure,
  Mine be thy love and thy love's use their treasure.

21

So is it not with me as with that Muse
Stirr'd by a painted beauty to his verse,
Who heaven itself for ornament doth use
And every fair with his fair doth rehearse;
Making a couplement of proud compare, [5]
With sun and moon, with earth and sea's rich gems,
With April's first-born flowers, and all things rare
That heaven's air in this huge rondure hems.
O' let me, true in love, but truly write,
And then believe me, my love is as fair
As any mother's child, though not so bright
As those gold candles fix'd in heaven's air:
  Let them say more than like of hearsay well;
  I will not praise that purpose not to sell.

22

My glass shall not persuade me I am old,
So long as youth and thou are of one date;
But when in thee time's furrows I behold,
Then look I death my days should expiate.
For all that beauty that doth cover thee
Is but the seemly raiment of my heart,
Which in thy breast doth live, as thine in me:
How can I then be elder than thou art?
O, therefore, love, be of thyself so wary
As I, not for myself, but for thee will;
Bearing thy heart, which I will keep so chary
As tender nurse her babe from faring ill.
  Presume not on thy heart when mine is slain;
  Thou gavest me thine, not to give back again.

23

As an unperfect actor on the stage
Who with his fear is put besides his part,
Or some fierce thing replete with too much rage,
Whose strength's abundance weakens his own heart.
So I, for fear of trust, forget to say
The perfect ceremony of love's rite,
And in mine own love's strength seem to decay,
O'ercharged with burden of mine own love's might.
O, let my books be then the eloquence
And dumb presagers of my speaking breast,
Who plead for love and look for recompense
More than that tongue that more hath more
    express'd.
  O, learn to read what silent love hath writ:
  To hear with eyes belongs to love's fine wit.

24

Mine eye hath play'd the painter and hath stell'd
Thy beauty's form in table of my heart;
My body is the frame wherein 'tis held,
And perspective it is the painter's art.
For through the painter must you see his skill,
To find where your true image pictured lies;
Which in my bosom's shop is hanging still,
That hath his windows glazed with thine eyes.
Now see what good turns eyes for eyes have done:
Mine eyes have drawn thy shape, and thine for me

Are windows to my breast, where-through the sun
Delights to peep, to gaze therein on thee;
 Yet eyes this cunning want to grace their art;
 They draw but what they see, know not the heart.

25

Let those who are in favour with their stars
Of public honour and proud titles boast
Whilst I, whom fortune of such triumph bars,
Unlook'd for joy in that I honour most.
Great princes' favourites their fair leaves spread
But as the marigold at the sun's eye,
And in themselves their pride lies buried,
For at a frown they in their glory die.
The painful warrior famoused for fight, [6]
After a thousand victories once foil'd,
Is from the book of honour razed quite,
And all the rest forgot for which he toil'd:
 Then happy I, that love and am beloved
 Where I may not remove nor be removed.

26

Lord of my love, to whom in vassalage
Thy merit hath my duty strongly knit,
To thee I send this written embassage,
To witness duty, not to show my wit:
Duty so great, which wit so poor as mine
May make seem bare, in wanting words to show it,
But that I hope some good conceit of thine
In thy soul's thought, all naked, will bestow it;
Till whatsoever star that guides my moving
Points on me graciously with fair aspect
And puts apparel on my tatter'd loving,
To show me worthy of thy sweet respect:
 Then may I dare to boast how I do love thee;
 Till then not show my head where thou mayst prove me.

27

Weary with toil, I haste me to my bed,
The dear repose for limbs with travel tired;
But then begins a journey in my head,
To work my mind, when body's work's expired:
For then my thoughts, from far where I abide,
Intend a zealous pilgrimage to thee,
And keep my drooping eyelids open wide,
Looking on darkness which the blind do see:
Save that my soul's imaginary sight
Presents thy shadow to my sightless view, [7]
Which, like a jewel hung in ghastly night,
Makes black night beauteous and her old face new.
 Lo! thus, by day my limbs, by night my mind,
 For thee and for myself no quiet find.

28

How can I then return in happy plight,
That am debarr'd the benefit of rest?
When day's oppression is not eased by night,
But day by night, and night by day, oppress'd?
And each, though enemies to either's reign,
Do in consent shake hands to torture me;
The one by toil, the other to complain
How far I toil, still farther off from thee.
I tell the day, to please them thou art bright
And dost him grace when clouds do blot the heaven:
So flatter I the swart-complexion'd night,
When sparkling stars twire not thou gild'st the even.
 But day doth daily draw my sorrows longer [8]
 And night doth nightly make grief's strength seem stronger.

29

When, in disgrace with fortune and men's eyes,
I all alone beweep my outcast state
And trouble deaf heaven with my bootless cries
And look upon myself and curse my fate,
Wishing me like to one more rich in hope,
Featured like him, like him with friends possess'd,
Desiring this man's art and that man's scope,
With what I most enjoy contented least;
Yet in these thoughts myself almost despising,
Haply I think on thee, and then my state,
Like to the lark at break of day arising
From sullen earth, sings hymns at heaven's gate;
 For thy sweet love remember'd such wealth brings
 That then I scorn to change my state with kings.

30

When to the sessions of sweet silent thought
I summon up remembrance of things past,
I sigh the lack of many a thing I sought,
And with old woes new wail my dear time's waste:
Then can I drown an eye, unused to flow,
For precious friends hid in death's dateless night,
And weep afresh love's long since cancell'd woe,
And moan the expense of many a vanish'd sight:
Then can I grieve at grievances foregone,
And heavily from woe to woe tell o'er

The sad account of fore-bemoaned moan,
Which I new pay as if not paid before.
  But if the while I think on thee, dear friend,
  All losses are restored and sorrows end.

31

Thy bosom is endeared with all hearts,
Which I by lacking have supposed dead,
And there reigns love and all love's loving parts,
And all those friends which I thought buried.
How many a holy and obsequious tear
Hath dear religious love stol'n from mine eye
As interest of the dead, which now appear
But things removed that hidden in thee lie! [9]
Thou art the grave where buried love doth live,
Hung with the trophies of my lovers gone,
Who all their parts of me to thee did give;
That due of many now is thine alone:
  Their images I loved I view in thee,
  And thou, all they, hast all the all of me.

32

If thou survive my well-contented day,
When that churl Death my bones with dust shall cover,
And shalt by fortune once more re-survey
These poor rude lines of thy deceased lover,
Compare them with the bettering of the time,
And though they be outstripp'd by every pen,
Reserve them for my love, not for their rhyme,
Exceeded by the height of happier men.
O, then vouchsafe me but this loving thought:
'Had my friend's Muse grown with this growing age,
A dearer birth than this his love had brought,
To march in ranks of better equipage:
  But since he died and poets better prove,
  Theirs for their style I'll read, his for his love.'

33

Full many a glorious morning have I seen
Flatter the mountain-tops with sovereign eye,
Kissing with golden face the meadows green,
Gilding pale streams with heavenly alchemy;
Anon permit the basest clouds to ride
With ugly rack on his celestial face,
And from the forlorn world his visage hide,
Stealing unseen to west with this disgrace:
Even so my sun one early morn did shine
With all-triumphant splendor on my brow;
But out, alack! he was but one hour mine;
The region cloud hath mask'd him from me now.
  Yet him for this my love no whit disdaineth;
  Suns of the world may stain when heaven's sun staineth.

34

Why didst thou promise such a beauteous day,
And make me travel forth without my cloak,
To let base clouds o'ertake me in my way,
Hiding thy bravery in their rotten smoke?
'Tis not enough that through the cloud thou break,
To dry the rain on my storm-beaten face,
For no man well of such a salve can speak
That heals the wound and cures not the disgrace:
Nor can thy shame give physic to my grief;
Though thou repent, yet I have still the loss: [10]
The offender's sorrow lends but weak relief
To him that bears the strong offence's cross.
  Ah! but those tears are pearl which thy love sheds, [11]
  And they are rich and ransom all ill deeds.

35

No more be grieved at that which thou hast done:
Roses have thorns, and silver fountains mud;
Clouds and eclipses stain both moon and sun,
And loathsome canker lives in sweetest bud.
All men make faults, and even I in this,
Authorizing thy trespass with compare,
Myself corrupting, salving thy amiss,
Excusing thy sins more than thy sins are;
For to thy sensual fault I bring in sense—
Thy adverse party is thy advocate—
And 'gainst myself a lawful plea commence:
Such civil war is in my love and hate
  That I an accessary needs must be
  To that sweet thief which sourly robs from me.

36

Let me confess that we two must be twain,
Although our undivided loves are one:
So shall those blots that do with me remain
Without thy help by me be borne alone.
In our two loves there is but one respect,
Though in our lives a separable spite,
Which though it alter not love's sole effect,
Yet doth it steal sweet hours from love's delight.
I may not evermore acknowledge thee,
Lest my bewailed guilt should do thee shame,

Nor thou with public kindness honour me,
Unless thou take that honour from thy name:
 But do not so; I love thee in such sort
 As, thou being mine, mine is thy good report.

37

As a decrepit father takes delight
To see his active child do deeds of youth,
So I, made lame by fortune's dearest spite,
Take all my comfort of thy worth and truth.
For whether beauty, birth, or wealth, or wit,
Or any of these all, or all, or more,
Entitled in thy parts do crowned sit,
I make my love engrafted to this store:
So then I am not lame, poor, nor despised,
Whilst that this shadow doth such substance give
That I in thy abundance am sufficed
And by a part of all thy glory live.
 Look, what is best, that best I wish in thee:
 This wish I have; then ten times happy me!

38

How can my Muse want subject to invent,
While thou dost breathe, that pour'st into my verse
Thine own sweet argument, too excellent
For every vulgar paper to rehearse?
O, give thyself the thanks, if aught in me
Worthy perusal stand against thy sight;
For who's so dumb that cannot write to thee,
When thou thyself dost give invention light?
Be thou the tenth Muse, ten times more in worth
Than those old nine which rhymers invocate;
And he that calls on thee, let him bring forth
Eternal numbers to outlive long date.
 If my slight Muse do please these curious days,
 The pain be mine, but thine shall be the praise.

39

O, how thy worth with manners may I sing,
When thou art all the better part of me?
What can mine own praise to mine own self bring?
And what is 't but mine own when I praise thee?
Even for this let us divided live,
And our dear love lose name of single one,
That by this separation I may give
That due to thee which thou deservest alone.
O absence, what a torment wouldst thou prove,
Were it not thy sour leisure gave sweet leave
To entertain the time with thoughts of love,
Which time and thoughts so sweetly doth deceive, [12]
 And that thou teachest how to make one twain,
 By praising him here who doth hence remain!

40

Take all my loves, my love, yea, take them all;
What hast thou then more than thou hadst before?
No love, my love, that thou mayst true love call;
All mine was thine before thou hadst this more.
Then if for my love thou my love receivest,
I cannot blame thee for my love thou usest;
But yet be blamed, if thou thyself deceivest [13]
By wilful taste of what thyself refusest.
I do forgive thy robbery, gentle thief,
Although thou steal thee all my poverty;
And yet, love knows, it is a greater grief
To bear love's wrong than hate's known injury.
 Lascivious grace, in whom all ill well shows,
 Kill me with spites; yet we must not be foes.

41

Those petty wrongs that liberty commits,
When I am sometime absent from thy heart,
Thy beauty and thy years full well befits,
For still temptation follows where thou art.
Gentle thou art and therefore to be won,
Beauteous thou art, therefore to be assailed;
And when a woman woos, what woman's son
Will sourly leave her till she have prevailed? [14]
Ay me! but yet thou mightest my seat forbear,
And chide try beauty and thy straying youth,
Who lead thee in their riot even there
Where thou art forced to break a twofold truth,
 Hers by thy beauty tempting her to thee,
 Thine, by thy beauty being false to me.

42

That thou hast her, it is not all my grief,
And yet it may be said I loved her dearly;
That she hath thee, is of my wailing chief,
A loss in love that touches me more nearly.
Loving offenders, thus I will excuse ye:
Thou dost love her, because thou knowst I love her;
And for my sake even so doth she abuse me,
Suffering my friend for my sake to approve her.
If I lose thee, my loss is my love's gain,
And losing her, my friend hath found that loss;
Both find each other, and I lose both twain,
And both for my sake lay on me this cross:

But here's the joy; my friend and I are one;
Sweet flattery! then she loves but me alone.

43

When most I wink, then do mine eyes best see,
For all the day they view things unrespected;
But when I sleep, in dreams they look on thee,
And darkly bright are bright in dark directed.
Then thou, whose shadow shadows doth make bright,
How would thy shadow's form form happy show
To the clear day with thy much clearer light,
When to unseeing eyes thy shade shines so!
How would, I say, mine eyes be blessed made
By looking on thee in the living day,
When in dead night thy fair imperfect shade
Through heavy sleep on sightless eyes doth stay!
All days are nights to see till I see thee,
And nights bright days when dreams do show thee me.

44

If the dull substance of my flesh were thought,
Injurious distance should not stop my way;
For then despite of space I would be brought,
From limits far remote where thou dost stay.
No matter then although my foot did stand
Upon the furthest earth removed from thee;
For nimble thought can jump both sea and land
As soon as think the place where he would be.
But ah! thought kills me that I am not thought,
To leap large lengths of miles when thou art gone,
But that so much of earth and water wrought
I must attend time's leisure with my moan,
Receiving nought by elements so slow
But heavy tears, badges of either's woe.

45

The other two, slight air and purging fire,
Are both with thee, wherever I abide;
The first my thought, the other my desire,
These present-absent with swift motion slide.
For when these quicker elements are gone
In tender embassy of love to thee,
My life, being made of four, with two alone
Sinks down to death, oppress'd with melancholy;
Until life's composition be recured
By those swift messengers return'd from thee,
Who even but now come back again, assured
Of thy fair health, recounting it to me:
This told, I joy; but then no longer glad,
I send them back again and straight grow sad.

46

Mine eye and heart are at a mortal war
How to divide the conquest of thy sight;
Mine eye my heart thy picture's sight would bar,
My heart mine eye the freedom of that right.
My heart doth plead that thou in him dost lie,—
A closet never pierced with crystal eyes—
But the defendant doth that plea deny
And says in him thy fair appearance lies.
To 'cide this title is impanneled
A quest of thoughts, all tenants to the heart,
And by their verdict is determined
The clear eye's moiety and the dear heart's part:
As thus; mine eye's due is thy outward part,
And my heart's right thy inward love of heart.

47

Betwixt mine eye and heart a league is took,
And each doth good turns now unto the other:
When that mine eye is famish'd for a look,
Or heart in love with sighs himself doth smother,
With my love's picture then my eye doth feast
And to the painted banquet bids my heart;
Another time mine eye is my heart's guest
And in his thoughts of love doth share a part:
So, either by thy picture or my love,
Thyself away art resent still with me;
For thou not farther than my thoughts canst move,
And I am still with them and they with thee;
Or, if they sleep, thy picture in my sight
Awakes my heart to heart's and eye's delight.

48

How careful was I, when I took my way,
Each trifle under truest bars to thrust,
That to my use it might unused stay
From hands of falsehood, in sure wards of trust!
But thou, to whom my jewels trifles are,
Most worthy of comfort, now my greatest grief,
Thou, best of dearest and mine only care,
Art left the prey of every vulgar thief.
Thee have I not lock'd up in any chest,
Save where thou art not, though I feel thou art,
Within the gentle closure of my breast,
From whence at pleasure thou mayst come and part;

And even thence thou wilt be stol'n, I fear,
For truth proves thievish for a prize so dear.

49

Against that time, if ever that time come,
When I shall see thee frown on my defects,
When as thy love hath cast his utmost sum,
Call'd to that audit by advised respects;
Against that time when thou shalt strangely pass
And scarcely greet me with that sun thine eye,
When love, converted from the thing it was,
Shall reasons find of settled gravity,—
Against that time do I ensconce me here
Within the knowledge of mine own desert, [16]
And this my hand against myself uprear,
To guard the lawful reasons on thy part:
To leave poor me thou hast the strength of laws,
Since why to love I can allege no cause.

50

How heavy do I journey on the way,
When what I seek, my weary travel's end,
Doth teach that ease and that repose to say
'Thus far the miles are measured from thy friend!'
The beast that bears me, tired with my woe,
Plods dully on, to bear that weight in me,
As if by some instinct the wretch did know
His rider loved not speed, being made from thee:
The bloody spur cannot provoke him on
That sometimes anger thrusts into his hide;
Which heavily he answers with a groan,
More sharp to me than spurring to his side;
For that same groan doth put this in my mind;
My grief lies onward and my joy behind.

51

Thus can my love excuse the slow offence
Of my dull bearer when from thee I speed:
From where thou art why should I haste me thence?
Till I return, of posting is no need.
O, what excuse will my poor beast then find,
When swift extremity can seem but slow?
Then should I spur, though mounted on the wind;
In winged speed no motion shall I know:
Then can no horse with my desire keep pace;
Therefore desire of perfect'st love being made,
Shall neigh—no dull flesh—in his fiery race; [17]
But love, for love, thus shall excuse my jade;
Since from thee going he went wilful-slow,
Towards thee I'll run, and give him leave to go.

52

So am I as the rich, whose blessed key
Can bring him to his sweet up-locked treasure,
The which he will not every hour survey,
For blunting the fine point of seldom pleasure.
Therefore are feasts so solemn and so rare,
Since, seldom coming, in the long year set,
Like stones of worth they thinly placed are,
Or captain jewels in the carcanet.
So is the time that keeps you as my chest,
Or as the wardrobe which the robe doth hide,
To make some special instant special blest,
By new unfolding his imprison'd pride.
Blessed are you, whose worthiness gives scope,
Being had, to triumph, being lack'd, to hope.

53

What is your substance, whereof are you made,
That millions of strange shadows on you tend?
Since every one hath, every one, one shade,
And you, but one, can every shadow lend.
Describe Adonis, and the counterfeit
Is poorly imitated after you;
On Helen's cheek all art of beauty set,
And you in Grecian tires are painted new:
Speak of the spring and foison of the year;
The one doth shadow of your beauty show,
The other as your bounty doth appear;
And you in every blessed shape we know.
In all external grace you have some part,
But you like none, none you, for constant heart.

54

O, how much more doth beauty beauteous seem
By that sweet ornament which truth doth give!
The rose looks fair, but fairer we it deem
For that sweet odour which doth in it live.
The canker-blooms have full as deep a dye
As the perfumed tincture of the roses,
Hang on such thorns and play as wantonly
When summer's breath their masked buds discloses:
But, for their virtue only is their show,
They live unwoo'd and unrespected fade,
Die to themselves. Sweet roses do not so;
Of their sweet deaths are sweetest odours made:
And so of you, beauteous and lovely youth,
When that shall fade, my verse distills your truth.

55

Not marble, nor the gilded monuments [18]
Of princes, shall outlive this powerful rhyme;
But you shall shine more bright in these contents
Than unswept stone besmear'd with sluttish time.
When wasteful war shall statues overturn,
And broils root out the work of masonry,
Nor Mars his sword nor war's quick fire shall burn
The living record of your memory.
'Gainst death and all-oblivious enmity
Shall you pace forth; your praise shall still find room
Even in the eyes of all posterity
That wear this world out to the ending doom.
So, till the judgment that yourself arise,
You live in this, and dwell in lover's eyes.

56

Sweet love, renew thy force; be it not said
Thy edge should blunter be than appetite,
Which but to-day by feeding is allay'd,
To-morrow sharpen'd in his former might:
So, love, be thou; although to-day thou fill
Thy hungry eyes even till they wink with fullness,
To-morrow see again, and do not kill
The spirit of love with a perpetual dullness.
Let this sad interim like the ocean be
Which parts the shore, where two contracted new
Come daily to the banks, that, when they see
Return of love, more blest may be the view;
Else call it winter, which being full of care [19]
Makes summer's welcome thrice more wish'd, more rare.

57

Being your slave, what should I do but tend
Upon the hours and times of your desire?
I have no precious time at all to spend,
Nor services to do, till you require.
Nor dare I chide the world-without-end hour
Whilst I, my sovereign, watch the clock for you,
Nor think the bitterness of absence sour
When you have bid your servant once adieu;
Nor dare I question with my jealous thought
Where you may be, or your affairs suppose,
But, like a sad slave, stay and think of nought
Save, where you are how happy you make those.
So true a fool is love that in your will, [20]
Though you do any thing, he thinks no ill.

58

That god forbid that made me first your slave,
I should in thought control your times of pleasure,
Or at your hand the account of hours to crave,
Being your vassal, bound to stay your leisure!
O, let me suffer, being at your beck,
The imprison'd absence of your liberty;
And patience, tame to sufferance, bide each check,
Without accusing you of injury.
Be where you list, your charter is so strong
That you yourself may privilege your time
To what you will; to you it doth belong
Yourself to pardon of self-doing crime.
I am to wait, though waiting so be hell;
Not blame your pleasure, be it ill or well.

59

If there be nothing new, but that which is
Hath been before, how are our brains beguiled,
Which, labouring for invention, bear amiss
The second burden of a former child!
O, that record could with a backward look,
Even of five hundred courses of the sun,
Show me your image in some antique book,
Since mind at first in character was done!
That I might see what the old world could say
To this composed wonder of your frame;
Whether we are mended, or whether better they,
Or whether revolution be the same.
O, sure I am, the wits of former days
To subjects worse have given admiring praise.

60

Like as the waves make towards the pebbled shore,
So do our minutes hasten to their end;
Each changing place with that which goes before,
In sequent toil all forwards do contend.
Nativity, once in the main of light,
Crawls to maturity, wherewith being crown'd,
Crooked elipses 'gainst his glory fight,
And Time that gave doth now his gift confound.
Time doth transfix the flourish set on youth
And delves the parallels in beauty's brow,
Feeds on the rarities of nature's truth,
And nothing stands but for his scythe to mow:
And yet to times in hope my verse shall stand,
Praising thy worth, despite his cruel hand.

61

Is it thy will thy image should keep open
My heavy eyelids to the weary night?
Dost thou desire my slumbers should be broken,
While shadows like to thee do mock my sight?
Is it thy spirit that thou send'st from thee
So far from home into my deeds to pry,
To find out shames and idle hours in me,
The scope and tenor of thy jealousy?
O, no! thy love, though much, is not so great:
It is my love that keeps mine eye awake;
Mine own true love that doth my rest defeat,
To play the watchman ever for thy sake:
For thee watch I whilst thou dost wake elsewhere,
From me far off, with others all too near.

62

Sin of self-love possesseth all mine eye
And all my soul and all my every part;
And for this sin there is no remedy,
It is so grounded inward in my heart.
Methinks no face so gracious is as mine,
No shape so true, no truth of such account;
And for myself mine own worth do define, [21]
As I all other in all worths surmount.
But when my glass shows me myself indeed,
Beated and chopp'd with tann'd antiquity,
Mine own self-love quite contrary I read;
Self so self-loving were iniquity.
'Tis thee, myself, that for myself I praise,
Painting my age with beauty of thy days.

63

Against my love shall be, as I am now,
With Time's injurious hand crush'd and o'er-worn;
When hours have drain'd his blood and fill'd his brow
With lines and wrinkles; when his youthful morn
Hath travell'd on to age's steepy night,
And all those beauties whereof now he's king
Are vanishing or vanish'd out of sight,
Stealing away the treasure of his spring;
For such a time do I now fortify
Against confounding age's cruel knife,
That he shall never cut from memory
My sweet love's beauty, though my lover's life:
His beauty shall in these black lines be seen,
And they shall live, and he in them still green.

64

When I have seen by Time's fell hand defaced
The rich proud cost of outworn buried age;
When sometime lofty towers I see down-razed
And brass eternal slave to mortal rage;
When I have seen the hungry ocean gain
Advantage on the kingdom of the shore,
And the firm soil win of the watery main,
Increasing store with loss and loss with store;
When I have seen such interchange of state,
Or state itself confounded to decay;
Ruin hath taught me thus to ruminate,
That Time will come and take my love away.
This thought is as a death, which cannot choose
But weep to have that which it fears to lose.

65

Since brass, nor stone, nor earth, nor boundless sea,
But sad mortality o'er-sways their power,
How with this rage shall beauty hold a plea,
Whose action is no stronger than a flower?
O, how shall summer's honey breath hold out
Against the wreckful siege of battering days,
When rocks impregnable are not so stout,
Nor gates of steel so strong, but Time decays?
O fearful meditation! where, alack,
Shall Time's best jewel from Time's chest lie hid?
Or what strong hand can hold his swift foot back?
Or who his spoil of beauty can forbid? [22]
O, none, unless this miracle have might,
That in black ink my love may still shine bright.

66

Tired with all these, for restful death I cry,
As, to behold desert a beggar born,
And needy nothing trimm'd in jollity,
And purest faith unhappily forsworn,
And gilded honour shamefully misplaced,
And maiden virtue rudely strumpeted,
And right perfection wrongfully disgraced,
And strength by limping sway disabled,
And art made tongue-tied by authority,
And folly doctor-like controlling skill,
And simple truth miscall'd simplicity,
And captive good attending captain ill:
Tired with all these, from these would I be gone,
Save that, to die, I leave my love alone.

67

Ah! wherefore with infection should he live,
And with his presence grace impiety,
That sin by him advantage should achieve
And lace itself with his society?
Why should false painting imitate his cheek
And steal dead seeing of his living hue?
Why should poor beauty indirectly seek
Roses of shadow, since his rose is true?
Why should he live, now Nature bankrupt is,
Beggar'd of blood to blush through lively veins?
For she hath no exchequer now but his,
And, proud of many, lives upon his gains.
O, him she stores, to show what wealth she had
In days long since, before these last so bad.

68

Thus is his cheek the map of days outworn,
When beauty lived and died as flowers do now,
Before the bastard signs of fair were born,
Or durst inhabit on a living brow;
Before the golden tresses of the dead,
The right of sepulchres, were shorn away,
To live a second life on second head;
Ere beauty's dead fleece made another gay:
In him those holy antique hours are seen,
Without all ornament, itself and true,
Making no summer of another's green,
Robbing no old to dress his beauty new;
And him as for a map doth Nature store,
To show false Art what beauty was of yore.

69

Those parts of thee that the world's eye doth view
Want nothing that the thought of hearts can mend;
All tongues, the voice of souls, give thee that due, [23]
Uttering bare truth, even so as foes commend.
Thy outward thus with outward praise is crown'd;
But those same tongues that give thee so thine own
In other accents do this praise confound
By seeing farther than the eye hath shown.
They look into the beauty of thy mind,
And that, in guess, they measure by thy deeds;
Then, churls, their thoughts, although their eyes were kind,
To thy fair flower add the rank smell of weeds:
But why thy odour matcheth not thy show,
The solve is this, that thou dost common grow.

70

That thou art blamed shall not be thy defect, [24]
For slander's mark was ever yet the fair;
The ornament of beauty is suspect,
A crow that flies in heaven's sweetest air.
So thou be good, slander doth but approve
Thy worth the greater, being woo'd of time; [25]
For canker vice the sweetest buds doth love,
And thou present'st a pure unstained prime.
Thou hast pass'd by the ambush of young days,
Either not assail'd or victor being charged;
Yet this thy praise cannot be so thy praise,
To tie up envy evermore enlarged:
If some suspect of ill mask'd not thy show,
Then thou alone kingdoms of hearts shouldst owe.

71

No longer mourn for me when I am dead
Then you shall hear the surly sullen bell
Give warning to the world that I am fled
From this vile world, with vilest worms to dwell:
Nay, if you read this line, remember not
The hand that writ it; for I love you so
That I in your sweet thoughts would be forgot
If thinking on me then should make you woe.
O, if, I say, you look upon this verse
When I perhaps compounded am with clay,
Do not so much as my poor name rehearse.
But let your love even with my life decay,
Lest the wise world should look into your moan
And mock you with me after I am gone.

72

O, lest the world should task you to recite
What merit lived in me, that you should love
After my death, dear love, forget me quite,
For you in me can nothing worthy prove;
Unless you would devise some virtuous lie,
To do more for me than mine own desert,
And hang more praise upon deceased I
Than niggard truth would willingly impart:
O, lest your true love may seem false in this,
That you for love speak well of me untrue,
My name be buried where my body is,
And live no more to shame nor me nor you.
For I am shamed by that which I bring forth,
And so should you, to love things nothing worth.

73

That time of year thou mayst in me behold
When yellow leaves, or none, or few, do hang
Upon those boughs which shake against the cold,
Bare ruin'd choirs, where late the sweet birds
  sang. [26]
In me thou see'st the twilight of such day
As after sunset fadeth in the west,
Which by and by black night doth take away,
Death's second self, that seals up all in rest.
In me thou see'st the glowing of such fire
That on the ashes of his youth doth lie,
As the death-bed whereon it must expire
Consumed with that which it was nourish'd by.
  This thou perceivest, which makes thy love more strong,
  To love that well which thou must leave ere long.

74

But be contented: when that fell arrest
Without all bail shall carry me away,
My life hath in this line some interest,
Which for memorial still with thee shall stay.
When thou reviewest this, thou dost review
The very part was consecrate to thee:
The earth can have but earth, which is his due;
My spirit is thine, the better part of me:
So then thou hast but lost the dregs of life,
The prey of worms, my body being dead,
The coward conquest of a wretch's knife,
Too base of thee to be remembered.
  The worth of that is that which it contains,
  And that is this, and this with thee remains. [27]

75

So are you to my thoughts as food to life,
Or as sweet-seasoned showers are to the ground;
And for the peace of you I hold such strife
As 'twixt a miser and his wealth is found;
Now proud as an enjoyer and anon
Doubting the filching age will steal his treasure,
Now counting best to be with you alone,
Then better'd that the world may see my pleasure;
Sometime all full with feasting on your sight
And by and by clean starved for a look;
Possessing or pursuing no delight,
Save what is had or must from you be took.
  Thus do I pine and surfeit day by day,
  Or gluttoning on all, or all away.

76

Why is my verse so barren of new pride,
So far from variation or quick change?
Why with the time do I not glance aside
To new-found methods and to compounds strange?
Why write I still all one, ever the same,
And keep invention in a noted weed,
That every word doth almost tell my name, [28]
Showing their birth and where they did proceed?
O, know, sweet love, I always write of you,
And you and love are still my argument;
So all my best is dressing old words new,
Spending again what is already spent:
  For as the sun is daily new and old,
  So is my love still telling what is told.

77 [29]

Thy glass will show thee how thy beauties wear,
Thy dial how thy precious minutes waste;
The vacant leaves thy mind's imprint will bear,
And of this book this learning mayst thou taste.
The wrinkles which thy glass will truly show
Of mouthed graves will give thee memory;
Thou by thy dial's shady stealth mayst know
Time's thievish progress to eternity.
Look, what thy memory can not contain
Commit to these waste blanks, and thou shalt find
Those children nursed, deliver'd from thy brain,
To take a new acquaintance of thy mind.
  These offices, so oft as thou wilt look,
  Shall profit thee and much enrich thy book.

78

So oft I invoked thee for my Muse
And found such fair assistance in my verse
As every alien pen hath got my use
And under thee their poesy disperse.
Thine eyes that taught the dumb on high to sing
And heavy ignorance aloft to fly
Have added feathers to the learned's wing
And given grace a double majesty.
Yet be most proud of that which I compile,
Whose influence is thine and born of thee:
In others' works thou dost but mend the style,
And arts with thy sweet graces graced be;
  But thou art all my art and dost advance
  As high as learning my rude ignorance.

79

Whilst I alone did call upon thy aid,
My verse alone had all thy gentle grace,
But now my gracious numbers are decay'd
And my sick Muse doth give another place.
I grant, sweet love, thy lovely argument
Deserves the travail of a worthier pen,
Yet what of thee thy poet doth invent
He robs thee of and pays it thee again.
He lends thee virtue and he stole that word
From thy behavior; beauty doth he give
And found it in thy cheek; he can afford
No praise to thee but what in thee doth live.
  Then thank him not for that which he doth say,
  Since what he owes thee thou thyself dost pay.

80

O, how I faint when I of you do write,
Knowing a better spirit doth use your name,
And in the praise thereof spends all his might,
To make me tongue-tied, speaking of your fame!
But since your worth, wide as the ocean is,
The humble as the proudest sail doth bear,
My saucy bark inferior far to his
On your broad main doth wilfully appear.
Your shallowest help will hold me up afloat,
Whilst he upon your soundless deep doth ride;
Or, being wreck'd, I am a worthless boat,
He of tall building and of goodly pride:
  Then if he thrive and I be cast away,
  The worst was this; my love was my decay.

81

Or I shall live your epitaph to make,
Or you survive when I in earth am rotten;
From hence your memory death cannot take,
Although in me each part will be forgotten.
Your name from hence immortal life shall have,
Though I, once gone, to all the world must die:
The earth can yield me but a common grave,
When you entombed in men's eyes shall lie.
Your monument shall be my gentle verse,
Which eyes not yet created shall o'er-read,
And tongues to be your being shall rehearse
When all the breathers of this world are dead;
  You still shall live— such virtue hath my pen—
  Where breath most breathes, even in the mouths of men.

82

I grant thou wert not married to my Muse
And therefore mayst without attaint o'erlook
The dedicated words which writers use
Of their fair subject, blessing every book.
Thou art as fair in knowledge as in hue,
Finding thy worth a limit past my praise,
And therefore art enforced to seek anew
Some fresher stamp of the time-bettering days.
And do so, love; yet when they have devised
What strained touches rhetoric can lend,
Thou truly fair wert truly sympathized
In true plain words by thy true-telling friend;
  And their gross painting might be better used
  Where cheeks need blood; in thee it is abused.

83

I never saw that you did painting need
And therefore to your fair no painting set;
I found, or thought I found, you did exceed
The barren tender of a poet's debt;
And therefore have I slept in your report,
That you yourself being extant well might show
How far a modern quill doth come too short,
Speaking of worth, what worth in you doth grow.
This silence for my sin you did impute,
Which shall be most my glory, being dumb;
For I impair not beauty being mute,
When others would give life and bring a tomb.
  There lives more life in one of your fair eyes
  Than both your poets can in praise devise.

84

Who is it that says most? which can say more
Than this rich praise, that you alone are you?
In whose confine immured is the store
Which should example where your equal grew.
Lean penury within that pen doth dwell
That to his subject lends not some small glory;
But he that writes of you, if he can tell
That you are you, so dignifies his story,
Let him but copy what in you is writ,
Not making worse what nature made so clear,
And such a counterpart shall fame his wit,
Making his style admired every where.
  You to your beauteous blessings add a curse,
  Being fond on praise, which makes your praises worse.

85

My tongue-tied Muse in manners holds her still,
While comments of your praise, richly compiled,
Reserve their character with golden quill [30]
And precious phrase by all the Muses filed.
I think good thoughts whilst other write good words,
And like unletter'd clerk still cry 'Amen'
To every hymn that able spirit affords
In polish'd form of well-refined pen.
Hearing you praised, I say ''Tis so, 'tis true,'
And to the most of praise add something more;
But that is in my thought, whose love to you,
Though words come hindmost, holds his rank before.
Then others for the breath of words respect,
Me for my dumb thoughts, speaking in effect.

86

Was it the proud full sail of his great verse,
Bound for the prize of all too precious you,
That did my ripe thoughts in my brain in-hearse,
Making their tomb the womb wherein they grew?
Was it his spirit, by spirits taught to write
Above a mortal pitch, that struck me dead?
No, neither he, nor his compeers by night
Giving him aid, my verse astonished.
He, nor that affable familiar ghost
Which nightly gulls him with intelligence,
As victors of my silence cannot boast;
I was not sick of any fear from thence:
But when your countenance fill'd up his line, [31]
Then lack'd I matter; that enfeebled mine.

87

Farewell! thou art too dear for my possessing,
And like enough thou know'st thy estimate:
The charter of thy worth gives thee releasing;
My bonds in thee are all determinate.
For how do I hold thee but by thy granting?
And for that riches where is my deserving?
The cause of this fair gift in me is wanting,
And so my patent back again is swerving.
Thyself thou gavest, thy own worth then not knowing,
Or me, to whom thou gavest it, else mistaking;
So thy great gift, upon misprision growing,
Comes home again, on better judgement making.
Thus have I had thee, as a dream doth flatter,
In sleep a king, but waking no such matter.

88

When thou shalt be disposed to set me light
And place my merit in the eye of scorn,
Upon thy side against myself I'll fight
And prove thee virtuous, though thou art forsworn.
With mine own weakness being best acquainted,
Upon thy part I can set down a story
Of faults conceal'd, wherein I am attainted,
That thou in losing me shalt win much glory:
And I by this will be a gainer too;
For bending all my loving thoughts on thee,
The injuries that to myself I do,
Doing thee vantage, double-vantage me.
Such is my love, to thee I so belong,
That for thy right myself will bear all wrong.

89

Say that thou didst forsake me for some fault,
And I will comment upon that offence;
Speak of my lameness, and I straight will halt,
Against thy reasons making no defence.
Thou canst not, love, disgrace me half so ill,
To set a form upon desired change,
As I'll myself disgrace: knowing thy will,
I will acquaintance strangle and look strange,
Be absent from thy walks, and in my tongue
Thy sweet beloved name no more shall dwell,
Lest I, too much profane, should do it wrong
And haply of our old acquaintance tell.
For thee against myself I'll vow debate,
For I must ne'er love him whom thou dost hate.

90

Then hate me when thou wilt; if ever, now;
Now, while the world is bent my deeds to cross,
Join with the spite of fortune, making me bow,
And do not drop in for an after-loss:
Ah, do not, when my heart hath 'scaped this sorrow,
Come in the rearward of a conquer'd woe;
Give not a windy night a rainy morrow,
To linger out a purposed overthrow.
If thou wilt leave me, do not leave me last,
When other petty griefs have done their spite,
But in the onset come; so shall I taste

At first the very worst of fortune's might,
  And other strains of woe, which now seem woe,
  Compared with loss of thee will not seem so.

91

Some glory in their birth, some in their skill,
Some in their wealth, some in their bodies' force,
Some in their garments, though new-fangled ill,
Some in their hawks and hounds, some in their
  horse;
And every humour hath his adjunct pleasure,
Wherein it finds a joy above the rest:
But these particulars are not my measure;
All these I better in one general best.
Thy love is better than high birth to me,
Richer than wealth, prouder than garments' cost,
Of more delight than hawks or horses be;
And having thee, of all men's pride I boast:
  Wretched in this alone, that thou mayst take
  All this sway and me most wretched make.

92

But do thy worst to steal thyself away,
For term of life thou art assured mine,
And life no longer than thy love will stay,
For it depends upon that love of thine.
Then need I not to fear the worst of wrongs,
When in the least of them my life hath end.
I see a better state to me belongs
Than that which on thy humour doth depend;
Thou canst not vex me with inconstant mind,
Since that my life on thy revolt doth lie.
O, what a happy title do I find,
Happy to have thy love, happy to die!
  But what's so blessed-fair that fears no blot?
  Thou mayst be false, and yet I know it not.

93

So shall I live, supposing thou art true,
Like a deceived husband; so love's face
May still seem love to me, though alter'd new;
Thy looks with me, thy heart in other place:
For there can live no hatred in thine eye,
Therefore in that I cannot know thy change.
In many's looks the false heart's history
Is writ in moods and frowns and wrinkles strange,
But heaven in thy creation did decree
That in thy face sweet love should ever dwell;
Whate'er thy thoughts or thy heart's workings be,
Thy looks should nothing thence but sweetness tell.
  How like Eve's apple doth thy beauty grow,
  If thy sweet virtue answer not thy show!

94 [32]

They that have power to hurt and will do none,
That do not do the thing they most do show,
Who, moving others, are themselves as stone,
Unmoved, cold, and to temptation slow,
They rightly do inherit heaven's graces
And husband nature's riches from expense;
They are the lords and owners of their faces,
Others but stewards of their excellence.
The summer's flower is to the summer sweet,
Though to itself it only live and die,
But if that flower with base infection meet,
The basest weed outbraves his dignity:
  For sweetest things turn sourest by their deeds;
  Lilies that fester smell far worse than weeds.

95

How sweet and lovely dost thou make the shame
Which, like a canker in the fragrant rose,
Doth spot the beauty of thy budding name!
O, in what sweets dont thou thy sins enclose!
That tongue that tells the story of thy days,
Making lascivious comments on thy sport,
Cannot dispraise but in a kind of praise;
Naming thy name blesses an ill report.
O, what a mansion have those vices got
Which for their habitation chose out thee,
Where beauty's veil doth cover every blot,
And all things turn to fair that eyes can see! [33]
  Take heed, dear heart, of this large privilege;
  The hardest knife ill-used doth lose his edge.

96

Some say thy fault is youth, some wantonness;
Some say thy grace is youth and gentle sport;
Both grace and faults are loved of more and less;
Thou makest faults graces that to thee resort.
As on the finger of a throned queen
The basest jewel will be well esteem'd,
So are those errors that in thee are seen
To truths translated and for true things deem'd.
How many lambs might the stern wolf betray,
If like a lamb he could his looks translate!

How many gazers mightst thou lead away,
If thou wouldst use the strength of all thy state!
But do not so; I love thee in such sort
As, thou being mine, mine is thy good report.

97

How like a winter hath my absence been
From thee, the pleasure of the fleeting year!
What freezings have I felt, what dark days seen!
What old December's bareness every where!
And yet this time removed was summer's time,
The teeming autumn, big with rich increase,
Bearing the wanton burthen of the prime,
Like widow'd wombs after their lords' decease:
Yet this abundant issue seem'd to me
But hope of orphans and unfather'd fruit;
For summer and his pleasures wait on thee,
And, thou away, the very birds are mute;
Or, if they sing, 'tis with so dull a cheer
That leaves look pale, dreading the winter's near.

98

From you have I been absent in the spring,
When proud-pied April dress'd in all his trim
Hath put a spirit of youth in every thing,
That heavy Saturn laugh'd and leap'd with him.
Yet nor the lays of birds nor the sweet smell
Of different flowers in odour and in hue
Could make me any summer's story tell,
Or from their proud lap pluck them where they grew;
Nor did I wonder at the lily's white,
Nor praise the deep vermilion in the rose;
They were but sweet, but figures of delight,
Drawn after you, you pattern of all those.
Yet seem'd it winter still, and, you away,
As with your shadow I with these did play:

99 [34]

The forward violet thus did I chide:
Sweet thief, whence didst thou steal thy sweet that smells,
If not from my love's breath? The purple pride
Which on thy soft cheek for complexion dwells
In my love's veins thou hast too grossly dyed.
The lily I condemned for thy hand,
And buds of marjoram had stol'n thy hair:
The roses fearfully on thorns did stand,
One blushing shame, another white despair;
A third, nor red nor white, had stol'n of both
And to his robbery had annex'd thy breath;
But, for his theft, in pride of all his growth
A vengeful canker eat him up to death.
More flowers I noted, yet I none could see
But sweet or colour it had stol'n from thee. [35]

100

Where art thou, Muse, that thou forget'st so long
To speak of that which gives thee all thy might?
Spend'st thou thy fury on some worthless song,
Darkening thy power to lend base subjects light?
Return, forgetful Muse, and straight redeem
In gentle numbers time so idly spent;
Sing to the ear that doth thy lays esteem
And gives thy pen both skill and argument.
Rise, resty Muse, my love's sweet face survey,
If Time have any wrinkle graven there;
If any, be a satire to decay,
And make Time's spoils despised every where.
Give my love fame faster than Time wastes life;
So thou prevent'st his scythe and crooked knife.

101

O truant Muse, what shall be thy amends
For thy neglect of truth in beauty dyed?
Both truth and beauty on my love depends;
So dost thou too, and therein dignified.
Make answer, Muse: wilt thou not haply say
'Truth needs no colour, with his colour fix'd;
Beauty no pencil, beauty's truth to lay;
But best is best, if never intermix'd?'
Because he needs no praise, wilt thou be dumb?
Excuse not silence so; for't lies in thee
To make him much outlive a gilded tomb,
And to be praised of ages yet to be.
Then do thy office, Muse; I teach thee how
To make him seem long hence as he shows now.

102

My love is strengthen'd, though more weak in seeming;
I love not less, though less the show appear:
That love is merchandized whose rich esteeming
The owner's tongue doth publish every where.
Our love was new and then but in the spring
When I was wont to greet it with my lays,
As Philomel in summer's front doth sing
And stops her pipe in growth of riper days: [36]

Not that the summer is less pleasant now
Than when her mournful hymns did hush the night,
But that wild music burthens every bough
And sweets grown common lose their dear delight.
  Therefore like her I sometime hold my tongue,
  Because I would not dull you with my song.

103

Alack, what poverty my Muse brings forth,
That having such a scope to show her pride,
The argument all bare is of more worth
Than when it hath my added praise beside!
O, blame me not, if I no more can write!
Look in your glass, and there appears a face
That over-goes my blunt invention quite,
Dulling my lines and doing me disgrace.
Were it not sinful then, striving to mend,
To mar the subject that before was well?
For to no other pass my verses tend
Than of your graces and your gifts to tell;
  And more, much more, than in my verse can sit
  Your own glass shows you when you look in it.

104

To me, fair friend, you never can be old,
For as you were when first your eye I eyed,
Such seems your beauty still. Three winters cold
Have from the forests shook three summers' pride,
Three beauteous springs to yellow autumn turn'd
In process of the seasons have I seen,
Three April perfumes in three hot Junes burn'd,
Since first I saw you fresh, which yet are green.
Ah! yet doth beauty, like a dial-hand,
Steal from his figure and no pace perceived;
So your sweet hue, which methinks still doth stand,
Hath motion and mine eye may be deceived:
  For fear of which, hear this, thou age unbred;
  Ere you were born was beauty's summer dead.

105

Let not my love be call'd idolatry,
Nor my beloved as an idol show,
Since all alike my songs and praises be
To one, of one, still such, and ever so.
Kind is my love to-day, to-morrow kind,
Still constant in a wondrous excellence;
Therefore my verse to constancy confined,
One thing expressing, leaves out difference.
'Fair, kind, and true' is all my argument,
'Fair, kind, and true' varying to other words;
And in this change is my invention spent,
Three themes in one, which wondrous scope affords.
  'Fair, kind, and true,' have often lived alone,
  Which three till now never kept seat in one.

106

When in the chronicle of wasted time
I see descriptions of the fairest wights,
And beauty making beautiful old rhyme
In praise of ladies dead and lovely knights,
Then, in the blazon of sweet beauty's best,
Of hand, of foot, of lip, of eye, of brow,
I see their antique pen would have express'd
Even such a beauty as you master now.
So all their praises are but prophecies
Of this our time, all you prefiguring;
And, for they look'd but with divining eyes,
They had not skill enough your worth to sing: [37]
  For we, which now behold these present days,
  Have eyes to wonder, but lack tongues to praise.

107 [38]

Not mine own fears, nor the prophetic soul
Of the wide world dreaming on things to come,
Can yet the lease of my true love control,
Supposed as forfeit to a confined doom.
The mortal moon hath her eclipse endured
And the sad augurs mock their own presage;
Incertainties now crown themselves assured
And peace proclaims olives of endless age.
Now with the drops of this most balmy time
My love looks fresh, and Death to me subscribes,
Since, spite of him, I'll live in this poor rhyme,
While he insults o'er dull and speechless tribes:
  And thou in this shalt find thy monument,
  When tyrants' crests and tombs of brass are spent.

108

What's in the brain that ink may character
Which hath not figured to thee my true spirit?
What's new to speak, what new to register, [39]
That may express my love or thy dear merit?
Nothing, sweet boy; but yet, like prayers divine,
I must each day say o'er the very same,
Counting no old thing old, thou mine, I thine,
Even as when first I hallow'd thy fair name.
So that eternal love in love's fresh case
Weighs not the dust and injury of age,

Nor gives to necessary wrinkles place,
But makes antiquity for aye his page,
  Finding the first conceit of love there bred
  Where time and outward form would show it dead.

109

O, never say that I was false of heart,
Though absence seem'd my flame to qualify.
As easy might I from myself depart
As from my soul, which in thy breast doth lie:
That is my home of love: if I have ranged,
Like him that travels I return again,
Just to the time, not with the time exchanged,
So that myself bring water for my stain.
Never believe, though in my nature reign'd
All frailties that besiege all kinds of blood,
That it could so preposterously be stain'd,
To leave for nothing all thy sum of good;
  For nothing this wide universe I call,
  Save thou, my rose; in it thou art my all.

110

Alas, 'tis true I have gone here and there
And made myself a motley to the view,
Gored mine own thoughts, sold cheap what is most dear,
Made old offences of affections new;
Most true it is that I have look'd on truth
Askance and strangely: but, by all above,
These blenches gave my heart another youth,
And worse essays proved thee my best of love.
Now all is done, have what shall have no end:
Mine appetite I never more will grind
On newer proof, to try an older friend,
A god in love, to whom I am confined.
  Then give me welcome, next my heaven the best,
  Even to thy pure and most most loving breast.

111

O, for my sake do you with Fortune chide,
The guilty goddess of my harmful deeds,
That did not better for my life provide
Than public means which public manners breeds.
Thence comes it that my name receives a brand,
And almost thence my nature is subdued
To what it works in, like the dyer's hand:
Pity me then and wish I were renew'd;
Whilst, like a willing patient, I will drink
Potions of eisel 'gainst my strong infection;
No bitterness that I will bitter think,
Nor double penance, to correct correction.
  Pity me then, dear friend, and I assure ye
  Even that your pity is enough to cure me.

112

Your love and pity doth the impression fill
Which vulgar scandal stamp'd upon my brow;
For what care I who calls me well or ill,
So you o'er-green my bad, my good allow?
You are my all the world, and I must strive
To know my shames and praises from your tongue;
None else to me, nor I to none alive,
That my steel'd sense or changes right or wrong. [40]
In so profound abysm I throw all care
Of others' voices, that my adder's sense
To critic and to flatterer stopped are.
Mark how with my neglect I do dispense:
  You are so strongly in my purpose bred
  That all the world besides methinks are dead. [41]

113

Since I left you, mine eye is in my mind;
And that which governs me to go about
Doth part his function and is partly blind,
Seems seeing, but effectually is out;
For it no form delivers to the heart
Of bird, of flower, or shape, which it doth latch: [42]
Of his quick objects hath the mind no part,
Nor his own vision holds what it doth catch;
For if it see the rudest or gentlest sight,
The most sweet favour or deformed'st creature,
The mountain or the sea, the day or night,
The crow or dove, it shapes them to your feature:
  Incapable of more, replete with you,
  My most true mind thus makes mine eye untrue. [43]

114

Or whether doth my mind, being crown'd with you,
Drink up the monarch's plague, this flattery?
Or whether shall I say, mine eye saith true,
And that your love taught it this alchemy,
To make of monsters and things indigest
Such cherubins as your sweet self resemble,
Creating every bad a perfect best,
As fast as objects to his beams assemble?
O,'tis the first; 'tis flattery in my seeing,
And my great mind most kingly drinks it up:
Mine eye well knows what with his gust is 'greeing,

And to his palate doth prepare the cup:
If it be poison'd, 'tis the lesser sin
That mine eye loves it and doth first begin.

115

Those lines that I before have writ do lie,
Even those that said I could not love you dearer:
Yet then my judgement knew no reason why
My most full flame should afterwards burn clearer.
But reckoning time, whose million'd accidents
Creep in 'twixt vows and change decrees of kings,
Tan sacred beauty, blunt the sharp'st intents,
Divert strong minds to the course of altering things;
Alas, why, fearing of time's tyranny,
Might I not then say 'Now I love you best,'
When I was certain o'er incertainty,
Crowning the present, doubting of the rest?
Love is a babe; then might I not say so,
To give full growth to that which still doth grow?

116

Let me not to the marriage of true minds
Admit impediments. Love is not love
Which alters when it alteration finds,
Or bends with the remover to remove:
O, no! it is an ever-fixed mark
That looks on tempests and is never shaken;
It is the star to every wandering bark,
Whose worth's unknown, although his height be taken.
Love's not Time's fool, though rosy lips and cheeks
Within his bending sickle's compass come;
Love alters not with his brief hours and weeks,
But bears it out even to the edge of doom.
If this be error and upon me proved,
I never writ, nor no man ever loved.

117

Accuse me thus: that I have scanted all
Wherein I should your great deserts repay,
Forgot upon your dearest love to call,
Whereto all bonds do tie me day by day;
That I have frequent been with unknown minds
And given to time your own dear-purchased right;
That I have hoisted sail to all the winds
Which should transport me farthest from your sight.
Book both my wilfulness and errors down
And on just proof surmise accumulate;
Bring me within the level of your frown,
But shoot not at me in your waken'd hate;
Since my appeal says I did strive to prove
The constancy and virtue of your love.

118

Like as, to make our appetites more keen,
With eager compounds we our palate urge,
As, to prevent our maladies unseen,
We sicken to shun sickness when we purge,
Even so, being full of your ne'er-cloying sweetness,
To bitter sauces did I frame my feeding
And, sick of welfare, found a kind of meetness
To be diseased ere that there was true needing.
Thus policy in love, to anticipate
The ills that were not, grew to faults assured
And brought to medicine a healthful state
Which, rank of goodness, would by ill be cured:
But thence I learn, and find the lesson true,
Drugs poison him that so fell sick of you.

119

What potions have I drunk of Siren tears,
Distill'd from limbecks foul as hell within,
Applying fears to hopes and hopes to fears,
Still losing when I saw myself to win!
What wretched errors hath my heart committed,
Whilst it hath thought itself so blessed never!
How have mine eyes out of their spheres been fitted
In the distraction of this madding fever!
O benefit of ill! now I find true
That better is by evil still made better;
And ruin'd love, when it is built anew,
Grows fairer than at first, more strong, far greater.
So I return rebuked to my content
And gain by ill thrice more than I have spent. [44]

120

That you were once unkind befriends me now,
And for that sorrow which I then did feel
Needs must I under my transgression bow,
Unless my nerves were brass or hammer'd steel.
For if you were by my unkindness shaken
As I by yours, you've pass'd a hell of time, [45]
And I, a tyrant, have no leisure taken
To weigh how once I suffer'd in your crime.
O, that our night of woe might have remember'd
My deepest sense, how hard true sorrow hits,
And soon to you, as you to me, then tender'd
The humble slave which wounded bosoms fits!

But that your trespass now becomes a fee;
Mine ransoms yours, and yours must ransom me.

121

'Tis better to be vile than vile esteem'd,
When not to be receives reproach of being,
And the just pleasure lost which is so deem'd
Not by our feeling but by others' seeing:
For why should others' false adulterate eyes
Give salutation to my sportive blood?
Or on my frailties why are frailer spies,
Which in their wills count bad what I think good?
No, I am that I am, and they that level
At my abuses reckon up their own:
I may be straight, though they themselves be bevel;
By their rank thoughts my deeds must not be shown;
Unless this general evil they maintain,
All men are bad, and in their badness reign.

122

Thy gift, thy tables, are within my brain
Full character'd with lasting memory,
Which shall above that idle rank remain
Beyond all date, even to eternity;
Or at the least, so long as brain and heart
Have faculty by nature to subsist;
Till each to razed oblivion yield his part
Of thee, thy record never can be miss'd.
That poor retention could not so much hold,
Nor need I tallies thy dear love to score;
Therefore to give them from me was I bold,
To trust those tables that receive thee more:
To keep an adjunct to remember thee
Were to import forgetfulness in me.

123

No, Time, thou shalt not boast that I do change:
Thy pyramids built up with newer might
To me are nothing novel, nothing strange;
They are but dressings of a former sight.
Our dates are brief, and therefore we admire
What thou dost foist upon us that is old,
And rather make them born to our desire [46]
Than think that we before have heard them told.
Thy registers and thee I both defy,
Not wondering at the present nor the past,
For thy records and what we see doth lie,
Made more or less by thy continual haste.
This I do vow and this shall ever be;
I will be true, despite thy scythe and thee.

124

If my dear love were but the child of state,
It might for Fortune's bastard be unfather'd',
As subject to Time's love or to Time's hate,
Weeds among weeds, or flowers with flowers gather'd.
No, it was builded far from accident;
It suffers not in smiling pomp, nor falls
Under the blow of thralled discontent,
Whereto the inviting time our fashion calls:
It fears not policy, that heretic,
Which works on leases of short-number'd hours,
But all alone stands hugely politic,
That it nor grows with heat nor drowns with showers.
To this I witness call the fools of time, [47]
Which die for goodness, who have lived for crime.

125

Were 't aught to me I bore the canopy,
With my extern the outward honouring,
Or laid great bases for eternity,
Which prove more short than waste or ruining?
Have I not seen dwellers on form and favour
Lose all, and more, by paying too much rent,
For compound sweet forgoing simple savour,
Pitiful thrivers, in their gazing spent?
No, let me be obsequious in thy heart,
And take thou my oblation, poor but free,
Which is not mix'd with seconds, knows no art,
But mutual render, only me for thee.
Hence, thou suborn'd informer; a true soul
When most impeach'd stands least in thy control.

126 [48]

O thou, my lovely boy, who in thy power
Dost hold Time's fickle glass, his sickle, hour; [49]
Who hast by waning grown, and therein show'st
Thy lovers withering as thy sweet self grow'st;
If Nature, sovereign mistress over wrack,
As thou goest onwards, still will pluck thee back,
She keeps thee to this purpose, that her skill
May time disgrace and wretched minutes kill.
Yet fear her, O thou minion of her pleasure!
She may detain, but not still keep, her treasure:

Her audit, though delay'd, answer'd must be,
And her quietus is to render thee.

127

In the old age black was not counted fair,
Or if it were, it bore not beauty's name;
But now is black beauty's successive heir,
And beauty slander'd with a bastard shame:
For since each hand hath put on nature's power,
Fairing the foul with art's false borrow'd face,
Sweet beauty hath no name, no holy bower,
But is profaned, if not lives in disgrace.
Therefore my mistress' brows are raven black,
Her eyes so suited, and they mourners seem [50]
At such who, not born fair, no beauty lack,
Slandering creation with a false esteem:
Yet so they mourn, becoming of their woe,
That every tongue says beauty should look so.

128

How oft, when thou, my music, music play'st,
Upon that blessed wood whose motion sounds
With thy sweet fingers, when thou gently sway'st
The wiry concord that mine ear confounds,
Do I envy those jacks that nimble leap
To kiss the tender inward of thy hand,
Whilst my poor lips, which should that harvest reap,
At the wood's boldness by thee blushing stand!
To be so tickled, they would change their state
And situation with those dancing chips,
O'er whom thy fingers walk with gentle gait,
Making dead wood more blest than living lips.
Since saucy jacks so happy are in this,
Give them thy fingers, me thy lips to kiss.

129

The expense of spirit in a waste of shame
Is lust in action; and till action, lust
Is perjured, murderous, bloody, full of blame,
Savage, extreme, rude, cruel, not to trust,
Enjoy'd no sooner but despised straight,
Past reason hunted, and no sooner had
Past reason hated, as a swallow'd bait
On purpose laid to make the taker mad;
Mad in pursuit and in possession so;
Had, having, and in quest to have, extreme;
A bliss in proof, and proved, a very woe; [51]
Before, a joy proposed; behind, a dream.
All this the world well knows; yet none knows well
To shun the heaven that leads men to this hell.

130

My mistress' eyes are nothing like the sun;
Coral is far more red than her lips' red;
If snow be white, why then her breasts are dun;
If hairs be wires, black wires grow on her head.
I have seen roses damask'd, red and white,
But no such roses see I in her cheeks;
And in some perfumes is there more delight
Than in the breath that from my mistress reeks.
I love to hear her speak, yet well I know
That music hath a far more pleasing sound;
I grant I never saw a goddess go;
My mistress, when she walks, treads on the ground:
And yet, by heaven, I think my love as rare
As any she belied with false compare.

131

Thou art as tyrannous, so as thou art,
As those whose beauties proudly make them cruel;
For well thou know'st to my dear doting heart
Thou art the fairest and most precious jewel.
Yet, in good faith, some say that thee behold
Thy face hath not the power to make love groan:
To say they err I dare not be so bold,
Although I swear it to myself alone.
And, to be sure that is not false I swear,
A thousand groans, but thinking on thy face,
One on another's neck, do witness bear
Thy black is fairest in my judgement's place.
In nothing art thou black save in thy deeds,
And thence this slander, as I think, proceeds.

132

Thine eyes I love, and they, as pitying me,
Knowing thy heart torments me with disdain,
Have put on black and loving mourners be,
Looking with pretty ruth upon my pain.
And truly not the morning sun of heaven
Better becomes the grey cheeks of the east,
Nor that full star that ushers in the even
Doth half that glory to the sober west,
As those two mourning eyes become thy face:
O, let it then as well beseem thy heart
To mourn for me, since mourning doth thee grace,
And suit thy pity like in every part.

Then will I swear beauty herself is black
And all they foul that thy complexion lack.

133

Beshrew that heart that makes my heart to groan
For that deep wound it gives my friend and me!
Is't not enough to torture me alone,
But slave to slavery my sweet'st friend must be?
Me from myself thy cruel eye hath taken,
And my next self thou harder hast engross'd:
Of him, myself, and thee, I am forsaken;
A torment thrice threefold thus to be cross'd.
Prison my heart in thy steel bosom's ward,
But then my friend's heart let my poor heart bail;
Whoe'er keeps me, let my heart be his guard;
Thou canst not then use rigour in my gaol:
And yet thou wilt; for I, being pent in thee,
Perforce am thine, and all that is in me.

134

So, now I have confess'd that he is thine,
And I myself am mortgaged to thy will,
Myself I'll forfeit, so that other mine
Thou wilt restore, to be my comfort still:
But thou wilt not, nor he will not be free,
For thou art covetous and he is kind;
He learn'd but surety-like to write for me
Under that bond that him as fast doth bind.
The statute of thy beauty thou wilt take,
Thou usurer, that put'st forth all to use,
And sue a friend came debtor for my sake;
So him I lose through my unkind abuse.
Him have I lost; thou hast both him and me:
He pays the whole, and yet am I not free.

135

Whoever hath her wish, thou hast thy 'Will,'
And 'Will' to boot, and 'Will' in overplus;
More than enough am I that vex thee still,
To thy sweet will making addition thus.
Wilt thou, whose will is large and spacious,
Not once vouchsafe to hide my will in thine?
Shall will in others seem right gracious,
And in my will no fair acceptance shine?
The sea, all water, yet receives rain still
And in abundance addeth to his store;
So thou, being rich in 'Will,' add to thy 'Will'
One will of mine, to make thy large 'Will' more.
Let no unkind, no fair beseechers kill; [52]
Think all but one, and me in that one 'Will.'

136

If thy soul cheque thee that I come so near,
Swear to thy blind soul that I was thy 'Will,'
And will, thy soul knows, is admitted there;
Thus far for love my love-suit, sweet, fulfil.
'Will' will fulfil the treasure of thy love,
Ay, fill it full with wills, and my will one.
In things of great receipt with ease we prove
Among a number one is reckon'd none:
Then in the number let me pass untold,
Though in thy stores' account I one must be;
For nothing hold me, so it please thee hold
That nothing me, a something sweet to thee:
Make but my name thy love, and love that still,
And then thou lovest me, for my name is 'Will.'

137 [53]

Thou blind fool, Love, what dost thou to mine eyes,
That they behold, and see not what they see?
They know what beauty is, see where it lies,
Yet what the best is take the worst to be.
If eyes corrupt by over-partial looks
Be anchor'd in the bay where all men ride,
Why of eyes' falsehood hast thou forged hooks,
Whereto the judgement of my heart is tied?
Why should my heart think that a several plot
Which my heart knows the wide world's common place?
Or mine eyes seeing this, say this is not,
To put fair truth upon so foul a face?
In things right true my heart and eyes have err'd,
And to this false plague are they now transferr'd.

138

When my love swears that she is made of truth
I do believe her, though I know she lies,
That she might think me some untutor'd youth,
Unlearned in the world's false subtleties.
Thus vainly thinking that she thinks me young,
Although she knows my days are past the best,
Simply I credit her false-speaking tongue:
On both sides thus is simple truth suppress'd.
But wherefore says she not she is unjust?
And wherefore say not I that I am old?
O, love's best habit is in seeming trust,

And age in love loves not to have years told:
  Therefore I lie with her and she with me,
  And in our faults by lies we flatter'd be.

139

O, call not me to justify the wrong
That thy unkindness lays upon my heart;
Wound me not with thine eye but with thy tongue;
Use power with power and slay me not by art.
Tell me thou lovest elsewhere, but in my sight,
Dear heart, forbear to glance thine eye aside:
What need'st thou wound with cunning when thy might
Is more than my o'er-press'd defence can bide?
Let me excuse thee: ah! my love well knows
Her pretty looks have been mine enemies,
And therefore from my face she turns my foes,
That they elsewhere might dart their injuries:
  Yet do not so; but since I am near slain,
  Kill me outright with looks and rid my pain.

140

Be wise as thou art cruel; do not press
My tongue-tied patience with too much disdain;
Lest sorrow lend me words and words express
The manner of my pity-wanting pain.
If I might teach thee wit, better it were,
Though not to love, yet, love, to tell me so;
As testy sick men, when their deaths be near,
No news but health from their physicians know;
For if I should despair, I should grow mad,
And in my madness might speak ill of thee:
Now this ill-wresting world is grown so bad,
Mad slanderers by mad ears believed be.
  That I may not be so, nor thou belied,
  Bear thine eyes straight, though thy proud heart go wide.

141

In faith, I do not love thee with mine eyes,
For they in thee a thousand errors note;
But 'tis my heart that loves what they despise,
Who in despite of view is pleased to dote;
Nor are mine ears with thy tongue's tune delighted,
Nor tender feeling, to base touches prone,
Nor taste, nor smell, desire to be invited
To any sensual feast with thee alone:
But my five wits nor my five senses can
Dissuade one foolish heart from serving thee,
Who leaves unsway'd the likeness of a man,
Thy proud hearts slave and vassal wretch to be:
  Only my plague thus far I count my gain,
  That she that makes me sin awards me pain.

142

Love is my sin and thy dear virtue hate,
Hate of my sin, grounded on sinful loving:
O, but with mine compare thou thine own state,
And thou shalt find it merits not reproving;
Or, if it do, not from those lips of thine,
That have profaned their scarlet ornaments [54]
And seal'd false bonds of love as oft as mine,
Robb'd others' beds' revenues of their rents.
Be it lawful I love thee, as thou lovest those
Whom thine eyes woo as mine importune thee:
Root pity in thy heart, that when it grows
Thy pity may deserve to pitied be.
  If thou dost seek to have what thou dost hide,
  By self-example mayst thou be denied!

143

Lo! as a careful housewife runs to catch [55]
One of her feather'd creatures broke away,
Sets down her babe and makes all swift dispatch
In pursuit of the thing she would have stay,
Whilst her neglected child holds her in chase,
Cries to catch her whose busy care is bent
To follow that which flies before her face,
Not prizing her poor infant's discontent;
So runn'st thou after that which flies from thee,
Whilst I thy babe chase thee afar behind;
But if thou catch thy hope, turn back to me,
And play the mother's part, kiss me, be kind:
  So will I pray that thou mayst have thy 'Will,' [56]
  If thou turn back, and my loud crying still.

144 [57]

Two loves I have of comfort and despair,
Which like two spirits do suggest me still:
The better angel is a man right fair,
The worser spirit a woman colour'd ill.
To win me soon to hell, my female evil
Tempteth my better angel from my side, [58]
And would corrupt my saint to be a devil,
Wooing his purity with her foul pride.
And whether that my angel be turn'd fiend [59]

Suspect I may yet, but not directly tell;
But being both from me, both to each friend,
I guess one angel in another's hell:
 Yet this shall I ne'er know, but live in doubt,
 Till my bad angel fire my good one out.

145 [60]

Those lips that Love's own hand did make
Breathed forth the sound that said 'I hate'
To me that languish'd for her sake;
But when she saw my woeful state,
Straight in her heart did mercy come,
Chiding that tongue that ever sweet
Was used in giving gentle doom,
And taught it thus anew to greet;
'I hate' she alter'd with an end,
That follow'd it as gentle day
Doth follow night, who like a fiend
From heaven to hell is flown away;
 'I hate' from hate away she threw,
 And saved my life, saying 'not you.'

146

Poor soul, the centre of my sinful earth, [61]
These rebel powers that thee array,
Why dost thou pine within and suffer dearth,
Painting thy outward walls so costly gay?
Why so large cost, having so short a lease,
Dost thou upon thy fading mansion spend?
Shall worms, inheritors of this excess,
Eat up thy charge? is this thy body's end?
Then, soul, live thou upon thy servant's loss,
And let that pine to aggravate thy store;
Buy terms divine in selling hours of dross;
Within be fed, without be rich no more:
 So shalt thou feed on Death, that feeds on men,
 And Death once dead, there's no more dying then.

147

My love is as a fever, longing still
For that which longer nurseth the disease,
Feeding on that which doth preserve the ill,
The uncertain sickly appetite to please.
My reason, the physician to my love,
Angry that his prescriptions are not kept,
Hath left me, and I desperate now approve
Desire is death, which physic did except.
Past cure I am, now reason is past care,
And frantic-mad with evermore unrest;
My thoughts and my discourse as madmen's are,
At random from the truth vainly express'd;
 For I have sworn thee fair and thought thee bright,
 Who art as black as hell, as dark as night.

148

O me, what eyes hath Love put in my head,
Which have no correspondence with true sight!
Or, if they have, where is my judgement fled,
That censures falsely what they see aright?
If that be fair whereon my false eyes dote,
What means the world to say it is not so?
If it be not, then love doth well denote
Love's eye is not so true as all men's 'No.'
How can it? O, how can Love's eye be true,
That is so vex'd with watching and with tears?
No marvel then, though I mistake my view;
The sun itself sees not till heaven clears.
 O cunning Love! with tears thou keep'st me blind,
 Lest eyes well-seeing thy foul faults should find.

149

Canst thou, O cruel! say I love thee not,
When I against myself with thee partake?
Do I not think on thee, when I forgot
Am of myself, all tyrant, for thy sake?
Who hateth thee that I do call my friend?
On whom frown'st thou that I do fawn upon?
Nay, if thou lour'st on me, do I not spend
Revenge upon myself with present moan?
What merit do I in myself respect,
That is so proud thy service to despise,
When all my best doth worship thy defect,
Commanded by the motion of thine eyes?
 But, love, hate on, for now I know thy mind;
 Those that can see thou lovest, and I am blind.

150

O, from what power hast thou this powerful might
With insufficiency my heart to sway?
To make me give the lie to my true sight,
And swear that brightness doth not grace the day?
Whence hast thou this becoming of things ill,
That in the very refuse of thy deeds
There is such strength and warrantise of skill
That, in my mind, thy worst all best exceeds?
Who taught thee how to make me love thee more
The more I hear and see just cause of hate?
O, though I love what others do abhor,

With others thou shouldst not abhor my state:
  If thy unworthiness raised love in me,
  More worthy I to be beloved of thee.

151

Love is too young to know what conscience is;
Yet who knows not conscience is born of love?
Then, gentle cheater, urge not my amiss,
Lest guilty of my faults thy sweet self prove:
For, thou betraying me, I do betray
My nobler part to my gross body's treason;
My soul doth tell my body that he may
Triumph in love; flesh stays no farther reason;
But, rising at thy name, doth point out thee
As his triumphant prize. Proud of this pride,
He is contented thy poor drudge to be,
To stand in thy affairs, fall by thy side.
  No want of conscience hold it that I call
  Her 'love' for whose dear love I rise and fall.

152

In loving thee thou know'st I am forsworn,
But thou art twice forsworn, to me love swearing,
In act thy bed-vow broke and new faith torn
In vowing new hate after new love bearing.
But why of two oaths' breach do I accuse thee,
When I break twenty? I am perjured most;
For all my vows are oaths but to misuse thee
And all my honest faith in thee is lost,
For I have sworn deep oaths of thy deep kindness,
Oaths of thy love, thy truth, thy constancy,
And, to enlighten thee, gave eyes to blindness,
Or made them swear against the thing they see;
  For I have sworn thee fair; more perjured I, [62]
  To swear against the truth so foul a lie!

153

Cupid laid by his brand, and fell asleep:
A maid of Dian's this advantage found,
And his love-kindling fire did quickly steep
In a cold valley-fountain of that ground;
Which borrow'd from this holy fire of Love
A dateless lively heat, still to endure,
And grew a seething bath, which yet men prove
Against strange maladies a sovereign cure.
But at my mistress' eye Love's brand new-fired,
The boy for trial needs would touch my breast;
I, sick withal, the help of bath desired,
And thither hied, a sad distemper'd guest,
  But found no cure: the bath for my help lies
  Where Cupid got new fire—my mistress' eyes.

154

The little Love-god lying once asleep
Laid by his side his heart-inflaming brand,
Whilst many nymphs that vow'd chaste life to keep
Came tripping by; but in her maiden hand
The fairest votary took up that fire
Which many legions of true hearts had warm'd;
And so the general of hot desire
Was sleeping by a virgin hand disarm'd.
This brand she quenched in a cool well by,
Which from Love's fire took heat perpetual,
Growing a bath and healthful remedy
For men diseased; but I, my mistress' thrall,
  Came there for cure, and this by that I prove,
  Love's fire heats water, water cools not love.

Notes

1. And … all; – so Malone. Quarto, *'And … or.'*
2. This, … pen; – Quarto. *'this (Time's pensel or my pupill pen).'* Massey conjectured *'this time's pencil, or my pupil pen';* this reading is accepted by several editors, who interpret the first clause to refer either to some particular artist, or to any painter of the time.
3. Fleet'st; – so Quarto; Dyce, *'fleets'* (rhyming with *'sweets'*); *cp.* VIII. 7.
4. Hue, all "hues"; – Quarto, *'hew all Hews'* (*Hews* in italics).
5. Couplement; – Quarto, *'coopelment.'*
6. Fight … quite; – Malone (Theobald conjectured); Quarto, *'worth … quite.'* Theobald conjectured *'worth … forth';* Capell MS., *'might … quite.'*
7. Thy; – Quarto, *'their';* a common mistake in the Sonnets, evidently due to the *'y'* being taken for *'e'* with the mark of contraction for *'ir.'*
8. Longer … strength seem stronger; – Capell MS. and Collier conjecture; Quarto, *'longer … length seeme stronger.'*
9. Thee; – Quarto, *'there.'*
10. Loss … cross; – Quarto, *'losse … losse.'*
11. Sheds; – Quarto, *'sheeds'* (rhyming with *'deeds'*).
12. Doth; – Quarto, *'dost.'*
13. Thyself; – Quarto, *'this selfe.'*
14. She have; – Tyrwhitt conjectured; Quarto, *'he haue';* Ewing, *'he has.'*
15. Not, – so ed. 1640; Quarto, *'nor.'*
16. Desert; – Quarto, *'desart'* (rhyming with *'part'*).
17. Neigh—no dull flesh— – (Malone); Quarto, *'naigh noe dull flesh';* probably the reading of the Quarto is correct. *'neigh'* = 'neigh after,' 'neigh to,' *cp.* "They were fed horses in the morning; everyone neighed after his neighbour's wife," Jeremiah v. 8.
18. Monuments; – Quarto, *'monument.'*

19. Or; – Tyrwhitt conjecture and Capell MS.; Quarto, *'As';* Anonymous conjecture, *'Ah!'; 'Else.'*
20. Will; – Quarto, *'Will';* Massey conjectured *"'Will.'"*
21. And for myself, i.e. – 'and for my own satisfaction,' or perhaps the words merely emphasize the statement.
22. Of; – Malone; Quarto, *'or';* Capell MS., *'o'er';* Gildon, *'on.'*
23. That due; – Capell MS. and Tyrwhitt conjecture; Quarto *'that end';* Sewell (ed. 2), *'thy due.'*
24. Art, – ed. 1640; Quarto, *'are.'*
25. Thy; – Capell MS.; Quarto, *'their.'*
26. Bare ruin'd choirs; – Quarto, *'Bare rn'wd quiers;'*
27. That is this, i.e. – my spirit is my poetry.
28. Tell. – Capell MS., Quarto, *'fel';* Lintott, *'fell';* Nicholson conjectured *'spell.'*
29. "Probably this sonnet was designed to accompany a present of a book consisting of blank paper" (Steevens).
30. Reserve their; – Tyler (Anon. conj. MS.), *'Rehearse thy,'* a more plausible reading than *'preserve their,' 'deserve their,'* &c., and other suggestions which have been advanced; there is probably some error in the text as printed.
31. Fill'd; – Quarto, *'fild';* Malone, *'fil'd.'*
32. Cp. – Edward III. ii. 1 (printed in 1596):—

"Poison shows worst in a golden cup;
Dark night seems darker by the lightning flash;
Lilies that fester seem far worse than weeds;
And every glory, that inclines to sin,
The same is treble by the opposite."

33. Turn; – Quarto, *'turnes.'*
34. A fifteen-lined sonnet; the first line serves as a sort of introduction, standing outside the sonnet.
35. Sweet; – S. Walker conjectured, *'scent.'*
36. Her, – Houseman; Quarto, *'his.'*
37. Skill; – Tyrwhitt conjecture and Capell MS.; Quarto, *'still.'*
38. It has been suggested that this is a possible allusion to the peace completed in 1609, which ended the war between Spain and the United Provinces; but this is merely a random suggestion.
39. New … new, – Malone; Quarto, *'new … now';* S. Walker conjectured *'now … now.'*
40. Or changes; – Malone conjectured *'e'er changes';* Knight conjectured *'so changes.'*
41. Besides methinks are, – Capell MS. and Steevens conjecture; Quarto, *'besides me thinkes y' are';* Dyce, *'besides methinks they're.'*
42. Latch; – Quarto, *'lack.'*
43. Maketh mine untrue; – so Quarto; Capell MS., and Malone conjecture *'makes mine eye untrue';* Collier conjectured *'maketh my eyne untrue';* Malone conjectured *'thy most true mind maketh mine untrue.'*
44. Ill, – Malone; Quarto, *'ills.'*
45. You've; – Quarto, *'y'haue.'*
46. Them, i.e. 'what thou dost foist upon us.' –
47. The fools of time, – &c. Tyler sees in these lines a reference to the popular repute of Essex as the "good earl," notwithstanding the "crimes" for which he and certainly his companions were executed; the allusion is probably more general, and perhaps, as Palgrave observes, to "the plotters and political martyrs of the time."
48. This short poem is of six rhymed couplets; it was evidently not intended to pass as an ordinary sonnet, though after the last line an omission of two lines is marked in the Quarto by two pairs of parentheses. It is the *envoy,* the conclusion of one series of sonnets.
49. Sickle, hour; – Quarto, *'sickle, hower';* perhaps we should read *'sickle hour';* other suggestions, unsatisfactory for the most part , are, *'fickle mower'; 'fickle hoar'; 'sickle hoar';* &c.
50. Eyes … eyes, – Quarto; Capell MS., *'eyes … hairs';* S. Walker and Delius conjecture *'hairs … eyes';* Staunton and Brae conjecture *'brows … eyes,'* &c.
51. Proved, a very, – Capell MS.; Quarto, *'proud and very.'*
52. No unkind, no; Dowden conjectured *'no unkind "No"';* Rosetti proposed *'skill,' i.e.* 'avail' instead of *'kill.'*
53. Cp. – PASSIONATE PILGRIM, i.
54. Cp. – EDWARD III. ii. 1:—*'His cheeks put on their scarlet ornaments.'*
55. Housewife; – Quarto, *'huswife.'*
56. Have thy "Will": i.e. – Shakespeare's friend Will, not himself.
57. Cp. – PASSIONATE PILGRIM, ii.
58. Side, – so Passionate Pilgrim, and Capell MS.; Quarto, *'sight.'*
59. Fiend; – Quarto, *'finde';* Passionate Pilgrim, *'feend.'*
60. The only sonnet in Shakespeare in eight-syllable verse.
61. Earth … these rebel; – Quarto, *'earth, My sinfull earth these rebbell';* Malone, *'earth, Fool'd by those rebel';* Steevens, *'earth, Starv'd by the rebel';* Dowden, *'earth [Press'd by] these rebel,'* &c. Probably any one of these readings comes near the original; in this case *array* = clothe. Ingleby renders the word "abuse, afflict, ill-treat"; he reads, *'leagu'd with,'* and takes the participle in close conjunction with *'earth.'* This rendering is ingenious, but very doubtful.
62. I; – Quarto, *'eye.'*

THE RAPE OF LUCRECE

TO THE
RIGHT HONORABLE HENRY WRIOTHESLY,
EARL OF SOUTHAMPTON, AND BARON OF TICHFIELD.

THE love I dedicate to your lordship is without end; whereof this pamphlet, without beginning, is but a superfluous moiety. The warrant I have of your honourable disposition, not the worth of my untutored lines, makes it assured of acceptance. What I have done is yours; what I have to do is yours; being part in all I have, devoted yours. Were my worth greater, my duty would show greater; meantime, as it is, it is bound to your lordship, to whom I wish long life, still lengthened with all happiness.

Your lordship's in all duty,
WILLIAM SHAKESPEARE.

LUCIUS TARQUINIUS, for his excessive pride surnamed Superbus, after he had caused his own father-in-law Servius Tullius to be cruelly murdered, and, contrary to the Roman laws and customs, not requiring or staying for the people's suffrages, had possessed himself of the kingdom, went, accompanied with his sons and other noblemen of Rome, to besiege Ardea. During which siege the principal men of the army meeting one evening at the tent of Sextus Tarquinius, the king's son, in their discourses after supper every one commended the virtues of his own wife; among whom Collatinus extolled the incomparable chastity of his wife Lucretia. In that pleasant humour they posted to Rome; and intending, by their secret and sudden arrival, to make trial of that which every one had before avouched, only Collatinus finds his wife, though it were late in the night, spinning amongst her maids: the other ladies were all found dancing and revelling, or in several disports. Whereupon the noblemen yielded Collatinus the victory, and his wife the fame. At that time Sextus Tarquinius being inflamed with Lucrece' beauty, yet smothering his passions for the present, departed with the rest back to the camp; from whence he shortly after privily withdrew himself, and was, according to his estate, royally entertained and lodged by Lucrece at Collatium. The same night he treacherously stealeth into her chamber, violently ravished her, and early in the morning speedeth away. Lucrece, in this lamentable plight, hastily dispatcheth messengers, one to Rome for her father, another to the camp for Collatine. They came, the one accompanied with Junius Brutus, the other with Publius Valerius; and finding Lucrece attired in mourning habit, demanded the cause of her sorrow. She, first taking an oath of them for her revenge, revealed the actor, and whole manner of his dealing, and withal suddenly stabbed herself. Which done, with one consent they all vowed to root out the whole hated family of the Tarquins; and bearing the dead body to Rome, Brutus acquainted the people with the doer and manner of the vile deed, with a bitter invective against the tyranny of the king: wherewith the people were so moved, that with one consent and a general acclamation the Tarquins were all exiled, and the state government changed from kings to consuls.

FROM the besieged Ardea all in post,
Borne by the trustless wings of false desire,
Lust-breathed Tarquin leaves the Roman host,
And to Collatium bears the lightless fire
Which, in pale embers hid, lurks to aspire
And girdle with embracing flames the waist
Of Collatine's fair love, Lucrece the chaste.

Haply that name of 'chaste' unhappily set [1]
This bateless edge on his keen appetite;
When Collatine unwisely did not let
To praise the clear unmatched red and white
Which triumph'd in that sky of his delight,
Where mortal stars, as bright as heaven's beauties,
With pure aspects did him peculiar duties.

For he the night before, in Tarquin's tent,
Unlock'd the treasure of his happy state;
What priceless wealth the heavens had him lent
In the possession of his beauteous mate;
Reckoning his fortune at such high-proud rate,
That kings might be espoused to more fame,
But king nor peer to such a peerless dame.

O happiness enjoy'd but of a few!
And, if possess'd, as soon decay'd and done
As is the morning's silver-melting dew [2]
Against the golden splendor of the sun!
An expired date, cancell'd ere well begun:
Honour and beauty, in the owner's arms,
Are weakly fortress'd from a world of harms.

Beauty itself doth of itself persuade
The eyes of men without an orator;
What needeth then apologies be made, [3]
To set forth that which is so singular?
Or why is Collatine the publisher
Of that rich jewel he should keep unknown
From thievish ears, because it is his own?

Perchance his boast of Lucrece' sovereignty
Suggested this proud issue of a king;
For by our ears our hearts oft tainted be:
Perchance that envy of so rich a thing,
Braving compare, disdainfully did sting
His high-pitch'd thoughts, that meaner men should vaunt
That golden hap which their superiors want.

But some untimely thought did instigate
His all-too-timeless speed, if none of those:
His honour, his affairs, his friends, his state,
Neglected all, with swift intent he goes
To quench the coal which in his liver glows.
O rash false heat, wrapp'd in repentant cold,
Thy hasty spring still blasts, and ne'er grows old!

When at Collatium this false lord arrived,
Well was he welcomed by the Roman dame,
Within whose face beauty and virtue strived
Which of them both should underprop her fame:
When virtue bragg'd, beauty would blush for shame;
When beauty boasted blushes, in despite
Virtue would stain that o'er with silver white. [4]

But beauty, in that white intituled,
From Venus' doves doth challenge that fair field:
Then virtue claims from beauty beauty's red,
Which virtue gave the golden age to gild
Their silver cheeks, and call'd it then their shield;
Teaching them thus to use it in the fight,
When shame assail'd, the red should fence the white.

This heraldry in Lucrece' face was seen,
Argued by beauty's red and virtue's white
Of either's colour was the other queen,
Proving from world's minority their right:
Yet their ambition makes them still to fight;
The sovereignty of either being so great,
That oft they interchange each other's seat.

Their silent war of lilies and of roses,
Which Tarquin view'd in her fair face's field,
In their pure ranks his traitor eye encloses;
Where, lest between them both it should be kill'd,
The coward captive vanquished doth yield
To those two armies that would let him go,
Rather than triumph in so false a foe.

Now thinks he that her husband's shallow tongue,—
The niggard prodigal that praised her so,—
In that high task hath done her beauty wrong,
Which far exceeds his barren skill to show:
Therefore that praise which Collatine doth owe
Enchanted Tarquin answers with surmise,
In silent wonder of still-gazing eyes.

This earthly saint, adored by this devil,
Little suspecteth the false worshipper;
For unstain'd thoughts do seldom dream on evil;
Birds never limed no secret bushes fear:

So guiltless she securely gives good cheer 91
And reverend welcome to her princely guest,
Whose inward ill no outward harm express'd:

For that he colour'd with his high estate,
Hiding base sin in plaits of majesty;
That nothing in him seem'd inordinate,
Save something too much wonder of his eye,
Which, having all, all could not satisfy;
But, poorly rich, so wanteth in his store,
That, cloy'd with much, he pineth still for more.

But she, that never coped with stranger eyes,
Could pick no meaning from their parling looks, 102
Nor read the subtle-shining secrecies
Writ in the glassy margents of such books:
She touch'd no unknown baits, nor fear'd no hooks;
Nor could she moralize his wanton sight,
More than his eyes were open'd to the light.

He stories to her ears her husband's fame,
Won in the fields of fruitful Italy;
And decks with praises Collatine's high name,
Made glorious by his manly chivalry
With bruised arms and wreaths of victory:
Her joy with heaved-up hand she doth express,
And, wordless, so greets heaven for his success.

Far from the purpose of his coming hither,
He makes excuses for his being there:
No cloudy show of stormy blustering weather
Doth yet in his fair welkin once appear;
Till sable Night, mother of Dread and Fear,
Upon the world dim darkness doth display,
And in her vaulty prison stows the Day.

For then is Tarquin brought unto his bed, 122
Intending weariness with heavy spright;
For, after supper, long he questioned
With modest Lucrece, and wore out the night:
Now leaden slumber with life's strength doth fight;
And every one to rest themselves betake,
Save thieves, and cares, and troubled minds, that wake.

As one of which doth Tarquin lie revolving
The sundry dangers of his will's obtaining;
Yet ever to obtain his will resolving,
Though weak-built hopes persuade him to abstaining: 134
Despair to gain doth traffic oft for gaining;
And when great treasure is the meed proposed,
Though death be adjunct, there's no death supposed.

Those that much covet are with gain so fond, [5]
For what they have not, that which they possess
They scatter and unloose it from their bond,
And so, by hoping more, they have but less;
Or, gaining more, the profit of excess
Is but to surfeit, and such griefs sustain,
That they prove bankrupt in this poor-rich gain. 145

The aim of all is but to nurse the life
With honour, wealth, and ease, in waning age;
And in this aim there is such thwarting strife,
That one for all, or all for one we gage;
As life for honour in fell battle's rage;
Honour for wealth; and oft that wealth doth cost
The death of all, and all together lost.

So that in venturing ill we leave to be
The things we are for that which we expect;
And this ambitious foul infirmity, 153
In having much, torments us with defect
Of that we have: so then we do neglect
The thing we have; and, all for want of wit,
Make something nothing by augmenting it.

Such hazard now must doting Tarquin make,
Pawning his honour to obtain his lust;
And for himself himself be must forsake:
Then where is truth, if there be no self-trust?
When shall he think to find a stranger just,
When he himself himself confounds, betrays
To slanderous tongues and wretched hateful days? 166

Now stole upon the time the dead of night,
When heavy sleep had closed up mortal eyes:
No comfortable star did lend his light,
No noise but owls' and wolves' death-boding cries;
Now serves the season that they may surprise
The silly lambs: pure thoughts are dead and still,
While lust and murder wake to stain and kill.

And now this lustful lord leap'd from his bed,
Throwing his mantle rudely o'er his arm; 175
Is madly toss'd between desire and dread;
Th' one sweetly flatters, th' other feareth harm;
But honest fear, bewitch'd with lust's foul charm,
Doth too too oft betake him to retire,
Beaten away by brain-sick rude desire.

His falchion on a flint he softly smiteth,
That from the cold stone sparks of fire do fly;
Whereat a waxen torch forthwith he lighteth,
Which must be lode-star to his lustful eye;
And to the flame thus speaks advisedly,
'As from this cold flint I enforced this fire,
So Lucrece must I force to my desire.'

Here pale with fear he doth premeditate
The dangers of his loathsome enterprise,
And in his inward mind he doth debate
What following sorrow may on this arise:
Then looking scornfully, he doth despise
His naked armour of still-slaughter'd lust,
And justly thus controls his thoughts unjust:

'Fair torch, burn out thy light, and lend it not
To darken her whose light excelleth thine:
And die, unhallow'd thoughts, before you blot
With your uncleanness that which is divine;
Offer pure incense to so pure a shrine:
Let fair humanity abhor the deed [6]
That spots and stains love's modest snow-white weed.

'O shame to knighthood and to shining arms!
O foul dishonour to my household's grave!
O impious act, including all foul harms!
A martial man to be soft fancy's slave!
True valour still a true respect should have;
Then my digression is so vile, so base,
That it will live engraven in my face.

'Yea, though I die, the scandal will survive,
And be an eye-sore in my golden coat;
Some loathsome dash the herald will contrive,
To cipher me how fondly I did dote;
That my posterity, shamed with the note,
Shall curse my bones, and hold it for no sin
To wish that I their father had not been.

'What win I, if I gain the thing I seek?
A dream, a breath, a froth of fleeting joy.
Who buys a minute's mirth to wail a week?
Or sells eternity to get a toy?
For one sweet grape who will the vine destroy?
Or what fond beggar, but to touch the crown,
Would with the sceptre straight be strucken down?

'If Collatinus dream of my intent,
Will he not wake, and in a desperate rage
Post hither, this vile purpose to prevent?
This siege that hath engirt his marriage,
This blur to youth, this sorrow to the sage,
This dying virtue, this surviving shame,
Whose crime will bear an ever-during blame?

'O, what excuse can my invention make,
When thou shalt charge me with so black a deed?
Will not my tongue be mute, my frail joints shake,
Mine eyes forego their light, my false heart bleed?
The guilt being great, the fear doth still exceed;
And extreme fear can neither fight nor fly,
But coward-like with trembling terror die.

'Had Collatinus kill'd my son or sire,
Or lain in ambush to betray my life,
Or were he not my dear friend, this desire
Might have excuse to work upon his wife,
As in revenge or quittal of such strife:
But as he is my kinsman, my dear friend,
The shame and fault finds no excuse nor end.

'Shameful it is; ay, if the fact be known: [7]
Hateful it is; there is no hate in loving:
I'll beg her love; but she is own:
The worst is but denial and reproving:
My will is strong, past reason's weak removing.
Who fears a sentence or an old man's saw
Shall by a painted cloth be kept in awe.'

Thus, graceless, holds he disputation
'Tween frozen conscience and hot-burning will,
And with good thoughts make dispensation,
Urging the worser sense for vantage still;
Which in a moment doth confound and kill
All pure effects, and doth so far proceed,
That what is vile shows like a virtuous deed.

Quoth he, 'She took me kindly by the hand,
And gazed for tidings in my eager eyes,
Fearing some hard news from the warlike band,
Where her beloved Collatinus lies.
O, how her fear did make her colour rise!
First red as roses that on lawn we lay,
Then white as lawn, the roses took away.

'And how her hand, in my hand being lock'd
Forced it to tremble with her loyal fear!
Which struck her sad, and then it faster rock'd,
Until her husband's welfare she did hear;
Whereat she smiled with so sweet a cheer,
That had Narcissus seen her as she stood,
Self-love had never drown'd him in the flood.

'Why hunt I then for colour or excuses?
All orators are dumb when beauty pleadeth;
Poor wretches have remorse in poor abuses;
Love thrives not in the heart that shadows dreadeth:
Affection is my captain, and he leadeth;
And when his gaudy banner is display'd,
The coward fights and will not be dismay'd.

'Then, childish fear, avaunt! debating, die!
Respect and reason, wait on wrinkled age!
My heart shall never countermand mine eye:
Sad pause and deep regard beseem the sage;
My part is youth, and beats these from the stage:
Desire my pilot is, beauty my prize;
Then who fears sinking where such treasure lies?'

As corn o'ergrown by weeds, so heedful fear
Is almost choked by unresisted lust.
Away he steals with open listening ear,
Full of foul hope and full of fond mistrust;
Both which, as servitors to the unjust,
So cross him with their opposite persuasion,
That now he vows a league, and now invasion.

Within his thought her heavenly image sits,
And in the self-same seat sits Collatine:
That eye which looks on her confounds his wits;
That eye which him beholds, as more divine,
Unto a view so false will not incline;
But with a pure appeal seeks to the heart,
Which once corrupted takes the worser part;

And therein heartens up his servile powers,
Who, flatter'd by their leader's jocund show,
Stuff up his lust, as minutes fill up hours;
And as their captain, so their pride doth grow.
Paying more slavish tribute than they owe.
By reprobate desire thus madly led,
The Roman lord marcheth to Lucrece' bed.

The locks between her chamber and his will,
Each one by him enforced, retires his ward;
But, as they open, they all rate his ill,
Which drives the creeping thief to some regard:
The threshold grates the door to have him heard;
Night-wandering weasels shriek to see him there;
They fright him, yet he still pursues his fear.

As each unwilling portal yields him way,
Through little vents and crannies of the place
The wind wars with his torch to make him stay,
And blows the smoke of it into his face,
Extinguishing his conduct in this case;
But his hot heart, which fond desire doth scorch,
Puffs forth another wind that fires the torch:

And being lighted, by the light he spies
Lucrece's glove, wherein her needle sticks:
He takes it from the rushes where it lies,
And griping it, the needle his finger pricks;
As who should say 'This glove to wanton tricks
Is not inured; return again in haste;
Thou see'st our mistress' ornaments are chaste.'

But all these poor forbiddings could not stay him;
He in the worst sense construes their denial:
The doors, the wind, the glove, that did delay him,
He takes for accidental things of trial;
Or as those bars which stop the hourly dial,
Who with a lingering slay his course doth let,
Till every minute pays the hour his debt.

'So, so,' quoth he, 'these lets attend the time,
Like little frosts that sometime threat the spring,
To add a more rejoicing to the prime,
And give the sneaped birds more cause to sing.
Pain pays the income of each precious thing;
Huge rocks, high winds, strong pirates, shelves and sands,
The merchant fears, ere rich at home he lands.'

Now is he come unto the chamber door,
That shuts him from the heaven of his thought,
Which with a yielding latch, and with no more,
Hath barr'd him from the blessed thing be sought.
So from himself impiety hath wrought,
That for his prey to pray he doth begin,
As if the heavens should countenance his sin.

But in the midst of his unfruitful prayer,
Having solicited th' eternal power
That his foul thoughts might compass his fair fair,
And they would stand auspicious to the hour,
Even there he starts: quoth he, 'I must deflower:
The powers to whom I pray abhor this fact,
How can they then assist me in the act?

'Then Love and Fortune be my gods, my guide!
My will is back'd with resolution:
Thoughts are but dreams till their effects be tried;
The blackest sin is clear'd with absolution;
Against love's fire fear's frost hath dissolution.

Into the camber wickedly he stalks.

The eye of heaven is out, and misty night
Covers the shame that follows sweet delight.'

This said, his guilty hand pluck'd up the latch,
And with his knee the door he opens wide.
The dove sleeps fast that this night-owl will catch:
Thus treason works ere traitors be espied.
Who sees the lurking serpent steps aside;
But she, sound sleeping, fearing no such thing,
Lies at the mercy of his mortal sting.

Into the chamber wickedly he stalks,
And gazeth on her yet unstained bed.
The curtains being close, about he walks,
Rolling his greedy eyeballs in his head:
By their high treason is his heart misled;
Which gives the watch-word to his hand full soon
To draw the cloud that hides the silver moon.

Look, as the fair and fiery-pointed sun,
Rushing from forth a cloud, bereaves our sight;
Even so, the curtain drawn, his eyes begun
To wink, being blinded with a greater light:
Whether it is that she reflects so bright,
That dazzleth them, or else some shame supposed;
But blind they are, and keep themselves enclosed.

O, had they in that darksome prison died!
Then had they seen the period of their ill;
Then Collatine again, by Lucrece' side,
In his clear bed might have reposed still:
But they must ope, this blessed league to kill;
And holy-thoughted Lucrece to their sight
Must sell her joy, her life, her world's delight.

Her lily hand her rosy cheek lies under,
Cozening the pillow of a lawful kiss;
Who, therefore angry, seems to part in sunder,
Swelling on either side to want his bliss;
Between whose hills her head entombed is:
Where, like a virtuous monument, she lies,
To be admired of lewd unhallow'd eyes.

Without the bed her other fair hand was,
On the green coverlet; whose perfect white
Show'd like an April daisy on the grass,
With pearly sweat, resembling dew of night.
Her eyes, like marigolds, had sheathed their light,
And canopied in darkness sweetly lay,
Till they might open to adorn the day.

Her hair, like golden threads, play'd with her breath;
O modest wantons! wanton modesty!
Showing life's triumph in the map of death,

And death's dim look in life's mortality:
Each in her sleep themselves so beautify,
As if between them twain there were no strife,
But that life lived in death, and death in life.

Her breasts, like ivory globes circled with blue,
A pair of maiden worlds unconquered,
Save of their lord no bearing yoke they knew,
And him by oath they truly honoured.
These worlds in Tarquin new ambition bred;
Who, like a foul ursurper, went about
From this fair throne to heave the owner out.

What could he see but mightily he noted?
What did he note but strongly he desired?
What he beheld, on that he firmly doted,
And in his will his wilful eye he tired.
With more than admiration he admired
Her azure veins, her alabaster skin,
Her coral lips, her snow-white dimpled chin.

As the grim lion fawneth o'er his prey,
Sharp hunger by the conquest satisfied,
So o'er this sleeping soul doth Tarquin stay,
His rage of lust by gazing qualified;
Slack'd, not suppress'd; for standing by her side,
His eye, which late this mutiny restrains,
Unto a greater uproar tempts his veins:

And they, like straggling slaves for pillage fighting,
Obdurate vassals fell exploits effecting,
In bloody death and ravishment delighting,
Nor children's tears nor mothers' groans respecting,
Swell in their pride, the onset still expecting:
Anon his beating heart, alarum striking,
Gives the hot charge and bids them do their liking.

His drumming heart cheers up his burning eye,
His eye commends the leading to his hand;
His hand, as proud of such a dignity,
Smoking with pride, march'd on to make his stand
On her bare breast, the heart of all her land;
Whose ranks of blue veins, as his hand did scale,
Left there round turrets destitute and pale.

They, mustering to the quiet cabinet
Where their dear governess and lady lies,
Do tell her she is dreadfully beset,
And fright her with confusion of their cries:
She, much amazed, breaks ope her lock'd-up eyes,
Who, peeping forth this tumult to behold,
Are by his flaming torch dimm'd and controll'd.

Imagine her as one in dead of night
From forth dull sleep by dreadful fancy waking,
That thinks she hath beheld some ghastly sprite,
Whose grim aspect sets every joint a-shaking;
What terror or 'tis! but she, in worser taking,
From sleep disturbed, heedfully doth view
The sight which makes supposed terror true.

Wrapp'd and confounded in a thousand fears,
Like to a new-kill'd bird she trembling lies;
She dares not look; yet, winking, there appears
Quick-shifting antics, ugly in her eyes:
Such shadows are the weak brain's forgeries;
Who, angry that the eyes fly from their lights,
In darkness daunts them with more dreadful sights.

His hand, that yet remains upon her breast,—
Rude ram, to batter such an ivory wall!—
May feel her heart-poor citizen!—distress'd,
Wounding itself to death, rise up and fall,
Beating her bulk, that his hand shakes withal.
This moves in him more rage and lesser pity,
To make the breach and enter this sweet city.

First, like a trumpet, doth his tongue begin
To sound a parley to his heartless foe;
Who o'er the white sheet peers her whiter chin,
The reason of this rash alarm to know,
Which he by dumb demeanor seeks to show;
But she with vehement prayers urgeth still
Under what colour he commits this ill.

Thus he replies: 'The colour in thy face,
That even for anger makes the lily pale,
And the red rose blush at her own disgrace,
Shall plead for me and tell my loving tale:
Under that colour am I come to scale
Thy never-conquer'd fort: the fault is thine,
For those thine eyes betray thee unto mine.

'Thus I forestall thee, if thou mean to chide:
Thy beauty hath ensnared thee to this night,
Where thou with patience must my will abide;
My will that marks thee for my earth's delight,
Which I to conquer sought with all my might;
But as reproof and reason beat it dead,
By thy bright beauty was it newly bred.

'I see what crosses my attempt will bring;
I know what thorns the growing rose defends;
I think the honey guarded with a sting;
All this beforehand counsel comprehends:

But will is deaf and hears no heedful friends;
Only he hath an eye to gaze on beauty,
And dotes on what he looks, 'gainst law or duty.

'I have debated, even in my soul,
What wrong, what shame, what sorrow I shall breed;
But nothing can affection's course control,
Or stop the headlong fury of his speed.
I know repentant tears ensue the deed,
Reproach, disdain, and deadly enmity;
Yet strive I to embrace mine infamy.'

This said, he shakes aloft his Roman blade,
Which, like a falcon towering in the skies,
Coucheth the fowl below with his wings' shade,
Whose crooked beak threats if he mount he dies:
So under his insulting falchion lies
Harmless Lucretia, marking what he tells
With trembling fear, as fowl hear falcon's bells.

'Lucrece,' quoth he, 'this night I must enjoy thee:
If thou deny, then force must work my way,
For in thy bed I purpose to destroy thee:
That done, some worthless slave of thine I'll slay,
To kill thine honour with thy life's decay;
And in thy dead arms do I mean to place him,
Swearing I slew him, seeing thee embrace him.

'So thy surviving husband shall remain
The scornful mark of every open eye;
Thy kinsmen hang their heads at this disdain,
Thy issue blurr'd with nameless bastardy:
And thou, the author of their obloquy,
Shalt have thy trespass cited up in rhymes,
And sung by children in succeeding times.

'But if thou yield, I rest thy secret friend:
The fault unknown is as a thought unacted;
A little harm done to a great good end
For lawful policy remains enacted.
The poisonous simple sometimes is compacted
In a pure compound; being so applied,
His venom in effect is purified.

'Then, for thy husband and thy children's sake,
Tender my suit: bequeath not to their lot
The shame that from them no device can take,
The blemish that will never be forgot;
Worse than a slavish wipe or birth-hour's blot:
For marks descried in men's nativity
Are nature's faults, not their own infamy.'

Here with a cockatrice' dead-killing eye
He rouseth up himself and makes a pause;
While she, the picture of pure piety,
Like a white hind under the gripe's sharp claws,
Pleads, in a wilderness where are no laws,
To the rough beast that knows no gentle right,
Nor aught obeys but his foul appetite.

But when a black-faced cloud the world doth threat,
In his dim mist the aspiring mountains hiding,
From earth's dark womb some gentle gust doth get,
Which blows these pitchy vapours from their biding,
Hindering their present fall by this dividing;
So his unhallow'd haste her words delays,
And moody Pluto winks while Orpheus plays.

Yet, foul night-working cat, he doth but dally,
While in his hold-fast foot the weak mouse panteth:
Her sad behavior feeds his vulture folly,
A swallowing gulf that even in plenty wanteth:
His ear her prayers admits, but his heart granteth
No penetrable entrance to her plaining:
Tears harden lust, though marble wear with raining.

Her pity-pleading eyes are sadly fixed
In the remorseless wrinkles of his face;
Her modest eloquence with sighs is mixed,
Which to her oratory adds more grace.
She puts the period often from his place;
And midst the sentence so her accent breaks,
That twice she doth begin ere once she speaks.

She conjures him by high almighty Jove,
By knighthood, gentry, and sweet friendship's oath,
By her untimely tears, her husband's love,
By holy human law, and common troth,
By heaven and earth, and all the power of both,
That to his borrow'd bed he make retire,
And stoop to honour, not to foul desire.

Quoth she, 'Reward not hospitality
With such black payment as thou hast pretended;
Mud not the fountain that gave drink to thee;
Mar not the thing that cannot be amended;
End thy ill aim before thy shoot be ended;
He is no woodman that doth bend his bow
To strike a poor unseasonable doe.

'My husband is thy friend; for his sake spare me:
Thyself art mighty; for thine own sake leave me:
Myself a weakling; do not then ensnare me:

Thou look'st not like deceit; do not deceive me.
My sighs, like whirlwinds, labour hence to heave thee:
If ever man were moved with woman's moans,
Be moved with my tears, my sighs, my groans:

'All which together, like a troubled ocean,
Beat at thy rocky and wreck-threatening heart,
To soften it with their continual motion;
For stones dissolved to water do convert.
O, if no harder than a stone thou art,
Melt at my tears, and be compassionate!
Soft pity enters at an iron gate.

'In Tarquin's likeness I did entertain thee:
Hast thou put on his shape to do him shame?
To all the host of heaven I complain me,
Thou wrong'st his honour, wound'st his princely name.
Thou art not what thou seem'st; and if the same,
Thou seem'st not what thou art, a god, a king;
For kings like gods should govern everything.

'How will thy shame be seeded in thine age,
When thus thy vices bud before thy spring!
If in thy hope thou darest do such outrage,
What darest thou not when once thou art a king?
O, be remember'd, no outrageous thing
From vassal actors can be wiped away;
Then kings' misdeeds cannot be hid in clay.

'This deed will make thee only loved for fear;
But happy monarchs still are fear'd for love:
With foul offenders thou perforce must bear,
When they in thee the like offences prove:
If but for fear of this, thy will remove;
For princes are the glass, the school, the book,
Where subjects' eyes do learn, do read, do look.

'And wilt thou be the school where Lust shall learn?
Must he in thee read lectures of such shame?
Wilt thou be glass wherein it shall discern
Authority for sin, warrant for blame,
To privilege dishonour in thy name?
Thou black'st reproach against long-living laud,
And makest fair reputation but a bawd.

'Hast thou command? by him that gave it thee,
From a pure heart command thy rebel will:
Draw not thy sword to guard iniquity,
For it was lent thee all that brood to kill.
Thy princely office how canst thou fulfil,
When, pattern'd by thy fault, foul sin may say,
He learn'd to sin, and thou didst teach the way?

'Think but how vile a spectacle it were,
To view thy present trespass in another.
Men's faults do seldom to themselves appear;
Their own transgressions partially they smother:
This guilt would seem death-worthy in thy brother.
O, how are they wrapp'd in with infamies
That from their own misdeeds askance their eyes! [8]

'To thee, to thee, my heaved-up hands appeal,
Not to seducing lust, thy rash relier:
I sue for exiled majesty's repeal;
Let him return, and flattering thoughts retire:
His true respect will prison false desire,
And wipe the dim mist from thy doting eyne,
That thou shalt see thy state and pity mine.'

'Have done,' quoth he: 'my uncontrolled tide
Turns not, but swells the higher by this let.
Small lights are soon blown out, huge fires abide,
And with the wind in greater fury fret:
The petty streams that pay a daily debt [9]
To their salt sovereign, with their fresh falls' haste
Add to his flow, but alter not his taste.'

'Thou art,' quoth she, 'a sea, a sovereign king;
And, lo, there falls into thy boundless flood
Black lust, dishonour, shame, misgoverning,
Who seek to stain the ocean of thy blood.
If all these pretty ills shall change thy good,
Thy sea within a puddle's womb is hearsed,
And not the puddle in thy sea dispersed.

'So shall these slaves be king, and thou their slave;
Thou nobly base, they basely dignified;
Thou their fair life, and they thy fouler grave:
Thou loathed in their shame, they in thy pride:
The lesser thing should not the greater hide;
The cedar stoops not to the base shrub's foot,
But low shrubs wither at the cedar's root.

'So let thy thoughts, low vassals to thy state'—
No more,' quoth he; 'by heaven, I will not hear thee:
Yield to my love; if not, enforced hate,
Instead of love's coy touch, shall rudely tear thee;
That done, despitefully I mean to bear thee
Unto the base bed of some rascal groom,
To be thy partner in this shameful doom.

This said, he sets his foot upon the light,
For light and lust are deadly enemies:
Shame folded up in blind concealing night,
When most unseen, then most doth tyrannize.
The wolf hath seized his prey, the poor lamb cries;
Till with her own white fleece her voice controll'd
Entombs her outcry in her lips' sweet fold:

For with the nightly linen that she wears
He pens her piteous clamours in her head;
Cooling his hot face in the chastest tears
That ever modest eyes with sorrow shed.
O, that prone lust should stain so pure a bed!
The spots whereof could weeping purify,
Her tears should drop on them perpetually.

But she hath lost a dearer thing than life,
And he hath won what he would lose again:
This forced league doth force a further strife;
This momentary joy breeds months of pain;
This hot desire converts to cold disdain:
Pure Chastity is rifled of her store,
And Lust, the thief, far poorer than before.

Look, as the full-fed hound or gorged hawk,
Unapt for tender smell or speedy flight,
Make slow pursuit, or altogether balk
The prey wherein by nature they delight;
So surfeit-taking Tarquin fares this night:
His taste delicious, in digestion souring,
Devours his will, that lived by foul devouring.

O, deeper sin than bottomless conceit
Can comprehend in still imagination!
Drunken Desire must vomit his receipt,
Ere he can see his own abomination.
While Lust is in his pride, no exclamation
Can curb his heat or rein his rash desire,
Till like a jade Self-will himself doth tire.

And then with lank and lean discolour'd cheek,
With heavy eye, knit brow, and strengthless pace,
Feeble Desire, all recreant, poor, and meek,
Like to a bankrupt beggar wails his case:
The flesh being proud, Desire doth fight with Grace,
For there it revels; and when that decays,
The guilty rebel for remission prays.

So fares it with this faultful lord of Rome,
Who this accomplishment so hotly chased;
For now against himself he sounds this doom,
That through the length of times he stands disgraced:
Besides, his soul's fair temple is defaced;
To whose weak ruins muster troops of cares,
To ask the spotted princess how she fares.

She says, her subjects with foul insurrection
Have batter'd down her consecrated wall,
And by their mortal fault brought in subjection
Her immortality, and made her thrall
To living death and pain perpetual:
Which in her prescience she controlled still,
But her foresight could not forestall their will.

Even in this thought through the dark night he stealeth,
A captive victor that hath lost in gain;
Bearing away the wound that nothing healeth,
The scar that will, despite of cure, remain;
Leaving his spoil perplex'd in greater pain.
She bears the load of lust he left behind,
And he the burden of a guilty mind.

He like a thievish dog creeps sadly thence;
She like a wearied lamb lies panting there;
He scowls and hates himself for his offence;
She, desperate, with her nails her flesh doth tear;
He faintly flies, sneaking with guilty fear;
She stays, exclaiming on the direful night;
He runs, and chides his vanish'd, loathed delight.

He thence departs a heavy convertite;
She there remains a hopeless castaway;
He in his speed looks for the morning light;
She prays she never may behold the day,
'For day,' quoth she, 'nights scapes doth open lay,
And my true eyes have never practised how
To cloak offences with a cunning brow.

They think not but that every eye can see
The same disgrace which they themselves behold;
And therefore would they still in darkness be,
To have their unseen sin remain untold;
For they their guilt with weeping will unfold,
And grave, like water that doth eat in steel,
Upon my cheeks what helpless shame I feel.'

Here she exclaims against repose and rest,
And bids her eyes hereafter still be blind.
She wakes her heart by beating on her breast,
And bids it leap from thence, where it may find
Some purer chest to close so pure a mind.
Frantic with grief thus breathes she forth her spite
Against the unseen secrecy of night:

'O comfort-killing Night, image of hell!
Dim register and notary of shame!
Black stage for tragedies and murders fell!
Vast sin-concealing chaos! nurse of blame!
Blind muffled bawd! dark harbour for defame!
 Grim cave of death! whispering conspirator
 With close-tongued treason and the ravisher!

'O hateful, vaporous, and foggy Night!
Since thou art guilty of my cureless crime,
Muster thy mists to meet the eastern light,
Make war against proportion'd course of time;
Or if thou wilt permit the sun to climb
 His wonted height, yet ere he go to bed,
 Knit poisonous clouds about his golden head.

'With rotten damps ravish the morning air;
Let their exhaled unwholesome breaths make sick
The life of purity, the supreme fair,
Ere he arrive his weary noon-tide prick;
And let thy misty vapours march so thick, [10]
 That in their smoky ranks his smother'd light
 May set at noon and make perpetual night.

'Were Tarquin Night, as he is but Night's child,
The silver-shining queen he would distain;
Her twinkling handmaids too, by him defiled,
Through Night's black bosom should not peep again:
So should I have co-partners in my pain;
 And fellowship in woe doth woe assuage,
 As palmers' chat makes short their pilgrimage.

'Where now I have no one to blush with me,
To cross their arms and hang their heads with mine,
To mask their brows and hide their infamy;
But I alone alone must sit and pine,
Seasoning the earth with showers of silver brine,
 Mingling my talk with tears, my grief with groans,
 Poor wasting monuments of lasting moans.

'O Night, thou furnace of foul-reeking smoke,
Let not the jealous Day behold that face
Which underneath thy black all-hiding cloak
Immodestly lies martyr'd with disgrace!
Keep still possession of thy gloomy place,
 That all the faults which in thy reign are made
 May likewise be sepulchred in thy shade!

'Make me not object to the tell-tale Day!
The light will show, character'd in my brow,
The story of sweet chastity's decay,
The impious breach of holy wedlock vow:
Yea the illiterate, that know not how
 To cipher what is writ in learned books,
 Will quote my loathsome trespass in my looks.

'The nurse, to still her child, will tell my story,
And fright her crying babe with Tarquin's name;
The orator, to deck his oratory,
Will couple my reproach to Tarquin's shame;
Feast-finding minstrels, tuning my defame,
 Will tie the hearers to attend each line,
 How Tarquin wronged me, I Collatine.

'Let my good name, that senseless reputation,
For Collatine's dear love be kept unspotted:
If that be made a theme for disputation,
The branches of another root are rotted
And undeserved reproach to him allotted
 That is as clear from this attaint of mine
 As I, ere this, was pure to Collatine.

'O unseen shame! invisible disgrace!
O unfelt sore! crest-wounding, private scar!
Reproach is stamp'd in Collatinus' face,
And Tarquin's eye may read the mot afar,
How he in peace is wounded, not in war.
 Alas, how many bear such shameful blows,
 Which not themselves, but he that gives them knows!

'If, Collatine, thine honour lay in me,
From me by strong assault it is bereft.
My honour lost, and I, a drone-like bee,
Have no perfection of my summer left,
But robb'd and ransack'd by injurious theft:
 In thy weak hive a wandering wasp hath crept,
 And suck'd the honey which thy chaste bee kept.

'Yet am I guilty of thy honour's wrack; [11]
Yet for thy honour did I entertain him;
Coming from thee, I could not put him back,
For it had been dishonour to disdain him:
Besides, of weariness he did complain him,
 And talk'd of virtue: O unlook'd-for evil,
 When virtue is profaned in such a devil!

'Why should the worm intrude the maiden bud?
Or hateful cuckoos hatch in sparrows' nests?
Or toads infect fair founts with venom mud?
Or tyrant folly lurk in gentle breasts?
Or kings be breakers of their own behests?
 But no perfection is so absolute,
 That some impurity doth not pollute.

'The aged man that coffers-up his gold
Is plagued with cramps and gouts and painful fits;
And scarce hath eyes his treasure to behold,
But like still-pining Tantalus he sits,
And useless barns the harvest of his wits;
Having no other pleasure of his gain
But torment that it cannot cure his pain.

'So then he hath it when he cannot use it,
And leaves it to be master'd by his young;
Who in their pride do presently abuse it:
Their father was too weak, and they too strong,
To hold their cursed-blessed fortune long.
The sweets we wish for turn to loathed sours
Even in the moment that we call them ours.

'Unruly blasts wait on the tender spring;
Unwholesome weeds take root with precious flowers;
The adder hisses where the sweet birds sing;
What virtue breeds iniquity devours:
We have no good that we can say is ours,
But ill-annexed Opportunity
Or kills his life or else his quality.

'O Opportunity, thy guilt is great!
'Tis thou that executest the traitor's treason:
Thou set'st the wolf where he the lamb may get;
Whoever plots the sin, thou 'point'st the season;
'Tis thou that spurn'st at right, at law, at reason;
And in thy shady cell, where none may spy him,
Sits Sin, to seize the souls that wander by him.

'Thou makest the vestal violate her oath;
Thou blow'st the fire when temperance is thaw'd;
Thou smother'st honesty, thou murder'st troth;
Thou foul abettor! thou notorious bawd!
Thou plantest scandal and displacest laud:
Thou ravisher, thou traitor, thou false thief,
Thy honey turns to gall, thy joy to grief!

'Thy secret pleasure turns to open shame,
Thy private feasting to a public fast,
Thy smoothing titles to a ragged name,
Thy sugar'd tongue to bitter wormwood taste:
Thy violent vanities can never last.
How comes it then, vile Opportunity,
Being so bad, such numbers seek for thee?

'When wilt thou be the humble suppliant's friend,
And bring him where his suit may be obtain'd?
When wilt thou sort an hour great strifes to end?
Or free that soul which wretchedness hath chain'd?
Give physic to the sick, ease to the pain'd?
The poor, lame, blind, halt, creep, cry out for thee;
But they ne'er meet with Opportunity.

'The patient dies while the physician sleeps;
The orphan pines while the oppressor feeds;
Justice is feasting while the widow weeps;
Advice is sporting while infection breeds:
Thou grant'st no time for charitable deeds:
Wrath, envy, treason, rape, and murder's rages,
Thy heinous hours wait on them as their pages.

'When Truth and Virtue have to do with thee,
A thousand crosses keep them from thy aid:
They buy thy help; but Sin ne'er gives a fee,
He gratis comes; and thou art well appaid
As well to hear as grant what he hath said.
My Collatine would else have come to me
When Tarquin did, but he was stay'd by thee.

Guilty thou art of murder and of theft,
Guilty of perjury and subornation,
Guilty of treason, forgery, and shift,
Guilty of incest, that abomination;
An accessary by thine inclination
To all sins past, and all that are to come,
From the creation to the general doom.

'Mis-shapen Time, copesmate of ugly Night,
Swift subtle post, carrier of grisly care,
Eater of youth, false slave to false delight,
Base watch of woes, sin's pack-horse, virtue's snare;
Thou nursest all and murder'st all that are:
O, hear me then, injurious, shifting Time! [12]
Be guilty of my death, since of my crime.

'Why hath thy servant, Opportunity,
Betray'd the hours thou gavest me to repose,
Cancell'd my fortunes, and enchained me
To endless date of never-ending woes?
Time's office is to fine the hate of foes;
To eat up errors by opinion bred,
Not spend the dowry of a lawful bed.

'Time's glory is to calm contending kings,
To unmask falsehood and bring truth to light,
To stamp the seal of time in aged things,
To wake the morn and sentinel the night,
To wrong the wronger till he render right,
To ruinate proud buildings with thy hours,
And smear with dust their glittering golden towers;

'To fill with worm-holes stately monuments,
To feed oblivion with decay of things,
To blot old books and alter their contents,
To pluck the quills from ancient ravens' wings,
To dry the old oak's sap and cherish springs,
To spoil antiquities of hammer'd steel, 970
And turn the giddy round of Fortune's wheel;

'To show the beldam daughters of her daughter,
To make the child a man, the man a child,
To slay the tiger that doth live by slaughter,
To tame the unicorn and lion wild,
To mock the subtle in themselves beguiled,
To cheer the ploughman with increaseful crops,
And waste huge stones with little water drops.

'Why work'st thou mischief in thy pilgrimage,
Unless thou couldst return to make amends?
One poor retiring minute in an age
Would purchase thee a thousand thousand friends,
Lending him wit that to bad debtors lends:
O, this dread night, wouldst thou one hour come back,
I could prevent this storm and shun thy wrack!

'Thou ceaseless lackey to eternity,
With some mischance cross Tarquin in his flight:
Devise extremes beyond extremity,
To make him curse this cursed crimeful night:
Let ghastly shadows his lewd eyes affright;
And the dire thought of his committed evil
Shape every bush a hideous shapeless devil.

'Disturb his hours of rest with restless trances,
Afflict him in his bed with bedrid groans;
Let there bechance him pitiful mischances,
To make him moan; but pity not his moans:
Stone him with harden'd hearts harder than stones;
And let mild women to him lose their mildness,
Wilder to him than tigers in their wildness.

'Let him have time to tear his curled hair, 1001
Let him have time against himself to rave,
Let him have time of Time's help to despair,
Let him have time to live a loathed slave,
Let him have time a beggar's orts to crave,
And time to see one that by alms doth live
Disdain to him disdained scraps to give.

'Let him have time to see his friends his foes,
And merry fools to mock at him resort;
Let him have time to mark how slow time goes
In time of sorrow, and how swift and short
His time of folly and his time of sport;
And ever let his unrecalling crime
Have time to wail th' abusing of his time.

'O Time, thou tutor both to good and bad,
Teach me to curse him that thou taught'st this ill!
At his own shadow let the thief run mad,
Himself himself seek every hour to kill!
Such wretched hands such wretched blood should spill; 1020
For who so base would such an office have
As slanderous deathsman to so base a slave?

'The baser is he, coming from a king,
To shame his hope with deeds degenerate:
The mightier man, the mightier is the thing
That makes him honour'd, or begets him hate;
For greatest scandal waits on greatest state.
The moon being clouded presently is miss'd,
But little stars may hide them when they list.

'The crow may bathe his coal-black wings in mire,
And unperceived fly with the filth away; 1031
But if the like the snow-white swan desire,
The stain upon his silver down will stay.
Poor grooms are sightless night, kings glorious day:
Gnats are unnoted wheresoe'er they fly,
But eagles gazed upon with every eye.

'Out, idle words, servants to shallow fools!
Unprofitable sounds, weak arbitrators!
Busy yourselves in skill-contending schools;
Debate where leisure serves with dull debaters;
To trembling clients be you mediators: 1042
For me, I force not argument a straw,
Since that my case is past the help of law.

'In vain I rail at Opportunity,
At Time, at Tarquin, and uncheerful Night;
In vain I cavil with mine infamy,
In vain I spurn at my confirm'd despite:
This helpless smoke of words doth me no right.
The remedy indeed to do me good
Is to let forth my foul-defiled blood.

'Poor hand, why quiver'st thou at this decree?
Honour thyself to rid me of this shame; 1053
For if I die, my honour lives in thee;
But if I live, thou livest in my defame:
Since thou couldst not defend thy loyal dame,

And wast afeard to scratch her wicked foe,
Kill both thyself and her for yielding so.'

This said, from her be-tumbled couch she starteth,
To find some desperate instrument of death:
But this no slaughterhouse no tool imparteth
To make more vent for passage of her breath;
Which, thronging through her lips, so vanisheth
As smoke from Aetna, that in air consumes,
Or that which from discharged cannon fumes.

'In vain,' quoth she, 'I live, and seek in vain
Some happy mean to end a hapless life.
I fear'd by Tarquin's falchion to be slain,
Yet for the self-same purpose seek a knife:
But when I fear'd I was a loyal wife:
So am I now: O no, that cannot be;
Of that true type hath Tarquin rifled me.

'O, that is gone for which I sought to live,
And therefore now I need not fear to die.
To clear this spot by death, at least I give
A badge of fame to slander's livery;
A dying life to living infamy:
Poor helpless help, the treasure stol'n away,
To burn the guiltless casket where it lay!

'Well, well, dear Collatine, thou shalt not know
The stained taste of violated troth;
I will not wrong thy true affection so,
To flatter thee with an infringed oath;
This bastard graff shall never come to growth:
He shall not boast who did thy stock pollute
That thou art doting father of his fruit.

'Nor shall he smile at thee in secret thought,
Nor laugh with his companions at thy state;
But thou shalt know thy interest was not bought
Basely with gold, but stol'n from forth thy gate.
For me, I am the mistress of my fate,
And with my trespass never will dispense,
Till life to death acquit my forced offence.

'I will not poison thee with my attaint,
Nor fold my fault in cleanly-coin'd excuses;
My sable ground of sin I will not paint,
To hide the truth of this false night's abuses:
My tongue shall utter all; mine eyes, like sluices,
As from a mountain-spring that feeds a dale,
Shall gush pure streams to purge my impure tale.'

By this, lamenting Philomel had ended
The well-tuned warble of her nightly sorrow,
And solemn night with slow sad gait descended
To ugly hell; when, lo, the blushing morrow
Lends light to all fair eyes that light will borrow:
But cloudy Lucrece shames herself to see,
And therefore still in night would cloister'd be.

Revealing day through every cranny spies,
And seems to point her out where she sits weeping;
To whom she sobbing speaks: 'O eye of eyes,
Why pry'st thou through my window? leave thy peeping:
Mock with thy tickling beams eyes that are sleeping:
Brand not my forehead with thy piercing light,
For day hath nought to do what's done by night.'

Thus cavils she with every thing she sees:
True grief is fond and testy as a child,
Who wayward once, his mood with nought agrees:
Old woes, not infant sorrows, bear them mild;
Continuance tames the one: the other wild,
Like an unpractised swimmer plunging still,
With too much labour drowns for want of skill.

So she, deep-drenched in a sea of care,
Holds disputation with each thing she views,
And to herself all sorrow doth compare;
No object but her passion's strength renews;
And as one shifts, another straight ensues:
Sometime her grief is dumb and hath no words;
Sometime 'tis mad and too much talk affords.

The little birds that tune their morning's joy
Make her moans mad with their sweet melody:
For mirth doth search the bottom of annoy;
Sad souls are slain in merry company;
Grief best is pleased with grief's society:
True sorrow then is feelingly sufficed
When with like semblance it is sympathized.

'Tis double death to drown in ken of shore;
He ten times pines that pines beholding food;
To see the salve doth make the wound ache more;
Great grief grieves most at that would do it good;
Deep woes roll forward like a gentle flood,
Who being stopp'd, the bounding banks o'erflows;
Grief dallied with nor law nor limit knows.

'You mocking-birds,' quoth she, 'your tunes entomb
Within your hollow-swelling feather'd breasts,
And in my hearing be you mute and dumb:
My restless discord loves no stops nor rests;
A woeful hostess brooks not merry guests:

Relish your nimble notes to pleasing ears;
Distress likes dumps when time is kept with tears.

'Come, Philomel, that sing'st of ravishment,
Make thy sad grove in my dishevell'd hair:
As the dank earth weeps at thy languishment,
So I at each sad strain will strain a tear,
And with deep groans the diapason bear;
For burden-wise I'll hum on Tarquin still,
While thou on Tereus descant'st better skill. [13]

'And whiles against a thorn thou bear'st thy part,
To keep thy sharp woes waking, wretched I,
To imitate thee well, against my heart
Will fix a sharp knife to affright mine eye;
Who, if it wink, shall thereon fall and die.
These means, as frets upon an instrument,
Shall tune our heart-strings to true languishment.

'And for, poor bird, thou sing'st not in the day,
As shaming any eye should thee behold,
Some dark deep desert, seated from the way,
That knows not parching heat nor freezing cold,
Will we find out; and there we will unfold
To creatures stern sad tunes, to change their kinds:
Since men prove beasts, let beasts bear gentle minds.'

As the poor frighted deer, that stands at gaze,
Wildly determining which way to fly,
Or one encompass'd with a winding maze,
That cannot tread the way out readily;
So with herself is she in mutiny,
To live or die which of the twain were better,
When life is shamed, and death reproach's debtor.

'To kill myself,' quoth she, 'alack, what were it,
But with my body my poor soul's pollution?
They that lose half with greater patience bear it
Than they whose whole is swallow'd in confusion.
That mother tries a merciless conclusion
Who, having two sweet babes, when death takes one,
Will slay the other and be nurse to none.

'My body or my soul, which was the dearer,
When the one pure, the other made divine?
Whose love of either to myself was nearer,
When both were kept for heaven and Collatine?
Ay me! the bark peel'd from the lofty pine,
His leaves will wither and his sap decay;
So must my soul, her bark being peel'd away.

'Her house is sack'd, her quiet interrupted,
Her mansion batter'd by the enemy;
Her sacred temple spotted, spoil'd, corrupted,
Grossly engirt with daring infamy:
Then let it not be call'd impiety,
If in this blemish'd fort I make some hole
Through which I may convey this troubled soul.

'Yet die I will not till my Collatine
Have heard the cause of my untimely death;
That he may vow, in that sad hour of mine,
Revenge on him that made me stop my breath.
My stained blood to Tarquin I'll bequeath,
Which by him tainted shall for him be spent,
And as his due writ in my testament.

'My honour I'll bequeath unto the knife
That wounds my body so dishonoured.
'Tis honour to deprive dishonour'd life;
The one will live, the other being dead:
So of shame's ashes shall my fame be bred;
For in my death I murder shameful scorn:
My shame so dead, mine honour is new-born.

'Dear lord of that dear jewel I have lost,
What legacy shall I bequeath to thee?
My resolution, love, shall be thy boast,
By whose example thou revenged mayest be.
How Tarquin must be used, read it in me:
Myself, thy friend, will kill myself, thy foe,
And for my sake serve thou false Tarquin so.

'This brief abridgement of my will I make:
My soul and body to the skies and ground;
My resolution, husband, do thou take;
Mine honour be the knife's that makes my wound;
My shame be his that did my fame confound;
And all my fame that lives disbursed be
To those that live, and think no shame of me.

'Thou, Collatine, shalt oversee this will;
How was I overseen that thou shalt see it!
My blood shall wash the slander of mine ill;
My life's foul deed, my life's fair end shall free it.
Faint not, faint heart, but stoutly say "So be it:"
Yield to my hand; my hand shall conquer thee:
Thou dead, both die, and both shall victors be.'

This Plot of death when sadly she had laid,
And wiped the brinish pearl from her bright eyes,
With untuned tongue she hoarsely calls her maid,
Whose swift obedience to her mistress hies;

For fleet-wing'd duty with thought's feathers flies.
Poor Lucrece' cheeks unto her maid seem so
As winter meads when sun doth melt their snow.

Her mistress she doth give demure good-morrow,
With soft-slow tongue, true mark of modesty,
And sorts a sad look to her lady's sorrow,
For why her face wore sorrow's livery;
But durst not ask of her audaciously
Why her two suns were cloud-eclipsed so,
Nor why her fair cheeks over-wash'd with woe.

But as the earth doth weep, the sun being set,
Each flower moisten'd like a melting eye;
Even so the maid with swelling drops gan wet
Her circled eyne, enforced by sympathy
Of those fair suns set in her mistress' sky,
Who in a salt-waved ocean quench their light,
Which makes the maid weep like the dewy night.

A pretty while these pretty creatures stand,
Like ivory conduits coral cisterns filling:
One justly weeps; the other takes in hand
No cause, but company, of her drops spilling:
Their gentle sex to weep are often willing;
Grieving themselves to guess at others' smarts,
And then they drown their eyes or break their hearts. 1264

For men have marble, women waxen, minds,
And therefore are they form'd as marble will;
The weak oppress'd, the impression of strange kinds
Is form'd in them by force, by fraud, or skill:
Then call them not the authors of their ill,
No more than wax shall be accounted evil
Wherein is stamp'd the semblance of a devil.

Their smoothness, like a goodly champaign plain,
Lays open all the little worms that creep;
In men, as in a rough-grown grove, remain
Cave-keeping evils that obscurely sleep: 1275
Through crystal walls each little mote will peep:
Though men can cover crimes with bold stern looks,
Poor women's faces are their own fault's books.

No man inveigh against the wither'd flower,
But chide rough winter that the flower hath kill'd:
Not that devour'd, but that which doth devour,
Is worthy blame. O, let it not be hild
Poor women's faults, that they are so fulfill'd
With men's abuses: those proud lords, to blame,
Make weak-made women tenants to their shame. 1286

The precedent whereof in Lucrece view,
Assail'd by night with circumstances strong
Of present death, and shame that might ensue
By that her death, to do her husband wrong:
Such danger to resistance did belong,
The dying fear through all her body spread;
And who cannot abuse a body dead?

By this, mild patience bid fair Lucrece speak
To the poor counterfeit of her complaining:
'My girl,' quoth she, 'on what occasion break
Those tears from thee, that down thy cheeks are raining? 1298
If thou dost weep for grief of my sustaining,
Know, gentle wench, it small avails my mood:
If tears could help, mine own would do me good.

'But tell me, girl, when went'—and there she stay'd
Till after a deep groan—'Tarquin from hence?'
'Madam, ere I was up,' replied the maid,
'The more to blame my sluggard negligence:
Yet with the fault I thus far can dispense;
Myself was stirring ere the break of day,
And, ere I rose, was Tarquin gone away.

'But, lady, if your maid may be so bold,
She would request to know your heaviness.'
'O, peace!' quoth Lucrece: 'if it should be told,
The repetition cannot make it less;
For more it is than I can well express:
And that deep torture may be call'd a hell
When more is felt than one hath power to tell.

'Go, get me hither paper, ink, and pen:
Yet save that labour, for I have them here.
What should I say? One of my husband's men
Bid thou be ready, by and by, to bear
A letter to my lord, my love, my dear:
Bid him with speed prepare to carry it;
The cause craves haste, and it will soon be writ.'

Her maid is gone, and she prepares to write,
First hovering o'er the paper with her quill:
Conceit and grief an eager combat fight;
What wit sets down is blotted straight with will;
This is too curious-good, this blunt and ill:
Much like a press of people at a door, 1328
Throng her inventions, which shall go before.

At last she thus begins: 'Thou worthy lord
Of that unworthy wife that greeteth thee,
Health to thy person! next vouchsafe t' afford—
If ever, love, thy Lucrece thou wilt see—
Some present speed to come and visit me.
So, I commend me from our house in grief:
My woes are tedious, though my words are brief.'

Here folds she up the tenor of her woe,
Her certain sorrow writ uncertainly.
By this short schedule Collatine may know
Her grief, but not her grief's true quality:
She dares not thereof make discovery,
Lest he should hold it her own gross abuse,
Ere she with blood had stain'd her stain'd excuse.

Besides, the life and feeling of her passion
She hoards, to spend when he is by to hear her:
When sighs and groans and tears may grace the fashion
Of her disgrace, the better so to clear her
From that suspicion which the world might bear her.
To shun this blot, she would not blot the letter
With words, till action might become them better.

To see sad sights moves more than hear them told:
For then eye interprets to the ear
The heavy motion that it doth behold,
When every part a part of woe doth bear.
'Tis but a part of sorrow that we hear:
Deep sounds make lesser noise than shallow fords,
And sorrow ebbs, being blown with wind of words. 1357

Her letter now is seal'd, and on it writ
'At Ardea to my lord with more than haste.'
The post attends, and she delivers it,
Charging the sour-faced groom to hie as fast
As lagging fowls before the northern blast:
Speed more than speed but dull and slow she deems:
Extremity still urgeth such extremes.

The homely villain court'sies to her low; [14]
And, blushing on her, with a steadfast eye
Receives the scroll without or yea or no, 1368
And forth with bashful innocence doth hie.
But they whose guilt within their bosoms lie
Imagine every eye beholds their blame;
For Lucrece thought he blush'd to her see shame:

When, silly groom! God wot, it was defect
Of spirit, Life, and bold audacity.
Such harmless creatures have a true respect
To talk in deeds, while others saucily
Promise more speed, but do it leisurely:
Even so this pattern of the worn-out age
Pawn'd honest looks, but laid no words to gage.

His kindled duty kindled her mistrust,
That two red fires in both their faces blazed;
She thought he blush'd, as knowing Tarquin's lust,
And, blushing with him, wistly on him gazed;
Her earnest eye did make him more amazed:
The more she saw the blood his cheeks replenish,
The more she thought he spied in her some blemish.

But long she thinks till he return again,
And yet the duteous vassal scarce is gone.
The weary time she cannot entertain,
For now 'tis stale to sigh, to weep, and groan:
So woe hath wearied woe, moan tired moan,
That she her plaints a little while doth stay,
Pausing for means to mourn some newer way.

At last she calls to mind where hangs a piece
Of skilful painting, made for Priam's Troy;
Before the which is drawn the power of Greece.
For Helen's rape the city to destroy, 1397
Threatening cloud-kissing Ilion with annoy;
Which the conceited painter drew so proud,
As heaven, it seem'd, to kiss the turrets bow'd.

A thousand lamentable objects there,
In scorn of nature, art gave lifeless life:
Many a dry drop seem'd a weeping tear,
Shed for the slaughter'd husband by the wife:
The red blood reek'd, to show the painter's strife;
The dying eyes gleam'd forth their ashy lights,
Like dying coals burnt out in tedious nights.

There might you see the labouring pioner
Begrimed with sweat, and smeared all with dust;
And from the towers of Troy there would appear
The very eyes of men through loop-holes thrust,
Gazing upon the Greeks with little lust:
Such sweet observance in this work was had,
That one might see those far-off eyes look sad.

In great commanders grace and majesty
You might behold, triumphing in their faces;
In youth, quick bearing and dexterity;
And here and there the painter interlaces 1418
Pale cowards, marching on with trembling paces;

Which heartless peasants did so well resemble,
That one would swear he saw them quake and tremble.

In Ajax and Ulysses, O, what art
Of physiognomy might one behold!
The face of either cipher'd either's heart;
Their face their manners most expressly told:
In Ajax' eyes blunt rage and rigor roll'd;
But the mild glance that sly Ulysses lent
Show'd deep regard and smiling government.

There pleading might you see grave Nestor stand,
As 'twere encouraging the Greeks to fight;
Making such sober action with his hand,
That it beguiled attention, charm'd the sight:
In speech, it seem'd, his beard, all silver white,
Wagg'd up and down, and from his lips did fly
Thin winding breath, which purl'd up to the sky.

About him were a press of gaping faces,
Which seem'd to swallow up his sound advice;
All jointly listening, but with several graces,
As if some mermaid did their ears entice,
Some high, some low, the painter was so nice;
The scalps of many, almost hid behind,
To jump up higher seem'd, to mock the mind.

Here one man's hand lean'd on another's head,
His nose being shadow'd by his neighbour's ear;
Here one being throng'd bears back, all boll'n and red;
Another smother'd seems to pelt and swear;
And in their rage such signs of rage they bear,
As, but for loss of Nestor's golden words,
It seem'd they would debate with angry swords.

For much imaginary work was there;
Conceit deceitful, so compact, so kind,
That for Achilles' image stood his spear,
Griped in an armed hand; himself, behind,
Was left unseen, save to the eye of mind:
A hand, a foot, a face, a leg, a head,
Stood for the whole to be imagined.

And from the walls of strong-besieged Troy
When their brave hope, bold Hector, march'd to field,
Stood many Trojan mothers, sharing joy
To see their youthful sons bright weapons wield;
And to their hope they such odd action yield,
That through their light joy seemed to appear,
Like bright things stain'd, a kind of heavy fear.

And from the strand of Dardan, where they fought,
To Simois' reedy banks the red blood ran,
Whose waves to imitate the battle sought
With swelling ridges; and their ranks began
To break upon the galled shore, and than
Retire again, till, meeting greater ranks,
They join and shoot their foam at Simois' banks.

To this well-painted piece is Lucrece come,
To find a face where all distress is stell'd.
Many she sees where cares have carved some,
But none where all distress and dolour dwell'd,
Till she despairing Hecuba beheld,
Staring on Priam's wounds with her old eyes,
Which bleeding under Pyrrhus' proud foot lies.

In her the painter had anatomized
Time's ruin, beauty's wreck, and grim care's reign:
Her cheeks with chaps and wrinkles were disguised;
Of what she was no semblance did remain:
Her blue blood changed to black in every vein,
Wanting the spring that those shrunk pipes had fed,
Show'd life imprison'd in a body dead.

On this sad shadow Lucrece spends her eyes,
And shapes her sorrow to the beldam's woes,
Who nothing wants to answer her but cries,
And bitter words to ban her cruel foes:
The painter was no god to lend her those;
And therefore Lucrece swears he did her wrong,
To give her so much grief and not a tongue.

'Poor instrument,' quoth she,'without a sound,
I'll tune thy woes with my lamenting tongue;
And drop sweet balm in Priam's painted wound,
And rail on Pyrrhus that hath done him wrong;
And with my tears quench Troy that burns so long;
And with my knife scratch out the angry eyes
Of all the Greeks that are thine enemies.

'Show me the strumpet that began this stir,
That with my nails her beauty I may tear.
Thy heat of lust, fond Paris, did incur
This load of wrath that burning Troy doth bear:
Thy eye kindled the fire that burneth here;
And here in Troy, for trespass of thine eye,
The sire, the son, the dame, and daughter die.

'Why should the private pleasure of some one
Become the public plague of many moe?
Let sin, alone committed, light alone
Upon his head that hath transgressed so;

Let guiltless souls be freed from guilty woe:
For one's offence why should so many fall,
To plague a private sin in general?

'Lo, here weeps Hecuba, here Priam dies,
Here manly Hector faints, here Troilus swounds,
Here friend by friend in bloody channel lies,
And friend to friend gives unadvised wounds,
And one man's lust these many lives confounds:
Had doting Priam cheque'd his son's desire,
Troy had been bright with fame and not with fire.' 1522

Here feelingly she weeps Troy's painted woes:
For sorrow, like a heavy-hanging bell,
Once set on ringing, with his own weight goes;
Then little strength rings out the doleful knell:
So Lucrece, set a-work, sad tales doth tell
To pencill'd pensiveness and colour'd sorrow;
She lends them words, and she their looks doth borrow.

She throws her eyes about the painting round,
And whom she finds forlorn she doth lament.
At last she sees a wretched image bound,
That piteous looks to Phrygian shepherds lent:
His face, though full of cares, yet show'd content;
Onward to Troy with the blunt swains he goes,
So mild, that Patience seem'd to scorn his woes.

In him the painter labour'd with his skill
To hide deceit, and give the harmless show
An humble gait, calm looks, eyes wailing still,
A brow unbent, that seem'd to welcome woe;
Cheeks neither red nor pale, but mingled so
That blushing red no guilty instance gave,
Nor ashy pale the fear that false hearts have.

But, like a constant and confirmed devil,
He entertain'd a show so seeming just,
And therein so ensconced his secret evil,
That jealousy itself could not mistrust
False-creeping craft and perjury should thrust
Into so bright a day such black-faced storms,
Or blot with hell-born sin such saint-like forms. 1552

The well-skill'd workman this mild image drew
For perjured Sinon, whose enchanting story
The credulous old Priam after slew;
Whose words like wildfire burnt the shining glory
Of rich-built Ilion, that the skies were sorry,
And little stars shot from their fixed places,
When their glass fell wherein they view'd their faces.

This picture she advisedly perused,
And chid the painter for his wondrous skill,
Saying, some shape in Sinon's was abused;
So fair a form lodged not a mind so ill: 1564
And still on him she gazed; and gazing still,
Such signs of truth in his plain face she spied,
That she concludes the picture was belied.

'It cannot be,' quoth she,'that so much guile'—
She would have said 'can lurk in such a look;'
But Tarquin's shape came in her mind the while,
And from her tongue 'can lurk' from 'cannot' took:
'It cannot be' she in that sense forsook,
And turn'd it thus,' It cannot be, I find,
But such a face should bear a wicked mind:

'For even as subtle Sinon here is painted.
So sober-sad, so weary, and so mild,
As if with grief or travail he had fainted,
To me came Tarquin armed; so beguiled
With outward honesty, but yet defiled
With inward vice: as Priam him did cherish,
So did I Tarquin; so my Troy did perish.

'Look, look, how listening Priam wets his eyes,
To see those borrow'd tears that Sinon sheds!
Priam, why art thou old and yet not wise?
For every tear he falls a Trojan bleeds:
His eye drops fire, no water thence proceeds;
Those round clear pearls of his, that move thy pity,
Are balls of quenchless fire to burn thy city.

'Such devils steal effects from lightless hell;
For Sinon in his fire doth quake with cold,
And in that cold hot-burning fire doth dwell;
These contraries such unity do hold,
Only to flatter fools and make them bold:
So Priam's trust false Sinon's tears doth flatter, 1595
That he finds means to burn his Troy with water.'

Here, all enraged, such passion her assails,
That patience is quite beaten from her breast.
She tears the senseless Sinon with her nails,
Comparing him to that unhappy guest
Whose deed hath made herself herself detest:
At last she smilingly with this gives o'er;
'Fool, fool!' quoth she, 'his wounds will not be sore.'

Thus ebbs and flows the current of her sorrow,
And time doth weary time with her complaining.
She looks for night, and then she longs for morrow,
And both she thinks too long with her remaining:
Short time seems long in sorrow's sharp sustaining:
Though woe be heavy, yet it seldom sleeps;
And they that watch see time how slow it creeps.

Which all this time hath overslipp'd her thought,
That she with painted images hath spent;
Being from the feeling of her own grief brought
By deep surmise of others' detriment;
Losing her woes in shows of discontent.
It easeth some, though none it ever cured,
To think their dolour others have endured.

But now the mindful messenger, come back,
Brings home his lord and other company;
Who finds his Lucrece clad in mourning black:
And round about her tear-stained eye
Blue circles stream'd; like rainbows in the sky:
These water-galls in her dim element
Foretell new storms to those already spent.

Which when her sad-beholding husband saw,
Amazedly in her sad face he stares:
Her eyes, though sod in tears, look'd red and raw,
Her lively colour kill'd with deadly cares.
He hath no power to ask her how she fares:
Both stood, like old acquaintance in a trance,
Met far from home, wondering each other's chance.

At last he takes her by the bloodless hand,
And thus begins: 'What uncouth ill event
Hath thee befall'n, that thou dost trembling stand?
Sweet love, what spite hath thy fair colour spent?
Why art thou thus attired in discontent?
Unmask, dear dear, this moody heaviness,
And tell thy grief, that we may give redress.'

Three times with sighs she gives her sorrow fire,
Ere once she can discharge one word of woe:
At length address'd to answer his desire,
She modestly prepares to let them know
Her honour is ta'en prisoner by the foe;
While Collatine and his consorted lords
With sad attention long to hear her words.

And now this pale swan in her watery nest
Begins the sad dirge of her certain ending;
'Few words,' quoth she, 'Shall fit the trespass best,
Where no excuse can give the fault amending:
In me moe woes than words are now depending;
And my laments would be drawn out too long,
To tell them all with one poor tired tongue.

'Then be this all the task it hath to say:
Dear husband, in the interest of thy bed
A stranger came, and on that pillow lay
Where thou was wont to rest thy weary head;
And what wrong else may be imagined
By foul enforcement might be done to me,
From that, alas, thy Lucrece is not free.

'For in the dreadful dead of dark midnight,
With shining falchion in my chamber came
A creeping creature, with a flaming light,
And softly cried "Awake, thou Roman dame,
And entertain my love; else lasting shame
On thee and thine this night I will inflict,
If thou my love's desire do contradict.

'For some hard-favour'd groom of thine,'
quoth he,
'Unless thou yoke thy liking to my will,
I'll murder straight, and then I'll slaughter thee
And swear I found you where you did fulfil
The loathsome act of lust, and so did kill
The lechers in their deed: this act will be
My fame and thy perpetual infamy."

'With this, I did begin to start and cry;
And then against my heart he sets his sword,
Swearing, unless I took all patiently,
I should not live to speak another word;
So should my shame still rest upon record,
And never be forgot in mighty Rome
Th' adulterate death of Lucrece and her groom.

'Mine enemy was strong, my poor self weak,
And far the weaker with so strong a fear:
My bloody judge forbade my tongue to speak;
No rightful plea might plead for justice there:
His scarlet lust came evidence to swear
That my poor beauty had purloin'd his eyes;
And when the judge is robb'd the prisoner dies.

'O, teach me how to make mine own excuse!
Or at the least this refuge let me find;
Though my gross blood be stain'd with this abuse,
Immaculate and spotless is my mind;
That was not forced; that never was inclined
To accessary yieldings, but still pure
Doth in her poison'd closet yet endure.'

Lo, here, the hopeless merchant of this loss,
With head declined, and voice damm'd up with woe, 1698
With sad set eyes, and wretched arms across, [15]
From lips new-waxen pale begins to blow
The grief away that stops his answer so:
But, wretched as he is, he strives in vain;
What he breathes out his breath drinks up again.

As through an arch the violent roaring tide
Outruns the eye that doth behold his haste,
Yet in the eddy boundeth in his pride 1706
Back to the strait that forced him on so fast;
In rage sent out, recall'd in rage, being past:
Even so his sighs, his sorrows, make a saw,
To push grief on, and back the same grief draw.

Which speechless woe of his poor she attendeth,
And his untimely frenzy thus awaketh:
'Dear lord, thy sorrow to my sorrow lendeth
Another power; no flood by raining slaketh.
My woe too sensible thy passion maketh
More feeling-painful: let it then suffice
To drown one woe, one pair of weeping eyes. 1717

'And for my sake, when I might charm thee so,
For she that was thy Lucrece, now attend me:
Be suddenly revenged on my foe,
Thine, mine, his own: suppose thou dost defend me
From what is past: the help that thou shalt lend me
Comes all too late, yet let the traitor die;
For sparing justice feeds iniquity.

'But ere I name him, you fair lords,' quoth she,
Speaking to those that came with Collatine,
'Shall plight your honourable faiths to me,
With swift pursuit to venge this wrong of mine;
For 'tis a meritorious fair design
To chase injustice with revengeful arms:
Knights, by their oaths, should right poor ladies' harms.'

At this request, with noble disposition
Each present lord began to promise aid,
As bound in knighthood to her imposition,
Longing to hear the hateful foe bewray'd.
But she, that yet her sad task hath not said,
The protestation stops. 'O, speak,' quoth she, 1738
'How may this forced stain be wiped from me?

'What is the quality of mine offence,
Being constrain'd with dreadful circumstance?
May my pure mind with the foul act dispense,
My low-declined honour to advance?
May any terms acquit me from this chance?
The poison'd fountain clears itself again;
And why not I from this compelled stain?'

With this, they all at once began to say, 1747
Her body's stain her mind untainted clears;
While with a joyless smile she turns away
The face, that map which deep impression bears
Of hard misfortune, carved in it with tears.
'No, no,' quoth she, 'no dame, hereafter living,
By my excuse shall claim excuse's giving.'

Here with a sigh, as if her heart would break,
She throws forth Tarquin's name: 'He, he,' she says,
But more than 'he' her poor tongue could not speak;
Till after many accents and delays,
Untimely breathings, sick and short assays,
She utters this, 'He, he, fair lords, 'tis he,
That guides this hand to give this wound to me.'

Even here she sheathed in her harmless breast
A harmful knife, that thence her soul unsheathed:
That blow did that it from the deep unrest
Of that polluted prison where it breathed:
Her contrite sighs unto the clouds bequeathed
Her winged sprite, and through her wounds doth fly
Life's lasting date from cancell'd destiny.

Stone-still, astonish'd with this deadly deed,
Stood Collatine and all his lordly crew; 1770
Till Lucrece' father, that beholds her bleed,
Himself on her self-slaughter'd body threw;
And from the purple fountain Brutus drew
The murderous knife, and, as it left the place,
Her blood, in poor revenge, held it in chase;

And bubbling from her breast, it doth divide
In two slow rivers, that the crimson blood
Circles her body in on every side,
Who, like a late-sack'd island, vastly stood
Bare and unpeopled in this fearful flood.
Some of her blood still pure and red remain'd,
And some look'd black, and that false Tarquin stain'd.

About the mourning and congealed face
Of that black blood a watery rigol goes,
Which seems to weep upon the tainted place:
And ever since, as pitying Lucrece' woes,

We will revenge the death of this true wife!

Corrupted blood some watery token shows;
 And blood untainted still doth red abide,
 Blushing at that which is so putrified.

'Daughter, dear daughter,' old Lucretius cries,
'That life was mine which thou hast here deprived.
If in the child the father's image lies,
Where shall I live now Lucrece is unlived?
Thou wast not to this end from me derived.
 If children pre-decease progenitors,
 We are their offspring, and they none of ours.

'Poor broken glass, I often did behold
In thy sweet semblance my old age new born;
But now that fresh fair mirror, dim and old,
Shows me a bare-boned death by time out-worn:
O, from thy cheeks my image thou hast torn,
 And shiver'd all the beauty of my glass,
 That I no more can see what once I was!

'O time, cease thou thy course and last no longer,
If they surcease to be that should survive.
Shall rotten death make conquest of the stronger
And leave the faltering feeble souls alive?
The old bees die, the young possess their hive:
 Then live, sweet Lucrece, live again and see
 Thy father die, and not thy father thee!'

By this, starts Collatine as from a dream,
And bids Lucretius give his sorrow place;
And then in key-cold Lucrece's bleeding stream
He falls, and bathes the pale fear in his face,
And counterfeits to die with her a space;
 Till manly shame bids him possess his breath
 And live to be revenged on her death.

The deep vexation of his inward soul
Hath served a dumb arrest upon his tongue;
Who, mad that sorrow should his use control,
Or keep him from heart-easing words so long,
Begins to talk; but through his lips do throng
 Weak words, so thick come in his poor heart's aid,
 That no man could distinguish what he said.

Yet sometime 'Tarquin' was pronounced plain,
But through his teeth, as if the name he tore.
This windy tempest, till it blow up rain,
Held back his sorrow's tide, to make it more;
At last it rains, and busy winds give o'er:
 Then son and father weep with equal strife
 Who should weep most, for daughter or for wife.

The one doth call her his, the other his,
Yet neither may possess the claim they lay.
The father says 'She's mine.' 'O, mine she is,'
Replies her husband: 'do not take away
My sorrow's interest; let no mourner say
 He weeps for her, for she was only mine,
 And only must be wail'd by Collatine.'

'O,' quoth Lucretius,' I did give that life
Which she too early and too late hath spill'd.'
'Woe, woe,' quoth Collatine, 'she was my wife,
I owed her, and 'tis mine that she hath kill'd.'

'My daughter' and 'my wife' with clamours fill'd
 The dispersed air, who, holding Lucrece' life,
 Answer'd their cries, 'my daughter' and 'my wife.'

Brutus, who pluck'd the knife from Lucrece's side,
Seeing such emulation in their woe,
Began to clothe his wit in state and pride,
Burying in Lucrece' wound his folly's show.
He with the Romans was esteemed so
 As silly-jeering idiots are with kings,
 For sportive words and uttering foolish things:

But now he throws that shallow habit by,
Wherein deep policy did him disguise;
And arm'd his long-hid wits advisedly,
To cheque the tears in Collatinus' eyes.
'Thou wronged lord of Rome,' quoth be, 'arise:
 Let my unsounded self, supposed a fool,
 Now set thy long-experienced wit to school.

'Why, Collatine, is woe the cure for woe?
Do wounds help wounds, or grief help grievous deeds?
Is it revenge to give thyself a blow
For his foul act by whom thy fair wife bleeds?
Such childish humour from weak minds proceeds:
 Thy wretched wife mistook the matter so,
 To slay herself, that should have slain her foe.

'Courageous Roman, do not steep thy heart
In such relenting dew of lamentations;
But kneel with me and help to bear thy part,
To rouse our Roman gods with invocations,
That they will suffer these abominations,
 Since Rome herself in them doth stand disgraced,
 By our strong arms from forth her fair streets chased.

'Now, by the Capitol that we adore,
And by this chaste blood so unjustly stain'd,
By heaven's fair sun that breeds the fat earth's store,
By all our country rights in Rome maintain'd,
And by chaste Lucrece's soul that late complain'd
 Her wrongs to us, and by this bloody knife,
 We will revenge the death of this true wife.'

This said, he struck his hand upon his breast,
And kiss'd the fatal knife, to end his vow;
And to his protestation urged the rest,
Who, wondering at him, did his words allow:
Then jointly to the ground their knees they bow;
 And that deep vow, which Brutus made before,
 He doth again repeat, and that they swore.

When they had sworn to this advised doom,
They did conclude to bear dead Lucrece thence;
To show her bleeding body thorough Rome,
And so to publish Tarquin's foul offence:
Which being done with speedy diligence,
 The Romans plausibly did give consent
 To Tarquin's everlasting banishment.

Notes

1. LUCRECE; 8. *'unhappily';* Quartos 1, 2, 3, *'unhap'ly.'*
2. Morning's; – Quarto 1 (Bodl. 1), *'morning.'*
3. Apologies; – Quarto 1 (Bodl. 1), *'appologie.'*
4. O'er; – Quartos 1, 2, 3, 'ore'; Quarto 4, *'or'e';* Malone (1780), *'or'* (*i.e.* gold).
5. Many emendations have been proposed to render clear the meaning of these lines, but no change is necessary: "the covetous have not, *i.e.* do not possess, that which they possess, longing for the possessions of others"; the second clause of line 137 is in apposition to the first.
6. Let; – Schmidt conjectured *'lest.'*
7. Ay, if; – early Quartos, *'I, if.'*
8. i.e. – "who, in consequence of their own misdeeds, look with indifference on the offences of others" (Schmidt).
9. Debt; – early Quartos, *'det'* (rhyming with *'fret'*); similarly 1. 696, *'balk';* Quartos, *'bauk'* (rhyming with *'hawk'*).
10. Misty; – Quartos 1, 2, *'mustie.'*
11. Guilty; – Malone, *'guiltless,'* but no change is necessary; Lucrece's self-reproach at first assigns the guilt to herself.
12. Perhaps we should read, *'injurious-shifting Time.'*
13. Descant'st; – Quartos, *'descants.'*
14. Court'sies; – Quartos, *'cursies.'*
15. Wretched; – S. Walker conjectured *'wreathed.'*

VENUS AND ADONIS

'Vilia miretur vulgus; mihi flavus Apollo
Pocula Castalia plena ministret aqua.'

TO THE
RIGHT HONOURABLE HENRY WRIOTHESLY,
EARL OF SOUTHAMPTON, AND BARON OF TICHFIELD.

RIGHT HONOURABLE,

I KNOW not how I shall offend in dedicating my unpolished lines to your lordship, nor how the world will censure me for choosing so strong a prop to support so weak a burden: only if your honour seem but pleased, I account myself highly praised, and vow to take advantage of all idle hours, till I have honoured you with some graver labour. But if the first heir of my invention prove deformed, I shall be sorry it had so noble a god-father, and never after ear so barren a land, for fear it yield me still so bad a harvest. I leave it to your honourable survey, and your honour to your heart's content; which I wish may always answer your own wish and the world's hopeful expectation.

Your honour's in all duty,
WILLIAM SHAKESPEARE.

EVEN as the sun with purple-colour'd face
Had ta'en his last leave of the weeping morn,
Rose-cheek'd Adonis hied him to the chase;
Hunting he loved, but love he laugh'd to scorn;
  Sick-thoughted Venus makes amain unto him,
  And like a bold-faced suitor 'gins to woo him.

'Thrice-fairer than myself,' thus she began,
'The field's chief flower, sweet above compare,
Stain to all nymphs, more lovely than a man,
More white and red than doves or roses are;
  Nature that made thee, with herself at strife,
  Saith that the world hath ending with thy life.

'Vouchsafe, thou wonder, to alight thy steed,
And rein his proud head to the saddle-bow;
If thou wilt deign this favour, for thy meed
A thousand honey secrets shalt thou know:
  Here come and sit, where never serpent hisses,
  And being set, I'll smother thee with kisses;

'And yet not cloy thy lips with loathed satiety,
But rather famish them amid their plenty,
Making them red and pale with fresh variety,
Ten kisses short as one, one long as twenty:
  A summer's day will seem an hour but short,
  Being wasted in such time-beguiling sport.'

With this she seizeth on his sweating palm,
The precedent of pith and livelihood,
And trembling in her passion, calls it balm,
Earth's sovereign salve to do a goddess good:
  Being so enraged, desire doth lend her force
  Courageously to pluck him from his horse.

Over one arm the lusty courser's rein,
Under her other was the tender boy,
Who blush'd and pouted in a dull disdain,
With leaden appetite, unapt to toy;
 She red and hot as coals of glowing fire,
 He red for shame, but frosty in desire.

The studded bridle on a ragged bough
Nimbly she fastens:—O, how quick is love!—
The steed is stalled up, and even now
To tie the rider she begins to prove:
 Backward she push'd him, as she would be thrust,
 And govern'd him in strength, though not in lust.

So soon was she along as he was down,
Each leaning on their elbows and their hips:
Now doth she stroke his cheek, now doth he frown,
And 'gins to chide, but soon she stops his lips;
And kissing speaks, with lustful language broken,
'If thou wilt chide, thy lips shall never open.'
He burns with bashful shame: she with her tears
Doth quench the maiden burning of his cheeks;
Then with her windy sighs and golden hairs
To fan and blow them dry again she seeks:
 He saith she is immodest, blames her 'miss;
 What follows more she murders with a kiss

Even as an empty eagle, sharp by fast,
Tires with her beak on feathers, flesh and bone,
Shaking her wings, devouring all in haste,
Till either gorge be stuff'd or prey be gone;
 Even so she kissed his brow, his cheek, his chin,
 And where she ends she doth anew begin.

Forced to content, but never to obey,
Panting he lies and breatheth in her face;
She feedeth on the steam as on a prey,
And calls it heavenly moisture, air of grace;
 Wishing her cheeks were gardens full of flowers,
 So they were dew'd with such distilling showers.

Look, how a bird lies tangled in a net,
So fasten'd in her arms Adonis lies;
Pure shame and awed resistance made him fret,
Which bred more beauty in his angry eyes:
 Rain added to a river that is rank
 Perforce will force it overflow the bank.

Still she entreats, and prettily entreats,
For to a pretty ear she tunes her tale;
Still is he sullen, still he lours and frets,
'Twixt crimson shame and anger ashy-pale:
 Being red, she loves him best; and being white,
 Her best is better'd with a more delight.

Look how he can, she cannot choose but love;
And by her fair immortal hand she swears,
From his soft bosom never to remove,
Till he take truce with her contending tears,
 Which long have rain'd, making her cheeks all wet;
 And one sweet kiss shall pay this countless debt.

Upon this promise did he raise his chin,
Like a dive-dapper peering through a wave,
Who, being look'd on, ducks as quickly in;
So offers he to give what she did crave;
 But when her lips were ready for his pay,
 He winks, and turns his lips another way.

Never did passenger in summer's heat
More thirst for drink than she for this good turn.
Her help she sees, but help she cannot get;
She bathes in water, yet her fire must burn:
 'O, pity,' 'gan she cry, 'flint-hearted boy!
 'Tis but a kiss I beg; why art thou coy?

'I have been woo'd, as I entreat thee now,
Even by the stern and direful god of war,
Whose sinewy neck in battle ne'er did bow,
Who conquers where he comes in every jar;
 Yet hath he been my captive and my slave,
 And begg'd for that which thou unask'd shalt have.

'Over my altars hath he hung his lance,
His batter'd shield, his uncontrolled crest,
And for my sake hath learn'd to sport and dance,
To toy, to wanton, dally, smile and jest,
 Scorning his churlish drum and ensign red,
 Making my arms his field, his tent my bed.

'Thus he that overruled I oversway'd,
Leading him prisoner in a red-rose chain:
Strong-tempered steel his stronger strength obey'd,
Yet was he servile to my coy disdain.
 O, be not proud, nor brag not of thy might,
 For mastering her that foil'd the god of fight!

'Touch but my lips with those fair lips of thine,—
Though mine be not so fair, yet are they red—
The kiss shall be thine own as well as mine.
What seest thou in the ground? hold up thy head:

Look in mine eye-balls, there thy beauty lies;
Then why not lips on lips, since eyes in eyes?

'Art thou ashamed to kiss? then wink again,
And I will wink; so shall the day seem night;
Love keeps his revels where they are but twain;
Be bold to play, our sport is not in sight:
These blue-vein'd violets whereon we lean
Never can blab, nor know not what we mean.

'The tender spring upon thy tempting lip
Shows thee unripe; yet mayst thou well be tasted:
Make use of time, let not advantage slip;
Beauty within itself should not be wasted: 130
Fair flowers that are not gather'd in their prime
Rot and consume themselves in little time.

'Were I hard-favour'd, foul, or wrinkled-old,
Ill-nurtured, crooked, churlish, harsh in voice,
O'erworn, despised, rheumatic and cold,
Thick-sighted, barren, lean and lacking juice,
Then mightst thou pause, for then I were not for thee;
But having no defects, why dost abhor me?

'Thou canst not see one wrinkle in my brow;
Mine eyes are gray and bright and quick in turning; 142
My beauty as the spring doth yearly grow,
My flesh is soft and plump, my marrow burning;
My smooth moist hand, were it with thy hand felt,
Would in thy palm dissolve, or seem to melt.

'Bid me discourse, I will enchant thine ear,
Or, like a fairy, trip upon the green,
Or, like a nymph, with long dishevell'd hair,
Dance on the sands, and yet no footing seen:
Love is a spirit all compact of fire,
Not gross to sink, but light, and will aspire.

'Witness this primrose bank whereon I lie;
These forceless flowers like sturdy trees support me;
Two strengthless doves will draw me through the sky,
From morn till night, even where I list to sport me:
Is love so light, sweet boy, and may it be
That thou shouldst think it heavy unto thee? [1]

'Is thine own heart to thine own face affected?
Can thy right hand seize love upon thy left?
Then woo thyself, be of thyself rejected,
Steal thine own freedom and complain on theft.
Narcissus so himself himself forsook, 163
And died to kiss his shadow in the brook.

'Torches are made to light, jewels to wear,
Dainties to taste, fresh beauty for the use,
Herbs for their smell, and sappy plants to bear,
Things growing to themselves are growth's abuse:
Seeds spring from seeds and beauty breedeth beauty;
Thou wast begot; to get it is thy duty.

'Upon the earth's increase why shouldst thou feed,
Unless the earth with thy increase be fed?
By law of nature thou art bound to breed, [2]
That thine may live when thou thyself art dead;
And so, in spite of death, thou dost survive,
In that thy likeness still is left alive.'

By this the love-sick queen began to sweat,
For where they lay the shadow had forsook them,
And Titan, tired in the mid-day heat,
With burning eye did hotly overlook them;
Wishing Adonis had his team to guide,
So he were like him and by Venus' side.

And now Adonis, with a lazy spright,
And with a heavy, dark, disliking eye,
His louring brows o'erwhelming his fair sight,
Like misty vapours when they blot the sky,
Souring his cheeks cries 'Fie, no more of love!
The sun doth burn my face; I must remove.'

'Ay me,' quoth Venus, 'young, and so unkind?
What bare excuses makest thou to be gone!
I'll sigh celestial breath, whose gentle wind
Shall cool the heat of this descending sun:
I'll make a shadow for thee of my hairs;
If they burn too, I'll quench them with my tears.

'The sun that shines from heaven shines but warm,
And, lo, I lie between that sun and thee:
The heat I have from thence doth little harm,
Thine eye darts forth the fire that burneth me;
And were I not immortal, life were done
Between this heavenly and earthly sun.

'Art thou obdurate, flinty, hard as steel,
Nay, more than flint, for stone at rain relenteth?
Art thou a woman's son, and canst not feel
What 'tis to love? how want of love tormenteth?
O, had thy mother borne so hard a mind,
She had not brought forth thee, but died unkind.

'What am I, that thou shouldst contemn me this?
Or what great danger dwells upon my suit?
What were thy lips the worse for one poor kiss?
Speak, fair; but speak fair words, or else be mute:
Give me one kiss, I'll give it thee again,
And one for interest, if thou wilt have twain.

'Fie, lifeless picture, cold and senseless stone, [3]
Well-painted idol, image dull and dead,
Statue contenting but the eye alone, [4]
Thing like a man, but of no woman bred!
Thou art no man, though of a man's complexion,
For men will kiss even by their own direction.'

This said, impatience chokes her pleading tongue,
And swelling passion doth provoke a pause;
Red cheeks and fiery eyes blaze forth her wrong;
Being judge in love, she cannot right her cause:
And now she weeps, and now she fain would speak,
And now her sobs do her intendments break.

Sometimes she shakes her head and then his hand,
Now gazeth she on him, now on the ground;
Sometimes her arms infold him like a band:
She would, he will not in her arms be bound;
And when from thence he struggles to be gone,
She locks her lily fingers one in one.

'Fondling,' she saith, 'since I have hemm'd thee here
Within the circuit of this ivory pale,
I'll be a park, and thou shalt be my deer; [5]
Feed where thou wilt, on mountain or in dale:
Graze on my lips; and if those hills be dry,
Stray lower, where the pleasant fountains lie.

'Within this limit is relief enough,
Sweet bottom-grass and high delightful plain,
Round rising hillocks, brakes obscure and rough,
To shelter thee from tempest and from rain:
Then be my deer, since I am such a park; [5]
No dog shall rouse thee, though a thousand bark.'

At this Adonis smiles as in disdain,
That in each cheek appears a pretty dimple:
Love made those hollows, if himself were slain,
He might be buried in a tomb so simple;
Foreknowing well, if there he came to lie,
Why, there Love lived and there he could not die.

These lovely caves, these round enchanting pits,
Open'd their mouths to swallow Venus' liking.
Being mad before, how doth she now for wits?
Struck dead at first, what needs a second striking?
Poor queen of love, in thine own law forlorn,
To love a cheek that smiles at thee in scorn!

Now which way shall she turn? what shall she say?
Her words are done, her woes are more increasing;
The time is spent, her object will away,
And from her twining arms doth urge releasing.
'Pity,' she cries, 'some favour, some remorse!'
Away he springs and hasteth to his horse.

But, lo, from forth a copse that neighbors by,
A breeding jennet, lusty, young and proud,
Adonis' trampling courser doth espy,
And forth she rushes, snorts and neighs aloud:
The strong-neck'd steed, being tied unto a tree,
Breaketh his rein, and to her straight goes he.

Imperiously he leaps, he neighs, he bounds,
And now his woven girths he breaks asunder;
The bearing earth with his hard hoof he wounds,
Whose hollow womb resounds like heaven's thunder;
The iron bit he crusheth 'tween his teeth,
Controlling what he was controlled with.

His ears up-prick'd; his braided hanging mane
Upon his compass'd crest now stand on end; [6]
His nostrils drink the air, and forth again,
As from a furnace, vapours doth he send:
His eye, which scornfully glisters like fire,
Shows his hot courage and his high desire.

Sometime he trots, as if he told the steps,
With gentle majesty and modest pride;
Anon he rears upright, curvets and leaps,
As who should say 'Lo, thus my strength is tried,
And this I do to captivate the eye
Of the fair breeder that is standing by.'

What recketh he his rider's angry stir, [7]
His flattering 'Holla,' or his 'Stand, I say'?
What cares he now for curb or pricking spur?
For rich caparisons or trapping gay?
He sees his love, and nothing else he sees,
For nothing else with his proud sight agrees.

Look, when a painter would surpass the life,
In limning out a well-proportion'd steed,
His art with nature's workmanship at strife,

As if the dead the living should exceed;
So did this horse excel a common one
In shape, in courage, colour, pace and bone.

Round-hoof'd, short-jointed, fetlocks shag and long,
Broad breast, full eye, small head and nostril wide,
High crest, short ears, straight legs and passing strong,
Thin mane, thick tail, broad buttock, tender hide:
Look, what a horse should have he did not lack,
Save a proud rider on so proud a back.

Sometime he scuds far off and there he stares;
Anon he starts at stirring of a feather;
To bid the wind a base he now prepares,
And whether he run or fly they know not whether; [8]
For through his mane and tail the high wind sings,
Fanning the hairs, who wave like feather'd wings.

He looks upon his love and neighs unto her;
She answers him as if she knew his mind:
Being proud, as females are, to see him woo her,
She puts on outward strangeness, seems unkind,
Spurns at his love and scorns the heat he feels,
Beating his kind embracements with her heels.

Then, like a melancholy malcontent,
He vails his tail that, like a falling plume,
Cool shadow to his melting buttock lent:
He stamps and bites the poor flies in his fume.
His love, perceiving how he is enraged,
Grew kinder, and his fury was assuaged.

His testy master goeth about to take him;
When, lo, the unback'd breeder, full of fear,
Jealous of catching, swiftly doth forsake him,
With her the horse, and left Adonis there:
As they were mad, unto the wood they hie them,
Out-stripping crows that strive to over-fly them.

All swoln with chafing, down Adonis sits,
Banning his boisterous and unruly beast:
And now the happy season once more fits,
That love-sick Love by pleading may be blest;
For lovers say, the heart hath treble wrong
When it is barr'd the aidance of the tongue.

An oven that is stopp'd, or river stay'd,
Burneth more hotly, swelleth with more rage:
So of concealed sorrow may be said;
Free vent of words love's fire doth assuage; [9]
But when the heart's attorney once is mute,
The client breaks, as desperate in his suit.

He sees her coming, and begins to glow,
Even as a dying coal revives with wind,
And with his bonnet hides his angry brow;
Looks on the dull earth with disturbed mind,
Taking no notice that she is so nigh,
For all askance he holds her in his eye.

O, what a sight it was, wistly to view
How she came stealing to the wayward boy!
To note the fighting conflict of her hue,
How white and red each other did destroy!
But now her cheek was pale, and by and by
It flash'd forth fire, as lightning from the sky.

Now was she just before him as he sat,
And like a lowly lover down she kneels;
With one fair hand she heaveth up his hat,
Her other tender hand his fair cheek feels: [10]
His tenderer cheek receives her soft hand's print,
As apt as new-fall'n snow takes any dint.

O, what a war of looks was then between them!
Her eyes petitioners to his eyes suing;
His eyes saw her eyes as they had not seen them;
Her eyes woo'd still, his eyes disdain'd the wooing:
And all this dumb play had his acts made plain
With tears, which, chorus-like, her eyes did rain.

Full gently now she takes him by the hand,
A lily prison'd in a gaol of snow, [11]
Or ivory in an alabaster band;
So white a friend engirts so white a foe:
This beauteous combat, wilful and unwilling,
Show'd like two silver doves that sit a-billing.

Once more the engine of her thoughts began:
'O fairest mover on this mortal round,
Would thou wert as I am, and I a man,
My heart all whole as thine, thy heart my wound;
For one sweet look thy help I would assure thee,
Though nothing but my body's bane would cure thee.'

'Give me my hand,' saith he, 'why dost thou feel it?'
'Give me my heart,' saith she, 'and thou shalt have it;
O, give it me, lest thy hard heart do steel it,
And being steel'd, soft sighs can never grave it:
Then love's deep groans I never shall regard,
Because Adonis' heart hath made mine hard.

'For shame,' he cries, 'let go, and let me go;
My day's delight is past, my horse is gone,

And 'tis your fault I am bereft him so:
I pray you hence, and leave me here alone;
For all my mind, my thought, my busy care,
Is how to get my palfrey from the mare.'

Thus she replies: 'Thy palfrey, as he should,
Welcomes the warm approach of sweet desire:
Affection is a coal that must be cool'd;
Else, suffer'd, it will set the heart on fire:
The sea hath bounds, but deep desire hath none;
Therefore no marvel though thy horse be gone.

'How like a jade he stood, tied to the tree,
Servilely master'd with a leathern rein! [12]
But when he saw his love, his youth's fair fee,
He held such petty bondage in disdain;
Throwing the base thong from his bending crest,
Enfranchising his mouth, his back, his breast.
'Who sees his true-love in her naked bed,
Teaching the sheets a whiter hue than white,
But, when his glutton eye so full hath fed,
His other agents aim at like delight?
Who is so faint, that dares not be so bold
To touch the fire, the weather being cold? [9]

'Let me excuse thy courser, gentle boy;
And learn of him, I heartily beseech thee,
To take advantage on presented joy;
Though I were dumb, yet his proceedings teach thee:
O, learn to love; the lesson is but plain,
And once made perfect, never lost again.'

'I know not love,' quoth he, 'nor will not know it,
Unless it be a boar, and then I chase it;
'Tis much to borrow, and I will not owe it;
My love to love is love but to disgrace it;
For I have heard it is a life in death,
That laughs and weeps, and all but with a breath.

'Who wears a garment shapeless and unfinish'd?
Who plucks the bud before one leaf put forth?
If springing things be any jot diminish'd,
They wither in their prime, prove nothing worth:
The colt that's back'd and burden'd being young
Loseth his pride and never waxeth strong.

'You hurt my hand with wringing; let us part,
And leave this idle theme, this bootless chat:
Remove your siege from my unyielding heart;
To love's alarms it will not ope the gate:
Dismiss your vows, your feigned tears, your flattery;
For where a heart is hard they make no battery.'

'What! canst thou talk?' quoth she, 'hast thou a tongue?
O, would thou hadst not, or I had no hearing!
Thy mermaid's voice hath done me double wrong; [13]
I had my load before, now press'd with bearing:
Melodious discord, heavenly tune harshsounding,
Ear's deep-sweet music, and heart's deep-sore wounding.

'Had I no eyes but ears, my ears would love
That inward beauty and invisible; [14]
Or were I deaf, thy outward parts would move
Each part in me that were but sensible:
Though neither eyes nor ears, to hear nor see,
Yet should I be in love by touching thee.

'Say, that the sense of feeling were bereft me,
And that I could not see, nor hear, nor touch,
And nothing but the very smell were left me,
Yet would my love to thee be still as much;
For from the stillitory of thy face excelling
Comes breath perfumed that breedeth love by smelling.

'But, O, what banquet wert thou to the taste,
Being nurse and feeder of the other four!
Would they not wish the feast might ever last,
And bid Suspicion double-lock the door,
Lest Jealousy, that sour unwelcome guest,
Should, by his stealing in, disturb the feast?'

Once more the ruby-colour'd portal open'd,
Which to his speech did honey passage yield;
Like a red morn, that ever yet betoken'd
Wreck to the seaman, tempest to the field, [15]
Sorrow to shepherds, woe unto the birds,
Gusts and foul flaws to herdmen and to herds.

This ill presage advisedly she marketh:
Even as the wind is hush'd before it raineth,
Or as the wolf doth grin before he barketh,
Or as the berry breaks before it staineth,
Or like the deadly bullet of a gun,
His meaning struck her ere his words begun.

And at his look she flatly falleth down,
For looks kill love and love by looks reviveth;
A smile recures the wounding of a frown;
But blessed bankrupt, that by love so thriveth! [16, 17]
The silly boy, believing she is dead,
Claps her pale cheek, till clapping makes it red;

And all amazed brake off his late intent,
For sharply he did think to reprehend her,

Which cunning love did wittily prevent:
Fair fall the wit that can so well defend her!
For on the grass she lies as she were slain,
Till his breath breatheth life in her again.

He wrings her nose, he strikes her on the cheeks,
He bends her fingers, holds her pulses hard,
He chafes her lips; a thousand ways he seeks
To mend the hurt that his unkindness marr'd:
He kisses her; and she, by her good will,
Will never rise, so he will kiss her still.
The night of sorrow now is turn'd to day:
Her two blue windows faintly she up-heaveth,
Like the fair sun, when in his fresh array
He cheers the morn and all the earth relieveth;
And as the bright sun glorifies the sky,
So is her face illumined with her eye;

Whose beams upon his hairless face are fix'd,
As if from thence they borrow'd all their shine.
Were never four such lamps together mix'd,
Had not his clouded with his brow's repine;
But hers, which through the crystal tears gave light,
Shone like the moon in water seen by night.

'O, where am I?' quoth she, 'in earth or heaven,
Or in the ocean drench'd, or in the fire?
What hour is this? or morn or weary even?
Do I delight to die, or life desire?
But now I lived, and life was death's annoy;
But now I died, and death was lively joy.

'O, thou didst kill me: kill me once again:
Thy eyes' shrewd tutor, that hard heart of thine,
Hath taught them scornful tricks and such disdain
That they have murder'd this poor heart of mine;
And these mine eyes, true leaders to their queen,
But for thy piteous lips no more had seen.

'Long may they kiss each other, for this cure!
O, never let their crimson liveries wear!
And as they last, their verdure still endure, [18]
To drive infection from the dangerous year!
That the star-gazers, having writ on death,
May say, the plague is banish'd by thy breath.

'Pure lips, sweet seals in my soft lips imprinted,
What bargains may I make, still to be sealing?
To sell myself I can be well contented,
So thou wilt buy and pay and use good dealing;
Which purchase if thou make, for fear of slips
Set thy seal-manual on my wax-red lips.

'A thousand kisses buys my heart from me;
And pay them at thy leisure, one by one.
What is ten hundred touches unto thee?
Are they not quickly told and quickly gone?
Say, for non-payment that the debt should double,

Is twenty hundred kisses such a trouble?
'Fair queen,' quoth he, 'if any love you owe me,
Measure my strangeness with my unripe years:
Before I know myself, seek not to know me;
No fisher but the ungrown fry forbears:
The mellow plum doth fall, the green sticks fast,
Or being early pluck'd is sour to taste.

'Look, the world's comforter, with weary gait, [19]
His day's hot task hath ended in the west;
The owl, night's herald, shrieks, "'Tis very late;"
The sheep are gone to fold, birds to their nest,
And coal-black clouds that shadow heaven's light
Do summon us to part and bid good night.

'Now let me say "Good night," and so say you;
If you will say so, you shall have a kiss.'
'Good night,' quoth she, and, ere he says 'Adieu,'
The honey fee of parting tender'd is:
Her arms do lend his neck a sweet embrace;
Incorporate then they seem; face grows to face.

Till, breathless, he disjoin'd, and backward drew
The heavenly moisture, that sweet coral mouth,
Whose precious taste her thirsty lips well knew,
Whereon they surfeit, yet complain on drouth:
He with her plenty press'd, she faint with dearth
Their lips together glued, fall to the earth.

Now quick desire hath caught the yielding prey, [20]
And glutton-like she feeds, yet never filleth;
Her lips are conquerors, his lips obey,
Paying what ransom the insulter willeth;
Whose vulture thought doth pitch the price so high,
That she will draw his lips' rich treasure dry:

And having felt the sweetness of the spoil,
With blindfold fury she begins to forage;
Her face doth reek and smoke, her blood doth boil,
And careless lust stirs up a desperate courage;
Planting oblivion, beating reason back,
Forgetting shame's pure blush and honour's wrack.

Hot, faint, and weary, with her hard embracing,
Like a wild bird being tamed with too much handling,

Or as the fleet-foot roe that's tired with chasing,
Or like the froward infant still'd with dandling,
He now obeys, and now no more resisteth,
While she takes all she can, not all she listeth.
What wax so frozen but dissolves with tempering,

And yields at last to every light impression?
Things out of hope are compass'd oft with venturing, [21]
Chiefly in love, whose leave exceeds commission:
Affection faints not like a pale-faced coward,
But then woos best when most his choice is froward.

When he did frown, O, had she then gave over,
Such nectar from his lips she had not suck'd.
Foul words and frowns must not repel a lover;
What though the rose have prickles, yet 'tis pluck'd:
Were beauty under twenty locks kept fast,
Yet love breaks through and picks them all at last.

For pity now she can no more detain him;
The poor fool prays her that he may depart:
She is resolved no longer to restrain him;
Bids him farewell, and look well to her heart,
The which, by Cupid's bow she doth protest,
He carries thence incaged in his breast.

'Sweet boy,' she says, 'this night I'll waste in sorrow,
For my sick heart commands mine eyes to watch.
Tell me, Love's master, shall we meet to-morrow?
Say, shall we? shall we? wilt thou make the match?'
He tells her, no; to-morrow he intends
To hunt the boar with certain of his friends.

'The boar!' quoth she; whereat a sudden pale,
Like lawn being spread upon the blushing rose,
Usurps her cheek; she trembles at his tale,
And on his neck her yoking arms she throws:
She sinketh down, still hanging by his neck,
He on her belly falls, she on her back.

Now is she in the very lists of love,
Her champion mounted for the hot encounter:
All is imaginary she doth prove,
He will not manage her, although he mount her;
That worse than Tantalus' is her annoy, [22]
To clip Elysium and to lack her joy.

Even as poor birds, deceived with painted grapes,
Do surfeit by the eye and pine the maw,
Even so she languisheth in her mishaps,
As those poor birds that helpless berries saw.
The warm effects which she in him finds missing
She seeks to kindle with continual kissing.

But all in vain; good queen, it will not be:
She hath assay'd as much as may be proved;
Her pleading hath deserved a greater fee;
She's Love, she loves, and yet she is not loved.
'Fie, fie,' he says, 'you crush me; let me go;
You have no reason to withhold me so.'

'Thou hadst been gone,' quoth she, 'sweet boy, ere this,
But that thou told'st me thou wouldst hunt the boar.
O, be advised! thou know'st not what it is
With javelin's point a churlish swine to gore,
Whose tushes never sheathed he whetteth still,
Like to a mortal butcher bent to kill.

'On his bow-back he hath a battle set
Of bristly pikes, that ever threat his foes;
His eyes, like glow-worms, shine when he doth fret;
His snout digs sepulchres where'er he goes;
Being moved, he strikes whate'er is in his way,
And whom he strikes his crooked tushes slay.

'His brawny sides, with hairy bristles arm'd,
Are better proof than thy spear's point can enter;
His short thick neck cannot be easily harm'd;
Being ireful, on the lion he will venture: [23]
The thorny brambles and embracing bushes,
As fearful of him, part, through whom he rushes.

'Alas, he nought esteems that face of thine,
To which Love's eyes pay tributary gazes; [24]
Nor thy soft hands, sweet lips and crystal eyne,
Whose full perfection all the world amazes;
But having thee at vantage,—wondrous dread!—
Would root these beauties as he roots the mead.

'O, let him keep his loathsome cabin still;
Beauty hath nought to do with such foul fiends:
Come not within his danger by thy will;
They that thrive well take counsel of their friends.
When thou didst name the boar, not to dissemble,
I fear'd thy fortune, and my joints did tremble.

'Didst thou not mark my face? was it not white?
Saw'st thou not signs of fear lurk in mine eye?
Grew I not faint? and fell I not downright?
Within my bosom, whereon thou dost lie,
My boding heart pants, beats, and takes no rest,
But, like an earthquake, shakes thee on my breast.

'For where Love reigns, disturbing Jealousy
Doth call himself Affection's sentinel;
Gives false alarms, suggesteth mutiny,
And in a peaceful hour doth cry "Kill, kill!"
Distempering gentle Love in his desire,
As air and water do abate the fire.

'This sour informer, this bate-breeding spy,
This canker that eats up Love's tender spring,
This carry-tale, dissentious Jealousy,
That sometime true news, sometime false doth bring,
Knocks at my heat and whispers in mine ear
That if I love thee, I thy death should fear:

'And more than so, presenteth to mine eye
The picture of an angry-chafing boar,
Under whose sharp fangs on his back doth lie
An image like thyself, all stain'd with gore;
Whose blood upon the fresh flowers being shed
Doth make them droop with grief and hang the head.

'What should I do, seeing thee so indeed,
That tremble at the imagination?
The thought of it doth make my faint heart bleed,
And fear doth teach it divination:
I prophesy thy death, my living sorrow,
If thou encounter with the boar to-morrow.

'But if thou needs wilt hunt, be ruled by me;
Uncouple at the timorous flying hare,
Or at the fox which lives by subtlety,
Or at the roe which no encounter dare:
Pursue these fearful creatures o'er the downs,
And on thy well-breath'd horse keep with thy
hounds.

'And when thou hast on foot the purblind hare,
Mark the poor wretch, to overshoot his troubles [25]
How he outruns the wind and with what care
He cranks and crosses with a thousand doubles:
The many musets through the which he goes
Are like a labyrinth to amaze his foes.

'Sometime he runs among a flock of sheep,
To make the cunning hounds mistake their smell,
And sometime where earth-delving conies keep,
To stop the loud pursuers in their yell,
And sometime sorteth with a herd of deer: [5]
Danger deviseth shifts; wit waits on fear:

'For there his smell with others being mingled,
The hot scent-snuffing hounds are driven to doubt,
Ceasing their clamorous cry till they have singled
With much ado the cold fault cleanly out;
Then do they spend their mouths: Echo replies,
As if another chase were in the skies.

'By this, poor Wat, far off upon a hill,
Stands on his hinder legs with listening ear,
To harken if his foes pursue him still:
Anon their loud alarums he doth hear;
And now his grief may be compared well
To one sore sick that hears the passing-bell.

'Then shalt thou see the dew-bedabbled wretch
Turn, and return, indenting with the way;
Each envious brier his weary legs doth scratch, [26]
Each shadow makes him stop, each murmur stay:
For misery is trodden on by many,
And being low never relieved by any.

'Lie quietly, and hear a little more;
Nay, do not struggle, for thou shalt not rise:
To make thee hate the hunting of the boar,
Unlike myself thou hear'st me moralize,
Applying this to that, and so to so;
For love can comment upon every woe.

Where did I leave?' 'No matter where;' quoth he,
Leave me, and then the story aptly ends:
The night is spent.' 'Why, what of that?' quoth she.
I am,' quoth he, 'expected of my friends;
And now 'tis dark, and going I shall fall.'
'In night,' quoth she, 'desire sees best of all

But if thou fall, O, then imagine this,
The earth, in love with thee, thy footing trips,
And all is but to rob thee of a kiss.
Rich preys make true men thieves; so do thy lips
Make modest Dian cloudy and forlorn,
Lest she should steal a kiss and die forsworn.

'Now of this dark night I perceive the reason:
Cynthia for shame obscures her silver shine,
Till forging Nature be condemn'd of treason,
For stealing moulds from heaven that were divine;
Wherein she framed thee in high heaven's despite,
To shame the sun by day and her by night.

And therefore hath she bribed the Destinies
To cross the curious workmanship of nature,
To mingle beauty with infirmities,
And pure perfection with impure defeature,

Making it subject to the tyranny
Of mad mischances and much misery;

'As burning fevers, agues pale and faint,
Life-poisoning pestilence and frenzies wood,
The marrow-eating sickness, whose attaint
Disorder breeds by heating of the blood:
Surfeits, imposthumes, grief, and damn'd despair, [27]
Swear Nature's death for framing thee so fair.

'And not the least of all these maladies
But in one minute's fight brings beauty under:
Both favour, savour, hue and qualities,
Whereat the impartial gazer late did wonder,
Are on the sudden wasted, thaw'd and done,
As mountain-snow melts with the midday sun.

'Therefore, despite of fruitless chastity,
Love-lacking vestals and self-loving nuns,
That on the earth would breed a scarcity
And barren dearth of daughters and of sons,
Be prodig3al: the lamp that burns by night
Dries up his oil to lend the world his light.

'What is thy body but a swallowing grave,
Seeming to bury that posterity
Which by the rights of time thou needs must have.
If thou destroy them not in dark obscurity?
If so, the world will hold thee in disdain,
Sith in thy pride so fair a hope is slain.

'So in thyself thyself art made away;
A mischief worse than civil home-bred strife,
Or theirs whose desperate hands themselves do slay,
Or butcher-sire that reaves his son of life.
Foul-cankering rust the hidden treasure frets,
But gold that's put to use more gold begets.'

'Nay, then,' quoth Adon, 'you will fall again
Into your idle over-handled theme:
The kiss I gave you is bestow'd in vain,
And all in vain you strive against the stream;
For, by this black-faced night, desire's foul nurse,
Your treatise makes me like you worse and worse.

If love lent you twenty thousand tongues,
And every tongue more moving than your own,
Bewitching like the wanton mermaid's songs,
Yet from mine ear the tempting tune is blown;
For know, my heart stands armed in mine ear,
And will not let a false sound enter there;

'Lest the deceiving harmony should run [28]
Into the quiet closure of my breast;
And then my little heart were quite undone,
In his bedchamber to be barr'd of rest.
No, lady, no; my heart longs not to groan,
But soundly sleeps, while now it sleeps alone.

'What have you urged that I cannot reprove?
The path is smooth that leadeth on to danger:
I hate not love, but your device in love,
That lends embracements unto every stranger.
You do it for increase: O strange excuse,
When reason is the bawd to lust's abuse!

'Call it not love, for Love to heaven is fled,
Since sweating Lust on earth usurp'd his name;
Under whose simple semblance he hath fed
Upon fresh beauty, blotting it with blame;
Which the hot tyrant stains and soon bereaves,
As caterpillars do the tender leaves.

'Love comforteth like sunshine after rain,
But Lust's effect is tempest after sun;
Love's gentle spring doth always fresh remain,
Lust's winter comes ere summer half be done:
Love surfeits not, Lust like a glutton dies;
Love is all truth, Lust full of forged lies.

'More I could tell, but more I dare not say;
The text is old, the orator too green.
Therefore, in sadness, now I will away;
My face is full of shame, my heart of teen:
Mine ears, that to your wanton talk attended,
Do burn themselves for having so offended.'

With this, he breaketh from the sweet embrace
Of those fair arms which bound him to her breast,
And homeward through the dark laund runs apace;
Leaves Love upon her back deeply distress'd.
Look, how a bright star shooteth from the sky,
So glides he in the night from Venus' eye.

Which after him she darts, as one on shore
Gazing upon a late-embarked friend,
Till the wild waves will have him seen no more,
Whose ridges with the meeting clouds contend:
So did the merciless and pitchy night
Fold in the object that did feed her sight.

Whereat amazed, as one that unaware
Hath dropp'd a precious jewel in the flood,
Or stonish'd as night-wanderers often are,
Their light blown out in some mistrustful wood,

Even so confounded in the dark she lay,
Having lost the fair discovery of her way.

And now she beats her heart, whereat it groans,
That all the neighbour caves, as seeming troubled,
Make verbal repetition of her moans;
Passion on passion deeply is redoubled: [29]
'Ay me!' she cries, and twenty times 'Woe, woe!'
And twenty echoes twenty times cry so.

She marking them begins a wailing note
And sings extemporally a woeful ditty;
How love makes young men thrall and old men dote;
How love is wise in folly, foolish-witty:
Her heavy anthem still concludes in woe,
And still the choir of echoes answer so.

Her song was tedious and outwore the night,
For lovers' hours are long, though seeming short:
If pleased themselves, others, they think, delight
In such-like circumstance, with such-like sport
Their copious stories oftentimes begun
End without audience and are never done.

For who hath she to spend the night withal
But idle sounds resembling parasites,
Like shrill-tongued tapsters answering every call,
Soothing the humour of fantastic wits?
She says ''Tis so:' they answer all ''Tis so;'
And would say after her, if she said 'No.'

Lo, here the gentle lark, weary of rest,
From his moist cabinet mounts up on high,
And wakes the morning, from whose silver breast
The sun ariseth in his majesty;
Who doth the world so gloriously behold
That cedar-tops and hills seem burnish'd gold.

Venus salutes him with this fair good-morrow:
'O thou clear god, and patron of all light,
From whom each lamp and shining star doth borrow
The beauteous influence that makes him bright,
There lives a son that suck'd an earthly mother,
May lend thee light, as thou dost lend to other.'

This said, she hasteth to a myrtle grove,
Musing the morning is so much o'erworn,
And yet she hears no tidings of her love:
She hearkens for his hounds and for his horn:
Anon she hears them chant it lustily,
And all in haste she coasteth to the cry.

And as she runs, the bushes in the way
Some catch her by the neck, some kiss her face,
Some twine about her thigh to make her stay:
She wildly breaketh from their strict embrace,
Like a milch doe, whose swelling dugs do ache,
Hasting to feed her fawn hid in some brake.

By this, she hears the hounds are at a bay;
Whereat she starts, like one that spies an adder
Wreathed up in fatal folds just in his way,
The fear whereof doth make him shake and shudder;
Even so the timorous yelping of the hounds
Appals her senses and her spirit confounds.

For now she knows it is no gentle chase,
But the blunt boar, rough bear, or lion proud,
Because the cry remaineth in one place,
Where fearfully the dogs exclaim aloud:
Finding their enemy to be so curst,
They all strain courtesy who shall cope him first.
This dismal cry rings sadly in her ear,
Through which it enters to surprise her heart;
Who, overcome by doubt and bloodless fear,
With cold-pale weakness numbs each feeling part:
Like soldiers, when their captain once doth yield,
They basely fly and dare not stay the field.

Thus stands she in a trembling ecstasy;
Till, cheering up her senses all dismay'd,
She tells them 'tis a causeless fantasy,
And childish error, that they are afraid;
Bids them leave quaking, bids them fear no more:—
And with that word she spied the hunted boar,

Whose frothy mouth, bepainted all with red,
Like milk and blood being mingled both together, [30]
A second fear through all her sinews spread,
Which madly hurries her she knows not whither:
This way runs, and now she will no further,
But back retires to rate the boar for murther.

A thousand spleens bear her a thousand ways;
She treads the path that she untreads again;
Her more than haste is mated with delays,
Like the proceedings of a drunken brain,
Full of respects, yet nought at all respecting;
In hand with all things, nought at all effecting.

Here kennell'd in a brake she finds a hound,
And asks the weary caitiff for his master,

And there another licking of his wound,
'Gainst venom'd sores the only sovereign plaster;
 And here she meets another sadly scowling,
 To whom she speaks, and he replies with howling.

When he hath ceased his ill-resounding noise,
Another flap-mouth'd mourner, black and grim,
Against the welkin volleys out his voice;
Another and another answer him,
 Clapping their proud tails to the ground below,
 Shaking their scratch'd ears, bleeding as they go.

Look, how the world's poor people are amazed
At apparitions, signs and prodigies,
Whereon with fearful eyes they long have gazed,
Infusing them with dreadful prophecies;
So she at these sad signs draws up her breath
And sighing it again, exclaims on Death.
'Hard-favour'd tyrant, ugly, meagre, lean,
Hateful divorce of love,'—thus chides she Death,—
'Grim-grinning ghost, earth's worm, what dost thou mean
To stifle beauty and to steal his breath,
 Who when he lived, his breath and beauty set
 Gloss on the rose, smell to the violet?

'If he be dead,—O no, it cannot be,
Seeing his beauty, thou shouldst strike at it:—
O yes, it may; thou hast no eyes to see,
But hatefully at random dost thou hit. [31]
 Thy mark is feeble age, but thy false dart
 Mistakes that aim and cleaves an infant's heart.

'Hadst thou but bid beware, then he had spoke,
And, hearing him, thy power had lost his power.
The Destinies will curse thee for this stroke;
They bid thee crop a weed, thou pluck'st a flower:
 Love's golden arrow at him should have fled,
 And not Death's ebon dart, to strike dead.

'Dost thou drink tears, that thou provokest such weeping?
What may a heavy groan advantage thee?
Why hast thou cast into eternal sleeping
Those eyes that taught all other eyes to see?
 Now Nature cares not for thy mortal vigour,
 Since her best work is ruin'd with thy rigour.'

Here overcome, as one full of despair,
She vail'd her eyelids, who, like sluices, stopt
The crystal tide that from her two cheeks fair
In the sweet channel of her bosom dropt;
 But through the flood-gates breaks the silver rain,
 And with his strong course opens them again.

O, how her eyes and tears did lend and borrow!
Her eyes seen in the tears, tears in her eye;
Both crystals, where they view'd each other's sorrow,
Sorrow that friendly sighs sought still to dry;
 But like a stormy day, now wind, now rain,
 Sighs dry her cheeks, tears make them wet again.

Variable passions throng her constant woe,
As striving who should best become her grief;
All entertain'd, each passion labours so,
That every present sorrow seemeth chief,
 But none is best: then join they all together,
 Like many clouds consulting for foul weather.

By this, far off she hears some huntsman hollo;
A nurse's song ne'er pleased her babe so well:
The dire imagination she did follow
This sound of hope doth labour to expel;
 For now reviving joy bids her rejoice,
 And flatters her it is Adonis' voice.

Whereat her tears began to turn their tide,
Being prison'd in her eye like pearls in glass;
Yet sometimes falls an orient drop beside,
Which her cheek melts, as scorning it should pass,
To wash the foul face of the sluttish ground,
Who is but drunken when she seemeth drown'd.

O hard-believing love, how strange it seems
Not to believe, and yet too credulous!
Thy weal and woe are both of them extremes;
Despair and hope makes thee ridiculous:
 The one doth flatter thee in thoughts unlikely,
 In likely thoughts the other kills thee quickly.

Now she unweaves the web that she hath wrought;
Adonis lives, and Death is not to blame;
It was not she that call'd him, all to naught: [32]
Now she adds honours to his hateful name;
 She clepes him king of graves and grave for kings,
 Imperious supreme of all mortal things.

'No, no,' quoth she, 'sweet Death, I did but jest;
Yet pardon me I felt a kind of fear
When as I met the boar, that bloody beast,
Which knows no pity, but is still severe;
Then, gentle shadow,—truth I must confess,—
I rail'd on thee, fearing my love's decease. [33]

'Tis not my fault: the boar provoked my tongue;
Be wreak'd on him, invisible commander;
'Tis he, foul creature, that hath done thee wrong;
I did but act, he's author of thy slander:
  Grief hath two tongues, and never woman yet
  Could rule them both without ten women's wit.'

Thus hoping that Adonis is alive,
Her rash suspect she doth extenuate;
And that his beauty may the better thrive,
With Death she humbly doth insinuate;
  Tells him of trophies, statues, tombs, and stories [34]
  His victories, his triumphs and his glories.

'O Jove,' quoth she, 'how much a fool was I
To be of such a weak and silly mind
To wail his death who lives and must not die
Till mutual overthrow of mortal kind!
  For he being dead, with him is beauty slain,
  And, beauty dead, black chaos comes again.

'Fie, fie, fond love, thou art so full of fear
As one with treasure laden, hemm'd with thieves;
Trifles, unwitnessed with eye or ear,
Thy coward heart with false bethinking grieves.'
  Even at this word she hears a merry horn,
  Whereat she leaps that was but late forlorn.

As falcon to the lure, away she flies;
The grass stoops not, she treads on it so light;
And in her haste unfortunately spies
The foul boar's conquest on her fair delight;
  Which seen, her eyes, as murder'd with the view,
  Like stars ashamed of day, themselves withdrew;

Or, as the snail, whose tender horns being hit,
Shrinks backward in his shelly cave with pain,
And there, all smother'd up, in shade doth sit,
Long after fearing to creep forth again;
  So, at his bloody view, her eyes are fled
  Into the deep dark cabins of her head:

Where they resign their office and their light
To the disposing of her troubled brain;
Who bids them still consort with ugly night, [35]
And never wound the heart with looks again;
  Who like a king perplexed in his throne,
  By their suggestion gives a deadly groan,

Whereat each tributary subject quakes;
As when the wind, imprison'd in the ground,
Struggling for passage, earth's foundation shakes,
Which with cold terror doth men's minds confound.
  This mutiny each part doth so surprise
  That from their dark beds once more leap her eyes;

And, being open'd, threw unwilling light
Upon the wide wound that the boar had trench'd
In his soft flank; whose wonted lily white
With purple tears, that his wound wept, was drench'd:
  No flower was nigh, no grass, herb, leaf, or weed,
  But stole his blood and seem'd with him to bleed.

This solemn sympathy poor Venus noteth;
Over one shoulder doth she hang her head;
Dumbly she passions, franticly she doteth;
She thinks he could not die, he is not dead:
  Her voice is stopt, her joints forget to bow;
  Her eyes are mad that they have wept till now.

Upon his hurt she looks so steadfastly,
That her sight dazzling makes the wound seem three;
And then she reprehends her mangling eye,
That makes more gashes where no breach should be:
  His face seems twain, each several limb is doubled; [36]
  For oft the eye mistakes, the brain being troubled.

'My tongue cannot express my grief for one,
And yet,' quoth she, 'behold two Adons dead!
My sighs are blown away, my salt tears gone,
Mine eyes are turn'd to fire, my heart to lead:
  Heavy heart's lead, melt at mine eyes' red fire!
  So shall I die by drops of hot desire.

'Alas, poor world, what treasure hast thou lost!
What face remains alive that's worth the viewing?
Whose tongue is music now? what canst thou boast
Of things long since, or any thing ensuing?
  The flowers are sweet, their colours fresh and trim;
  But true-sweet beauty lived and died with him.

'Bonnet nor veil henceforth no creature wear!
Nor sun nor wind will ever strive to kiss you:
Having no fair to lose, you need not fear;
The sun doth scorn you and the wind doth hiss you:
  But when Adonis lived, sun and sharp air
  Lurk'd like two thieves, to rob him of his fair:

'And therefore would he put his bonnet on,
Under whose brim the gaudy sun would peep;

'Alas, poor world, what treasure hast thou lost!

The wind would blow it off and, being gone,
Play with his locks: then would Adonis weep;
 And straight, in pity of his tender years,
 They both would strive who first should dry his tears.

To see his face the lion walk'd along
Behind some hedge, because he would not fear him;
To recreate himself when he hath sung,
The tiger would be tame and gently hear him;
 If he had spoke, the wolf would leave his prey
 And never fright the silly lamb that day.

'When he beheld his shadow in the brook,
The fishes spread on it their golden gills;
When he was by, the birds such pleasure took,
That some would sing, some other in their bills
 Would bring him mulberries and ripe-red cherries;
 He fed them with his sight, they him with berries.

'But this foul, grim, and urchin-snouted boar,
Whose downward eye still looketh for a grave,
Ne'er saw the beauteous livery that he wore;
Witness the entertainment that he gave:
 If he did see his face, why then I know
 He thought to kiss him, and hath kill'd him so.

''Tis true, 'tis true; thus was Adonis slain:
He ran upon the boar with his sharp spear,
Who did not whet his teeth at him again,
But by a kiss thought to persuade him there;
 And nuzzling in his flank, the loving swine
 Sheathed unaware the tusk in his soft groin.

'Had I been tooth'd like him, I must confess,[37]
With kissing him I should have kill'd him first;
But he is dead, and never did he bless
My youth with his; the more am I accurst.'
 With this, she falleth in the place she stood,
 And stains her face with his congealed blood.

She looks upon his lips, and they are pale;
She takes him by the hand, and that is cold;
She whispers in his ears a heavy tale,
As if they heard the woeful words she told;
 She lifts the coffer-lids that close his eyes,
 Where, lo, two lamps, burnt out, in darkness lies;

Two glasses, where herself herself beheld
A thousand times, and now no more reflect;
Their virtue lost, wherein they late excell'd,
And every beauty robb'd of his effect:
 'Wonder of time,' quoth she, 'this is my spite,
 That, thou being dead, the day should yet be light.

'Since thou art dead, lo, here I prophesy:
Sorrow on love hereafter shall attend:

It shall be waited on with jealousy,
Find sweet beginning, but unsavoury end,
Ne'er settled equally, but high or low,
That all love's pleasure shall not match his woe. 1163
'It shall be fickle, false and full of fraud,
Bud and be blasted in a breathing-while;
The bottom poison, and the top o'er straw'd
With sweets that shall the truest sight beguile:
 The strongest body shall it make most weak,
 Strike the wise dumb and teach the fool to speak.

'It shall be sparing and too full of riot,
Teaching decrepit age to tread the measures;
The staring ruffian shall it keep in quiet,
Pluck down the rich, enrich the poor with treasures; 1174
 It shall be raging-mad and silly-mild,
 Make the young old, the old become a child.

'It shall suspect where is no cause of fear;
It shall not fear where it should most mistrust;
It shall be merciful and too severe, [38]
And most deceiving when it seems most just;
 Perverse it shall be where it shows most toward,
 Put fear to valour, courage to the coward.

'It shall be cause of war and dire events,
And set dissension 'twixt the son and sire;
Subject and servile to all discontents, [39]
As dry combustious matter is to fire:
 Sith in his prime Death doth my love destroy,
 They that love best their loves shall not enjoy.'

By this, the boy that by her side lay kill'd
Was melted like a vapour from her sight,
And in his blood that on the ground lay spill'd,
A purple flower sprung up, chequer'd with white,
 Resembling well his pale cheeks and the blood
 Which in round drops upon their whiteness stood. 1195

She bows her head, the new-sprung flower to smell,
Comparing it to her Adonis' breath,
And says, within her bosom it shall dwell,
Since he himself is reft from her by death:
 She crops the stalk, and in the breach appears
 Green dropping sap, which she compares to tears.

'Poor flower,' quoth she, 'this was thy father's guise—
Sweet issue of a more sweet-smelling sire—
For every little grief to wet his eyes:
To grow unto himself was his desire, 1205
 And so 'tis thine; but know, it is as good
 To wither in my breast as in his blood.

'Here was thy father's bed, here in my breast;
Thou art the next of blood, and 'tis thy right:
Lo, in this hollow cradle take thy rest,
My throbbing heart shall rock thee day and night:
 There shall not be one minute in an hour
 Wherein I will not kiss my sweet love's flower.'

Thus weary of the world, away she hies,
And yokes her silver doves; by whose swift aid
Their mistress, mounted, through the empty skies 1217
In her light chariot quickly is convey'd;
Holding their course to Paphos, where their queen
Means to immure herself and not be seen.

Notes

1. VENUS AND ADONIS; 156. *'shouldst'*; Quarto 1, *'should.'*
2. Cp. – Sonnet I.
3. Lifeless; – Quartos 1, 2, 3, *'liuelesse.'*
4. Statue; – Quartos 1, 2, 3, *'Statüe'*; *cp.* 1. 1013; Quartos 3, 4, *'statües.'*
5. Deer; – Quartos 1, 2, 3, *'deare.'*
6. Stand, – so Quartos 1-4; the rest *'stands.'*
7. Stir; – Quartos 1, 2, 3, *'sturre.'*
8. And whether; – Quartos, *'And where'* (*i.e. 'wher'er'*).
9. Fire; – Quartos 1, 2, 3, *'fier'*; but *'fire,'* 1. 494 (rhyming with *'desire'*).
10. Tenderer; – Quarto 1, *'tendrer'*; the rest, *'tender.'*
11. Goal; – Quartos, *'gaile'*; *'Iaile.'*
12. Master'd; – Quartos 1, 2, 3, *'maister'd'*; *cp.* 1. 114; *'mastering'*; Quartos 1, 2, 3, *'maistring.'*
 ——, *'rein'*; Quartos 1-10, *'raine.'*
13. Mermaid's; – early Quartos, *'marmaides'*; *'marmaids'*; *cp.* 1. 777; Quartos 1, 2, 3, *'marmaids'*; Quarto 4, *'mirmaides.'*
14. Invisible; – Steevens conjectured *'invincible.'*
15. Wreck; – Quartos, *'wracke,' 'wrack'* (*cp.* 1. 558).
16. Bankrupt; – Quartos, *'bankrout,' 'banckrout,' 'banquerout.'*
17. Love; – S. Walker conjectured *'loss.'*
18. Verdure; – Quartos 1, 2, 3, *'verdour.'*
19. Gait; – Quartos, *'gate.'*
20. Prey; – Quartos, *'pray'* (though rhyming with 'obey'); so *'prayes,'* 1. 724, and *'pray'*; (rhyming with *'day'*), 1. 1097.
21. Venturing; – Quartos, *'ventring.'*
22. Tantalus; – Quartos, *'Tantalus.'*
23. Venture; – Quartos, *'venter'* (rhyming with *'enter'*).
24. Eyes pay; – Quartos 1, 2, *'eye paies.'*
25. Overshoot, – Steevens conjecture; Quartos 1, 2, 3, *'overshut.'*
26. Doth; – Quartos 1, 2, 3, *'do.'*
27. Imposthumes; – Quartos, *'impostumes.'*
28. Run; – Quartos 1, 2, 3, *'ronne'* (rhyming with *'undone'*).
29. Deeply; – S. Walker conjectured *'doubly.'*

30. Together; – Quartos, *'togither'* (rhyming with *'whither'*); *sp.* 1. 971; Quartos 1, 2, 3, *'all together'* (rhyming with *'weather'*); Quarto 4, *'altogither.'*
31. Random; – Quartos 1-4, *'randon.'*
32. All to nought – (rhyming with *'wrought'*); Dyce, *'all-to naught';* Delius, *'all-to naught.'*
33. Decease; – early Quartos, *'decesse'* (rhyming with *'confess'*).
34. Stories His; – Theobald's conjecture; Quartos, *'stories, His.'*
35. Ugly; – Quarto 1, *'oughly.'*
36. Limb; – Quartos, *'lim.'*
37. Been; – Quarto 1, *'bin.'*
38. Severe; – early Quartos, *'seveare'* (rhyming with *'fear'*).
39. Servile; – Quartos 1, 2, *'seruill'; cp.* line 392, *'servilely';* Quartos 1, 2, 3, *'seruilly.'*

THE PHOENIX AND THE TURTLE

LET the bird of loudest lay,
On the sole Arabian tree,
Herald sad and trumpet be,
To whose sound chaste wings obey.

But thou shrieking harbinger,
Foul precurrer of the fiend,
Augur of the fever's end,
To this troop come thou not near!

From this session interdict
Every fowl of tyrant wing,
Save the eagle, feath'red king;
Keep the obsequy so strict.

Let the priest in surplice white,
That defunctive music can,
Be the death-divining swan,
Lest the requiem lack his right.

And thou treble-dated crow,
That thy sable gender mak'st
With the breath thou giv'st and tak'st,
'Mongst our mourners shalt thou go.

Here the anthem doth commence:
Love and Constancy is dead;
Phoenix and the turtle fled
In a mutual flame from hence.

So they lov'd, as love in twain
Had the essence but in one;
Two distincts, division none:
Number there in love was slain.

Hearts remote, yet not asunder;
Distance, and no space was seen
'Twixt this turtle and his queen:
But in them, it were a wonder.

So between them love did shine,
That the turtle saw his right
Flaming in the phoenix' sight;
Either was the other's mine.

Property was thus appalled,
That the self was not the same;
Single nature's double name
Neither two nor one was called.

Reason, in itself confounded,
Saw division grow together,
To themselves yet either neither,
Simple were so well compounded,

That it cried, "How true a twain
Seemeth this concordant one!
Love hath reason, Reason none,
If what parts can so remain."

Whereupon it made this threne
To the phoenix and the dove,
Co-supremes and stars of love,
As chorus to their tragic scene.

THRENOS

Beauth, Truth, and Rarity,
Grace in all simplicity,
Here enclos'd, in cinders lie.

Death is now the phoenix' nest;
And the turtle's loyal breast
To eternity doth rest;

Leaving no posterity:
'Twas not their infirmity,
It was married chastity.

Truth may seem, but cannot be;
Beauty brag, but 't is not she;
Truth and Beauty buried be.

To this urn let those repair
That are either true or fair;
For these dead birds sigh a prayer.

THE PASSIONATE PILGRIM

1 [1]

WHEN my love swears that she is made of truth,
I do believe her, though I know she lies,
That she might think me some untutor'd youth,
Unskilful in the world's false forgeries.
Thus vainly thinking that she thinks me young,
Although I know my years be past the best,
I smiling credit her false-speaking tongue,
Outfacing faults in love with love's ill rest.
But wherefore says my love that she is young?
And wherefore say not I that I am old?
O, love's best habit is a soothing tongue,
And age, in love, loves not to have years told.
Therefore I'll lie with love, and love with me,
Since that our faults in love thus smother'd be.

2

Two loves I have, of comfort and despair,
That like two spirits do suggest me still;
My better angel is a man right fair,
My worser spirit a woman colour'd ill.
To win me soon to hell, my female evil
Tempteth my better angel from my side,
And would corrupt my saint to be a devil,
Wooing his purity with her fair pride.
And whether that my angel be turn'd fiend,
Suspect I may, yet not directly tell:
For being both to me, both to each friend,
I guess one angel in another's hell:
The truth I shall not know, but live in doubt,
Till my bad angel fire my good one out.

3 [2]

Did not the heavenly rhetoric of thine eye,
'Gainst whom the world could not hold argument,
Persuade my heart to this false perjury?
Vows for thee broke deserve not punishment.
A woman I forswore; but I will prove,
Thou being a goddess, I forswore not thee:
My vow was earthly, thou a heavenly love;
Thy grace being gain'd cures all disgrace in me.
My vow was breath, and breath a vapour is;
Then, thou fair sun, that on this earth doth shine,
Exhale this vapour vow; in thee it is:
If broken, then it is no fault of mine.
If by me broke, what fool is not so wise
To break an oath, to win a paradise?

4

Sweet Cytherea, sitting by a brook
With young Adonis, lovely, fresh, and green,
Did court the lad with many a lovely look,
Such looks as none could look but beauty's queen.
She told him stories to delight his ear;
She show'd him favours to allure his eye;
To win his heart, she touch'd him here and there,—
Touches so soft still conquer chastity.
But whether unripe years did want conceit,
Or he refused to take her figured proffer,
The tender nibbler would not touch the bait,
But smile and jest at every gentle offer:
Then fell she on her back, fair queen, and toward:
He rose and ran away; ah, fool too froward!

5

If love make me forsworn, how shall I swear to love?
O never faith could hold, if not to beauty vow'd:
Though to myself forsworn, to thee I'll constant prove;
Those thoughts, to me like oaks, to thee like osiers bow'd.
Study his bias leaves, and makes his book thine eyes,
Where all those pleasures live that art can comprehend.
If knowledge be the mark, to know thee shall suffice;
Well learned is that tongue that well can thee commend;
All ignorant that soul that sees thee without wonder;
Which is to me some praise, that I thy parts admire:
Thine eye Jove's lightning seems, thy voice his dreadful thunder,
Which, not to anger bent, is music and sweet fire.
 Celestial as thou art, O do not love that wrong,
 To sing heaven's praise with such an earthly tongue.

6

Scarce had the sun dried up the dewy morn,
And scarce the herd gone to the hedge for shade,
When Cytherea, all in love forlorn,
A longing tarriance for Adonis made
Under an osier growing by a brook,
A brook where Adon used to cool his spleen:
Hot was the day; she hotter that did look
For his approach, that often there had been.
Anon he comes, and throws his mantle by,
And stood stark naked on the brook's green brim:
The sun look'd on the world with glorious eye,
Yet not so wistly as this queen on him.
 He, spying her, bounced in, whereas he stood:
 'O Jove,' quoth she, 'why was not I a flood!'

7

Fair is my love, but not so fair as fickle;
Mild as a dove, but neither true nor trusty;
Brighter than glass, and yet, as glass is, brittle;
Softer than wax, and yet, as iron, rusty:
A lily pale, with damask dye to grace her,
None fairer, nor none falser to deface her.
Her lips to mine how often hath she joined,
Between each kiss her oaths of true love swearing!
How many tales to please me hath she coined,
Dreading my love, the loss thereof still fearing!
Yet in the midst of all her pure protestings,
Her faith, her oaths, her tears, and all were jestings.
She burn'd with love, as straw with fire flameth;
She burn'd out love, as soon as straw outburneth;
She framed the love, and yet she foil'd the framing;
She bade love last, and yet she fell a-turning.
 Was this a lover, or a lecher whether?
 Bad in the best, though excellent in neither.

8

If music and sweet poetry agree,
As they must needs, the sister and the brother,
Then must the love be great 'twixt thee and me,
Because thou lovest the one, and I the other.
Dowland to thee is dear, whose heavenly touch [3]
Upon the lute doth ravish human sense;
Spenser to me, whose deep conceit is such
As, passing all conceit, needs no defence.
Thou lovest to hear the sweet melodious sound
That Phoebus' lute, the queen of music, makes;
And I in deep delight am chiefly drown'd
Whenas himself to singing he betakes.
 One god is god of both, as poets feign;
 One knight loves both, and both in thee remain.

9

Fair was the morn when the fair queen of love,

* * * * * *

Paler for sorrow than her milk-white dove,
For Adon's sake, a youngster proud and wild;
Her stand she takes upon a steep-up hill:
Anon Adonis comes with horn and hounds;
She, silly queen, with more than love's good will,
Forbade the boy he should not pass those grounds:
'Once,' quoth she, 'did I see a fair sweet youth
Here in these brakes deep-wounded with a boar,
Deep in the thigh, a spectacle of ruth!
See, in my thigh,' quoth she, 'here was the sore.'
 She showed hers: he saw more wounds than one,
 And blushing fled, and left her all alone.

10

Sweet rose, fair flower, untimely pluck'd, soon vaded,
Pluck'd in the bud, and vaded in the spring!
Bright orient pearl, alack, too timely shaded!
Fair creature, kill'd too soon by death's sharp sting!
Like a green plum that hangs upon a tree,

And falls, through wind, before the fall should be.
I weep for thee, and yet no cause I have;
For why thou left'st me nothing in thy will:
And yet thou left'st me more than I did crave;
For why I craved nothing of thee still:
O yes, dear friend, I pardon crave of thee,
Thy discontent thou didst bequeath to me.

11

Venus, with young Adonis sitting by her
Under a myrtle shade, began to woo him:
She told the youngling how god Mars did try her,
And as he fell to her, so fell she to him.
'Even thus,' quoth she, 'the warlike god embraced me,'
And then she clipp'd Adonis in her arms;
'Even thus,' quoth she, 'the warlike god unlaced me,'
As if the boy should use like loving charms;
'Even thus,' quoth she, 'he seized on my lips,'
And with her lips on his did act the seizure:
And as she fetched breath, away he skips,
And would not take her meaning nor her pleasure.
Ah, that I had my lady at this bay,
To kiss and clip me till I run away!

12

Crabbed age and youth cannot live together:
Youth is full of pleasance, age is full of care;
Youth like summer morn, age like winter weather;
Youth like summer brave, age like winter bare.
Youth is full of sport, age's breath is short;
Youth is nimble, age is lame;
Youth is hot and bold, age is weak and cold;
Youth is wild, and age is tame.
Age, I do abhor thee; youth, I do adore thee;
O, my love, my love is young!
Age, I do defy thee: O, sweet shepherd, hie thee,
For methinks thou stay'st too long, [4]

13 [5]

Beauty is but a vain and doubtful good;
A shining gloss that vadeth suddenly;
A flower that dies when first it gins to bud;
A brittle glass that's broken presently:
A doubtful good, a gloss, a glass, a flower,
Lost, vaded, broken, dead within an hour.
And as goods lost are seld or never found,
As vaded gloss no rubbing will refresh,
As flowers dead lie wither'd on the ground,
As broken glass no cement can redress,
So beauty blemish'd once's for ever lost,
In spite of physic, painting, pain and cost.

14

Good night, good rest. Ah, neither be my share:
She bade good night that kept my rest away;
And daff'd me to a cabin hang'd with care,
To descant on the doubts of my decay.
'Farewell,' quoth she, 'and come again to-morrow:'
Fare well I could not, for I supp'd with sorrow.
Yet at my parting sweetly did she smile,
In scorn or friendship, nill I construe whether:
'T may be, she joy'd to jest at my exile,
'T may be, again to make me wander thither:
'Wander,' a word for shadows like myself,
As take the pain, but cannot pluck the pelf.

15

Lord, how mine eyes throw gazes to the east!
My heart doth charge the watch; the morning rise
Doth cite each moving sense from idle rest.
Not daring trust the office of mine eyes,
While Philomela sits and sings, I sit and mark,
And wish her lays were tuned like the lark;
For she doth welcome daylight with her ditty,
And drives away dark dismal-dreaming night: [6]
The night so pack'd, I post unto my pretty;
Heart hath his hope, and eyes their wished sight;
Sorrow changed to solace, solace mix'd with sorrow;
For why, she sigh'd and bade me come to-morrow.
Were I with her, the night would post too soon;
But now are minutes added to the hours;
To spite me now, each minute seems a moon;
Yet not for me, shine sun to succour flowers!
Pack night, peep day; good day, of night now borrow:
Short, night, to-night, and length thyself to-morrow.

Notes

1. THE PASSIONATE PILGRIM: I., II.; *cp.* SONNETS, cxxxviii., cxliv.
2. cp. – LOVE'S LABOUR LOST, IV. iii. 60–73; IV. ii. 109–122; IV. iii. 101–120.
3. John Dowland was one of the most famous of Elizabethan musicians; his song-books appeared in 1597, 1600, and 1603; his *"Pilgrim's Solace,"* 1612.

There are many references to him in Elizabethan and later literature, more especially to his *'Lachrymae, or, Seven Tears figured in seven heavenlie Pavans'* (1605); (*cp.* Bullen's *Lyrics from Elizabethan Song-Books*).

4. Stay'st; – old eds. *'staies.'*
5. Two copies of this poem "from a corrected MS." were printed in *Gent. Mag.* xx. 521; xxx. 39; the variants do not improve the poem.
6. And drives; – perhaps we should read, *'And daylight drives'* (Anon. conj.).

SONNETS TO SUNDRY NOTES OF MUSIC

16

It was a lording's daughter, the fairest one of three,
That liked of her master as well as well might be,
Till looking on an Englishman, the fair'st that eye could see,
Her fancy fell a-turning.
Long was the combat doubtful that love with love did fight,
To leave the master loveless, or kill the gallant knight:
To put in practise either, alas, it was a spite
Unto the silly damsel!
But one must be refused; more mickle was the pain
That nothing could be used to turn them both to gain, 231
For of the two the trusty knight was wounded with disdain:
Alas, she could not help it!
Thus art with arms contending was victor of the day,
Which by a gift of learning did bear the maid away:
Then, lullaby, the learned man hath got the lady gay;
For now my song is ended.

17 [1]

On a day, alack the day!
Love, whose month was ever May,
Spied a blossom passing fair,
Playing in the wanton air: 242
Through the velvet leaves the wind,
All unseen, gan passage find;
That the lover, sick to death,
Wish'd himself the heaven's breath,
'Air,' quoth he, 'thy cheeks may blow;
Air, would I might triumph so!
But, alas! my hand hath sworn
Ne'er to pluck thee from thy thorn:
Vow, alack! for youth unmeet:
Youth, so apt to pluck a sweet. 252
Thou for whom Jove would swear
Juno but an Ethiope were;
And deny himself for Jove,
Turning mortal for thy love.'

18

My flocks feed not,
My ewes breed not,
My rams speed not,
All is amiss:
Love's denying, [2]
Faith's defying,
Heart's renying, [3]
Causer of this. 264
All my merry jigs are quite forgot,
All my lady's love is lost, God wot:
Where her faith was firmly fix'd in love,
There a nay is placed without remove.
One silly cross
Wrought all my loss;
O frowning Fortune, cursed, fickle dame!
For now I see 272
Inconstancy
More in women than in men remain.
In black mourn I,
All fears scorn I,

Love hath forlorn me, [4]
Living in thrall:
Heart is bleeding,
All help needing,
O cruel speeding,
Fraughted with gall.
My shepherd's pipe can sound no deal;
My wether's bell rings doleful knell;
My curtail dog, that wont to have play'd
Plays not at all, but seems afraid;
My sighs so deep [5]
Procure to weep,
In howling wise, to see my doleful plight.
How sighs resound
Through heartless ground,
Like a thousand vanquish'd men in bloody fight!
Clear wells spring not,
Sweet birds sing not,
Green plants bring not
Forth their dye;
Herds stand weeping,
Flocks all sleeping,
Nymphs back peeping [6]
Fearfully:
All our pleasure known to us poor swains,
All our merry meetings on the plains,
All our evening sport from us is fled,
All our love is lost, for Love is dead.
Farewell, sweet lass,
Thy like ne'er was
For a sweet content, the cause of all my moan:
Poor Corydon
Must live alone;
Other help for him I see that there is none.

19

When as thine eye hath chose the dame,
And stall'd the deer that thou shouldst strike,
Let reason rule things worthy blame,
As well as fancy partial might: [7]
Take counsel of some wiser head,
Neither too young nor yet unwed.
And when thou comest thy tale to tell,
Smooth not thy tongue with filed talk,
Lest she some subtle practise smell,—
A cripple soon can find a halt;—
But plainly say thou lovest her well,
And set thy person forth to sell.
What though her frowning brows be bent,
Her cloudy looks will calm ere night:
And then too late she will repent
That thus dissembled her delight;
And twice desire, ere it be day,
That which with scorn she put away.
What though she strive to try her strength,
And ban and brawl, and say thee nay,
Her feeble force will yield at length,
When craft hath taught her thus to say,
'Had women been so strong as men,
In faith, you had not had it then.'
And to her will frame all thy ways;
Spare not to spend, and chiefly there
Where thy desert may merit praise,
By ringing in thy lady's ear:
The strongest castle, tower, and town,
The golden bullet beats it down.
Serve always with assured trust,
And in thy suit be humble true;
Unless thy lady prove unjust,
Press never thou to choose anew:
When time shall serve, be thou not slack
To proffer, though she put thee back.
The wiles and guiles that women work,
Dissembled with an outward show,
The tricks and toys that in them lurk,
The cock that treads them shall not know.
Have you not heard it said full oft,
A woman's nay doth stand for nought?
Think women still to strive with men,
To sin and never for to saint:
There is no heaven, by holy then, [8]
When time with age doth them attaint.
Were kisses all the joys in bed,
One woman would another wed.
But, soft! enough, too much, I fear;
Lest that my mistress hear my song,
She will not stick to round me i' the ear,
To teach my tongue to be so long:
Yet will she blush, here be it said,
To hear her secrets so bewray'd.

20

Live with me, and be my love, [9]
And we will all the pleasures prove
That hills and valleys, dales and fields,

And all the craggy mountains yields.
There will we sit upon the rocks,
And see the shepherds feed their flocks,
By shallow rivers, by whose falls
Melodious birds sing madrigals.
There will I make thee a bed of roses,
With a thousand fragrant posies,
A cap of flowers, and a kirtle
Embroider'd all with leaves of myrtle.
A belt of straw and ivy buds,
With coral clasps and amber studs;
And if these pleasures may thee move,
Then live with me and be my love.
LOVE'S ANSWER.
If that the world and love were young,
And truth in every shepherd's tongue,
These pretty pleasures might me move
To live with thee and be thy love.

21

As it fell upon a day
In the merry month of May,
Sitting in a pleasant shade
Which a grove of myrtles made,
Beasts did leap, and birds did sing,
Trees did grow, and plants did spring;
Every thing did banish moan,
Save the nightingale alone:
She, poor bird, as all forlorn,
Lean'd her breast up-till a thorn
And there sung the dolefull'st ditty,
That to hear it was great pity:
'Fie, fie, fie,' now would she cry;
'Tereu, tereu!' by and by;
That to hear her so complain,
Scarce I could from tears refrain;
For her griefs, so lively shown,
Made me think upon mine own.
Ah, thought I, thou mourn'st in vain!
None takes pity on thy pain:
Senseless trees they cannot hear thee;
Ruthless beasts they will not cheer thee:
King Pandion he is dead;
All thy friends are lapp'd in lead;
All thy fellow birds do sing,
Careless of thy sorrowing.
Even so, poor bird, like thee,
None alive will pity me.
Whilst as fickle Fortune smiled,
Thou and I were both beguiled.
Every one that flatters thee
Is no friend in misery.
Words are easy, like the wind;
Faithful friends are hard to find:
Every man will be thy friend
Whilst thou hast wherewith to spend;
But if store of crowns be scant,
No man will supply thy want.
If that one be prodigal,
Bountiful they will him call,
And with such-like flattering,
'Pity but he were a king;'
If he be addict to vice,
Quickly him they will entice;
If to women he be bent,
They have at commandement:
But if Fortune once do frown,
Then farewell his great renown;
They that fawn'd on him before
Use his company no more.
He that is thy friend indeed,
He will help thee in thy need:
If thou sorrow, he will weep;
If thou wake, he cannot sleep;
Thus of every grief in heart
He with thee doth bear a part.
These are certain signs to know
Faithful friend from flattering foe.

Notes

1. cp. – LOVE'S LABOUR LOST, IV. iii. 60–73; IV. ii. 109–122; IV. iii. 101–120.
2. Love's denying; – Malone's conjecture; old eds., *'Love is dying'; England's Helicon, 'Love is denying.'*
3. Renying; – ed. 1599, *'nenying.'*
4. Love hath forlorn me; – Steevens conjectured *'Love forlorn I.'*
5. My sighs . . . Procure to'; – ed. 1599, 1612, *'With sighes . . . procures to';* the reading of the text is Malone's.
6. Back peeping; – edd. 1599, 1612, *'blacke peeping.'*
7. Fancy, partial wight; – Capell MS. and Malone conjecture withdrawn; edd. 1599, 1612, *'fancy (party all might)';* ed. 1640, *'fancy (partly all might)';* Malone (from MS. copy), *'fancy, partial like,'* Collier (from MS. copy), *'partial fancy like';* Steevens conjectured *'fancy, partial tike';* Furnivall conjectured *'fancy's partial might.'*
8. There is no heaven, by holy then; – the line has been variously emended; Malone reads from an old MS.:—

"Here is no heaven; they holy then
Begin, when," &c.

No satisfactory emendation has been proposed, and perhaps the original reading may be allowed to stand without the comma after *'heaven':—'there is no heaven by holy then,' i.e.* "by that holy time"; others suggest, *'be holy then,'* or *'by the holy then,'* &c.

9. Live with me, and be my love; – in *England's Helicon* and other early versions the line runs, *'Come live with me,'* &c., and in this way it is usually quoted. Two verses found in *England's Helicon* are omitted in the present version, but included in the 1640 ed., where *"Love's Answer"* is also in six quatrains; the additional matter was evidently also derived from *England's Helicon.* After 1. 12 the following lines are inserted:—

"A gown made of the finest wool,
Which from our pretty Lambs we pull.
Fair lined slippers for the cold,
With buckles of the purest gold."

The last stanza runs thus:—

*"The shepherd's swains shall dance and sing**
For thy delight each May morning;
If these delights thy mind may move,
Then live with me and be my love."

A LOVER'S COMPLAINT

FROM off a hill whose concave womb reworded
A plaintful story from a sistering vale,
My spirits to attend this double voice accorded,
And down I laid to list the sad-tuned tale;
Ere long espied a fickle maid full pale,
Tearing of papers, breaking rings a-twain,
Storming her world with sorrow's wind and rain.

Upon her head a platted hive of straw,
Which fortified her visage from the sun,
Whereon the thought might think sometime it saw
The carcass of a beauty spent and done:
Time had not scythed all that youth begun, [1]
Nor youth all quit; but, spite of heaven's fell rage,
Some beauty peep'd through lattice of sear'd age.

Oft did she heave her napkin to her eyne,
Which on it had conceited characters,
Laundering the silken figures in the brine
That season'd woe had pelleted in tears,
And often reading what contents it bears;
As often shrieking undistinguish'd woe,
In clamours of all size, both high and low.

Sometimes her levell'd eyes their carriage ride,
As they did battery to the spheres intend;
Sometime diverted their poor balls are tied
To the orbed earth; sometimes they do extend
Their view right on; anon their gazes lend
To every place at once, and, nowhere fix'd,
The mind and sight distractedly commix'd.

Her hair, nor loose nor tied in formal plat,
Proclaim'd in her a careless hand of pride
For some, untuck'd, descended her sheaved hat,
Hanging her pale and pined cheek beside;
Some in her threaden fillet still did bide,
And true to bondage would not break from thence,
Though slackly braided in loose negligence.

A thousand favours from a maund she drew
Of amber, crystal, and of beaded jet, [2]
Which one by one she in a river threw,
Upon whose weeping margent she was set; [3]
Like usury, applying wet to wet,
Or monarch's hands that let not bounty fall
Where want cries some, but where excess begs all.
Of folded schedules had she many a one,
Which she perused, sigh'd, tore, and gave the flood;
Crack'd many a ring of posied gold and bone,
Bidding them find their sepulchres in mud;
Found yet moe letters sadly penn'd in blood,
With sleided silk feat and affectedly
Enswathed, and seal'd to curious secrecy.

These often bathed she in her fluxive eyes,
And often kiss'd, and often 'gan to tear; [4]
Cried 'O false blood, thou register of lies,
What unapproved witness dost thou bear!
Ink would have seem'd more black and damned here!'
This said, in top of rage the lines she rents,
Big discontent so breaking their contents.

A reverend man that grazed his cattle nigh—
Sometime a blusterer, that the ruffle knew
Of court, of city, and had let go by
The swiftest hours, observed as they flew—[5]
Towards this afflicted fancy fastly drew,
And, privileged by age, desires to know
In brief the grounds and motives of her woe.

So slides he down upon his grained bat,
And comely-distant sits he by her side;
When he again desires her, being sat,
Her grievance with his hearing to divide:
If that from him there may be aught applied
Which may her suffering ecstasy assuage,
'Tis promised in the charity of age.

'Father,' she says, 'though in me you behold
The injury of many a blasting hour,
Let it not tell your judgment I am old;
Not age, but sorrow, over me hath power:
I might as yet have been a spreading flower,
Fresh to myself, If I had self-applied
Love to myself and to no love beside.

'But, woe is me! too early I attended
A youthful suit— it was to gain my grace—
Of one by nature's outwards so commended,
That maidens' eyes stuck over all his face:
Love lack'd a dwelling, and made him her place;
And when in his fair parts she did abide,
She was new lodged and newly deified.

'His browny locks did hang in crooked curls;
And every light occasion of the wind
Upon his lips their silken parcels hurls.
What's sweet to do, to do will aptly find:
Each eye that saw him did enchant the mind,
For on his visage was in little drawn
What largeness thinks in Paradise was sawn.
'Small show of man was yet upon his chin;
His phoenix down began but to appear
Like unshorn velvet on that termless skin
Whose bare out-bragg'd the web it seem'd to wear:
Yet show'd his visage by that cost more dear;
And nice affections wavering stood in doubt
If best were as it was, or best without.

'His qualities were beauteous as his form,
For maiden-tongued he was, and thereof free;
Yet, if men moved him, was he such a storm
As oft 'twixt May and April is to see,
When winds breathe sweet, untidy though they be.
His rudeness so with his authorized youth
Did livery falseness in a pride of truth.

'Well could he ride, and often men would say
'That horse his mettle from his rider takes:
Proud of subjection, noble by the sway,
What rounds, what bounds, what course, what stop he makes!'
And controversy hence a question takes,
Whether the horse by him became his deed,
Or he his manage by the well-doing steed.[6]

'But quickly on this side the verdict went:
His real habitude gave life and grace
To appertainings and to ornament,
Accomplish'd in himself, not in his case:
All aids, themselves made fairer by their place,
Came for additions; yet their purposed trim[7]
Pieced not his grace, but were all graced by him.

'So on the tip of his subduing tongue
All kinds of arguments and question deep,
All replication prompt, and reason strong,
For his advantage still did wake and sleep:
To make the weeper laugh, the laugher weep,
He had the dialect and different skill,
Catching all passions in his craft of will:

'That he did in the general bosom reign
Of young, of old; and sexes both enchanted,
To dwell with him in thoughts, or to remain
In personal duty, following where he haunted:
Consents bewitch'd, ere he desire, have granted;
And dialogued for him what he would say,
Ask'd their own wills, and made their wills obey.

'Many there were that did his picture get,
To serve their eyes, and in it put their mind;
Like fools that in th' imagination set
The goodly objects which abroad they find
Of lands and mansions, theirs in thought assign'd;
And labouring in moe pleasures to bestow them
Than the true gouty landlord which doth owe them:
'So many have, that never touch'd his hand,
Sweetly supposed them mistress of his heart.
My woeful self, that did in freedom stand,
And was my own fee-simple, not in part,

What with his art in youth, and youth in art,
Threw my affections in his charmed power,
Reserved the stalk and gave him all my flower.

'Yet did I not, as some my equals did,
Demand of him, nor being desired yielded;
Finding myself in honour so forbid,
With safest distance I mine honour shielded:
Experience for me many bulwarks builded
Of proofs new-bleeding, which remain'd the foil
Of this false jewel, and his amorous spoil.

'But, ah, who ever shunn'd by precedent
The destined ill she must herself assay?
Or forced examples, 'gainst her own content,
To put the by-past perils in her way?
Counsel may stop awhile what will not stay;
For when we rage, advice is often seen
By blunting us to make our wits more keen.

'Nor gives it satisfaction to our blood,
That we must curb it upon others' proof;
To be forbod the sweets that seem so good, [8]
For fear of harms that preach in our behoof.
O appetite, from judgment stand aloof!
The one a palate hath that needs will taste,
Though Reason weep, and cry, "It is thy last."

'For further I could say "This man's untrue,"
And knew the patterns of his foul beguiling;
Heard where his plants in others' orchards grew,
Saw how deceits were gilded in his smiling;
Knew vows were ever brokers to defiling;
Thought characters and words merely but art,

And bastards of his foul adulterate heart.
'And long upon these terms I held my city,
Till thus he gan besiege me: "Gentle maid,
Have of my suffering youth some feeling pity,
And be not of my holy vows afraid:
That's to ye sworn to none was ever said;
For feasts of love I have been call'd unto,
Till now did ne'er invite, nor never woo. [9]

'All my offences that abroad you see
Are errors of the blood, none of the mind;
Love made them not: with acture they may be,
Where neither party is nor true nor kind:
They sought their shame that so their shame did
find;
And so much less of shame in me remains,
By how much of me their reproach contains.

'Among the many that mine eyes have seen,
Not one whose flame my heart so much as warm'd,
Or my affection put to the smallest teen,
Or any of my leisures ever charm'd:
Harm have I done to them, but ne'er was harm'd;
Kept hearts in liveries, but mine own was free,
And reign'd, commanding in his monarchy.

'Look here, what tributes wounded fancies sent me,
Of paled pearls and rubies red as blood;
Figuring that they their passions likewise lent me
Of grief and blushes, aptly understood
In bloodless white and the encrimson'd mood;
Effects of terror and dear modesty,
Encamp'd in hearts, but fighting outwardly.

'And, lo, behold these talents of their hair,
With twisted metal amorously impleach'd,
I have received from many a several fair,
Their kind acceptance weepingly beseech'd,
With the annexions of fair gems enrich'd,
And deep-brain'd sonnets that did amplify
Each stone's dear nature, worth, and quality.

'The diamond,—why, 'twas beautiful and hard,
Whereto his invised properties did tend;
The deep-green emerald, in whose fresh regard
Weak sights their sickly radiance do amend;
The heaven-hued sapphire and the opal blend
With objects manifold: each several stone,
With wit well blazon'd, smiled or made some moan.

'Lo, all these trophies of affections hot,
Of pensived and subdued desires the tender,
Nature hath charged me that I hoard them not,
But yield them up where I myself must render,
That is, to you, my origin and ender;
For these, of force, must your oblations be,
Since I their altar, you enpatron me.

'O, then, advance of yours that phraseless hand,
Whose white weighs down the airy scale of praise;
Take all these similes to your own command,
Hallow'd with sighs that burning lungs did raise; [10]
What me your minister, for you obeys,
Works under you; and to your audit comes
Their distract parcels in combined sums.

'Lo, this device was sent me from a nun,
Or sister sanctified, of holiest note;
Which late her noble suit in court did shun,
Whose rarest havings made the blossoms dote;
For she was sought by spirits of richest coat,
But kept cold distance, and did thence remove,
To spend her living in eternal love.

'But, O my sweet, what labour is't to leave
The thing we have not, mastering what not strives,
Playing the place which did no form receive, [11]
Playing patient sports in unconstrained gyves?
She that her fame so to herself contrives,
The scars of battle 'scapeth by the flight,
And makes her absence valiant, not her might.

'O, pardon me, in that my boast is true:
The accident which brought me to her eye
Upon the moment did her force subdue,
And now she would the caged cloister fly:
Religious love put out Religion's eye:
Not to be tempted, would she be immured,
And now, to tempt, all liberty procured.

'How mighty then you are, O, hear me tell!
The broken bosoms that to me belong
Have emptied all their fountains in my well,
And mine I pour your ocean all among:
I strong o'er them, and you o'er me being strong,
Must for your victory us all congest,
As compound love to physic your cold breast.

'My parts had power to charm a sacred nun, [12]
Who, disciplined, ay, dieted in grace, [13]
Believed her eyes when they to assail begun,
All vows and consecrations giving place:
O most potential love! vow, bond, nor space,
In thee hath neither sting, knot, nor confine,
For thou art all, and all things else are thine.

'When thou impressest, what are precepts worth
Of stale example? When thou wilt inflame,
How coldly those impediments stand forth
Of wealth, of filial fear, law, kindred, fame!
Love's arms are peace, 'gainst rule, 'gainst sense,
'gainst shame, [14]
And sweetens, in the suffering pangs it bears,
The aloes of all forces, shocks, and fears.

'Now all these hearts that do on mine depend,
Feeling it break, with bleeding groans they pine;
And supplicant their sighs to you extend,
To leave the battery that you make 'gainst mine,
Lending soft audience to my sweet design,
And credent soul to that strong-bonded oath
That shall prefer and undertake my troth."
'This said, his watery eyes he did dismount,
Whose sights till then were levell'd on my face;
Each cheek a river running from a fount
With brinish current downward flow'd apace:
O, how the channel to the stream gave grace!
Who glazed with crystal gate the glowing roses [15]
That flame through water which their hue encloses.

'O father, what a hell of witchcraft lies
In the small orb of one particular tear!
But with the inundation of the eyes
What rocky heart to water will not wear?
What breast so cold that is not warmed here?
O cleft effect! cold modesty, hot wrath,
Both fire from hence and chill extincture hath.

'For, lo, his passion, but an art of craft,
Even there resolved my reason into tears;
There my white stole of chastity I daff'd,
Shook off my sober guards and civil fears;
Appear to him, as he to me appears,
All melting; though our drops this difference
bore,
His poison'd me, and mine did him restore.

'In him a plenitude of subtle matter,
Applied to cautels, all strange forms receives,
Of burning blushes, or of weeping water,
Or swooning paleness; and he takes and leaves,
In either's aptness, as it best deceives,
To blush at speeches rank, to weep at woes,
Or to turn white and swoon at tragic shows: [16]

'That not a heart which in his level came
Could 'scape the hail of his all-hurting aim,
Showing fair nature is both kind and tame;
And, veil'd in them, did win whom he would maim:
Against the thing he sought he would exclaim;
When he most burn'd in heart-wish'd luxury,
He preach'd pure maid, and praised cold chastity.

'Thus merely with the garment of a Grace
The naked and concealed fiend he cover'd
That th' unexperient gave the tempter place,
Which like a cherubin above them hover'd.
Who, young and simple, would not be so lover'd?

Ay me! I fell; and yet do question make
What I should do again for such a sake.

'O, that infected moisture of his eye,
O, that false fire which in his cheek so glow'd,
O, that forced thunder from his heart did fly,
O, that sad breath his spongy lungs bestow'd,
O, all that borrow'd motion seeming owed,
Would yet again betray the fore-betray'd,
And new pervert a reconciled maid!' 334

Notes

1. A LOVER'S COMPLAINT; 12. 'scythed'; – Quarto, *'sithed.'*
2. Beaded; – Quarto, *'bedded'* (? = "imbedded, set").
3. Weeping margent; – Malone conjectured *'margent weeping.'*
4. 'Gan to tear; – Quarto, *'gaue to teare';* Gildon, *'gave a tear.'*
5. Observed as they flew; – the clause is probably connected with 'hours'; "the reverend man had not let the swift hours pass by without gaining some knowledge of the world"; it is possible, however, that *'they'* refers to the torn-up letters.
6. Manage; – Quarto, *'mannad'g.'*
7. Came; – Sewell's correction; Quarto, *'can';* Sewell's 2nd ed., *'can for additions get their purpose trim.'*
8. Woe; – Quarto, *'vow.'*
9. Sweets that seem; – Quarto, *'sweets that seemes';* Capell MS., *'sweet that seems.'*
10. Hallow'd; – Quarto, *hollowed';* Sewell's correction.
11. Playing the place; – some error due to the printer has spoilt the line; the first word of the line has been caught up by the compositor's eye from the first of the next line, or *vice versa:* the most ingenious and plausible emendation is *'paling'* for *'playing.'*
12. Nun; – Quarto, *'Sunne.'*
13. Ay; – Quarto, *'I.'*
14. Love's arms are peace; – so Quarto; Capell MS. and Malone conjecture, *'proof'* for *'peace,'* a plausible change, if any is necessary; other readings are:—*'Love aims at peace'; 'Love charms our peace'; 'Love aims a piece';* &c.
15. Who glaz'd with crystal gate; – Malone, *'who, glaz'd with crystal, gate'* (*i.e. gate* = "the ancient perfect tense of the verb *to get,"* *flame* being its object).
16. Swound – Quarto, *'sound,' cp.* 305, *'swounding';* Quarto, *'sounding.'*

GLOSSARY

ABATE: to shorten, to cast down, to blunt
ABATEMENT: diminution
ABIDE: to sojourn, to expiate (a corruption of 'Aby')
ABLE: to uphold
ABRIDGEMENT: a short play
ABROOK: to brook, abide
ABSEY-BOOK: a primer
ABSOLUTE: positive, certain, complete
ABUSE: to deceive
ABUSE: deception
ABY: to expiate a fault
ABYSM: abyss
ACCITE: to cite, summon
ACCUSE: accusation
ACHIEVE: to obtain
ACKNOWN: 'to be acknown' is to acknowledge
ACQUITTANCE: a receipt or discharge
ACTION-TAKING: litigious
ACTURE: action
ADDITION: title, attribute
ADDRESS: to prepare oneself
ADDRESSED: prepared
ADVANCE: to prefer, promote to honor
ADVERTISEMENT: admonition
ADVERTISING: attentive
ADVICE: consideration, discretion
ADVISE: sometimes *neuter*, sometimes *reflective* to consider, reflect
ADVISED: considerate
ADVOCATION: pleading, advocacy
AFEARD: afraid
AFFECT: to love
AFFEERED: assessed, confirmed
AFRONT: in front
AFFY: to affiance, to trust
AGAZED: looking in amazement
AGLET-BABY: the small figure engraved on a jewel
AGNISE: to acknowledge, confess
A-GOOD: a good deal, plenteously
A-HOLD: a sea-term
AIERY: the nest of a bird of prey
AIM: a guess
ALDER-LIEFEST: most loved of all
ALE: alehouse
ALLOW: to approve
ALLOWANCE: approval
AMES-ACE: two aces, the lowest throw of the dice
AMORT: dead, dejected
AN: if
ANCHOR: an anchorite, hermit
ANCIENT: an ensign bearer
ANGEL: a coin, so called because it bore the image of an angel
ANIGHT: by night
ANSWER: retaliation
ANTHROPOPHAGINIAN: a cannibal
ANTICK: the fool in the old plays
ANTRE: a cave
APPARENT: heir-apparent
APPEAL: accusation, to accuse
APPEARED: made apparent
APPLE-JOHN: a kind of apple
APPOINTMENT: preparation
APPREHENSION: opinion
APPREHENSIVE: apt to apprehend or understand
APPROBATION: probation
APPROOF: approbation, proof
APPROVE: to prove, to justify, make good
APPROVER: one who proves or tries
ARCH: chief
ARGAL: a ridiculous word intended for the Latin ergo
ARGENTINE: silver
ARGIER: Algiers
ARGOSY: originally a vessel of Ragusa or Ragosa, a Ragosine; hence any ship of burden
ARGUMENT: subject
ARMIGERO: a mistake for Armiger, the Latin for Esquire
AROINT: found only in the imperat, mood, get thee gone
A-ROW: in a row
ARTICULATE: to enter into articles of agreement, to exhibit in articles
ASK: to require
ASPECT: regard, looks
ASPERSION: sprinkling; hence blessing because before the Reformation benediction was generally accompanied by sprinkling of holy water
ASSAY: to attempt, test, make proof of
ASSINEGO: an ass
ASSUBJUGATE: to subjugate

ASSURANCE: deed of assurance
ASSURED: betrothed
ATOMY: an atom, used in contempt of a small person
ATONE: to put people at one, to reconcile, to agree
ATTACH: to seize, lay hold on
ATTASKED: taken to task, reprehended
ATTEND: to listen to
ATTENT: attentive
ATTORNEY: an agent, to employ as an agent, to perform by an agent
AUDACIOUS: spirited, daring, but without any note of blame attached to it
AUGUR: augury
AUTHENTIC: clothed with authority
AVAUNT: be gone, a word of abhorrence
AVE: the Latin for hail; hence acclamation
AVE-MARY: the angelic salutation addressed to the B. Virgin Mary
AVERRING: confirming
AWFUL: worshipful
AWKWARD: contrary

BACCARE: keep back
BACKWARD: the hinder part; hence, when applied to time, the past
BALKED: heaped, as on a ridge
BALLOW: a cudgel
BALM: the oil of consecration
BAN: to curse
BANK: to sail by the banks
BARM: yeast
BARN: a child
BARNACLE: a shell-fish, supposed to produce the sea-bird of the same name
BASE: a game, sometimes called Prisoners' base
BASES: an embroidered mantle worn by knights on horseback, and reaching from the middle to below the knees
BASILISK: a kind of ordnance
BASTA: (Italian), enough
BASTARD: raisin wine
BAT-FOWLING: catching birds with a clapnet by night
BATE: to flutter as a hawk, to except, to abate
BATLET: a small bat, used for beating clothes
BATTLE: army
BAVIN: a piece of waste wood, applied contemptuously to anything worthless
BAWCOCK: a fine fellow
BAY: the space between the main timbers of the roof
BEADSMAN: one who bids bedes, that is, prays prayers for another
BEARING-CLOTH: a rich cloth in which children were wrapt at their christening
BEAT: to flutter as a falcon, to meditate, consider earnestly
BEAVER: the lower part of a helmet
BEETLE: a mallet
BEING: dwelling
BEING: since, inasmuch as
BE-METE: to measure
BE-MOILED: daubed with dirt
BENDING: stooping under a weight
BENVENUTO: (Italian), welcome
BERGOMASK: a rustic dance
BESHREW: evil befal
BESTRAUGHT: distraught, distracted
BETEEM: to pour out
BETID: happened
BEZONIAN: a beggarly fellow
BIDING: abiding-place
BIGGEN: a night-cap
BILBERRY: the whortleberry
BILBO: a sword, from Bilboa, a town in Spain where they were made
BILBOES: fetters or stocks
BILL: a bill-hook, a weapon
BIN: been, are
BALLOW: a cudgel
BIRD-BOLT: a bolt to be shot from a crossbow at birds
BIRDING: hawking at partridges
BISSON: blind
BLANK: the white mark in the middle of a target; hence, metaphorically, that which is aimed at
BLENCH: to start aside, flinch
BLENT: blended
BLOOD-BOLTERED: smeared with blood
BLOW: to inflate
BOARD: to accost
BOB: a blow, metaph, a sarcasm, to strike, metaph, to ridicule, or to obtain by raillery
BODGE: to botch, bungle
BODIKIN: a corrupt word used as an oath
BOITIER VERT (FRENCH): green box
BOLD: to embolden
BOLLEN: swollen
BOLTER: a sieve
BOLTED: sifted, refined
BOLTING-HUTCH: a hutch in which meal was sifted
BOMBARD: a barrel, a drunkard
BOMBAST: padding
BONA-ROBA: a harlot
BOND: that to which one is bound
BOOK: a paper of conditions
BOOT: help, use, to help, to avail
BOOTLESS: without boot or advantage, useless
BOOTS: bots, a kind of worm
BORE: caliber of a gun; hence, metaph, size, weight, importance
BOSKY: covered with underwood
BOSOM: wish, heart's desire
BOTS: worms which infest horses
BOURN: a boundary, a brook
BRACE: armor for the arm, state of defence
BRACH: a hound bitch
BRAID: deceitful
BRAVE: handsome, well-dressed, boast
BRAVERY: finery, boastfulness
BRAWL: a kind of dance
BREED-BATE: a breeder of debate, a fomenter of quarrels
BREAST: voice
BREATHE: to exercise
BREATHING: exercising
BREECHING: liable to be whipt
BREESE: the gadfly
BRIDE-BUCK: a buck given away in presents
BRING: to attend one on a journey
BROCK: a badger, a term of contempt
BROKE: to act as a procurer
BROKEN: having lost some teeth by age
BROKEN MUSIC: the music of stringed instruments
BROKER: an agent

BROTHERHOOD: trading company
BROWNIST: a sectary, a follower of Brown, the founder of the Independents
BRUIT: noise, report, rumor, to noise abroad
BRUSH: rude assault
BUCK: suds or lye for washing clothes in
BUCK-BASKET: the basket in which clothes are carried to be washed
BUCKING: washing
BUCK-WASHING: washing in lye
BUG: a bugbear, a sceptre
BULLY-ROOK: a bragging cheater
BURGONET: a kind of helmet
BURST: to break
BUSKY: bushy
BUTT-SHAFT: a light arrow for shooting at a butt
BUXOM: obedient
BY'RLAKIN: by our little Lady: an oath

CADDIS: worsted galloon, so called because it resembles the caddis-worm
CADE: a cask or barrel
CAGE: a prison
CAIN-COLORED: red (applied to hair)
CAITIFF: a captive, a slave; hence, a witch
CALCULATE: prophesy
CALIVER: a hand-gun
CALLET: a trull
CALLING: appellation
CALM: qualm
CAN: to know, be skillful in
CANARY: a wine brought from the Canary Islands
CANDLE-WASTERS: persons who sit up all night to drink
CANAKIN: a little can
CANKER: a caterpillar, the dog-rose
CANSTICK: a candlestick
CANTLE: a slice, corner
CANTON: a canto
CANVAS: to sift; hence, metaphorically, to prove
CAPABLE: intelligent, capable of inheriting, ample, capacious
CAPITULATE: make head
CAPOCCHIA: a simpleton
CAPRICIO: (Italian), caprice
CAPRICIOUS: lascivious
CAPTIOUS: capacious
CARACK: a large ship of burden
CARBONADO: meat scotched for broiling
CARBONADO: to scotch for broiling
CARD: the paper on which the points of the compass are marked under the mariner's needle
CAREIRE: the curvetting of a horse
CARKANET: a necklace
CARL: a churl
CARLOT: a churl
CASTILIAN: a native of Castile; used as a cant term
CASTILIANO VULGO: a cant term, meaning, apparently, to use discreet language
CATALAN: a native of Cathay, a cant word
CATLING: cat-gut
CAVALERO: a cavalier, gentleman
CAVIARE: the roe of sturgeon pickled, a delicacy not appreciated by the vulgar
CAUTEL: deceit
CAUTELOUS: insidious
CEASE: decease
CEASE: put off, made to cease
CENSURE: judgment
CENSURE: to judge, criticise
CENTURY: a hundred of anything, whether men, prayers, or anything else
CEREMONY: a ceremonial vestment, religious rite, or anything ceremonial
CERTES: certainly
CESS: rate, reckoning
CHACE: a term at tennis
CHAMBER: a species of great gun
CHAMBERER: an effeminate man
CHANSON: a song
CHARACT: affected quality
CHARACTER: a letter, handwriting
CHARACTER: to carve or engrave
CHARACTERY: handwriting, that which is written
CHARE: a turn of work
CHARGE-HOUSE: a free-school
CHARLES' WAIN: the constellation called also Ursa Major, or the Great Bear
CHARNECO: a species of sweet wine
CHAUDRON: entrails
CHEATER: for escheator, an officer who collected the fines to be paid into the Exchequer, a decoy
CHECK: a technical term in falconry; when a falcon flies at a bird which is not her proper game she is said to check at it
CHECKS: perhaps intended for ethics
CHEER: fortune, countenance
CHERRY-PIT: a game played with cherrystones
CHEVERIL: kid leather
CHEWIT: cough
CHILDING: pregnant
CH'ILL: vulgar for 'I will.'
CHIRURGEONLY: in a manner becoming a surgeon
CHOPIN: a high shoe or clog
CHRISTOM: clothed with a chrisom, the white garment which used to be put on newly-baptized children
CHRISTENDOM: the state of being a Christian, name
CHUCK: chicken, a term of endearment
CHUFF: a coarse blunt clown
CINQUE PACE: a kind of dance
CIPHER: to decipher
CIRCUMSTANCE: an argument
CITAL: recital
CITE: to incite
CITTERN: a guitar
CLACK-DISH: a beggar's dish
CLAP I' THE CLOUT: to shoot an arrow into the bull's eye of the target
CLAW: to flatter
CLEPE: to call
CLIFF: clef, the key in music
CLING: to starve
CLINQUANT: glittering
CLIP: to embrace, to enclose
CLOUT: the mark in the middle of a target
COAST: to advance
COBLOAF: a big loaf
COCK: a cock boat, a euphemism for God
COCK-AND-PIE: an oath
COCKLE: tares or darnel

COCKNEY: a cock
COCK-SHUT-TIME: the twilight when cocks and hens go to roost
COG: to cheat, dissemble
COGNIZANCE: badge, token
COIGN: projecting corner stone
COIL: tumult, turmoil
COLLECTION: drawing a conclusion
COLLIED: blackened
COLOR: pretence
COLORABLE: specious
COLT: to defraud, befool
CO-MART: a joint bargain
COMBINATE: betrothed
COMBINE: to bind
COMMODITY: interest, profit
COMMONTY: used ludicrously for comedy.
COMPACT: compacted, composed
COMPARATIVE: rival
COMPARE: comparison
COMPASSIONATE: moving comparison
COMPETITOR: one who seeks the same thing, an associate in any object
COMPLEMENT: accomplishment
COMPLEXION: passion
COMPOSE: to agree
COMPOSITION: composition
COMPTIBLE: tractable
CON: to learn by heart, to acknowledge
CONCEIT: conception, opinion, fancy
CONCUPY: concubine
CONDITION: temper, quality
CONDOLEMENT: grief
CONDUCT: escort
CONFECT: to make up into sweetmeats
CONFOUND: to consume, destroy
CONJECT: conjecture
CONSIGN: to sign a common bond, to confederate
CONSORT: company
CONSORT: to accompany
CONSTANCY: consistency
CONSTANT: settled, determined
CONSTANTLY: firmly
CONSTER: to construe
CONTEMPTIBLE: contemptuous
CONTINENT: that which contains anything, that which is contained
CONTINUATE: uninterrupted
CONTRACTION: the marriage contract
CONTRARY: to oppose
CONTRIVE: to conspire, to wear away
CONTROL: to confute
CONVENT: to convene, summon, to be convenient
CONVERT: to change
CONVERTITE: a convert
CONVEY: to manage, to filch
CONVEYANCE: theft, fraud
CONVICT: convicted
CONVICTED: overpowered, vanquished, a doubtful word
CONVINCE: to conquer, subdue
CONVIVE: to feast together
CONVOY: escort
CONY-CATCH: to cheat
CONY-CATCHING: poaching, pilfering
COOLING CARD: used metaphorically for an insurmountable obstacle
COPATAIN HAT: a high-crowned hat
COPE: to reward, to give in return
COPPED: rising to a cop or head
COPY: theme
CORAGIO (Italian): courage!
CORAM: an ignorant mistake for Quorum
CORANTO: a lively dance
CORINTH: a cant term for a brothel
CORINTHIAN: a wencher
CORKY: dry like cork
CORNUTO (ITALIAN): a cuckold
COROLLARY: a surplus
CORPORAL: corporeal, bodily
CORPORAL OF THE FIELD: an aide-de-camp
CORRIVAL: rival
COSTARD: the head
COSTER-MONGER: peddling, mercenary
COT-QUEAN: an effeminate man, molly-coddle
COTE: a cottage, to quote, instance
COTE: to come alongside, overtake
COUCHINGS: crouchings
COUNTERVAIL: to counterpoise, outweigh
COUNTRY: belonging to one's country
COUPLEMENT: union
COURT HOLY-WATER: flattery
COUNT CONFECT: a nobleman composed of affectation
COUNTENANCE: fair shew
COUNTERFEIT: portrait, a piece of base coin
COUNTERPOINT: a counterpane
COUNTY: count, earl
COVENT: a convent
COVER: to lay the table for dinner
COWISH: cowardly
COWL-STAFF: the staff on which a vessel is supported between two men
COX MY PASSION: an oath, a euphemism for 'God's Passion.'
COY: to stroke, fondle, to condescend with difficulty
COYSTRILL: a kestril, a cowardly kind of hawk
COZEN: to cheat
COZENAGE: cheating
COZENER: a cheater
COZIER: a tailor
CRACK: to boast, a loud noise, clap, a forward boy
CRACKER: boaster
CRACK-HEMP: a gallows-bird
CRANK: a winding passage
CRANKING: winding
CRANTS: garlands, a doubtful word
CRARE: a ship of burden
CRAVEN: a dunghill cock
CREATE: formed, compounded
CREDENT: creditable, credible, credulous
CREDIT: report
CRESCIVE: increasing
CRESTLESS: not entitled to bear arms, lowborn
CRISP: curled, winding
CROSS: a piece of money, so called because coin was formerly stamped with a cross
CROW-KEEPER: one who scares crows
CROWNER: a coroner
CROWNET: a coronet
CRY: the yelping of hounds, a pack of hounds, a company, used contemptuously
CRY AIM: to encourage
CUE: the last words of an actor's speech, which is the signal for the next actor to begin
CUISSES: pieces of armor to cover the thighs

CULLION: a base fellow
CUNNING: skill, skillful
CURB: to bend, truckle
CURRENTS: occurrences
CURST: petulant, shrewish
CURSTNESS: shrewishness
CURTAIL: a cur
CURTAL: a docked horse
CURTAL-AXE: a cutlass
CUSTALORUM: a ludicrous mistake for Custos Rotulorum
CUSTARD-COFFIN: the crust of a custard-pudding
CUSTOMER: a common woman
CUT: a cheat, 'to draw cuts' is to draw lots
CYPRESS: a kind of crape

DAFF: to befool, to put off; this seems to be a corruption of 'doff.'
DAMN: to condemn
DANGER: reach, control, power
DANSKER: a Dane
DARE: to challenge
DARKLING: in the dark
DARRAIGN: to set in array
DAUB: to disguise
DAUBERY: imposition
DAY-WOMAN: a dairy-maid
DEAR: dire, that which has to do with the affections, piteous, important
DEARN: lonely. (Gower)
DEBOSHED: debauched, drunken
DECK: to bedew, this is probably a form of the verb 'to drag,' now a provincial word
DECK: a pack of cards
DECLINE: to enumerate, as in going through the cases of a noun
DECLINED: fallen
DEEM: doom, judgment
DEFEAT: to undo, destroy, destruction
DEFEATURE: disfigurement
DEFENCE: art of fencing
DEFEND: to forbid
DEFENSIBLE: having the power to defend
DEFTLY: dexterously
DEFY: renounce
DEGREES: a step
DELAY: to let slip by delaying
DEMERIT: merit, desert
DEMURELY: solemnly
DENAY: denial
DENIER: the 12th part of a French sol
DENOTEMENT: marking, note or manifestation
DENY: to refuse
DEPART: departure, to part
DEPARTING: parting, separation
DEPEND: to be in service
DERIVED: born, descended
DEROGATE: degraded
DESCANT: a variation upon a melody, hence, metaphorically, a comment on a given theme
DESIGN: to draw up articles
DESPATCH: to deprive, bereave
DESPERATE: determined, bold
DETECT: to charge, blame
DETERMINE: to conclude
DICH: optative mood, perhaps contracted for 'do it.'
DIET: food regulated by the rules of medicine
DIET: to have one's food regulated by the rules of medicine
DIFFUSED: confused
DIGRESSING: transgressing, going out of the right way
DIGRESSION: transgression
DIG-YOU-GOOD-DEN: give you good evening
DILDO: the chorus or burden of a song
DINT: stroke
DIRECTION: judgment, skill
DISABLE: to disparage
DISAPPOINTED: unprepared
DISCASE: to undress
DISCONTENT: a malcontent
DISCOURSE: power of reasoning
DISDAINED: disdainful
DISLIMN: to disfigure, transform
DISME: a tenth or tithe
DISPARK: to destroy a park
DISPONGE: to squeeze out as from a sponge
DISPOSE: disposal
DISPOSE: to conspire
DISPOSITION: maintenance
DISPUTABLE: disputation
DISPUTE: to argue, examine
DISSEMBLY: used ridiculously for assembly
DISTASTE: to corrupt
DISTEMPERED: discontented
DISTRACTION: a detached troop or company of soldiers
DISTRAUGHT: distracted, mad
DIVERTED: turned from the natural course
DIVISION: a phrase or passage in a melody
DIVULGED: published, spoken of
DOFF: to do off, strip., to put off with an excuse
DOIT: a small Dutch coin
DOLE: portion dealt, grief, lamentation
DON: to do on, put on
DONE: 'done to death,' put to death
DOTANT: one who dotes, a dotard
DOUT: to do out, quench
DOWLAS: a kind of coarse sacking
DOWLE: the swirl of a feather
DOWN-GYVED: hanging down like gyves or fetters
DRAB: a harlot
DRABBING: whoring
DRAUGHT: a privy
DRAWN: having his sword drawn
DRAWN: drunk, having taken a good draught
DRIBBLING: weak
DRIVE: to rush impetuously
DROLLERY: a puppet-show
DRUMBLE: to dawdle
DRY: thirsty
DUC-DAME: perhaps the Latin duc-ad-me, bring him to me
DUDGEON: a dagger
DULL: soothing
DULLARD: a dull person
DUMP: complaint
DUP: to do up, lift up

EAGER: sour, harsh, biting
EANLING: a yeanling, a lamb
EAR: to plough
ECHE: to eke out. (Gower)
ECSTASY: madness
EFT: ready, convenient
EISEL: vinegar
ELD: old age
EMBOSSED: swollen into protuberances, covered with foam
EMBOWELLED: disembowelled, emptied
EMBRASURE: embrace
EMINENCE: exalted station
EMPERY: empire

EMULATION: jealousy, mutiny
EMULOUS: jealous
ENCAVE: to place oneself in a cave
END: 'Still an end,' continually for ever
ENFEOFF: to place in possession in fee simple
ENGINE: a machine of war
ENGLUT: to swallow speedily
ENGROSS: to make gross or fat
ENGROSSMENT: immoderate acquisition
ENKINDLE: to make keen
ENMEW: to shut up, as a hawk is shut up in a mew
ENSCONCE: to cover as with a fort
ENSEAMED: fat, rank
ENSHIELD: hidden
ENTERTAIN: encounter, experience
ENTERTAINMENT: treatment, a disposition to entertain a proposal, service
ENTREATMENTS: interviews
EPHESIAN: interviews
EPHESIAN: a toper, a cant term
EQUIPAGE: attendance
EREWHILE: a short time since
ESCOT: to pay a man's reckoning, to maintain
ESPERANCE: hope, used as a war-cry
ESPIAL: a scout or spy
ESTIMATION: conjecture
ESTRIDGE: ostridge
ETERNE: eternal
EVEN: coequal
EVEN: to equal
EXAMINE: to question
EXCREMENT: that which grows outwardly from the body and has no sensation like the hair or nails, any outward show
EXECUTOR: an executioner
EXEMPT: excluded
EXERCISE: a religious service
EXHALE: to hale or draw out, to draw the sword
EXHIBITION: allowance, tension
EXIGENT: death, ending
EXION: ridiculously used for 'action.'
EXPECT: expectation
EXPEDIENCE: expedition, undertaking, haste
EXPEDIENT: expeditious, swift
EXPIATE: completed
EXPOSTULATE: to expound, discuss
EXPOSTURE: exposure
EXPRESS: to reveal
EXPULSE: to expel
EXSUFFICATE: that which has been hissed off, contemptible
EXTEND: to seize
EXTENT: a seizure
EXTERN: outward
EXTIRP: to extirpate
EXTRACTING: distracting
EXTRAUGHT: extracted, descended
EXTRAVAGANT: foreign, wandering
EXTREMES: extravagance of conduct, extremities
EYAS: a nestling hawk
EYAS-MUSKET: a nestling of the musket or merlin, the smallest species of British hawk
EYE: a glance, œillad
EYE: a shade of color, as in shot silk
EYNE: eyes

FACINOROUS: wicked
FACT: guilt
FACTIOUS: instant, importunate
FACULTY: essential virtue or power
FADGE: to suit
FADING: a kind of ending to a song
FAIN: glad, gladly
FAIR: beauty
FAITOR: a traitor
FALL: to let fall
FALLOW: fawn-colored
FALSE: falsehood
FALSING: deceptive
FAMILIAR: a familiar spirit
FANCY-FREE: untouched by love
FANG: to seize in the teeth
FANTASTIC: a fantastical person
FAP: drunk
FAR: farther
FARCED: stuffed
FARDEL: a burden
FARTUOUS: used ridiculously for 'virtuous.'
FAST: assuredly, unalterably
FAT: dull
FAVOR: countenance, complexion, quality
FEAR: the object of fear, to affright
FEARFUL: subject to fear, timorous
FEAT: dexterous
FEAT: to make fine
FEATER: more neatly
FEATLY: nimbly, daintily
FEATURE: beauty
FEDERARY: confederate
FEE-GRIEF: a grief held, as it were, in fee-simple, or the peculiar property of him who possesses it
FEEDER: agent, servant
FEERE: a companion, husband
FEHEMENTLY: used ridiculously for 'vehemently.'
FELL: the hide
FENCE: art or skill in defence
FEODARY: one who holds an estate by suit or service to a superior lord; hence one who acts under the direction of another
FESTER: to rankle, grow virulent
FESTINATELY: quickly
FET: fetched
FICO: a fig
FIELDED: in the field of battle
FIG: to insult
FIGHTS: clothes hung round a ship to conceal the men from the enemy
FILE: a list or catalogue
FILE: to defile, to smooth or polish, to make even
FILL-HORSE: shaft-horse
FILLS: the shafts
FILTH: a whore
FINE: end, to make fine or specious
FINELESS: endless
FIRAGO: ridiculously used for 'Virago.'
FIRE-DRAKE: Will o' the Wisp
FIRE-NEW: with the glitter of novelty on, like newly-forged metal
FIRK: to chastise
FIT: canto or division of a song, a trick or habit
FITCHEW: a polecat
FIVES: a disease incident to horses
FLAP-DRAGON: raisins in burning brandy
FLAP-JACK: a pan-cake
FLAT: certain
FLATNESS: lowness, depth
FLAW: a gust of wind, sudden emotion or the cause of it
FLAW: to make a flaw in, to break
FLECKED: spotted, streaked

FLEET: to float, to pass away, to pass the time
FLEETING: inconstant
FLESHMENT: the act of fleshing the sword, hence the first feat of arms
FLEWED: furnished with hang lips, as hounds are
FLIGHT: a particular mode of practising archery
FLIRT-GILL: a light woman
FLOURISH: an ornament
FLOURISH: to ornament, disguise with ornament
FLOTE: wave, sea
FLUSH: fresh, full of vigor
FOIL: defeat, disadvantage
FOIN: to fence, fight
FOISON: plenty
FOND: foolish, foolishly affectionate
FOOT-CLOTH: a saddle-cloth hanging down to the ground
FOR: for that, because
FORBID: accursed, outlawed
FORBODE: forbidden
FORCE: to stuff, for 'farce.'
FORCED: falsely attributed
FORDO: to kill, destroy, to weary
FORFEND: forbid
FOREIGN: obliged to live abroad
FOREPAST: former
FORESLOW: to delay
FORGETIVE: inventive
FORKED: horned
FORMAL: regular, retaining its proper and essential characteristic
FORSPENT: exhausted, weary
FORSPEAK: to speak against
FORTHRIGHT: a straight path; forthrights and meanders, straight paths and crooked ones
FORWEARY: to weary, exhaust
FOSSET-SELLER: one who sells the pipes inserted into a vessel to give vent to the liquor, and stopped by a spigot
FOX: a sword; a cant word
FOX-SHIP: the cunning of the fox
FRAMPOLD: peevish, unquiet
FRANK: the feeding place of swine
FRANKED: confined
FRANKLIN: a freeholder, a small squire
FRAUGHT: freighted
FRAUGHTAGE: freight
FRAUGHTING: of to fraught; loading or constituting the cargo of a ship
FRESH: a spring of fresh water
FRET: the stop of a guitar
FRET: to wear away, to variegate
FRIEND: to befriend
FRIPPERY: an old-clothes shop
FROM: contrary to
FRONT: to affront, oppose
FRONTIER: opposition
FRONTLET: that which is worn on the forehead
FRUSH: to break or bruise
FRUSTRATE: frustrated
FUB OFF: to put off
FULFILL: to fill full
FULL: complete.
FULLAM: a loaded die
FULSOME: lustful
FURNITOR: furnitory, an herb
FURNISHED: equipped

GABERDINE: a loose outer coat, or smock frock
GAD: a pointed instrument, a goad, upon the gad, with impetuous haste, upon the spur of the moment
GAIN-GIVING: misgiving
GAIT: going, steps
GALLIARD: a kind of dance
GALLIASSE: a kind of ship
GALLIMAUFRY: a ridiculous medley
GALLOW: to scare
GALLOWGLASS: the irregular infantry of Ireland, and the Highlands of Scotland
GAMESTER: a frolicsome person, a loose woman
GARBOIL: disorder, uproar
GARISH: gaudy, staring
GARNER: to lay by, as corn in a barn
GAST: frightened
GAUDY: festive
GAZE: an object of wonder
GEAR: matter of business of any kind
GECK: a fool
GENERAL: the generality, common people
GENERATIONS: children
GENEROSITY: noble birth
GENEROUS: noble
GENTILITY: good manners
GENTLE: gentlefolk, noble, to ennoble
GENTRY: complaisance, conduct becoming gentlefolk
GERMAN: akin, appropriate
GERMEN: seed, embryo
GEST: period
GIB: a he-cat
GIFTS: talents, endowment
GIGLOT: a wanton girl
GILDER: a coin of the value of or
GILT: money, state of wealth
GIMMAL: double
GIMMOR: contrivance
GING: gang
GIRD: to gibe
GIRD: a sarcasm or gibe
GLEEK: to scoff, a scoff
GLOSE: to comment; hence, to be garrulous
GLUT: to swallow
GNARL: to snarl
GOOD-DEED: indeed
GOOD-DEN: good-evening, contracted from 'Good-even.'
GOOD-YEAR OR GOOD-JER: a corruption of the French goujere; the venereal disease
GORBELLIED: corpulent
GOVERNMENT: discretion
GOURD: a species of game of chance
GOUT: a drop
GRACIOUS: abounding in grace Divine
GRAINED: engrained
GRAMERCY: grand mercy, much thanks
GRANGE: the farmstead attached to a monastery, a solitary farm-house
GRATILLITY: used ridiculously for 'gratuity.'
GRATULATE: to congratulate
GRAVE: to bury
GREASILY: grossly
GREEK: a bawd
GREEN: immature, fresh, unused
GREENLY: foolishly
GREET: to weep
GRIZE: a step
GROSSLY: palpably
GROUNDLING: one who sits in the pit of a theatre
GROWING: accruing
GUARD: decoration, to decorate

GUARDAGE: guardianship
GUINEA-HEN: the pitando, a cant term
GULES: red, a term in heraldry
GULF: the throat
GUN-STONE: a cannon ball
GUST: taste, relish
GYVE: to fetter

HACK: to become common
HAGGARD: a wild or unreclaimed hawk
HAG-SEED: seed or offspring of a hag
HAIR: course, order, grain
HALIDOM: holiness, sanctification, Christian fellowship; used as an oath, and analogous to 'By my faith.'
HALL: an open space to dance in
HALLOWMAS: All Hallow's Day
HAP: chance, fortune
HAPPILY: accidentally
HANDSAW: perhaps a corruption of Heronshaw; a hern
HARDIMENT: defiance, brave deeds
HARLOCK: charlock, wild mustard
HARRY: to annoy, harass
HAVING: property, fortune
HAVIOUR: behavior
HAUGHT: haughty
HAUNT: company
HAY: a term in fencing
HEADY: violent, headlong
HEAT: 'to heat,' heated
HEBENON: hebane
HEFT: a heaving
HEFT: furnished with a handle: hence, metaphorically, finished off, delicately formed
HELM: to steer, manage
HENCE: henceforward
HENCHMAN: a page or attendant
HENT: to seize, take
HERMIT: a beadsman, one bound to pray for another
HEST: command
HIGH: used in composition with adjectives to heighten or emphasize their signification, as, high-fantastical
HIGHT: called
HILD: held
HILDING: a paltry fellow
HINT: suggestion
HIREN: a prostitute, with a pun on the word 'iron.'
HIT: to agree
HOISE: to hoist, heave up on high
HOIST: hoisted
HOLP: to help; helped
HOME: to the utmost
HONEST: chaste
HONESTY: chastity
HONEY-STALKS: the red clover
HOODMAN-BLIND: the game now called blind-man's-buff
HORN-MAD: probably, that is, brain-mad
HOROLOGE: a clock
HOT-HOUSE: a brothel
HOX: to hamstring
HUGGER-MUGGER: secresy
HULL: to drift on the sea like a wrecked ship
HUMOROUS: fitful, or, perhaps, hurried
HUNT-COUNTER: to follow the scent the wrong way
HUNTS-UP: a holla used in hunting when the game was on foot
HURLY: noise, confusion
HURTLE: to clash
HURTLING: noise, confusion
HUSBANDRY: frugality, management
HUSWIFE: a jilt

ICE-BROOK: an icy-cold brook
I'FECKS: in faith, a euphemism
IGNOMY: ignominy
IMAGE: representation
IMBARE: to bare, lay open
IMMEDIACY: close connexion
IMMOMENT: unimportant
IMP: to graft, to splice a falcon's broken feathers
IMP: a scion, a child
IMPAWN: to stake, compromise
IMPEACH: to bring into question, impeachment
IMPEACHMENT: cause of censure, hindrance
IMPERCEIVERANT: dull of perception
IMPETICOS: to pocket
IMPORTANCE: importunity
IMPORTANT: importunate
IMPORTING: significant
IMPOSE: imposition, meaning command or task imposed upon any one
IMPOSITION: command
IMPRESE: a device with a motto
IMPRESS: to compel to serve
INCAPABLE: unconscious
INCARNARDINE: to dye red
INCENSED: incited, egged on
INCH-MEAL: by inch-meal, by portions of inches
INCLINING: compliant, inclination
INCLIP: to embrace
INCLUDE: conclude
INCONY: fine, delicate
INCORRECT: ill-regulated
IND: India
INDENT: to compound or bargain
INDEX: a preface
INDIFFERENT: ordinary
INDIGEST: disordered
INDITE: to invite, to convict
INDUCTION: introduction, beginning
INDURANCE: delay
INFINITE: infinite power
INGRAFT: to engraff, engrafted
INHABITABLE: uninhabitable
INHERIT: to possess
INHOOPED: penned up in hoops
INKHORN-MATE: a contemptuous term for an ecclesiastic, or man of learning
INKLE: a kind of narrow fillet or tape
INLAND: civilized, well-educated
INLY: inwardly
INQUISITION: enquiry
INSANE: that which causes insanity
INSCONCE: to arm, fortify
INSTANCE: example, information, reason, proof
INTEND: to pretend
INTENDING: regarding
INTENDMENT: intention
INTENTIVELY: attentively
INTERESSED: allied
INTERMISSION: pause, delay
INTRENCHMENT: not capable of being cut
INTRINSE: intricate
INTRINSICATE: intricate
INVENTION: imagination
INWARD: an intimate friend, intimate
INWARDNESS: intimacy

IRREGULOUS: lawless, licentious
ITERATION: reiteration

JACK: a mean fellow
JACK-A-LENT: a puppet thrown at in Lent
JACK GUARDANT: a jack in office
JADE: to whip, to treat with contempt
JAR: the ticking of a clock
JAR: to tick as a clock
JAUNCE: to prance
JESS: a strap of leather attached to the talons of a hawk, by which it is held on the fist
JEST: to tilt in a tournament
JET: to strut
JOVIAL: appertaining to Jove
JOURNAL: daily
JUDICIOUS: critical
JUMP: to agree, to hazard, hazard, exactly, nicely
JUSTICER: a judge, magistrate
JUT: to encroach
JUTTY: a projection, to jut out beyond
JUVENAL: youth, young man

KAM: crooked
KECKSY: hemlock
KEECH: a lump of tallow
KEEL: to skim
KEEP: to restrain
KEISAR: Caesar, Emperor
KERN: the rude foot soldiers of the Irish
KIBE: a chillblain
KICKSHAW: a made dish
KICKSY WICKSY: a wife, used in disdain
KILN-HOLE: the ash-hole under a kiln
KIND: nature
KINDLE: to bring forth young; used only of beasts
KINDLESS: unnatural
KINDLY: natural
KIRTLE: a gown
KNAVE: a boy, a serving-man
KNAP: to snap, crack
KNOT: a figure in garden beds
KNOW: to acknowledge

LABRAS: lips
LACED-MUTTON: a courtezan
LAG: the lowest of the people
LAG: late, behindhand
LAKIN: ladykin, little lady, an endearing term applied to the Virgin Mary in the oath, 'By our lakin.'
LAND-DAMN: perhaps to extirpate; Hanmer thinks it means to kill by stopping the urine
LAPSED: taken, apprehended
LARGE: licentious, free
LARGESS: a present
LASS-LORN: deserted by a mistress
LATCH: to smear, to catch
LATED: belated
LATTEN: made of brass
LAUND: lawn
LAVOLTA: a dance
LAY: wager
LEAGUE: besieging army
LEASING: lying
LEATHER-COATS: a kind of apple
LEECH: a physician
LEER: countenance, complexion
LEET: a manor court
LEGERITY: lightness
LEGE: to allege
LEIGER: an ambassador resident abroad
LEMAN: a lover or mistress
LENTEN: meagre, that which may be eaten in Lent
L'ENVOY: the farewell or moral at the end of a tale or poem
LET: to hinder, to hinder
LET: hindrance
LETHE: death
LEVEL: to aim, that which is aimed at
LEWD: ignorant, foolish
LEWDLY: wickedly
LEWDSTER: a lewd person
LIBBARD: a leopard
LIBERAL: licentious
LIBERTY: libertinism
LICENSE: licentiousness
LIEF: dear
LIFTER: a thief
LIGHT O' LOVE: a tune so called
LIGHTLY: easily, generally
LIKE: to please, to liken, compare, likely
LIKELIHOOD: promise, appearance
LIKING: condition
LIMBECK: an alembick, a still
LIMBO: or Limbo patrum, the place where good men under the Old Test. were believed to be imprisoned till released by Christ after his crucifixion
LIME: bird-lime
LIMN: to draw
LINE: to entangle as with bird-lime, to smear with bird-lime, to mix lime with beer or other liquor
LINE: to cover on the inside, to strengthen by inner works
LINSTOCK: a staff with a match at the end of it, used by gunners in firing cannon
LIST: a margin, hence a bound or enclosure
LITHER: lazy
LITTLE: miniature
LIVELIHOOD: appearance of life
LIVERY: a law phrase, signifying the act of delivering a freehold into the possession of the heir or purchaser
LIVING: lively, convincing
LOACH: a fish so called
LOB: a looby
LOCKRAM: a sort of coarse linen
LODE-STAR: the leading-star, pole-star
LOFFE: to laugh
LOGGATS: the game called nine-pins
LONGLY: longingly
LOOF: to luff, bring a vessel up to the wind
LOON: a low contemptible fellow
LOT: a prize in a lottery
LOTTERY: that which falls to a man by lot
LOWT: a clown
LOWT: to treat one as a lowt, with contempt
LOZEL: a spendthrift
LUBBER: a leopard
LUCE: the pike or jack, a fresh-water fish
LUMPISH: dull, dejected
LUNES: fits of lunacy
LURCH: to defeat, to win
LURCH: to shift, to play tricks
LURE: a thing stuffed to resemble a bird with which the falconer allures a hawk
LUSH: juicy, luxuriant

LUSTIG: lusty, cheerful
LUXURIOUS: lascivious
LUXURY: lust
LYM: a limer or slow hound

MADE: having his fortune made
MAGNIFICO: the chief magistrate at Venice
MAGOT-PIE: a magpie, a pie which feeds on magots
MAILED: covered as with a coat of mail
MAIN-COURSE: a sea-term
MAKE: to do up, bar, to do
MALKIN: a familiar name for Mary; hence a servant wench
MALLECHO: mischief
MAMMERING: hesitating
MAMMETS: a woman's breasts, a doll
MAMMOCK: to break, tear
MAN: to tame a hawk
MANAGE: management
MANDRAGORA, MANDRAKE: a plant of soporiferous quality, supposed to resemble a man
MANKIND: having a masculine nature
MARCHES: frontiers, borders
MARCHPANE: a kind of sweet biscuit
MARGENT: margin
MARRY TRAP: an oath
MARTLEMAS: the Feast of St. Martin, which occurs on the 11th of Nov. when the fine weather generally ends; hence applied to an old man
MATCH: an appointment
MATE: to confound, dismay
MEACOCK: tame, cowardly
MEALED: mingled
MEAN: instrument used to promote an end
MEAN: the tenor part in a harmony
MEAN: opportunity, power
MEASURE: reach, a stately dance
MEAZEL: a leper, spoken in contempt of a mean person
MEDAL: a portrait in a locket
MEDICINE: a physician
MEED: reward, hire
MEHERCLE: by Hercules
MEINY: retinue
MELL: to mix, to meddle
MEMORIZE: to cause to be remembered
MEPHISTOPHILUS: the name of a familiar spirit
MERCATANTE: (Italian), a foreign trader
MERELY: simply, absolutely
MESS: a company of four
METAPHYSICAL: supernatural
METE-YARD: measuring-wand
MEW UP: to confine
MICHER: a truant
MICKLE: much
MILL-SIXPENCE: a milled sixpence
MINCE: to do any thing affectedly
MINCING: affected
MISCREATE: illegitimate
MISDOUBT: to suspect
MISERY: avarice
MISPRISE: to despise, to mistake
MISPRISION: mistake
MISSIVE: messenger
MISTEMPERED: angry
MISTHINK: to think ill of
MISTRESS: the jack in bowling
MOBLED: muffled
MODERN: commonplace
MODULE: a model, image
MOE: more, of frequent occurrence
MOIETY: a portion
MOME: a stupid person
MOMENTARY: momentary
MONTHS-MIND: a monthly commemoration of the dead, but used ludicrously to mean a great mind or strong desire
MOOD: anger
MOON-CALF: a nick-name applied to Caliban
MOONISH: inconstant
MOP: nod
MORISCO: a Moor
MORRIS-PIKE: Moorish-pike
MORT: death, applied to animals of the chase
MORT-DU-VINAIGRE: (French), a ridiculous oath
MORTAL: fatal, deadly, murderous
MORTIFIED: ascetic
MOSE: a doubtful word, applied to some disease in a horse
MOTION: solicitation, emotion, a puppet
MOTIVE: one who moves, that which moves
MOTLEY: used as the many-colored coat of a fool, a fool
MOTLEY-MINDED: foolish
MOUSE-HUNT: a weasel
MOW: to make grimaces
MOY: a coin, probably a moidore
MUCH: significant of contempt, used ironically
MURE: a wall
MUST: a scramble
MUTINE: to mutiny, a mutineer

NAPKIN: a handkerchief
NATURAL: an idiot
NAYWARD: towards denial, a catch-word, by-word
NEB: the beak
NEELD: a needle
NEIF: hand
NEPHEW: a grandson
NETHER-STOCKS: stockings
NEXT: nearest
NICE: foolish
NICK: score or reckoning
NICK: to brand with folly
NIGHTED: black as night
NIGHT-RULE: nightly solemnity
NINE MEN'S MORRIS: a place set apart for a Moorish dance by nine men
NINNY: a fool, jester
NOBILITY: nobleness
NOBLE: a coin, worth
NODDY: a dolt
NONCE: for the nonce, corrupted from 'for then once,' for the occasion
NOOK-SHOTTEN: indented with bays and creeks
NOURISH: a nurse
NOVUM: a game at dice
NOWL: head
NUTHOOK: a hook for pulling down nuts, hence a thief

O: a circle
OAR: to row as with oars
OBSEQUIOUS: behaving as becomes one who attends funeral obsequies
OBSEQUIOUSLY: funereally
OBSTACLE: ridiculously used for 'obstinate.'

OCCUPATION: persons occupied in business
OCCURRENT: an incident
OD'S BODY, OD'S HEARTLINGS, OD'S PITTIKINS, OD'S PLESSED WILL: 'Od's in these and all similar exclamations is a euphemism for 'God's.'
OEILLIAD: an amorous glance
O'ERPARTED: having too important a part to act
O'ER-RAUGHT: overreached, overtasked
OFFERING: challenging
OFFICE: benefit, kindness, use, function
OLD: a cant term for great, as we say fine, or pretty
ONCE: some time
ONEYER: a banker, a doubtful word
OPE: open
OPE: to open, to open
OPEN: plain, public, to give tongue as a hound
OPERANT: active
OPINIONED: used ridiculously for pinioned
OPPOSITE: adversary
OPPOSITION: combat
OR: before
ORDER: measures
ORDINANCE: rank, order
ORGULOUS: proud
ORT: leaving, refuse
OSTENT: show, appearance
OSTENTATION: show, appearance
OUNCE: a beast of prey of the tiger kind
OUPHE: a fairy
OUSEL-COCK: the blackbird
OUT: all out, fully
OUT-LOOK: to face down
OUTWARD: not in the secret of affairs, outside
OWE: to own

PACK: to practice unlawful confederacy
PACK: a number of people confederated
PADDOCK: a toad
PAID: punished
PALABRAS: words, a cant term, from the Spanish
PALE: to enclose
PALL: to wrap as with a pall
PALLED: impaired
PALMER: one who bears a palm-branch, in token of having made a pilgrimage to Palestine
PALMY: victorious
PARCELLED: belonging to individuals
PARD: the leopard
PARITOR: an apparitor
PARLE: talk
PARLOUS: perilous, keen, shrewd
PARTED: endowed, gifted
PARTIZAN: a pike
PASH: the face
PASH: to strike violently, to bruise, crush
PASS: to practice, to surpass expectation
PASSANT: a term of heraldry, applied to animals represented on the shield as passing by at a trot
PASSING: surpassingly, exceedingly
PASSION: to have feelings
PASSIONATE: to suffer
PASSY-MEASURE: a kind of dance
PASTRY: the room where pastry was made
PATCH: a mean fellow
PATCHED: dressed in motley
PATCHERY: trickery
PATH: to walk
PATHETICAL: affected, hypocritical
PATIENT: to make patient, to compose
PATINE: the metal disc on which the bread is placed in the administration of the Eucharist
PATTERN: to give an example of, afford a pattern for
PAUCA VERBA: few words
PAUCAS: few, a cant term
PAVIN: a dance
PAX: a small image of Christ
PAY: to despatch
PEAT: a term of endearment for a child
PEDASCULE: a pedant, schoolmaster
PEER: to peep out
PEIZE: to balance, weigh down
PELTING: paltry
PERDU: lost
PERDURABLE: durable
PERDY: a euphemism for Par Dieu
PERFECT: certain
PERFECT: to inform perfectly
PERIAPTS: charms worn round the neck
PERJURE: a perjured person
PERSEVER: to persevere
PERSPECTIVE: a telescope, or some sort of optical glass
PEW-FELLOW: a comrade
PHEEZE: to comb, fleece, curry
PIA-MATER: the membrane covering the brain, the brain itself
PICK: to pitch, throw.
PICKED: chosen, selected
PICKERS (*and* STEALERS): the fingers, used ridiculously
PICKING: insignificant
PICKT-HATCH: a place noted for brothels
PIED: motley-coated, wearing the motley coat of a jester
PIELED: shaven
PIGHT: pitched
PILCHER: a scabbard
PILL: to pillage
PIN: a malady of the eyes, the centre of a target
PINFOLD: a pound, a place to confine lost cattle
PIONED: digged
PLACKET: a petticoat-front
PLAIN SONG: a simple air
PLAITED: intricate
PLANCHED: made of boards
PLANTATION: colonizing, planting a colony
PLAUSIVE: plausible
PLEACHED: interwoven
POINT: a lace furnished with a tag by which the breeches were held up
POINT-DE-VICE: derived from the French, faultless
POISE: balance, doubt
POLLED: bare
POMANDER: a perfumed ball
POMEWATER: a kind of apple
POOR-JOHN: a herring
POPINJAY: a parrot
PORT: pomp, state
PORT: a gate
PORTABLE: bearable
PORTANCE: conduct, behavior
POSSESS: to inform

POTCH: to push violently
POTENT: a potentate
POUNCET-BOX: a box for holding perfumes
POWER: forces, army
PRACTICE: wicked stratagem
PRACTISANT: a confederate
PRANK: to dress up
PRECEPT: a justice's summons
PRECIOUSLY: in business of great importance
PREGNANT: fertile of invention, ready, obvious
PRENOMINATE: to name beforehand, to prophesy
PRE-ORDINANCE: old-established law
PRESENCE: the presence-chamber, high bearing
PREST: ready
PRETENCE: design
PRETEND: to portend, to intend
PREVENT: to anticipate
PRICK: the mark denoting the hour on a dial
PRICK: to incite, to choose by pricking a hole with a pin opposite the name
PRICK-SONG: music sung in parts by note
PRICKET: a stag of two years
PRIDE: heat
PRIG: to steal
PRIME: rank, lecherous
PRIMER: more-important
PRIMERO: a game at cards
PRINCIPALITY: that which holds the highest place
PRINCOX: a coxcomb
PRISER: a prize-fighter
PROCURE: to bring
PROFACE: much good may it do you
PROFANE: outspoken
PROGRESS: a royal ceremonial journey
PROJECT: to shape or contrive
PROMPTURE: suggestion
PRONE: ready, willing
PROOF: strength of manhood
PROPAGATE: to advance, to forward
PROPAGATION: obtaining
PROPER-FALSE: natural falsehood
PROPERTIED: endowed with the properties of
PROPERTIES: scenes, dresses, &c. used in a theatre
PROPERTY: to take possession of
PROPOSE: to suppose, for the sake of argument, to converse
PROPOSE: conversation
PROROGUE: to defer
PROVAND: provender
PROVISION: forecast
PUCELLE: a virgin, the name given to Joan of Arc
PUDENCY: modesty
PUGGING: thieving
PUN: to pound
PURCHASE: to acquire, win
PURCHASE: gain, winnings
PUT: to compel
PUTTER-ON: an instigator
PUTTER-OUT: one who lends money at interest
PUTTING-ON: instigation
PUTTOCK: a kite

QUAIL: to faint, be languid, be afraid, to cause to quail
QUAINT: curiously beautiful
QUAKE: to cause to quake or tremble
QUALIFY: to moderate
QUALITY: those of the same nature, rank or condition
QUARREL: a suit, cause
QUARRY: game, a heap of game
QUART D'ÉCU: a quarter crown
QUARTER: the post allotted to a soldier
QUAT: a pimple; used in contempt of a person
QUEASY: squeamish, unsettled
QUELL: murder
QUENCH: to grow cool
QUERN: a hand-mill
QUEST: enquiry, search, inquest, jury
QUESTRIST: one who goes in search of another
QUICK: so far gone in pregnancy that the child is alive
QUICKEN: to come to life
QUIDDITY: QUIDDIT.} a subtle question
QUILLET: quidlibet, a subtle case in law
QUINTAIN: a post for tilting at
QUIP: sharp jest, a taunt
QUIRE: to sing in concert
QUIT: to requite, respond
QUIT: past tense of the verb to quit, quitted
QUITANCE: requital
QUIVER: active
QUOTE: to note

RABATO: a ruff
RABBIT-SUCKER: a weasel
RACE: breed; inherited nature
RACK: wreck, to enhance the price of anything, to drive as clouds
RAG: a term of contempt applied to persons
RAKE: to cover
RAPT: transported with emotion
RAPTURE: a fit
RASCAL: a lean deer
RASH: quick, violent
RATE: opinion, judgment, to assign, to value, to scold
RATOLORUM: a ludicrous mistake for Rotulorum
RAVIN: ravenous
RAVIN: to devour
RAUGHT: past tense of to reach
RAWLY: inadequately
RAWNESS: unprovided state
RAYED: arrayed, served
RAZED: slashed
REAR-MOUSE: the bat
REBATE: to deprive of keenness
REBECK: a three stringed fiddle
RECEIPT: money received
RECEIVING: capacity
RECHEAT: a point of the chase to call back the hounds
RECORD: to sing
RECORDER: a flute
RECURE: to cure, recover
RED-LATTICE: suitable to an ale-house, because ale-houses had commonly red lattices
RED PLAGUE: erysipelas
REDUCE: to bring back
REECHY: smoky, dirty
REFELL: to refute
REFER: to reserve to
REGIMENT: government
REGREET: a salutation
REGREET: to salute
REGUERDON: requital
RELATIVE: applicable
REMEMBER: to remind
REMORSE: pity

REMORSEFUL: full of pity, compassionate
REMOTION: removal
REMOVED: sequestered, remote
RENDER: to describe you
RENDER: account
RENEGE: to renounce, to deny
REPAIR: to renovate, comfort
REPEAL: to reverse the sentence of exile
REPROOF: confutation
REPUGN: to resist
REQUIEM: mass for the dead, so called because it begins with the words, Requiem eternam dona eis, Domine
RESOLVE: to satisfy, to dissolve
RESPECT: consideration
RESPECTIVE: respectful, thoughtful
RESPECTIVE: corresponding
RESPECTIVELY: respectfully
RETAILED: handed down
RETIRE: retreat
RETIRE: to draw back
REVERB: to echo
REVOLT: a rebel
RIB: to enclose as within ribs
RID: to destroy
RIFT: to split, a split
RIGGISH: wanton
RIGOL: a circle
RIPE: drunk
RIVAGE: the shore
RIVAL: a partner
RIVALITY: equal rank
RIVE: to fire
ROAD: the high road, applied to a common woman (traviata)
ROISTING: roistering, violent
ROMAGE: unusual stir
RONYON: a term of contempt applied to a woman
ROOD: the crucifix
ROOK: a cheater
ROPERY: roguery
ROPE-TRICKS: tricks such as are played by a rope-dancer
ROUND: to whisper, to become great with child, to finish off
ROUND: a diadem
ROUND: unceremonious
ROUNDEL: a dance or song
ROUNDURE: an enclosure
ROUSE: carousal
ROYNISH: mangy
RUBIOUS: ruddy
RUDDOCK: the redbreast
RUSH: to push
RUSHLING: rustling

SACRIFICIAL: reverent, as words used in religious worship
SACRING-BELL: the little bell rung at mass to give notice that the elements are consecrated
SAD: serious
SADLY: seriously
SADNESS: seriousness
SAFE: to make safe
SAG: to hang down
SALT: lascivious
SALT: taste
SANDED: marked with yellow spots
SANS: without
SAUCY: lascivious
SAW: moral saying
SAY: silken
SAY: assay, taste, relish
SCAFFOLDAGE: the gallery of a theatre
SCALD: scurvy, scabby
SCALE: to weigh in scales
SCALL: a scab, a word of reproach
SCAMBLE: to scramble
SCAMEL: probably a misprint for sea-mel, sea-mew
SCAN: to examine subtly
SCANT: to cut short, to spare
SCANT: scanty, short, scarcely
SCANTLING: a small portion
SCAPE: to escape
SCAPE: a sally
SCATHE: injury
SCATHE: to injure
SCATHFUL: destructive
SCONCE: the head
SCOTCH: to bruise or cut slightly
SCRIMER: a fencer
SCROYLE: a scabby fellow
SCULL: a shoal of fish
SCURVY: scabby; metaph, mean
SEAL: to set one's seal to a deed; hence, to confirm
SEAM: fat
SEAMY: showing the seam or sewing
SEAR: scorched, withered, to stigmatise
SEARCH: to probe; hence, to apply a healing remedy
SEATED: fixed, confirmed
SECT: a slip or scion, a political party
SECURELY: inconsiderately
SEEL: to close
SEELING: closing, blinding
SEEMING: seemly, becomingly
SEEMING: outward manner and appearance
SEEN: versed, instructed
SELD: seldom
SELF-BOUNTY: native goodness
SEMBLABLY: alike
SENIORY: seniority
SENNET: a flourish of trumpets
SEPULCHRE: to bury
SEQUESTRATION: separation
SERE: dry
SERJEANT: a bailiff
SERPIGO: a cutaneous disease
SERVICEABLE: 'serviceable vows,' vows that you will do her service, or be her servant
SETEBOS: the name of a fiend
SETTER: one who watches travellers to give information to thieves
SEVERAL: land which is not common but appropriated
SHAME: to be ashamed
SHAME: modesty
SHARDS: shreds, broken fragments of pottery
SHARDS: the wing cases of beetles; hence 'sharded.' and 'shard-bone.'
SHARKED: snatched up, as a shark does his prey
SHEEN: brilliancy
SHEER: pure, unmixed
SHENT: rebuked, blamed, hurt
SHERIFF'S-POST: a post at the door of a sheriff, to which royal proclamations were fixed
SHIVE: slice
SHOT: the reckoning at an ale-house
SHOUGHS: shaggy dogs
SHOULDERED: A doubtful word
SHOVEL-BOARD: game played by sliding metal pieces along a board at a mark
SHREWD: mischievous
SHRIFT: confession, absolution
SHRIVE: to confess
SHRIVING-TIME: time for confession
SHROUD: to enshroud oneself, cover oneself up

SIDE-SLEEVES: loose hanging sleeves
SIEGE: seat, stool, rank
SIGHT: an aperture in a helmet
SIGHTLESS: invisible, unsightly
SIGN: to give an omen
SILLY: simple, rustic
SIMULAR: counterfeit, feigned
SINGLE: feeble
SIR: a title applied to a bachelor of arts at the Universities
SITH: since
SITHENCE: since
SIZES: allowances
SKAINS-MATES: scapegraces
SKILL: to be of importance
SKILLESS: ignorant
SKIMBLE-SKAMBLE: rambling, disjointed
SKINKER: a drawer of liquor
SKIRR: to scour
SLACK: slacken
SLAVE: to turn to slavish uses
SLEAVE: floss-silk
SLEDDED: sledged
SLEIDED: untwisted, raw, applied to silk. (Gower)
SLEIGHTS: artifices
SLICE:
SLIPPER: slippery
SLIPS: a kind of noose, or leash, a piece of base money
SLIVER: to slice
SLIVER: a slice
SLOPS: loose breeches
SLUBBER: to slur over.
SMIRCHED: smeared, soiled
SMOOTH: to flatter
SMOOTHED: flattered, fawned upon
SNEAP: taunt, sarcasm
SNEAPED: pinched
SNEAPING:
SNECK-UP: go hang!
SNUFF: anger, 'to take in snuff' is to take offence
SOFTLY: gently
SOIL: spot, taint
SOLICIT: solicitation
SOLIDARE: a small coin
SOLVE: solution
SOMETIMES: formerly
SOOTH: truth, conciliation
SOOTH: true
SOREL: a buck of the third year
SORRIEST: most sorrowful
SORRY: sorrowful, dismal
SORT: a company, rank, condition, lot, 'In a sort,' in a manner
SORT: to choose, to suit, to consort
SOT: fool
SOUL-FEARING: soul-terrifying
SOWL: to lug, drag
SOWTER: name of a dog
SPECIALTY: a special contract
SPED: settled, done for
SPEED: fortune
SPERR: to bolt, fasten
SPIAL: spy
SPILL: to destroy
SPILTH: spilling
SPLEEN: violent haste, used of the lightning flash
SPRAG: quick
SPRING: shoot, bud, beginning
SPRINGHALT: stringhalt, a disease of horses
SPRITED: haunted
SPURS: roots of trees
SQUANDERED: scattered
SQUARE: to quarrel, the front part of a woman's dress, stomacher, equitable
SQUARER: quarreller
SQUASH: an unripe peascod
SQUIER: a square or rule
SQUINY: to squint
STAGGERS: a disease in horses, attended with giddiness: hence any bewildering distress
STAIN: to disfigure
STALE: a decoy, a gull, a prostitute
STALE: to make stale, deprive anything of its freshness
STAND UPON: to be incumbent on
STANIEL: an inferior kind of hawk
STARK: stiff
STARKLY: stiffly
STATE: a canopied chair
STATION: attitude, act of standing
STATIST: a statesman
STATUA: a statue
STATUE: image, picture
STATUTE: security, obligation
STATUTE-CAPS: woollen caps worn by citizens
STAY: a check
STEAD: to profit
STELLED: (a doubtful word) set or fixed
STERNAGE: steerage, course
STICKLER: an arbitrator in combats
STIGMATIC: a deformed person
STIGMATICAL: deformed
STILL: constant, constantly
STILLY: softly
STINT: to stop, to stop
STITHY: a smith's forge, to forge
STOCCADO: a stoccata, or thrust in fencing
STOCK: a stocking
STOMACH: courage, stubbornness, appetite, inclination
STONE-BOW: a cross-bow for throwing stones
STOUP: a cup
STOUT: strong, healthy
STOVER: folder
STRACHY: A word of doubtful meaning
STRAIGHT: immediately
STRAIN: lineage, disposition
STRAITED: straitened
STRANGE: foreign, coy, reserved, marvellous
STRANGENESS: coyness, reserve
STRANGER: foreigner
STRAPPADO: a kind of punishment
STRICTURE: strictness
STROSSERS: trowsers
STUCK: a thrust of a sword.
STUCK IN: corruption of stoccata
STUFF: baggage, material, substance
STUFFED: filled, stored
STY: to lodge as in a sty
SUBSCRIBE: to yield, to succumb
SUCCESS: issue, consequence, succession
SUCCESSIVE: succeeding
SUCCESSIVELY: in succession
SUDDEN: hasty, rash
SUDDENLY: hastily
SUFFERANCE: suffering
SUGGEST: to tempt, entice
SUGGESTION: temptation, enticement
SUITED: dressed
SULLEN: doleful, melancholy.
SUMPTER: a horse that carries provisions on a journey
SUPPOSE: a trick, imposition
SUPPOSED: counterfeit
SURCEASE: to cease
SURCEASE: cessation, end
SURPRISE: to capture by surprise

SUR-REINED: over-worked
SUSPECT: suspicion
SUSPIRE: to breathe
SWABBER: a sweeper of the deck of a ship
SWARTH: black, black quantity of grass cut down by one sweep of the scythe
SWASHER: swaggerer
SWASHING: dashing, smashing
SWATH: The same as 'swarth.'
SWATHLING: swaddling
SWAY: to move on
SWEAR: to adjure
SWEAR OVER: to out-swear
SWIFT: ready, quick
SWINGE-BUCKLER: a bully

TABLE: a tablet, note-book
TABLE-BOOK: note-book
TABLES: the game of backgammon, a note book
TABOR: a small side-drum
TABORER: a player on the tabor
TABOURINE: tambourine, drum
TAG: the rabble
TAINT: tainted
TAINTURE: defilement
TAKE: to infect, blast, bewitch
TAKE IN: to conquer
TAKE OUT: to copy
TAKE UP: to borrow money, or buy on credit, to make up a quarrel
TAKING: infection, malignant influence
TAKING UP: buying on credit
TALL: strong, valiant
TALE: counting, reckoning
TALLOW-CATCH: a lump of tallow
TANG: twang, sound, to sound
TANLING: anything tanned by the sun
TARRE: to excite, urge on
TARRIANCE: delay
TARTAR: Tartarus
TASK: to tax, challenge
TASKING: challenging
TASTE: to try
TAWDRY-LACE: a rustic necklace
TAXATION: satire, sarcasm
TAXING: satire
TEEN: grief
TELL: to count
TEMPER: to mix
TEMPERANCE: temperature
TEMPERED: mixed
TEND: to attend to
TENDER: to hold, to esteem, to have consideration for
TENT: to probe as a wound, a probe for searching a wound
TERCEL: the male of the goshawk
TERMAGANT: a ranting character in old plays
TESTED: pure, assayed
TESTERN: to reward with a tester, or sixpence
THARBOROUGH: (corrupted from 'third-borough') a constable
THEORICK: theory
THEWES: sinews, muscles
THICK: rapidly.
THICK-PLEACHED: thickly intertwined
THIRD-BOROUGH: a constable
THOUGHT: anxiety, grief, so 'to take thoughts' is to give way to grief
THARSONICAL: boastful
THREE-MAN BEETLE: a wooden mallet worked by three men
THREE-MAN-SONG-MEN: singers of glees in three parts
THREE-PILE: three-piled velvet
THRENE: lament
THRID: thread, fibre
THROE: to put in agonies
THRUM: the tufted end of a thread in weaving
THRUMMED: made of coarse ends or tufts
TICKLE: ticklish
TIGHT: nimble, active
TIGHTLY: briskly, promptly
TIKE: a cur
TILLY-VALLY: an exclamation of contempt
TILTH: tillage
TIMELESS: untimely
TINET: stain, dye
TIRE: attire, head-dress
TIRE: to tear as a bird of prey, hence, metaphorically, to feed
TIRE: to attire, dress
TOD: to yield a tod of wool
TOKENS: plague spots
TOKENED: marked with plague spots
TOLL: to exact toll, to pay toll
TOO TOO: excessively
TOPLESS: supreme, without superior
TOUCH: touchstone for testing gold, trait, an acute feeling
TOUCHED: pricked
TOUSE: to pull, drag
TOWARDS: nearly ready
TOYS: trifles, foolish tricks
TRADE: beaten path
TRANECT: a ferry
TRASH: to check, as a huntsman his hounds
TRANSLATED: transformed
TRAVAIL: labor, toil
TRAY-TRIP: an old game played with dice
TREACHERS: traitors
TREATIES: entreaties
TRENCHED: carved
TRICK: technically, a copy of a coat of arms; hence, any peculiarity which distinguishes voice or feature
TRICK: to dress up
TRICKED: blazoned
TRICKING: ornament
TRICKSY: elegantly quaint
TRIPLE: third
TROJAN: a cant word for a thief
TROL-MY-DAMES: the name of a game; also called pigeon-holes
TROTH-PLIGHT: betrothed
TROW: to trust, think
TRUE: honest
TRUNDLE-TAIL: a long-tailed dog
TUCKET-SONANCE: a flourish on the trumpet
TUNDISH: a funnel
TURLYGOOD: a name adopted by bedlam-beggars
TURN: to modulate
TWANGLING: twanging
TWIGGEN: made of twigs, wicker
TWILLED: A doubtful word
TWINK: a twinkling
TWIRE: to peep, twinkle

UMBERED: stained, dark, as with umber
UNANELED: without extreme unction
UNAVOIDED: unavoidable
UNBARBED: untrimmed
UNBATED: unblunted
UNBOLT: to disclose
UNBOLTED: unsifted, unrefined
UNBREATHED: unpractised

UNCAPE: to throw off the hounds
UNCHARGED: undefended, applied to the gates of a city
UNCLEW: to unravel, undo
UNCOINED: unalloyed, unfeigned
UNDERGO: to undertake
UNDERTAKER: one who takes up another's quarrel
UNDER-WROUGHT: undermined
UNEATH: hardly
UNEXPRESSIVE: inexpressible
UNFAIR: to deprive of beauty
UNHAPPILY: censoriously
UNHAPPY: mischievous
UNHATCHED: undisclosed
UNHOUSELED: without receiving the sacrament
UNIMPROVED: unreproved
UNION: a pearl
UNJUST: dishonest
UNKIND: unnatural
UNLIVED: bereft of life
UNMANNED: untamed, applied to a hawk
UNOWED: unowned
UNPREGNANT: stupid
UNPROPER: common to all
UNQUESTIONABLE: not inquisitive
UNREADY: undressed
UNRESPECTIVE: inconsiderate
UNSISTING: unresting
UNSTANCHED: incontinent
UNTEMPERING: unsoftening
UNTENTED: unsearchable
UNTRADED: unused, uncommon
UNTRIMMED: spoiled of grace or ornament
UNTRUE: untruth
UNVALUED: invaluable
UNSPRING REEL: a boisterous dance
URCHIN: the hedge-hog
USANCE: usury
USE: interest
UTIS: riotous merriment, which accompanied the eighth day of a festival
UTTER: to expel, put forth
UTTERANCE: extremity

VADE: to fade
VAIL: to lower
VAILING: lowering
VAINNESS: vanity
VALANCED: adorned with a valance or fringe; applied to the beard
VALIDITY: value
VANTAGE: advantage
VANTBRACE: armor for the front of the arm
VARLET: a servant, valet
VAST: properly a waste-place, metaphorically, the dead of night, a gulf
VASTIDITY: immensity
VASTLY: like a waste
VASTY: vast, waste
VAUNT: the van, that which precedes
VAUNT-COURIERS: forerunners
VAWARD: the van, vanguard, advanced guard of an army, hence, metaphorically, the first of anything
VEGETIVES: herbs
VELURE: velvet
VELVET-GUARDS: literally, velvet trimmings; applied metaphorically to the citizens who wore them
VENEW: a bout in fencing, metaphorically applied to repartee and sallies of wit
VENEY: a bout at fencing
VENGE: to avenge
VENTAGES: holes in a flute or flageolet
VERBAL: wordy
VERY: true, real
VIA: off with you!
VICE: to screw, the buffoon in the old morality plays
VIE: to challenge; a term at cards, to play as for a wager
VIEWLESS: invisible
VILLAIN: a lowborn man
VINEWED: mouldy
VIOL-DE-GAMBOYS: a bass viol
VIRGINALLING: playing as on the virginals, a kind of a spinet
VIRTUE: the essential excellence
VIRTUOUS: excellent, endowed with virtues
VIZAMENT: advisement
VOLUBLE: fickle
VOLUNTARY: volunteer
VOTARIST: votary, one who has taken a vow
VULGAR: the common people, common
VULGARLY: publicly

WAFT: to wave, beckon, to turn
WAFTAGE: passage
WAFTURE: waving, beckoning
WAGE: to reward as with wages
WAILFUL: lamentable
WAIST: the middle of a ship
WANNION: 'With a wannion' = 'with a vengeance.'
WAPPENED: withered, overworn
WARD: guard, prison
WARDEN: a large pear used for baking
WARDER: truncheon
WARN: to summon
WASSAIL: a drinking bout, festivity
WAT: a familiar word for a hare
WATCH: a watch light
WATCH: to tame by keeping constantly awake
WATER-GALL: a secondary rainbow
WATER-WORK: painting in distemper
WATER-RUG: a kind of dog
WAX: to grow
WAXEN: perhaps, to hiccough
WEALTH: weal, advantage
WEAR: fashion
WEATHER-FEND: to defend from the weather
WEB AND PIN: the cataract in the eye
WEE: small, tiny
WEED: garment
WEE: to think
WEET: to wit, know
WEIGH OUT: to outweigh
WELKIN: the sky
WELKIN: sky-blue
WELL-LIKING: in good condition
WELL SAID: well done!
WEND: to go
WESAND: the wind-pipe
WHELK: a weal
WHELKED: marked with whelks or protuberances
WHEN AS: when
WHEN: an exclamation of impatience
WHERE: whereas, a place
WHIFFLER: an officer who clears the way in processions
WHILE-ERE: a little while ago
WHILES: until

WHIP-STOCK: handle of a whip
WHIST: hushed, silent
WHITE: the centre of an archery butt
WHITING-TIME: bleaching time
WHITSTER: bleacher
WHITELEY: pale-faced, a doubtful word
WHITTLE: a clasp knife
WHOO-BUB: hubbub
WHOOP: to cry out with astonishment
WICKED: noisome, baneful
WIDOW: to give a jointure to
WIDOWHOOD: widow's jointure
WIGHT: person
WILD: weald
WILDERNESS: wildness
WIMPLED: veiled, hooded
WINDOW-BARS: lattice-work across a woman's stomacher
WINDRING: winding
WINTER-GROUND: to protect (a plant) from frost
WIS: in the compound 'I wis,' certainly
WISH: to commend
WISTLY: wistfully
WIT: knowledge, wisdom
WITHOUT: beyond
WITS: five, the five senses
WITTOL: a contented cuckold
WITTY: intelligent
WOMAN-TIRED: hen-pecked
WONDERED: marvellously gifted
WOOD: mad
WOODCOCK: a simpleton
WOODMAN: a forester, huntsman, a cant term for a wencher
WOOLWARD: shirtless
WORD: to flatter or put off with words, to repeat the words of a song
WORLD: 'To go to the *world* is to get married, so 'a woman of the *world*' is a married woman
WORM: a serpent
WORSER: worse
WORSHIP: to honor
WORTH: wealth, fortune
WORTS: cabbages
WOT: to know
WOUND: twisted about
WREAK: vengeance, to avenge
WREAKFUL: revengeful, avenging
WREST: an instrument used for tuning a harp
WRIT: gospel, truth. (Gower)
WRITHLED: shrivelled
WROTH: calamity, misfortune
WRY: to swerve
WRUNG: twisted, strained

YARE: ready, used as an int., 'be' being understood
YARELY: readily
Y-CLAD: clad
Y-CLEPED: called, named
YEARN: to grieve, vex
YELLOWNESS: jealousy
YELLOWS: a disease of horses
YEOMAN: a sheriff's officer
YIELD: to reward, to report
YOND: and yonder

ZANY: a clown, gull

INDEX OF CHARACTERS